# WORLD CIVILIZATIONS

## Spanish/English Guided Reading Workbook

# Contents/Contenido

# How to Use this Book/Cómo usar este libro

The *Spanish/English Guided Reading Workbook* was developed to help you get the most from your reading. Using this book will help you master world history content while developing your reading and vocabulary skills. Reviewing the next few pages before getting started will make you aware of the many useful features in this book./El *Spanish/English Guided Reading Workbook* fue diseñado para ayudarte a sacar el máximo provecho de tu lectura. Este libro te ayudará a dominar el contenido del curso sobre historia mundial mientras desarrollas tus destrezas de lectura y vocabulario. Antes de comenzar, revisa las páginas que siguen para conocer las distintas características útiles del libro.

*Lesson summary pages allow you to interact with the content and key terms and people from each lesson of a module. The summaries explain each lesson of your textbook in a way that is easy to understand./Las páginas de resumen de la lección te permiten relacionarte fácilmente con el contenido y las personas y palabras clave de cada lección de un módulo. Los resúmenes explican cada lección de tu libro de texto para que sea fácil de comprender.*

**Lesson numbers make it easy to find your place in the workbook./Los números de lección hacen que sea fácil saber en qué parte del libro estás.**

**The Main Ideas statements help focus your attention as you read the summaries./Las oraciones de Ideas principales te ayudan a concentrar tu atención a medida que lees los resúmenes.**

**Definitions for the Key Terms and People from your textbook are given./Se dan las definiciones de las Personas y palabras clave de tu libro de texto.**

**Headings under each lesson summary match those in your textbook. This will help you find the material you need./Los títulos dentro de cada resumen de la lección coinciden con los de tu libro de texto. Esto te ayudará a encontrar el material que necesitas.**

---

Name/Nombre_____ Class/Clase_____ Date/Fecha_____

**Ancient India/La antigua India**

Lesson/Lección 5

**MAIN IDEAS/IDEAS PRINCIPALES**

**1.** The Mauryan Empire unified most of India./El Imperio mauryano unificó la mayor parte de la India.

**2.** Gupta rulers promoted Hinduism in their empire./Los gobernantes de la dinastía Gupta fomentaron el hinduismo en su imperio.

### Key Terms and People/Personas y palabras clave

**Candragupta Maurya/Candragupta Maurya** Indian military leader who first unified India and founded the Mauryan Empire/líder militar indio, el primero en unificar la India y fundador del Imperio mauryano

**Asoka/Asoka** Candragupta's grandson and last ruler of the Mauryan Empire/nieto de Candragupta y último gobernante del Imperio mauryano

**Candra Gupta II/Candra Gupta II** ruler who brought great prosperity and stability to India/gobernante que le dio gran prosperidad y estabilidad a la India

### Lesson Summary/Resumen de la lección

**MAURYAN EMPIRE UNIFIES INDIA/EL IMPERIO MAURYANO UNIFICA LA INDIA**

Under Aryan rule, India was divided into several states with no central leader. Then, in the 320s BC, an Indian military leader named **Candragupta Maurya** seized control of the entire northern part of India. The Mauryan Empire lasted for 150 years./Bajo el dominio ario, la India estaba dividida en varios estados sin un líder central. Entonces, en la década de 320 a. C., un líder militar indio llamado **Candragupta Maurya** tomó el control de toda la parte norte de la India. El Imperio mauryano duró 150 años.

Candragupta's complex government included a huge army and a network of spies. He taxed the population heavily for the protection he offered. Eventually, Candragupta became a Jainist monk and gave up his throne to his son. His family continued to expand the Indian empire./El complejo gobierno de Candragupta contaba

> Which Indian leader unified northern India in the 320s BC?/¿Qué líder indio unificó el norte de la India en la década de 320 a. C.?

> What is the relationship between Candragupta's government and heavy taxes?/¿Qué relación hay entre el gobierno de Candragupta y los impuestos altos?
> _____
> _____
> _____
> _____

---

**The Key Terms and People from your textbook have been boldfaced, allowing you to quickly find and study them./Las Personas y palabras clave de tu libro de texto están en negrita, para ayudarte a encontrarlas rápidamente y estudiarlas.**

Name/Nombre_____ Class/Clase _____ Date/Fecha_____

Lesson/Lección 5, *continued/continuación*

con un inmenso ejército y una red de espías. El soberano cobraba impuestos altos a la población a cambio de protección. Con el tiempo, Candragupta se convirtió en un monje jainista y cedió el trono a su hijo. Su familia continuó expandiendo el Imperio indio.

Candragupta's grandson, **Asoka,** was the strongest ruler of the Mauryan dynasty. The empire thrived under his rule. But eventually, tired of bloodshed and war, Asoka converted to Buddhism. He devoted the rest of his rule to improving the lives of his people by building roads, hospitals, and even universities. Asoka also sent Buddhist missionaries to other countries. The rest of the family, however, did not follow Asoka's example. When Asoka died, his sons struggled for power and foreign invaders threatened the country. The Mauryan Empire fell in 184 BC and India divided into smaller states for about 500 years. The spread of Buddhism steadily increased, while Hinduism declined./El nieto de Candragupta, **Asoka,** fue el gobernante más poderoso de la dinastía mauryana. Bajo su gobierno, el imperio prosperó. Sin embargo, con el paso del tiempo, y cansado de las muertes y las guerras, Asoka se convirtió al budismo. Envió misioneros budistas a otros países y dedicó el resto de su mandato a mejorar la vida de su pueblo mediante la construcción de caminos, hospitales e incluso universidades. No obstante, el resto de la familia no siguió el ejemplo de Asoka. Después de su muerte, sus hijos lucharon por el poder y el país se vio amenazado por invasores extranjeros. El Imperio mauryano cayó en el año 184 a. C. y la India se dividió en estados más pequeños que duraron unos 500 años. El budismo siguió expandiéndose, mientras que el hinduismo comenzó a decaer.

How did India's government change after the death of Asoka?/¿En qué cambió el gobierno de la India tras la muerte de Asoka?

_____
_____
_____
_____
_____

© Houghton Mifflin Harcourt Publishing Company

113    Spanish/English Guided Reading Workbook

**As you read each summary, be sure to complete the questions and activities in the margin boxes. They help you check your reading comprehension and track important content./Al leer cada resumen, asegúrate de completar las preguntas y actividades de los recuadros del margen. Te ayudarán a comprobar tu comprensión y a seguir la información importante.**

*Each lesson has at least one vocabulary activity that will help you demonstrate your understanding of the key terms and people introduced in the lesson./Cada lección tiene por lo menos una actividad de vocabulario que te ayudará a demostrar tu comprensión de las personas y palabras clave que se enseñaron en la lección.*

**The Challenge Activity provides an opportunity for you to apply important critical thinking skills using the content that you learned in the lesson./La Actividad avanzada te ofrece la oportunidad de aplicar importantes destrezas de pensamiento crítico utilizando la información que aprendiste en la lección.**

**Some activities have a word bank. You can use it to help find answers or complete writing activities./Algunas actividades tienen un banco de palabras. Puedes usarlo para hallar respuestas o para completar las actividades de escritura.**

**Various types of activities help you check your knowledge of key terms and people./Distintos tipos de actividades te ayudan a comprobar tu conocimiento de las personas y palabras clave.**

---

Name/Nombre_____ Class/Clase_____ Date/Fecha_____

Lesson/Lección 5, *continued/continuación*

fines del siglo 5 agotaron los recursos del imperio. La India volvió a dividirse en pequeños estados.

**CHALLENGE ACTIVITY/ACTIVIDAD AVANZADA**
**Critical Thinking: Make Inferences/Pensamiento crítico: Hacer inferencias** Asoka was strongly influenced by Buddhism. Candra Gupta II followed Hinduism. Choose one of these kings and write an essay explaining how his religion affected his point of view and his decisions during his reign./Asoka estaba fuertemente influenciado por el budismo. Candra Gupta II seguía el hinduismo. Elige a uno de estos líderes y escribe un ensayo en el que expliques cómo su religión influyó en su punto de vista y en las decisiones que tomó durante su gobierno.

| Asoka/Asoka | Candra Gupta II/Candra Gupta II | Candragupta Maurya/Candragupta Maurya |
|---|---|---|
| establish/establece | Gupta Dynasty/dinastía Gupta | Huns/hunos |

**DIRECTIONS/INSTRUCCIONES** Read each sentence and fill in the blank with the word in the word pair that best completes the sentence./Lee cada oración y escribe en el espacio en blanco la palabra del par de palabras que mejor la completa.

1. Under Emperor _____, Indian civilization reached a high point. The empire's economy strengthened and people prospered. **(Candra Gupta II/Candragupta Maurya)**/Durante el gobierno del emperador _____, la civilización india alcanzó su apogeo. La economía del imperio se fortaleció y la gente prosperó. **(Candra Gupta II/Candragupta Maurya)**

2. _____ was the strongest ruler of the Mauryan dynasty. Later, he converted to Buddhism and worked toward improving the lives of his people. **(Asoka/Huns)**/_____ fue el gobernante más poderoso de la dinastía mauryana. Más tarde, se convirtió al budismo y se esforzó por mejorar la vida de su pueblo. **(Asoka/Hunos)**

115  Spanish/English Guided Reading Workbook

Name/Nombre_____ Class/Clase _____ Date/Fecha_____

Lesson/Lección 5, *continued/continuación*

3. The Mauryan Empire was founded by _____, who ruled with a complex government that included a network of spies and a huge army. **(Candra Gupta II/Candragupta Maurya)**/El Imperio mauryano fue fundado por _____, cuyo complejo gobierno contaba con una red de espías y un inmenso ejército. **(Candra Gupta II/Candragupta Maurya)**

4. When the _____ from Central Asia invaded India, it led to the end of the Gupta Dynasty. **(Asoka/Huns)**/Cuando los _____ de Asia Central invadieron la India, la dinastía Gupta llegó a su fin. **(Asoka/hunos)**

5. Under the _____, Hinduism became popular again, but the rulers also supported Buddhism and Jainism. **(Gupta Dynasty/Huns)**/Bajo el gobierno de _____, el hinduismo volvió a generalizarse, pero los gobernantes también apoyaban el budismo y el jainismo. **(la dinastía Gupta/los hunos)**

**DIRECTIONS/INSTRUCCIONES** Use the vocabulary terms from the word list to write a summary of the Mauryan Empire and the Gupta Dynasty./Usa el vocabulario de la lista de palabras para escribir un resumen del Imperio mauryano y la dinastía Gupta.

_____
_____
_____
_____
_____
_____
_____
_____
_____
_____
_____
_____

**Writing activities require you to include Key Terms and People in what you write. Remember to check to make sure that you are using the terms and names correctly./Las actividades de escritura requieren que incluyas las Personas y palabras clave en lo que escribes. Recuerda revisar tu trabajo para asegurarte de que estás usando las palabras y los nombres correctamente.**

# Uncovering the Past/Descubrir el pasado

## Lesson/Lección 1

**MAIN IDEAS/IDEAS PRINCIPALES**

1. History is the study of the past./La historia es el estudio del pasado.
2. We can improve our understanding of people's actions and beliefs through the study of history./Al estudiar la historia, podemos comprender mejor los actos y las creencias de las personas.
3. Historians use clues from various sources to learn about the past./Los historiadores usan pistas de diversas fuentes para aprender acerca del pasado.

## Key Terms and People/Personas y palabras clave

**history/historia** the study of the past/el estudio del pasado

**culture/cultura** the knowledge, beliefs, customs, and values of a group of people/ los conocimientos, las creencias, las costumbres y los valores de un grupo de personas

**archaeology/arqueología** the study of the past based on what people left behind/ el estudio del pasado a partir de lo que dejaron los pueblos antiguos

**fossil/fósil** a part or imprint of something that was once alive/una parte o una huella de un ser que alguna vez estuvo vivo

**artifacts/artefactos** objects created by and used by humans/objetos creados y usados por los seres humanos

**primary source/fuente primaria** an account of an event created by someone who took part in or witnessed the event/el relato de un suceso narrado por alguien que participó o fue testigo del mismo

**secondary source/fuente secundaria** information gathered by someone who did not take part in or witness an event/información reunida por alguien que no participó ni fue testigo del suceso al que se refiere

## Lesson Summary/Resumen de la lección

### THE STUDY OF THE PAST/EL ESTUDIO DEL PASADO

**History** is the study of the past. Historians are people who study history. Historians want to know how people lived and why they did the things they did. They try to learn about the problems people faced and how they found solutions. They are interested in how people lived their daily lives. They study the past to understand people's culture. **Culture** is the knowledge, beliefs, customs, and values of a group of people./La **historia** es el estudio del pasado. Los historiadores son las personas que estudian la historia. Quieren saber cómo vivían los pueblos en el pasado y por qué

> What do we call people who study how people lived in the past?/¿Cómo se llama a las personas que estudian la forma en que vivían los pueblos del pasado?
>
> _____
> _____
> _____

Lesson/Lección 1, *continued*/*continuación*

hicieron las cosas que hicieron. Buscan aprender sobre los problemas que debieron afrontar y las soluciones que idearon. Los historiadores se interesan en saber cómo era la vida cotidiana en el pasado. Estudian el pasado para comprender las culturas. La **cultura** son los conocimientos, las creencias, las costumbres y los valores de un grupo de personas.

The study of the past based on what people left behind is called **archaeology** (ahr-kee-AH-luh-jee). Archaeologists explore places where people once lived, worked, or fought. They examine the things that people left in these places to learn about how these people lived./El estudio del pasado a partir de lo que dejaron los pueblos antiguos se llama **arqueología.** Los arqueólogos exploran los lugares en los que alguna vez vivieron, trabajaron o lucharon las personas. Examinan los objetos que dejaron en esos lugares para descubrir cómo vivían.

> **Underline the sentence that tells why archaeologists examine the things that people left behind./**Subraya la oración que explica por qué los arqueólogos examinan los objetos que dejaron los pueblos antiguos.

## UNDERSTANDING THROUGH HISTORY/
## COMPRENDER A TRAVÉS DE LA HISTORIA

Understanding the past helps you understand the world today. History can even teach you about yourself. What if you did not know about your own past? You would not know what makes you proud about yourself. You would not know what mistakes you should not repeat./Entender el pasado nos ayuda a comprender el mundo actual. La historia incluso puede enseñarnos acerca de nosotros mismos. ¿Qué pasaría si no conocieras tu propio pasado? No sabrías qué cosas te pueden enorgullecer de ti mismo. Tampoco sabrías qué errores tienes que tratar de no repetir.

> **How can studying history teach you about yourself?/**¿De qué manera estudiar la historia puede enseñarte cosas sobre ti mismo?
>
> _____
> _____
> _____
> _____

History is just as important for groups. What would happen if countries had no record of their past? People would not remember their nation's great triumphs or tragedies. History shapes our identity and teaches us the values that we share./La historia tiene la misma importancia para los grupos de personas. ¿Qué pasaría si los países no tuvieran un registro de su pasado? Las personas no recordarían los grandes triunfos de su nación ni sus tragedias. La historia conforma nuestra identidad y nos enseña los valores que compartimos.

History also teaches about cultures that are unlike your own. Learning other people's stories can help you respect and understand different opinions. You also learn to understand how today's events are shaped by events of the past. History encourages you to ask important questions./La historia también nos enseña sobre culturas diferentes a la nuestra. Aprender sobre la historia de otros pueblos puede ayudarte a respetar y entender otras opiniones. También permite comprender cómo los sucesos del pasado afectan los sucesos actuales. La historia te incentiva a hacer preguntas importantes.

> **Underline the sentence that explains why history helps you relate more easily to people of different backgrounds./Subraya la oración que explica por qué la historia te ayuda a relacionarte más fácilmente con personas que tienen un origen diferente.**

## USING CLUES/USAR PISTAS

We learn about history from a variety of sources. **Fossils**, such as bones or footprints preserved in rock, give us clues to life very long ago. **Artifacts,** such as tools, coins, or pottery, also give us information. People invented writing about 5,000 years ago. Since then, laws, poems, speeches, letters, and other things have been written. People have learned from these written sources. Writing can be a **primary source,** which was written by someone who took part in or witnessed an event. Writing can also be a **secondary source,** which is information gathered by someone who did not take part in or witness an event./Aprendemos sobre la historia a partir de diversas fuentes. Los **fósiles,** como los huesos o las huellas preservadas en las rocas, dan pistas sobre los seres que vivieron hace mucho tiempo. Diferentes **artefactos,** como herramientas, monedas u objetos de cerámica, también nos brindan información. La escritura se inventó hace unos 5,000 años. Desde entonces, se han escrito leyes, poemas, discursos y cartas, entre otros. Las personas han aprendido mucho de estas fuentes escritas. Los textos pueden ser **fuentes primarias,** es decir, que fueron escritos por alguien que participó en un suceso o fue testigo del mismo. También pueden ser **fuentes secundarias,** es decir, información reunida por alguien que no participó ni fue testigo del suceso al que se refiere.

> **What sources give us clues to life very long ago?/¿Qué fuentes nos brindan información sobre cómo era la vida hace mucho tiempo?**
>
> _____
>
> _____

## CHALLENGE ACTIVITY/ACTIVIDAD AVANZADA

**Critical Thinking: Make Inferences/Pensamiento crítico: Hacer inferencias** Imagine a tribe or group of people that might have lived a long time ago. Write a short essay about its culture./ Imagina una tribu o un grupo de personas que pudiera haber vivido hace mucho tiempo. Escribe un breve ensayo sobre su cultura.

| archaeology/ arqueología | artifacts/ artefactos | culture/ cultura | fossil/ fósil |
|---|---|---|---|
| history/ historia | primary source/ fuente primaria | secondary source/ fuente secundaria | |

**DIRECTIONS/INSTRUCCIONES** Use the seven vocabulary terms from the lesson to write a summary of what you learned in the lesson./Usa los siete términos de vocabulario de la lección para escribir un resumen de lo que aprendiste en la lección.

**DIRECTIONS/INSTRUCCIONES** On the line provided before each statement, write **T** if a statement is true and **F** if a statement is false. If the statement is false, write the correct term on the line after each sentence that makes the sentence a true statement./En la línea que precede a cada enunciado, escribe **V** si el enunciado es verdadero y **F** si es falso. Si el enunciado es falso, escribe en la línea que sigue a la oración el término correcto que lo hace verdadero.

_____ 1. A <u>fossil</u> is a part or imprint of something that was once alive./ <u>Un fósil</u> es una parte o una huella de algo que alguna vez estuvo vivo.

_____

_____ 2. A <u>primary source</u> is information gathered by someone who did not take part in or witness an event./<u>Una fuente primaria</u> es información reunida por alguien que no participó ni fue testigo de un suceso.

_____

_____ 3. <u>Artifacts</u> are objects that were created and used by humans./<u>Los artefactos</u> son objetos creados y usados por seres humanos.

_____

Lesson/Lección 1, *continued*/*continuación*

_____ 4. A <u>secondary source</u> is an account of an event created by someone who took part in or witnessed the event./<u>Una fuente secundaria</u> es un relato de un suceso narrado por alguien que participó o fue testigo del mismo.

_____

_____ 5. The study of the past is called <u>history</u>./El estudio del pasado se llama <u>historia</u>.

_____

_____ 6. The study of the past based on what people left behind is called <u>history</u>./El estudio del pasado a partir de lo que dejaron los pueblos antiguos se llama <u>historia</u>.

_____

## Uncovering the Past/Descubrir el pasado

**MAIN IDEAS/IDEAS PRINCIPALES**

1. Geography is the study of places and people./La geografía es el estudio de los lugares y las personas.

2. Studying location is important to both physical and human geography./Estudiar la ubicación es importante para la geografía física y la geografía humana.

3. Geography and history are closely connected./La geografía y la historia tienen una relación muy estrecha.

## Key Terms and People/Personas y palabras clave

**geography/geografía** the study of the earth's physical and cultural features/ el estudio de las características físicas y culturales de la Tierra

**environment/medio ambiente** all the living and nonliving things that affect life in an area/todos los seres vivos y elementos inertes que afectan la vida en una zona

**landforms/accidentes geográficos** the natural features of the land's surface/ las características naturales de la superficie de la Tierra

**climate/clima** the pattern of weather conditions in a certain area over a long period of time/el patrón del estado del tiempo en un área determinada durante un largo período de tiempo

**region/región** area with one or more features that make it different from surrounding areas/área con una o más características que la diferencian de las áreas circundantes

**resources/recursos** materials found in the earth that people need and value/ materiales que se encuentran en la tierra y que las personas necesitan y valoran

## Lesson Summary/Resumen de la lección

### STUDYING PLACES AND PEOPLE/ESTUDIAR LUGARES Y PERSONAS

Historians study geography to understand where events took place and who was there. **Geography** is the earth's physical and cultural features. It includes mountains, rivers, people, cities, and countries./Los historiadores estudian la geografía para comprender dónde ocurrieron los sucesos y quiénes se encontraban allí. La **geografía** comprende las características físicas y culturales de la Tierra. Abarca montañas, ríos, personas, ciudades y países.

> **What subject helps historians understand where events took place?/ ¿Qué disciplina ayuda a los historiadores a conocer los lugares donde ocurrieron los sucesos?**
>
> _____

Geography has two main areas of study. Physical geography is the study of the earth's land and features. Human geography is the study of people and the places where they live. Physical geographers study the **environment,** which includes all the living and nonliving things that affect life in an area. The environment is shaped by the physical processes of weathering, erosion, and pollution. The most important features for physical geographers are **landforms,** the natural features of the land's surface. Physical geographers also study **climate,** the pattern of weather conditions in a certain area over a long period of time./La geografía posee dos ramas de estudio principales. La geografía física es el estudio de la configuración del terreno y sus características. La geografía humana es el estudio de las personas y los lugares en los que habitan. Los geógrafos físicos estudian el **medio ambiente,** que incluye todos los seres vivos y elementos inertes que afectan la vida en una zona. El medio ambiente se conforma a través de los procesos físicos de meteorización, erosión y contaminación. Las características más importantes para los geógrafos físicos son los **accidentes geográficos,** es decir, las formaciones naturales de la superficie terrestre. Los geógrafos físicos también estudian el **clima,** o el patrón del estado del tiempo en un área determinada durante un largo período de tiempo.

Specialists in human geography study many interesting questions about how people and the environment affect each other./Los especialistas en geografía humana estudian muchas cuestiones interesantes sobre cómo las personas influyen en el medio ambiente y viceversa.

> **What are the two main areas of study in geography?/¿Cuáles son las dos ramas de estudio principales de la geografía?**
>
> _____
>
> _____

> **Underline the sentence that explains what climate is./** Subraya la oración que explica qué es el clima.

## STUDYING LOCATION/ESTUDIAR LA UBICACIÓN

No two places are exactly alike. That is why geographers try to understand how different locations can affect human populations, or groups of people. Geographers use maps to study and compare locations. A map is a drawing of an area. Some maps show physical features, such as mountains, forests, and rivers. Other maps show cities and the boundaries of states or countries. Studying location is often helped by learning about **regions,** or areas with one or more features that make them different from surrounding areas./No existen dos lugares exactamente iguales. Por esa razón, los geógrafos intentan comprender cómo la ubicación puede afectar a las poblaciones humanas, o grupos de personas. Los geógrafos usan mapas para estudiar y comparar ubicaciones. Un mapa es el dibujo de un área. Algunos mapas muestran características físicas, como montañas, bosques y ríos. Otros muestran las ciudades y los límites de los estados o países. Para estudiar ubicaciones, es útil conocer las características de las distintas **regiones,** o áreas con una o más características que las diferencian de las áreas circundantes.

> **What are maps used for?/¿Para qué sirven los mapas?**
> _____
> _____

## GEOGRAPHY AND HISTORY/GEOGRAFÍA E HISTORIA

Geography gives us clues about the people and places that came before us. We can piece together information about past cultures by knowing where people lived and what the area was like./ La geografía nos brinda pistas sobre las personas y los lugares que existieron antes que nosotros. Al conocer dónde vivieron las personas y las características de ese lugar, podemos reunir información sobre las culturas del pasado.

Early people settled in places that were rich in resources. **Resources** are materials that are found

> **Underline the sentence that explains how geography gives us clues about the past./Subraya la oración que explica de qué manera la geografía nos brinda pistas sobre el pasado.**

Lesson/Lección 2, *continued/continuación*

in the earth that people need and value. They include water, animals, fertile land, stone for tools, and metals. Resources influence the development of cultures and the growth of civilizations and societies. For example, early societies formed along rivers. The relationship between geography and people is not one sided. People have influenced their environments positively by planting trees. They have influenced the environment negatively by creating wastelands where forests once existed./ Los pueblos primitivos se establecían en lugares ricos en recursos. Los **recursos** son materiales que se encuentran en la tierra y que las personas necesitan y valoran, como el agua, los animales, la tierra fértil, las piedras para fabricar herramientas o los metales. Los recursos afectan el desarrollo de las culturas y el crecimiento de las civilizaciones y sociedades. Por ejemplo, las sociedades primitivas se formaban a orillas de los ríos. La relación entre la geografía y las personas no es unilateral. Las personas han influido positivamente en el medio ambiente al plantar árboles. En cambio, lo han afectado de manera negativa al transformar bosques en terrenos baldíos.

> **Why might early societies have formed along rivers?/ ¿Cuál podría ser la razón por la cual las sociedades primitivas se desarrollaban a orillas de los ríos?**
>
> _____
>
> _____
>
> _____

## CHALLENGE ACTIVITY/ACTIVIDAD AVANZADA

**Critical Thinking: Design/Pensamiento crítico: Diseñar** Draw a map of an imaginary country or region. Include features such as mountains, rivers, and cities./Dibuja un mapa de un país o una región imaginaria. Incluye características geográficas, como montañas, ríos y ciudades.

| climate/clima | environment/medio ambiente | geography/geografía |
| landforms/accidentes geográficos | region/región | resources/recursos |

**DIRECTIONS/INSTRUCCIONES** Look up the vocabulary terms in the word bank in a dictionary. Write the dictionary definition of the word that is closest to the definition used in your textbook./Busca en un diccionario los términos de vocabulario del banco de palabras. Escribe la definición del diccionario más cercana a la definición que aparece en tu libro de texto.

1. climate/clima _____

_____

_____

2. environment/medio ambiente _____

_____

_____

3. geography/geografía _____

_____

_____

4. landforms/accidentes geográficos _____

_____

_____

5. region/región _____

_____

_____

6. resources/recursos _____

_____

_____

_____

## Uncovering the Past/Descubrir el pasado

### Lesson/Lección 3

**MAIN IDEAS/IDEAS PRINCIPALES**

1. The main problem in economics is scarcity./El principal problema de la economía es la escasez.

2. Businesses and countries have to make decisions about economic resources./Las empresas y los países deben tomar decisiones sobre los recursos económicos.

3. Businesses and other organizations help people meet their needs and wants./Las empresas y otras organizaciones ayudan a que las personas satisfagan sus deseos y necesidades.

4. Money is used as a medium of exchange, a store of value, and a unit of account./El dinero se usa como medio de intercambio, reserva de valor y unidad de cuenta.

5. Economics helps explain events in world history./La economía ayuda a explicar muchos sucesos de la historia mundial.

## Key Terms and People/Personas y palabras clave

**economy/economía** a system of producing, selling, and buying goods and services/sistema de producción, venta y compra de bienes y servicios

**scarcity/escasez** not enough resources to meet people's wants/falta de recursos suficientes para satisfacer los deseos de las personas

**profit/ganancia** the money an individual or business has left after paying expenses/el dinero que le queda a un individuo o negocio después de pagar los gastos

**entrepreneur/empresario** a person who organizes, manages, and assumes the risk of a business/persona que organiza, administra y asume el riesgo de un negocio

**mixed economy/economía mixta** economy in which businesses are free to operate but they must obey a government's laws and rules/economía en la cual las empresas pueden operar con libertad, pero deben obedecer las leyes y normas que establece el gobierno

**trade/comercio** the activity of buying, selling, or exchanging goods and services/la actividad de comprar, vender o intercambiar bienes y servicios

**wealth/riqueza** the value of all possessions that a person or country has/el valor de todas las cosas que tiene una persona o un país

# Lesson Summary/Resumen de la lección
## ECONOMIC FUNDAMENTALS/PRINCIPIOS DE LA ECONOMÍA

An **economy** is a system of producing, selling, and buying goods and services. A main economic problem is **scarcity,** or not enough resources to meet people's wants. It forces them to make choices about what they want. The laws of supply and demand determine the price of a good or service./ Una **economía** es un sistema de producción, venta y compra de bienes y servicios. Uno de los principales problemas de la economía es la **escasez,** es decir, la falta de recursos suficientes para satisfacer los deseos de las personas. Esto obliga a las personas a elegir entre las cosas que desean. Las leyes de la oferta y la demanda determinan el precio de un bien o servicio.

> Why is scarcity a main economic problem?/¿Por qué la escasez es uno de los principales problemas de la economía?
>
> _____
> _____
> _____
> _____

**Profit** is money left over after expenses have been paid. Profit and saving money are incentives for people to buy and sell goods and services./La **ganancia** es el dinero que queda después de pagar los gastos. Obtener ganancias y ahorrar dinero son incentivos para que las personas compren y vendan bienes y servicios.

## SYSTEMS TO ORGANIZE RESOURCES/ SISTEMAS PARA ORGANIZAR LOS RECURSOS

Businesses have to make choices about factors of production. These factors are: natural resources, capital, labor, and **entrepreneurs,** people who organize, manage, and assume business risk./ Las empresas deben tomar decisiones sobre los diferentes factores de producción. Estos factores son los recursos naturales, el capital, la mano de obra y los **empresarios,** que son las personas que organizan, administran, y asumen los riesgos de un negocio.

> Underline the phrase that explains what entrepreneurs do./Subraya la frase que explica lo que hace un empresario.

**Lesson/Lección 3**, *continued/continuación*

Countries make production choices, too. Their economic system addresses how they distribute economic resources. Types of economies are traditional, command, and market. Today, many countries follow a **mixed economy.** Businesses are basically free to operate as they wish, but they must follow government laws and rules./Los países también toman decisiones sobre la producción. El sistema económico de un país determina cómo se distribuyen los recursos económicos. Algunos sistemas económicos son el tradicional, el planificado y el de mercado. En la actualidad, muchos países se rigen por una **economía mixta.** En ella, las empresas pueden operar con libertad, pero deben obedecer las leyes y normas que establece el gobierno.

> **What is an advantage of following a mixed economy?/¿Cuál es una ventaja de la economía mixta?**
>
> _____
>
> _____

## NEEDS AND WANTS/DESEOS Y NECESIDADES

Today, large businesses aid the economy. They have the resources and tools to produce goods people need and want. The government and nonprofit organizations also help meet people's needs and wants./En la actualidad, las grandes empresas contribuyen a la economía. Tienen los recursos y las herramientas para producir los bienes que las personas necesitan y desean. El gobierno y las organizaciones sin fines de lucro también ayudan a que las personas satisfagan sus deseos y necesidades.

## MONEY AND TRADE/DINERO Y COMERCIO

**Trade** is buying, selling, or exchanging goods and services. Early trade was called the barter system. Over time, trade routes formed, such as the Silk Road. Trade led to the exchange of languages, religions, tools, and inventions. With more trading, it became harder to agree on the value of products. So countries began to use money as a medium of exchange. Money is a form of wealth. **Wealth** is the value of all possessions that a person or country has./El **comercio** es la actividad de comprar, vender o intercambiar bienes y servicios. En la antigüedad, el comercio estaba basado en el sistema de trueque. Con el tiempo, se formaron rutas comerciales, como la Ruta de la Seda. El comercio dio lugar al intercambio de idiomas, religiones, herramientas e inventos. Pero al aumentar el comercio, se volvió más difícil acordar el valor de los productos, por lo que los países comenzaron a usar el dinero como medio de intercambio. El dinero es una forma de riqueza. La **riqueza** es el valor de todas las cosas que tiene una persona o un país.

> Why did money become a medium of exchange?/¿Por qué el dinero se convirtió en un medio de intercambio?
>
> _____
>
> _____
>
> _____
>
> _____

## THE IMPORTANCE OF ECONOMICS/LA IMPORTANCIA DE LA ECONOMÍA

Studying economics can help people make everyday decisions about money. It can also help people interpret the past, explain the present, and predict future consequences of economic decisions. Economic growth has been affected by the discovery of new resources and expansion, which increased trade. It also has been helped by technology and education, which increased productivity./Estudiar la economía nos puede servir para tomar decisiones cotidianas sobre el dinero. También nos puede ayudar a interpretar el pasado, explicar el presente y predecir las consecuencias que tendrán nuestras decisiones económicas en el futuro. El crecimiento económico se ha visto afectado por el descubrimiento de nuevos recursos y por la expansión, que hicieron crecer el comercio. También se ha visto beneficiado por la tecnología y la educación, que aumentaron la productividad.

> Underline the factors that have helped economic growth./Subraya los factores que han contribuido al crecimiento económico.

## CHALLENGE ACTIVITY/ACTIVIDAD AVANZADA
**Critical Thinking: Identify Cause and Effect/**
**Pensamiento crítico: Identificar causa y efecto** What is
the effect of scarcity? Write a short essay about why
scarcity is likely to continue to exist./¿Cuál es el efecto
de la escasez? Escribe un breve ensayo acerca de por
qué es probable que la escasez siga existiendo.

**DIRECTIONS/INSTRUCCIONES** Write a word that has a similar
meaning, or synonym, for the term given./Escribe un sinónimo
de los siguientes términos, es decir, una palabra que tenga un
significado similar.

1. entrepreneur/empresario _____

2. profit/ganancia _____

3. scarcity/escasez _____

4. trade/comercio _____

**DIRECTIONS/INSTRUCCIONES** Read each sentence and fill in
the blank with the word in the word pair that best completes
the sentence./Lee cada oración y escribe en el espacio en blanco
la palabra del par de palabras que mejor la completa.

5. The value of all possessions that a person or country has is called
_____. **(money/wealth)**/El valor de todas las cosas que tiene una
persona o un país se llama _____. **(dinero/riqueza)**

6. In a _____ economy, businesses are basically free to operate as
they please but must obey laws and government rules. **(mixed/traditional)**/
En una economía _____, las empresas pueden operar con libertad,
pero deben obedecer las leyes y normas que establece el gobierno.
**(mixta/tradicional)**

7. The activity of buying, selling, or exchanging goods and services is known
as _____. **(scarcity/trade)**/La actividad de comprar, vender o
intercambiar bienes y servicios se conoce como _____.
**(escasez/comercio)**

8.  The _____ is a system of producing, selling, and buying goods and services. **(profit/economy)**/Se llama _____ al sistema de producción, venta y compra de bienes y servicios. **(ganancia/economía)**

9.  _____ occurs when there are not enough resources to meet people's wants. **(wealth/scarcity)**/La _____ ocurre cuando no hay suficientes recursos para satisfacer los deseos de las personas. **(riqueza/escasez)**

10. When a business or individual has money left after expenses have been paid, that person or business has made a _____. **(profit/trade)**/Cuando a un negocio o un individuo le queda dinero después de pagar los gastos, esa persona o negocio ha obtenido _____. **(ganancia/comercio)**

## Uncovering the Past/Descubrir el pasado

**MAIN IDEAS/IDEAS PRINCIPALES**

1. A country's government affects the lives of its people./El gobierno de un país influye en la vida de sus habitantes.

2. There have been many different forms of government throughout history./Han existido muchas formas diferentes de gobierno a lo largo de la historia.

3. Governments have a role to play in the economy, including providing services and collecting taxes./Los gobiernos cumplen una función en la economía, como brindar servicios y recaudar impuestos.

## Key Terms and People/Personas y palabras clave

**civics/Educación Cívica** the study of citizenship and government/el estudio de la ciudadanía y el gobierno

**government/gobierno** the organizations and individuals who have the right to rule over a group of people/las organizaciones y los individuos que tienen el derecho a gobernar a un grupo de personas

**constitution/constitución** a written plan of government/un plan escrito de gobierno

**democracy/democracia** the people either rule directly or they elect officials who act on their behalf/las personas ejercen el poder directamente o eligen funcionarios que actúan en su nombre

**republic/república** a system of government in which people elect representatives to carry on the work of government/sistema de gobierno en el que las personas eligen representantes que desempeñen la tarea de gobernar

**tax/impuesto** a charge people pay to a government/un cargo que pagan las personas a un gobierno

## Lesson Summary/Resumen de la lección

### NEED FOR GOVERNMENTS/NECESIDAD DE TENER GOBIERNO

**Civics** is the study of citizenship and government. A person who is a citizen is legally recognized by his or her country. The **government** is the organizations and individuals who have the right to rule over the people. Government provides a way for people to unite, solve problems, and cooperate. Government makes people's lives safer and easier./La **Educación Cívica** es el estudio de la

What makes a person a citizen of a country?/¿Qué hace que una persona sea ciudadana de un país?

_____

_____

_____

**Lesson/Lección 4,** *continued/continuación*

ciudadanía y el gobierno. Un ciudadano es una persona legalmente reconocida por su país. El **gobierno** son las organizaciones y los individuos que tienen el derecho a gobernar a las personas. El gobierno ayuda a que las personas se unan, resuelvan problemas y cooperen entre sí. También hace que la vida de las personas sea más fácil y segura.

Government provides services such as establishing schools and providing police and fire departments. It creates highways between its borders and establishes a system of money./El gobierno brinda servicios, como escuelas, policías y cuerpos de bomberos. Construye caminos dentro de sus fronteras y establece un sistema monetario.

Government provides laws for society. Many countries are ruled by a written plan of government, or a **constitution.** It describes the government's purpose and how it will be organized. Laws cannot go against it, and they must be recorded so people know about them. Many laws guarantee freedoms, such as freedom of speech, press, and religion./El gobierno proporciona leyes para la sociedad. Muchos países se rigen por un plan escrito de gobierno, o **constitución.** La constitución describe el propósito del gobierno y cómo será organizado. Las leyes no pueden contradecir la constitución y deben registrarse por escrito para que las personas las conozcan. Muchas leyes garantizan libertades, como la libertad de expresión, de prensa y de religión o culto.

## FORMS OF GOVERNMENT/FORMAS DE GOBIERNO

Some governments are nondemocratic, so citizens do not have the power to rule. Other governments are democratic. In a **democracy,** the people either rule directly or elect officials

---

List three ways governments affect people./Menciona tres formas en las que los gobiernos influyen en la vida de las personas.

_____

_____

_____

---

Underline the sentence that describes what laws may guarantee./Subraya la oración que describe qué pueden garantizar las leyes.

---

Why might it be better to live in a democracy instead of a nondemocratic government?/¿Por qué será mejor vivir en una democracia que bajo un gobierno no democrático?

_____

_____

_____

_____

_____

who act for them./Algunos gobiernos no son
democráticos, por lo que los ciudadanos no
tiene el poder de gobernar. Otros gobiernos
sí son democráticos. En una **democracia,** las
personas ejercen el poder directamente o bien
eligen funcionarios que actúan en su nombre.

Democracy began in Athens in ancient Greece.
Then, for a time, Rome had a republic. In a
**republic,** the people agree to be ruled by their
elected leaders. The United States is a republic. In
European countries, governments were monarchies
ruled by a king or queen. Then in 1215, Britain's
King John was forced to sign the Magna Carta. It
protected the rights of English citizens. In the 17th
and 18th centuries, John Locke and others said
people were born equal with natural rights. These
ideas inspired Americans to fight for independence
from Great Britain./La democracia comenzó en
Atenas, en la antigua Grecia. Luego, por un
tiempo, Roma tuvo una república. En una
**república,** las personas aceptan ser gobernadas
por los líderes que eligen. Los Estados Unidos
son una república. En los países europeos, los
gobiernos eran monarquías conducidas por un rey
o una reina. Pero, en 1215, el rey Juan de Inglaterra
fue obligado a firmar la Carta Magna, la cual
protegía los derechos de los ciudadanos ingleses.
En los siglos 17 y 18, John Locke, entre otros, dijo
que todas las personas nacen iguales y con los
mismos derechos naturales. Estas ideas inspiraron
a los estadounidenses a luchar por independizarse
de Gran Bretaña.

> **Underline the sentences that tells the ideas that inspired America to seek its independence from Great Britain./Subraya las oraciones que contienen las ideas que inspiraron a los estadounidenses a independizarse de Gran Bretaña.**

> **What is the government's role in the economy?/¿Cuál es el papel del gobierno en la economía?**
> _____
> _____
> _____
> _____
> _____

## THE ROLE OF GOVERNMENT IN THE ECONOMY/ EL PAPEL DEL GOBIERNO EN LA ECONOMÍA

Governments influence economics, because they
determine how goods and services are produced
and distributed. Many democracies have market
or mixed economies./El gobierno influye en
la economía, porque determina cómo se

producen y distribuyen los bienes y servicios. Muchas democracias tienen economías de mercado o mixtas.

To be able to provide services and protection, governments collect taxes. A **tax** is a charge people pay to a government. Governments may also participate in economies by making trade laws. They do this to protect jobs and industries from foreign competition. Even still, most governments support international trade./Para poder dar servicios y protección, el gobierno recauda impuestos. Un **impuesto** es un cargo que las personas pagan a un gobierno. El gobierno también puede participar en la economía dictando leyes que regulen el comercio. De esta manera, protege los puestos de trabajo y las industrias frente a la competencia de otros países. Aun así, la mayoría de los gobiernos apoyan el comercio internacional.

## CHALLENGE ACTIVITY/ACTIVIDAD AVANZADA

**Critical Thinking: Develop/Pensamiento crítico: Desarrollar** Imagine a country that has just become independent. Draft a constitution to protect its citizens./Imagina un país que acaba de independizarse. Escribe el borrador de una constitución para proteger a sus ciudadanos.

| | | |
|---|---|---|
| civics/Educación Cívica | constitution/constitución | democracy/democracia |
| government/gobierno | republic/república | tax/impuesto |

**DIRECTIONS/INSTRUCCIONES** Match the terms on the left to their definitions on the right. Write the correct letter on the line before each term./Une los términos de la izquierda con las definiciones de la derecha. Escribe la letra correcta en la línea que precede a cada término.

_____ 1. civics/
Educación
Cívica

a. the people either rule directly or they elect officials who act for them/las personas ejercen el poder directamente o bien eligen funcionarios que actúan en su nombre

_____ 2. tax/impuesto

b. a written plan of government/un plan escrito de gobierno

_____ 3. government/
gobierno

c. the study of citizenship and government/ el estudio de la ciudadanía y el gobierno

_____ 4. democracy/
democracia

d. system of government in which people elect representatives to carry on the work of government for them/sistema de gobierno en el que las personas eligen representantes para que desempeñen la tarea de gobernar en su nombre

_____ 5. republic/
república

e. the organizations and individuals who have the right to rule over a group of people/las organizaciones y los individuos que tienen el derecho a gobernar a un grupo de personas

_____ 6. constitution/
constitución

f. a charge people pay to a government/cargo que pagan las personas a un gobierno

**DIRECTIONS/INSTRUCCIONES** On the line provided before each statement, write **T** if a statement is true and **F** if a statement is false. If the statement is false, write the correct term on the line after each sentence that makes the sentence a true statement./En la línea que precede a cada enunciado, escribe **V** si el enunciado es verdadero y **F** si es falso. Si el enunciado es falso, escribe en la línea que sigue a la oración el término correcto que lo hace verdadero.

_____ 7. A <u>republic</u> is a written plan of government./<u>Una república</u> es un plan escrito de gobierno.

_____

_____ 8. A <u>tax</u> is a charge people pay to a government./<u>Un impuesto</u> es un cargo que pagan las personas a un gobierno.

_____

_____ 9. <u>Democracy</u> is the study of citizenship and government./<u>La democracia</u> es el estudio de la ciudadanía y el gobierno.

_____

# The Stone Ages and Early Cultures/Las Edades de Piedra y las primeras culturas

## Lesson/Lección 1

**MAIN IDEAS/IDEAS PRINCIPALES**

1. Scientists study the remains of early humans to learn about prehistory./Los científicos estudian los restos de los primeros seres humanos para aprender sobre la prehistoria.
2. Hominids and early humans first appeared in East Africa millions of years ago./Los homínidos y los primeros seres humanos aparecieron por primera vez en África oriental hace millones de años.
3. Stone Age tools grew more complex as time passed./Las herramientas de la Edad de Piedra se volvieron más complejas con el paso del tiempo.
4. Hunter-gatherer societies developed language, art, and religion./Las sociedades de cazadores y recolectores desarrollaron el lenguaje, el arte y la religión.

## Key Terms and People/Personas y palabras clave

**prehistory/prehistoria** the time before there was writing/período anterior a la escritura

**hominid/homínido** an early ancestor of humans/antepasado remoto de los seres humanos

**ancestor/antepasado** a relative who lived in the past/pariente que vivió en el pasado

**tool/herramienta** any handheld object that has been modified to help a person accomplish a task/cualquier objeto manual que sirve para ayudar a una persona a realizar una tarea

**Paleolithic Era/el Paleolítico** the first part of the Stone Age/primera etapa de la Edad de Piedra

**society/sociedad** a community of people who share a common culture/comunidad de personas que comparten una misma cultura

**hunter-gatherers/cazadores y recolectores** people who hunt animals and gather wild plants, seeds, fruits, and nuts to survive/personas que cazan animales y recolectan plantas silvestres, semillas, frutos y nueces para sobrevivir

## Lesson Summary/Resumen de la lección

### SCIENTISTS STUDY REMAINS/LOS CIENTÍFICOS ESTUDIAN LOS RESTOS

Humans have lived on the earth for more than a million years, but writing was not invented until about 5,000 years ago. Historians call the time before writing **prehistory.** Historic time periods began when people started writing letters, words, and numbers. To study prehistory, historians rely on the work of other experts./Los seres humanos viven en la Tierra desde hace más de un millón de años, pero la escritura se inventó hace apenas unos 5,000 años. Los historiadores llaman **prehistoria** al período anterior a la escritura. Los períodos históricos comenzaron cuando las personas empezaron a escribir letras, palabras y números. Para estudiar la prehistoria, los historiadores se basan en el trabajo de otros expertos.

> **Why is prehistory different from historic time periods?/** ¿En qué se diferencia la prehistoria de los períodos históricos?
>
> _____
> _____
> _____
> _____
> _____

Archaeologists have found old bones that appear to belong to **hominids,** early **ancestors** of humans. Discoveries of ancient bones give us information about early humans and their ancestors, but not all scientists agree on the meaning of these discoveries. Geographers and other types of scientists study prehistory, too, to learn about human migration./Los arqueólogos han encontrado huesos antiguos que parecen haber pertenecido a **homínidos, antepasados** remotos de los seres humanos. Los descubrimientos de huesos antiguos nos dan información sobre los primeros seres humanos y sus antepasados, pero no todos los científicos están de acuerdo en cuanto al significado de esos descubrimientos. Los geógrafos y otros tipos de científicos también estudian la prehistoria para aprender sobre las migraciones humanas.

## HOMINIDS AND EARLY HUMANS/HOMÍNIDOS Y PRIMEROS SERES HUMANOS

As time passed, hominids became more like modern humans. Many scientists think that the first modern humans appeared in Africa about 200,000 years ago. Scientists call these early humans *homo sapiens,* or "wise man." Every person alive today belongs to this group./

> **What do scientists call modern humans?/**¿Qué nombre dan los científicos a los seres humanos modernos?
>
> _____

Con el paso del tiempo, los homínidos se fueron pareciendo más a los seres humanos modernos. Muchos científicos creen que los primeros seres humanos modernos aparecieron en África hace unos 200,000 años. Los científicos los llaman *homo sapiens*, que significa "hombre sabio". Todas las personas que viven en la actualidad pertenecen a ese grupo.

## STONE AGE TOOLS/HERRAMIENTAS DE LA EDAD DE PIEDRA

During the **Paleolithic** (pay-lee-uh-LI-thik) **Era,** the first part of the Stone Age, people used sharpened stones as **tools.** Stone tools were probably used to cut, chop, and scrape roots, bones, or meat. Later, people made tools out of flint. They also learned how to attach wooden handles to sharp stones to make hand axes and spears./Durante el **Paleolítico,** la primera etapa de la Edad de Piedra, las personas usaban piedras afiladas a modo de **herramientas.** Las herramientas de piedra probablemente se utilizaban para cortar, picar y raspar raíces, huesos o carne. Más adelante, las personas comenzaron a fabricar herramientas de pedernal. También aprendieron a añadir mangos de madera a las piedras afiladas para fabricar lanzas y hachas de mano.

> What is one advantage to attaching a wooden handle to a stone tool? Draw a picture if it will help you visualize the tool./¿Cuál es una de las ventajas de añadir un mango de madera a una herramienta de piedra? Haz un dibujo si te ayuda a visualizar la herramienta.
>
> _____
> _____
> _____
> _____
> _____

## HUNTER-GATHERER SOCIETIES/SOCIEDADES DE CAZADORES Y RECOLECTORES

Anthropologists believe that early humans lived in small groups of **hunter-gatherers.** In these **societies,** men hunted and women collected plants to eat and took care of children. Children also did things to help. These societies developed cultures with language, art, and religion. Language developed as a way to communicate and resolve problems like how to distribute food. Scholars are not sure why societies developed

> What cultural element did Stone Age societies develop as a means of communicating and resolving issues?/¿Qué elemento cultural desarrollaron las sociedades de la Edad de Piedra para comunicarse y resolver problemas?
>
> _____

art and religion./Los antropólogos creen que los primeros seres humanos vivían en grupos pequeños de **cazadores y recolectores.** En esas **sociedades,** los hombres cazaban y las mujeres recolectaban plantas para comer y cuidaban a los niños. Los niños también ayudaban. Esas sociedades desarrollaron culturas con un lenguaje, un arte y una religión. El lenguaje surgió como una forma de comunicarse y de resolver problemas tales como·la distribución de los alimentos. Los expertos tienen dudas acerca de por qué surgieron el arte y la religión.

## CHALLENGE ACTIVITY/ACTIVIDAD AVANZADA

**Critical Thinking: Draw Conclusions/Pensamiento crítico: Sacar conclusiones** Many years from now, an archaeologist discovers your house with nothing in it but old furniture, appliances, tools, and bits of clothing. Write a short essay describing some conclusions the archaeologist might draw from these artifacts./Dentro de muchos años, un arqueólogo descubre tu casa y solo encuentra muebles viejos, electrodomésticos, herramientas y algo de ropa. Escribe un ensayo breve en el que describas algunas de las conclusiones que el arqueólogo podría sacar a partir de esos artefactos.

Lesson/Lección 1, *continued*/*continuación*

| ancestor/ antepasado | hominid/ homínido | hunter-gatherers/ cazadores y recolectores | Paleolithic Era/ el Paleolítico |
| prehistory/ prehistoria | society/ sociedad | tool/herramienta | |

**DIRECTIONS/INSTRUCCIONES** Write a word or short phrase that has the same meaning as the term given./Escribe una palabra o frase breve que tenga el mismo significado que el término dado.

1. ancestor/antepasado _____

2. hominid/homínido _____

3. hunter-gatherers/cazadores y recolectores _____

4. Paleolithic Era/el Paleolítico _____

5. prehistory/prehistoria _____

6. society/sociedad _____

7. tool/herramienta _____

**DIRECTIONS/INSTRUCCIONES** Choose five of the vocabulary words from the word bank. Use these words to write a summary of what you learned in the lesson./Escoge cinco de las palabras de vocabulario del banco de palabras. Úsalas para escribir un resumen de lo que aprendiste en la lección.

_____

_____

_____

_____

_____

_____

Name/Nombre_____ Class/Clase_____ Date/Fecha_____

# The Stone Ages and Early Cultures/Las Edades de Piedra y las primeras culturas

### Lesson/Lección 2

**MAIN IDEAS/IDEAS PRINCIPALES**

1. People moved out of Africa as the earth's climates changed./Los seres humanos se fueron de África debido a los cambios climáticos que tuvieron lugar en la Tierra.

2. People adapted to new environments by making clothing and new types of tools./Los seres humanos se adaptaron a los nuevos ambientes fabricando vestimentas y nuevos tipos de herramientas.

## Key Terms and People/Personas y palabras clave

**migrate/migrar** move to a new place/trasladarse a otro lugar

**ice ages/Edades de Hielo** long periods of freezing weather/largos períodos de clima helado

**land bridge/puente terrestre** a strip of land connecting two continents/franja de tierra que conecta dos continentes

**Mesolithic Era/el Mesolítico** the middle part of the Stone Age, from about 10,000 years ago to about 5,000 years ago/etapa intermedia de la Edad de Piedra, que abarcó desde hace unos 10,000 años hasta hace unos 5,000 años

## Lesson Summary/Resumen de la lección

**PEOPLE MOVE OUT OF AFRICA/EL SER HUMANO SE VA DE ÁFRICA**

About 1.6 million years ago, many places around the world began to experience **ice ages,** or long periods of freezing weather. In response to these changes, many hominids and early humans **migrated** from Africa to Asia and eventually spread to India, China, Southeast Asia, and Europe. The ice ages ended about 10,000 years ago./Hace aproximadamente 1.6 millones de años, muchos lugares del mundo comenzaron a entrar en las **Edades de Hielo,** o largos períodos de clima helado. En respuesta a esos cambios, muchos de los homínidos y de los primeros seres humanos **migraron** de África a Asia y, con el tiempo, llegaron a la India, China, el sudeste asiático y Europa. Las Edades de Hielo terminaron hace aproximadamente 10,000 años.

During the ice ages, huge sheets of ice formed from ocean water covered much of the Earth's land. These ice sheets caused ocean levels to be lower than they are now. Many areas that are now under water were dry land then. Scientists think that in some places the ocean level dropped and exposed **land bridges** between continents./Durante las Edades de Hielo, gigantescas capas de hielo formadas con el agua de los océanos cubrían gran parte de la superficie terrestre. Esas capas de hielo hacían que los niveles de agua de los océanos fueran más bajos de lo que son en la actualidad. Muchas áreas que actualmente se encuentran bajo agua eran tierra seca en aquel entonces. Los científicos creen que, en algunos lugares, el nivel de los océanos bajó y dejó al descubierto **puentes terrestres** entre los continentes.

Scientists also agree that it took people hundreds of thousands of years to migrate around the world. First, early hominids migrated from Africa to Asia. Then these ancestors of modern humans went to Southeast Asia and Europe./Los científicos también creen que los seres humanos tardaron cientos de miles de años en migrar por todo el mundo. Primero, los antiguos homínidos migraron de África a Asia. Luego, estos antepasados de los seres humanos modernos se trasladaron al sudeste asiático y Europa.

Humans began to migrate around 100,000 years ago. They moved from East Africa to southern Africa and Asia. Most scholars believe the first people used a land bridge to cross from Asia to North America. They also went to Australia, but scientists are not sure how they were able to get there. Early humans often migrated because the climate changed, and they needed to find new food sources./Los seres humanos comenzaron a migrar hace unos 100,000 años. Se trasladaron de África oriental al sur de África y a Asia. La

---

**What is one thing that happened to Earth during the ice ages?/¿Cuál es una de las cosas que sucedieron en la Tierra durante las Edades de Hielo?**

_____
_____
_____
_____
_____
_____
_____
_____

---

**How long did it take for Stone Age people to migrate around the world?/¿Cuánto tardaron los seres humanos de la Edad de Piedra en migrar por todo el mundo?**

_____
_____

---

**Why did early humans often migrate?/¿Por qué los primeros seres humanos a menudo migraban?**

_____
_____
_____

mayoría de los expertos creen que los primeros
pobladores usaron un puente de tierra para cruzar
de Asia a América del Norte. También llegaron a
Australia, pero los científicos no saben con certeza
cómo lo hicieron. Los primeros seres humanos
migraban a menudo porque el clima cambiaba y
necesitaban hallar nuevas fuentes de alimento.

## PEOPLE ADAPT TO NEW ENVIRONMENTS/ EL SER HUMANO SE ADAPTA A LOS NUEVOS AMBIENTES

Early people had to learn to adapt to new
environments. The places to which they migrated
were often much colder than the places they
left and often had new plants and animals./Los
primeros seres humanos tuvieron que aprender
a adaptarse a los nuevos ambientes. Los lugares
a los que migraban solían ser mucho más fríos
que los lugares de los que provenían y solían
tener plantas y animales diferentes.

To keep warm, they learned to sew animal
skins together to make clothing. At first they
took shelter in caves. When they moved to areas
with no caves, they built their own shelters. At
first these shelters were pits in the ground with
roofs of branches and leaves. Later, people
learned to build more permanent structures with
wood, stone, clay, or other materials, even bones
from large animals such as mammoths./Para
abrigarse, aprendieron a coser las pieles de los
animales para hacer vestimentas. Al principio, se
refugiaban en cuevas. Cuando se trasladaban a
lugares donde no había cuevas, construían sus
propios refugios. Al principio, esos refugios eran
pozos en el suelo con techos de ramas y hojas.
Más adelante, los seres humanos aprendieron a
construir estructuras más permanentes con
madera, piedra, arcilla y otros materiales, incluso
huesos de animales grandes como el mamut.

> **What materials did early humans use to build more permanent structures?/ ¿Qué materiales usaron los primeros seres humanos para construir estructuras más permanentes?**
>
> _____
>
> _____

People also began to make new types of tools.
These tools were smaller and more complex than
tools from the Paleolithic Era. They defined the
**Mesolithic** (me-zuh-LI-thik) **Era,** which began
more than 10,000 years ago and lasted to about
5,000 years ago in some places. These new tools
included hooks and spears for fishing, and bows
and arrows for hunting./Los seres humanos
también comenzaron a fabricar nuevos tipos
de herramientas, más pequeñas y complejas
que las del Paleolítico. Esas herramientas
definieron al **Mesolítico,** que comenzó hace
más de 10,000 años y en algunos lugares duró
hasta hace unos 5,000 años. Entre las nuevas
herramientas había anzuelos y lanzas para
pescar, así como arcos y flechas para cazar.

People in the Mesolithic Era also developed
new technologies to improve their lives. For
example, they learned how to make pots from
clay and how to hollow out logs to make canoes./
Los seres humanos del Mesolítico también
desarrollaron nuevas tecnologías para mejorar
su calidad de vida. Por ejemplo, aprendieron
a hacer vasijas de arcilla y a ahuecar troncos
para hacer canoas.

> **How did early humans make canoes?/¿Cómo fabricaban canoas los primeros seres humanos?**
> _____
> _____

## CHALLENGE ACTIVITY/ACTIVIDAD AVANZADA
**Critical Thinking: Design/Pensamiento crítico:
Diseñar** Draw a building plan with written
instructions for a Mesolithic dwelling./Dibuja
el plano de una vivienda del Mesolítico e incluye
indicaciones escritas.

| ice ages/las Edades de Hielo | land bridge/ puente terrestre | Mesolithic Era/ el Mesolítico | migrate/migrar |

**DIRECTIONS/INSTRUCCIONES** Read each sentence and fill in the blank with the word from the word bank that best completes the sentence./Lee cada oración y escribe en el espacio en blanco la palabra del banco de palabras que mejor la completa.

1. During the _____, people made tools that were smaller and more complex than those made during the Old Stone Age./Durante _____, los seres humanos fabricaron herramientas más pequeñas y complejas que las de la Antigua Edad de Piedra.

2. During the _____, huge sheets of ice were formed from ocean water, so ocean levels were lower than they are now./Durante _____, el agua de los océanos formó gigantescas capas de hielo, por lo que los niveles de los océanos eran más bajos que en la actualidad.

3. A _____ is a strip of land that connects two continents./ Un _____ es una franja de tierra que conecta dos continentes.

4. In response to the Earth's changing climate and geography, people began to _____./Los seres humanos comenzaron a _____ en respuesta a los cambios climáticos y geográficos de la Tierra.

**DIRECTIONS/INSTRUCCIONES** Write three adjectives or descriptive phrases that describe the term./Escribe tres adjetivos o frases descriptivas que describan el término.

5. land bridge/puente terrestre _____

_____

6. migrate/migrar _____

_____

## The Stone Ages and Early Cultures/Las Edades de Piedra y las primeras culturas

**MAIN IDEAS/IDEAS PRINCIPALES**
1. The first farmers learned to grow plants and raise animals in the New Stone Age./Durante la Nueva Edad de Piedra, los primeros agricultores aprendieron a cultivar plantas y a criar animales.
2. Farming changed societies and the way people lived./La agricultura transformó las sociedades y la forma de vida de las personas.

## Key Terms and People/Personas y palabras clave

**Neolithic Era/el Neolítico** the New Stone Age, which began about 10,000 years ago in Southwest Asia and much later in other places/la Nueva Edad de Piedra, que comenzó hace unos 10,000 años en el sudoeste asiático y mucho más tarde en otros lugares

**domestication/domesticación** the process of changing plants or animals to make them more useful to humans/el proceso de modificar las plantas o los animales para que sean más útiles para los seres humanos

**agriculture/agricultura** the development of farming from the domestication of plants/la producción de cultivos a partir de la domesticación de las plantas

**megaliths/megalitos** huge stones used as monuments or sites for religious gatherings/enormes piedras utilizadas como monumentos o sitios para reuniones religiosas

## Lesson Summary/Resumen de la lección
### THE FIRST FARMERS/LOS PRIMEROS AGRICULTORES

A warming trend brought an end to the ice ages, and new plants began to grow in some areas. Throughout Southwest Asia, people came to depend on wild barley and wheat for food. People soon learned that they could plant seeds to grow their own crops. This shift from food gathering to food producing defined the **Neolithic** (nee-uh-LI-thik) **Era.**/La temperatura empezó a subir y puso fin a las Edades de Hielo. En algunos lugares, empezaron a crecer plantas nuevas. En el suroeste asiático, las personas comenzaron a depender de la cebada y el trigo silvestres como forma de

> **What change defined a shift during the Neolithic Era?/¿Qué cambio definió el Neolítico?**
>
> _____
> _____
> _____

alimentación. Pronto descubrieron que podían plantar semillas para producir sus propios cultivos. Ese cambio de la recolección a la producción de alimentos definió al **Neolítico.**

This **domestication** of plants led to the development of **agriculture,** or farming. The first farmers also learned to domesticate animals. Instead of following wild herds, they could now keep sheep and goats for milk, food, and wool. People could also use large animals like cattle to carry loads or to pull large tools used in farming. Domestication greatly improved people's chances of surviving./La **domesticación** de las plantas condujo al desarrollo de la **agricultura,** o producción de cultivos. Los primeros agricultores también aprendieron a domesticar animales. En vez de seguir manadas salvajes, ahora podían criar ovejas y cabras para obtener leche, alimento y lana. También podían usar animales grandes, como el ganado, para transportar cargas o arrastrar las grandes herramientas que utilizaban en las tareas agrícolas. La domesticación mejoró enormemente las probabilidades de supervivencia del ser humano.

| What were three tasks for which early people used domesticated animals?/ ¿Para qué tres tareas utilizaban los primeros seres humanos a los animales domesticados? |
| --- |
| _____ |
| _____ |
| _____ |
| _____ |

## FARMING CHANGES SOCIETIES/LA AGRICULTURA TRANSFORMA LAS SOCIEDADES

With survival more certain, people could focus on activities other than finding food. People began to make clothing from plant fibers, wool, and animal skins. As early farmers learned to control their own food production and to make better shelters and clothing, populations grew. People began to build permanent settlements. In some areas, farming communities developed into towns./Con la supervivencia más asegurada, las personas pudieron concentrarse en actividades que no fueran la constante búsqueda de

| What materials were first used by Neolithic people to make clothing?/¿Qué materiales se usaron por primera vez en el Neolítico para hacer ropa? |
| --- |
| _____ |
| _____ |
| _____ |

alimentos. Comenzaron a fabricar prendas
con fibras vegetales, lana y pieles de animales.
A medida que los primeros agricultores
aprendían a controlar su propia producción
de alimentos y a fabricar mejores refugios y
ropa, las poblaciones fueron creciendo.
Comenzaron a construirse asentamientos
permanentes. En algunos lugares, las
comunidades agrícolas crecieron hasta
convertirse en aldeas.

Neolithic communities like Çatal Hüyük and
Jericho had traditional economies. People made
decisions based on customs and beliefs passed
down from generation to generation. They
decided things like which crops to plant and how
to distribute them./Las comunidades neolíticas
como Çatal Hüyük y Jericó tenían economías
tradicionales. Las personas tomaban decisiones
basándose en costumbres y creencias que se
transmitían de generación en generación.
Decidían cuestiones tales como qué cultivos
plantar y cómo distribuirlos.

Farmers stored food in large pits because they
began to have an extra amount of it. This surplus
made barter possible. People would barter when
they would trade goods and services for other
goods and services./Los agricultores comenzaron
a almacenar alimentos en grandes pozos debido
a que empezaron a producir más de lo necesario.
Ese excedente posibilitó el trueque, mediante el
cual las personas intercambiaban bienes y
servicios por otros bienes y servicios.

Some groups gathered to perform religious
ceremonies around huge stone monuments called
**megaliths.** These people probably believed in gods
and goddesses associated with air, water, fire,
earth, and animals. Scholars also believe that

| What would people do during barter?/¿En qué consistía el trueque? |
| --- |
| _____ |
| _____ |
| _____ |
| _____ |

some prehistoric people prayed to their ancestors or buried their bones in the floors of homes./ Algunos grupos se reunían para celebrar ceremonias religiosas en torno a enormes monumentos de piedra llamados **megalitos.** Es probable que esas personas creyeran en dioses y diosas relacionados con el aire, el agua, el fuego, la tierra y los animales. Los expertos también sostienen que algunos pueblos prehistóricos rezaban a sus antepasados o enterraban sus huesos bajo el suelo de sus hogares.

Archaeologists have found clues about prehistoric governments. Çatal Hüyük did not appear to have a leader, but men and women seemed to have been treated equally. Jericho had a wall around it. This likely means the city had a government. A person or group probably had to give directions for the wall./Los arqueólogos han hallado pistas sobre la existencia de gobiernos prehistóricos. Çatal Hüyük no parece haber tenido un líder, pero se cree que los hombres y las mujeres recibían el mismo trato. Jericó estaba amurallada, lo que posiblemente significa que la ciudad tenía un gobierno: es probable que una persona o un grupo haya dado instrucciones para la construcción del muro.

> What clues have given archaeologists information about the governments of Çatal Hüyük and Jericho?/ ¿Qué pistas han dado información a los arqueólogos sobre el gobierno en Çatal Hüyük y Jericó?
>
> _____
> _____
> _____
> _____
> _____

## CHALLENGE ACTIVITY/ACTIVIDAD AVANZADA

**Critical Thinking: Evaluate/Pensamiento crítico: Evaluar** Use the Internet or a library to research theories about how the megaliths at Stonehenge in England were built. Then write your own theory./Investiga en Internet o en una biblioteca teorías sobre cómo se construyeron los megalitos de Stonehenge, Inglaterra. Luego, escribe tu propia teoría al respecto.

**DIRECTIONS/INSTRUCCIONES** On the line provided before each
statement, write **T** if a statement is true and **F** if a statement is false.
If the statement is false, write the correct term on the line after each
sentence that makes the sentence a true statement./En la línea que
precede a cada enunciado, escribe **V** si el enunciado es verdadero
y **F** si es falso. Si el enunciado es falso, escribe en la línea que sigue
a la oración el término correcto que lo hace verdadero.

_____ 1. <u>Mammoths</u> are large stones that were used in religious ceremonies as
monuments./<u>Los mamuts</u> son grandes piedras que se utilizaban como
monumentos en las ceremonias religiosas.

_____

_____ 2. <u>Domestication</u> is the process of changing plants and animals to make
them more useful to humans./<u>La domesticación</u> es el proceso de
modificar las plantas y los animales para que sean más útiles para los
seres humanos.

_____

_____ 3. During the <u>Neolithic Era</u>, or New Stone Age, people planted seeds
to grow their own crops and depended on wild barley and wheat for
food./Durante <u>el Neolítico</u>, o la Nueva Edad de Piedra, las personas
plantaban semillas para producir sus propios cultivos y dependían de
la cebada y el trigo silvestres como forma de alimentación.

_____

_____ 4. With the development of <u>agriculture</u>, or farming, people had to decide
things like which crops to plant and how to distribute them./Con el
desarrollo de <u>la agricultura</u>, o producción de cultivos, las personas
tuvieron que comenzar a decidir cuestiones tales como qué cultivos
plantar y cómo distribuirlos.

_____

## The Fertile Crescent, Mesopotamia, and the Persian Empire/La Media Luna Fértil, Mesopotamia y el Imperio persa

### Lesson/Lección 1

**MAIN IDEAS/IDEAS PRINCIPALES**

1. The rivers of Southwest Asia supported the growth of civilization./Los ríos del suroeste asiático fueron la base para el crecimiento de la civilización.

2. New farming techniques led to the growth of cities./Las nuevas técnicas agrícolas condujeron al crecimiento de las ciudades.

## Key Terms and People/Personas y palabras clave

**Fertile Crescent/Media Luna Fértil** a large arc of rich farmland extending from the Persian Gulf to the Mediterranean Sea/amplio arco de tierras ricas para el cultivo que se extiende desde el golfo Pérsico hasta el mar Mediterráneo

**silt/cieno** a mix of rich soil and small rocks/mezcla de suelo fértil y rocas pequeñas

**civilization/civilización** an organized group of people (society) that live in an area and work to improve their way of life/grupo organizado de personas (sociedad) que habitan en una misma región y buscan mejorar su modo de vida

**irrigation/irrigación** a way of supplying water to an area of land/modo de suministrar agua a un terreno

**canals/canales** human-made waterways/vías acuáticas construidas por el ser humano

**surplus/excedente** more of something than is needed/más de lo que se necesita de una cosa

**division of labor/división del trabajo** an arrangement in which people specialize in specific tasks/sistema de organización en el que las personas se especializan en tareas específicas

## Lesson Summary/Resumen de la lección

### RIVERS SUPPORT THE GROWTH OF CIVILIZATION/LOS RÍOS SON LA BASE PARA EL CRECIMIENTO DE LA CIVILIZACIÓN

Early peoples settled where crops would grow. Crops usually grew well near rivers, where water was available and regular floods made the soil rich./Los primeros pueblos se asentaban donde crecían los cultivos. Por lo general, estos prosperaban cerca de los ríos, donde había agua

disponible y las frecuentes inundaciones
enriquecían el suelo.

Mesopotamia, part of the region known as the
**Fertile Crescent** in Southwest Asia, lay between
the Tigris and Euphrates rivers. Every year,
floods on the rivers brought **silt.** The fertile silt
made the land ideal for farming./Mesopotamia,
parte de la región conocida como la **Media Luna
Fértil,** se extendía entre los ríos Tigris y Éufrates,
en el suroeste asiático. Todos los años, las
inundaciones provocadas por los ríos traían
**cieno.** El cieno fértil hacía que el terreno fuera
ideal para la agricultura.

Hunter-gatherer groups first settled in
Mesopotamia more than 12,000 years ago. Over
time, these people learned how to work together
to control floods. They planted crops and grew
their own food./Hace más de 12,000 años, se
asentaron en Mesopotamia los primeros grupos
de cazadores y recolectores. Con el tiempo,
aprendieron a trabajar en conjunto para
controlar las inundaciones. Allí sembraban y
cultivaban sus propios alimentos.

Farm settlements formed in Mesopotamia as
early as 7000 BC. Farmers grew wheat, barley,
and other grains. Livestock, birds, and fish
were also sources of food. Plentiful food led
to population growth and villages formed.
Eventually, these early villages developed into
the world's first **civilization.**/Ya hacia 7000 a. C.
habían comenzado a surgir en Mesopotamia
los primeros asentamientos agrícolas. Los
agricultores cultivaban trigo, cebada y otros
cereales. El ganado, las aves y los peces también
eran fuentes de alimento. La abundancia de
alimento permitió que las poblaciones crecieran
y se formaron aldeas. Con el tiempo, aquellas
primeras aldeas se convirtieron en la primera
**civilización** del mundo.

> *Mesopotamia* means
> "between the rivers" in
> Greek. To which two rivers
> does the name of the
> region refer?/ En griego,
> *Mesopotamia* significa
> "entre los ríos". ¿A qué
> dos ríos se refiere el
> nombre de la región?
>
> _____
>
> _____

> List two grains grown by
> Mesopotamian farmers./
> Menciona dos tipos de
> cereales cultivados por
> los agricultores de
> Mesopotamia.
>
> _____
>
> _____

## FARMING AND CITIES/AGRICULTURA Y CIUDADES

Early farmers faced the challenge of learning how to control the flow of river water to their fields in both rainy and dry seasons. Flooding destroyed crops, killed livestock, and washed away homes. When water levels were too low, crops dried up./Los primeros agricultores enfrentaron el desafío de aprender a controlar la corriente del agua que llegaba de los ríos hasta sus campos, tanto en las temporadas de lluvia como en las de sequía. Las inundaciones destruían los cultivos, mataban el ganado y arrasaban las casas. Y cuando los niveles de agua eran demasiado bajos, los cultivos se secaban.

> Underline the sentence that lists some of the problems caused by flooding./Subraya la oración en la que se mencionan algunos de los problemas causados por las inundaciones.

To solve their problems, Mesopotamians used **irrigation.** They dug out large storage basins to hold water supplies. Then they dug **canals** that connected these basins to a network of ditches. These ditches brought water to the fields and watered grazing areas for cattle and sheep./Para resolver estos problemas, los habitantes de Mesopotamia recurrieron a la **irrigación.** Cavaron grandes fosas para almacenar agua. Luego cavaron **canales** que conectaban esas fosas con una red de acequias. Las acequias llevaban el agua a los campos y regaban las áreas de pastoreo del ganado.

> From where did the water collected in the storage basins come?/¿De dónde provenía el agua que se almacenaba en las fosas?
> _____
> _____

Because irrigation made farmers more productive, they produced a **surplus.** Some people became free to do other jobs. For the first time, people became crafts persons, religious leaders, and government workers. A **division of labor** developed./Con la irrigación, aumentó la productividad de los agricultores y se generó un **excedente.** Eso permitió que algunas personas quedaran libres para hacer otras tareas. Por primera vez, hubo artesanos, líderes religiosos y funcionarios gubernamentales. Así surgió la **división del trabajo.**

Mesopotamian settlements grew in size and complexity. Most people continued to work in farming jobs. However, cities became important places. People traded goods in cities. Cities became the political, religious, cultural, and economic centers of Mesopotamian civilization./ Los asentamientos de Mesopotamia crecieron en tamaño y complejidad. La mayoría de las personas continuaron dedicándose a tareas agrícolas. Sin embargo, las ciudades se convirtieron en lugares importantes donde se intercambiaban bienes. Las ciudades se convirtieron en los centros políticos, religiosos, culturales y económicos de la civilización mesopotámica.

> **Which places in Mesopotamia became the centers of civilization?/ ¿Qué lugares de Mesopotamia se convirtieron en los centros de la civilización?**
>
> _____
>
> _____

## CHALLENGE ACTIVITY/ACTIVIDAD AVANZADA

**Critical Thinking: Develop/Pensamiento crítico: Desarrollar** Write a proposal for an irrigation system that will divert floodwaters and benefit riverbank farmers./Escribe una propuesta para montar un sistema de irrigación que desvíe el agua de las crecidas y beneficie a los agricultores asentados en las orillas de los ríos.

| | | |
|---|---|---|
| canals/canales | civilization/civilización | division of labor/<br>división del trabajo |
| Fertile Crescent/Media<br>Luna Fértil | irrigation/irrigación | silt/cieno |
| | surplus/excedente | |

**DIRECTIONS/INSTRUCCIONES** Use the vocabulary terms in the word bank to write how Mesopotamia came to have cities./ Usa el vocabulario del banco de palabras para escribir acerca de cómo surgieron las ciudades en Mesopotamia.

_____

_____

_____

_____

_____

_____

**DIRECTIONS/INSTRUCCIONES** Look at each set of three vocabulary terms following each number. On the line provided, write the letter of the term that does not relate to the others./Observa cada conjunto de tres términos de vocabulario que aparece después de cada número. En el espacio en blanco, escribe la letra del término que no tiene relación con los demás.

_____ 1. a. irrigation/irrigación    b. silt/cieno    c. canal/canal

_____ 2. a. surplus/excedente    b. division of labor/<br>división del trabajo    c. Fertile Crescent/<br>Media Luna<br>Fértil

_____ 3. a. Fertile Crescent/<br>Media Luna Fértil    b. civilization/<br>civilización    c. division of labor/<br>división del<br>trabajo

# The Fertile Crescent, Mesopotamia, and the Persian Empire/La Media Luna Fértil, Mesopotamia y el Imperio persa

### Lesson/Lección 2

**MAIN IDEAS/IDEAS PRINCIPALES**

1. The Sumerians created the world's first advanced society./Los sumerios crearon la primera sociedad avanzada del mundo.
2. Religion played a major role in Sumerian society./La religión desempeñó un rol importante en la sociedad sumeria.
3. The Sumerians invented the world's first writing system./Los sumerios inventaron el primer sistema de escritura del mundo.
4. Technical advances and inventions changed Sumerian lives./Los adelantos técnicos y los inventos cambiaron la vida de los sumerios.
5. Many types of art developed in Sumer./En Sumeria se desarrollaron muchos tipos de arte.

## Key Terms and People/Personas y palabras clave

**rural/rural** having to do with the countryside/relacionado con el campo

**urban/urbano** having to do with the city/relacionado con la ciudad

**city-state/ciudad estado** a political unit consisting of a city and the surrounding countryside/unidad política formada por una ciudad y las tierras de los alrededores

**Gilgamesh/Gilgamesh** an Uruk king who became a legend in Sumerian literature/ rey de Uruk que se convirtió en una leyenda de la literatura sumeria

**Sargon/Sargón** Akkadian emperor who defeated Sumer and built the world's first empire/emperador acadio que venció a Sumeria y fundó el primer imperio

**empire/imperio** land with different territories and peoples under a single rule/ región que reúne diferentes territorios y pueblos bajo un mismo gobierno

**polytheism/politeísmo** the worship of many gods/veneración de muchos dioses

**priests/sacerdotes** people who performed religious ceremonies/personas que llevaban a cabo las ceremonias religiosas

**social hierarchy/jerarquía social** a division of society by rank or class/división de la sociedad en rangos o clases

**cuneiform/cuneiforme** world's first system of writing/primer sistema de escritura

**pictographs/pictogramas** picture symbols/símbolos representados con dibujos

**scribe/escriba** writer and record keeper/copista y encargado de llevar registros

**epics/epopeyas** long poems that tell the stories of heroes/poemas largos que narran las hazañas de héroes

**architecture/arquitectura** the science of building/la ciencia de la construcción

**ziggurat/zigurat** a pyramid-shaped temple tower/templo con forma de pirámide

## Lesson Summary/Resumen de la lección
### AN ADVANCED SOCIETY/UNA SOCIEDAD AVANZADA

In southern Mesopotamia in about 3000 BC, people known as the Sumerians (soo-MER-ee-unz) created an advanced society. Most people in Sumer (soo-muhr) lived in **rural** areas, but they were governed from **urban,** or city, areas. The size of these **city-states** depended on its military strength. Stronger city-states controlled larger areas. Individual city-states gained and lost power over time. For 1,000 years, the city-states of Uruk and Ur fought for power. One Uruk king, **Gilgamesh,** became a legend in Sumerian literature./En el sur de Mesopotamia, hacia el año 3000 a. C., el pueblo conocido como los sumerios creó una sociedad avanzada. La mayoría de los habitantes de Sumeria vivían en zonas **rurales,** pero sus gobernantes estaban en las zonas **urbanas,** es decir, en las ciudades. El tamaño de las **ciudades estado** dependía de su poderío militar: las ciudades estado más poderosas controlaban las regiones más grandes. Las diferentes ciudades estado fueron ganando y perdiendo poder con el paso del tiempo. Durante 1,000 años, las ciudades estado de Uruk y Ur se disputaron el poder. Un rey de Uruk, **Gilgamesh,** se convirtió en una leyenda de la literatura sumeria.

Around 2300 BC, **Sargon** was the leader of the Akkadians (uh-KAY-dee-uhns), a people who lived to the north of Sumer. Sargon built a large army and defeated all the city-states of Sumer as well as all of northern Mesopotamia. He established the world's first **empire.** It stretched from the Persian Gulf to the Mediterranean Sea and lasted about 150 years./Alrededor del año 2300 a. C., **Sargón** era el líder de los acadios, un pueblo que vivía al norte de Sumeria. Sargón organizó un ejército de grandes dimensiones,

> Why do you think governments are usually located in cities?/¿Por qué crees que los gobiernos suelen estar ubicados en las ciudades?
>
> _____
> _____
> _____
> _____

venció a todas las ciudades estado de Sumeria y se apoderó también de todo el norte de Mesopotamia. Así fundó el primer **imperio** del mundo, que se extendía desde el golfo Pérsico hasta el mar Mediterráneo y que duró aproximadamente 150 años.

## RELIGION SHAPES SOCIETY/LA RELIGIÓN INFLUYE EN LA SOCIEDAD

Religion played an important role in nearly every aspect of Sumerian public and private life. Sumerians practiced **polytheism,** the worship of many gods. They believed that their gods had enormous powers bringing either illness or good health and wealth. Every area of life depended on pleasing the gods. Each city-state had one god as its special protector. People relied on **priests** to help them gain the gods' favor. Priests interpreted the wishes of the gods and made offerings to them./La religión desempeñó un papel importante en casi todos los aspectos de la vida pública y privada de los sumerios. Los sumerios practicaban el **politeísmo,** es decir, la veneración de muchos dioses. Creían que sus dioses tenían enormes poderes, que les permitían provocar enfermedades o traer buena salud y riqueza. Todos los aspectos de la vida se centraban en complacer a los dioses. Cada ciudad estado tenía un dios protector. Las personas recurrían a los **sacerdotes** para obtener el favor de los dioses. Los sacerdotes interpretaban los deseos de los dioses y les hacían ofrendas.

A **social hierarchy** developed in Sumerian city-states. Kings were at the top. Priests and nobles followed. The middle ranks included skilled craftspeople, merchants, and traders. Traders had a great impact as they traded grain for precious metals and lumber. Farmers and laborers made up the large working class. Slaves were at the bottom

> What type of religion did the Sumerians practice?/ ¿Qué tipo de religión practicaban los sumerios?
>
> _____

> In Sumerian religious practice, what did priests do to try to please the gods?/En la práctica religiosa sumeria, ¿qué hacían los sacerdotes para intentar complacer a los dioses?
>
> _____

> Which two groups formed the Sumerian upper classes?/¿Cuáles eran los dos grupos que formaban las clases altas sumerias?
>
> _____
>
> _____

of the social order. Most women were limited to the home and raising children; some upper-class women were educated and even became priestesses./En las ciudades estado sumerias se desarrolló una **jerarquía social.** Los reyes se encontraban en la parte superior. Les seguían los sacerdotes y los nobles. En los rangos intermedios estaban los artesanos especializados, los mercaderes y los comerciantes. Estos últimos tenían una gran influencia, ya que intercambiaban granos por metales preciosos y madera. Los agricultores y los obreros constituían la extensa clase trabajadora. Los esclavos estaban en el escalón más bajo del orden social. La mayoría de las mujeres estaban confinadas al hogar y a la crianza de los hijos. Sin embargo, algunas mujeres de las clases altas recibían educación e incluso llegaban a convertirse en sacerdotisas.

## THE INVENTION OF WRITING/INVENCIÓN DE LA ESCRITURA

The Sumerians developed **cuneiform** (kyoo-NEE-uh-fohrm), the world's first system of writing. They used sharp tools to make symbols on clay tablets. Earlier writing was **pictographs,** or picture symbols. In cuneiform, symbols could also be syllables or basic parts of words. At first, Sumerian **scribes** used cuneiform for business records. Later, they wrote works on history, law, math, and even literature. Some were **epics,** long poems about heroes./Los sumerios desarrollaron la escritura **cuneiforme,** el primer sistema de escritura del mundo. Usaban instrumentos afilados para marcar símbolos en tablillas de arcilla. Las formas de escritura anteriores consitían en símbolos representads con dibujos llamados **pictogramas.** En la escritura cuneiforme, los símbolos también podían ser sílabas o partes básicas de una palabra. En un principio, los **escribas** sumerios usaban la

> How was cuneiform different from pictographs?/ ¿En qué se diferenciaba la escritura cuneiforme de los pictogramas?
>
> _____
> _____
> _____
> _____

escritura cuneiforme para llevar registros comerciales. Luego, comenzaron a escribir sobre historia, derecho, matemáticas y hasta obras de literatura como las **epopeyas,** o poemas largos sobre héroes.

## ADVANCES AND INVENTIONS/ADELANTOS E INVENTOS

The Sumerians invented many important tools. They were the first to build wheeled vehicles like carts and wagons. They invented the ox-drawn plow and greatly improved farm production. They built sewers under city streets and learned to use bronze to make strong tools. They also excelled in math and science, developing the clock and calendar we use today./Los sumerios inventaron muchas herramientas importantes. Fueron los primeros en construir vehículos con ruedas, como carros y carretas. Inventaron el arado tirado por bueyes y mejoraron enormemente la producción agrícola. Construyeron alcantarillados debajo de las calles de las ciudades y aprendieron a usar el bronce para fabricar herramientas resistentes. También se destacaron en matemáticas y ciencias: desarrollaron el reloj y el calendario que usamos en la actualidad.

> **List three items the Sumerians invented./ Enumera tres cosas que inventaron los sumerios.**
>
> _____
> _____
> _____
> _____
> _____

## THE ARTS OF SUMER/ARTES EN SUMERIA

Sumerian remains reveal great skills in the fields of art, metalwork, and **architecture.** Artists and craftspeople created statues in clay as well as jewelry made from imported gold, silver and gems. A special art form, the cylinder seal, was a stone engraved with designs for rolling over wet clay to decorate objects or to "sign" documents. A pyramid-shaped **ziggurat** rose above each city. Most people lived in one-story houses with rooms arranged around a small courtyard./Los restos de la civilización sumeria revelan que los

> **Which Sumerian skill or invention do you think was most important to Sumerian society?/¿Qué habilidad o invento de los sumerios crees que fue el más importante para la sociedad sumeria?**
>
> _____
> _____
> _____

sumerios eran muy hábiles para el arte, el trabajo en metal y la **arquitectura.** Los artistas y los artesanos creaban estatuas de arcilla y joyería hecha con materiales importados, como oro, plata y gemas. Una forma de arte especial, el sello cilíndrico, consistía en una piedra grabada con diseños que se hacía rodar sobre arcilla húmeda para decorar objetos o para "firmar" documentos. Un **zigurat** en forma de pirámide se erguía sobre cada ciudad. La mayoría de las personas vivían en casas de una planta con habitaciones distribuidas alrededor de un patio pequeño.

## CHALLENGE ACTIVITY/ACTIVIDAD AVANZADA

**Critical Thinking: Compare/Pensamiento crítico: Comparar** Consider the invention of writing and of the wheel. As you go through a normal day, keep a list of the things you do that rely on one of these two inventions./Piensa en los inventos de la escritura y la rueda. Haz una lista de las cosas que haces en un día normal para las que necesitas alguno de estos dos inventos.

| | | | |
|---|---|---|---|
| architecture/ arquitectura | city-state/ una ciudad estado | cuneiform/ cuneiforme | empire/ imperio |
| epics/epopeyas | Gilgamesh/Gilgamesh | impact/impacto | pictographs/ pictogramas |
| polytheism/ politeísmo | priests/los sacerdotes | rural/rurales | Sargon/ Sargón |
| scribe/escriba | social hierarchy/ la jerarquía social | urban/urbano | ziggurat/ el zigurat |

**DIRECTIONS/INSTRUCCIONES** Read each sentence and fill in the blank with a word from the word bank that best completes the sentence./Lee cada oración y escribe en el espacio en blanco la palabra del banco de palabras que mejor la completa.

1. Land with different territories and peoples under a single rule is called an _____./Una región con diferentes territorios y pueblos reunidos bajo un mismo gobierno se llama _____.

2. _____ is a division of society by rank or class./_____ es la división de la sociedad en rangos o clases.

3. Countryside areas are considered to be _____./Las zonas de campo se denominan zonas _____.

4. _____ are people who perform religious ceremonies./_____ son las personas que celebran las ceremonias religiosas.

5. A _____ consists of a city, which is the political center, and the surrounding countryside./_____ consiste en una ciudad, que es el centro político, y las tierras de sus alrededores.

6. The practice of worshipping many gods is called _____./La práctica de venerar a muchos dioses se llama _____.

7. The temple's _____ was taller than all of the other buildings in the city./_____ del templo era más alto que los demás edificios de la ciudad.

8. Trade had a positive _____ on Sumerian society, allowing artists to be more creative./El comercio tuvo un _____ positivo en la sociedad sumeria, lo que les permitió a los artistas ser más creativos.

9. Scribes wrote on clay tablets using _____ in order to keep business records./Los escribas usaban la escritura _____ para llevar registro de las actividades comerciales en tabletas de arcilla.

## The Fertile Crescent, Mesopotamia, and the Persian Empire/La Media Luna Fértil, Mesopotamia y el Imperio persa

### Lesson/Lección 3

**MAIN IDEAS/IDEAS PRINCIPALES**
1. The Babylonians conquered Mesopotamia and created a code of law./ Los babilonios conquistaron Mesopotamia y crearon un código de leyes.
2. Invasions of Mesopotamia changed the region's culture./Las invasiones que sufrió Mesopotamia cambiaron la cultura de la región.

## Key Terms and People/Personas y palabras clave

**monarch/monarca** a ruler of a kingdom or empire/gobernante de un reino o imperio

**Hammurabi/Hammurabi** the city of Babylon's greatest monarch/ciudad del monarca más importante de Babilonia

**Hammurabi's Code/Código de Hammurabi** the earliest known written collection of laws, comprising 282 laws that dealt with almost every part of daily life/ la colección de leyes escritas más antigua que se conoce, compuesta de 282 leyes que trataban sobre casi todos los aspectos de la vida cotidiana

**chariot/carro de guerra** a wheeled, horse-drawn battle cart/carro de batalla con ruedas y tirado por caballos

**Nebuchadnezzar/Nabucodonosor** the Chaldean king who rebuilt Babylon/ rey caldeo que reconstruyó Babilonia

## Lesson Summary/Resumen de la lección

### THE BABYLONIANS CONQUER MESOPOTAMIA/ LOS BABILONIOS CONQUISTAN MESOPOTAMIA

By 1800 BC, a powerful government had arisen in Babylon, an old Sumerian city on the Euphrates. Babylon's greatest **monarch** (MAH-nark), **Hammurabi,** had conquered all of Mesopotamia./Hacia 1800 a. C., un poderoso gobierno había surgido en Babilonia, una antigua ciudad sumeria a orillas del Éufrates. El **monarca** más importante de Babilonia, **Hammurabi,** había conquistado toda Mesopotamia.

> On what river was the city of Babylon located?/ ¿A orillas de qué río se encontraba la ciudad de Babilonia?
>
> _____

Hammurabi was not just a brilliant war leader. During his 42-year reign, Hammurabi oversaw many building and irrigation projects, improved the tax collection system, and brought prosperity through increased trade. He is most famous, however, for **Hammurabi's Code,** the earliest known written collection of laws. It contained laws on everything from trade, loans, and theft to injury, marriage, and murder. Some of its ideas are still found in laws today. The code was important not only for how thorough it was, but also because it was written down for all to see./ Hammurabi no solo fue un brillante líder de guerra. Durante su gobierno de 42 años, supervisó muchos proyectos de construcción e irrigación, mejoró el sistema de recaudación de impuestos y generó prosperidad gracias al crecimiento del comercio. Sin embargo, es famoso principalmente por haber creado el **Código de Hammurabi,** la colección de leyes escritas más antigua que se conoce. El Código contenía leyes sobre todo tipo de aspectos, desde el comercio, los préstamos y los robos hasta los daños y perjuicios, el matrimonio y el asesinato. Algunos de sus conceptos aún se reflejan en las leyes actuales. El Código era importante no solo por lo exhaustivo que era, sino también porque estaba escrito, de modo que todos pudieran consultarlo.

> **Why do you think it is important for laws to be written down?/¿Por qué crees que es importante que las leyes estén escritas?**
>
> _____
> _____
> _____
> _____
> _____
> _____

## INVASIONS OF MESOPOTAMIA/INVASIONES A MESOPOTAMIA

Several other civilizations developed in and around the Fertile Crescent. As their armies battled one another for Mesopotamia's fertile land, control of the region passed from one empire to another. The Hittites of Asia Minor captured Babylon in 1595 BC with strong well-made iron weapons and the skillful use of the **chariot** on the battlefield. Soon the Hittite king was killed, and the Kassites captured Babylon and ruled for almost 400 years./Varias civilizaciones más surgieron en la Media Luna

Fértil y sus alrededores. Mientras los ejércitos se disputaban las fértiles tierras de Mesopotamia, el control de la región pasaba de un imperio a otro. Los hititas de Asia Menor conquistaron Babilonia en el año 1595 a. C. gracias a sus armas de hierro, resistentes y bien fabricadas, y a su hábil manejo del **carro de guerra** en el campo de batalla. Poco después, el rey hitita fue asesinado y los casitas conquistaron Babilonia y reinaron durante casi 400 años.

In the 1200s BC, the Assyrians briefly took over Babylon but were overrun by invaders. It took 300 years, but by around 900 BC they were the next group to conquer all of the Fertile Crescent and parts of Asia Minor and Egypt. The key to their success was their strong, fierce army. They also used iron weapons and chariots. They were well organized. Every soldier knew his role./En el siglo 13 a. C., los asirios dominaron Babilonia por un breve período, pero fueron invadidos por otros pueblos. Habrían de transcurrir 300 años más hasta que, hacia el año 900 a. C., se convirtieran en el siguiente pueblo en conquistar toda la Media Luna Fértil y partes de Asia Menor y Egipto. La clave de su éxito fue su imponente ejército. Además, los asirios usaban armas de hierro y carros de guerra, y estaban bien organizados. Cada soldado sabía qué papel debía desempeñar.

The Assyrians ruled from Nineveh (NI-nuh-vuh), a city in the north. They collected taxes, enforced laws, and raised troops through local leaders. The Assyrians also built roads to link distant parts of the empire. One Assyrian king built a royal library with tens of thousands of cuneiform tablets./La base del gobierno asirio se encontraba en Nínive, una ciudad del norte. Los asirios recaudaban impuestos, aplicaban leyes y reclutaban tropas a través de los líderes locales.

> **Name four groups that conquered all of Mesopotamia after the Babylonians./Menciona cuatro pueblos que conquistaron toda Mesopotamia después de los babilonios.**
>
> _____
>
> _____
>
> _____

También construyeron caminos para conectar partes distantes del imperio. Un rey asirio construyó una biblioteca real con decenas de miles de tablillas de escritura cuneiforme.

A series of wars started in 652 BC. In 612, BC the Chaldeans, a group from the Syrian Desert, conquered the Assyrians and set up a new empire of their own./En el año 652 a. C. se desató una serie de guerras. En 612 a. C., los caldeos, un pueblo proveniente del desierto sirio, conquistaron a los asirios y fundaron su propio imperio.

**Nebuchadnezzar** (neb-uh-kuhd-NEZ-uhr), the most famous Chaldean king, rebuilt Babylon into a beautiful city. According to legend, his grand palace featured the famous Hanging Gardens. The Chaldeans revived Sumerian culture and made notable advances in astronomy and mathematics./**Nabucodonosor,** el rey caldeo más famoso, reconstruyó Babilonia y la convirtió en una hermosa ciudad. Según cuenta la leyenda, en su gran palacio estaban los famosos jardines colgantes. Los caldeos revitalizaron la cultura sumeria e hicieron notables avances en astronomía y matemáticas.

> **Which older Mesopotamian civilization did the Chaldeans admire and study?/¿Qué civilización mesopotámica más antigua admiraban y estudiaban los caldeos?**
>
> _____
>
> _____

## CHALLENGE ACTIVITY/ACTIVIDAD AVANZADA

**Critical Thinking: Sequence/Pensamiento crítico: Hacer una secuencia** Make a timeline with approximate dates showing the various empires and invasions that characterized the history of Mesopotamia up to the time of the Chaldeans./ Haz una línea cronológica con fechas aproximadas que incluya los diferentes imperios y las distintas invasiones que caracterizaron la historia de Mesopotamia hasta la época de los caldeos.

| chariot/carro de guerra | Hammurabi/ Hammurabi | Hammurabi's Code/ Código de Hammurabi |
| monarch/monarca | Nebuchadnezzar/ Nabucodonosor | |

**DIRECTIONS/INSTRUCCIONES** Read each sentence and fill in
the blank with the word in the word pair that best completes
the sentence./Lee cada oración y escribe en el espacio en blanco
la palabra del par de palabras que mejor la completa.

1. _____ was the most famous Chaldean king who rebuilt
   Babylon into a beautiful city and whose palace was famous for the Hanging
   Gardens. **(Hammurabi/Nebuchadnezzar)**/_____ fue el
   rey caldeo más famoso que reconstruyó Babilonia y la convirtió en una
   hermosa ciudad, y cuyo palacio se hizo famoso por sus jardines colgantes..
   **(Hammurabi/Nabucodonosor)**

2. A powerful ruler of a kingdom or empire is known as a _____.
   **(monarch/chariot)**/El poderoso gobernante de un reino o imperio se
   denomina _____. **(monarca/carro de guerra)**

3. _____ was a brilliant military leader who brought
   all of Mesopotamia into the Babylonian Empire. **(Nebuchadnezzar/
   Hammurabi)**/_____ fue un brillante líder militar que
   reunió toda Mesopotamia bajo el Imperio babilónico. **(Nabucodonosor/
   Hammurabi)**

4. The Hittites skillfully used the _____, a wheeled, horse-
   drawn battle cart, to move quickly around the battlefield and fire arrows
   at their enemy. **(chariot/monarch)**/Los hititas eran diestros en el uso del
   _____, un vehículo de batalla con ruedas tirado por
   caballos, para moverse rápidamente por el campo de batalla y disparar
   flechas al enemigo. **(carro de guerra/monarca)**

5. _____ was famous for his code of laws, which dealt
   with almost every part of daily life and was written down for all to see.
   **(Nebuchadnezzar/Hammurabi)**/_____ se hizo famoso por
   su código de leyes, que trataban sobre casi todos los aspectos de la vida
   cotidiana y estaban escritas, de modo que todos pudieran consultarlas.
   **(Nabucodonosor/Hammurabi)**

**DIRECTIONS/INSTRUCCIONES** On the line provided before each statement, write **T** if a statement is true and **F** if a statement is false. If the statement is false, write the correct term on the line after each sentence that makes the sentence a true statement./En la línea que precede a cada enunciado, escribe **V** si el enunciado es verdadero y **F** si es falso. Si el enunciado es falso, escribe en la línea que sigue a la oración el término correcto que lo hace verdadero.

_____ 6. The Hittite soldiers used the <u>monarch</u> in their battles to capture Babylon./Los soldados hititas usaron <u>el monarca</u> en sus batallas para conquistar Babilonia.

_____

_____ 7. Under the laws of <u>Nebuchadnezzar</u>, injuring a rich man brought a greater penalty than injuring a poor man./Según las leyes de <u>Nabucodonosor</u>, causar daños o perjuicios a un hombre rico tenía una pena mayor que causar daños o perjucios a un hombre pobre.

_____

# The Fertile Crescent, Mesopotamia, and the Persian Empire/La Media Luna Fértil, Mesopotamia y el Imperio persa

## Lesson/Lección 4

**MAIN IDEAS/IDEAS PRINCIPALES**
1. The Phoenicians built a trading society in the eastern Mediterranean region./ Los fenicios desarrollaron una sociedad comercial en la región del este del Mediterráneo.
2. Phoenicians developed one of the world's first alphabets./Los fenicios crearon uno de los primeros alfabetos del mundo.

## Key Terms and People/Personas y palabras clave

**alphabet/alfabeto** a set of letters than can be combined to form written words/ conjunto de letras que pueden combinarse para formar palabras escritas

## Lesson Summary/Resumen de la lección

### PHOENICIA/FENICIA

A land known as Phoenicia, at the western end of the Fertile Crescent along the Mediterranean Sea, created a wealthy trading society. Major Phoenician city-states, including Byblos, Sidon, and Tyre, began as early as 3000 BC. At times controlled by Egyptians and Hittites, by 1200 BC the Phoenician cities formed a loose association of city-states, each ruled by its own king. Phoenicia was conquered by the Persian Empire in 538 BC./ En una tierra llamada Fenicia, situada en el extremo occidental de la Media Luna Fértil, a orillas del mar Mediterráneo, se creó una próspera sociedad cuya economía estaba basada en el comercio. Las principales ciudades estado fenicias, como Biblos, Sidón y Tiro, ya habían surgido aproximadamente en 3000 a. C. Hacia 1200 a. C. las ciudades fenicias, que en diferentes períodos habían estado bajo el control de los egipcios y los hititas, formaron una asociación poco definida de ciudades estado, cada una gobernada por su propio rey. Fenicia fue conquistada por el Imperio persa en el año 538 a. C.

> On what body of water were most Phoenician city-states located?/¿A orillas de qué masa de agua estaban ubicadas la mayoría de las ciudades estado fenicias?
>
> _____
>
> _____

Phoenicia had few resources other than cedar trees to trade. But its location was valuable. Its city-states connected Mediterranean Sea routes with land routes into the Fertile Crescent. Phoenician leaders looked to the sea to trade and expand their economy./Fenicia tenía pocos recursos comerciales más allá de los árboles de cedro, pero su ubicación era valiosa. Sus ciudades estado conectaban rutas del mar Mediterráneo con rutas terrestres de la Media Luna Fértil. Los líderes fenicios recurrieron al mar para comerciar y expandir su economía.

## PHOENICIAN TRADE AND CULTURE/COMERCIO Y CULTURA FENICIOS

Fleets of fast Phoenician trading ships sailed all around the Mediterranean Sea and even into the Atlantic Ocean through the Strait of Gibraltar. The Phoenicians built trade networks and founded new cities. Many became expert sailors, and they built ships with both sails and oars. They founded colonies along their trade routes. Carthage (KAHR-thij), on the northern coast of Africa, was the most famous and powerful city on the Mediterranean./Los fenicios navegaron por todo el mar Mediterráneo en sus flotas de rápidos barcos construidos para el comercio y hasta se adentraron en el océano Atlántico a través del estrecho de Gibraltar. Los fenicios tendieron redes comerciales y fundaron ciudades. Muchos se volvieron navegantes expertos y construyeron embarcaciones de vela y remo. Fundaron colonias a lo largo de sus rutas comerciales. Cartago, en la costa norte de África, fue la ciudad más famosa y poderosa del Mediterráneo.

Phoenicia grew wealthy from its trade. They traded silverwork, ivory carvings, and slaves. After the invention of glassblowing, beautiful glass objects were traded. Phoenicians made a

> Underline the sentence that explains what Phoenicians did with their resources./ Subraya la oración en la que se explica qué hacían los fenicios con sus recursos.

purple dye from a type of shellfish and traded cloth dyed with this purple color. Phoenicians used their goods to trade for resources that were not local to them, such as ivory, gold, copper, tin, and iron./Gracias al comercio, Fenicia prosperó. Los fenicios comerciaban con artículos de plata, esculturas de marfil y esclavos. Tras la invención del soplado de vidrio, también comerciaron con hermosos objetos de vidrio. Los fenicios hacían una tintura de color morado a partir de un tipo de molusco y comerciaban con telas teñidas de ese color. Intercambiaban sus productos por recursos de los que no disponían en su región, como marfil, oro, cobre, estaño y hierro.

The Phoenicians made several important contributions to early civilization. They created trade and communication routes throughout the Mediterranean area. Different cultures came to know one another better as they exchanged goods. To navigate the Mediterranean Sea they learned to use Polaris, the North Star, to make sure they were moving in the right direction./ Los fenicios hicieron muchas contribuciones importantes a los inicios de la civilización. Crearon rutas comerciales y de comunicación a lo largo de toda la región del Mediterráneo. Gracias al intercambio de bienes, diferentes culturas llegaron a conocerse mejor. Para navegar por el mar Mediterráneo, los fenicios aprendieron a usar la Estrella del Norte, o Polaris, para verificar que estuvieran avanzando en la dirección correcta.

The Phoenicians' most important achievement, however, was the development of one of the world's first alphabets. The Phoenician **alphabet** was a set of 22 letters that could be combined to form words. Instead of pictographs or cuneiform to communicate ideas, the alphabet made it easier to use writing to communicate big ideas.

> **Circle the three forms of writing used by early civilizations./Encierra en un círculo las tres formas de escritura que usaban las primeras civilizaciones.**

Later civilizations, including our own, have
benefited from this development. The English
and Spanish alphabets are based on the
Phoenician alphabet./Sin embargo, el logro más
importante de los fenicios fue el desarrollo de
uno de los primeros alfabetos del mundo. El
**alfabeto** fenicio era un conjunto de 22 letras que
podían combinarse para formar palabras. A
diferencia de los pictogramas o de la escritura
cuneiforme, el alfabeto facilitaba el uso de la
escritura para comunicar ideas importantes.
Civilizaciones posteriores, incluida la nuestra, se
han beneficiado de este desarrollo. El alfabeto
inglés y el español se basan en el alfabeto fenicio.

## CHALLENGE ACTIVITY/ACTIVIDAD AVANZADA
**Critical Thinking: Evaluate/Pensamiento crítico:
Evaluar** Consider this statement: The invention
of the alphabet was the Phoenicians' most
important achievement. Write a paragraph
explaining why you agree or disagree./Lee el
siguiente enunciado: La invención del alfabeto
fue el logro más importante de los fenicios.
Escribe un párrafo en el que expliques por
qué estás o no de acuerdo con ese enunciado.

| | | |
|---|---|---|
| alphabet/alfabeto | Carthage/Cartago | cuneiform/escritura cuneiforme |
| fleet/flota | navigate/navegar | Polaris/Polaris |

**DIRECTIONS/INSTRUCCIONES** Read each sentence and fill in
the blank with the word in the word pair that best completes
the sentence./Lee cada oración y escribe en el espacio en blanco
la palabra del par de palabras que mejor la completa.

1. Sailors safely arrived at ports because they learned to track the location of
   the star named _____. **(Carthage/Polaris)**/Los navegantes
   lograban llegar a los puertos porque aprendieron a guiarse por la ubicación
   de la estrella llamada _____. **(Cartago/Polaris)**

2. A set of letters that can be combined together to form words is known as an _____, which was developed by the Phoenician traders. **(alphabet/cuneiform)**/Un conjunto de letras que pueden combinarse para formar palabras, como el que desarrollaron los comerciantes fenicios, se denomina _____. **(alfabeto/escritura cuneiforme)**

3. Phoenicians could successfully _____ their ships to many ports on the Mediterranean Sea. **(navigate/fleet)**/Los fenicios lograban _____ con sus barcos hasta muchos puertos del mar Mediterráneo. **(navegar/flota)**

4. The Phoenicians had a large _____ of ships to trade goods all along the Mediterranean Sea. **(navigate/fleet)**/Los fenicios contaban con una gran _____ de barcos para comerciar con bienes por todo el mar Mediterráneo. **(navegar/flota)**

**DIRECTIONS/INSTRUCCIONES** On the line provided before each statement, write **T** if a statement is true and **F** if a statement is false. If the statement is false, write the correct term on the line after each sentence that makes the sentence a true statement./En la línea que precede a cada enunciado, escribe **V** si el enunciado es verdadero y **F** si es falso. Si el enunciado es falso, escribe en la línea que sigue a la oración el término correcto que lo hace verdadero.

_____ 5. The Phoenicians wrote using <u>cuneiform</u> to record their trades./Los fenicios usaban <u>la escritura cuneiforme</u> para llevar un registro de sus actividades comerciales.

_____

_____ 6. The port of <u>Polaris</u> on the north coast of Africa was a famous Phoenician center of trade on the Mediterranean./El puerto de <u>Polaris</u>, en la costa norte de África, era un famoso centro comercial fenicio a orillas del Mediterráneo.

_____

_____ 7. The <u>alphabet</u> developed by the Phoenicians is similar to the one we use today./<u>El alfabeto</u> desarrollado por los fenicios se parece al que utilizamos en la actualidad.

_____

## The Fertile Crescent, Mesopotamia, and the Persian Empire/La Media Luna Fértil, Mesopotamia y el Imperio persa

### Lesson/Lección 5

**MAIN IDEAS/IDEAS PRINCIPALES**
1. Persia became an empire under Cyrus the Great./Persia se convirtió en imperio durante el gobierno de Ciro el Grande.
2. The Persian Empire grew stronger under Darius I./El Imperio persa se fortaleció durante el gobierno de Darío I.
3. The Persians fought Greece twice in the Persian Wars./Los persas lucharon contra Grecia dos veces en las Guerras Médicas.

## Key Terms and People/Personas y palabras clave

**cavalry/caballería** a unit of soldiers mounted on horses/unidad de soldados a caballo

**Cyrus the Great/Ciro el Grande** founder of the Persian Empire/fundador del Imperio persa

**Darius I/Darío I** Persian emperor who organized and expanded the empire/emperador persa que organizó y expandió el imperio

**Persian Wars/Guerras Médicas** a series of wars between Persia and Greece beginning in 490 BC/serie de guerras entre Persia y Grecia que comenzaron en 490 a. C.

**Xerxes I/Jerjes I** Persian emperor who led the second invasion of Greece in 480 BC/emperador persa que dirigió la segunda invasión a Grecia en 480 a. C.

## Lesson Summary/Resumen de la lección

### PERSIA BECOMES AN EMPIRE/PERSIA SE CONVIERTE EN IMPERIO

Early in their history, the Persians often fought other peoples of Southwest Asia. In 550 BC, the Persian leader Cyrus II won independence from a people called the Medes (MEEDZ). He went on to conquer almost all of Southwest Asia. His well-organized and loyal army included a powerful **cavalry** that charged the enemy and used arrows. Cyrus II let the people he conquered keep their own customs. As a result, few people rebelled and the empire remained strong. By the time he died around 529 BC, Cyrus ruled the largest empire

> Underline the sentence that explains strategies Cyrus II used to make his army strong./Subraya la oración en la que se explican las estrategias de Ciro II para fortalecer su ejército.

the world had ever seen. He became known in history as **Cyrus the Great.**/En sus orígenes, los persas a menudo luchaban contra otros pueblos del suroeste asiático. En el año 550 a. C., el líder persa Ciro II logró independizarse de un pueblo llamado los medos y conquistar casi todo el suroeste asiático. Tenía un ejército bien organizado y leal con una poderosa **caballería** que cargaba contra el enemigo y usaba flechas. Ciro II permitía que los pueblos que conquistaba conservaran sus costumbres. Como resultado, pocos pueblos se rebelaban, y así el imperio se mantuvo fuerte. Al momento de su muerte, hacia el año 529 a. C., Ciro gobernaba el imperio más grande conocido hasta entonces. Pasó a la historia como **Ciro el Grande.**

> **Why do you think Cyrus II became known as Cyrus "the Great"?/¿Por qué crees que Ciro II pasó a la historia como Ciro "el Grande"?**
>
> _____
> _____
> _____
> _____
> _____

## THE PERSIAN EMPIRE GROWS STRONGER/ EL IMPERIO PERSA SE FORTALECE

**Darius I** seized power when the death of Cyrus's son left Persia without a clear leader. Darius organized the empire by dividing it into 20 provinces. Then he chose governors called satraps (SAY-traps) to rule the provinces for him. Darius expanded the Persian Empire eastward to the Indus Valley and westward into Southeastern Europe. He called himself king of kings to remind other rulers of his power./**Darío I** tomó el poder cuando, al morir el hijo de Ciro, Persia se quedó sin un líder claro. Darío organizó el imperio dividiéndolo en 20 provincias. Luego, eligió gobernadores llamados sátrapas para que gobernaran las provincias en su nombre. Expandió el Imperio persa en dirección este hacia el valle del Indo y en dirección oeste, hacia el sureste de Europa. Se hizo llamar "rey de reyes" para recordarles a otros gobernantes lo poderoso que era.

During his rule, Persia made advances in art and architecture. Darius's improvements to Persian society included roads that messengers used to travel quickly throughout Persia. Darius built a new capital called Persepolis that he filled with artwork, including carvings and statues made with gold, silver, and jewels./Durante el reinado de Darío, Persia desarrolló el arte y la arquitectura. Una de las mejoras que introdujo Darío en la sociedad persa fue la construcción de caminos que los mensajeros usaban para viajar rápidamente a través de Persia. Darío construyó una nueva capital llamada Persépolis, que llenó con obras de arte, como esculturas y estatuas realizadas con oro, plata y joyas.

During his reign, a popular new religion called Zoroastrianism (zawr-uh-WAS-tree-uh-nih-zuhm) arose in Persia. This religion taught that the forces of good and evil were fighting for control of the universe./Durante su reinado surgió en Persia una nueva religión popular llamada zoroastrismo, que enseñaba que las fuerzas del bien y del mal se disputaban el control del universo.

> **What new religion arose during the reign of Darius?/¿Qué nueva religión surgió durante el reinado de Darío?**
>
> _____

## THE PERSIANS FIGHT GREECE/LOS PERSAS LUCHAN CONTRA GRECIA

In 499 BC, several Greek cities in Asia Minor (in what is now Turkey) rebelled against Persian rule. They were joined by a few city-states from mainland Greece. The Persians put down the revolt, but nine years later Darius invaded Greece and began the **Persian Wars.** The Greeks won the first battle at Marathon because they had better weapons and armor./En el año 499 a. C., varias ciudades griegas de Asia Menor (en la actual Turquía) se rebelaron contra el dominio persa. Algunas ciudades estado de la Grecia continental

> **Underline the sentence that explains why the Greeks defeated the Persians at the Battle of Marathon./Subraya la oración en la que se explica por qué los griegos derrotaron a los persas en la Batalla de Maratón.**

se les unieron. Los persas sofocaron la revuelta pero, nueve años más tarde, Darío invadió Grecia y dio comienzo a las **Guerras Médicas.** Los griegos ganaron la primera batalla en Maratón porque tenían mejores armas y armaduras.

Ten years later, Darius's son, **Xerxes I** (ZUHRK-seez), sent another army into Greece. The city-states of Athens and Sparta joined forces to defend Greece. Despite a brave stand by the Spartans at Thermopylae (thuhr-MAH-puh-lee), the Persians succeeded in attacking and burning Athens. However, in the subsequent battles of Salamis (SAH-luh-muhs) and Plataea (pluh-TEE-uh), the Greeks overcame the Persians and brought an end to the wars. The Greeks had defeated a powerful foe and defended their homeland./Diez años después, el hijo de Darío, **Jerjes I,** envió otro ejército a Grecia. Las ciudades estado de Atenas y Esparta se unieron para defender a Grecia. A pesar de la valiente resistencia de los espartanos en Termópilas, los persas lograron atacar e incendiar Atenas. Sin embargo, en las subsiguientes batallas de Salamina y Platea, los griegos vencieron a los persas y pusieron fin a las guerras. Habían logrado derrotar a un rival poderoso y defender su patria.

> **Who won the Persian Wars?**/¿Quién ganó las Guerras Médicas?
> _____

## CHALLENGE ACTIVITY/ACTIVIDAD AVANZADA

**Critical Thinking: Make Inferences/Pensamiento crítico: Hacer inferencias** Draw a simple map of a location where three armed soldiers could prevent an entire army of foot-soldiers from moving forward./Dibuja un mapa sencillo de un lugar en el que tres soldados armados podrían evitar el avance de un ejército entero de soldados de infantería.

**DIRECTIONS/INSTRUCCIONES** Read each sentence and fill in the blank with a choice from the word pair that best completes each sentence./Lee cada oración y escribe en el espacio en blanco una de las palabras del par de palabras que mejor la completa.

1. _____ let conquered people keep their own customs in the hope that this would make them less likely to rebel. **(Cyrus the Great/ Darius I)**/_____ les permitía a los pueblos conquistados conservar sus propias costumbres para que fuera menos probable que se rebelaran. **(Ciro el Grande/Darío I)**

2. A unit of soldiers mounted on horseback is called a _____. **(cavalry/satrap)**/Una unidad de soldados a caballo se llama _____. **(caballería/sátrapa)**

3. After Cyrus the Great's son died, _____ claimed the Persian throne and killed all of his rivals, after which he restored order in Persia. **(Darius I/Xerxes I)**/Tras la muerte del hijo de Ciro el Grande, _____ reclamó el trono persa, mató a todos sus rivales y restableció el orden en Persia. **(Darío I/Jerjes I)**

4. Greece fought off two major Persian invasions in the _____. **(Battle of Salamis/Persian Wars)**/Grecia repelió dos importantes invasiones persas en _____. **(la Batalla de Salamina/las Guerras Médicas)**

5. Darius I organized the Persian Empire by dividing it into 20 provinces ruled over by governors called _____. **(cavalry/satraps)**/Darío I organizó el Imperio persa dividiéndolo en 20 provincias regidas por gobernadores llamados _____. **(caballería/sátrapas)**

**DIRECTIONS/INSTRUCCIONES** Write three adjectives or a descriptive phrase to describe the term or person./Escribe tres adjetivos o una frase descriptiva que describan el término o la persona.

6. cavalry/caballería _____

7. Cyrus the Great/Ciro el Grande _____

8. Darius I/Darío I _____

9. Persian Wars/Guerras Médicas _____

10. Xerxes I/Jerjes I _____

## Kingdoms of the Nile/Reinos del Nilo

---

**MAIN IDEAS/IDEAS PRINCIPALES**

1. Egypt was called "the gift of the Nile" because the Nile River was so important./Egipto fue llamado "el regalo del Nilo" por la importancia del río Nilo.
2. Civilization developed after people began farming along the Nile./La civilización se desarrolló una vez que se comenzó a cultivar a orillas del Nilo.
3. Strong kings unified all of Egypt./Reyes poderosos unificaron todo Egipto.

## Key Terms and People/Personas y palabras clave

**cataracts/cataratas** steep river rapids, almost impossible to sail by boat/rápidos empinados de un río por los que es casi imposible navegar en barco

**delta/delta** triangle-shaped area of land made of soil deposited by a river/ terreno de forma triangular compuesto por los sedimentos que deposita un río

**Menes/Menes** Egyptian leader who united both Upper and Lower Egypt into one kingdom/líder egipcio que unificó el Alto Egipto y el Bajo Egipto en un mismo reino

**pharaoh/faraón** ruler of unified Egypt, literally means "great house"/soberano del Egipto unificado; literalmente significa "casa grande"

**dynasty/dinastía** series of rulers from the same family/serie de gobernantes que pertenecen a la misma familia

## Lesson Summary/Resumen de la lección

### THE GIFT OF THE NILE/REGALO DEL NILO

The existence of Egypt was based solely around the Nile, the world's longest river. The Nile carries water from central Africa through a vast stretch of desert land. The river was so important that the Greek writer Herodotus called Egypt "the gift of the Nile."/La vida en Egipto se desarrollaba únicamente alrededor del Nilo, el río más largo del mundo. El Nilo fluye desde el centro de África y atraviesa un extenso tramo del desierto. Este río era tan importante que el escritor griego Heródoto llamó a Egipto "el regalo del Nilo".

> **Why is a river a "gift" to a desert land?/¿Por qué se considera que un río es un "regalo" para un terreno desértico?**
>
> _____
> _____

Ancient Egypt developed along a 750-mile stretch of the Nile and was originally organized into two kingdoms—Upper Egypt and Lower Egypt. The Nile flowed through the desert of Upper Egypt. This kingdom was located upriver in relation to the Nile's flow. Lower Egypt was the northern region and was located down river./ El antiguo Egipto se desarrolló a lo largo de un tramo del Nilo que abarcaba 750 millas y estaba organizado, inicialmente, en dos reinos: el Alto Egipto y el Bajo Egipto. El Nilo fluía por el desierto del Alto Egipto. Dicho reino estaba ubicado río arriba respecto de la corriente del Nilo. El Bajo Egipto era la región del norte y estaba ubicado río abajo.

**Cataracts,** or steep rapids, marked the southern border of Upper Egypt. Lower Egypt was centered in the river **delta,** a triangle-shaped area of land made of soil deposited by the river. In midsummer, the Nile would flood Upper Egypt, and in the fall the river would flood Lower Egypt. This made sure that the farmland would stay moist and fertile from rich silt. Because the land surrounding the Nile Valley was arid desert, this watered area made farming possible in Egypt./La frontera sur del Alto Egipto estaba delimitada por **cataratas**, es decir, por rápidos empinados. El Bajo Egipto se centraba en el **delta** del río, un terreno de forma triangular compuesto por los sedimentos que deposita el río. En pleno verano, el Nilo inundaba el Alto Egipto y, durante el otoño, inundaba el Bajo Egipto. Esto garantizaba que las tierras de cultivo se mantuvieran húmedas y fértiles gracias al sedimento que servía de fertilizante. Como el terreno que rodeaba el valle del Nilo era desértico, esta zona húmeda posibilitaba la agricultura en Egipto.

**Why were the Nile's floods so important in Ancient Egypt?/¿Por qué eran tan importantes los desbordes del Nilo en el antiguo Egipto?**

_____
_____
_____
_____
_____
_____

## CIVILIZATION DEVELOPS IN EGYPT/ DESARROLLO DE LA CIVILIZACIÓN EN EGIPTO

With dry desert all around, it is no wonder that ancient settlers were attracted to this abundant and protected area of fertile farmland. Hunter-gatherers first moved to the area around 12,000 years ago and found plenty of wild animals, plants, and fish to hunt and eat. By 4500 BC, farmers were living in villages and growing wheat and barley. They also raised cattle and sheep, while hunters trapped wild geese and ducks along the banks of the Nile./No es de extrañar que, rodeados de desierto, los antiguos pobladores se hayan sentido atraídos a esta zona abundante y protegida con tierras de cultivo fértiles. Los cazadores y recolectores se trasladaron por primera vez a la zona hace unos 12,000 años y encontraron una gran cantidad de animales salvajes, plantas y peces para cazar y comer. Hacia el año 4500 a. C., los agricultores vivían en aldeas y cultivaban trigo y cebada. También se dedicaban a la cría de ganado y ovejas, mientras que los cazadores cazaban gansos y patos salvajes a orillas del Nilo.

> **What did hunter-gatherers find when they moved to the Nile Valley?/¿Qué encontraron los cazadores y recolectores cuando se trasladaron al valle del Nilo?**
>
> _____
> _____
> _____

Egypt had natural barriers, so it was a hard place to invade. Egyptian villages grew and became organized into two kingdoms. The capital of Lower Egypt was located in the northwest Nile Delta at a town called Pe. The capital city of Upper Egypt was called Nekhen. It was located on the west bank of the Nile./ Egipto tenía fronteras naturales, por lo que era difícil de invadir. Las aldeas egipcias crecieron y se organizaron en dos reinos. La capital del Bajo Egipto estaba ubicada en el noroeste del delta del Nilo, en un pueblo llamado Pe. La capital del Alto Egipto se llamaba Nekhen y estaba ubicada en la ribera oeste del Nilo.

## KINGS UNIFY EGYPT/LOS REYES UNIFICAN EGIPTO

Around 3100 BC, **Menes** (MEE-neez), the king of Upper Egypt, invaded Lower Egypt. He married a princess there in order to unite the two kingdoms under his rule. Menes was the first **pharaoh**, which literally means ruler of a "great house." He also started the first Egyptian **dynasty**, or series of rulers from the same family. He built a new capital city, Memphis, which became a popular cultural center. His dynasty ruled for nearly 200 years./ Cerca del año 3100 a. C., **Menes,** el rey del Alto Egipto, invadió el Bajo Egipto, donde se casó con una princesa para unificar los dos reinos y gobernarlos. Menes fue el primer **faraón,** que literalmente significa soberano de una "casa grande". También comenzó la primera **dinastía** egipcia, es decir, una serie de gobernantes que pertenecen a la misma familia. Construyó una capital nueva, Menfis, que se convirtió en un popular centro cultural. Su dinastía reinó durante casi 200 años.

> Why do you think Menes united Egypt's two kingdoms?/¿Por qué crees que Menes unificó los dos reinos de Egipto?
>
> _____
>
> _____
>
> _____
>
> _____

## CHALLENGE ACTIVITY/ACTIVIDAD AVANZADA

**Critical Thinking: Elaborate/Pensamiento crítico: Profundizar** Powerful leaders like Menes unite territories and people under one organization. Imagine that you are an ancient Egyptian interested in becoming a leader. Write a speech explaining what would make you a powerful person fit for ruling a large village./Los líderes poderosos como Menes unifican territorios y pueblos bajo una misma organización. Imagina que vives en el antiguo Egipto y que quieres convertirte en líder. Escribe un discurso en el que expliques qué cualidades posees que te ayudarían a convertirte en una persona poderosa, apta para gobernar un pueblo con muchos habitantes.

**DIRECTIONS/INSTRUCCIONES** On the line provided before each statement, write **T** if a statement is true and **F** if a statement is false. If the statement is false, write the correct term on the line after each sentence that makes the sentence a true statement./En la línea que precede a cada enunciado, escribe **V** si el enunciado es verdadero y **F** si es falso. Si el enunciado es falso, escribe en la línea que sigue a la oración el término correcto que lo hace verdadero.

_____ 1. Cataracts are triangle-shaped areas of land made of soil that is deposited by a river./Las cataratas son terrenos de forma triangular compuestos por los sedimentos que deposita un río.

_____

_____ 2. Deltas are steep rapids that made sailing portions of rivers such as the Nile very difficult./Los deltas son rápidos empinados que dificultan la navegación en algunos tramos de los ríos, como el río Nilo.

_____

_____ 3. Menes was a leader who united Upper and Lower Egypt into one kingdom./Menes fue un líder que unificó el Alto Egipto y el Bajo Egipto en un mismo reino.

_____

_____ 4. Menes founded Egypt's first pharaoh, a series of rulers from the same family./Menes fundó el primer faraón de Egipto, una serie de gobernantes que pertenecen a la misma familia.

_____

_____ 5. Historians consider Menes to be Egypt's first dynasty, the title used by the rulers of Egypt./Los historiadores consideran que Menes fue la primera dinastía de Egipto, un título que usaban los soberanos egipcios.

_____

## Kingdoms of the Nile/Reinos del Nilo

### Lesson/Lección 2

**MAIN IDEAS/IDEAS PRINCIPALES**
1. Life in the Old Kingdom was influenced by pharaohs, roles in society, and trade./Los faraones, los roles sociales y el comercio influían en la vida en el Imperio Antiguo.
2. Religion shaped Egyptian life./La religión dominaba la vida egipcia.
3. The pyramids were built as huge tombs for Egyptian pharaohs./Las pirámides eran tumbas gigantescas construidas para los faraones egipcios.

## Key Terms and People/Personas y palabras clave

**Old Kingdom/Imperio Antiguo** the third Egyptian dynasty, which lasted nearly 500 years/tercera dinastía de Egipto, que duró casi 500 años

**theocracy/teocracia** a government where religious leaders have power to make, approve, or enforce laws/forma de gobierno en la que los líderes religiosos tienen el poder de crear, aprobar y hacer respetar las leyes

**Khufu/Keops** the most famous pharaoh of the Old Kingdom/el faraón más conocido del Imperio Antiguo

**nobles/nobles** people from rich and powerful families/personas provenientes de familias ricas y poderosas

**afterlife/vida después de la muerte** life after death, a widely held ancient Egyptian belief/una antigua creencia egipcia muy arraigada

**mummies/momias** dead bodies preserved by wrapping them in cloth/cadáveres que se preservan envueltos en tela

**elite/élite** people of wealth and power/personas ricas y poderosas

**pyramids/pirámides** huge stone tombs with four triangle-shaped walls that meet at a top point/tumbas gigantescas de piedra con cuatro paredes triangulares que se juntan en un punto en la parte superior

**engineering/ingeniería** application of scientific knowledge for practical purposes/aplicación de los conocimientos científicos para fines prácticos

## Lesson Summary/Resumen de la lección

**LIFE IN THE OLD KINGDOM/VIDA EN EL IMPERIO ANTIGUO**

Around 2700 BC, the Third Dynasty, or the **Old Kingdom,** came to power in Egypt. During the next 500 years, the Egyptians developed a

**theocracy.** Religious leaders had power to make, approve, or enforce laws in this government. Egyptians believed the pharaoh was both a king and a god. The most famous pharaoh of the Old Kingdom was **Khufu.** Many monuments were built to him./Hacia el año 2700 a. C., la tercera dinastía, o el **Imperio Antiguo,** llegó al poder en Egipto. Durante los siguientes 500 años, los egipcios desarrollaron una **teocracia.** Con ese sistema de gobierno, los líderes religiosos tenían el poder de crear, aprobar y hacer respetar las leyes. Los egipcios creían que el faraón era un rey y también un dios. El faraón más conocido del Imperio Antiguo fue **Keops.** En su honor se construyeron muchos monumentos.

Egyptians believed that a well-ordered society would keep their kingdom strong. Social classes developed. The pharaoh was at the top and **nobles** from rich and powerful families made up the upper class. The middle class included lesser government officials, scribes, and rich craftspeople. Most people, including farmers, belonged to the lower class. Lower-class people were often used by the pharaoh as laborers./Los egipcios pensaban que una sociedad bien ordenada garantizaba la fuerza del reino. Surgieron las clases sociales; el faraón estaba en la parte superior y los **nobles** de familias ricas y poderosas componían la clase alta. La clase media incluía a funcionarios menores del gobierno, escribas y artesanos ricos. La mayoría de las personas, entre ellos los agricultores, pertenecían a la clase baja. El faraón a menudo empleaba a la clase baja como mano de obra.

Trade also developed during the Old Kingdom. Traders sailed on the Mediterranean and south on the Nile and the Red Sea to acquire gold, copper, ivory, slaves, wood, and stone./ Durante el Imperio Antiguo también se

---

**Why was there no distinction between religion and politics in Egypt's Old Kingdom?**/ ¿Por qué no había distinción entre la religión y la política en el Imperio Antiguo de Egipto?

_____

_____

_____

_____

_____

---

**Of the upper, middle, and lower classes, which was the largest in ancient Egypt?**/De las clases alta, media y baja, ¿cuál era la más numerosa en el antiguo Egipto?

_____

_____

desarrolló el comercio. Los comerciantes navegaban por el Mediterráneo y hacia el sur por el Nilo y el mar Rojo para adquirir oro, cobre, marfil, esclavos, madera y piedra.

## RELIGION AND EGYPTIAN LIFE/RELIGIÓN Y VIDA COTIDIANA EN EGIPTO

Officials in the Old Kingdom expected everyone to worship the same gods. Over time certain cities built temples and were associated with particular gods. The Egyptians had gods for nearly everything./Los funcionarios del Imperio Antiguo querían que todos adoraran a los mismos dioses. Con el tiempo, ciertas ciudades construyeron templos y comenzaron a estar vinculadas con determinados dioses. Los egipcios tenían dioses para casi todo.

There was also much focus on the **afterlife**. Each person's *ka* (KAH), or life force, existed after death but remained linked to the body. To keep the *ka* from suffering, the Egyptians developed a method called embalming to preserve bodies. Royalty and other members of the **elite** had their bodies preserved as **mummies,** specially treated bodies wrapped in cloth./La **vida después de la muerte** era un concepto muy importante en Egipto. El *ka* (o fuerza vital) de la persona subsistía después de la muerte, pero permanecía vinculado al cuerpo. Para evitar que el *ka* sufriera, los egipcios desarrollaron un método de preservación de los cadáveres llamado embalsamamiento. La realeza y otros miembos de la élite ordenaban preservar sus cuerpos en forma de **momias,** cadáveres especialmente tratados y envueltos en tela.

> **What is the *ka*?/¿Qué es el *ka*?**
> _____
> _____

## THE PYRAMIDS/PIRÁMIDES

**Pyramids,** spectacular stone monuments, were built to house dead rulers. Many pyramids are still standing today, amazing reminders of Egyptian **engineering.**/Las **pirámides,** impresionantes monumentos de piedra, se construían para albergar a los soberanos muertos. Muchas pirámides aún continúan en pie, increíbles vestigios de la **ingeniería** egipcia.

> **Why do you think the Egyptians believed that royal burial sites were so important?/¿Por qué crees que los egipcios daban tanta importancia al lugar donde enterraban a sus reyes?**
>
> _____
> _____
> _____
> _____
> _____
> _____

## CHALLENGE ACTIVITY/ACTIVIDAD AVANZADA

**Critical Thinking: Make Judgments/Pensamiento crítico: Dar opiniones** Write a one-page essay considering whether a god-king pharaoh ruling today would be loved or hated by his people./ Escribe un ensayo de una página en el que reflexiones acerca de si, en la actualidad, la gente amaría u odiaría a un faraón rey-dios.

## DIRECTIONS/INSTRUCCIONES Write two adjectives or descriptive phrases that describe the term./Escribe dos adjetivos o frases descriptivas que describan el término.

1. afterlife/vida después de la muerte _____

2. elite/élite _____

3. engineering/ingeniería _____

_____

4. Khufu/Keops _____

5. mummies/momias _____

_____

6. nobles/nobles _____

7. Old Kingdom/Imperio Antiguo _____

8. pyramids/pirámides _____

_____

9. theocracy/teocracia _____

## Kingdoms of the Nile/Reinos del Nilo

**MAIN IDEAS/IDEAS PRINCIPALES**

1. The Middle Kingdom was a period of stable government between periods of disorder./El Imperio Medio fue un período de estabilidad en el gobierno entre períodos de disturbios.

2. The New Kingdom was the peak of Egyptian trade and military power, but its greatness did not last./El Imperio Nuevo fue la época de apogeo del comercio y el poderío militar egipcios, pero su esplendor no duró.

3. Work and daily life were different among Egypt's social classes./El trabajo y la vida cotidiana en Egipto variaban según las clases sociales.

## Key Terms and People/Personas y palabras clave

**Middle Kingdom/Imperio Medio** period of stability and order in ancient Egypt between about 2050 and 1750 BC/período de estabilidad y orden en el antiguo Egipto que se extendió entre los años 2050 y 1750 a. C.

**New Kingdom/Imperio Nuevo** the height of Egypt's power and glory, between 1550 and 1050 BC/período de apogeo del poderío y la gloria de Egipto, entre los años 1550 y 1050 a. C.

**trade routes/rutas comerciales** paths followed by traders/trayectos que seguían los comerciantes

**Queen Hatshepsut/reina Hatshepsut** New Kingdom ruler renowned for expanding Egyptian trade/soberana del Imperio Nuevo, célebre por expandir el comercio egipcio

**Ramses the Great/Ramsés el Grande** important New Kingdom pharaoh who defended Egypt from invaders and strengthened defenses/faraón importante del Imperio Nuevo que defendió a Egipto de los invasores y fortaleció las defensas

## Lesson Summary/Resumen de la lección

### THE MIDDLE KINGDOM/IMPERIO MEDIO

The Old Kingdom ended with the pharaohs in debt. Ambitious nobles serving in government positions managed to take power from the pharaohs and rule for nearly 160 years. Egypt had no central ruler during this time. Finally, a powerful pharaoh regained control around 2050 BC and started a peaceful period of rule.

| Who ruled Egypt before the Middle Kingdom began?/¿Quiénes gobernaron Egipto antes de que comenzara el Imperio Medio? |
| --- |
| _____ |
| _____ |
| _____ |

This era was called the **Middle Kingdom** and lasted until Southwest Asian invaders conquered Lower Egypt around 1750 BC./Al final del Imperio Antiguo, los faraones estaban endeudados. Los nobles ambiciosos que cumplían funciones gubernamentales lograron quitarles el poder a los faraones y gobernaron durante casi 160 años. Durante este período, Egipto no tuvo ningún soberano central. Finalmente, un faraón poderoso recuperó el control cerca del año 2050 a. C. y así comenzó un período de reinado pacífico. Esta época se llamó **Imperio Medio** y duró hasta que los invasores del suroeste asiático conquistaron el Bajo Egipto, cerca del año 1750 a. C.

## THE NEW KINGDOM/IMPERIO NUEVO

When an Egyptian named Ahmose (AHM-ohs) drove away the invaders and declared himself king of Egypt in 1550 BC, he began Egypt's eighteenth dynasty and the start of the **New Kingdom.** Responding to invasions, Egypt took control of possible invasion routes and quickly became the leading military power in the region, with an empire extending from the Euphrates River in the northeast to Nubia in the south. These conquests also made Egypt rich, through gifts and vastly expanded **trade routes.** One particular ruler, **Queen Hatshepsut,** was active in establishing new paths for traders./Un egipcio llamado Amosis expulsó a los invasores y se declaró rey de Egipto en el año 1550 a. C. Así, fundó la decimoctava dinastía de Egipto y dio comienzo al **Imperio Nuevo.** En respuesta a las invasiones, Egipto tomó el control de las posibles rutas de invasión y pronto se convirtió en la

> **Why did Egypt become the leading military power in the region?/¿Por qué Egipto se convirtió en la potencia militar más importante de la región?**
>
> _____
>
> _____

potencia militar más importante de la región. El imperio se extendía desde el río Éufrates en el noreste hasta Nubia en el sur. Estas conquistas también enriquecieron a Egipto, gracias a las ofrendas y a la enorme expansión de las **rutas comerciales.** Una soberana en particular, la **reina Hatshepsut,** trabajó para crear nuevas rutas para los comerciantes.

Despite the strong leadership of **Ramses the Great,** a tide of invasions from the west and Southwest Asia eventually reduced Egypt to violence and disorder./A pesar del liderazgo firme de **Ramsés el Grande,** una oleada de invasiones provenientes del oeste y el suroeste asiático terminó por sumir a Egipto en la violencia y los disturbios.

## WORK AND DAILY LIFE/TRABAJO Y VIDA COTIDIANA

During the Middle and New Kingdoms daily life in Egypt did not change very much. The population continued to grow and become more complex. Professional and skilled workers like scribes, artisans, artists, and architects were honored. These roles in society were usually passed on in families, with young boys learning a trade from their fathers./Durante los Imperios Medio y Nuevo, la vida cotidiana en Egipto no cambió mucho. La población siguió creciendo y se tornó más compleja. Se honraba a los profesionales y a los trabajadores especializados, como los escribas, los artesanos, los artistas y los arquitectos. Estos roles sociales solían transmitirse dentro de las familias, al aprender los jóvenes del oficio de sus padres.

> **What sort of workers were respected in ancient Egyptian society?/¿Qué tipos de trabajadores eran respetados en la sociedad del antiguo Egipto?**
>
> _____
>
> _____

Farmers and peasants made up the vast majority of the population. In addition to hard work on the land, they were required to pay taxes and were subject to special labor duty at any time. Only slaves were beneath them in social status./La gran mayoría de la población estaba compuesta por agricultores y campesinos. Además de tener que trabajar intensamente la tierra, tenían que pagar impuestos y podían ser sometidos a realizar trabajos especiales en cualquier momento. Únicamente los esclavos estaban por debajo de ellos en la escala social.

Most Egyptian families lived in their own homes. Boys were expected to marry young and start their own families. Women focused on the home, but many also had other jobs. Egyptian women had the legal rights to own property, make contracts, and divorce their husbands./La mayoría de las familias egipcias tenían casas propias. Se esperaba que los varones se casaran jóvenes y formaran sus propias familias. Las mujeres se dedicaban al hogar, pero muchas también tenían otros trabajos. Las mujeres egipcias tenían derecho a la propiedad, a realizar contratos y a divorciarse de sus esposos.

> **What was daily life like in Egypt for farmers and peasants?/¿Cómo era la vida cotidiana de los agricultores y los campesinos en Egipto?**
>
> _____
>
> _____
>
> _____
>
> _____
>
> _____

## CHALLENGE ACTIVITY/ACTIVIDAD AVANZADA

**Critical Thinking: Design/Pensamiento crítico: Diseñar** Design an ancient Egyptian "job want ad" and then write a letter to a potential employer explaining why you should be hired./Diseña un anuncio clasificado para un trabajo en el antiguo Egipto y escribe una carta a un posible empleador en la que expliques por qué debería contratarte.

| | | |
|---|---|---|
| Middle Kingdom/ Imperio Medio | Queen Hatshepsut/reina Hatshepsut | trade routes/rutas comerciales |
| New Kingdom/Imperio Nuevo | Ramses the Great/Ramsés el Grande | |

**DIRECTIONS/INSTRUCCIONES** Read each sentence and choose the correct term from the word bank to replace the underlined phrase. Write the term in the space provided and then define the term in your own words./Lee cada oración y escoge del banco de palabras el término correcto para reemplazar la frase subrayada. Escribe el término en el espacio en blanco y, luego, defínelo con tus propias palabras.

1. Queen Hatshepsut could not stop invasions from the west and Southwest Asia./La reina Hatshepsut no pudo detener las invasiones provenientes del oeste y el suroeste asiático. _____

   Your definition:/Tu definición: _____

   _____

2. Ahmose's dynasty began the Middle Kingdom./La dinastía de Amosis dio comienzo al Imperio Medio. _____

   Your definition:/Tu definición: _____

   _____

3. One ruler who worked to increase Egyptian trade was Ramses the Great./ Un soberano que trabajó para aumentar el comercio en Egipto fue Ramsés el Grande. _____

   Your definition:/Tu definición: _____

   _____

4. Paths followed by traders are New Kingdoms./Los recorridos que siguen los comerciantes se llaman Imperios Nuevos. _____

   Your definition:/Tu definición: _____

   _____

5. The period during which Egypt had a peaceful period of rule is called the <u>trade routes</u>./El período durante el cual reinó la paz en Egipto se denomina <u>rutas comerciales</u>. _____

Your definition:/Tu definición: _____

_____

# Kingdoms of the Nile/Reinos del Nilo

## Lesson/Lección 4

**MAIN IDEAS/IDEAS PRINCIPALES**
1. Egyptian writing used hieroglyphics./En la escritura egipcia se usaban jeroglíficos.
2. Egypt's great temples were lavishly decorated./Los grandes templos egipcios tenían decoraciones suntuosas.
3. Egyptian art filled tombs./Las tumbas estaban decoradas con arte egipcio.

## Key Terms and People/Personas y palabras clave

**hieroglyphics/jeroglíficos** Egyptian writing system, one of the world's first, which used symbols/sistema de escritura egipcio, uno de los primeros del mundo, que usaba símbolos

**papyrus/papiro** long-lasting, paperlike substance made from reeds/sustancia duradera similar al papel que se fabrica a partir de juncos

**Rosetta Stone/piedra de Rosetta** a stone slab discovered in 1799 that was inscribed with hieroglyphics and their Greek meanings/bloque de piedra descubierto en 1799 que tiene inscripciones jeroglíficas y sus significados en griego

**sphinxes/esfinges** huge ancient Egyptian statues of imaginary creatures with the heads of people or animals and bodies of lions/estatuas gigantescas del antiguo Egipto que representan criaturas imaginarias con cabeza humana o de animales y cuerpo de león

**obelisk/obelisco** a tall, four-sided pillar that is pointed on top/pilar alto de cuatro caras que termina en punta

**King Tutankhamen/rey Tutankamón** a pharaoh whose tomb was untouched by raiders, leaving much information about Egyptian art and burial practices/faraón cuya tumba no fue saqueada por los ladrones, gracias a lo cual se pudo obtener mucha información sobre las prácticas de sepultura y el arte egipcios

## Lesson Summary/Resumen de la lección

### EGYPTIAN WRITING/ESCRITURA EGIPCIA

Egyptians invented one of the world's first writing systems, using a series of more than 600 images, symbols, and pictures called **hieroglyphics** (hy-ruh-GLIH-fiks). Each symbol represented one or more sounds in the Egyptian language./Los egipcios inventaron uno de los primeros sistemas de escritura del mundo a partir de una serie de más de 600 imágenes, símbolos y figuras llamados **jeroglíficos.** Cada símbolo representaba uno o más sonidos del idioma egipcio.

At first, hieroglyphics were carved in stone. Later they were written with brushes and ink on **papyrus** (puh-PY-ruhs). It was made by pressing layers of reeds together and pounding them into sheets./En un principio, los jeroglíficos se tallaban en piedra. Más adelante, se escribían con pinceles y tinta en **papiros.** Para hacer papiros, se ejercía presión sobre varias capas de junco, que se machacaban hasta reducirlas a una lámina.

Because papyrus didn't decay, many ancient Egyptian texts still survive, including government records, science texts, and literary works, such as *The Book of the Dead.* The discovery of the **Rosetta Stone** in 1799 provided the key to reading Egyptian writing because its text was inscribed both in hieroglyphics and Greek./Como los papiros no se descompusieron, muchos textos del antiguo Egipto se conservan en la actualidad, entre ellos, registros gubernamentales, textos científicos y obras literarias, como *El libro de los muertos.* El descubrimiento de la **piedra de Rosetta** en 1799 brindó la clave para descifrar la escritura egipcia porque, además de jeroglíficos, tenía inscripciones en griego.

The Egyptians created two 12-month calendars. One was based on the moon and the other on the sun. The solar calendar was more accurate./Los egipcios crearon dos calendarios de 12 meses: uno se basaba en la luna y otro, en el sol. El calendario solar era más preciso.

> **How was papyrus made?/ ¿Cómo se fabricaba el papiro?**
> _____
> _____
> _____

> **What language helped scholars to understand the meaning of hieroglyphics on the Rosetta Stone?/ ¿Qué idioma ayudó a los estudiosos a comprender el significado de los jeroglíficos de la piedra de Rosetta?**
> _____

## EGYPT'S GREAT TEMPLES/GRANDES TEMPLOS EGIPCIOS

Egyptian architects are known for designing magnificent temples. These structures were the homes of the gods. Temples were lavishly decorated with numerous statues and beautifully painted walls and pillars. **Sphinxes** and **obelisks** were usually found near the entrances to the temples./Los arquitectos egipcios son conocidos por diseñar templos magníficos. Dichas estructuras eran el hogar de los dioses. Los templos tenían decoraciones suntuosas con numerosas estatuas y hermosas pinturas en las paredes y las columnas. Cerca de las entradas de los templos solía haber **esfinges** y **obeliscos.**

## EGYPTIAN ART/ARTE EGIPCIO

Many great works are found in either the temples or the tombs of the pharaohs. Most Egyptians, however, never saw these paintings, because only kings, priests, or other important people could enter these places./Tanto en los templos como en las tumbas de los faraones, se pueden encontrar muchas obras de arte increíbles. Sin embargo, la mayoría de los egipcios nunca vieron esas pinturas porque únicamente los reyes, los sacerdotes y otras personas importantes podían entrar a esos lugares.

Egyptian paintings depict a variety of subjects, like royal events, religious rituals, and daily life. The paintings also have a particular style. People are drawn as if they were twisting as they walked. They are shown in different sizes depending upon their stature in society. In contrast, animals appear more realistically. The Egyptians were also skilled stone and metal workers, creating beautiful statues and jewelry./Las pinturas egipcias representan una variedad de temas, como acontecimientos de la realeza, rituales religiosos y la vida cotidiana. Las pinturas también tienen un estilo particular. Las personas

> **Why did only some people get to see ancient Egyptian sculptures and paintings?/** ¿Por qué solo algunas personas pudieron ver las esculturas y pinturas egipcias antiguas?
>
> _____
> _____
> _____
> _____
> _____
> _____

> **What determined a person's size in an Egyptian painting?/** ¿Qué determinaba el tamaño de una persona en una pintura egipcia?
>
> _____
> _____

están dibujadas como si caminaran torciendo la cintura y su tamaño varía según su posición social. Los animales, en cambio, están representados de manera más realista. Los egipcios también eran expertos en el trabajo con piedras y metales, y crearon estatuas y joyas bellísimas.

Much of what we know about Egyptian art and burial practices comes from the tomb of **King Tutankhamen.** It was one of the few Egyptian tombs that was left untouched by raiders looking for valuables. The tomb was discovered in 1922./Mucho de lo que sabemos sobre las prácticas de sepultura y el arte egipcios proviene de la tumba del **rey Tutankamón,** pues es una de las pocas tumbas egipcias que no fue saqueada por los ladrones que buscaban objetos de valor. La tumba fue descubierta en 1922.

> **Why is King Tutankhamen's tomb so important for the study of Egyptian history?/ ¿Por qué es tan importante la tumba de Tutankamón para el estudio de la historia de Egipto?**
>
> _____
> _____
> _____
> _____

## CHALLENGE ACTIVITY/ACTIVIDAD AVANZADA

**Critical Thinking: Analyze/Pensamiento crítico: Analizar** Using the library or an online resource, find a key to translate Egyptian hieroglyphics into English. Write a message using hieroglyphics and trade off with another student to see if you can read each other's messages. Provide a copy of your message and the translation to your teacher./Usa la biblioteca o recursos en línea para buscar una clave que permita traducir jeroglíficos egipcios al español. Escribe un mensaje con jeroglíficos e intercámbialo con un compañero para ver si pueden descifrar los mensajes. Entrega una copia de tu mensaje y de tu traducción a tu maestro.

Lesson/Lección 4, *continued*/*continuación*

| | | |
|---|---|---|
| hieroglyphics/jeroglíficos | obelisk/obelisco | Rosetta Stone/piedra de Rosetta |
| King Tutankhamen/rey Tutankamón | papyrus/papiro | sphinxes/esfinges |

**DIRECTIONS/INSTRUCCIONES** Read each sentence and fill in the blank with the word in the word pair that best completes the sentence./Lee cada oración y escribe en el espacio en blanco la palabra del par de palabras que mejor la completa.

1. _____ is a long-lasting, paperlike substance made from reeds. **(Sphinxes/Papyrus)**/_____ es una sustancia duradera similar al papel que se fabrica a partir de juncos. **(La esfinge/ El papiro)**

2. The Egyptian writing system is known as _____. **(obelisk/hieroglyphics)**/El sistema de escritura egipcio se conoce como _____. **(obelisco/jeroglífico)**

3. The tomb of _____ was one of the few Egyptian tombs left untouched by raiders. **(King Tutankhamen/Rosetta Stone)**/La tumba _____ es una de las pocas tumbas egipcias que no fueron saqueadas por los ladrones. **(del rey Tutankamón/de la piedra de Rosetta)**

4. The _____ had hieroglyphics inscribed on it and became the key to deciphering Egyptian writing. **(obelisk/Rosetta Stone)**/_____ tenía inscripciones jeroglíficas y brindó la clave para descifrar la escritura egipcia. **(El obelisco/La piedra de Rosetta)**

5. _____ were imaginary creatures with the bodies of lions and the heads of people. **(Sphinxes/Papyruses)**/_____ eran criaturas imaginarias que tenían cuerpo de león y cabeza humana. **(Las esfinges/Los papiros)**

6. A(n) _____ is a tall, four-sided pillar that is pointed on top. **(obelisk/sphinx)**/_____ es un pilar alto de cuatro caras que termina en punta. **(Un obelisco/Una esfinge)**

# Kingdoms of the Nile/Reinos del Nilo

## Lesson/Lección 5

**MAIN IDEAS/IDEAS PRINCIPALES**
1. The geography of early Nubia helped civilization develop there./La geografía de la antigua Nubia ayudó a que se desarrollara una civilización allí.
2. Kush and Egypt traded, but they also fought./Kush y Egipto tenían relaciones comerciales, pero también se enfrentaban en combate.
3. Later Kush became a trading power with a unique culture./Más adelante, Kush se convirtió en una potencia comercial con una cultura singular.
4. Both internal and external conflicts led to the decline of Kush and Aksum./ Conflictos internos y externos llevaron a la decadencia de Kush y Aksum.

## Key Terms and People/Personas y palabras clave

**Piankhi/Pianjy** Kushite king who conquered all of Egypt/rey kushita que conquistó todo Egipto

**trade network/red comercial** a system of people in different lands who trade goods back and forth/sistema en el que personas de distintos territorios intercambian productos

**merchants/mercaderes** traders/comerciantes

**exports/exportaciones** items sent for sale in other countries or regions/ productos que se venden a otros países o regiones

**imports/importaciones** goods brought in from other countries or regions/ productos que se traen de otros países o regiones

**Queen Shanakhdakheto/reina Shanakdakhete** the first woman to rule Kush/ primera mujer que gobernó Kush

**Aksum/Aksum** an ancient kingdom located near the Red Sea in northeast Africa/reino antiguo situado cerca del mar Rojo en el noreste de África

**King Ezana/rey Ezana** Aksumite king who destroyed Meroë and took over the kingdom of Kush/rey de Aksum que destruyó Meroe y se apoderó del reino de Kush

## Lesson Summary/Resumen de la lección

### THE GEOGRAPHY OF EARLY NUBIA/GEOGRAFÍA DE LA ANTIGUA NUBIA

The kingdom of Kush developed in Nubia, south of Egypt. Just as in Egypt, yearly Nile floods provided fertile soil and farming thrived. The area was also rich in gold, copper, and stone. Kerma (KAR-muh), the capital city on the Nile, was protected by a cataract, or stretch of shallow rapids./El reino de Kush se desarrolló en Nubia, al sur de Egipto. Al igual que en Egipto, las crecidas anuales del Nilo aportaban tierras fértiles, y la agricultura prosperó. En la zona también abundaban el oro, el cobre y la piedra. Kerma, la capital ubicada a orillas del Nilo, estaba protegida por una catarata, es decir, por un tramo de rápidos poco profundos.

> **How was Kush like Egypt?/** **¿En qué se parecía Kush a Egipto?**
> _____
> _____
> _____

## KUSH AND EGYPT/KUSH Y EGIPTO

Kush and Egypt were trading partners. The Kushites sent Egypt gold, copper, ebony, ivory, and slaves. At times, Kush and Egypt were at war. By around 850 BC, Kush had freed itself from Egypt and was a power again. During the 700s under the king Kashta, the Kushites began to invade Egypt. Kashta's son, **Piankhi** (PYANG-kee), conquered all of Egypt by the time he died. Piankhi's brother became pharaoh of the Kushite dynasty. Egyptian culture thrived. But by 670 BC, Assyrians invaded Egypt. Their iron weapons were better than Kush's bronze weapons. Kush lost control of Egypt./Kush y Egipto eran socios comerciales. Los kushitas enviaban oro, cobre, ébano, marfil y esclavos a Egipto. A veces, Kush y Egipto entraban en guerra. Aproximadamente hacia el año 850 a. C., Kush se había liberado de Egipto y se había vuelto a convertir en una potencia. Durante el siglo 8 a. C., bajo el dominio del rey Kashta, los kushitas comenzaron a invadir Egipto. Al momento de su muerte, el hijo de Kashta, **Pianjy,** había conquistado todo Egipto. El hermano de Pianjy se convirtió en faraón de la dinastía kushita. La cultura egipcia prosperó, pero hacia el año 670 a. C. los asirios

> **What made Assyrian weapons better than Kushite weapons?/¿Por qué las armas de Asiria eran mejores que las de Kush?**
> _____
> _____
> _____

invadieron Egipto. Sus armas de hierro eran mejores que las armas de bronce del reino de Kush. Así, Kush perdió el control de Egipto.

## LATER KUSH/AÑOS POSTERIORES DE KUSH

Meroë (MER-oh-wee) became the center of a **trade network.** Africa's first iron industry developed here because iron ore and wood for fuel were available. Egyptian and Greek **merchants** shipped goods from Kush and sent them to the Mediterranean and beyond. Kush's **exports** included gold, pottery, iron tools, ivory, and slaves. **Imports** included luxury items from Egypt, Asia, and the Mediterranean./Meroe se convirtió en el centro de una **red comercial.** Allí se desarrolló la primera industria del hierro de África porque era fácil conseguir mineral de hierro y madera como combustible. Los **mercaderes** de Egipto y Grecia despachaban productos desde Kush y los enviaban al Mediterráneo y más allá. Las **exportaciones** de Kush incluían oro, cerámica, herramientas de hierro, marfil y esclavos. Las **importaciones** incluían objetos lujosos de Egipto, Asia y el Mediterráneo.

> **What items did Kush export?/¿Qué productos exportaba Kush?**
> _____
> _____

The Kushites worshipped their own gods and developed their own writing. Women were active in society, and some rose to positions of authority. **Queen Shanakhdakheto** (shah-nahk-dah-KEE-toh) was the first of many women who ruled Kush./Los kushitas adoraban a sus propios dioses y desarrollaron su propia escritura. Las mujeres participaban en la sociedad y algunas ocuparon puestos de autoridad. La **reina Shanakdakhete** fue la primera de muchas mujeres en gobernar Kush.

> **What was the role of women in Kushite society?/¿Cuál era el papel de las mujeres en la sociedad kushita?**
> _____
> _____
> _____
> _____

## THE DECLINE OF KUSH/DECADENCIA DE KUSH

By the AD 300s, another trading center, **Aksum** (AHK-soom), located in what is now Eritrea, began competing with Kush for trade. The Aksum leader **King Ezana** (AY-zah-nah) invaded, and Kush fell./ Hacia el siglo 4 d. C., otro centro comercial, **Aksum,** ubicado en lo que hoy es Eritrea, comenzó a competir con Kush por la actividad comercial. El líder de Aksum, el **rey Ezana,** invadió Kush y tomó posesión del reino.

Aksum became a major trading power. Traders also brought new beliefs, such as Christianity. In the late 300s, King Ezana made Christianity the official religion. Aksum was never conquered, but it became cut off from its allies. The people of Aksum then retreated to Ethiopia./Aksum se convirtió en una potencia comercial muy importante. Los comerciantes también introdujeron creencias nuevas, como el cristianismo. A fines del siglo 4, el rey Ezana adoptó el cristianismo como religión oficial. El reino de Aksum nunca fue conquistado, pero quedó aislado de sus aliados. Luego, los habitantes de Aksum se retiraron a Etiopía.

> Circle the name and kingdom of the ruler who eventually defeated Kush./ Encierra en un círculo el nombre y el reino del soberano que finalmente derrotó a Kush.

## CHALLENGE ACTIVITY/ACTIVIDAD AVANZADA

**Critical Thinking: Summarize/Pensamiento crítico: Resumir** Pretend you are a Kushite leader in 850 BC. Write a short essay summarizing the details of a plan to defeat Egypt./Imagina que eres un líder kushita que vive en el año 850 a. C. Escribe un ensayo breve en el que resumas los detalles de un plan para derrotar a Egipto.

**DIRECTIONS/INSTRUCCIONES** Look at each set of four vocabulary terms. On the line provided, write the letter of the term that does not relate to the others./Observa cada conjunto de cuatro términos de vocabulario. En el espacio en blanco, escribe la letra del término que no tiene relación con los demás.

_____ 1. a. Piankhi/Pianjy
b. an Egyptian/un egipcio
c. son of Kashta/hijo de Kashta
d. a Kushite/un kushita

_____ 2. a. Piankhi/Pianjy
b. trade network/red comercial
c. Meroë/Meroe
d. a system of people in different lands who trade goods/sistema en el que personas de diferentes territorios intercambian productos

_____ 3. a. merchants/mercaderes
b. traders/comerciantes
c. Egyptian and Greek/egipcios y griegos
d. King Ezana/rey Ezana

_____ 4. a. imports/importaciones
b. exports/exportaciones
c. goods brought in/productos que se introducen en un país
d. fine jewelry and luxury items/joyas finas y objetos de lujo

_____ 5. a. imports/importaciones
b. exports/exportaciones
c. items sent out/productos que se envían a otro país
d. gold and slaves/oro y esclavos

_____ 6. a. King Ezana/rey Ezana
b. first woman to rule Kush/primera mujer que gobernó Kush
c. 170 BC to 150 BC/desde el 170 a. C. hasta el 150 a. C.
d. Queen Shanakhdakheto/reina Shanakdakhete

_____ 7. a. King Ezana/rey Ezana
b. Queen Shanakhdakheto/reina Shanakdakhete
c. King of Aksum/rey de Aksum
d. destroyed Meroë/destrucción de Meroe

_____ 8. a. in northeast Africa/en el noreste de África
b. near the Red Sea/cerca del mar Rojo
c. ruled by women/gobernado por mujeres
d. an ancient kingdom/reino antiguo

## Ancient India/La antigua India

**MAIN IDEAS/IDEAS PRINCIPALES**
1. The geography of India includes high mountains, great rivers and heavy seasonal rain./La geografía de la India incluye montañas altas, grandes ríos y lluvias estacionales intensas.
2. Harappan civilization developed along the Indus River./La civilización harappa se desarrolló a orillas del río Indo.

## Key Terms and People/Personas y palabras clave

**subcontinent/subcontinente** a large landmass smaller than a continent/gran masa de tierra de menor tamaño que un continente

**monsoons/monzones** seasonal wind patterns that cause wet and dry seasons/patrones estacionales de viento que causan las estaciones secas y húmedas

**seal/sello** a stamped image with images of humans and animals/imagen estampada con figuras humanas y de animales

## Lesson Summary/Resumen de la lección
### GEOGRAPHY OF INDIA/GEOGRAFÍA DE LA INDIA

India is home to one of the world's earliest civilizations. India is so huge it's called a **subcontinent**, which is a large landmass that is smaller than a continent. A subcontinent is usually separated from a continent by physical features, such as mountains. The world's highest mountains, the Himalayas, are in India. India also has a vast desert, many fertile plains, and rugged plateaus. The Indus River, which flows from the Himalayas and is located mainly in present-day Pakistan, is the cradle of ancient Indian civilization. As in Egypt and Mesopotamia, the flooding river created fertile plains where people first settled. The Ganges River is shorter than the Indus, but it flows through a fertile and populated area. It has been used for irrigation since early times. The Ganges has long been used for transportation, and today it is an important source of hydroelectric power.

> Underline India's geographic features./Subraya los accidentes geográficos de la India.

> Circle the name of the world's highest mountains./Encierra en un círculo el nombre de la cordillera más alta del mundo.

> What effect do monsoons have on India's climate?/¿Qué efecto tienen los monzones en el clima de la India?
>
> _____
>
> _____

India's hot and humid climate is heavily influenced by **monsoons**, wind patterns that cause wet and dry seasons./En la India, surgió una de las primeras civilizaciones del mundo. La India es un país tan grande que se le considera un **subcontinente**, es decir, una gran masa de tierra de menor tamaño que un continente. Muchas veces, los subcontinentes están separados del resto del continente por características físicas como las montañas. En la India, está la cordillera más alta del mundo: el Himalaya. La India también tiene un gran desierto, muchas llanuras fértiles y mesetas irregulares. El río Indo, que nace en el Himalaya y atraviesa la mayor parte del territorio actual de Pakistán, fue la cuna de la antigua civilización india. Al igual que en Egipto y Mesopotamia, las inundaciones del río crearon llanuras fértiles en las que surgieron los primeros asentamientos. El río Ganges es más corto que el Indo, pero atraviesa una zona fértil y poblada. Este río se usa para irrigación desde tiempos remotos. También se usa para el transporte desde hace mucho tiempo y, en la actualidad, es una importante fuente de energía hidroeléctrica. El clima caluroso y húmedo de la India recibe la influencia de los **monzones,** patrones de viento que causan las estaciones secas y húmedas.

## HARAPPAN CIVILIZATION/CIVILIZACIÓN HARAPPA

India's first-known civilization that grew up in the Indus River Valley is called the Harappan (huh-RA-puhn) civilization. It is named after the modern city of Harappa, Pakistan. Archaeologists believe Harappans thrived between 2300 and 1700 BC. In fact, most information about Harappans comes from the ruins of Harappa and another major city, Mohenjo Daro (mo-HEN-joh DAR-oh). Both cities were on the Indus and were more than 300 miles apart. Each city was well planned with a large fortress nearby that could easily oversee the city streets. The buildings were built of brick made from mud left by the river flooding. Both cities had public wells. Harappan farmers used irrigation to help produce a surplus of food./La civilización harappa fue la primera civilización que se conoce de la India y se desarrolló en el valle del Indo. Debe su nombre a la actual ciudad de Harappa, en Pakistán. Los arqueólogos creen que esta civilización tuvo su apogeo entre los años 2300 y 1700 a. C. De hecho, la mayor parte de la información sobre los harappas se obtuvo de las ruinas de Harappa y Mohenjo Daro, otra ciudad importante. Ambas ciudades estaban sobre el río Indo, y se encontraban a más de 300 millas de distancia una de otra. Las dos estaban bien planificadas: tenían cerca una gran fortaleza desde la que se podían ver las calles de la ciudad. Las construcciones eran de ladrillos que se hacían con el barro que dejaban las inundaciones del río. Ambas ciudades tenían pozos de agua públicos. Los agricultores harappas irrigaban sus cultivos para producir un excedente de alimentos.

The cities were very advanced. Most houses had indoor plumbing. The Harappans developed beautiful artisan crafts and a system of weights and measures. **Seals,** stamped images with figures of humans and animals, may mean they were religious. They also developed India's first writing system, but scholars have not yet learned to read it./Las ciudades eran muy avanzadas. La mayoría de las casas tenían instalaciones de agua. Los harappas confeccionaban hermosas artesanías y contaban con un sistema de pesos y medidas. Se han encontrado **sellos,** o imágenes estampadas con figuras humanas y de animales, que podrían indicar que eran religiosos. Los harappas también desarrollaron el primer sistema de escritura de la

> **Why was it an advantage for the streets of Mohenjo Daro and Harappa to be viewed from a fortress?/ ¿Por qué era una ventaja que las calles de Mohenjo Daro y Harappa se pudieran ver desde una fortaleza?**
>
> _____
> _____
> _____
> _____

India, pero los estudiosos aún no han podido descifrarlo.

Little is known about Harappan society. We do know that they traded with other regions, because Harappan seals have been found in Mesopotamia. The Persian Gulf may have been a sea trade route. It's also unclear why the Harappan civilization ended by the early 1700s BC./Se sabe muy poco acerca de la sociedad harappa. Lo que sí sabemos es que comerciaban con otras regiones, pues se han hallado sellos harappas en Mesopotamia. Es probable que el golfo Pérsico haya sido una ruta comercial marítima. Se desconoce la razón por la que la civilización harappa llegó a su fin cerca del año 1700 a. C.

> **Why do we know so little about the Harappans?/¿Por qué sabemos tan poco sobre los harappas?**
>
> _____
> _____
> _____
> _____
> _____
> _____

## CHALLENGE ACTIVITY/ACTIVIDAD AVANZADA

**Critical Thinking: Make Inferences/Pensamiento crítico: Hacer inferencias** Write a short essay explaining what you think might have happened to the Harappan civilization./Escribe un ensayo breve en el que expliques qué crees que pasó con la civilización harappa.

## DIRECTIONS/INSTRUCCIONES Write a word or phrase that has the same meaning as the term given./Escribe una palabra o frase que tenga el mismo significado que el término dado.

1. monsoons/monzones _____

   _____

2. seals/sellos _____

   _____

3. subcontinent/subcontinente_____

   _____

**DIRECTIONS/INSTRUCCIONES** Read each sentence and fill in the blank with the word in the word pair that best completes the sentence./Lee cada oración y escribe en el espacio en blanco la palabra del par de palabras que mejor la completa.

4. The _____ civilization was India's first civilization. **(Mesopotamian/ Harappan)**/La civilización _____ fue la primera civilización de la India. **(mesopotámica/harappa)**

5. The _____, which are located in northern India, are the highest mountains in the world. **(Ganges/Himalayas)**/El _____, en el norte de la India, es la cordillera más alta del mundo. **(Ganges/Himalaya)**

6. The longest river that flows out of the Himalaya mountain range is the _____ River. **(Ganges/Indus)**/El río más largo que nace en la cordillera del Himalaya es el río _____. **(Ganges/Indo)**

7. A _____ is usually separated from the rest of the continent by physical features, such as mountains. **(monsoon/subcontinent)**/Los _____ suelen estar separados del resto del continente por características físicas como las montañas. **(monzones/subcontinentes)**

8. In the summertime, _____ blow into India from the ocean, bringing heavy rains that can cause terrible floods. **(monsoons/seals)**/En el verano, los _____ soplan hacia la India desde el océano, lo que genera lluvias intensas que causan inundaciones catastróficas. **(monzones/sellos)**

9. Today the _____ River is an important source of _____ power. **(Ganges/Indus) (human/hydroelectric)**/En la actualidad, el río _____ es una fuente importante de energía _____. **(Ganges/Indo) (humana/hidroeléctrica)**

10. Harappan _____ have been found in Mesopotamian cities, showing that the people traded goods with other civilizations. **(monsoons/seals)**/Se han hallado _____ harappas en ciudades de Mesopotamia, lo que indica que los harappas comerciaban con otras civilizaciones. **(monzones/sellos)**

11. Little is known about the _____ civilization because scholars have not yet learned to read their writing system. **(Indian/Harappan)**/Se sabe muy poco sobre la civilización _____, ya que los estudiosos aún no han descifrado su sistema de escritura. **(india/harappa)**

# Ancient India/La antigua India

**MAIN IDEAS/IDEAS PRINCIPALES**
1. The Aryan migration to India changed the region's civilization./La migración de los arios hacia la India provocó cambios en la civilización de la región.
2. The Aryans practiced a religion known as Brahmanism./Los arios practicaban una religión conocida como brahmanismo.
3. Indian society divided into distinct groups under the Aryans./Bajo el dominio ario, la sociedad india se dividió en grupos bien definidos.

## Key Terms and People/Personas y palabras clave

**Sanskrit/sánscrito** ancient India's most important language, on which the Hindi language is based/el idioma más importante de la antigua India, del cual derivó el idioma hindi

**caste system/sistema de castas** a division of Indian society into groups based on a person's birth, wealth, or occupation/división de la sociedad india en grupos según el origen, la riqueza o la ocupación de cada persona

## Lesson Summary/Resumen de la lección

### ARYAN MIGRATION/MIGRACIÓN ARIA

Following the Harappan civilization, the Aryans (AIR-ee-uhnz), nomads from Central Asia, moved into the Indus Valley in the 2000s BC. Aryans were originally from the Caspian Sea in Central Asia, and over the centuries they became the dominant group in India. Unlike the Harappans, they did not build big cities but lived in small communities based on family ties, each run by a local leader, or raja./Después de la civilización harappa, el valle del Indo fue poblado por los arios, nómadas de Asia Central, alrededor del año 2000 a. C. Los arios eran originarios del mar Caspio en Asia Central y, con el paso de los siglos, se convirtieron en el grupo dominante de la India. A diferencia de los harappas, los arios no construyeron grandes ciudades, sino que vivían en comunidades pequeñas basadas en los lazos familiares. Cada comunidad estaba administrada por un líder del lugar, o rajá.

The Aryans spoke **Sanskrit** and developed a rich tradition of poems and hymns, but they did not have a writing system. Instead, their works survived from generation to generation by word of mouth. Aryans eventually figured out how to write Sanskrit to keep records. The lasting influence of these early written works made Sanskrit the most important language of ancient India. Much of what we know about the early Aryans comes to us through Sanskrit works. Sanskrit is no longer spoken today, but it is the root of many modern South Asian languages, including Hindi./Los arios hablaban en **sánscrito** y tenían una rica tradición de poemas e himnos, pero no tenían un sistema de escritura. Sin embargo, sus obras sobrevivieron gracias a la transmisión oral de una generación a la otra. Con el tiempo, los arios desarrollaron una forma de escritura en sánscrito para llevar registros. La influencia duradera de estas primeras obras escritas hizo del sánscrito el idioma más importante de la antigua India. Gran parte de lo que sabemos sobre los primeros arios proviene de las obras escritas en sánscrito. Esta lengua ya no se habla en la actualidad, pero dio origen a muchas lenguas modernas del sur de Asia, incluido el idioma hindi.

> **The early Aryans had a rich and expressive language, but they did not write. How did they preserve their poems and their history without writing?/Los primeros arios tenían una lengua rica y expresiva, pero no escribían. ¿Cómo hicieron para preservar sus poemas y su historia sin la escritura?**
>
> _____
>
> _____

## BRAHMANISM/BRAHMANISMO

The religion practiced by the Aryan priests became known as Brahmanism. Their religion was based on the Vedas, first passed down orally and then written. They contained ancient sacred hymns and poems. Over time, Aryan Brahmins and scholars wrote their thoughts about the Vedas, which were compiled into Vedic texts. The texts described rituals, explained how to perform sacrifices, and offered reflections from religious scholars./La religión que practicaban los

> **Underline what the Vedic texts contained./Subraya lo que contenían los textos védicos.**

sacerdotes arios se conoció como brahmanismo.
Se basaba en los Vedas, que en un principio se
trasmitieron oralmente y luego de forma escrita.
Los Vedas contenían himnos y poemas sagrados
de la Antigüedad. Con el paso del tiempo, los
brahmanes y los eruditos arios empezaron a
escribir sus ideas sobre los Vedas, que fueron
recopiladas en textos védicos. En estos textos se
describían rituales, se explicaba cómo realizar
sacrificios y se ofrecían reflexiones de los
estudiosos religiosos.

In the later Vedic period between 800 BC and
500 BC, communities switched from a focus on
family identity to identifying themselves by where
they lived. Rajas became more like powerful
chiefs. Chiefs gave sacrifices of wealth to priests
to be more powerful and to be close to the
gods./A fines del período védico, entre los años
800 y 500 a. C., las comunidades pasaron de
tener una identidad familiar a identificarse con
el lugar donde vivían. Los rajás se parecían cada
vez más a jefes poderosos. Los jefes ofrecían sus
bienes como sacrificio a los sacerdotes para
tener más poder y estar cerca de los dioses.

## INDIAN SOCIETY DIVIDES/LA SOCIEDAD INDIA SE DIVIDE

Aryan society was divided into social classes.
There were four main groups called *varnas*. The
Brahmins (BRAH-muhns) were priests and were
the highest ranking *varna*. The Kshatriyas (KSHA-
tree-uhs) were rulers and warriors. The Vaisyas
(VYSH-yuhs) were farmers, craftspeople, and
traders. The Sudras (SOO-drahs) were laborers
and non-Aryans./La sociedad aria estaba
dividida en clases sociales. Había cuatro grupos
principales, llamados *varnas*. Los brahmanes
eran sacerdotes y pertenecían a la *varna* superior.
Los chatrias eran gobernantes y guerreros.

> **Number the Aryan varnas in order of their social rank, with one (1) being highest and four (4) being the lowest./Coloca un número para ordenar los varnas arios según su rango social, desde el más alto (1) hasta el más bajo (4).**
> ____ **Brahmins/brahmanes**
> ____ **Sudras/sudras**
> ____ **Kshatriyas/chatrias**
> ____ **Vaisyas/vaisias**

Los vaisias eran agricultores, artesanos y comerciantes. Los sudras eran los obreros y los no arios.

The **caste system** became more complex, dividing Indian society into groups based on birth, wealth, or occupation, and it determined people's place in society. Castes increased in number and the Aryans created sutras, or guides, listing rules of behavior. One group did not belong to any caste and was called the untouchables./El **sistema de castas** se volvió cada vez más complejo y comenzó a dividir a la sociedad india en grupos según el origen, la riqueza o la ocupación. El sistema de castas determinaba el lugar de cada persona en la sociedad. La cantidad de castas aumentó y los arios crearon sutras, o guías, que enumeraban reglas de conducta. Había un grupo que no pertenecía a ninguna casta: los intocables.

> **In ancient India, how was a person's caste determined?/ En la antigua India, ¿cómo se determinaba la casta de una persona?**
>
> _____
> _____
> _____

## CHALLENGE ACTIVITY/ACTIVIDAD AVANZADA

**Critical Thinking: Interpret/Pensamiento crítico: Interpretar** The caste system in Indian society became more complex over time. Why did this happen? Write a letter to a friend explaining why you believe this may have happened./El sistema de castas de la sociedad india se volvió cada vez más complejo. ¿Por qué sucedió esto? Escribe una carta a un amigo en la que expliques por qué crees que pudo haber pasado eso.

**DIRECTIONS/INSTRUCCIONES** On the line provided before each statement, write **T** if a statement is true and **F** if a statement is false. If the statement is false, write the correct term on the line after each sentence that makes the sentence a true statement./En la línea que precede a cada enunciado, escribe **V** si el enunciado es verdadero y **F** si es falso. Si el enunciado es falso, escribe en la línea que sigue a la oración el término correcto que lo hace verdadero.

_____ 1. Ancient writings known as the <u>Sanskrit</u> include poems, hymns, myths, and rituals./<u>Los sánscritos</u> son escritos antiguos que incluyen poemas, himnos, mitos y rituales.

_____

_____ 2. The leader of each village was given the title of <u>raja</u>./El líder de cada aldea recibía el título de <u>rajá</u>.

_____

_____ 3. Sanskrit was the language of the <u>Harappan civilization</u>./El sánscrito era el idioma de la <u>civilización harappa</u>.

_____

_____ 4. Today <u>Sanskrit</u> is no longer a spoken language, but the modern Hindi language is based on it./En la actualidad ya no se habla el <u>sánscrito</u>, pero el idioma hindi derivó de él.

_____

_____ 5. The early caste system divided Aryan society into four social classes called <u>Sudras</u>./El primer sistema de castas dividió a la sociedad aria en cuatro clases sociales llamadas <u>sudras</u>.

_____

_____ 6. Brahmanism was practiced by <u>Harappan</u> priests who based their religion on the Vedas./El brahmanismo era practicado por los sacerdotes <u>harappas</u>, que basaban su religión en los Vedas.

_____

_____ 7. The <u>caste system</u> came to divide Indian society into groups based on birth, wealth, or occupation./<u>El sistema de castas</u> llegó a dividir a la sociedad india en grupos según el origen, la riqueza o la ocupación.

_____

_____ 8. To keep the social classes distinct, the Aryans wrote guides called <u>Vaisyas</u> that listed all the rules for the caste system./Para que la división en clases sociales estuviera bien definida, los arios escribieron guías llamadas <u>vaisias</u> en las que se enumeraban todas las reglas del sistema de castas.

_____

## Ancient India/La antigua India

**MAIN IDEAS/IDEAS PRINCIPALES**
1. Hinduism developed out of Brahmanism and influences from other cultures./ El hinduismo se desarrolló a partir del brahmanismo y de las influencias de otras culturas.
2. A few groups reacted to Hinduism by breaking away to form their own religions./Algunos grupos se separaron del hinduismo y formaron sus propias religiones.

# Key Terms and People/Personas y palabras clave

**Hinduism/hinduismo** the most widespread religion in India today/la religión de mayor difusión en la India en la actualidad

**reincarnation/reencarnación** the belief that the soul, once a person dies, is reborn in another person/creencia de que, después de que una persona muere, el alma vuelve a nacer en otra persona

**karma/karma** the effects that good or bad actions have on a person's soul/las consecuencias que tienen las buenas o las malas acciones en el alma de una persona

**samskaras/samskaras** rites of passage to prepare a person for an event or next stage in life/ritos de paso para preparar a una persona para un evento o para su próxima etapa de la vida

**Jainism/jainismo** a nonviolent religion based on the teachings of Mahavira/ religión no violenta que se basa en las enseñanzas de Mahavira

**Mahavira/Mahavira** founder of Jainism who taught four basic nonviolent principles to follow/fundador del jainismo, quien enseñaba cuatro principios básicos de la no violencia

**nonviolence/no violencia** the avoidance of violent actions/la práctica de evitar las acciones violentas

**Sikhism/sijismo** monotheistic religion founded in India in the 1400s/religión monoteísta fundada en la India en el siglo 15

**Guru Nanak/Guru Nanak** teacher whose blending of religious ideas from Islam, Hinduism, and other religions came to be called Sikhism/maestro cuya fusión de ideas religiosas provenientes del islam, el hinduismo y otras religiones se denominó sijismo

# Lesson Summary/Resumen de la lección
## HINDUISM DEVELOPS/DESARROLLO DEL HINDUISMO

**Hinduism** is India's largest religion today. It developed from Brahmanism and ideas from other cultures. Hindus believe that there are many gods but all gods are part of a universal spirit called Brahman. Hindus believe everyone has a soul, or *atman*, inside them and the soul longs to join with Brahman. This happens when the soul recognizes that the world we live in is an illusion. Hindus believe this understanding takes several lifetimes, so **reincarnation,** or rebirth, is necessary. The form you take when you are reborn depends upon your **karma,** the effect your actions in life have on your soul. Those who build good karma by good actions are reborn to higher castes. Those who create bad karma by evil actions are reborn into lower castes. Hinduism teaches that each person has a *dharma*, a set of spiritual duties to fulfill in each life. By teaching people to accept their station in life, Hinduism helped to keep the caste system in place./El **hinduismo** es la religión mayoritaria de la India en la actualidad. Se desarrolló a partir del brahmanismo y de las ideas de otras culturas. Los hindúes creen que existen muchos dioses, pero que todos ellos forman parte de un espíritu universal llamado Brahman. Los hindúes creen que todas las personas tienen un alma, o *atman*, y que esta desea unirse con Brahman. Esta unión sucede cuando el alma reconoce que el mundo en el que vivimos es una ilusión. Los hindúes creen que esta comprensión tarda varias vidas en llegar, de modo que es necesaria la **reencarnación,** es decir, el renacimiento. La forma que se toma al renacer depende del **karma,** que es la consecuencia que tienen en el alma las acciones de una persona.

> **Underline the Hindu name for the soul./**Subraya el nombre que se le da al alma en el hinduismo.

> **What is karma?/**¿Qué es el karma?
> _____
> _____
> _____
> _____
> _____

Quienes desarrollan un buen karma mediante buenas acciones vuelven a nacer en castas superiores. En cambio, quienes generan mal karma mediante actos malvados vuelven a nacer en castas inferiores. El hinduismo enseña que cada persona tiene un *dharma*, o conjunto de deberes espirituales que debe cumplir en cada vida. Al enseñar a las personas a aceptar su condición en la vida, el hinduismo contribuyó a mantener en pie el sistema de castas.

Rituals and ceremonies have always been important parts of Hinduism. **Samskaras,** rites of passage to prepare a person for a special event or for his or her next stage in life, are still important today./Los rituales y las ceremonias siempre han sido una parte importante del hinduismo. Aún hoy son importantes los **samskaras,** ritos de paso para preparar a una persona para un evento especial o para la próxima etapa de su vida.

Hinduism spread throughout Southeast Asia, mostly due to traders exchanging goods, and then through colonization when Hindus went to work in British and Dutch colonies./El hinduismo se difundió a través del sureste asiático en gran parte gracias a los comerciantes y luego mediante la colonización, cuando los hindúes fueron a trabajar a las colonias británicas y neerlandesas.

## GROUPS REACT TO HINDUISM/ALGUNOS GRUPOS REACCIONAN AL HINDUISMO

The religions of **Jainism** and **Sikhism** developed in reaction to Hinduism. Jainism is based upon the teachings of **Mahavira,** who taught four basic principles: injure no life, tell the truth, do not steal, and own no property. Jains practice **nonviolence**, meaning they avoid violent actions because they believe that everything is alive and

> Underline the four main teachings of Jainism./ Subraya las cuatro enseñanzas principales del jainismo.

**Lesson/Lección 3,** *continued/continuación*

part of the cycle of rebirth. The Sanskrit word
for nonviolence is *ahimsa* (uh-HIM-sah)./El
**jainismo** y el **sijismo** son religiones que surgieron
como reacción al hinduismo. El jainismo se basa
en las enseñanzas de **Mahavira,** quien predicaba
cuatro principios básicos: no hacer daño a
ninguna forma de vida, decir la verdad, no robar
y no tener posesiones. Los jainas practican la **no
violencia,** es decir, evitan los actos violentos ya
que creen que todo tiene vida y que todo forma
parte del ciclo de renacimiento. En sánscrito, no
violencia se decía *ahimsa.*

Sikhism was founded centuries after Jainism,
based on the teachings of **Guru Nanak.** It is
monotheistic, which means Sikhs believe in one
god. Sikhims blends elements of Hinduism and
other religions, including Islam./El sijismo fue
fundado siglos después del jainismo y se basó
en las enseñanzas de **Guru Nanak.** Se trata de
una religión monoteísta, lo que significa que los
sijes creen en un solo dios. El sijismo combina
elementos del hinduismo y de otras religiones,
incluido el islam.

> **What does** *monotheistic*
> **mean?/¿Qué significa**
> *monoteísta*?
>
> _____
>
> _____
>
> _____

## CHALLENGE ACTIVITY/ACTIVIDAD AVANZADA

**Critical Thinking: Make Inferences/Pensamiento
crítico: Hacer inferencias** The idea of *ahimsa*
has proved popular with reformers through the
centuries. Write a one-page essay explaining why
this might be so./La idea de *ahimsa* ha sido bien
recibida por diferentes reformistas a través de los
siglos. Escribe un ensayo de una página en el que
expliques por qué crees que esto fue así.

**DIRECTIONS/INSTRUCCIONES** On the line provided before each statement, write **T** if a statement is true and **F** if a statement is false. If the statement is false, write the correct term on the line after each sentence that makes the sentence a true statement./En la línea que precede a cada enunciado, escribe **V** si el enunciado es verdadero y **F** si es falso. Si el enunciado es falso, escribe en la línea que sigue a la oración el término correcto que lo hace verdadero.

_____ 1. The force created by a person's actions is called <u>karma</u>./La fuerza creada por las acciones de una persona se llama <u>karma</u>.

_____

_____ 2. <u>Hinduism</u> is based on four major principles: injure no life, tell the truth, do not steal, and own no property./<u>El hinduismo</u> se basa en cuatro principios básicos: no hacer daño a ninguna forma de vida, decir la verdad, no robar y no tener posesiones.

_____

_____ 3. <u>Hinduism</u>, the largest religion in India, teaches that each person has a *dharma*, spiritual duties to fulfill in each life./<u>El hinduismo</u>, la religión mayoritaria de la India, enseña que cada persona tiene un *dharma*, o deberes espirituales que debe cumplir en cada vida.

_____

_____ 4. <u>Nonviolence</u> is the avoidance of violent actions, which was practiced by the Jains./<u>La no violencia</u> es la práctica de evitar las acciones violentas y era practicada por los jainas.

_____

_____ 5. Hindus believe that souls are born and reborn many times, each time into a new body, in a process called <u>reincarnation</u>./Los hindúes creen que el alma nace y vuelve a nacer muchas veces, cada vez en un cuerpo distinto, en un proceso llamado <u>reencarnación</u>.

_____

_____ 6. According to Hindu teachings, everyone has a soul, or *<u>atman</u>*, inside them./Según las enseñanzas hindúes, todas las personas tienen un alma, o *<u>atman</u>*.

_____

_____ 7. <u>Hinduism</u> is based on the teachings of a man named Guru Nanak./
<u>El hinduismo</u> se basa en las enseñanzas de un hombre llamado
Guru Nanak.

_____

_____ 8. Hindus believe that a person's ultimate goal should be to reunite the
soul with <u>karma</u>, the universal spirit./Los hindúes creen que el objetivo
final de una persona debe ser que su alma se reencuentre con <u>el karma</u>,
el espíritu universal.

_____

## Ancient India/La antigua India

**MAIN IDEAS/IDEAS PRINCIPALES**

1. Siddhartha Gautama searched for wisdom in many ways./Sidarta Gautama buscaba la sabiduría de distintas maneras.
2. The teachings of Buddhism deal with finding peace./Las enseñanzas del budismo están relacionadas con la búsqueda de la paz.
3. Buddhism spread far from where it began in India./El budismo se extendió más allá de la India, donde se originó.

# Key Terms and People/Personas y palabras clave

**fasting/ayunar** going without food/dejar de comer

**meditation/meditación** focusing the mind on spiritual ideas/la práctica de enfocar la mente en ideas espirituales

**the Buddha/Buda** founder of Buddhism, born an Indian prince named Siddhartha Gautama/fundador del budismo, nacido como el príncipe indio Sidarta Gautama

**Buddhism/budismo** religion based on the teachings of the Buddha/religión basada en las enseñanzas de Buda

**nirvana/nirvana** a state of perfect peace/estado de paz perfecta

**missionaries/misioneros** people who spread and teach religious beliefs/personas que difunden y enseñan las creencias religiosas

# Lesson Summary/Resumen de la lección

### SIDDARTHA'S SEARCH FOR WISDOM/SIDARTA BUSCA LA SABIDURÍA

Not everyone in India accepted Hinduism. In the late 500s BC, a major new religion began to develop from questions posed by a young prince named Siddhartha Gautama (si-DAHR-tuh GAU-tuh-muh). Siddhartha was born to a wealthy family and led a life of comfort, but he wondered at the pain and suffering he saw all around him. By the age of 30, Siddhartha left his home and family to travel India. He talked to many priests and wise people, but he was not satisfied with their answers./En la India, no todos aceptaban el hinduismo. Hacia fines del siglo 6 a. C., comenzó

> **Why did Prince Siddhartha leave a comfortable home and loving family?/¿Por qué el príncipe Sidarta abandonó su vida llena de comodidades y a su querida familia?**
>
> _____
> _____
> _____
> _____

a desarrollarse una importante religión a partir de
los cuestionamientos de un joven príncipe llamado
Sidarta Gautama. Sidarta pertenecía a una familia
adinerada y tenía una vida llena de comodidades.
Sin embargo, el dolor y el sufrimiento que veía a
su alrededor lo inquietaban. A los 30 años, Sidarta
dejó su hogar y a su familia para viajar por la
India. Conversó con muchos sacerdotes y sabios,
pero no quedó satisfecho con sus respuestas.

Siddhartha did not give up. He wandered for
years throughout India trying to free himself
from daily concerns by **fasting** and **meditating.**
After six years, Siddhartha sat down under a tree
near the town of Gaya and meditated for seven
weeks. He came up with an answer to what causes
human suffering. Suffering is caused by wanting
what one does not have, wanting to keep what
one likes and already has, and not wanting what
one dislikes but has. He began to travel and teach
his ideas, and was soon called **the Buddha,** or
"Enlightened One." From his teachings sprang
the religion **Buddhism.**/Sidarta no se rindió.
Deambuló durante años por toda la India
intentando liberarse de las preocupaciones diarias
mediante el **ayuno** y la **meditación.** Después de seis
años, Sidarta se sentó bajo un árbol cerca de la
ciudad de Gaya y meditó durante siete semanas.
Entonces, dio con las causas del sufrimiento de
los seres humanos: desear lo que no se tiene,
desear retener lo que a uno le gusta y ya tiene,
y no desear lo que a uno no le gusta pero tiene.
Sidarta empezó a viajar para enseñar sus ideas,
y pronto se le llamó **Buda,** o "el iluminado".
De sus enseñanzas surgió la religión conocida
como **budismo.**

> Underline what Siddhartha believed to be the three causes of human suffering./Subraya las tres causas del sufrimiento humano, según Sidarta.

## TEACHINGS OF BUDDHISM/ENSEÑANZAS DEL BUDISMO

Buddhism is intent on relieving human suffering.
It is based upon the Four Noble Truths. These

truths are: suffering and unhappiness are a part of life; suffering stems from our desire for pleasure and material goods; people can overcome their desires and reach **nirvana,** a state of perfect peace, which ends the cycle of reincarnation; and people can overcome desire and ignorance by following an eightfold path to nirvana./El budismo intenta aliviar el sufrimiento humano. Se basa en las Cuatro Nobles Verdades: el sufrimiento y la infelicidad son parte de la vida; el sufrimiento surge de nuestro deseo de placer y bienes materiales; es posible dominar los propios deseos y alcanzar el **nirvana,** un estado de paz perfecta que finaliza el ciclo de reencarnación; y es posible superar el deseo y la ignorancia siguiendo un camino óctuple hacia el nirvana.

> **Underline the name of the central teachings of Buddhism./Subraya el nombre de las enseñanzas fundamentales del budismo.**

These teachings were similar to some Hindu concepts but went against some traditional Hindu ideas. Buddhism questioned the need for animal sacrifice and challenged the authority of the Brahmins, the Hindu priests. The Buddha said that each individual could reach salvation on his or her own. Buddhism also opposed the caste system./Aunque estas enseñanzas eran similares a algunos conceptos del hinduismo, estaban en contra de algunas de las ideas tradicionales de esa religión. El budismo cuestionaba la necesidad del sacrificio de animales y desafiaba la autoridad de los brahmanes, los sacerdotes hindúes. Buda decía que cada individuo podía lograr la salvación por sus propios medios. El budismo también se oponía al sistema de castas.

> **What is one difference between Buddhism and Hinduism?/¿Cuál es una de las diferencias entre el budismo y el hinduismo?**
>
> _____
> _____
> _____
> _____
> _____
> _____

## BUDDHISM SPREADS/EXPANSIÓN DEL BUDISMO

Buddhism spread quickly throughout India to eventually become a major global religion. With the help of Indian king Asoka, Buddhist **missionaries** were sent to other countries to teach their religious beliefs. Buddhism quickly took hold in neighboring countries like Nepal, Sri Lanka, and China. Buddhism soon became very influential in Japan and Korea. Over time, two branches of Buddhism developed—Theravada and Mahayana./El budismo se extendió con rapidez por toda la India y, con el tiempo, llegó a ser una de las religiones más importantes del mundo. Con la ayuda del rey indio Asoka, se enviaron **misioneros** budistas a otros países para enseñar sus creencias religiosas. En poco tiempo, el budismo ganó adeptos en países vecinos como Nepal, Sri Lanka y China, y comenzó a tener mucha influencia en Japón y Corea. Con el tiempo, surgieron dos ramas: theravada y mahayana.

> **Name three countries to which Buddhism spread./** Menciona tres países en los que se difundió el budismo.
>
> _____
>
> _____
>
> _____

## CHALLENGE ACTIVITY/ ACTIVIDAD AVANZADA

**Critical Thinking: Make Inferences/ Pensamiento crítico: Hacer inferencias** Could you leave your family, home, and everything you know to preach what you believe to be a spiritual truth? What do you think inspired the Buddha to do so? Write a short essay in which you explain his choice./¿Serías capaz de dejar a tu familia, tu hogar y todo lo que conoces para predicar lo que consideras una verdad espiritual? ¿Qué piensas que inspiró a Buda a hacerlo? Escribe un ensayo breve en él que expliques su decisión.

| | | |
|---|---|---|
| Buddha/ Buda | Buddhism/ budismo | fasting/ ayuno |
| meditation/ meditación | missionaries/ misioneros | nirvana/ nirvana |

**DIRECTIONS/ INSTRUCCIONES** Answer each question by writing a sentence that contains at least one word from the word bank./ Responde cada pregunta con una oración que contenga al menos una palabra del banco de palabras.

1. According to Buddhist teachings, if people can overcome their desires and ignorance, they will reach what?/Según las enseñanzas del budismo, si las personas pueden superar sus deseos y su ignorancia, ¿qué lograrán?

2. What did Siddhartha do to free his mind from daily concerns?/¿Qué hizo Sidarta para liberar su mente de las preocupaciones diarias?

_____

3. Who did the king send to spread the religious beliefs of Buddhism?/ ¿A quiénes envió el rey para que difundieran las creencias religiosas del budismo?

_____

4. What is the term that means "Enlightened One"?/¿Qué palabra significa "el iluminado"?

_____

5. What is the religion based on the teachings of Siddhartha Gautama?/¿Qué religión se basa en las enseñanzas de Sidarta Gautama?

_____

**DIRECTIONS/INSTRUCCIONES** On the line provided before each statement, write **T** if a statement is true and **F** if a statement is false. If the statement is false, write the correct term on the line after each sentence that makes the sentence a true statement./En la línea que precede a cada enunciado, escribe **V** si el enunciado es verdadero y **F** si es falso. Si el enunciado es falso, escribe en la línea que sigue a la oración el término correcto que lo hace verdadero.

_____ 6. The Buddha taught that anyone could achieve <u>meditation</u> no matter what caste the person had belonged to in life./Buda enseñaba que cualquier persona podía lograr <u>la meditación</u>, sin importar a qué casta había pertenecido en vida.

_____

_____ 7. <u>Buddhism</u> split into two major branches called Theravada and Mahayana./<u>El budismo</u> se separó en dos ramas principales llamadas theravada y mahayana.

_____

_____ 8. <u>Nirvana</u> traveled throughout Asia, eventually spreading Buddhism to China, Korea, and Japan./<u>Nirvana</u> viajó por toda Asia y difundió el budismo en China, Corea y Japón.

_____

## Ancient India/La antigua India

**MAIN IDEAS/IDEAS PRINCIPALES**
1. The Mauryan Empire unified most of India./El Imperio mauryano unificó la mayor parte de la India.
2. Gupta rulers promoted Hinduism in their empire./Los gobernantes de la dinastía Gupta fomentaron el hinduismo en su imperio.

## Key Terms and People/Personas y palabras clave

**Candragupta Maurya/Candragupta Maurya** Indian military leader who first unified India and founded the Mauryan Empire/líder militar indio, el primero en unificar la India y fundador del.Imperio mauryano

**Asoka/Asoka** Candragupta's grandson and last ruler of the Mauryan Empire/ nieto de Candragupta y último gobernante del Imperio mauryano

**Candra Gupta II/Candra Gupta II** ruler who brought great prosperity and stability to India/gobernante que le dio gran prosperidad y estabilidad a la India

## Lesson Summary/Resumen de la lección

**MAURYAN EMPIRE UNIFIES INDIA/EL IMPERIO MAURYANO UNIFICA LA INDIA**

Under Aryan rule, India was divided into several states with no central leader. Then, in the 320s BC, an Indian military leader named **Candragupta Maurya** seized control of the entire northern part of India. The Mauryan Empire lasted for 150 years./Bajo el dominio ario, la India estaba dividida en varios estados sin un líder central. Entonces, en la década de 320 a. C., un líder militar indio llamado **Candragupta Maurya** tomó el control de toda la parte norte de la India. El Imperio mauryano duró 150 años.

Candragupta's complex government included a huge army and a network of spies. He taxed the population heavily for the protection he offered. Eventually, Candragupta became a Jainist monk and gave up his throne to his son. His family continued to expand the Indian empire./El complejo gobierno de Candragupta contaba

> Which Indian leader unified northern India in the 320s BC?/¿Qué líder indio unificó el norte de la India en la década de 320 a. C.?
>
> _____
> _____

> What is the relationship between Candragupta's government and heavy taxes?/¿Qué relación hay entre el gobierno de Candragupta y los impuestos altos?
>
> _____
> _____
> _____
> _____

con un inmenso ejército y una red de espías. El soberano cobraba impuestos altos a la población a cambio de protección. Con el tiempo, Candragupta se convirtió en un monje jainista y cedió el trono a su hijo. Su familia continuó expandiendo el Imperio indio.

Candragupta's grandson, **Asoka,** was the strongest ruler of the Mauryan dynasty. The empire thrived under his rule. But eventually, tired of bloodshed and war, Asoka converted to Buddhism. He devoted the rest of his rule to improving the lives of his people by building roads, hospitals, and even universities. Asoka also sent Buddhist missionaries to other countries. The rest of the family, however, did not follow Asoka's example. When Asoka died, his sons struggled for power and foreign invaders threatened the country. The Mauryan Empire fell in 184 BC and India divided into smaller states for about 500 years. The spread of Buddhism steadily increased, while Hinduism declined./El nieto de Candragupta, **Asoka,** fue el gobernante más poderoso de la dinastía mauryana. Bajo su gobierno, el imperio prosperó. Sin embargo, con el paso del tiempo, y cansado de las muertes y las guerras, Asoka se convirtió al budismo. Envió misioneros budistas a otros países y dedicó el resto de su mandato a mejorar la vida de su pueblo mediante la construcción de caminos, hospitales e incluso universidades. No obstante, el resto de la familia no siguió el ejemplo de Asoka. Después de su muerte, sus hijos lucharon por el poder y el país se vio amenazado por invasores extranjeros. El Imperio mauryano cayó en el año 184 a. C. y la India se dividió en estados más pequeños que duraron unos 500 años. El budismo siguió expandiéndose, mientras que el hinduismo comenzó a decaer.

> **How did India's government change after the death of Asoka?/¿En qué cambió el gobierno de la India tras la muerte de Asoka?**
>
> _____
> _____
> _____
> _____
> _____

## GUPTA RULERS PROMOTE HINDUISM/LOS GOBERNANTES DE LA DINASTÍA GUPTA FOMENTAN EL HINDUISMO

A new dynasty was established in India. During the AD 300s, the Gupta Dynasty once again rose to unite and build the prosperity of India. Not only did the Guptas control India's military, they were devout Hindus and encouraged the revival of Hindu traditions and writings. They believed the social order of the caste system would keep their dynasty strong. The Guptas, however, also supported Jainism and Buddhism./En la India se estableció una nueva dinastía. Durante el siglo 4 d. C., la dinastía Gupta volvió a unir a la India y a traerle prosperidad. Los Gupta no solo controlaban al ejército indio, sino que eran hindúes devotos y fomentaban el restablecimiento de las tradiciones y las escrituras hindúes. Creían que el orden social del sistema de castas mantendría a su dinastía fuerte. Sin embargo, los Gupta también apoyaban el jainismo y el budismo.

> Underline the name of the dynasty that reunited India and revived Hindu traditions./Subraya el nombre de la dinastía que volvió a unir a la India y revivió las tradiciones hindúes.

Indian civilization reached a high point under **Candra Gupta II** (not related to Candragupta Maurya). He poured money and resources into strengthening the country's borders, as well as promoting the arts, literature, and religion./La civilización india alcanzó su apogeo bajo el dominio de **Candra Gupta II** (que no tenía parentesco con Candragupta Maurya). Candra Gupta II destinó dinero y recursos al fortalecimiento de las fronteras, así como a promover el arte, la literatura y la religión.

The Gupta Dynasty lasted until fierce attacks by the Huns from Central Asia during the late 400s drained the empire of its resources. India broke up once again into a patchwork of small states./La dinastía Gupta perduró hasta que los feroces ataques de los hunos de Asia Central a

fines del siglo 5 agotaron los recursos del imperio.
La India volvió a dividirse en pequeños estados.

## CHALLENGE ACTIVITY/ ACTIVIDAD AVANZADA

**Critical Thinking: Make Inferences/ Pensamiento crítico: Hacer inferencias** Asoka was strongly influenced by Buddhism. Candra Gupta II followed Hinduism. Choose one of these kings and write an essay explaining how his religion affected his point of view and his decisions during his reign./ Asoka estaba fuertemente influenciado por el budismo. Candra Gupta II seguía el hinduismo. Elige a uno de estos líderes y escribe un ensayo en el que expliques cómo su religión influyó en su punto de vista y en las decisiones que tomó durante su gobierno.

| Asoka/ Asoka | Candra Gupta II/ Candra Gupta II | Candragupta Maurya/ Candragupta Maurya |
|---|---|---|
| establish/ establece | Gupta Dynasty/ dinastía Gupta | Huns/ hunos |

**DIRECTIONS/ INSTRUCCIONES** Read each sentence and fill in the blank with the word in the word pair that best completes the sentence./ Lee cada oración y escribe en el espacio en blanco la palabra del par de palabras que mejor la completa.

1. Under Emperor _____, Indian civilization reached a high point. The empire's economy strengthened and people prospered. **(Candra Gupta II/Candragupta Maurya)/** Durante el gobierno del emperador _____, la civilización india alcanzó su apogeo. La economía del imperio se fortaleció y la gente prosperó. **(Candra Gupta II/Candragupta Maurya)**

2. _____ was the strongest ruler of the Mauryan dynasty. Later, he converted to Buddhism and worked toward improving the lives of his people. **(Asoka/Huns)/** _____ fue el gobernante más poderoso de la dinastía mauryana. Más tarde, se convirtió al budismo y se esforzó por mejorar la vida de su pueblo. **(Asoka/Hunos)**

3. The Mauryan Empire was founded by _____, who ruled with a complex government that included a network of spies and a huge army. **(Candra Gupta II/Candragupta Maurya)**/El Imperio mauryano fue fundado por _____, cuyo complejo gobierno contaba con una red de espías y un inmenso ejército. **(Candra Gupta II/Candragupta Maurya)**

4. When the _____ from Central Asia invaded India, it led to the end of the Gupta Dynasty. **(Asoka/Huns)**/Cuando los _____ de Asia Central invadieron la India, la dinastía Gupta llegó a su fin. **(Asoka/hunos)**

5. Under the _____, Hinduism became popular again, but the rulers also supported Buddhism and Jainism. **(Gupta Dynasty/Huns)**/Bajo el gobierno de _____, el hinduismo volvió a generalizarse, pero los gobernantes también apoyaban el budismo y el jainismo. **(la dinastía Gupta/los hunos)**

**DIRECTIONS/INSTRUCCIONES** Use the vocabulary terms from the word list to write a summary of the Mauryan Empire and the Gupta Dynasty./Usa el vocabulario de la lista de palabras para escribir un resumen del Imperio mauryano y la dinastía Gupta.

_____

_____

_____

_____

_____

_____

_____

_____

_____

_____

## Ancient India/La antigua India

**MAIN IDEAS/IDEAS PRINCIPALES**

1. Indian artists created great works of religious art./Los artistas indios crearon grandes obras de arte religioso.

2. Sanskrit literature flourished during the Gupta period./La literatura en sánscrito floreció durante el período de los Gupta.

3. The Indians made scientific advances in metalworking, medicine, and other sciences./Los indios lograron adelantos científicos en el trabajo con metales, la medicina y otras ciencias.

## Key Terms and People/Personas y palabras clave

**metallurgy/metalurgia** the science of working with metals/ciencia de trabajar con metales

**alloy/aleación** a mixture of two or more metals/mezcla de dos o más metales

**Hindu-Arabic numerals/números indoarábigos** the numbering system invented by Indian mathematicians and brought to Europe by Arabs; the numbers we use today/sistema numérico que usamos hoy en día, inventado por los matemáticos indios y llevado a Europa por los árabes

**inoculation/inoculación** a method of injecting a person with a small dose of a virus to help him or her build up defenses to a disease/método que consiste en inyectar una pequeña dosis de un virus a una persona para ayudarla a generar defensas contra una enfermedad

**astronomy/astronomía** the study of stars and planets/estudio de las estrellas y los planetas

## Lesson Summary/Resumen de la lección

### RELIGIOUS ART/ARTE RELIGIOSO

Both the Mauryan and Guptan empires unified India and created a stable environment where artists, writers, scholars, and scientists could thrive. Their works are still admired today. Much of the Indian art from this period was religious, inspired by both Hindu and Buddhist teachings. Many beautiful temples were built during this time and decorated with elaborate wood and stone carvings./Tanto el Imperio mauryano como el Imperio gupta unificaron la India y generaron un entorno estable en el que pudieron prosperar

What was the main inspiration for art and literature during the Mauryan and Guptan empires?/¿Cuál fue la principal inspiración del arte y la literatura durante los Imperios mauryano y gupta?

_____

_____

_____

_____

**Lesson/Lección 6,** *continued/continuación*

los artistas, los escritores, los eruditos y los
científicos. Las obras creadas aún hoy generan
admiración. Gran parte del arte indio de este
período era religioso y estaba inspirado en las
enseñanzas hinduistas y budistas. En esta época,
se erigieron muchos templos hermosos que se
adornaron con piedra y madera talladas.

## SANSKRIT LITERATURE/LITERATURA EN SÁNSCRITO

Great works of literature were written in
Sanskrit, the ancient Aryan language, during
the Gupta Dynasty. The best-known works
are the *Mahabharata* (muh-HAH-BAH-ruh-tuh)
and the *Ramayana* (rah-MAH-yuh-nuh). The
*Mahabharata*, a long story about the struggle
between two families for control of a kingdom,
is considered a classic Hindu text. The most
famous passage of the *Mahabharata* is called the
*Bhagavad Gita* (BUG-uh-vuhd GEE-tah). The
*Ramayana* is the story of the Prince Rama, a
human incarnation of one of the three major
Hindu gods, Vishnu, who fights demons and
marries the beautiful Princess Sita./Durante la
dinastía Gupta, las grandes obras literarias se
escribían en sánscrito, el antiguo idioma ario.
Las obras más conocidas son el *Mahabharata*
y el *Ramayana*. El *Mahabharata*, un extenso
relato sobre la lucha entre dos familias por el
control de un reino, es un clásico de la literatura
hindú. El pasaje más famoso del *Mahabharata*
se llama *Bhagavad Gita*. El Ramayana cuenta
la historia del príncipe Rama, la encarnación
humana de uno de los tres dioses principales del
hinduismo, Vishnu, quien enfrenta a demonios
y se casa con la hermosa princesa Sita.

> **In what language were literary works from the Gupta period written?/¿En qué idioma se escribieron las obras literarias del período de los Gupta?**
>
> _____
>
> _____

## SCIENTIFIC ADVANCES/ADELANTOS CIENTÍFICOS

Scientific and scholarly work also blossomed during the early Indian empires. Most prominent was the development of **metallurgy,** the science of working with metals. Indian technicians and engineers made strong tools and weapons. They also invented processes for creating **alloys.** Alloys, such as steel or bronze, may be stronger or more useful than pure metals like iron or copper./ Durante los primeros imperios indios, también prosperó el trabajo de científicos y estudiosos. El avance más importante fue el desarrollo de la **metalurgia,** la ciencia de trabajar con metales. Los técnicos e ingenieros indios fabricaron armas y herramientas resistentes, y también inventaron procesos para la creación de **aleaciones.** Las aleaciones, como el acero o el bronce, pueden resultar más resistentes o útiles que los metales puros como el hierro o el cobre.

> **What is the science of working with metals called?/¿Cómo se llama la ciencia de trabajar con metales?**
> _____

The numbers we use today, called **Hindu-Arabic numerals,** were first developed by Indian mathematicians and brought to Europe by Arabs. They also created the concept of zero, upon which all modern mathematics is based./ Los números que usamos en la actualidad, conocidos como **números indoarábigo**s, fueron desarrollados por matemáticos indios y llevados a Europa por los árabes. Los indios también inventaron el concepto del cero, sobre el que se basa la matemática moderna.

> **What important mathematical concept did Indians create?/¿Qué importante concepto matemático inventaron los indios?**
> _____

Other sciences also benefited from this period of Indian history. In medicine, Indians developed the technique of **inoculation,** which is injecting a person with a small dose of a virus to help him or her build up defenses to a disease. Doctors could even perform certain surgeries. India's fascination with **astronomy,** the study of stars and planets, led to the discovery of seven of the planets in our solar system./Otras ciencias

> **Indians at this period did not have telescopes. How do you think they discovered planets?/Los indios de este período no tenían telescopios. ¿Cómo crees que descubrieron los planetas?**
> _____
> _____
> _____
> _____
> _____
> _____
> _____
> _____
> _____
> _____

también se beneficiaron en este período de la historia de la India. En el campo de la medicina, los indios desarrollaron la técnica de la **inoculación,** que consiste en inyectar una pequeña dosis de un virus a una persona para ayudarla a generar defensas contra una enfermedad. Los médicos también realizaban ciertas cirugías. La fascinación de la India por la **astronomía,** el estudio de las estrellas y los planetas, condujo al descubrimiento de siete de los planetas que conforman el sistema solar.

## CHALLENGE ACTIVITY/ACTIVIDAD AVANZADA

**Critical Thinking: Make Inferences/Pensamiento crítico: Hacer inferencias** Our modern society borrows significantly from the scientific and mathematical achievements of the early Indian empires. Write a short play, story, or essay describing how our modern world might look without these inventions./Nuestra sociedad actual se nutrió considerablemente de los logros científicos y matemáticos de los primeros imperios de la India. Escribe una obra de teatro, un cuento o un ensayo breve para describir cómo sería el mundo moderno sin estos inventos.

## DIRECTIONS/INSTRUCCIONES Write a word or phrase that has the same meaning as the term given./Escribe una palabra o frase breve que tenga el mismo significado que el término dado.

1. alloy/aleación _____

   _____

2. astronomy/astronomía _____

   _____

3. Hindu-Arabic numerals/números indoarábigos _____

   _____

4. inoculation/inoculación _____

_____

5. metallurgy/metalurgia _____

_____

**DIRECTIONS/INSTRUCCIONES** Read each sentence and fill in the blank with the term in the word pair that best completes the sentence./Lee cada oración y escribe en el espacio en blanco la palabra del par de palabras que mejor la completa.

6. Identifying seven of the planets in our solar system is one accomplishment early Indians made in the field of _____. **(astronomy/metallurgy)/** Uno de los logros de la antigua civilización india en el campo de la _____ fue la identificación de siete planetas de nuestro sistema solar. **(astronomía/metalurgia)**

7. Indian doctors knew how to protect people against disease through _____. **(alloy/inoculation)/**Los médicos indios sabían cómo proteger a las personas de las enfermedades a través de la _____. **(aleación/inoculación)**

8. Ancient Indians were masters of _____ and knew processes for mixing metals to create an _____. **(astronomy/metallurgy) (alloy/ inoculation)**/Los antiguos indios eran expertos en _____ y conocían procesos para mezclar metales y así crear una _____. **(astronomía/ metalurgia) (aleación/inoculación)**

9. The _____ is one of Hinduism's most famous texts. (***Bhagavad Gita*/ Hindu-Arabic numerals)/**_____ es el nombre de uno de los textos más famosos del hinduismo. (***Bhagavad Gita*/Números indoarábigos)**

10. The numbers we use today are called _____ because they were created by Indian scholars and brought to Europe by the Arabs. (***Bhagavad Gita*/Hindu-Arabic numerals)/**Los números que usamos en la actualidad se llaman _____ porque fueron inventados por eruditos indios y llevados a Europa por los árabes. (***Bhagavad Gita*/números indoarábigos)**

## Ancient China/La antigua China

**MAIN IDEAS/IDEAS PRINCIPALES**
1. China's physical geography made farming possible but travel and communication difficult./La geografía física de China hizo posible la agricultura, pero dificultó los viajes y las comunicaciones.
2. Civilization began in China along the Huang He and Chang Jiang rivers./ En China, la civilización comenzó a desarrollarse a orillas de los ríos Huang He y Chang Jiang.
3. China's first dynasties helped Chinese society develop and made many other achievements./Las primeras dinastías de China contribuyeron al desarrollo de la sociedad china y obtuvieron muchos otros logros.

## Key Terms and People/Personas y palabras clave

**jade/jade** a hard gemstone/piedra preciosa muy dura

**oracle/oráculo** a prediction/predicción

## Lesson Summary/Resumen de la lección
### CHINA'S PHYSICAL GEOGRAPHY/GEOGRAFÍA FÍSICA DE CHINA

China is a large country—about the same size as the United States. It has many geographical features that affected Chinese civilization. Some features separated China from the rest of the world. An example is the Gobi, a desert that spreads over much of China's north. Some features separated groups of people within China. These include rugged mountains on the western frontier. /China es un país extenso; tiene aproximadamente el mismo tamaño que los Estados Unidos. Posee muchas características geográficas que influyeron en la civilización china. Algunas de estas características la separaron del resto del mundo. Un ejemplo es el desierto de Gobi, que ocupa gran parte del norte de China. Otras características, como las escarpadas montañas de la frontera occidental, separaron a grupos de personas dentro de la misma China.

> **In which part of China is the Gobi?/¿En qué parte de China se encuentra el desierto de Gobi?**
>
> _____

Low-lying plains in the east form one of the world's largest farming regions. Weather patterns vary widely across China. Two great rivers flow from west to east, the Huang He, or Yellow River, and the Chang Jiang, or Yangzi River. These rivers helped connect people in the east with the west./ Las llanuras bajas del este conforman una de las regiones agrícolas más grandes del mundo. Los patrones climáticos varían considerablemente a lo largo y a lo ancho de China. Dos grandes ríos fluyen de oeste a este: el río Huang He, o río Amarillo, y el río Chang Jiang, o río Yangtsé. Estos ríos permitieron que los habitantes del este se vincularan con los del oeste.

> **Underline the names of the features that helped connect people in the eastern part of China with those in western China./** Subraya los nombres de las características geográficas que contribuyeron a que los habitantes del este de China se vincularan con los del oeste.

## CIVILIZATION BEGINS/INICIOS DE LA CIVILIZACIÓN

Like other ancient peoples, people in China first settled along rivers. By 7000 BC, farmers grew rice in the Chang Jiang Valley. Along the Huang He, they grew millet and wheat. They also fished and hunted and raised pigs and sheep. Separate cultures developed along the rivers. As populations grew, villages spread. A social order developed. Graves of the rich often had objects made from **jade**./Al igual que otros pueblos antiguos, los primeros habitantes de China se establecieron a orillas de los ríos. Hacia el año 7000 a. C., los agricultores cultivaban arroz en el valle del Chang Jiang. A orillas del Huang He, en cambio, cultivaban mijo y trigo. También pescaban y cazaban, además de criar cerdos y ovejas. Diferentes culturas se desarrollaron a orillas de los ríos. A medida que la población crecía, las aldeas comenzaron a expandirse. Surgió un orden social. Las personas adineradas a menudo tenían objetos hechos de **jade** en sus tumbas.

> **Where did the Chinese first grow rice?/¿Dónde cultivaron arroz por primera vez los chinos?**
>
> _____
>
> _____

## CHINA'S FIRST DYNASTIES/PRIMERAS DINASTÍAS DE CHINA

Societies along the Huang He grew larger and more complex. Around 2200 BC, a legendary emperor called Yu the Great is said to have founded the Xia (SHAH) dynasty. It is believed that the first flood control channels were built during the Xia dynasty./Las sociedades que se encontraban a lo largo del Huang He se volvieron más extensas y complejas. Se cree que, alrededor del año 2200 a. C., un emperador legendario llamado Yu el Grande fundó la dinastía Xia. Aparentemente, durante esta dinastía se construyeron los primeros canales para contener inundaciones.

> **Under which dynasty were the first flood control channels built in China?/¿Durante qué dinastía se construyeron los primeros canales para contener inundaciones?**
>
> _____

The first dynasty for which there is clear evidence is the Shang. It was established by the 1500s BC. The Shang ruler and his family were at the top of the social order. Nobles and warrior leaders also had high rank. Artisans came next. They lived in groups depending on what they did for a living. Farmers were below artisans. They worked hard but had little wealth. Slaves, the lowest rank, provided an important source of labor./La primera dinastía de la cual se tiene evidencia clara es la de los Shang, establecida en el siglo 16 a. C. El monarca shang y su familia se encontraban en la cima de la escala social. Los nobles y los líderes guerreros también pertenecían a las clases altas. Luego venían los artesanos, que vivían en grupos conformados según el trabajo que hacían. Los agricultores estaban por debajo de los artesanos. Trabajaban mucho, pero tenían pocas riquezas. Los esclavos, la clase más baja, constituían una importante fuente de mano de obra.

The Shang made many advances, including China's first writing system. The Chinese symbols that are used today are based on the pictographs and symbols of the Shang period. Priests carved questions about the future on bones or shells, which were then heated, causing them to crack. The priests believed they could "read" these cracks to predict the future. So the bones were called **oracle** bones./Los Shang tuvieron muchos logros, entre ellos el primer sistema de escritura de China. Los símbolos chinos que se usan en la actualidad se basan en los pictogramas y símbolos del período shang. Los sacerdotes tallaban preguntas sobre el futuro en huesos o en caparazones que luego calentaban hasta que les salían grietas. Los sacerdotes creían que podían "leer" esas grietas para predecir el futuro. Por ello, a esos huesos les llamaban huesos del **oráculo.**

> **Which dynasty created China's writing system?/**¿Qué dinastía creó el primer sistema de escritura de China?
> _____

Artisans made bronze containers for cooking and religious ceremonies. They made ornaments, knives, and axes from jade. The military developed war chariots and bronze body armor. Shang astrologers developed a calendar based on sun and moon cycles./Los artesanos fabricaban recipientes de bronce para cocinar y para usar en las ceremonias religiosas. Hacían adornos, cuchillos y hachas de jade. Los militares construyeron carros de guerra y armaduras de bronce. Los astrólogos shang crearon un calendario basado en los ciclos del Sol y la Luna.

> **Underline some achievements of Shang artisans./**Subraya algunos logros de los artesanos shang.

## CHALLENGE ACTIVITY/ACTIVIDAD AVANZADA

**Critical Thinking: Interpret/Pensamiento crítico: Interpretar** Using the library or online resources, study ancient Chinese writing. Use some of these symbols to illustrate something you have learned

about China and its culture./Usa la biblioteca
o recursos en línea para estudiar la antigua
escritura china. Usa algunos de los símbolos
para ilustrar algo que hayas aprendido sobre
China y su cultura.

**DIRECTIONS/INSTRUCCIONES** Read each sentence and fill in
the blank with the term in the word pair that best completes the
sentence./Lee cada oración y escribe en el espacio en blanco la
palabra del par de palabras que mejor la completa.

1. One of the physical barriers that separates China from the outside world
   is a desert called the _____. **(Gobi/Huang He)**/Una de
   las barreras físicas que separa a China del mundo exterior es el desierto de
   _____. **(Gobi/Huang He)**

2. Farmers grew millet and wheat along the _____, or
   Yellow River. **(Gobi/Huang He)**/Los agricultores cultivaban mijo y trigo a
   orillas del río _____, o río Amarillo. **(Gobi/Huang He)**

3. An indication of a social order was that the graves of many rich people had
   objects made of _____. **(oracle/jade)**/Un indicio de que
   existía un orden social era que las tumbas de muchas personas adineradas
   contenían objetos hechos de _____. **(oráculo/jade)**

4. A legendary emperor, Yu the Great, is believed to have founded the
   _____ dynasty around 2200 BC. **(Xia/Shang)**/
   Se cree que un emperador legendario, Yu el Grande, fundó la dinastía
   _____ alrededor del año 2200 a. C. **(Xia/Shang)**

5. The _____ dynasty made many advances, including
   China's first writing system. **(Xia/Shang)**/La dinastía _____
   tuvo muchos logros, entre ellos el primer sistema de escritura de China.
   **(Xia/Shang)**

6. _____ bones were pieces of bone or shell that Chinese
   priests believed they could "read" to predict the future. **(Oracle/Jade)**/Los
   huesos del _____ eran pedazos de hueso o caparazones
   que los sacerdotes chinos creían poder "leer" para predecir el futuro.
   **(oráculo/jade)**

7. The Shang social order had the ruler and nobles at the top and _____ in the middle. **(warrior leaders/artisans)**/En el orden social de los Shang, el monarca y los nobles se encontraban en lo más alto y los _____ estaban en el medio. **(líderes guerreros/artesanos)**

8. China's first writing system used _____, symbols that express words or ideas. **(pictographs/jade)**/El primer sistema de escritura de China consistía en _____, o símbolos que expresan palabras o ideas. **(pictogramas/jades)**

**DIRECTIONS/INSTRUCCIONES** Look at each set of three vocabulary terms following each number. On the line provided, write the letter of the term that does not relate to the others./Observa el conjunto de tres términos de vocabulario que aparece después de cada número. En el espacio en blanco, escribe la letra del término que no tiene relación con los demás.

_____ 9. a. Chang Jiang/     b. jade/jade     c. Huang He/
         Chang Jiang                                      Huang He

_____ 10. a. Gobi/Gobi     b. Shang/Shang     c. Xia/Xia

## Ancient China/La antigua China

**MAIN IDEAS/IDEAS PRINCIPALES**

1. The Zhou dynasty expanded China but then declined./La dinastía Zhou expandió las fronteras de China, pero luego entró en decadencia.
2. Confucius offered ideas to bring order to Chinese society./Confucio propuso ideas para restablecer el orden en la sociedad china.
3. Daoism and Legalism also gained followers./El taoísmo y el legalismo también ganaron adeptos.

## Key Terms and People/Personas y palabras clave

**lords/señores feudales** people of high rank/personas de alto nivel social

**peasants/campesinos** farmers with small farms/agricultores con pequeñas parcelas de tierra

**Confucius/Confucio** the most influential teacher in Chinese history/el maestro más influyente de la historia china

**ethics/ética** moral values/valores morales

**Confucianism/confucianismo** the ideas of Confucius/las ideas de Confucio

**Daoism/taoísmo** an early Chinese belief that stressed living in harmony with the guiding force of all reality/antiguo sistema de creencias chino que enfatizaba la importancia de vivir en armonía con la fuerza que guía toda la realidad

**Laozi/Laozi** the most famous Daoist teacher/el maestro taoísta más conocido

**Legalism/legalismo** an early Chinese belief that people were bad by nature and needed to be controlled/antiguo sistema de creencias chino que sostenía que las personas eran malas por naturaleza y debían ser controladas

## Lesson Summary/Resumen de la lección

### THE ZHOU DYNASTY/LA DINASTÍA ZHOU

The Zhou (JOH) came from an area west of the Shang kingdom. The Zhou overthrew the Shang during the 1100s BC. The Zhou expanded its territory east and northwest. Then its army moved south to the Chang Jiang river. The Zhou established a new political order. The king granted land to **lords,** or people of high rank. They paid taxes and provided soldiers to the king. **Peasants,** farmers with small farms, received a

> How did the Zhou establish their rule throughout China?/¿Cómo establecieron los Zhou su gobierno en toda China?
>
> _____
> _____
> _____

small plot of land and had to farm additional land for a noble. The social system brought order for a time. However, the loyalty of the lords gradually lessened. Eventually, they began to fight each other. Family structure, which had been the foundation of Chinese life for centuries, was severely weakened. By the 400s BC, China had entered an era called the Warring States period./Los Zhou provenían de un área ubicada al oeste del reino Shang y derrocaron a la dinastía Shang en el siglo 12 a. C. Los Zhou expandieron su territorio hacia el este y el noroeste. Luego desplazaron su ejército hacia el sur hasta el río Chang Jiang. Los Zhou establecieron un nuevo orden político. El rey entregaba tierras a los **señores feudales,** o personas de alto nivel social. Los señores feudales pagaban impuestos y proporcionaban soldados al rey. Los **campesinos,** agricultores con pequeñas parcelas de tierra, recibían un lote para ellos y debían cultivar otras tierras para un noble. El sistema social mantuvo el orden por un tiempo, pero la lealtad de los señores feudales fue disminuyendo poco a poco. Con el tiempo, comenzaron a luchar unos contra otros. La estructura familiar, que durante siglos había sido la base de la vida china, se debilitó enormemente. Hacia el siglo 5 a. C., ya China había entrado en lo que se llamó el periodo de los Reinos Combatientes.

> **What kind of wars existed during the Warring States period? Why?/¿Qué tipo de guerras tuvieron lugar durante el período de los Reinos Combatientes? ¿Por qué?**
>
> _____
> _____
> _____
> _____

## CONFUCIUS AND SOCIETY/CONFUCIO Y LA SOCIEDAD

Toward the end of the Zhou period, the most influential teacher in Chinese history, **Confucius,** traveled through China. He taught that order in society stems from **ethics,** or moral values. He wanted China to return to the ideas and practices from a time when people knew their proper roles in society. **Confucianism** has been a guiding force

> **What was Confucius's goal?/¿Cuál era el objetivo de Confucio?**
>
> _____
> _____
> _____
> _____

in human behavior and religious understanding in China through the centuries./Hacia finales del período de los Zhou, el maestro más influyente de la historia china, **Confucio,** viajaba por toda China. Enseñaba que el orden social proviene de la **ética,** o valores morales. Quería que China regresara a las ideas y las prácticas de la época en que las personas sabían cuál era su papel en la sociedad. El **confucianismo** es una fuerza que ha guiado la conducta humana y las creencias religiosas en China a través de los siglos.

## DAOISM AND LEGALISM/TAOÍSMO Y LEGALISMO

Around the same time as Confucianism, other influential beliefs arose in China. **Daoism** (DOW-ih-ZUM) stressed living in harmony with the Dao, the guiding force of all reality. Daoists believed that people should be like water and simply let things flow in a natural way. They regarded humans as just a part of nature, not better than any other thing. **Laozi** was the most famous Daoist teacher. /Casi al mismo tiempo que el confucianismo, surgieron otras creencias influyentes en China. El **taoísmo** enfatizaba la creencia de que se debe vivir en armonía con el Tao, la fuerza que guía toda la realidad. Para los taoístas, las personas debían ser como el agua y simplemente dejar que las cosas fluyeran de manera natural. Consideraban a los seres humanos como una parte más de la naturaleza, no mejores que el resto de ella. **Laozi** fue el maestro taoísta más famoso.

> Underline the sentence that describes the way Daoists regard human life./Subraya la oración que describe la manera en la que los taoístas consideraban al ser humano.

   **Legalism** is different from both Daoism and Confucianism. Legalists believed that society needed strict laws to control people. They believed in unity, efficiency, and punishment for bad conduct. They wanted the empire to continue to expand, so they urged the state to always be prepared for war. Legalists were the first to put their ideas into practice throughout China./El **legalismo** es diferente del taoísmo y del confucianismo. Los legalistas sostenían que la sociedad necesitaba leyes estrictas para controlar a las personas. Creían en la unidad, la eficiencia y el castigo de la mala conducta. Querían que el imperio continuara expandiéndose, por lo que instaban al Estado a que siempre estuviera preparado para la guerra. Los legalistas fueron los primeros en llevar a la práctica sus ideas en toda China.

> **Why did Legalists want the state to always be prepared for war?/¿Por qué los legalistas querían que el Estado siempre estuviera preparado para la guerra?**
>
> _____
>
> _____

## CHALLENGE ACTIVITY/ACTIVIDAD AVANZADA

**Critical Thinking: Summarize/Pensamiento crítico: Resumir** Write a short play with two characters, a Daoist and a Legalist. Make sure each character clearly expresses his or her views on behavior, society, and government./Escribe una obra de teatro breve con dos personajes: un taoísta y un legalista. Asegúrate de que cada personaje exprese claramente sus puntos de vista sobre la conducta, la sociedad y el gobierno.

| Confucianism/ confucianismo | Confucius/ Confucio | Daoism/ taoísmo | ethics/ética |
|---|---|---|---|
| Laozi/Laozi | Legalism/ legalismo | lords/señores feudales | peasant/ campesino |

**DIRECTIONS/INSTRUCCIONES** Choose five of the vocabulary words from the word bank. On a separate sheet of paper, use these words to write a letter that relates to the lesson./Escoge cinco de las palabras de vocabulario del banco de palabras. Úsalas para escribir en una hoja aparte una carta que se relacione con la lección.

**DIRECTIONS/INSTRUCCIONES** Look at each set of three
vocabulary terms following each number. On the line provided,
write the letter of the term that does not relate to the others./
Observa el conjunto de tres términos de vocabulario que aparece
después de cada número. En el espacio en blanco, escribe la letra
del término que no tiene relación con los demás.

_____ 1. a. ethics/ética      b. Confucius/Confucio    c. lords/señores
                                                              feudales

_____ 2. a. lords/señores      b. Daoism/taoísmo        c. Laozi/Laozi
              feudales

_____ 3. a. peasant/           b. lords/señores         c. Confucianism/
              campesino             feudales                 confucianismo

**DIRECTIONS/INSTRUCCIONES** On the line provided before each
statement, write **T** if a statement is true and **F** if a statement is false.
If the statement is false, write the correct term on the line after each
sentence that makes the sentence a true statement./En la línea que
precede a cada enunciado, escribe **V** si el enunciado es verdadero
y **F** si es falso. Si el enunciado es falso, escribe en la línea que
sigue a la oración el término correcto que lo hace verdadero.

_____ 4. <u>Peasants</u>, or farmers with small farms, were at the bottom of the social
             order during the Zhou dynasty./<u>Los campesinos,</u> o agricultores con
             pequeñas parcelas de tierra, estaban en la parte más baja del orden
             social durante la dinastía Zhou.

             _____

_____ 5. <u>Daoism</u> was the belief that people were bad by nature and needed to
             be controlled through strict laws and punishments./<u>El taoísmo</u> era la
             creencia de que las personas eran malas por naturaleza y debían ser
             controladas mediante leyes estrictas y castigos.

             _____

_____ 6. <u>Confucianism</u> stressed living in harmony with the Dao, the guiding
             force of all reality./<u>El confucianismo</u> enfatizaba la importancia de
             vivir en armonía con el Tao, la fuerza que guía toda la realidad.

             _____

## Ancient China/La antigua China

**MAIN IDEAS/IDEAS PRINCIPALES**
1. The first Qin emperor created a strong but strict government./El primer emperador de la dinastía Qin instauró un gobierno fuerte, pero estricto.
2. A unified China was created through Qin policies and achievements./La unificación de China ocurrió gracias a las políticas y los logros de la dinastía Qin.

## Key Terms and People/Personas y palabras clave

**Shi Huangdi/Shi Huangdi** the first emperor of the Qin dynasty/el primer emperador de la dinastía Qin

**Great Wall/Gran Muralla** a barrier across China's northern frontier/barrera construida a lo largo de la frontera norte de China

## Lesson Summary/Resumen de la lección

### THE QIN EMPEROR'S STRONG GOVERNMENT/ EL GOBIERNO FUERTE DEL EMPERADOR QIN

The Warring States period marked a time in China when several states battled each other for power. One state, the Qin (CHIN), built a strong army that defeated the armies of the other states. In 221 BC, the Qin king Ying Zheng unified China. He gave himself the title **Shi Huangdi** (SHEE hwahng-dee), which means "first emperor."/El período de los Reinos Combatientes marcó una época en China durante la cual varios estados lucharon entre sí por el poder. El estado de Qin reunió un poderoso ejército que derrotó a los demás estados. En el año 221 a. C., el rey Qin Ying Zheng logró unificar China. Se dio a sí mismo el nombre de **Shi Huangdi,** que significa "primer emperador".

Shi Huangdi was a follower of Legalist beliefs. He created a strong government with strict laws and severe punishments. He ordered the burning of all writings that did not agree with Legalism./ Shi Huangdi era partidario de las ideas legalistas. Instauró un gobierno fuerte con leyes estrictas y

> How did Shi Huangdi's rule demonstrate his Legalist beliefs?/¿Cómo puso en práctica el gobierno de Shi Huangdi sus ideas legalistas?
>
> _____
> _____
> _____
> _____

castigos severos. Mandó a quemar todos los
libros que no coincidieran con el legalismo.

Shi Huangdi took land and power away
from the lords. He made commoners work on
government building projects. He divided China
into districts, each with its own governor. This
helped Shi Huangdi enforce taxes and a strict
chain of command./Shi Huangdi les quitó las
tierras y el poder a los señores feudales. Puso a
los plebeyos a trabajar en obras de construcción
para el gobierno. Dividió a China en distritos,
cada uno con su propio gobernador. Esto le
permitió a Shi Huangdi cobrar impuestos y
establecer una estricta cadena de mando.

> **List three ways Shi Huangdi unified China./Enumera tres maneras en las que Shi Huangdi unificó China.**
>
> _____
> _____
> _____
> _____
> _____
> _____
> _____

## A UNIFIED CHINA/UNA CHINA UNIFICADA

Qin rule brought other major changes to China.
Under Shi Huangdi, new policies and
achievements united the Chinese people. The
emperor set up a uniform system of law. Rules
and punishments were to be the same in all parts
of the empire. He also standardized the written
language. People everywhere were required to
write using the same set of symbols. People from
different regions could now communicate with
one another in writing. This gave them a sense
of shared culture and a common identity./El
gobierno de la dinastía Qin también introdujo
otros cambios importantes en China. Bajo el
gobierno de Shi Huangdi, nuevas políticas y
logros unieron al pueblo chino. El emperador
estableció un sistema jurídico uniforme. Las leyes
y los castigos eran los mismos en todo el imperio.
También normalizó el lenguaje escrito. Todos
los habitantes debían usar el mismo conjunto
de símbolos para escribir. Así, las personas que
vivían en regiones diferentes podían comunicarse
por escrito. Esto les dio un sentido de cultura
compartida y una identidad común.

Lesson/Lección 3, *continued*/*continuación*

Shi Huangdi also set up a new monetary system. Standardized gold and copper coins became the currency for all of China. Weights and measures were also standardized. With all these changes and the unified writing system, trade became much easier. A new network of highways connected the capital to every part of the empire. Workers built canals to connect the country's rivers. Goods could be shipped faster and easier from north to south. Also, an irrigation system was built to make more land good for farming. Parts of the Qin irrigation system are still used today./Shi Huangdi también estableció un nuevo sistema monetario. Las monedas estandarizadas de oro y cobre se convirtieron en la moneda de uso corriente en toda China. También se uniformaron los pesos y las medidas. Con todos estos cambios y el sistema de escritura unificado, el comercio se volvió mucho más fácil. Una nueva red de carreteras conectó a la capital con todos los puntos del imperio. Los trabajadores construyeron canales para conectar los ríos del país y poder transportar los productos de norte a sur con mayor facilidad y rapidez. Además, se construyó un sistema de riego para lograr que se pudieran cultivar más tierras. En la actualidad, todavía se usan partes del sistema de riego de la dinastía Qin.

Shi Huangdi wanted to keep fierce nomads from the north from invading China. So he completed the **Great Wall,** a barrier across China's northern frontier. This was a major Qin achievement. The Qin connected earlier pieces of the wall to form a long, unbroken structure. Building the wall required years of labor from hundreds of thousands of soldiers and workers. Many of them died building the wall./

---

**Give three reasons why trade became easier under the Qin./**Menciona tres razones por las que el comercio se volvió más fácil durante la dinastía Qin.

_____
_____
_____
_____
_____
_____

---

**What was the purpose of the Great Wall?/**¿Con qué propósito se construyó la Gran Muralla?

_____
_____
_____

---

Shi Huangdi quería evitar que los temibles nómadas del norte invadieran China, así que terminó de construir la **Gran Muralla,** una barrera que se extendía a lo largo de la frontera norte. Este fue uno de los principales logros de la dinastía Qin. Los Qin unieron partes de antiguas murallas y así formaron una extensa estructura continua. Se necesitaron años de trabajo de cientos de miles de soldados y trabajadores. Muchos de ellos murieron durante la construcción de la muralla.

Although he unified China, many Chinese people hated Shi Huangdi's harsh ways. When he died in 210 BC, rebel forces formed across the country. One group attacked the Qin capital, and the new emperor surrendered. The Qin palace burned to the ground. Qin authority had disappeared. With no central government, China fell into civil war./Aunque Shi Huangdi unificó China, muchos chinos odiaban los severos métodos del emperador. Cuando este murió en el año 210 a. C., surgieron fuerzas rebeldes en todo el país. Un grupo atacó la capital qin y el nuevo emperador se rindió. El palacio qin fue quemado y quedó completamente destruido. La autoridad qin había desaparecido. Sin gobierno central, China se sumió en una guerra civil.

## CHALLENGE ACTIVITY/ACTIVIDAD AVANZADA
**Critical Thinking: Make Judgments/Pensamiento crítico: Dar opiniones** If you had lived in China during the Qin dynasty, would you have joined a rebel group to overthrow the government? Be sure to consider the ideas of Confucianism and Daoism in your answer./Si hubieras vivido en China durante la dinastía Qin, ¿te habrías unido a un grupo rebelde para derrocar el gobierno? Asegúrate de tomar en cuenta las ideas del confucianismo y del taoísmo al dar tu respuesta.

**DIRECTIONS/INSTRUCCIONES** On the line provided before each statement, write **T** if a statement is true and **F** if a statement is false. If the statement is false, write the correct term on the line after each sentence that makes the sentence a true statement./En la línea que precede a cada enunciado, escribe **V** si el enunciado es verdadero y **F** si es falso. Si el enunciado es falso, escribe en la línea que sigue a la oración el término correcto que lo hace verdadero.

_____ 1. The emperor who unified China gave himself the title <u>Qin dynasty</u>, which means "first emperor."/El emperador que unificó China se dio a sí mismo el nombre de <u>dinastía Qin</u>, que significa "primer emperador".

_____

_____ 2. <u>Shi Huangdi</u> was a follower of Legalist political beliefs. He created a strong government with strict laws and severe punishments./<u>Shi Huangdi</u> era partidario de las ideas políticas legalistas. Instauró un gobierno fuerte con leyes estrictas y castigos severos.

_____

_____ 3. Under the <u>Qin dynasty</u>, China was unified, a network of roads and canals was built, and the written language was standardized./Bajo el gobierno de <u>la dinastía Qin</u>, se unificó China, se construyó una red de carreteras y canales, y se normalizó el lenguaje escrito.

_____

| Great Wall/ | Qin dynasty/ | Shi Huangdi/ |
|---|---|---|
| Gran Muralla | dinastía Qin | Shi Huangdi |

**DIRECTIONS/INSTRUCCIONES** Answer each question by writing a sentence that contains at least one word from the word bank./ Responde cada pregunta con una oración que contenga al menos una palabra del banco de palabras.

4. Who ordered the destruction of all the writings that did not agree with Legalism?/¿Quién ordenó la destrucción de todos los textos que no coincidían con el legalismo?

_____

_____

5. What was the massive building project undertaken that required the labor of hundreds of thousands of soldiers and workers?/¿Cuál fue el enorme proyecto de construcción que requirió la mano de obra de cientos de miles de soldados y trabajadores?

_____

_____

# Ancient China/La antigua China

**MAIN IDEAS/IDEAS PRINCIPALES**

1. Han dynasty government was based on the ideas of Confucius./El gobierno de la dinastía Han se basó en las ideas de Confucio.
2. Family life was supported and strengthened in Han China./La vida familiar recibió apoyo y se fortaleció en el período de los Han.
3. The Han made many achievements in art, literature, and learning./La dinastía Han alcanzó muchos logros en el arte, la literatura y el conocimiento.
4. Buddhism spread to China along the trade routes from other lands./El budismo llegó a China a través de rutas comerciales desde otras tierras.

## Key Terms and People/Personas y palabras clave

**sundial/reloj de sol** a device that uses the position of shadows cast by the sun to tell time/aparato que utiliza la posición de las sombras que proyecta el sol para indicar la hora

**seismograph/sismógrafo** a device that measures the strength of an earthquake/aparato que mide la intensidad de un terremoto

**acupuncture/acupuntura** the practice of inserting needles through the skin at specific points to cure disease or relieve pain/práctica que consiste en insertar agujas en la piel en puntos específicos para curar enfermedades o aliviar el dolor

**silk/seda** a soft, light, highly valued fabric/tela suave y liviana muy apreciada

**diffusion/difusión** the spread of ideas, goods, and technology from one culture to another/propagación de ideas, bienes y tecnología de una cultura a otra

## Lesson Summary/Resumen de la lección

**HAN DYNASTY GOVERNMENT/GOBIERNO DE LA DINASTÍA HAN**

After the end of the Qin dynasty, Liu Bang (LEE-OO BANG) won control of China. He lowered farmers' taxes and made punishments less severe. His government was based on that of the Qin. His successor, Wudi (WOO-DEE), made Confucianism the official government policy. A person had to pass a test based on Confucianism to get a government job./Tras la caída de la dinastía

Qin, Liu Bang tomó el control de China. Bajó los impuestos que pagaban los agricultores y moderó los castigos. Tomó el gobierno qin como base. Su sucesor, Wudi, convirtió el confucianismo en la política de gobierno oficial de China. Para obtener un puesto gubernamental, había que aprobar un examen basado en esa doctrina.

| What was one aspect of the Qin government that the Han changed?/¿Cuál fue un aspecto del gobierno qin que cambió la dinastía Han? |
| --- |

## FAMILY LIFE/VIDA FAMILIAR

A class structure took hold during Han rule. Peasants were the second class in this Confucian system. Merchants were the lowest class because they only bought and sold what others made. This social division did not indicate wealth though. Peasants were still poor and merchants were still rich./Durante el gobierno de los Han, se estableció una estructura de clases. En este sistema confuciano, los campesinos conformaban la segunda clase social. Los comerciantes eran la clase más baja porque solo compraban y vendían lo que otros producían. Sin embargo, esta división social no era indicador de la riqueza. Los campesinos seguían siendo pobres mientras que los comerciantes seguían siendo ricos.

| Underline the sentence that explains why Confucian thinking devalues merchants./Subraya la oración que explica por qué las ideas de Confucio restan valor a los comerciantes. |
| --- |

During Wudi's reign, children were taught to respect their elders and the father had absolute power. Chinese parents valued boys more highly than girls. Some women, however, gained power and could influence their sons' families. An older widow might become the head of the family./Durante el gobierno de Wudi, a los niños se les enseñaba a respetar a los mayores y el padre tenía el poder absoluto. Los hijos varones eran más valorados que las hijas mujeres. Sin embargo, algunas mujeres lograban un poder propio que les permitía ejercer influencia en la familia de sus hijos varones. Las viudas de cierta edad podían incluso convertirse en cabezas de familia.

| Underline the sentence that explains which women could become heads of families./Subraya la oración que explica qué mujeres podían convertirse en cabezas de familia. |
| --- |

## HAN ACHIEVEMENTS/LOGROS DE LA DINASTÍA HAN

During Han rule, art and literature thrived and inventors developed many useful devices. Artists painted portraits. Poets developed new styles of verse. A historian wrote a history of China up to the Han dynasty. The Han Chinese also invented paper. Other innovations were the **sundial,** the **seismograph,** and the Chinese medical practice of **acupuncture** (AK-yoo-punk-cher). These and other Han inventions and advances are still used today./ Durante el gobierno de la dinastía Han, el arte y la literatura florecieron y se inventaron muchos aparatos útiles. Los artistas pintaron retratos y los poetas desarrollaron nuevos estilos de versos. Un historiador escribió una historia de China hasta la época de la dinastía Han. Los chinos de este período también crearon el papel. Otras innovaciones fueron el **reloj de sol,** el **sismógrafo** y una práctica médica china llamada **acupuntura.** Estos inventos, así como otros inventos y avances de la dinastía Han, se siguen utilizando en la actualidad.

> Which Han dynasty invention made books possible?/¿Qué invento de la dinastía Han hizo posibles los libros?
>
> _____

Advances in manufacturing, such as the iron plow and wheelbarrow, increased productivity. **Silk** production also increased. Weavers used foot-powered looms to weave fabric. Silk garments were expensive. The Chinese were determined to keep their process for making silk a secret./Avances en la manufactura, como el arado de hierro y la carretilla, aumentaron la productividad. La producción de **seda** también aumentó. Los tejedores usaban telares que funcionaban a pedal para tejer la tela. La ropa de seda era cara. Los chinos estaban decididos a mantener en secreto su proceso de producción de seda.

> Why do you think it was important to keep the silk production process a secret?/¿Por qué crees que era importante mantener en secreto el proceso de producción de la seda?
>
> _____
> _____
> _____
> _____

Lesson/Lección 4, *continued*/*continuación*

## BUDDHISM COMES TO CHINA/EL BUDISMO LLEGA A CHINA

Over time, the Han government became less stable. Buddhism seemed to offer more hope than Confucianism or Daoism. It offered a rebirth and a relief from suffering./Con el tiempo, el gobierno de la dinastía Han se volvió inestable. El budismo parecía ofrecer más esperanzas que el confucianismo o el taoísmo, ya que ofrecía un renacimiento y el alivio del sufrimiento.

Buddhism caught on in China with both the poor and the upper classes. Buddhism's introduction to China is an example of **diffusion,** the spread of ideas from one culture to another. Chinese culture changed in response to it./El budismo se hizo popular en China entre los pobres y en las clases altas. La introducción del budismo en China es un ejemplo de **difusión,** o la propagación de ideas de una cultura a otra. La cultura china cambió en respuesta al budismo.

> **Why did Buddhism become popular in China?/¿Por qué el budismo tuvo amplia aceptación en China?**
>
> _____
>
> _____
>
> _____
>
> _____
>
> _____

## CHALLENGE ACTIVITY/ACTIVIDAD AVANZADA

**Critical Thinking: Evaluate/Pensamiento crítico: Evaluar** Do you think the Han dynasty would have flourished as well if the Qin had not set up a strong government? Write a brief essay providing your point of view./¿Crees que la dinastía Han habría florecido de igual manera si la dinastía Qin no hubiera establecido un gobierno fuerte? Escribe un ensayo breve con tu punto de vista.

**DIRECTIONS/INSTRUCCIONES** Write a word or phrase
to describe the term given./Escribe una palabra o una frase
que describa el término dado.

1. acupuncture/acupuntura _____

   _____

2. seismograph/sismógrafo_____

3. sundial/reloj de sol _____

4. diffusion/difusión _____

5. silk/seda_____

**DIRECTIONS/INSTRUCCIONES** Read each sentence and fill in
the blank with the word in the word pair that best completes
the sentence./Lee cada oración y escribe en el espacio en blanco
la palabra del par de palabras que mejor la completa.

6. _____ became the first Han emperor by winning
   control of China after the fall of the Qin dynasty. **(Wudi/Liu Bang)**/
   _____ se convirtió en el primer emperador de la
   dinastía Han al tomar control de China después de la caída de la
   dinastía Qin. **(Wudi/Liu Bang)**

7. Under the _____ dynasty, the Chinese made advances
   in art, literature, medicine, and science. **(Qin/Han)**/Bajo el gobierno de la
   dinastía _____, los chinos lograron grandes avances
   en el arte, la literatura, la medicina y las ciencias. **(Qin/Han)**

8. The spread of ideas, goods, and technology from one culture to another
   is _____. **(diffusion/innovation)**/La propagación
   de ideas, bienes y tecnología de una cultura a otra se llama
   _____. **(difusión/innovación)**

9. A soft, light, highly valued fabric is called _____.
   **(silk/acupuncture)**/La _____ es una tela suave,
   liviana y de gran valor. **(seda/acupuntura)**

**DIRECTIONS/INSTRUCCIONES** Look at each set of three vocabulary terms following each number. On the line provided, write the letter of the term that does not relate to the others./ Observa cada conjunto de tres términos de vocabulario que aparecen después de cada número. En el espacio en blanco, escribe la letra del término que no tiene relación con los demás.

_____10. a. acupuncture/          b. paper/papel          c. Great Wall/
           acupuntura                                      Gran Muralla

_____11. a. Buddhism/           b. diffusion/           c. Liu Bang/Liu
           budismo                 difusión                Bang

_____12. a. Han/Han             b. Qin/Qin              c. iron plow/
                                                          arado de hierro

## Ancient China/La antigua China

**MAIN IDEAS/IDEAS PRINCIPALES**
1. Trade routes linked China with the Middle East and Rome./Las rutas comerciales conectaron a China con el Oriente Medio y Roma.
2. The most famous trade route was known as the Silk Road./La ruta comercial más famosa era conocida como la Ruta de la Seda.

## Key Terms and People/Personas y palabras clave

**Silk Road/Ruta de la Seda** a network of trade routes between China and the Mediterranean Sea/red de rutas comerciales que se extendían desde China hasta el mar Mediterráneo

## Lesson Summary/Resumen de la lección

### EXPANSION OF TRADE/EXPANSIÓN DEL COMERCIO

During the Han dynasty, Chinese goods, especially silk fabric and fine pottery, were highly valued by people in other lands. So the value of these goods outside China helped increase trade./ Durante la dinastía Han, los productos chinos, en particular la seda y la porcelana fina, eran muy valorados en otras tierras. El valor que se daba a estos productos fuera de China contribuyó a lograr un aumento en el comercio.

Powerful Han armies expanded into Central Asia, Vietnam, and Korea. Han rulers believed that other ethnic groups outside of China were inferior to the Chinese. So Han armies brought Chinese culture into these societies. They also stabilized the region, which made the transport of goods over trade routes safer. Trade increased as China's leaders realized they could make a profit by bringing silk to Central Asia. Then they traded it for horses. The Central Asian people then took the silk west and traded it for other products./Los poderosos ejércitos de la dinastía

> **What led to an increase in trade outside China?/¿Cuál fue la causa del aumento en el comercio fuera de China?**
> _____
> _____
> _____

> **Underline the sentence that explains why Han armies brought Chinese culture into areas outside of China./Subraya la oración que explica por qué los ejércitos de la dinastía Han llevaron la cultura china fuera de China.**

Han se expandieron hasta Asia Central, Vietnam y Corea. Los gobernantes de la dinastía Han consideraban que los grupos étnicos que vivían fuera de China eran inferiores a los chinos. Por eso, los ejércitos llevaron la cultura china a esas sociedades. También estabilizaron la región, lo cual hizo que fuera más seguro transportar productos por las rutas comerciales. El comercio aumentó cuando los gobernantes de China se dieron cuenta de que podían obtener buenas ganancias si llevaban la seda a Asia Central, donde la intercambiaban por caballos. Los habitantes de Asia Central luego llevaban la seda hacia el oeste y la intercambiaban por otros productos.

In 139 BC, Emperor Wudi wanted to establish alliances with an enemy group. He sent one of his generals to these western lands. However, the general was imprisoned and did not return for 13 years. Then he told of great wealth and large horses in Central Asia. Wudi sent an army there to conquer the lands. The empire grew, and trade routes developed to the west. The Chinese extended the Great Wall to protect their land and trade routes. Along the trade routes, trading posts and farming settlements developed. This led to the rise of cities in western China./En el año 139 a. C., el emperador Wudi quiso establecer alianzas con un grupo enemigo. Para ello, envió a uno de sus generales a tierras occidentales. Sin embargo, el general fue tomado prisionero y tardó 13 años en regresar. Entonces, describió las grandes riquezas y los enormes caballos que había en Asia Central. Wudi envió un ejército a conquistar esas tierras. El imperio se expandió y las rutas comerciales se extendieron hacia el oeste. Los chinos extendieron la Gran Muralla para proteger su territorio y las rutas

> **What caused cities to grow in western China?/¿Qué causó el surgimiento de las ciudades en el oeste de China?**
>
> _____
> _____
> _____
> _____

comerciales. A lo largo de estas rutas, se fundaron
puestos comerciales y asentamientos agrícolas, lo
que llevó al surgimiento de ciudades en el oeste
de China.

## TRADE ALONG THE SILK ROAD/COMERCIO EN LA RUTA DE LA SEDA

Traders used a series of overland routes to take
Chinese goods to distant lands. The most famous
trade route was known as the **Silk Road.** Most
merchants traveled only a small part of the Silk
Road, selling their goods along the way to other
traders. Then when they reached Central Asia,
these traders sold their goods to other local
traders who took the goods the rest of the way./
Los comerciantes llevaban bienes chinos a tierras
lejanas usando una serie de rutas terrestres. La
ruta comercial más famosa era conocida como la
**Ruta de la Seda.** La mayoría de los comerciantes
solo recorrían una pequeña parte de la Ruta
de la Seda y, en el camino, iban vendiendo sus
bienes a otros comerciantes. Luego, al llegar a
Asia Central, estos comerciantes vendían sus
bienes a otros comerciantes locales, que los
transportaban el resto del camino.

> **What was the most famous overland trade route that the Chinese used to take goods to distant lands?/** ¿Cuál era la ruta comercial terrestre más famosa que usaban los chinos para transportar bienes a tierras lejanas?
>
> _____

Traveling the Silk Road was difficult and risky,
so traders formed groups for protection. Traders
also faced icy blizzards, desert heat, and
sandstorms. However, the Silk Road was worth
the many risks. Silk was so popular in Rome,
for example, that China grew wealthy just from
trading with Romans. Traders also returned
from Rome with gold, silver, precious stones,
and horses./Viajar por la Ruta de la Seda era
difícil y peligroso, por lo que los comerciantes
se juntaban en grupos para protegerse. También
tenían que enfrentar las heladas tormentas de
nieve, el calor del desierto y las tormentas de

> **Underline the sentences that explain why traveling the Silk Road was worth the risks traders faced./** Subraya las oraciones que explican por qué valía la pena viajar por la Ruta de la Seda, a pesar de los peligros que enfrentaban los comerciantes.

arena. Sin embargo, valía la pena correr tales riesgos por la Ruta de la Seda. La seda era tan popular en Roma, por ejemplo, que China se enriqueció solo por comerciar con los romanos. Además, los comerciantes volvían de Roma con oro, plata, piedras preciosas y caballos.

The exchange of goods along the Silk Road led to a wider world economy. Goods from Europe and Africa went to China, and Chinese goods went west. In addition to goods, the Silk Road also caused people to exchange knowledge and inventions. People had to learn new languages to communicate with traders from different cultures. People from different places talked to one another and exchanged knowledge of the arts and science./El intercambio de bienes por la Ruta de la Seda dio lugar a una economía mundial más amplia. Los bienes de Europa y África iban a China, y los bienes chinos viajaban hacia el oeste. Además de bienes, la Ruta de la Seda permitió que se intercambiaran conocimientos e inventos. Los comerciantes tenían que aprender otros idiomas para comunicarse con comerciantes de diferentes culturas. Así, personas de distintos lugares hablaban entre sí e intercambiaban conocimientos sobre las artes y las ciencias.

Advanced technologies such as paper making and irrigation systems spread across Asia and beyond by way of the Silk Road. Religion also spread because of trade routes. Buddhism came from India to China by way of the Silk Road./Tecnologías avanzadas como la producción de papel y los sistemas de riego se difundieron por Asia y más allá de Asia por medio de la Ruta de la Seda. La religión también se difundió gracias a las rutas comerciales. El budismo llegó de la India a China a través de esta ruta.

---

**List three examples that demonstrate the spread of knowledge and technology along the Silk Road./** Enumera tres ejemplos que demuestren la difusión de conocimiento y tecnología gracias a la Ruta de la Seda.

_____
_____
_____
_____
_____

---

During the Han period, few foreigners traveled to China. However, trade brought foreign ideas and technology./Durante el período de los Han, pocos extranjeros viajaron a China. Sin embargo, el comercio llevó a China ideas y tecnología de otros lugares.

## CHALLENGE ACTIVITY/ACTIVIDAD AVANZADA

**Critical Thinking: Summarize/Pensamiento crítico: Resumir** Imagine that you are an experienced Chinese trader on the Silk Road. Write a short advertisement for an assistant trader. Be sure to include the benefits of the job./Imagina que eres un experimentado comerciante chino que transita por la Ruta de la Seda. Escribe un breve anuncio para reclutar un asistente. Asegúrate de incluir los beneficios del empleo.

**DIRECTIONS/INSTRUCCIONES** Use the vocabulary term *Silk Road* to write a poem about what you learned in the lesson./Usa el término de vocabulario *Ruta de la Seda* para escribir un poema sobre lo que aprendiste en la lección.

_____

_____

_____

_____

_____

_____

**DIRECTIONS/INSTRUCCIONES** On the line before each statement, write **T** if the statement is true and **F** if the statement is false. If the statement is false, change the underlined term to make the sentence true. Then write the correct term on the line after the sentence./En la línea que precede a cada enunciado, escribe **V** si el enunciado es verdadero y **F** si es falso. Si el enunciado es falso, cambia el término subrayado para que el enunciado sea verdadero. Luego escribe el término correcto en la línea que sigue al enunciado.

_____ 1. The Chinese extended the Silk Road to protect its land and trade routes./Los chinos extendieron la Ruta de la Seda para proteger su territorio y las rutas comerciales.

_____

_____ 2. During the Han dynasty, silk and pottery were highly valued by Romans./Durante la dinastía Han, la seda y la porcelana eran bienes altamente valorados por los romanos.

_____

_____ 3. The Silk Road was a network of routes westward between China and the Mediterranean Sea./La Ruta de la Seda era una red de rutas que se extendía hacia el oeste y conectaba China con el mar Mediterráneo.

_____

_____ 4. Traders returned from Vietnam with gold, silver, precious stones, and horses./Los comerciantes volvían de Vietnam con oro, plata, piedras preciosas y caballos.

_____

## The Hebrews and Judaism/Los hebreos y el judaísmo

### Lesson/Lección 1

**MAIN IDEAS/IDEAS PRINCIPALES**

1. Abraham led the Hebrews to Canaan and to a new religion, and Moses led the Israelites out of slavery in Egypt./Abraham condujo a los hebreos a Canaán y estableció una nueva religión; Moisés liberó a los israelitas de la esclavitud a la que estaban sometidos en Egipto.

2. Strong kings united the Israelites to fight off invaders./Los israelitas tuvieron reyes poderosos que unieron al pueblo para combatir a los enemigos que buscaban invadirlos.

3. Invaders conquered and ruled the Israelites after their kingdom broke apart./Tras la división del reino de Israel, los israelitas fueron conquistados y gobernados por distintos invasores.

4. Some women in Israelite society made great contributions to their history./Algunas mujeres de la sociedad israelita hicieron grandes aportes a la historia de su pueblo.

## Key Terms and People/Personas y palabras clave

**Judaism/judaísmo** the religion of the Hebrews/la religión de los hebreos

**Abraham/Abraham** the biblical father of the Hebrew people/el patriarca bíblico del pueblo hebreo

**Moses/Moisés** Hebrew leader who led the Israelites out of slavery in Egypt/líder hebreo que liberó a los israelitas de la esclavitud a la que estaban sometidos en Egipto

**Exodus/Éxodo** the journey the Israelites made from Egypt to Canaan, led by Moses/viaje que los israelitas hicieron desde Egipto hasta Canaán, guiados por Moisés

**Ten Commandments/Diez Mandamientos** moral code of laws that God handed down to Moses/código moral de leyes que Dios entregó a Moisés

**David/David** former shepherd who became king after the death of Saul, Israel's first king/pastor que se convirtió en rey tras la muerte de Saúl, el primer rey de Israel

**Solomon/Salomón** David's son; became king of the Israelites/hijo de David; fue rey de los israelitas

**Diaspora/diáspora** the dispersal of the Jews outside of Israel and Judah/la dispersión de los judíos fuera de Israel y Judá

# Lesson Summary/Resumen de la lección

## ABRAHAM AND MOSES LEAD THEIR PEOPLE/
## ABRAHAM Y MOISÉS GUÍAN A SU PUEBLO

A people called the Hebrews (HEE-brooz) appeared in Southwest Asia sometime between 2000 and 1500 BC. Their writings describe the laws of their religion, **Judaism** (JOO-dee-i-zuhm). The Hebrew Bible, or Torah, traces the Hebrews back to a man named **Abraham.** The Hebrew Bible says that God told Abraham to leave his home. God promised to lead him to a new land and to make his children into a mighty nation. Abraham moved to Canaan (KAY-nuhn) where the Hebrews lived for many years./Entre los años 2000 y 1500 a. C., se estableció en el suroeste de Asia un pueblo conocido como los hebreos. Sus escritos describen los principios de su religión, el **judaísmo.** De acuerdo con la Biblia hebrea, o Torá, el pueblo hebreo desciende de un hombre llamado **Abraham.** Según narra la Biblia hebrea, Dios le ordenó a Abraham que abandonara su hogar, y le prometió que lo guiaría hacia una nueva tierra y que sus hijos fundarían una nación poderosa. Abraham se estableció en Canaán, y allí vivieron los hebreos durante muchos años.

> **Circle the name of the people who appeared in Southwest Asia sometime between 2000 and 1500 BC./Encierra en un círculo el nombre del pueblo que se estableció en el suroeste de Asia entre los años 2000 y 1500 a. C.**

> **Underline the promise that God made to Abraham. Where did Abraham move?/Subraya la promesa que Dios le hizo a Abraham. ¿Dónde se estableció Abraham?**

> _____

Some of Abraham's descendents, the Israelites, later moved to Egypt. In time, Egypt's ruler, the pharaoh, made them slaves. In the 1200s BC, God told a leader named **Moses** to lead the Israelites out of Egypt. Moses went to the pharaoh and demanded that the Israelites be freed. The pharaoh agreed only after a series of plagues, or disasters, struck Egypt./Posteriormente, algunos de los descendientes de Abraham, los israelitas, se trasladaron a Egipto. Tiempo después, el gobernante egipcio, o faraón, los sometió a la esclavitud. En el siglo 13 a. C., Dios le encomendó a un líder llamado **Moisés**

que sacara a los israelitas de Egipto. Moisés se
presentó ante el faraón y le exigió la liberación
de los israelitas. El faraón aceptó solo después
de que una series de plagas, o catástrofes,
azotaran Egipto.

Moses led his people on a journey called the
**Exodus.** The Israelites believed that they had
been set free because God was watching over
them. The Bible says that during this journey,
God gave Moses two stone tablets with laws
written on them. They were known as the
**Ten Commandments.** According to them, the
Israelites were to worship only one God and
were to value human life, self-control, and
justice. After 40 years in exile, the Israelites
reached Canaan./El pueblo hebreo inició
entonces un viaje, llamado **Éxodo,** guiado
por Moisés. Los israelitas creían que habían sido
liberados porque Dios velaba por ellos. Según
se relata en la Biblia, durante ese viaje Dios
le entregó a Moisés dos tablas de piedra. En
ellas estaban escritas las leyes conocidas como
los **Diez Mandamientos.** Estas leyes establecían
que los israelitas debían rendir culto solo a
Dios, además de valorar la vida humana, el
autocontrol y la justicia. Después de 40 años
en el exilio, los israelitas llegaron a Canaán.

| Why was Moses an important Israelite leader?/¿Por qué Moisés fue un líder importante de los israelitas? |
|---|
| _____ |
| _____ |

| What three basic values are emphasized in the Ten Commandments?/¿Cuáles son los tres valores fundamentales que se destacan en los Diez Mandamientos? |
|---|
| _____ |
| _____ |

## KINGS UNITE THE ISRAELITES/REYES UNEN A LOS ISRAELITAS

**Saul,** after fighting the Philistines (FI-li-steenz),
became the first king of Israel. After he died, a
former shepherd named **David** became king.
David was well-loved. He defeated the Philistines
and other enemies. He captured the city of
Jerusalem. It became Israel's new capital. David's
son **Solomon** (SAHL-uh-muhn) became the next
king around 965 BC. He was a strong king. He
built a great temple in Jerusalem. It became the

| Circle the names of the first three kings of Israel. Which king built a temple?/Encierra en un círculo el nombre de los tres primeros reyes de Israel. ¿Cuál de ellos mandó a construir un templo? |
|---|
| _____ |
| _____ |

center of the Israelites' religious life./Después
de luchar contra los filisteos, **Saúl** se convirtió
en el primer rey de Israel. Tras su muerte, subió
al trono un pastor llamado **David.** David fue
un rey querido por el pueblo. Derrotó a los
filisteos y a otros enemigos, y tomó la ciudad
de Jerusalén, que se convirtió en la nueva capital
de Israel. El hijo de David, **Salomón,** llegó al
trono alrededor del año 965 a. C. Salomón fue
un rey poderoso. Mandó a construir un gran
templo en Jerusalén, que se convirtió en el
centro de la vida religiosa de los israelitas.

## INVADERS CONQUER AND RULE/
## INVASORES CONQUISTAN Y GOBIERNAN

Soon after Solomon's death in 930 BC, Israel
split into two kingdoms, Israel and Judah
(JOO-duh). The people of Judah were known
as Jews. Over the centuries, the Jewish people
were often conquered and enslaved. Jerusalem
was conquered by the Greeks during the 330s
BC. Judah regained independence for a time,
but was conquered again in 63 BC, this time by
the Romans. The dispersal of the Jews outside
of Israel and Judah is known as the **Diaspora.**/
Poco después de la muerte de Salomón, en
930 a. C., Israel se dividió en dos reinos: Israel
y Judá. Los habitantes de Judá eran conocidos
como los judíos. A lo largo de los siglos, el pueblo
judío fue conquistado y sometido a la esclavitud
en muchas ocasiones. Jerusalén fue conquistada
por los griegos durante la década de 330 a. C. El
reino de Judá logró recuperar su independencia
por un tiempo, pero en el año 63 a. C. cayó bajo
el dominio romano. La dispersión de los judíos
fuera de Israel y Judá se conoce como **diáspora.**

## WOMEN IN ISRAELITE SOCIETY/LAS MUJERES EN LA SOCIEDAD ISRAELITA

Although men dominated Israelite society, some Israelite and Jewish women made great contributions to the culture./Si bien los hombres dominaban la sociedad israelita, algunas mujeres israelitas y judías hicieron grandes aportes a la cultura de su pueblo.

## CHALLENGE ACTIVITY/ACTIVIDAD AVANZADA

**Critical Thinking: Make Inferences/Pensamiento crítico: Hacer inferencias** Write a set of ten commandments that reflects the responsibilities and rights of students and faculty for your school./Escribe diez mandamientos que reflejen los deberes y derechos de los estudiantes y los docentes de tu escuela.

**DIRECTIONS/INSTRUCCIONES** Read each sentence and fill in the blank with the word in the word pair that best completes the sentence./Lee cada oración y escribe en el espacio en blanco la palabra del par de palabras que mejor la completa.

1. After King Saul died, _____ became the new king of Israel. **(David/Solomon)**/Tras la muerte del rey Saúl, _____ se convirtió en el nuevo rey de Israel. **(David/Salomón)**

2. _____ led the Israelites out of Egypt, which freed them from slavery under the pharaoh. **(Moses/Abraham)**/ _____ sacó a los israelitas de Egipto, y así pudieron liberarse de la esclavitud a la que estaban sometidos bajo el gobierno del faraón. **(Moisés/Abraham)**

3. The _____, a code of moral laws, has helped shape the development of Israelite and Jewish society over time. **(Judaism/Ten Commandments)**/El código de leyes morales conocido como _____ ha sido determinante en el desarrollo de la sociedad israelita y judía a lo largo del tiempo. **(judaísmo/los Diez Mandamientos)**

4. The Hebrews trace their ancestry back to a man named
   _____. **(Abraham/David)**/Los hebreos descienden
   de un hombre llamado _____. **(Abraham/David)**

**DIRECTIONS/INSTRUCCIONES** Write three adjectives or
a descriptive phrase to describe the term or person./Escribe
tres adjetivos o una frase descriptiva para describir el término
o persona.

5. Diaspora/diáspora _____

6. Exodus/Éxodo _____

7. Judaism/judaísmo_____

8. Solomon/Salomón _____

9. Ten Commandments/Diez Mandamientos _____

## The Hebrews and Judaism/Los hebreos y el judaísmo

### Lesson/Lección 2

**MAIN IDEAS/IDEAS PRINCIPALES**

1. Belief in God, commitment to education and justice, and observance of the law anchor Jewish society./La fe en Dios, el compromiso con la educación y la justicia y el respeto por la ley son los pilares de la sociedad judía.

2. Jewish beliefs are listed in the Torah, the Hebrew Bible, and the Commentaries./Las creencias judías están contenidas en la Torá, la Biblia hebrea, y en los Comentarios.

3. The Dead Sea Scrolls reveal many past Jewish beliefs./Los Manuscritos del Mar Muerto revelan muchas de las antiguas creencias del pueblo judío.

4. The ideas of Judaism helped shape later cultures./Las ideas del judaísmo tuvieron gran influencia sobre culturas posteriores.

## Key Terms and People/Personas y palabras clave

**monotheism/monoteísmo** belief in only one god/creencia de que existe un solo dios

**Torah/Torá** the sacred text of Judaism/el texto sagrado del judaísmo

**synagogue/sinagoga** Jewish house of worship/lugar de culto de los judíos

**prophets/profetas** people said to receive messages from God to be taught to others/personas que, según se cree, reciben mensajes de Dios que deben transmitir a los demás

**Talmud/Talmud** commentaries, stories, and folklore recorded to explain Jewish laws/comentarios, relatos y tradiciones escritos con el fin de explicar las leyes judías

**Dead Sea Scrolls/Manuscritos del Mar Muerto** writings by Jews who lived about 2,000 years ago/escritos de judíos que vivieron hace aproximadamente 2,000 años

## Lesson Summary/Resumen de la lección

**JEWISH BELIEFS ANCHOR THEIR SOCIETY/**
**LAS CREENCIAS SON LA BASE**
**DE LA SOCIEDAD JUDÍA**

Jewish society is founded upon religion. Judaism's central concepts are belief in God, education, justice and righteousness, and observance of religious and moral law./La base de la sociedad judía es la religión. Los conceptos

> **Underline the four core values of Judaism./**
> **Subraya los cuatro valores fundamentales del judaísmo.**

fundamentales del judaísmo son la fe en Dios, la educación, la justicia y la rectitud, y el respeto por las leyes religiosas y morales.

Judaism is the oldest known religion to practice **monotheism,** the belief in only one God. The Hebrew name for God is YHWH. The Jews say their history was guided through God's relationship with Abraham, Moses, and other leaders. Moral and religious laws, believed to be handed down from God, have guided Jewish society throughout their history and continue to do so today./El judaísmo es la religión monoteísta más antigua que se conoce. El **monoteísmo** es la creencia de que existe un solo Dios. El nombre hebreo de Dios es YHWH. Según los judíos, la historia de su pueblo está afianzada en la relación de Dios con Abraham, Moisés y otros líderes. Las leyes morales y religiosas, que los judíos creen haber recibido de Dios, han guiado a la sociedad judía a lo largo de su historia, y siguen haciéndolo hoy en día.

Besides the Ten Commandments, Jews believe that Moses recorded a whole set of laws governing Jewish behavior. These are called Mosaic laws. They set down rules for everything, including what to eat, when to work, and how to pray. Today, Orthodox Jews continue to follow all of the Mosaic laws. Reform Jews choose not to follow many of the ancient rules. Conservative Jews fall in between./Los judíos creen que, además de recibir los Diez Mandamientos, Moisés recopiló un conjunto de leyes que rigen la conducta judía. Ese conjunto de leyes se conoce como ley mosaica, y regula todo tipo de cuestiones como, por ejemplo, qué comer, cuándo trabajar y cómo rezar. En la actualidad, los judíos ortodoxos siguen viviendo de acuerdo con las leyes mosaicas. En cambio, los judíos

> **What is monotheism?/**
> **¿Qué es el monoteísmo?**
> _____
> _____

reformistas respetan solo algunas de esas leyes.
Por su parte, los judíos conservadores mantienen
una posición intermedia.

## TEXTS LIST JEWISH BELIEFS/CREENCIAS JUDÍAS EN LOS TEXTOS

The laws and principles of Judaism are written
down in sacred texts. The most important text is
the **Torah.** The five books of the Torah record
most of the laws and the history of Judaism until
the death of Moses. Every **synagogue,** or place of
Jewish worship, has at least one Torah./Las leyes
y los principios del judaísmo están escritos en
textos sagrados. El más importante de estos
textos es la **Torá.** Los cinco libros de la Torá
registran la mayor parte de las leyes y la historia
del judaísmo hasta la muerte de Moisés. Cada
**sinagoga,** o lugar de culto judío, cuenta con
al menos una Torá.

> Circle the name of the most important sacred Jewish text./Encierra en un círculo el nombre del texto sagrado más importante del judaísmo.

The Torah is one of the three parts of the
Hebrew Bible, or Tanakh (tah-NAKH). The second
part contains messages from **prophets,** people
who are said to have received messages directly
from God. The third part is a collection of
poems, songs, stories, lessons, and histories./
La Torá es una de las tres partes de la Biblia
hebrea, o Tanaj. La segunda parte contiene
mensajes de los **profetas,** personas que, según
se cree, han recibido mensajes directamente de
Dios. La tercera parte es una compilación de
poemas, canciones, relatos, lecciones e historias.

The **Talmud** is a collection of commentaries,
folktales, and stories written by scholars. These
are intended to help people understand and
analyze the laws described in the Hebrew Bible./
El **Talmud** es un conjunto de comentarios,
cuentos populares y relatos escritos por sabios
para ayudar a las personas a comprender y
analizar las leyes descritas en la Biblia hebrea.

> What is in the Talmud?/
> ¿Qué contiene el Talmud?
> _____
> _____
> _____
> _____

## SCROLLS REVEAL PAST BELIEFS/MANUSCRITOS REVELAN CREENCIAS DEL PASADO

Another set of ancient texts, the **Dead Sea Scrolls,** was discovered in 1947. These scrolls, written by Jewish scholars about 2,000 years ago, contain commentaries and stories, and they offer more information about ancient Jewish life./En 1947 se descubrió otra colección de textos antiguos, conocidos como los **Manuscritos del Mar Muerto.** Dichos manuscritos, escritos por sabios judíos hace aproximadamente 2,000 años, contienen comentarios y relatos, y brindan más información sobre la vida de los judíos en la antigüedad.

## JUDAISM AND LATER CULTURES/EL JUDAÍSMO Y LAS CULTURAS POSTERIORES

Jewish ideas helped shape two other major world religions, Christianity and Islam. In addition, the Ten Commandments are reflected in our laws and in modern society's rules of behavior./ Las ideas del judaísmo han sido de gran influencia para otras dos grandes religiones del mundo: el cristianismo y el islam. Asimismo, los Diez Mandamientos se ven reflejados en nuestras leyes y en las normas de conducta de la sociedad moderna.

## CHALLENGE ACTIVITY/ACTIVIDAD AVANZADA

**Critical Thinking: Draw Inferences/Pensamiento crítico: Hacer inferencias** Pretend you are a writer contributing to a modern-day Talmud of American life. Write a short story illustrating how one of the Ten Commandments is followed today./ Imagina que eres un escritor que colabora en la creación de un Talmud de la vida estadounidense actual. Escribe un cuento que muestre cómo se sigue hoy en día uno de los Diez Mandamientos.

**DIRECTIONS/INSTRUCCIONES** On the line provided before each statement, write **T** if a statement is true and **F** if a statement is false. If the statement is false, change the underlined term to make the statement true. Write the correct term on the line provided./En la línea que precede a cada enunciado, escribe **V** si el enunciado es verdadero y **F** si es falso. Si el enunciado es falso, cambia el término subrayado para que el enunciado sea verdadero. Escribe el término correcto en la línea que sigue al enunciado.

_____ 1. The Talmud is a sacred text of Judaism and one of the three parts of the Hebrew Bible./El Talmud es un texto sagrado del judaísmo y una de las tres partes de la Biblia hebrea.

_____

_____ 2. Historians have learned much about the ancient laws and history of Judaism by studying the Torah./Los historiadores han aprendido mucho sobre la historia y las leyes antiguas del judaísmo estudiando la Torá.

_____

_____ 3. Orthodox Jews strictly follow a set of laws, known as Mosaic law, that guide many areas of their daily lives./Los judíos ortodoxos cumplen estrictamente un conjunto de leyes conocido como ley mosaica, que rige muchos aspectos de su vida cotidiana.

_____

_____ 4. Prophets are people who are said to have received messages from God to be taught to others./Los profetas son personas que, según se cree, han recibido mensajes de Dios que deben transmitir a los demás.

_____

_____ 5. Texts related to Judaism include the Torah, the Talmud, and the Dead Sea Scrolls./Entre los textos relacionados con el judaísmo, se encuentran la Torá, el Talmud y los Manuscritos del Mar Muerto.

_____

**DIRECTIONS/INSTRUCCIONES** Write a word or short phrase that
has the same meaning as the term given./Escribe una palabra o frase
breve que tenga el mismo significado que el término dado.

6. monotheism/monoteísmo _____

7. sacred/sagrado _____

8. synagogue/sinagoga _____

## The Hebrews and Judaism/Los hebreos y el judaísmo

### Lesson/Lección 3

**MAIN IDEAS/IDEAS PRINCIPALES**

1. Revolt, defeat, and migration led to great changes in Jewish culture./Las rebeliones, las derrotas y las migraciones produjeron grandes cambios en la cultura judía.

2. Because Jews settled in different parts of the world, two cultural traditions formed./Debido a que los judíos se establecieron en diferentes partes del mundo, surgieron dos tradiciones culturales diferentes.

3. Jewish traditions and holy days celebrate the history and religion of the Jews./Mediante las tradiciones y los días sagrados, los judíos celebran su historia y su religión.

## Key Terms and People/Personas y palabras clave

**Zealots/zelotes** Jews who rebelled against their Roman rulers/judíos que se rebelaron contra los gobernantes romanos

**rabbis/rabinos** teachers who guide Jews in their religious lives/maestros que guían a los judíos en su vida religiosa

**Passover/Pascua judía** a time for Jews to remember the Exodus/período en que los judíos recuerdan el Éxodo

**High Holy Days/Santos Días Supremos** the two most sacred Jewish holidays, Rosh Hashanah and Yom Kippur/los dos días de fiesta más sagrados para los judíos: Rosh Hashaná y Yom Kippur

## Lesson Summary/Resumen de la lección

### REVOLT, DEFEAT, AND MIGRATION/REBELIÓN, DERROTA Y MIGRACIÓN

The teachings of Judaism helped unite the ancient Jews. But many Jews were unhappy with the Roman rule of Jerusalem. Tensions increased. Some Jews refused to obey Roman officials. In AD 66, a group called the **Zealots** (ZE-luhts) led a rebellion against Rome. After four years of fierce fighting, the rebellion failed. The Jews' Second Temple of Jerusalem was destroyed in AD 70. The Romans put down another Jewish rebellion 60 years later. After this uprising, Jews were banned from living in Jerusalem, so they migrated to other parts of the world./

> **Why did the Zealots revolt?/¿Por qué se rebelaron los zelotes?**
>
> _____
>
> _____
>
> _____
>
> _____

Las enseñanzas del judaísmo ayudaron a unir a
los antiguos judíos. Sin embargo, muchos de ellos
no estaban conformes con el gobierno romano de
Jerusalén. Las tensiones aumentaron. Algunos
judíos se negaban a obedecer a los funcionarios
romanos. En el año 66 d. C., un grupo conocido
como los **zelotes** encabezó una rebelión contra
Roma. Después de cuatro años de duros
enfrentamientos, la rebelión fracasó. En el año
70 d. C., el Segundo Templo judío de Jerusalén
fue destruido. Sesenta años más tarde, los
romanos sofocaron otra rebelión judía. Después
de esa rebelión, a los judíos se les prohibió vivir
en Jerusalén, por los que debieron emigrar a
otras partes del mundo.

## TWO CULTURAL TRADITIONS/
## DOS TRADICIONES CULTURALES

Because Jews could not worship at a central temple
anymore, their traditions changed. Everywhere
Jews went, they built local temples. They also
appointed **rabbis,** religious leaders responsible for
teaching Judaism. Even with a similar culture and
background, Jewish traditions grew differently
depending on where they moved. Two major Jewish
cultures developed that still exist today./Como
los judíos ya no podían practicar su religión en
un templo central, sus tradiciones cambiaron.
Comenzaron a construir templos locales en cada
uno de los lugares adonde se asentaban. También
designaron **rabinos,** líderes religiosos responsables
de transmitir las enseñanzas del judaísmo. A pesar
de tener un origen y una cultura similares, las
tradiciones judías se desarrollaron de manera
diferente según el lugar donde se estableciera
cada grupo de judíos. Así, surgieron dentro del
judaísmo dos importantes tradiciones culturales
que aún existen en la actualidad.

> **Underline the definition of
> *rabbis* in the summary./
> Subraya la definición de
> *rabinos* en el resumen.**

The Ashkenazim (ahsh-kuh-NAH-zuhm) are descended from Jews who moved to France, Germany, and Eastern Europe. These Jews maintained separate customs from the region's other residents. They even developed Yiddish, their own language./Los askenazíes descienden de los judíos que emigraron a Francia, Alemania y Europa oriental. Estos judíos conservaron costumbres diferentes de las de los demás habitantes de la región, e incluso desarrollaron su propio idioma, el yiddish.

The Sephardim (suh-FAHR-duhm) moved to Spain and Portugal. Unlike the Ashkenazim, these Jews mixed with their non-Jewish neighbors. This melding of language and culture produced a Jewish golden age in Spain and Portugal when many Jews contributed to artistic achievement and scientific discovery./Los sefardíes emigraron a España y Portugal. A diferencia de los askenazíes, ellos se mezclaron con sus vecinos no judíos. Esta fusión de lenguas y culturas produjo una edad de oro judía en España y Portugal, en la que muchos judíos hicieron importantes contribuciones en el campo de las artes y las ciencias.

> **What was the main difference between the Ashkenazim and the Sephardim?/¿Cuál era la principal diferencia entre los askenazíes y los sefardíes?**
>
> _____
>
> _____
>
> _____
>
> _____

## TRADITIONS AND HOLY DAYS/TRADICIONES Y DÍAS SAGRADOS

No matter where Jews live, common traditions and holy days help them maintain and celebrate their long history. Many of these holidays honor the Jews' freedom. **Passover,** for example, celebrates the Jews' flight from slavery in Egypt during the Exodus. Hanukkah commemorates the rededication of the Temple of Jerusalem during the Maccabbees' successful revolt against the Greeks in 160 BC./Independientemente del lugar donde vivan, los judíos se unen en la celebración de sus tradiciones y días sagrados,

y eso los ayuda a recordar su larga historia.
Muchos de estos días de fiesta celebran la
libertad del pueblo judío. En la **Pascua judía,**
por ejemplo, se conmemora el Éxodo, la huida
de la esclavitud en Egipto. En Janucá se celebra
la reinauguración del templo de Jerusalén
durante la exitosa rebelión de los macabeos
contra los griegos en el año 160 a. C.

The most important holidays are the **High
Holy Days.** These days are Rosh Hashanah
(rahsh uh-SHAH-nuh), which celebrates the Jewish
New Year, and Yom Kippur (yohm ki-POOHR),
when Jews ask God to forgive their sins./Los días
de fiesta más importantes para los judíos son los
**Santos Días Supremos:** Rosh Hashaná, en el que
se celebra el Año Nuevo judío, y Yom Kippur,
el día en que los judíos le piden a Dios que
perdone sus pecados.

> **What is the proper name
> for the Jewish New Year?/
> ¿Cómo se llama el Año
> Nuevo judío?**
>
> _____

## CHALLENGE ACTIVITY/ACTIVIDAD AVANZADA

**Critical Thinking: Draw Inferences/Pensamiento
crítico: Hacer inferencias** Imagine that you are
living in Jerusalem during Roman rule. Write a
letter to your relatives explaining the difficulties
the Zealots faced and why they rebelled./Imagina
que vives en la Jerusalén gobernada por los
romanos. Escribe una carta a tus parientes en la
que expliques qué dificultades sufrían los zelotes
y las razones por las que decidieron rebelarse.

| Hanukkah/<br>Janucá | High Holy Days/<br>Santos Días Supremos | Masada/Masada | Passover/<br>Pascua judía |
|---|---|---|---|
| Rabbis/<br>rabinos | Rosh Hashanah/<br>Rosh Hashaná | Yom Kippur/<br>Yom Kippur | Zealots/zelotes |

**DIRECTIONS/INSTRUCCIONES** Choose the correct term from the word bank to replace the underlined phrase in each sentence below. Write the term in the space provided and then define the term in your own words./Escoge del banco de palabras el término correcto para reemplazar la frase subrayada en cada una de las siguientes oraciones. Escribe el término en el espacio en blanco y, luego, defínelo con tus propias palabras.

1. The rebellion led by <u>this group</u> resulted in the destruction of the Second Temple of Jerusalem and in the death or enslavement of many Jews./La rebelión iniciada por <u>este grupo</u> trajo como consecuencia la destrucción del Segundo Templo de Jerusalén y la muerte o esclavitud de muchos judíos. _____
Your definition/Tu definición: _____

2. <u>This event</u> commemorates the Jews' flight from slavery./<u>Este suceso</u> conmemora la liberación de los judíos de la esclavitud. _____
Your definition/Tu definición: _____

3. After the Romans banned Jews from Jerusalem, <u>these individuals</u> helped shape how Judaism was practiced for the next several centuries./Después de que los romanos prohibieron a los judíos vivir en Jerusalén, <u>estas personas</u> fueron importantes para definir cómo se practicaría el judaísmo en los siglos siguientes. _____

Your definition/Tu definición: _____

4. During <u>this sacred period</u>, Jews celebrate the start of a new year in the Jewish calendar and ask God to forgive their sins./En <u>estos días de fiesta</u>, los judíos celebran el comienzo de un nuevo año en su calendario y le piden a Dios que perdone sus pecados. _____
Your definition:/Tu definición: _____
_____

## Ancient Greece/La antigua Grecia

**MAIN IDEAS/IDEAS PRINCIPALES**

1. Geography helped shape early Greek civilization./La geografía influyó en el desarrollo de la antigua civilización griega.
2. Trading cultures developed in the Minoan and Mycenaean civilizations./En las civilizaciones minoica y micénica se desarrollaron culturas comerciales.
3. The Greeks created city-states for protection and security./Los griegos crearon ciudades estado para obtener protección y seguridad.

## Key Terms and People/Personas y palabras clave

**polis/polis** Greek word for city-state/palabra griega para designar una ciudad estado

**acropolis/acrópolis** a fortress atop a tall hill in the center of the city-states/ fortaleza construida en la cima de una colina alta en el centro de las ciudades estado

## Lesson Summary/Resumen de la lección
### GEOGRAPHY SHAPES GREEK CIVILIZATION/ LA GEOGRAFÍA INFLUYE EN LA CIVILIZACIÓN GRIEGA

The Greeks lived on rocky, mountainous lands, located on a peninsula surrounded by the Mediterranean, Ionian, and Aegean seas. The peninsula has an irregular shape. Many islands lie off the mainland. This area was the home of one of the world's greatest civilizations./Los griegos vivían en tierras rocosas y montañosas, ubicadas en una península rodeada por los mares Mediterráneo, Jónico y Egeo. La península tiene forma irregular y hay muchas islas a su alrededor. Esta región fue el hogar de una de las civilizaciones más importantes del mundo.

The few small valleys and plains of Greece provided farmland, and that is where people settled. These communities were separated by steep mountains, so there was little contact between groups. The villages created separate governments./Los valles y las llanuras de Grecia,

> Underline the names of the three seas that surrounded the Greek peninsula./ Subraya los nombres de los tres mares que rodeaban la península griega.

> Why did separate governments develop in ancient Greece?/¿Por qué había gobiernos separados en la antigua Grecia?
>
> _____
> _____
> _____
> _____
> _____

escasos y pequeños, servían como tierras de
cultivo; y allí se asentaron los pobladores. Estas
comunidades estaban separadas por montañas
escarpadas, por lo tanto, había poco contacto entre
los grupos. Cada aldea creó su propio gobierno.

Because they were surrounded by water, the
Greeks became skilled shipbuilders and sailors.
The Greeks were exposed to other cultures when
they sailed to other lands./Al estar rodeados
de agua, los griegos se convirtieron en hábiles
marineros y constructores de barcos. Los griegos
conocieron otras culturas cuando comenzaron
a navegar a otras tierras.

## TRADING CULTURES DEVELOP/SE DESARROLLAN CULTURAS COMERCIALES

Many cultures settled and grew in early Greece.
The earliest, with the greatest influence, were the
Minoans and the Mycenaeans. By 2000 BC, these
two cultures had built advanced societies on the
island of Crete. The Minoans were known as the
best shipbuilders of their time. They used ships
mainly for trading purposes. A volcano that
erupted in the 1600s BC may have led to the
end of the Minoan civilization./Muchas culturas
se establecieron y desarrollaron en la antigua
Grecia. Las primeras y más influyentes fueron la
minoica y la micénica. Hacia el año 2000 a. C.,
estas dos culturas ya habían desarrollado
sociedades avanzadas en la isla de Creta. Los
minoicos eran conocidos por ser los mejores
constructores de barcos de su época. Usaban
los barcos principalmente para el comercio.
Se cree que un volcán que hizo erupción en el
siglo 17 a. C. destruyó la civilización minoica.

The Mycenaeans spoke the language that
became Greek. While the Minoans were building
ships, the Mycenaeans were building fortresses on

the Greek mainland. The Mycenaeans eventually took over the trade routes once sailed by the Minoans. The Mycenaeans set up a powerful trading network on the Mediterranean and Black seas. In the 1200s BC, Mycenaean society also fell prey to earthquakes and invaders. Greece entered a period called the Dark Age./Los micénicos hablaban el idioma que luego se convirtió en el griego. Mientras los minoicos construían barcos, los micénicos construían fortalezas en tierra firme griega. Con el tiempo, los micénicos comenzaron a usar las rutas comerciales por las que una vez habían navegado los minoicos. Los micénicos establecieron una poderosa red comercial en los mares Mediterráneo y Negro. En el siglo 13 a. C., la sociedad micénica también fue víctima de terremotos e invasores. Grecia entró en un período llamado la Edad Oscura.

> While the Minoans built
>
> _____ ,
>
> the Mycenaeans built
>
> _____ ./
> Mientras que los minoicos construían
>
> _____ ,
>
> los micénicos construían
>
> _____ .

## GREEKS CREATE CITY-STATES/LOS GRIEGOS CREAN CIUDADES ESTADO

After 300 years of war and disorder, communities began to band together for stability and protection. They created the **polis,** or city-state. This marked the beginning of the Greek classical era, a time when some city-states became more powerful./Después de 300 años de guerras y desorden, las comunidades comenzaron a unirse en busca de estabilidad y protección. Crearon entonces la **polis,** o ciudad estado. Esto marcó el comienzo de la época clásica de Grecia, época en la que algunas ciudades estado se volvieron más poderosas.

The Greeks often built a city-state around a fortress perched atop a high hill called an **acropolis.** Walls surrounded many of these cities. Much of daily life centered on the agora, or marketplace, where politics and shopping shared the stage. As stability returned, some of the

> What features of the polis made it a safe, protected place to live and conduct business?/¿Qué características de la polis la hacían un lugar seguro y protegido para vivir y hacer negocios?
>
> _____
>
> _____
>
> _____
>
> _____
>
> _____

Greek city-states formed colonies in foreign lands. Early colonies included the locations of modern-day Istanbul in Turkey, Marseilles in France, and Naples in Italy. This created further independence for these city-states, and some city-states became great trading centers./Los griegos solían construir las ciudades estado alrededor de una fortaleza situada en la cima de una colina alta llamada **acrópolis.** Muchas de estas ciudades estaban rodeadas por muros. Gran parte de la vida cotidiana giraba en torno al ágora, o plaza del mercado, donde convivían la política y el comercio. Al regresar la estabilidad, algunas de las ciudades estado griegas establecieron colonias en tierras extranjeras. Entre las primeras colonias se encuentran las ciudades actuales de Estambul en Turquía, Marsella en Francia y Nápoles en Italia. Esto les dio mayor independencia a las ciudades estado y algunas de ellas se convirtieron en importantes centros de comercio.

## CHALLENGE ACTIVITY/ACTIVIDAD AVANZADA

**Critical Thinking: Make Inferences/Pensamiento crítico: Hacer inferencias** You are a leader of an ancient Greek polis dealing with all the same problems and circumstances the real city-states of the time faced. Write your own set of laws that would improve both security and quality of life for the citizens who live there./Eres el líder de una antigua polis griega que enfrenta los mismos problemas y circunstancias que las ciudades estado reales de la época. Escribe tu propio conjunto de leyes que mejorarían tanto la seguridad como la calidad de vida de los ciudadanos que viven allí.

**DIRECTIONS/INTRUCCIONES** Read each sentence and fill in the blank with the word in the word pair that best completes the sentence./Lee cada oración y escribe en el espacio en blanco la palabra del par de palabras que mejor la completa.

1. After the Dark Age, Greeks began to set up city-states and entered a period of great achievements known as Greece's _____ era. **(classical/peninsula)**/Después de la Edad Oscura, los griegos comenzaron a establecer ciudades estado y entraron en un período de grandes logros conocido como la época _____ de Grecia. **(clásica/península)**

2. The town around the _____ was surrounded by walls for protection. **(acropolis/colony)**/La ciudad se construía alrededor de la _____ y estaba rodeada por muros que la protegían. **(acrópolis/colonia)**

3. The _____ often served as a central place for Greeks to meet and hold assemblies. **(acropolis/agora)**/_____ era un lugar central donde los griegos a menudo se reunían y celebraban asambleas. **(La acrópolis/El ágora)**

4. The mainland of Greece is a _____, land surrounded by water on three sides. **(peninsula/polis)**/Grecia continental es una _____, es decir, una porción de tierra rodeada de agua por tres lados. **(península/polis)**

5. The Greek _____ provided security, stability, and identity to the people who lived there. **(acropolis/polis)**/_____ griega proporcionaba seguridad, estabilidad e identidad a las personas que vivían allí. **(La acrópolis/La polis)**

**DIRECTIONS/INSTRUCCIONES** Write a word that has a similar meaning to the term given./Escribe una palabra que tenga un significado parecido al del término dado.

6. acropolis/acrópolis _____

7. agora/ágora _____

8. polis/polis _____

**DIRECTIONS/INSTRUCCIONES** Write three adjectives
or a descriptive phrase to describe the term given./Escribe
tres adjetivos o una frase descriptiva que describan el
término dado.

9. influence/influencia _____

10. peninsula/península _____

# Ancient Greece/La antigua Grecia

**MAIN IDEAS/IDEAS PRINCIPALES**
1. Aristocrats and tyrants ruled early Athens./La antigua Atenas era gobernada por aristócratas y tiranos.
2. Athens created the world's first democracy./Atenas creó la primera democracia del mundo.
3. Ancient democracy was different from modern democracy./La democracia antigua era distinta de la democracia moderna.

## Key Terms and People/Personas y palabras clave

**democracy/democracia** type of government in which people rule themselves/ tipo de gobierno en el que el pueblo se gobierna a sí mismo

**aristocrats/aristócratas** rich landowners/terratenientes ricos

**oligarchy/oligarquía** government in which only a few people have power/ gobierno en el que solo unas pocas personas tienen el poder

**aristocracy/aristocracia** society ruled by rich landowners/sociedad gobernada por los terratenientes ricos

**citizens/ciudadanos** people with the right to participate in government/personas que tienen el derecho de participar en el gobierno

**tyrant/tirano** leader who rules by the use of force/líder que gobierna mediante el uso de la fuerza

**Pericles/Pericles** Athenian leader who ruled at the height of Athenian democracy/líder ateniense que gobernó en el apogeo de la democracia ateniense

## Lesson Summary/Resumen de la lección

### ARISTOCRATS AND TYRANTS RULE/GOBIERNO DE ARISTÓCRATAS Y TIRANOS

The city of Athens in Greece is the birthplace of **democracy.** Democracy is a form of a government in which people rule themselves. Athens was ruled first by kings, and then by an oligarchy of **aristocrats,** or rich landowners. Athenian society was also known as an **aristocracy** because only people in the highest social class had power. In the 600s BC, rebels

> **Circle two ways that Athens was ruled before democracy./Encierra en un círculo dos maneras en que Atenas fue gobernada antes de la democracia.**

tried to overthrow the aristocrats and failed.
Several rulers followed. First was Draco, who
was unpopular due to his overly strict laws.
Next was Solon, who ruled that all free men
were **citizens** who had a right to participate in
government. Then Peisistratus, the first **tyrant,**
became a leader of Athens by force. After he
died, rebellious aristocrats regained control of
the city of Athens./La ciudad de Atenas, en
Grecia, es el lugar donde nació la **democracia.** La
democracia es una forma de gobierno en la que
el pueblo se gobierna a sí mismo. Atenas fue
gobernada primero por reyes y luego por una
oligarquía de **aristócratas,** o terratenientes ricos.
La sociedad ateniense también era conocida
como una **aristocracia** porque solo las personas
de la clase social más alta tenían el poder. En el
siglo 7 a. C., un grupo de rebeldes intentaron
derrocar a los aristócratas, pero fallaron. Luego
siguieron varios gobernantes. Primero estuvo
Dracón, quien fue un gobernante odiado debido
a sus leyes excesivamente estrictas. Su sucesor,
Solón, dispuso que todos los hombres libres
eran **ciudadanos** que tenían el derecho de
participar en el gobierno. Luego Pisístrato, el
primer **tirano,** se convirtió en líder de Atenas
por medio de la fuerza. Después de su muerte,
los aristócratas rebeldes recuperaron el control
de la ciudad de Atenas.

> **Who was the first tyrant of Athens?**/¿Quién fue el primer tirano de Atenas?
>
> _____

## ATHENS CREATES DEMOCRACY/ATENAS CREA LA DEMOCRACIA

The leader Cleisthenes introduced democracy
to Athens in 500 BC when he overthrew the
aristocratic leaders by using popular support.
Citizens had the right to participate in the
assembly that created laws. Assemblies were
held outdoors, and anyone could give a speech

before voting. Often, either too many or not enough people would come to an assembly, so Athenians selected city officials to vote. Citizens gradually gained more power./El líder Clístenes introdujo la democracia en Atenas en el 500 a. C., cuando derrocó a los líderes aristocráticos con el apoyo popular. Los ciudadanos tenían el derecho de participar en la asamblea que creaba las leyes. Las asambleas se celebraban al aire libre y cualquier persona podía dar un discurso antes de la votación. A veces, había demasiadas personas o muy pocas en la asamblea, por lo cual los atenienses seleccionaban funcionarios de la ciudad para que votaran. Los ciudadanos gradualmente fueron obteniendo más poder.

Athenian democracy reached its height with **Pericles,** who led the government from 460 to 429 BC. Democracy all but ended when Athens was conquered by Macedonia in the 330s BC. The Macedonian king wanted to make his own laws./La democracia ateniense alcanzó su apogeo con **Pericles,** quien gobernó desde el 460 hasta el 429 a. C. La democracia estuvo a punto de llegar a su fin cuando Atenas fue conquistada por Macedonia en la década del año 330 a. C. El rey macedonio quería dictar sus propias leyes.

> **What do you think is the major disadvantage of allowing every citizen to participate in lawmaking?/¿Cuál crees que es la principal desventaja de permitir que todos los ciudadanos participen en la creación de las leyes?**
>
> _____
> _____
> _____
> _____

## ANCIENT DEMOCRACY DIFFERS FROM MODERN DEMOCRACY/LA DEMOCRACIA ANTIGUA ES DISTINTA DE LA DEMOCRACIA MODERNA

Although citizenship was very limited, Athens had a direct democracy, in which every citizen could participate and the majority ruled. The United States operates as a representative government, in which citizens elect people to represent them./A pesar de que la ciudadanía era muy limitada, Atenas tenía una democracia directa, en la que

> **What type of democracy is practiced in the United States today?/¿Qué tipo de democracia se practica en los Estados Unidos en la actualidad?**
>
> _____
> _____

cada ciudadano podía participar y la mayoría
decidía. Los Estados Unidos funcionan como un
gobierno representativo, en el que los ciudadanos
eligen a sus representantes.

## CHALLENGE ACTIVITY/ACTIVIDAD AVANZADA

**Critical Thinking: Compare/Pensamiento crítico:
Comparar** Create a chart showing the differences
between direct and representative democracy./Crea
un cuadro en el que se muestren las diferencias entre
la democracia directa y la democracia representativa.

**DIRECTIONS/INSTRUCCIONES** On the line before each statement,
write **T** if the statement is true and **F** if the statement is false. If the
statement is false, change the underlined term to make the statement
true. Then write the correct term on the line after the statement./En
la línea que precede a cada enunciado, escribe **V** si el enunciado es
verdadero y **F** si es falso. Si el enunciado es falso, cambia el término
subrayado para que el enunciado sea verdadero. Luego escribe el
término correcto en la línea que sigue al enunciado.

_____ 1. An <u>oligarchy</u> is a government in which only a few people have power./
<u>Una oligarquía</u> es un gobierno en el que solo unas pocas personas
tienen el poder.

_____

_____ 2. Greece is considered the birthplace of <u>democracy</u>, which is a type of
government in which people rule themselves./Se considera que Grecia
es el lugar donde nació <u>la democracia</u>, que es un tipo de gobierno en
el que el pueblo se gobierna a sí mismo.

_____

_____ 3. Democracy in Athens reached its height under the rule of a brilliant
elected leader named <u>Cleisthenes</u>./La democracia de Atenas llegó a
su apogeo bajo el gobierno de un brillante líder elegido por el pueblo
que se llamaba <u>Clístenes</u>.

_____

_____ 4. In the 590s BC, a leader named Solon ruled that all free men living in Athens were <u>aristocrats</u>./En la década del año 590 a. C., un líder llamado Solón dispuso que todos los hombres libres que vivían en Atenas eran <u>aristócratas</u>.

_____

_____ 5. The oligarchy in Athens lasted until one noble overthrew the government and ruled it alone as a <u>tyrant</u>./La oligarquía de Atenas duró hasta que un noble derrocó al gobierno y gobernó solo como <u>tirano</u>.

_____

**DIRECTIONS/INSTRUCCIONES** Look at each set of vocabulary terms following each number. On the line provided, write the letter of the term that does not relate to the others./Observa el conjunto de términos de vocabulario que aparece después de cada número. En el espacio en blanco, escribe la letra del término que no tiene relación con los demás.

_____ 6. a. democracy/democracia      b. oligarchy/oligarquía
        c. tyranny/tiranía            d. Pericles/Pericles

_____ 7. a. oligarchy/oligarquía      b. aristocrats/aristócratas
        c. democracy/democracia    d. aristocracy/aristocracia

## Ancient Greece/La antigua Grecia

**MAIN IDEAS/IDEAS PRINCIPALES**

1. The Spartans built a military society to provide security and protection./ Los espartanos crearon una sociedad militar para brindar seguridad y protección.

2. The Athenians admired the mind and the arts in addition to physical abilities./ Los atenienses admiraban el intelecto y las artes, además de las habilidades físicas.

3. Sparta and Athens fought over who should have power and influence in Greece./Esparta y Atenas luchaban para establecer quién debía tener poder e influencia en Grecia.

## Key Terms and People/Personas y palabras clave

**alliance/alianza** an agreement to work together/acuerdo para trabajar de manera conjunta

**Peloponnesian War/Guerra del Peloponeso** a war between the two great Greek city-states of Athens and Sparta in the 400s BC/guerra entre las dos grandes ciudades estado griegas de Atenas y Esparta en el siglo 5 a. C.

## Lesson Summary/Resumen de la lección

### SPARTANS BUILD A MILITARY SOCIETY/LOS ESPARTANOS CREAN UNA SOCIEDAD MILITAR

Spartan life was dominated by the army. The city-state of Sparta's social system was created by a man named Lycurgus (ly-KUHR-guhs) after a slave revolt. He increased the military's role. Courage and strength were the highest values. Boys who were healthy at birth were trained from an early age to be soldiers. Boys ran, jumped, swam, and threw javelins to increase their strength. Men between the ages of 20 and 30 lived in army barracks and only occasionally visited their families. Spartan men stayed in the army until they turned 60./La vida de los espartanos estaba dominada por el ejército. El sistema social de la ciudad estado de Esparta fue creado por un hombre llamado Licurgo después de una revuelta de esclavos. Licurgo amplió el rol del ejército.

> **What were the highest values in Spartan society?/¿Cuáles eran los valores más importantes en la sociedad espartana?**
>
> _____
>
> _____
>
> _____

La valentía y la fuerza eran los valores más importantes. Los niños varones que eran saludables al nacer recibían entrenamiento para ser soldados desde muy pequeños. Corrían, saltaban, nadaban y practicaban el lanzamiento de jabalina para aumentar su fuerza. Los hombres de entre 20 y 30 años vivían en barracas del ejército y solo ocasionalmente visitaban a sus familias. Los hombres espartanos permanecían en servicio en el ejército hasta los 60 años de edad.

Spartan men were often away at war, so Spartan women had more rights than other Greek women. Women owned much of the land in Sparta and ran their households. Women also learned how to run, jump, wrestle, and throw javelins. Spartans believed this would help women bear healthy children./Como los hombres espartanos frecuentemente estaban lejos en las guerras, las mujeres espartanas tenían más derechos que otras mujeres griegas. Las mujeres eran dueñas de gran parte de las tierras de Esparta y manejaban sus hogares. También aprendían a correr, saltar, luchar y lanzar la jabalina. Los espartanos creían que esto ayudaba a las mujeres a tener niños saludables.

Sparta was ruled by two kings who jointly led the army. Elected officials ran Sparta's day-to-day activities and handled dealings between Sparta and other city-states. Slaves grew the city's crops and did many other jobs. Fear of the army kept slaves from rebelling./Esparta era gobernada por dos reyes que dirigían el ejército de manera conjunta. Las actividades diarias de Esparta, así como los asuntos entre Esparta y otras ciudades estado, estaban a cargo de funcionarios electos. Los esclavos se encargaban de los cultivos de la ciudad y de muchas tareas. El miedo al ejército evitaba que los esclavos se rebelaran.

> **Underline why Spartan women had more rights than other Greek women./ Subraya por qué las mujeres espartanas tenían más derechos que otras mujeres griegas.**

## ATHENIANS ADMIRE THE MIND/LOS ATENIENSES ADMIRAN EL INTELECTO

Sparta's main rival in Greece was Athens. Although Athens had a powerful military and valued physical training, the Athenians also prized education, clear thinking, and the arts. They believed that educated men made the best citizens./El rival principal de Esparta en Grecia era Atenas. A pesar de que Atenas tenía un ejército poderoso y valoraba el entrenamiento físico, los atenienses también daban mucha importancia a la educación, la claridad de pensamiento y las artes. Creían que los hombres educados eran los mejores ciudadanos.

> **Underline the sentence that explains why the Athenians valued education./**Subraya la oración en la que se explica por qué los atenienses valoraban la educación.

Many Athenian students learned to read, write, and count as well as sing and play musical instruments. Boys from rich families often had private tutors who taught them philosophy, geometry, astronomy, and public speaking. Boys from poor families, however, did not receive much education, and very few girls were educated. Despite Athens's reputation for freedom and democracy, Athenian women had almost no rights at all./Muchos estudiantes atenienses aprendían a leer, escribir y contar, así como a cantar y tocar instrumentos musicales. Los niños varones de familias ricas tenían tutores privados que les enseñaban filosofía, geometría, astronomía y oratoria. Sin embargo, los niños varones de familias pobres no recibían mucha educación y las niñas la recibían en muy pocos casos. A pesar de la reputación que Atenas tenía por la libertad y la democracia, las mujeres atenienses tenían muy pocos derechos.

> **Who received the most education in the city-state of Athens and why?/**¿Quiénes recibían más educación en la ciudad estado de Atenas y por qué?
>
> _____
> _____
> _____
> _____
> _____

## SPARTA AND ATHENS FIGHT/ESPARTA Y ATENAS SE ENFRENTAN

After the Persian Wars, many Greek city-states joined an **alliance** to help defend one another and

protect trade. With its navy protecting the islands,
Athens was the most powerful member of the
league. Soon Athenians began to treat other
city-states as their subjects. In 431 BC, Sparta
and other cities formed the Delian League
and declared war on Athens. In the long
**Peloponnesian War** that followed, the Athenians
won at first but were forced to surrender in
404 BC. For about the next 30 years, the Spartans
controlled nearly all of Greece, but resentment
from other city-states led to a long period of
war that weakened all of Greece and left it
open to attack from outside./Después de las
Guerras Médicas, muchas ciudades estado
griegas formaron una **alianza** para defenderse
mutuamente y proteger el comercio. Atenas,
con su armada custodiando las islas, era el
miembro más poderoso de la liga. Muy pronto
los atenienses comenzaron a tratar a otras
ciudades estado como sus súbditos. En el
431 a. C., Esparta y otras ciudades formaron
la Liga de Delos y le declararon la guerra a
Atenas. Esto dio lugar a la **Guerra del Peloponeso.**
En un principio, los atenienses iban ganando,
pero tuvieron que rendirse en el 404 a. C. Durante
los siguientes 30 años aproximadamente, los
espartanos controlaron casi toda Grecia, pero
el resentimiento de otras ciudades estado llevó
a un largo periodo de guerras que debilitó a
toda Grecia y la dejó expuesta a ataques desde
el exterior.

> **Circle the noun that
> describes the popular
> feeling that undermined the
> power of Sparta./**Encierra
> en un círculo el sustantivo
> que describe el sentimiento
> popular que debilitó el
> poder de Esparta.

## CHALLENGE ACTIVITY/ACTIVIDAD AVANZADA
**Critical Thinking: Make Inferences/Pensamiento
crítico: Hacer inferencias** Imagine you live in
Sparta or Athens after the Persian Wars. Write a
poem or a song expressing how it feels to live in
that city-state./Imagina que vives en Esparta o en

Atenas después de las Guerras Médicas. Escribe
un poema o una canción que exprese cómo se
siente vivir en esa ciudad estado.

| | | | |
|---|---|---|---|
| alliance/ alianza | Athens/Atenas | city-states/ciudades estado | Delian League/ Liga de Delos |
| influence/ influencia | Peloponnesian League/ Liga del Peloponeso | Peloponnesian War/Guerra del Peloponeso | Sparta/Esparta |

**DIRECTIONS/INSTRUCCIONES** Use the vocabulary terms in the
word list above to write a summary of the conflicts that occurred
between Athens and Sparta./Usa el vocabulario de la lista de
palabras de arriba para escribir un resumen de los conflictos entre
Atenas y Esparta.

_____

_____

_____

_____

_____

_____

_____

_____

**DIRECTIONS/INSTRUCCIONES** Write three descriptive words or
phrases that describe each term./Escribe tres palabras o frases
descriptivas para describir cada término.

1. Athens/Atenas_____

2. Sparta/Esparta _____

# Ancient Greece/La antigua Grecia

**MAIN IDEAS/IDEAS PRINCIPALES**

1. The Greeks created myths to explain the world./Los griegos crearon mitos para explicar el mundo.

2. Ancient Greek literature provides some of the world's greatest poems and stories./Algunos de los mejores poemas y relatos del mundo pertenecen a la literatura de la antigua Grecia.

3. Greek literature lives on and influences our world even today./La literatura griega perdura e influye en nuestro mundo aún hoy.

## Key Terms and People/Personas y palabras clave

**mythology/mitología** body of stories about gods or heroes that tries to explain how the world works/conjunto de relatos sobre dioses y héroes que tratan de explicar cómo funciona el mundo

**Homer/Homero** author of two great epic poems, the *Iliad* and the *Odyssey*/autor de dos grandes poemas épicos: *La Ilíada* y *La Odisea*

**Sappho/Safo** most famous lyrical poet of ancient Greece/la poetisa lírica más famosa de la antigua Grecia

**Aesop/Esopo** author of the world's most famous set of fables/autor de las fábulas más famosas del mundo

**fables/fábulas** short stories that offer lessons on living/relatos breves que dan enseñanzas de vida

## Lesson Summary/Resumen de la lección

### MYTHS EXPLAIN THE WORLD/LOS MITOS EXPLICAN EL MUNDO

Instead of science, the ancient Greeks used **mythology**—stories about gods or heroes—to try to explain how the world works. The Greeks believed that the gods caused natural events, from the rising of the moon to thunderstorms. Everything was attributed to the gods, from disasters to daily events./En lugar de usar la ciencia, los antiguos griegos usaban la **mitología,** es decir, historias sobre dioses y héroes, para tratar de explicar cómo funciona el mundo. Los griegos creían que los dioses producían los hechos de la naturaleza, desde la salida de la luna hasta las

> **Underline what the Greeks believed to be caused by the gods./Subraya lo que, según los griegos, era causado por los dioses.**

tormentas. Todo era atribuido a los dioses, desde los desastres hasta los hechos cotidianos.

The Greeks believed that Demeter, the goddess of agriculture, caused the seasons. Hades, the god of the underworld, kidnapped Demeter's daughter. He eventually agreed to give her daughter back for half of the year. Because of Demeter's grief, when her daughter was not with her the plants did not grow, causing winter./ Los griegos creían que Deméter, la diosa de la agricultura, causaba las estaciones. Hades, el dios del inframundo, raptó a la hija de Deméter, aunque finalmente aceptó que regresara durante la mitad del año. Debido a la pena que sentía Deméter cuando su hija no estaba con ella, sus plantas no crecían, y eso provocaba el invierno.

Some myths told not of gods but of heroes. Each city had its own hero, real or fictional, who would slay terrible monsters. The most famous Greek hero was Hercules. The Greeks loved to tell these stories./Algunos mitos no contaban historias de dioses, sino de héroes. Cada ciudad tenía su propio héroe, real o ficticio, que mataba a monstruos terribles. El héroe griego más famoso era Hércules. A los griegos les encantaba contar estas historias.

| According to Greek mythology, which season was caused by Demeter not having her daughter?/De acuerdo con la mitología griega, ¿qué estación se produjo por la ausencia de la hija de Deméter? |
| --- |
| _____ _____ |

## ANCIENT GREEK LITERATURE/LITERATURA DE LA ANTIGUA GRECIA

Greek writers produced great works of literature and the world's most famous stories. Among the earliest and most influential are the epic poems the *Iliad* and the *Odyssey* by the poet **Homer.** Scholars are not sure if Homer actually existed, but the poems are central to Greek lore and education. The *Iliad* tells the story of the last years of the Trojan War. The *Odyssey* describes the Greek hero Odysseus's long journey home after the war./Los escritores griegos produjeron

| If Homer did not exist, how do you think the Iliad and the Odyssey were composed?/Si Homero no existió, ¿cómo crees que fueron creadas La Ilíada y La Odisea? |
| --- |
| _____ _____ _____ _____ _____ |

**Lesson/Lección 4,** *continued/continuación*

grandes obras literarias y los relatos más famosos del mundo. Entre los más antiguos y más influyentes se encuentran los poemas épicos *La Ilíada* y *La Odisea*, del poeta **Homero.** Aunque no se sabe si Homero realmente existió, sus poemas fueron fundamentales para la sabiduría tradicional y la educación griegas. *La Ilíada* cuenta la historia de los últimos años de la Guerra de Troya. *La Odisea* describe el largo viaje de regreso a casa del héroe griego Odiseo después de la guerra.

Other forms of literature were also popular. Lyric poetry, recited by the poet while playing the lyre, was especially prized. The most famous lyric poet was a woman, **Sappho.** Also popular were **fables,** or short stories that offer lessons on life. The most famous fable writer was **Aesop** (EE-sahp), who may have lived around 500 BC. Aesop's fables are still commonly told today./ También había otras formas literarias muy populares. La poesía lírica, que el poeta recitaba mientras tocaba la lira, era muy preciada. La poetisa lírica más famosa era una mujer: **Safo.** También eran populares las **fábulas,** o relatos breves que ofrecen enseñanzas de vida. El escritor de fábulas más famoso fue **Esopo,** que se cree que vivió alrededor del año 500 a. C. Las fábulas de Esopo se siguen contando aún hoy en día.

| What is lyric poetry?/¿Qué es la poesía lírica? |
| --- |
| _____ |
| _____ |
| _____ |

## GREEK LITERATURE LIVES/LA LITERATURA GRIEGA VIVE

Greek literature, language, and art have had a great influence on modern culture. The English language contains Greek expressions. A long journey, for example, is called an "odyssey" after Odysseus. Many places are named after Greek gods. Greek myths and stories have inspired painters, writers, and filmmakers for centuries./ La literatura, el idioma y el arte griegos han

| Titans were large and powerful gods in Greek myth. What word in English is derived from this group of Greek gods?/Los titanes eran dioses poderosos y de gran tamaño de la mitología griega. ¿Qué otra palabra del español deriva de este grupo de dioses griegos? |
| --- |
| _____ |

tenido una gran influencia en la cultura moderna.
El español contiene expresiones griegas. A un
largo viaje, por ejemplo, se le llama "odisea"
por Odiseo. Muchos lugares llevan el nombre
de dioses griegos. Los mitos y relatos griegos
han inspirado a pintores, escritores y cineastas
durante siglos.

Greeks created drama, or plays, as part of
religious ceremonies to honor their gods and
heroes. Greeks also were among the first to write
about history, believing people learn from the
past. One early historian, Thucydides, tried to
be neutral, not taking sides, in his historical
account of a war. Later historians often modeled
their works on his./Los griegos crearon el arte
dramático, o teatro, como parte de las
ceremonias religiosas para honrar a sus dioses
y héroes. Los griegos también estuvieron entre
los primeros en escribir sobre historia, porque
creían que las personas aprendían del pasado.
Un historiador antiguo, Tucídides, intentó ser
neutral, no tomar bandos, al hacer el relato
histórico de las guerras. Los historiadores
posteriores a menudo se basaban en sus obras.

## CHALLENGE ACTIVITY/ACTIVIDAD AVANZADA

**Critical Thinking: Elaborate/Pensamiento crítico:
Profundizar** Greek literature has influenced our
modern culture. Write a paragraph describing
how Greek literature, language, or art may have
influenced you./La literatura griega ha influido
en nuestra cultura moderna. Escribe un párrafo
en el que describas de qué manera la literatura,
el idioma o el arte griegos pueden haber influido
en tu vida.

| Achilles/Aquiles | Aesop/Esopo | fables/fábulas | Hercules/Hércules |
|---|---|---|---|
| Homer/Homero | mythology/mitología | neutral/neutral | Zeus/Zeus |

**DIRECTIONS/INSTRUCCIONES** Answer each question by writing a sentence that contains at least one word from the word bank. Not all words are used./Responde cada pregunta con una oración que contenga al menos una palabra del banco de palabras. No se usan todas las palabras.

1. What is the modern expression that refers to a person's weak spot and is based on a figure from Greek mythology?/¿Qué expresión moderna se refiere al punto débil de una persona y se basa en una figura de la mitología griega?

   _____

   _____

2. What was one way that Greek writers taught people important lessons about life?/¿Cuál era una manera en que los escritores griegos les enseñaban a las personas lecciones importantes sobre la vida?

   _____

   _____

3. How did the ancient Greeks explain weather, seasons, and natural disasters?/¿Cómo explicaban los antiguos griegos el clima, las estaciones y los desastres naturales?

   _____

   _____

4. What famous Greek hero fought monsters and killed the nine-headed hydra?/¿Qué famoso héroe griego luchó contra monstruos y mató a la hidra de nueve cabezas?

   _____

   _____

5. What was special about the historical work of the Greek historian Thucydides?/¿Qué tenían de especial las obras del historiador griego Tucídides?

   _____

   _____

   _____

# Ancient Greece/La antigua Grecia

### Lesson/Lección 5

**MAIN IDEAS/IDEAS PRINCIPALES**
1. The Greeks made great contributions to the arts./Los griegos hicieron grandes contribuciones a las artes.
2. The teachings of Socrates, Plato, and Aristotle are the basis of modern philosophy./Las enseñanzas de Sócrates, Platón y Aristóteles son la base de la filosofía moderna.
3. In science, the Greeks made key discoveries in math, medicine, and engineering./En el campo de la ciencia, los griegos hicieron descubrimientos clave en las matemáticas, la medicina y la ingeniería.

## Key Terms and People/Personas y palabras clave

**Socrates/Sócrates** the first of the great Greek thinkers and teachers/el primero de los grandes pensadores y maestros griegos

**Plato/Platón** teacher and thinker, student of Socrates, and founder of the Academy/maestro y pensador, discípulo de Sócrates y fundador de la Academia

**Aristotle/Aristóteles** philosopher who taught that people should live lives of moderation based on reason/filósofo que enseñó que las personas debían vivir con moderación y basarse en la razón

**reason/razón** clear and ordered thinking/pensamiento claro y ordenado

**Euclid/Euclides** great and influential mathematician/gran matemático influyente

**Hippocrates/Hipócrates** great Greek doctor who taught how to treat disease by understanding what caused illness/gran médico griego que enseñó a tratar las enfermedades mediante la comprensión de sus causas

## Lesson Summary/Resumen de la lección

### THE ARTS/LAS ARTES

The ancient Greeks were master artists. Their paintings and statues have been admired for thousands of years. Greek sculptors studied the human body, especially how it looks when it is moving. They used what they learned when they carved stone and marble statues. Greek artists painted detailed scenes on vases, pots, and other vessels. The remains of Greek architecture show

> Which three art forms are mentioned in this paragraph?/¿Cuáles son las tres formas de arte que se mencionan en este párrafo?
>
> _____
>
> _____
>
> _____

how much care the Greeks took in designing their buildings so they would reflect the beauty and greatness of their cities./Los antiguos griegos eran artistas distinguidos. Sus pinturas y estatuas han despertado admiración durante miles de años. Los escultores griegos estudiaban el cuerpo humano, en especial el aspecto que tenía en movimiento. Luego usaban lo que aprendían para tallar estatuas de piedra y mármol. Los artistas griegos pintaban escenas detalladas en jarrones, vasijas y otros recipientes. Los restos de la arquitectura griega muestran el gran cuidado que tenían los griegos al diseñar sus construcciones para que reflejaran la belleza y la grandeza de sus ciudades.

## PHILOSOPHY/FILOSOFÍA

The ancient Greeks worshipped gods and goddesses whose actions explained many of the mysteries of the world. But around 500 BC a few people began to think about other explanations. We call these people philosophers. Philosophers believe in the power of the human mind to think, explain, and understand life./Los antiguos griegos adoraban a dioses y diosas cuyas acciones explicaban muchos de los misterios del mundo. Sin embargo, alrededor del 500 a. C., algunos comenzaron a pensar en otras explicaciones. Estas personas se conocen como filósofos. Los filósofos creen en el poder de la mente humana para pensar, explicar y comprender la vida.

Three Greek philosophers' teachings are at the root of modern philosophy and science. These men thought about the world and searched for knowledge, wisdom, and truth. **Socrates** (SAHK-ruh-teez) believed that people must never stop looking for knowledge. He taught by asking questions. When people answered, he challenged their answers with more questions. This style of teaching is now called the Socratic method. His

> **Underline the sentence that explains what philosophers believe in./**Subraya la oración que explica en qué creían los filósofos.

> **What would Socrates say about learning?/**¿Qué diría Sócrates sobre el aprendizaje?
>
> _____
> _____
> _____
> _____

student **Plato** (PLAYT-oh) created a school called the Academy to which students, philosophers, and scientists could come to discuss ideas. Plato's student **Aristotle** (ar-uh-STAH-tuhl) taught that people should live lives of moderation, or balance. He believed that moderation was based on **reason.** Aristotle also made great advances in the field of logic, the process of making inferences./Las enseñanzas de tres filósofos griegos conforman la base de la filosofía y la ciencia modernas. Estos hombres pensaban acerca del mundo y buscaban el conocimiento, la sabiduría y la verdad. **Sócrates** creía que el ser humano nunca debía dejar de buscar el conocimiento. Enseñaba por medio de preguntas. Cuando le contestaban, cuestionaba esas respuestas haciendo más preguntas. Este estilo de enseñanza ahora se conoce como método socrático. Su discípulo **Platón** creó una escuela llamada la Academia, a la que estudiantes, filósofos y científicos podían ir para discutir ideas. Aristóteles, discípulo de Platón, enseñaba que las personas debían vivir una vida de moderación, o equilibrio. Creía que la moderación se basaba en la razón. Aristóteles también introdujo grandes adelantos en el campo de la lógica, que es el proceso de hacer inferencias.

## SCIENCE/CIENCIA

Many of the rules we still use today to measure and calculate were first developed by Greek mathematicians like **Euclid** (YOO-kluhd), who is best known for his work in geometry. Greek doctors like **Hippocrates** (hip-AHK-ruh-teez) wanted to cure diseases and keep people healthy. He is known today for his ideas about how doctors should behave. Greek inventors also made many discoveries that are still in use, such as practical devices like water screws, which bring water up from a lower level to a higher one./

> **Do you think doctors today have the same basic beliefs about medicine as Hippocrates did? Why or why not?/¿Crees que los médicos de hoy en día tienen las mismas creencias básicas sobre la medicina que tenía Hipócrates? ¿Por qué?**
>
> _____
> _____
> _____
> _____
> _____
> _____
> _____

Muchas de las reglas que aún usamos para medir
y calcular fueron desarrolladas inicialmente
por los matemáticos griegos, como **Euclides,**
conocido por su trabajo en la geometría. Los
grandes médicos griegos, como **Hipócrates,**
querían curar enfermedades y cuidar la salud
de las personas. Hoy se le conoce por sus ideas
sobre la manera en que los médicos deben
comportarse. Los inventores griegos también
hicieron descubrimientos que todavía usamos:
artefactos prácticos como el tornillo de
Arquímedes, que eleva el agua de un nivel
bajo a uno más alto.

## CHALLENGE ACTIVITY/ACTIVIDAD AVANZADA

**Critical Thinking: Summarize/Pensamiento crítico:**
**Resumir** Create a list showing contributions ancient
Greeks made to modern culture. Include the name
or names of people who are credited with each
contribution./Haz una lista de contribuciones que
los antiguos griegos hicieron a la cultura moderna.
Incluye el nombre o los nombres de las personas
a quienes se les atribuye cada contribución.

**DIRECTIONS/INSTRUCCIONES** On the line provided before each
statement, write **T** if a statement is true and **F** if a statement is false.
If the statement is false, write the correct term on the line after each
sentence that makes the sentence a true statement./En la línea que
precede a cada enunciado, escribe **V** si el enunciado es verdadero
y **F** si es falso. Si el enunciado es falso, escribe en la línea que sigue
a la oración el término correcto que lo hace verdadero.

_____ 1. The Parthenon, a beautiful temple to the goddess Athena, was one
of the most impressive of all ancient Greek buildings./El Partenón,
un hermoso templo dedicado a la diosa Atenea, fue uno de los
edificios más impactantes de toda la antigua Grecia.

_____

_____ 2. The Greek philosopher <u>Archimedes</u> taught by asking questions that challenged people to think about their beliefs./El filósofo griego <u>Arquímedes</u> enseñaba por medio de preguntas que incitaban a las personas a pensar sobre sus creencias.

_____

_____ 3. The Greek philosopher <u>Plato</u> taught that people should live lives of moderation, or balance, based on reason./El filósofo griego <u>Platón</u> enseñaba que las personas debían vivir una vida de moderación, o equilibrio, basada en la razón.

_____

_____ 4. The Greek scientist <u>Hippocrates</u> devoted his life to studying mathematics and developed many of the geometry rules used today./El científico griego <u>Hipócrates</u> dedicó su vida a estudiar las matemáticas y desarrolló muchas de las reglas de la geometría que se usan hoy en día.

_____

**DIRECTIONS/INSTRUCCIONES** Write three words or descriptive phrases that describe each person./Escribe tres palabras o frases descriptivas que describan a cada persona.

5. Socrates/Sócrates _____

_____

6. Plato/Platón _____

_____

7. Aristotle/Aristóteles _____

_____

8. Euclid/Euclides _____

_____

# The Hellenistic World/El mundo helenístico

**MAIN IDEAS/IDEAS PRINCIPALES**

1. Macedonia conquered Greece in the 300s BC./Macedonia conquistó Grecia en el siglo 4 a. C.

2. Alexander the Great built an empire that united parts of Europe, Asia, and Egypt./Alejandro Magno creó un imperio que unió partes de Europa, Asia y Egipto.

3. Alexander spread Greek cultural influences throughout his empire./Alejandro difundió influencias de la cultura griega en todo su imperio.

## Key Terms and People/Personas y palabras clave

**Philip II/Filipo II** powerful king of Macedonia/poderoso rey de Macedonia

**phalanx/falange** a group of warriors who stood close together in a square/grupo de guerreros que forman un cuadrado compacto

**Alexander the Great/Alejandro Magno** king of Macedonia who built the largest empire the world had ever seen/rey de Macedonia que creó el mayor imperio conocido hasta entonces en el mundo

**Hellenistic/helenística** name for the blended culture that developed in Alexander's empire/nombre con el que se designa a la mezcla de culturas que surgió en el imperio de Alejandro

## Lesson Summary/Resumen de la lección

### MACEDONIA CONQUERS GREECE/MACEDONIA CONQUISTA GRECIA

About 360 BC, **Philip II** of Macedonia invaded Athens and won easily. The rest of Greece surrendered. Philip's victory resulted from his military strategy and weaponry. For instance, he extended the Greek idea of the **phalanx** (FAY-langks) by giving each soldier spears longer than their opponents'. Philip planned to conquer Persia, but he was murdered in 336 BC and his throne passed to his 20-year-old son Alexander./Alrededor del año 360 a. C., **Filipo II** de Macedonia invadió Atenas y no tardó en conquistarla. El resto de Grecia se rindió.

| How was Philip II able to conquer Athens so easily?/¿Por qué le resultó tan fácil a Filipo II conquistar Atenas? |
|---|
| _____ |
| _____ |
| _____ |
| _____ |

Filipo obtuvo la victoria gracias a su estrategia
militar y su armamento. Por ejemplo, mejoró
el concepto griego de **falange** al darle a cada
soldado lanzas más largas que las de sus
oponentes. Filipo tenía planeado conquistar
Persia, pero fue asesinado en el año 336 a. C.
y, como resultado, su hijo Alejandro, que en
ese momento tenía 20 años, subió al trono.

## ALEXANDER BUILDS AN EMPIRE/ALEJANDRO CREA UN IMPERIO

When Philip died, the people of the Greek city
of Thebes rebelled. Alexander attacked Thebes
and enslaved the Theban people. He used Thebes
as an example of what would happen if any other
Greek cities rebelled against him. Alexander went
on to defeat the Persians time after time and to
conquer Egypt. He became ruler of what had
been the Persian empire. Before his death at
33 years of age, **Alexander the Great** (as he came
to be called) had built an empire stretching from
Asia Minor west to India and to Egypt in the
south. This was the largest empire the world had
ever seen. He ruled as an absolute dictator—
whatever he said was law. With no individual
rights under a dictatorship, Alexander often
punished people with death. Leaders who
governed poorly or were dishonest were
executed./Cuando murió Filipo, los habitantes
de la ciudad griega de Tebas se rebelaron.
Alejandro atacó Tebas y esclavizó al pueblo
tebano. Usó a Tebas como ejemplo de lo que
les ocurriría a las demás ciudades griegas si se
rebelaban. Luego, Alejandro derrotó a los persas
en numerosas batallas y conquistó Egipto. Se
convirtió en soberano de lo que había sido el
imperio persa. Antes de su muerte a los 33 años,

> **How did Alexander respond to the Theban rebellion?/¿Cuál fue la respuesta de Alejandro ante la rebelión de Tebas?**
> _____
> _____
> _____
> _____

**Alejandro Magno** (como se le conocía) había creado un imperio que se extendía hacia el oeste desde Asia Menor hasta la India y hasta Egipto en el sur: era el mayor imperio que el mundo había conocido jamás. Alejandro gobernaba como dictador absoluto: su palabra era la ley. Debido a que en las dictaduras no existen los derechos individuales, Alejandro a menudo imponía condenas a muerte. A los líderes que tomaban malas decisiones de gobierno o eran deshonestos se los ejecutaba.

## SPREADING GREEK CULTURE/DIFUSIÓN DE LA CULTURA GRIEGA

Alexander admired Greek culture and worked to spread Greek influence by founding cities in the lands he conquered. He modeled the cities after the cities of Greece, and he encouraged Greek settlers to move to these new cities. As a result, Greek became a common language throughout Alexander's empire. Even as he supported the spread of Greek culture, however, Alexander encouraged common people to keep their own customs and traditions. The new, blended culture that developed is called **Hellenistic.** It was not purely Greek. It combined elements of Persian, Egyptian, Syrian, and other cultures with Greek ideas./Alejandro admiraba la cultura griega y se dedicó a difundir las influencias griegas mediante la fundación de ciudades en las tierras que conquistaba. Construyó las ciudades siguiendo el modelo de las ciudades griegas y fomentó el traslado de habitantes griegos a esas nuevas ciudades. Como resultado, el griego se convirtió en una lengua común en todo el imperio de Alejandro. Sin embargo, aunque Alejandro apoyaba la difusión de la cultura

> Underline the sentence that explains why Greek became a common language throughout Alexander's empire./Subraya la oración que explica por qué el griego se convirtió en una lengua común en todo el imperio de Alejandro.

> Why is Hellenistic culture called a "blended" culture?/ ¿Por qué se dice que la cultura helenística era una "mezcla de culturas"?
>
> _____
> _____
> _____
> _____
> _____
> _____

griega, permitía que los pueblos conservaran sus propias costumbres y tradiciones. La nueva mezcla de culturas que surgió se conoció como **helenística.** No era puramente griega: era una combinación de elementos persas, egipcios, sirios y de otras culturas con ideas griegas.

Literature remained a popular art form during the Hellenistic period. Menander was the leading poet and dramatist of the Hellenistic period. He wrote over 100 plays, most of which were comedies. Another important and well-educated poet was Callimachus, who lived in the Egyptian city of Alexandria. Writers of this period wrote histories, biographies, and novels./Durante el período helenístico, la literatura siguió siendo un medio artístico popular. Menandro fue el principal poeta y dramaturgo de este período: escribió más de 100 obras de teatro, muchas de ellas comedias. Otro poeta importante e instruido fue Calímaco, que vivía en la ciudad egipcia de Alejandría. Los escritores de este período escribieron crónicas históricas, biografías y novelas.

## CHALLENGE ACTIVITY/ACTIVIDAD AVANZADA
**Critical Thinking: Make Inferences/Pensamiento crítico: Hacer inferencias**  Write a short essay that characterizes the United States as a blended culture./ Escribe un ensayo breve en el que se describa a los Estados Unidos como una mezcla de culturas.

| Alexander the Great/<br>Alejandro Magno | elements/<br>elementos | Macedonians/<br>macedonios |
| Hellenistic/helenística | Persia/Persia | phalanx/falange |
| Philip II/Filipo II | strategies/estrategias | spears/lanzas |

**DIRECTIONS/INSTRUCCIONES** Answer each question by writing
a sentence that contains at least one word from the word bank./
Responde cada pregunta con una oración que contenga al menos
una palabra del banco de palabras.

1. How was Philip II able to defeat the Greeks?/¿De qué manera Filipo II
logró derrotar a los griegos?

_____

_____

_____

2. What advantage did the soldiers in Philip's army have?/¿Qué ventaja tenían
los soldados del ejército de Filipo?

_____

_____

_____

3. What Macedonian leader is considered one of the greatest conquerors
in history? Why?/¿Qué líder macedonio es considerado uno de los
conquistadores más importantes de la historia? ¿Por qué?

_____

_____

_____

4. What new blended culture developed in Alexander the Great's empire, and
what did this culture combine?/¿Qué mezcla de culturas se desarrolló en el
imperio de Alejandro Magno y qué aspectos se combinaban?

_____

_____

_____

# The Hellenistic World/El mundo helenístico

## Lesson/Lección 2

**MAIN IDEAS/IDEAS PRINCIPALES**

1. Three powerful generals divided Alexander's empire among themselves, establishing Hellenistic Macedonia, Hellenistic Syria, and Hellenistic Egypt./Tres poderosos generales se dividieron el imperio de Alejandro. Así surgieron la Macedonia helenística, la Siria helenística y el Egipto helenístico.

2. A uniform system of trade developed throughout the Hellenistic kingdoms, with a common language, culture, and coinage./Los reinos helenísticos desarrollaron un sistema de comercio uniforme, con una lengua, una cultura y una moneda en común.

## Key Terms and People/Personas y palabras clave

**Antigonus/Antígono** a powerful general of Alexander's who became the king of Macedonia/poderoso general de Alejandro que se convirtió en rey de Macedonia

**Seleucus/Seleuco** a powerful general who seized most of Alexander's Asian conquests/poderoso general que acaparó la mayor parte de los territorios asiáticos conquistados por Alejandro

**Ptolemy/Ptolomeo** a powerful general of Alexander's who ruled Egypt and whose dynasty became the most powerful and wealthiest of Hellenistic kingdoms/poderoso general de Alejandro que gobernó Egipto y cuya dinastía se convirtió en la más poderosa y próspera de los reinos helenísticos

**Cleopatra VII/Cleopatra VII** the last and most famous Ptolemaic ruler of Egypt/la última y más famosa soberana ptolemaica de Egipto

## Lesson Summary/Resumen de la lección

### THREE HELLENISTIC KINGDOMS/TRES REINOS HELENÍSTICOS

After Alexander died, there was no obvious heir to his kingdom. So his generals fought for power. The empire was divided among three generals./Tras la muerte de Alejandro, el reino quedó sin un heredero definido, por lo que sus generales se disputaron el poder. El imperio se dividió entre tres generales.

**Antigonus** became the king of Alexander's homeland, Macedonia, which included Greece.

Lesson/Lección 2, *continued*/*continuación*

It had the weakest government. Macedonia had trouble defending itself from the many revolts of the Greeks. Rome's armies conquered the Antigonid dynasty in the mid-100s BC./**Antígono** se convirtió en rey de Macedonia, la tierra natal de Alejandro, que incluía a Grecia. De los tres reinos, Macedonia tenía el gobierno más débil. Tenía dificultades para defenderse de las muchas rebeliones de los griegos. Los ejércitos romanos conquistaron la dinastía antigónida a mediados del siglo 2 a. C.

**Why were Rome's armies able to conquer the Antigonid dynasty?/¿Por qué los ejércitos romanos pudieron conquistar la dinastía antigónida?**

_____
_____
_____
_____

**Seleucus** seized control of most of Alexander's Asian conquests, including Persia. This empire was larger than Macedonia and was difficult to control. It was spread out and was home to many different people with different customs. The capital was far from some parts of the kingdom, so people ignored the king. Seleucid rulers were eventually conquered by Rome in the 60s BC./ **Seleuco** acaparó el control de la mayor parte de los territorios asiáticos conquistados por Alejandro, entre los que se incluía Persia. Este imperio, mayor que Macedonia, era difícil de controlar. Abarcaba un territorio amplio y alojaba a muchos pueblos distintos con costumbres diferentes. La capital se hallaba lejos de algunas partes del reino y, por lo tanto, la gente hacía caso omiso al rey. Los gobernantes seléucidos fueron conquistados por Roma en la década del 60 a. C.

**What problems existed in the Seleucid kingdom?/ ¿Qué problemas existieron en el reino seléucido?**

_____
_____
_____
_____

**Ptolemy** became ruler of Egypt. His dynasty, the Ptolemaic, was the most powerful and wealthiest of the Hellenistic kingdoms. He was called "pharaoh" to gain him the support of the Egyptians. He ruled from Alexandria, one of the ancient world's greatest cities. It had the world's largest library and the Museum, a place for scholars and artists. Even this stable and prosperous kingdom, though, came into conflict

**Underline the sentence that provides some reasons for Alexandria being considered a great city./ Subraya la oración que presenta algunas de las razones por las que se consideraba a Alejandría una ciudad importante.**

with other powers, especially Rome. It lasted longer than the other kingdoms. But after the death of the last and most famous Ptolemaic ruler, **Cleopatra VII,** the Romans took control of Egypt./**Ptolomeo** se convirtió en gobernante de Egipto. Su dinastía, la ptolemaica, fue la más poderosa y próspera de los reinos helenísticos. Se hizo llamar "faraón" para ganarse el apoyo de los egipcios. Gobernaba desde Alejandría, una de las ciudades más importantes del mundo antiguo, donde estaba la biblioteca más grande del mundo y el Museo, un espacio para estudiosos y artistas. Sin embargo, ese reino estable y próspero entró en conflicto con otras potencias, en particular con Roma. Duró más que los otros imperios, pero tras la muerte de **Cleopatra VII,** la última y más famosa soberana ptolemaica, los romanos tomaron el control de Egipto.

## GOVERNMENT AND ECONOMY/GOBIERNO Y ECONOMÍA

Alexander had ruled without limits on his power, as did the Hellenistic rulers. Rule passed down within their families. Only men could be kings in Macedonia and the Seleucid kingdom. A few women became pharaohs in Egypt, such as Cleopatra VII./Al igual que Alejandro, los gobernantes helenísticos tenían poderes ilimitados. El mando se pasaba de un familiar a otro. Solo los hombres podían reinar en Macedonia y el reino seléucido. Egipto, en cambio, tuvo algunas faraonas, como Cleopatra VII.

Hellenistic rulers relied on Greek advisors. Together, they strengthened their economies, built and repaired roads and irrigation systems, promoted manufacturing and trade, and supported the arts. Large cities grew as kings

> How was rule in Egypt different from rule in Macedonia and the Seleucid kingdom?/¿Qué diferencia había entre el gobierno de Egipto y los gobiernos de Macedonia y el reino seléucido?
>
> _____
>
> _____

Lesson/Lección 2, *continued*/*continuación*

became wealthy from the taxes./Los gobernantes helenísticos tenían asesores griegos. Con su colaboración, fortalecieron sus economías, construyeron y repararon las carreteras y los sistemas de irrigación, promovieron la industria y el comercio y fomentaron las artes. Las ciudades comenzaron a crecer y los reyes se enriquecieron gracias a la recaudación de impuestos.

Throughout the Hellenistic region, the people followed a uniform system of trade. They shared a common culture and used a form of Greek as their common language. They continued to use standard coins from Alexander's time. They built trade networks with other civilizations. For example, China could send silk to the Hellenistic kingdoms, and they could send other goods back to China./Los pueblos de toda la región helenística tenían un sistema uniforme de comercio. Compartían la misma cultura y usaban una variedad del griego como lengua común. Siguieron utilizando las monedas de la época de Alejandro y establecieron redes comerciales con otras civilizaciones: por ejemplo, China podía enviar seda a los reinos helenísticos, y desde allí podían enviarse otros artículos a China.

> **What made trade so successful throughout the Hellenistic region?/¿Por qué prosperó tanto el comercio en la región helenística?**
>
> _____
> _____
> _____
> _____
> _____

## CHALLENGE ACTIVITY/ACTIVIDAD AVANZADA

**Critical Thinking: Make Judgments/Pensamiento crítico: Dar opiniones** Consider the three Hellenistic kingdoms Alexander's successors ruled. Choose the kingdom that you believe was the most successful. Write a short essay that supports your choice./Piensa en los tres reinos helenísticos gobernados por los sucesores de Alejandro. Escoge el reino que crees que tuvo el mayor éxito. Escribe un ensayo breve en el que respaldes tu elección.

| Antigonus/Antígono | Cleopatra VII/Cleopatra VII |
|---|---|
| Ptolemy/Ptolomeo | Seleucus/Seleuco |

**DIRECTIONS/INSTRUCCIONES** Answer each question by writing
a sentence that contains at least one word from the word bank./
Responde cada pregunta con una oración que contenga al menos
una palabra del banco de palabras.

1. Who was a female pharaoh who was the last and the most famous ruler
   of Egypt?/¿Qué faraona fue la última y más famosa soberana de Egipto?

   _____

   _____

2. Who took control of most of Alexander's Asian conquests?/¿Quién tomó el
   control de la mayoría de los territorios asiáticos conquistados por Alejandro?

   _____

   _____

3. Who formed the most powerful and wealthiest of Hellenistic kingdoms?/
   ¿Quién fundó el más poderoso y próspero de los reinos helenísticos?

   _____

   _____

4. Who became king of Macedonia?/¿Quién se convirtió en rey de Macedonia?

   _____

   _____

Lesson/Lección 2, *continued*/*continuación*

**DIRECTIONS/INSTRUCCIONES** Use the vocabulary terms from the lesson to write a short summary of the Hellenistic World after Alexander./Usa los términos de vocabulario de la lección para escribir un resumen breve del mundo helenístico después de Alejandro.

_____

_____

_____

_____

_____

_____

# The Hellenistic World/El mundo helenístico

## Lesson/Lección 3

### MAIN IDEAS/IDEAS PRINCIPALES

1. Greek-influenced culture was most noticeable in the cities, while rural areas tended to be more traditional./La influencia griega en la cultura era más visible en las ciudades, mientras que las zonas rurales solían ser más tradicionales.

2. Hellenistic art and architecture demonstrated Greek influences but had their own unique touches./El arte y la arquitectura helenísticos demostraban la influencia griega, pero tenían sus propios elementos distintivos.

## Key Terms and People/Personas y palabras clave

**Aristarchus/Aristarco** an astronomer who was the first person to propose that the earth moves around the sun/astrónomo; fue el primero en postular que la Tierra gira alrededor del Sol

## Lesson Summary/Resumen de la lección

### SOCIETY AND DAILY LIFE/SOCIEDAD Y VIDA COTIDIANA

Alexander introduced Greek customs into his empire, but he did not force people to follow them. So his kingdoms had a blended Hellenistic, or Greek-inspired, culture. Hellenistic Egypt was a blend of Greek and traditional Egyptian culture./Alejandro llevó las costumbres griegas a su imperio, pero no obligó a los pueblos a adoptarlas. Por eso, sus reinos tenían una cultura helenística mixta, inspirada en la cultura griega. El Egipto helenístico era una mezcla de la cultura griega y la cultura egipcia tradicional.

Greek influence was found in cities. The Greek language was used for government. People followed Greek-type laws. Buildings resembled ones found in Greek city-states. The upper class wore Greek-style clothing and followed Greek philosophy./La influencia griega era más evidente en las ciudades. En el gobierno se usaba la lengua griega, y los ciudadanos adoptaban leyes similares a las griegas. Los edificios se parecían a los de las

> **Why did Alexander's kingdoms have a Greek-inspired, or blended, Hellenistic culture?/¿Por qué los reinos de Alejandro tenían una cultura helenística mixta, inspirada en la cultura griega?**
>
> _____
> _____
> _____
> _____
> _____

ciudades estado griegas. La clase alta se vestía
al estilo griego y adoptaba la filosofía griega.

Alexandria, Egypt, was an example of a
Greek-style Hellenistic city. It had buildings that
reflected Greek taste and technological skill. The
Pharos, a lighthouse more than 350 feet tall,
towered over the city. It was one of the wonders
of the ancient world. Alexandria also had the
greatest collection of Greek and Hellenistic
knowledge in its library./Alejandría, en Egipto,
fue un ejemplo de una ciudad helenística de estilo
griego. Sus edificios estaban construidos según
los gustos y las destrezas tecnológicas de los
griegos. El Faro de Alejandría, un faro de más de
350 pies de altura que se erguía sobre la ciudad,
fue una de las maravillas del mundo antiguo.
Además, la biblioteca de Alejandría albergaba
la mayor colección de conocimientos griegos
y helenísticos.

Rural areas showed little Greek influence,
though. People spoke their own native languages
and followed their own religions. Their dress and
buildings remained the same. These areas
followed traditional Egyptian laws./Sin embargo,
en las zonas rurales no se percibía la influencia
griega. Los habitantes hablaban su lengua nativa
y tenían su propia religión. Ni su vestimenta ni
sus edificios cambiaron. Además, esas zonas
se regían por las leyes egipcias tradicionales.

In Greek city-states, women had few rights.
Over time, women in Hellenistic culture could
be educated, own property, and run businesses./
En las ciudades estado griegas, las mujeres tenían
pocos derechos. Con el tiempo, las mujeres de
la cultura helenística pudieron acceder a la
educación, tener propiedades y realizar
actividades comerciales.

> **How were rural areas different from Hellenistic cities?/¿En qué se diferenciaban las zonas rurales de las ciudades helenísticas?**
>
> _____
> _____
> _____
> _____
> _____
> _____
> _____

## CULTURE AND ACHIEVEMENTS/CULTURA Y LOGROS

Hellenistic art and architecture were inspired by Greek works. However, artists added their own unique style. For example, Hellenistic buildings were larger than Greek buildings had been. These large buildings were symbols of the rulers' power./El arte y la arquitectura helenísticos se inspiraban en las obras griegas. Sin embargo, los artistas añadían su estilo particular. Por ejemplo, los edificios helenísticos eran más grandes que los griegos. Simbolizaban el poder de los gobernantes.

> **Underline the sentence that offers a reason why Hellenistic buildings were so large./Subraya la oración en la que se presenta una razón por la cual los edificios helenísticos eran tan grandes.**

Hellenistic artists wanted their works to appear more natural than Greek works. A Greek statue might show a formal pose such as a king seated on a throne. In contrast, a Hellenistic sculpture might show a subject in an active and natural pose./Los artistas helenísticos querían que sus obras tuvieran una apariencia más natural que las obras griegas. Por ejemplo, mientras que en una obra de arte griega se mostraba una pose formal, como un rey en su trono, en una escultura helenística podía representarse a un sujeto en una pose activa y natural.

Religion inspired artistic expression in the Ptolemaic kingdom. The people worshipped both Greek and Egyptian gods, so artists made statues of both sets of gods. Hellenistic philosophers considered ways people could be happy and other worldly issues. Diogenes founded Cynicism, which said people should live according to nature. Pyrrho founded Skepticism, which said people can never know how things really are. Epicurus founded Epicureanism, which said people should avoid pain and pursue pleasure. Zeno founded Stoicism, which said that all people have a role to play in society./En el

> **Hellenistic artists made statues of both Greek and Egyptian gods. What does this fact indicate?/Los artistas helenísticos hacían estatuas de dioses griegos y egipcios. ¿Qué indica este dato?**
> _____
> _____
> _____

reino ptolemaico, la expresión artística se inspiraba en la religión. Como el pueblo adoraba a dioses griegos y egipcios, los artistas hacían esculturas de los dioses de las dos religiones. Los filósofos helenísticos reflexionaban sobre cómo podía alcanzarse la felicidad y otros asuntos mundanos. Diógenes fundó el cinismo, que postulaba que la vida de las personas debía regirse por las leyes naturales. Pirro fundó el escepticismo, que postulaba que no es posible saber cómo son las cosas en realidad. Epicuro fundó el epicureísmo, que postulaba que las personas deben evitar el dolor y buscar el placer. Zenón fundó el estoicismo, que postulaba que todas las personas desempeñan un papel en la sociedad.

Some Hellenistic thinkers were interested in the physical world, so they studied science. They conducted experiments and invented items to make people's lives easier. The greatest Hellenistic inventor, Archimedes, created a device to help farmers bring water uphill to their fields. Some scientists made advances in mathematics and astronomy. Euclid described basic ideas about geometry. Astronomer **Aristarchus** first proposed that the earth moves around the sun./Algunos pensadores helenísticos se interesaron por el mundo físico y estudiaron las ciencias. Llevaron a cabo experimentos e inventaron artículos diseñados para facilitar la vida de las personas. El inventor helenístico más importante, Arquímedes, creó un artefacto que ayudaba a los agricultores a llevar agua a las partes altas de sus campos. Algunos científicos hicieron avances en matemáticas y astronomía. Euclides describió algunas ideas básicas de geometría. El astrónomo **Aristarco** fue el primero en postular que la Tierra gira alrededor del Sol.

> **What made Aristarchus an important Hellenistic scientist?/¿Por qué Aristarco fue un científico helenístico importante?**
>
> _____
> _____
> _____
> _____

## CHALLENGE ACTIVITY/ACTIVIDAD AVANZADA

**Critical Thinking: Contrast/Pensamiento crítico: Contrastar** Hellenistic art and architecture took its inspiration from the Greeks. However, the Hellenistic style incorporated its own ideas. Write a short essay that describes what made Hellenistic works different from Greek style./El arte y la arquitectura helenísticos estaban inspirados en el arte y la arquitectura griegos. Sin embargo, el estilo helenístico incorporaba ideas propias. Escribe un ensayo breve en el que describas las diferencias entre las obras de arte helenísticas y el estilo griego.

**DIRECTIONS/INSTRUCCIONES** Write a word or descriptive phrase to describe each place, term, group, or person./Escribe una palabra o frase descriptiva que describa cada lugar, término, grupo o persona.

1. Greek-style Hellenistic city/Una ciudad helenística de estilo griego _____

_____

_____

2. Hellenistic rural areas/Las zonas rurales helenísticas _____

_____

_____

3. Hellenistic women/Las mujeres del período helenístico _____

_____

_____

4. Hellenistic art/El arte helenístico _____

_____

5. The Pharos/El Faro de Alejandría _____

_____

_____

6. Archimedes/Arquímedes _____
   _____
   _____

7. Aristarchus/Aristarco_____
   _____

8. Hellenistic philosophers/Los filósofos helenísticos _____
   _____
   _____

## Ancient Rome/La antigua Roma

**MAIN IDEAS/IDEAS PRINCIPALES**

1. The geography of Italy made land travel difficult but helped the Romans prosper./La geografía de Italia dificultaba los viajes por tierra, pero ayudó a los romanos a prosperar.

2. Ancient historians were very interested in Rome's legendary history./Los antiguos historiadores estaban muy interesados en la legendaria historia de Roma.

3. Once a monarchy, Rome created a republic./Roma, que una vez fue una monarquía, creó una república.

## Key Terms and People/Personas y palabras clave

**Aeneas/Eneas** great Trojan hero who fled Troy for Italy in a journey told in Virgil's *Aeneid*/gran héroe troyano que huyó de Troya a Italia en un viaje que se narra en la *Eneida* de Virgilio

**Romulus and Remus/Rómulo y Remo** legendary twin brothers who are said to have founded Rome/legendarios hermanos gemelos que, según se dice, fundaron Roma

**republic/república** government in which people elect leaders to govern them/ sistema de gobierno en el que las personas eligen líderes para que las gobiernen

**dictator/dictador** ruler with almost absolute power, elected during time of war/ gobernante con poder casi absoluto, elegido durante un período de guerra

**Cincinnatus/Cincinato** famous dictator who defeated a powerful enemy and then resigned his powers/famoso dictador que derrotó a un poderoso enemigo y luego renunció a sus poderes

**plebeians/plebeyos** common people of Rome/gente común de Roma

**patricians/patricios** powerful nobles of Rome/nobles poderosos de Roma

## Lesson Summary/Resumen de la lección

### THE GEOGRAPHY OF ITALY/LA GEOGRAFÍA DE ITALIA

Rome grew from a small town on the Tiber River to become a great power. Rome conquered Greece, Egypt, and Asia Minor. Rome's central location and good climate were factors in its success. Because most of Italy is surrounded by water, Romans could easily travel by sea. The mountains in the north made it difficult to travel over land, so it was hard for others to invade. The warm dry weather resulted in high crop yields, so the Romans had plenty of food./Roma era un pequeño pueblo a orillas del río Tíber que llegó a convertirse en una gran potencia. Conquistó Grecia, Egipto y Asia Menor. La ubicación céntrica de Roma y su buen clima influyeron en su éxito. Como la mayor parte de Italia está rodeada de agua, los romanos podían viajar por mar con facilidad. Las montañas del norte dificultaban los viajes por tierra, por lo que era complicado para otros pueblos invadir Italia. El clima cálido y seco favorecía el crecimiento de los cultivos, por lo que los romanos tenían alimentos en abundancia.

> **How did Italy's geography help the rise of Rome?/¿De qué manera la geografía de Italia contribuyó al crecimiento de Roma?**
>
> _____
> _____
> _____
> _____

## ROME'S LEGENDARY ORIGINS/LOS LEGENDARIOS ORÍGENES DE ROMA

Rome's beginnings are a mystery. Some ruins suggest that people lived there as early as 800 BC. Romans wanted a glorious past, so they created stories and legends about their history./Los comienzos de Roma son un misterio. Algunas ruinas sugieren que ya vivían personas allí en el año 800 a. C. Los romanos querían tener un pasado glorioso, así que crearon relatos y leyendas sobre su historia.

> **Why did the Romans make up stories and legends about their history?/¿Por qué los romanos inventaron relatos y leyendas sobre su historia?**
>
> _____
> _____

The Romans believed their history began with the great Trojan hero **Aeneas** (i-NEE-uhs). Aeneas fled Troy when the Greeks destroyed the city during the Trojan War. He formed an alliance with a people called the Latins and went to Italy. This story is told in the *Aeneid* (i-NEE-id), an epic poem written by a poet named Virgil (VUHR-juhl) around 20 BC./Los romanos creían que su historia comenzó con el gran héroe troyano **Eneas,** quien huyó de Troya cuando los griegos destruyeron la ciudad durante la Guerra de Troya. Eneas se alió con un pueblo conocido como los latinos y se fue a Italia. Esta historia se narra en la *Eneida*, una epopeya escrita por un poeta llamado Virgilio alrededor del año 20 a. C.

According to legend, Rome was founded by twin brothers, **Romulus** (RAHM-yuh-luhs) and **Remus** (REE-muhs). Romulus killed Remus. Then he built Rome and became its first king. Historians believe Rome was founded sometime between 800 and 700 BC. Early Rome was ruled by kings until 509 BC./Según la leyenda, Roma fue fundada por los hermanos gemelos **Rómulo** y **Remo.** Rómulo mató a Remo. Luego, construyó Roma y se convirtió en su primer rey. Los historiadores creen que Roma fue fundada en algún momento entre los años 800 y 700 a. C. La antigua Roma fue gobernada por reyes hasta el año 509 a. C.

> **Which of the two brothers named the city of Rome after himself?/¿Cuál de los dos hermanos dio su nombre a la ciudad de Roma?**
>
> _____
>
> _____

## THE EARLY REPUBLIC/LOS PRIMEROS AÑOS DE LA REPÚBLICA

The Romans created a **republic** so people could elect leaders to govern them. They voted once a year to prevent any one person from having too much power. However, most officials were wealthy, so other people had little say in the republic./Los romanos crearon una **república** para que las personas pudieran elegir líderes que las gobernaran. Votaban una vez al año para evitar que una sola persona tuviera demasiado poder. Sin embargo, la mayoría de los funcionarios eran adinerados, por lo que las demás personas tenían poca voz en la república.

Rome faced many challenges, such as being at war with nearby countries. To lead the country during war, the Romans chose **dictators,** rulers with almost absolute power. Dictators stayed in power for only six months. The most famous dictator was **Cincinnatus** (sin-suh-NAT-uhs), a farmer elected to defeat a major enemy. He resigned as dictator right after the war and went back to his farm./Roma enfrentó muchos retos, como estar en guerra con los países cercanos. Los romanos elegían **dictadores,** gobernantes con poder casi absoluto, para que gobernaran el país durante los períodos de guerra. Los dictadores permanecían en el poder durante solo seis meses. El dictador más famoso fue **Cincinato,** un agricultor que fue elegido para derrotar a un importante enemigo. Después de la guerra, renunció a ser dictador y regresó a su granja.

Within Rome, the **plebeians,** or common people, worked for change. Only the city's **patricians,** the wealthy citizens, could be elected to rule Rome. When the plebeians elected their own officials, the patricians changed the government to avoid a split./En Roma, los **plebeyos,** o gente común, querían un cambio. Solo los **patricios** de la ciudad, los ciudadanos adinerados, podían ser elegidos para gobernar Roma. Cuando los plebeyos eligieron a sus propios funcionarios, los patricios cambiaron la forma de gobierno para evitar una división.

> Why do you think Rome's patricians were so concerned when the plebeians elected their own council?/¿Por qué crees que los patricios de Roma se preocuparon tanto cuando los plebeyos eligieron su propio consejo?
>
> _____
> _____
> _____

## CHALLENGE ACTIVITY/ACTIVIDAD AVANZADA

**Critical Thinking: Summarize/Pensamiento crítico: Resumir** Imagine you are a Roman plebeian. Write a campaign speech saying why people should elect you to office—even though your position has no official power. Your speech should be historically accurate./Imagina que eres un plebeyo romano. Escribe un discurso de campaña en el que expliques por qué deberían elegirte para ser funcionario, aunque tu cargo no tenga poder oficial. Tu discurso debe ser preciso desde el punto de vista histórico.

**DIRECTIONS/INSTRUCCIONES** On the line provided before each statement, write **T** if a statement is true and **F** if a statement is false. If the statement is false, write the correct term on the line after each sentence that makes the sentence a true statement./En la línea que precede a cada enunciado, escribe **V** si el enunciado es verdadero y **F** si es falso. Si el enunciado es falso, escribe en la línea que sigue a la oración el término correcto que lo hace verdadero.

_____ 1. According to legend, <u>Cincinnatus</u> was chosen as dictator to lead the Roman army and quickly defeated his foes./Según la leyenda, <u>Cincinato</u> fue elegido como dictador para dirigir el ejército romano y rápidamente derrotó a sus enemigos.

_____

_____ 2. The Romans chose <u>patricians</u> to lead the city during difficult wars; however, these officials could remain in power for only six months./Los romanos elegían a <u>patricios</u> para que gobernaran la ciudad durante las guerras difíciles, pero esos funcionarios podían permanecer en el poder durante solo seis meses.

_____

_____ 3. <u>Romulus</u> was a legendary hero from Troy who fled to Italy and allied himself with a people called the Latins./<u>Rómulo</u> fue un legendario héroe de Troya que huyó a Italia y se alió con un pueblo conocido como los latinos.

_____

_____ 4. In a <u>republic</u>, people elect leaders to represent them in government./En una <u>república</u>, las personas eligen líderes para que las representen en el gobierno.

_____

_____ 5. The richer, more powerful citizens of Rome were called <u>patricians</u> and were originally the only ones who could be elected to office./A los ciudadanos más adinerados y poderosos de Roma se les llamaba <u>patricios</u> y eran originalmente los únicos que podían ser elegidos para ocupar un cargo.

_____

Lesson/Lección 1, *continued*/*continuación*

---

_____ 6. <u>Plebeians</u> were the common people of Rome, a group that wanted more of a say in how Rome was run./<u>Los plebeyos</u> eran la gente común de Roma, un grupo que quería tener más voz en cómo se gobernaba Roma.

_____

_____ 7. A ruler with almost unlimited power is called a <u>dictator</u>./Un gobernante con poder casi ilimitado se llama <u>dictador</u>.

_____

_____ 8. After <u>Cincinnatus</u> killed his brother, he named the city they built after himself./Después de matar a su hermano, <u>Cincinato</u> le dio su nombre a la ciudad que construyeron.

_____

# Ancient Rome/La antigua Roma

**MAIN IDEAS/IDEAS PRINCIPALES**

1. Roman government was made up of three parts that worked together to run the city./El gobierno romano estaba compuesto de tres partes que trabajaban juntas para gobernar la ciudad.

2. Roman life was shaped by laws, government, and social order./La vida en Roma estaba determinada por las leyes, el gobierno y el orden social.

3. Written laws helped keep order in Rome./Las leyes escritas contribuyeron a mantener el orden en Roma.

4. The late republic period saw the growth of territory and trade./Durante los últimos años de la República se produjo un crecimiento del territorio y del comercio.

5. Rome expanded its territory by conquering other lands./Roma expandió su territorio mediante la conquista de otras tierras.

## Key Terms and People/Personas y palabras clave

**magistrates/magistrados** elected officials/funcionarios electos

**consuls/cónsules** two most powerful elected officials/los dos funcionarios electos más poderosos

**Roman Senate/Senado romano** council of wealthy and powerful Romans that advised officials/consejo de romanos adinerados y poderosos que asesoraban a los funcionarios

**majority rule/gobierno de la mayoría** the largest group has the power to decide government actions/el grupo más grande tiene el poder para decidir las acciones del gobierno

**veto/vetar** to prohibit an official action/prohibir una acción oficial

**Latin/latín** language spoken by the ancient Romans/idioma hablado por los antiguos romanos

**checks and balances/control y compensación de poderes** methods of balancing power/métodos para equilibrar la distribución del poder

**Forum/foro** Rome's public meeting place/lugar público de reunión en Roma

**legions/legiones** groups of up to 6,000 soldiers/grupos de hasta 6,000 soldados

**Punic Wars/Guerras Púnicas** a series of wars between Rome and Carthage/serie de guerras entre Roma y Cartago

**Hannibal/Aníbal** brilliant Carthaginian general who attacked the city of Rome/brillante general cartaginense que atacó la ciudad de Roma

## Lesson Summary/Resumen de la lección
### ROMAN GOVERNMENT/EL GOBIERNO ROMANO

During the 400s BC, so the plebeians did not overthrow the government, the patricians created positions for them. A three-part, or tripartite, government was formed. First, there were elected officials, or **magistrates.** The two most powerful magistrates were **consuls.** The second part was the **Roman Senate,** a council of wealthy and powerful Romans that advised leaders. The third part was assemblies and tribunes. The assemblies' primary job was to elect magistrates. The tribunes governed by **majority rule,** so the group with the most members made the decisions. They could **veto,** or prohibit, government actions. *Veto* means "I forbid" in **Latin,** the Romans' language. **Checks and balances** kept any part from being too powerful./Durante el siglo 5 a. C., para que los plebeyos no derrocaran al gobierno, los patricios crearon puestos para ellos. Se estableció un gobierno de tres partes, o tripartito. La primera parte estaba formada por los funcionarios electos, o **magistrados.** Los dos magistrados más poderosos eran los **cónsules.** La segunda parte estaba formada por el **Senado romano,** un consejo de romanos adinerados y poderosos que asesoraban a los líderes. La tercera parte estaba formada por las asambleas y los tribunos. La función principal de las asambleas era elegir a los magistrados. Los tribunos aplicaban el **gobierno de la mayoría,** según el cual el grupo con el mayor número de miembros tomaba las decisiones. Los tribunos podían vetar, o prohibir, las acciones del gobierno. La palabra *veto* quiere decir "yo prohíbo" en **latín,** el idioma de los antiguos romanos. El sistema de **control y compensación de poderes** evitaba que alguna de las partes tuviera demasiado poder.

> **Why might the Romans have created a tripartite government?/¿Por qué crees que los romanos crearon un gobierno tripartito?**
>
> _____
> _____
> _____

> **Underline the name given to the most powerful magistrates in Rome./Subraya el nombre que se daba a los magistrados más poderosos de Roma.**

> **Underline what the word *veto* means in Latin./Subraya el significado de la palabra *veto* en latín.**

## WRITTEN LAWS KEEP ORDER/LAS LEYES ESCRITAS MANTIENEN EL ORDEN

Rome's officials followed the rule of law, the belief that all people must follow set rules. In 450 BC, Rome's law code was written on twelve tablets and displayed in the **Forum,** Rome's public meeting place. The Law of the Twelve Tables became the basis of Roman law./Los funcionarios de Roma se regían por el imperio de la ley, es decir, la creencia de que todas las personas deben cumplir las reglas establecidas. En el año 450 a. C., el código legal de Roma se escribió en doce tablas y se exhibió en el **foro,** el lugar público de reunión de Roma. La Ley de las Doce Tablas se convirtió en la base del derecho romano.

> What was the official name of Rome's first set of written laws?/¿Cuál era el nombre oficial del primer conjunto de leyes escritas de Roma?
>
> _____
>
> _____

## LIFE IN ANCIENT ROME/LA VIDA EN LA ANTIGUA ROMA

Women in ancient Rome ran the household and took care of children. Children played games and had pets. Generally, only the children in rich families went to school./En la antigua Roma, las mujeres se ocupaban de la casa y cuidaban a los hijos, que jugaban y tenían mascotas. Por lo general, solo los hijos de las familias adineradas iban a la escuela.

The Roman Forum was the heart of Rome. Government buildings and temples were there./El foro romano era el corazón de Roma. Allí se encontraban los edificios del gobierno y los templos.

## GROWTH OF TERRITORY AND TRADE/ EXPANSIÓN DEL TERRITORIO Y EL COMERCIO

Roman territory grew as the Romans fought off attacks. Rome's soldiers were organized into **legions,** or groups of up to 6,000 men. The army could fight together or break up into smaller

> What might be the military advantage of an army with both small units and large units?/¿Cuál podría ser la ventaja militar de un ejército con unidades tanto pequeñas como grandes?
>
> _____
>
> _____
>
> _____
>
> _____
>
> _____

Lesson/Lección 2, *continued*/*continuación*

groups. This contributed to Rome's success./El
territorio romano se expandió a medida que los
romanos luchaban para repeler los ataques. Los
soldados de Roma estaban organizados en
**legiones,** o grupos de hasta 6,000 hombres. El
ejército podía pelear unido o dividirse en grupos
más pequeños. Esto contribuyó al éxito de Roma.

Trade grew around Rome. Rome coined copper
and silver money, which was used in the region./
El comercio creció alrededor de Roma. Roma
acuñaba monedas de cobre y de plata, que se
usaban en la región.

## ROME GROWS BEYOND ITALY/ROMA CRECE MÁS ALLÁ DE ITALIA

The Roman army fought the **Punic Wars** with
Carthage, the capital of a Phoenician civilization.
Carthage's brilliant general **Hannibal** led an attack,
but Rome conquered Carthage. It also took over
Gaul, Greece, and parts of Asia. The Romans
adopted much of the Greek culture./El ejército
romano luchó en las **Guerras Púnicas** contra
Cartago, la capital de una civilización fenicia. El
brillante general cartaginense **Aníbal** encabezó
un ataque, pero Roma conquistó Cartago. Roma
también conquistó Galia, Grecia y partes de
Asia. Los romanos adoptaron gran parte de la
cultura griega.

> How did the Romans benefit from conquering Greece?/¿De qué manera se beneficiaron los romanos con la conquista de Grecia?
>
> _____
>
> _____
>
> _____
>
> _____

## CHALLENGE ACTIVITY/ACTIVIDAD AVANZADA

**Critical Thinking: Evaluate/Pensamiento crítico:
Evaluar** Use reference sources to find some
Roman laws. Rewrite any laws you think are
unfair. Then explain why you made the changes.
Discuss whether those laws should apply today./
Usa fuentes de referencia para hallar algunas
leyes romanas. Reescribe las leyes que consideres
injustas y explica por qué hiciste los cambios.
Comenta si esas leyes deberían aplicarse en
la actualidad.

| checks and balances/ control y compensación de poderes | consuls/ cónsules | Forum/foro | Hannibal/Aníbal |
|---|---|---|---|
| Latin/el latín | legions/legiones | magistrates/ magistrados | majority rule/el gobierno de la mayoría |
| Punic Wars/las Guerras Púnicas | rule of law/el imperio de la ley | Roman Senate/ el Senado romano | veto/vetar |

**DIRECTIONS/INSTRUCCIONES** Read each sentence and fill in the blank with a word from the word bank that best completes the sentence./Lee cada oración y escribe en el espacio en blanco la palabra del banco de palabras que mejor la completa.

1. The first tables of Rome's written law code were displayed in the public square called the _____./Las primeras tablas del código legal escrito de Roma se exhibieron en la plaza pública llamada _____.

2. The tribunes had the ability to _____, or prohibit, actions by other government officials./Los tribunos podían _____, o prohibir, las acciones de otros funcionarios del gobierno.

3. Rome's elected officials were called _____./Los funcionarios electos de Roma se llamaban _____.

4. Through the use of _____, one part of government cannot become more powerful than other parts of the government./Mediante el sistema de _____, ninguna parte del gobierno puede tener más poder que las otras.

5. The most powerful officials in Rome were called _____./ Los funcionarios más poderosos de Roma se llamaban _____.

6. The Romans' language was _____./El idioma de los romanos era _____.

7. The _____ was a council of wealthy and powerful Romans that advised the city's leaders./ _____ era un consejo de romanos adinerados y poderosos que asesoraban a los líderes de la ciudad.

8. The brilliant general from Carthage who led an attack against Rome during the Punic Wars was _____./El brillante general de Cartago que encabezó un ataque contra Roma durante las Guerras Púnicas fue _____.

9. Rome's soldiers were organized into _____, which were groups of up to 6,000 men./Los soldados de Roma estaban organizados en _____, que eran grupos de hasta 6,000 hombres.

10. The largest group of tribunes had the power to decide government actions because that part of government was governed by _____./ El grupo más grande de tribunos tenía el poder para decidir las acciones del gobierno porque esa parte del gobierno se regía por _____.

11. Wars fought by the Roman army against Carthage were the _____./Las guerras en las que el ejército romano luchó contra Cartago fueron _____.

12. The belief that all people must follow an established set of rules is known as the _____./La creencia de que todas las personas deben cumplir un conjunto de reglas establecidas se conoce como _____.

# Ancient Rome/La antigua Roma

**MAIN IDEAS/IDEAS PRINCIPALES**

**1.** Several crises struck the republic in later years./Varias crisis golpearon a la República en sus últimos años.

**2.** As Rome descended into chaos, many called for change in government./A medida que Roma se sumía en el caos, muchos pedían un cambio de gobierno.

**3.** Julius Caesar rose to power and became the sole ruler of Rome./Julio César ascendió al poder y se convirtió en el único gobernante de Roma.

**4.** Augustus became Rome's first emperor after defeating Caesar's killers and his own former allies./Augusto se convirtió en el primer emperador de Roma después de derrotar a los asesinos de César y a sus propios antiguos aliados.

# Key Terms and People/Personas y palabras clave

**Gaius Marius/Cayo Mario** consul and general who encouraged poor people to join the army, creating a force more loyal to him than to Rome/cónsul y general que animó a los pobres a unirse al ejército y creó, así, una fuerza que le era más leal a él que a Roma

**Lucius Cornelius Sulla/Lucio Cornelio Sila** rival of Marius who raised his own army to defeat Marius and take control of Rome/rival de Mario que reclutó su propio ejército para derrotar a Mario y tomar el control de Roma

**Spartacus/Espartaco** slave and former gladiator who led an uprising of slaves/ esclavo y antiguo gladiador que encabezó una rebelión de esclavos

**Cicero/Cicerón** a gifted philosopher and orator/talentoso filósofo y orador

**orator/orador** a public speaker/persona que habla en público

**Julius Caesar/Julio César** Roman general who became dictator for life/general romano que se convirtió en dictador de por vida

**Pompey/Pompeyo** a powerful man in Rome who fought against the Roman Senate/poderoso hombre de Roma que luchó contra el Senado romano

**Brutus/Bruto** a young Senator who was once a friend and ally of Caesar's/ senador joven que alguna vez fue amigo y aliado de César

**Marc Antony/Marco Antonio** Caesar's former assistant who took control of Roman politics/antiguo asistente de César que tomó el control de la política romana

**Augustus/Augusto** the first emperor of Rome/primer emperador de Roma

**Cleopatra/Cleopatra** the queen of Egypt/reina de Egipto

# Lesson Summary/Resumen de la lección

## CRISES STRIKE THE REPUBLIC/LAS CRISIS GOLPEAN A LA REPÚBLICA

As Rome's territory grew, so did its problems. Some leaders tried to ease tensions between the rich and poor, but wealthy citizens opposed their ideas. **Gaius Marius,** a consul, encouraged poor people to join the army. The purpose of his decision was to keep poor citizens happy. The troops became more loyal to Marius than to Rome. Then **Lucius Cornelius Sulla** also raised an army. He and Marius fought, which led to civil war. Sulla killed Marius and became dictator. A former gladiator, **Spartacus,** led a slave uprising. He was eventually killed./A medida que el territorio de Roma crecía, también crecían sus problemas. Algunos líderes intentaron suavizar las tensiones entre los ricos y los pobres, pero los ciudadanos adinerados se opusieron a sus ideas. **Cayo Mario,** un cónsul, animó a los pobres a unirse al ejército con el objetivo de mantenerlos contentos. Las tropas se volvieron más leales a Mario que a Roma. Luego, **Lucio Cornelio Sila** también reclutó un ejército. Él y Mario se enfrentaron, lo que desató una guerra civil. Sila mató a Mario y se convirtió en dictador. **Espartaco,** un antiguo gladiador, encabezó una rebelión de esclavos. Al final fue asesinado.

> **Why do you think the poor and unemployed respected Gaius Marius?**/¿Por qué crees que los pobres y los desempleados respetaban a Cayo Mario?
>
> _____
> _____
> _____
> _____
> _____

> **What effect did conflicts and a slave uprising have on Rome?**/¿De qué manera los conflictos y la rebelión de los esclavos afectaron a Roma?
>
> _____
> _____

## THE CALL FOR CHANGE/EL LLAMADO AL CAMBIO

Rome in the 70s BC was dangerous. Generals and politicians went to war to gain more power. People who were unemployed rioted for food. Some Romans tried to stop the chaos in the government. For example, **Cicero,** an **orator,** asked Romans to limit the generals' power and return power to the Senate. But Rome's government stayed the same./Entre los años

70 y 60 a. C., Roma era un lugar peligroso. Los generales y los políticos iban a la guerra para obtener más poder. Las personas desempleadas causaban disturbios para obtener alimentos. Algunos romanos intentaron frenar el caos en el gobierno. Por ejemplo, **Cicerón,** un **orador,** pidió a los romanos que limitaran el poder de los generales y devolvieran el poder al Senado. Pero el gobierno de Roma no cambió.

> **What actions did Cicero ask Romans to take?/**¿Qué les pidió Cicerón a los romanos?
>
> _____
>
> _____
>
> _____

## CAESAR'S RISE TO POWER/EL ASCENSO DE CÉSAR AL PODER

Then another powerful general, **Julius Caesar,** made an agreement with **Pompey,** a powerful Roman, to fight the Senate. Eventually, Caesar became dictator for life. People resented his rise to power. On March 15 in 44 BC, a group of senators stabbed him to death. **Brutus,** a young senator and former ally of Caesar's, was one of the attackers./Más tarde, otro poderoso general, **Julio César,** llegó a un acuerdo con **Pompeyo,** un importante romano, para luchar contra el Senado. Al final, César se convirtió en dictador de por vida. A la gente le molestaba su ascenso al poder. El 15 de marzo del año 44 a. C., un grupo de senadores lo asesinó a puñaladas. **Bruto,** un joven senador que anteriormente había sido aliado de César, fue uno de los atacantes.

## AUGUSTUS THE EMPEROR/AUGUSTO, EL EMPERADOR

Caesar's former assistant, **Marc Antony,** and Octavian, later renamed Augustus, took charge of Roman politics. They defeated Caesar's killers, who then killed themselves. Octavian returned to Italy while Antony headed east to fight Rome's enemies. Antony met **Cleopatra,** the queen of Egypt, and the two fell in love. Octavian and Antony soon became enemies. In 31 BC,

> **Underline the name of the person with whom Antony fell in love./**Subraya el nombre de la persona de quien se enamoró Antonio.

Lesson/Lección 3, *continued*/*continuación*

Octavian defeated Antony's fleet. Antony escaped and returned to Cleopatra. They killed themselves to avoid capture. Then Octavian ruled Rome. He claimed that he was giving his power to the Senate. But he took the name **Augustus** and became the Roman emperor./**Marco Antonio,** el antiguo asistente de César, y Octaviano, que más tarde adoptó el nombre de Augusto, se hicieron cargo de la política romana. Derrotaron a los asesinos de César, que luego se suicidaron. Octaviano regresó a Italia, mientras que Antonio se dirigió al este para luchar contra los enemigos de Roma. Antonio conoció a **Cleopatra,** reina de Egipto, y ambos se enamoraron. Octaviano y Antonio pronto pasaron a ser enemigos. En el año 31 a. C., Octaviano derrotó a la flota de Antonio. Antonio huyó y regresó con Cleopatra, pero ambos se suicidaron para evitar que los capturaran. Luego, Octaviano gobernó Roma. Anunció que renunciaría a su poder para dárselo al Senado, pero adoptó el nombre de **Augusto** y se convirtió en emperador de Roma.

> **Who was Augustus and how did he come to power?/¿Quién era Augusto y cómo llegó al poder?**
>
> _____
> _____
> _____
> _____
> _____
> _____
> _____

## CHALLENGE ACTIVITY/ACTIVIDAD AVANZADA

**Critical Thinking: Make Inferences/Pensamiento crítico: Hacer inferencias** Spartacus's rebellion had an impact on Roman history. Use the Internet to learn more about it. Then write an essay evaluating how one person can affect the course of history, using Spartacus as an example./La rebelión de Espartaco tuvo grandes repercusiones en la historia romana. Consulta la Internet para aprender más sobre ella. Luego, escribe un ensayo en el que evalúes cómo una persona puede cambiar el curso de la historia, tomando el caso de Espartaco como ejemplo.

**DIRECTIONS/INSTRUCCIONES** Read each sentence and fill in the blank with the name in the pair that best completes the sentence./ Lee cada oración y escribe en el espacio en blanco el nombre del par de nombres que mejor la completa.

1. Slaves led by _____ fought against the Roman army but were eventually defeated. **(Cicero/Spartacus)**/Los esclavos encabezados por _____ lucharon contra el ejército romano, pero al final fueron derrotados. **(Cicerón/Espartaco)**

2. To help grow an army, _____ encouraged poor people to join the army. **(Lucius Cornelius Sulla/Gaius Marius)**/Con el objetivo de reclutar un ejército, _____ animó a los pobres a unirse al ejército. **(Lucio Cornelio Sila/Cayo Mario)**

3. In hopes of returning power to the Senate, _____ asked Romans to limit the generals' power. **(Cicero/Pompey)**/Con la esperanza de devolver el poder al Senado, _____ pidió a los romanos que limitaran el poder de los generales. **(Cicerón/Pompeyo)**

4. _____ became dictator for life, but was eventually stabbed to death on March 15 in 44 BC. **(Brutus/Julius Caesar)**/_____ se convirtió en dictador de por vida, pero al final fue asesinado a puñaladas el 15 de marzo del año 44 a. C. **(Bruto/Julio César)**

5. After civil war, _____ named himself dictator of Rome. **(Spartacus/Lucius Cornelius Sulla)**/Después de la guerra civil, _____ se proclamó dictador de Roma. **(Espartaco/Lucio Cornelio Sila)**

6. The former ally of Caesar, _____, betrayed Caesar when he joined other senators in attacking the ruler. **(Brutus/Marc Antony)**/El antiguo aliado de César, _____, traicionó a César al aliarse con otros senadores para atacar al gobernante. **(Bruto/Marco Antonio)**

7. Caesar's former assistant who took control of Roman politics and then fell in love with the queen of Egypt was _____. **(Octavian/Marc Antony)**/El antiguo asistente de César que tomó el control de la política romana y luego se enamoró de la reina de Egipto fue _____. **(Octaviano/Marco Antonio)**

8. _____ changed his name from Octavian when he became
   the Roman emperor. **(Augustus/Julius Caesar)**/_____se
   cambió el nombre, que era Octaviano, cuando se convirtió en emperador
   de Roma. **(Augusto/Julio César)**

**DIRECTIONS/INSTRUCCIONES** Look at each set of three vocabulary
terms following each number. On the line provided, write the letter of
the term that does not relate to the others./Observa cada conjunto de
tres términos de vocabulario que aparece después de cada número. En
el espacio en blanco, escribe la letra del término que no tiene relación
con los demás.

____  9. a. Gaius Marius/     b. Lucius Cornelius Sulla/   c. Spartacus/Espartaco
           Cayo Mario            Lucio Cornelio Sila

____ 10. a. Julius Caesar/    b. Cicero/Cicerón           c. Augustus/Augusto
           Julio César

## Ancient Rome/La antigua Roma

**MAIN IDEAS/IDEAS PRINCIPALES**

1. The Roman Empire expanded to control the entire Mediterranean world./El Imperio romano se expandió y llegó a controlar todo el mundo mediterráneo.

2. Trade increased in Rome, both within the empire and with other people./El comercio aumentó en Roma, tanto dentro del imperio como con otros pueblos.

3. The Pax Romana was a period of peace and prosperity in the cities and the country./La Pax Romana fue un período de paz y prosperidad en las ciudades y en el país.

4. The Romans were very religious and worshipped many gods./Los romanos eran muy religiosos y rendían culto a muchos dioses.

## Key Terms and People/Personas y palabras clave

**Hadrian/Adriano** the emperor under whom the Romans conquered most of the island of Britain/emperador bajo cuyo mando los romanos conquistaron la mayor parte de la isla de Britania

**provinces/provincias** the areas outside of Italy that the Romans controlled/ regiones fuera de Italia controladas por los romanos

**currency/moneda** money/dinero

**Pax Romana/Pax Romana** the Roman Peace, a peaceful period in Rome's history/paz romana, un período de paz en la historia de Roma

**villas/villas** country homes belonging to rich Romans/casas de campo de los romanos adinerados

## Lesson Summary/Resumen de la lección

### THE EMPIRE EXPANDS/EL IMPERIO SE EXPANDE

Rome ruled most of the Mediterranean world when it became an empire. Within 150 years it controlled large areas of Europe, Africa, and Asia. The empire expanded through military might. It expanded to control hostile neighbors and prevent attacks. It also conquered for economic reasons, because conquered people had to pay taxes. In addition, many territories had gold, good farmland, and other resources./ Roma gobernaba la mayor parte del mundo mediterráneo cuando se convirtió en un imperio. Al cabo de 150 años, controlaba grandes áreas

> **Underline the sentence that tells the areas that Rome controlled./**Subraya la oración en la que se mencionan las áreas que controlaba Roma.

de Europa, África y Asia. El imperio se expandió gracias a su poderío militar. Llegó a controlar a vecinos hostiles y a prevenir ataques. El imperio también conquistaba por razones económicas, ya que los pueblos conquistados debían pagar impuestos. Además, muchos territorios tenían oro, buenas tierras de labranza y otros recursos.

> **What are three reasons why the empire expanded?/** Menciona tres razones por las que se expandió el imperio.
>
> _____
> _____
> _____
> _____
> _____

The empire grew after Augustus died. By the early 100s, the Romans had taken over Gaul and much of central Europe. By the time of the emperor **Hadrian,** the Romans had conquered most of Britain. Its people, the Celts, had fought fiercely but lost. The Romans had also taken over Asia Minor, the eastern coast of the Mediterranean, and all of the northern African coast. Romans called the Mediterranean *Mare Nostrum*, meaning "Our Sea."/El imperio creció después de la muerte de Augusto. Para comienzos del siglo 2, los romanos ya habían tomado el control de Galia y de gran parte del centro de Europa. Para la época del emperador **Adriano,** los romanos habían conquistado la mayor parte de Britania. Los celtas, el pueblo de Britania, habían luchado ferozmente pero habían perdido. Los romanos también habían conquistado Asia Menor, la costa este del Mediterráneo y toda la costa norte de África. Ellos llamaban al Mediterráneo *Mare Nostrum*, que significa "nuestro mar".

## TRADE INCREASES/EL COMERCIO AUMENTA

As the empire expanded, Romans wanted foreign goods. Traders went to the **provinces** to bring back metals, cloth, and food. In return, the Romans traded jewelry, glass, and clothing. Traders went to eastern Africa, India, and what is now Vietnam for other goods. Some went to China for silk. Romans used money, or **currency.** The empire had a uniform currency so trade could grow./

> **What did traders find in the provinces?/**¿Qué hallaban los comerciantes en las provincias?
>
> _____

A medida que el imperio se expandía, los romanos querían obtener bienes del exterior. Los comerciantes viajaban a las **provincias** en busca de metales, telas y alimentos, que intercambiaban por joyas, vidrio y vestimentas. Los comerciantes viabajan al este de África, la India y lo que hoy es Vietnam en busca de otros bienes. Algunos viajaban a China en busca de seda. Los romanos usaban su propio dinero, o **moneda.** El imperio tenía una moneda única para que el comercio pudiera crecer.

> **Why do you think a uniform currency helped trade grow?/¿Por qué crees que una moneda única contribuyó al crecimiento del comercio?**
>
> _____
> _____
> _____

## THE PAX ROMANA/LA PAX ROMANA

The **Pax Romana,** or Roman Peace, lasted about 200 years. It was a time of peace and prosperity, and the population grew. An effect of the time was an improvement in the people's quality of life./La **Pax Romana,** o paz romana, duró unos 200 años. Fue un período de paz y prosperidad, durante el cual la población creció y la calidad de vida de las personas mejoró.

Many people in cities were wealthy, but others lived in crowded apartment buildings. Many people lived in rural areas and were farmers. Some spoke languages other than Latin and did not follow Roman customs. **Villas**, or country homes, were scattered among the farms. Wealthy Romans used villas when they wanted a break from the city./Muchas de las personas que vivían en las ciudades eran adineradas, pero otras vivían hacinadas en edificios de apartamentos. Muchas personas vivían en áreas rurales y eran agricultores. Algunos no hablaban latín y no seguían las costumbres romanas. Las **villas,** o casas de campo, estaban diseminadas entre las granjas. Los romanos adinerados iban a las villas cuando querían tomarse un descanso de la ciudad.

## ROMANS ALLOW MANY RELIGIONS/
## LOS ROMANOS PERMITEN MUCHAS RELIGIONES

The Romans were religious. Myths about Rome's founding and rulers often connected past rulers to a god or goddess. Many of Rome's most popular gods came from people they had conquered. For example, many Romans worshipped Greece's Olympian gods because they had learned about Greek mythology. These gods became Rome's main gods, but with different names. Roman mythology influences culture today, as evidenced by our planets being named after Roman gods./Los romanos eran religiosos. Los mitos sobre la fundación y los gobernantes de Roma solían relacionar a los antiguos gobernantes con un dios o una diosa. Muchos de los dioses más populares de Roma provenían de los pueblos que habían conquistado. Por ejemplo, muchos romanos rendían culto a los dioses del Olimpo griego porque habían aprendido sobre la mitología griega. Esos dioses se convirtieron en los dioses principales de Roma, pero con distintos nombres. En la actualidad, la mitología romana influye en nuestra cultura, tal como lo demuestra el hecho de que nuestros planetas lleven nombres de dioses romanos.

> Where did many of Rome's most popular gods originate?/¿Dónde tenían su origen la mayoría de los dioses más populares de Roma?
>
> _____
>
> _____

> Underline a way in which Roman mythology influences culture today./Subraya una manera en que la mitología romana influye en la cultura actual.

## CHALLENGE ACTIVITY/ACTIVIDAD AVANZADA

**Critical Thinking: Elaborate/Pensamiento crítico: Profundizar** Use reference sources to find out more about Hadrian. Write an essay describing his achievements and their effect on the Roman Empire./Usa fuentes de referencia para averiguar más sobre Adriano. Escribe un ensayo en el que describas sus logros y las repercusiones que tuvieron en el Imperio romano.

**DIRECTIONS/INSTRUCCIONES** Write a descriptive phrase to describe each term./Escribe una frase descriptiva para describir cada término.

1. Hadrian/Adriano _____

_____

2. provinces/provincias _____

_____

3. currency/moneda _____

_____

4. Pax Romana/Pax Romana _____

_____

5. villas/villas _____

_____

**DIRECTIONS/INSTRUCCIONES** Use at least three of the vocabulary words **provinces, Hadrian, villas, currency,** and **Pax Romana** to write a letter that relates to the lesson./Usa al menos tres de las palabras de vocabulario **provincias, Adriano, villas, moneda** y **Pax Romana** para escribir una carta relacionada con la lección.

_____

_____

_____

_____

_____

_____

_____

_____

_____

## Ancient Rome/La antigua Roma

**MAIN IDEAS/IDEAS PRINCIPALES**

1. Many problems threatened the Roman Empire, leading one emperor to divide it in half./Debido a la gran cantidad de problemas que amenazaban al Imperio romano, un emperador lo dividió en dos.
2. Barbarians invaded Rome in the 300s and 400s./Los bárbaros invadieron Roma en los siglos 4 y 5.
3. Many factors contributed to Rome's fall./Muchos factores contribuyeron a la caída de Roma.

## Key Terms and People/Personas y palabras clave

**Diocletian/Diocleciano** emperor who divided the Roman Empire into two parts/ emperador que dividió el Imperio romano en dos

**Clovis/Clodoveo** Frankish king who built a huge kingdom in Gaul/rey de los francos que construyó un enorme reino en Galia

**Attila/Atila** fearsome Hun leader who attacked Rome's eastern empire/temible líder huno que atacó el Imperio romano de Oriente

**corruption/corrupción** decay in people's values/decadencia de los valores de las personas

## Lesson Summary/Resumen de la lección

### PROBLEMS THREATEN THE EMPIRE/PROBLEMAS AMENAZAN EL IMPERIO

At its height, the Roman Empire included all the land around the Mediterranean Sea. But by the end of the 100s, emperors had to give up some land./En su máximo esplendor, el Imperio romano incluía todas las tierras que rodean el mar Mediterráneo. Sin embargo, hacia fines del siglo 2, los emperadores tuvieron que renunciar a algunas tierras.

Rome had to defend itself from attacks from the north and the east. Problems came from within the empire, too. Disease killed many people. Taxes were high. Food was scarce because many farmers went to war. To increase food production, Germanic farmers were invited to

> **Name three problems facing the Roman Empire in the late 100s./Menciona tres problemas que enfrentaba el Imperio romano a fines del siglo 2.**
>
> _____
> _____
> _____
> _____
> _____

work on Roman lands, but they were not loyal to Rome./Roma tenía que defenderse de ataques que provenían del norte y el este. También había problemas dentro del imperio. Las enfermedades causaban la muerte de muchas personas. Los impuestos eran altos. La comida escaseaba porque muchos agricultores iban a la guerra. Para aumentar la producción de alimentos, se invitó a agricultores germanos a trabajar en tierras romanas, pero ellos no eran leales a Roma.

The emperor **Diocletian** took power in the late 200s. He divided the empire and ruled the east while a co-emperor ruled the west. The emperor Constantine reunited the empire. He moved the capital from Rome to Constantinople in the east. Constantinople had strategic importance because trade routes passed through it. Also, the city was hard to attack because it could be reached by land from only one direction./El emperador **Diocleciano** tomó el poder a fines del siglo 3. Dividió el imperio y gobernó la parte este, mientras que un coemperador gobernó la parte oeste. El emperador Constantino reunificó el imperio y trasladó la capital de Roma a Constantinopla, en el este. Constantinopla tenía una importancia estratégica porque las rutas comerciales pasaban por allí. Además, no era sencillo atacar la ciudad, porque solo se podía llegar a ella por tierra desde una dirección.

> **Which emperor divided the Roman Empire? Which emperor reunited it?**/¿Qué emperador dividió el Imperio romano? ¿Qué emperador lo reunificó?
>
> _____
>
> _____

## BARBARIANS INVADE ROME/LOS BÁRBAROS INVADEN ROMA

Once the capital moved to the east, barbarians attacked Roman territory in the north. During the late 300s, a fierce group from Central Asia called the Huns began attacking a group called the Goths. The Goths were forced into Roman territory. The Roman rulers kept the Goths in control and even paid them not to attack.

However in the end, the Goths destroyed Rome./
Una vez que la capital se trasladó al este, los
bárbaros atacaron el territorio romano por el
norte. A fines del siglo 4, un temible grupo de
Asia Central conocido como los hunos comenzó
a atacar a un grupo conocido como los godos,
que se vieron obligados a entrar en territorio
romano. Los gobernantes romanos mantuvieron
a los godos bajo control e incluso les pagaron
para que no los atacaran. Sin embargo, al final,
los godos destruyeron Roma.

After the destruction of Rome, the Vandals
invaded Spain. The Angles, Saxons, and Jutes
invaded Britain. The Franks invaded Gaul. The
Frankish king **Clovis,** who was a Christian, was
one of the most powerful German kings. He built
a large kingdom in Gaul. Meanwhile, the Huns
were under a new leader named **Attila.** He was a
brilliant leader and raided Roman territory in the
east. Rome's leaders were too weak to survive the
attacks. In 476, a barbarian leader overthrew
the Roman emperor and declared himself king.
This ended the western empire./Después de la
destrucción de Roma, los vándalos invadieron
España. Los anglos, sajones y jutos invadieron
Britania. Los francos invadieron Galia. El rey de
los francos, **Clodoveo,** que era cristiano, era uno
de los reyes germanos más poderosos. Construyó
un gran reino en Galia. Mientras tanto, los hunos
tenían un nuevo líder llamado **Atila.** Atila era un
líder brillante, y atacó el territorio romano por el
este. Los líderes de Roma eran demasiado débiles
para sobrevivir a los ataques. En el año 476, un
líder bárbaro derrocó al emperador romano y se
proclamó rey. Ese hecho puso fin al Imperio
romano de Occidente.

> **What role might the Huns have played in the Goths' destruction of Rome?/**
> **¿Qué papel crees que desempeñaron los hunos en la destrucción de Roma por parte de los godos?**
>
> _____
> _____
> _____
> _____

> **Underline the name of the leader of the Huns./**
> **Subraya el nombre del líder de los hunos.**

## FACTORS IN ROME'S FALL/FACTORES DE LA CAÍDA DE ROMA

Barbarian invasions are often considered the cause of Rome's decline. However, the vast size of the empire contributed to its fall as well. Its government suffered from **corruption,** or the decay of people's values. As problems continued, wealthy landowners left Rome. Life became more difficult for those who remained. The population decreased, and schools closed. However, taxes and prices soared, so more people became poor. By the end of the 400s, Rome was not the city it had once been. The empire collapsed around it./
Se suele considerar que las invasiones bárbaras fueron la causa de la decadencia de Roma. Sin embargo, la gran extensión del imperio también contribuyó a su caída. En el gobierno había **corrupción,** o decadencia de los valores de las personas. A medida que los problemas continuaban, los terratenientes adinerados se fueron marchando de Roma. La vida se volvió más complicada para aquellos que se quedaron. La población disminuyó y muchas escuelas cerraron. Por el contrario, los impuestos y los precios se dispararon, por lo que más personas se volvieron pobres. A fines del siglo 5, Roma ya no era la ciudad que una vez había sido. El imperio se derrumbaba a su alrededor.

> **What are two factors that led to the weakening of the Roman Empire?/¿Cuáles fueron dos de los factores que causaron el debilitamiento del Imperio romano?**
>
> _____
>
> _____
>
> _____

## CHALLENGE ACTIVITY/ACTIVIDAD AVANZADA

**Critical Thinking: Evaluate/Pensamiento crítico: Evaluar** Do you think the rulers of the Roman Empire could have done anything to stop the empire's collapse? Write a one-page essay explaining your answer./¿Crees que los gobernantes del Imperio romano podrían haber hecho algo para detener la caída del imperio? Escribe un ensayo de una página de longitud en el que expliques tu respuesta.

| | |
|---|---|
| Attila/Atila | Clovis/Clodoveo |
| corruption/corrupción | Diocletian/ Diocleciano |

**DIRECTIONS/INSTRUCCIONES** Answer each question by writing
a sentence that contains at least one word from the word bank./
Responde cada pregunta con una oración que contenga al
menos una palabra del banco de palabras.

1. Who divided the Roman Empire in the late 200s?/¿Quién dividió el Imperio
romano a fines del siglo 3?

_____

_____

2. Who was the fearsome leader of the Huns?/¿Quién era el temible líder de
los hunos?

_____

_____

3. What do we call the decay of people's values?/¿Qué nombre se da a la
decadencia de los valores de las personas?

_____

_____

4. Who was the Frankish king who built a huge kingdom in Gaul?/¿Quién era
el rey de los francos que construyó un enorme reino en Galia?

_____

_____

**DIRECTIONS/INSTRUCCIONES** Look at each set of vocabulary
terms following each number. On the line provided, write the
letter of the term that does not relate to the others./Observa
el conjunto de términos de vocabulario que aparece después
de cada número. En el espacio en blanco, escribe la letra del
término que no tiene relación con los demás.

_____ 5. a. Constantine/    b. Diocletian/    c. Clovis/Clodoveo
            Constantino      Diocleciano

_____ 6. a. Franks/francos    b. Attila/Atila    c. Huns/hunos

# Ancient Rome/La antigua Roma

## Lesson/Lección 6

**MAIN IDEAS/IDEAS PRINCIPALES**

1. The Romans looked for ways to use science and engineering to improve their lives./Los romanos buscaron maneras de usar la ciencia y la ingeniería para mejorar su vida.

2. Roman architecture and art were largely based on Greek ideas./La arquitectura y el arte romanos se basaron, en gran medida, en ideas griegas.

3. Roman literature and language have influenced how people write and speak./La literatura y la lengua de los romanos han influido en nuestra forma de escribir y hablar.

4. Roman law serves as a model for modern law codes around the world./El derecho romano sirve de modelo para los códigos de leyes modernos de todo el mundo.

5. Romans made important contributions to philosophy and history./Los romanos hicieron contribuciones importantes a la filosofía y la historia.

# Key Terms and People/Personas y palabras clave

**Galen/Galeno** Greek doctor who lived in the Roman Empire in the AD 100s/ médico griego que vivió en el Imperio romano en el siglo 2 d. C.

**aqueduct/acueducto** a raised channel used to carry water from mountains into cities/canal elevado que se usa para trasportar agua de las montañas a las ciudades

**Virgil/Virgilio** an author who wrote a great epic about the founding of Rome, the *Aeneid*/autor de la *Eneida,* una gran epopeya sobre la fundación de Roma

**Ovid/Ovidio** a poet who wrote about Roman mythology/poeta que escribió sobre la mitología romana

**satire/sátira** style of writing that pokes fun at people or society/estilo de escritura que consiste en burlarse de las personas o de la sociedad

**Romance languages/lenguas romances** the languages that developed from Latin, including Italian, French, Spanish, Portuguese, and Romanian/lenguas que surgieron a partir del latín, entre ellas el italiano, el francés, el español, el portugués y el rumano

**civil law/derecho civil** a legal system based on a written code of laws/sistema legal basado en un código de leyes escritas

# Lesson Summary/Resumen de la lección

## ROMAN SCIENCE AND ENGINEERING/CIENCIA E INGENIERÍA ROMANAS

Romans used engineering and science for practical purposes so they could improve their lives. They studied stars to produce a calendar. They studied plants to grow better crops. A Greek surgeon living in the empire, **Galen,** made discoveries about the body. Doctors based their ideas on his work for centuries. The Romans developed materials such as cement to make their structures last. They used arches in **aqueducts,** or channels that carry water from mountains to cities. Builders combined the arch to create a vault, a set of arches that supports a building's roof. They created large, open spaces within buildings. Roman buildings were larger than any created before./Los romanos usaron la ingeniería y la ciencia con fines prácticos para mejorar su vida. Estudiaron las estrellas para crear un calendario, y estudiaron las plantas para producir mejores cultivos. **Galeno,** un cirujano griego que vivía en el imperio, hizo descubrimientos sobre el cuerpo humano. Los médicos basaron sus ideas en su obra durante siglos. Los romanos desarrollaron materiales como el cemento para que sus estructuras fueran duraderas. Usaron arcos en los **acueductos,** es decir, los canales que transportan agua de las montañas a las ciudades. Combinaron los arcos para crear una bóveda, o un conjunto de arcos que sostiene el techo de un edificio. Crearon grandes espacios abiertos dentro de los edificios. Las construcciones romanas eran más grandes que ningún otro edificio anterior.

---

> **For what reason did the Romans use engineering and science?/¿Con qué propósito usaron los romanos la ingeniería y la ciencia?**
>
> _____
>
> _____
>
> _____

> **Underline the sentence that explains what helped Roman buildings last a long time./Subraya la oración en la que se explica qué contribuyó a que los edificios romanos fueran duraderos.**

## ARCHITECTURE AND ART/ARQUITECTURA Y ARTE

Roman architecture was influenced by earlier Greek designs. Similar to the Greeks, Romans used columns to make public buildings look stately and impressive. However, Roman engineering allowed them to create much larger buildings./La arquitectura romana recibió la influencia de los antiguos diseños griegos. Al igual que los griegos, los romanos usaban columnas para hacer que los edificios públicos se vieran majestuosos e imponentes. Sin embargo, la ingeniería romana les permitió crear edificios mucho más grandes.

Roman artists used mosaics for decoration on walls or floors. Frescoes also decorated walls. Roman sculptures were either original or copies of older Greek works. Since many original Greek works were destroyed, Roman copies provided the world with knowledge of the Greek masterpieces./Los artistas romanos usaban mosaicos para decorar las paredes o los pisos. También usaban frescos para decorar las paredes. Algunas esculturas romanas eran piezas originales y otras eran copias de obras griegas más antiguas. Como muchas de las obras griegas originales fueron destruidas, las copias romanas permitieron que el mundo conociera las obras maestras griegas.

> **How did Roman engineering improve on Greek architecture?/¿De qué manera la ingeniería romana mejoró la arquitectura griega?**
>
> _____
> _____
> _____
> _____
> _____

> **What might have happened if the Romans had not been influenced by Greek sculptures?/¿Qué podría haber sucedido si los romanos no hubieran recibido la influencia de las esculturas griegas?**
>
> _____
> _____
> _____
> _____

## LITERATURE AND LANGUAGE/LITERATURA Y LENGUA

**Virgil** wrote a great epic, the *Aeneid*, about the founding of Rome. **Ovid** wrote poems about Roman mythology. Romans excelled in **satire,** writing that pokes fun at people or society. Many works served as models for modern works. Roman poets wrote in Latin. Today, languages that developed from Latin are called **Romance languages** because they share many elements

with each other and with Latin./**Virgilio** escribió
la *Eneida,* una gran epopeya sobre la fundación
de Roma. **Ovidio** escribió poemas sobre la
mitología romana. Los romanos se destacaron
en la **sátira**, es decir, la escritura que consiste en
burlarse de las personas o de la sociedad. Muchas
obras sirvieron de modelo para las obras
modernas. Los poetas romanos escribían en latín.
En la actualidad, las lenguas que surgieron a
partir del latín se conocen como **lenguas romances**
porque comparten muchos elementos entre sí y
con el latín.

## THE BEGINNINGS OF CIVIL LAW/LOS COMIENZOS DEL DERECHO CIVIL

**Civil law,** a legal system based on a written code
of laws, was inspired by Roman law, which was
enforced throughout the empire. Most European
nations today are ruled by civil law./El **derecho
civil,** un sistema legal basado en un código de
leyes escritas, se inspiró en el derecho romano,
que se aplicaba en todo el imperio. En la
actualidad, la mayoría de las naciones europeas
se rigen por sistemas de derecho civil.

> **Why do you think civil law continues today in most of Europe?/¿Por qué crees que el derecho civil continúa usándose en la actualidad en la mayoría de los países de Europa?**
>
> _____
> _____
> _____
> _____

## PHILOSOPHY AND HISTORY/FILOSOFÍA E HISTORIA

Greek philosophy and the way Greeks wrote
about history influenced the Romans. They
also studied about their own history. They
documented the way the republic and the empire
changed over time./La filosofía griega y la
manera en que los griegos escribieron sobre la
historia influyó en los romanos. Ellos también
estudiaron su propia historia. Documentaron
la manera en que la República y el Imperio
cambiaron con el paso del tiempo.

## CHALLENGE ACTIVITY/ACTIVIDAD AVANZADA

**Critical Thinking: Make Judgments/Pensamiento crítico: Dar opiniones** Which of the following was the greatest Roman contribution to today's world: engineering, science, architecture, poetry, language, or law? Write a speech defending your view./¿Cuál de las siguientes fue la mayor contribución de los romanos al mundo actual: la ingeniería, la ciencia, la arquitectura, la poesía, la lengua o el derecho? Escribe un discurso en el que defiendas tu opinión.

**DIRECTIONS/INSTRUCCIONES** Match the terms in the first column with the correct definition from the second column by placing the letter of the correct definition in the space provided before each term./Une los términos de la primera columna con su definición correcta en la segunda columna. Escribe la letra de la definición correcta en el espacio que precede a cada término.

_____ 1. civil law/derecho civil

_____ 2. Galen/Galeno

_____ 3. satire/sátira

_____ 4. Romance languages/ lenguas romances

_____ 5. Virgil/Virgilio

a. style of writing that pokes fun at people or society/estilo de escritura que consiste en burlarse de las personas o de la sociedad

b. author who wrote a great epic about the founding of Rome/autor que escribió una gran epopeya sobre la fundación de Roma

c. Greek doctor who lived in the Roman Empire and made discoveries about the body/médico griego que vivió en el Imperio romano e hizo descubrimientos sobre el cuerpo

d. a set of arches that supports the roof of a building/conjunto de arcos que sostienen el techo de un edificio

e. a legal system based on a written code of laws/sistema legal basado en un código de leyes escritas

_____ 6. aqueduct/acueducto

f. poet who wrote about Roman mythology/ poeta que escribió sobre la mitología romana

_____ 7. vault/bóveda

g. a raised channel used to carry water from mountains into cities/canal elevado que se usa para transportar agua de las montañas a las ciudades

_____ 8. Ovid/Ovidio

h. the languages that developed from Latin/ lenguas que surgieron a partir del latín

**DIRECTIONS/INSTRUCCIONES** Look at each set of vocabulary terms following each number. On the line provided, write the letter of the term that does not relate to the others./Observa el conjunto de términos de vocabulario que aparece después de cada número. En el espacio en blanco, escribe la letra del término que no tiene relación con los demás.

_____ 9. a. Galen/Galeno        b. Virgil/Virgilio        c. Ovid/Ovidio

_____10. a. vault/bóveda        b. aqueduct/acueducto        c. satire/sátira

# The Growth of Christianity/La expansión del cristianismo

## Lesson/Lección 1

**MAIN IDEAS/IDEAS PRINCIPALES**

1. The Romans allowed many religions to be practiced in their empire./Los romanos permitieron que se practicaran muchas religiones en su imperio.
2. Jews and Romans clashed over religious and political ideas./Los judíos y los romanos tuvieron enfrentamientos por sus ideas políticas y religiosas.
3. The roots of Christianity had appeared in Judea by the end of the first century BC./Las raíces del cristianismo ya habían aparecido en Judea hacia fines del primer siglo a. C.

## Key Terms and People/Personas y palabras clave

**Christianity/cristianismo** religion based on the life and teachings of Jesus of Nazareth/religión basada en la vida y las enseñanzas de Jesús de Nazaret

**Jesus of Nazareth/Jesús de Nazaret** founder of Christianity/fundador del cristianismo

**Messiah/Mesías** leader Jews believed would return and restore the greatness of Israel/líder que, según creían los judíos, regresaría y restituiría la grandeza de Israel

**John the Baptist/Juan el Bautista** famous Jewish prophet who traveled throughout Judea to announce the Messiah was coming/famoso profeta judío que viajó por toda Judea para anunciar la llegada del Mesías

## Lesson Summary/Resumen de la lección

### ROMAN IDEAS ABOUT RELIGION/IDEAS ROMANAS SOBRE LA RELIGIÓN

Roman religion had many gods, but the Roman Empire did allow most conquered people to keep their own religions. The empire often built temples to honor Roman gods. These structures were called pantheons. Romans also built temples to the gods of new religions, so religious knowledge spread through the empire./La religión romana tenía muchos dioses; sin embargo, el Imperio romano permitió que la mayoría de los pueblos conquistados conservaran sus religiones. El imperio solía construir templos

> **Which two groups of gods had temples built for them?/¿En honor a qué dos grupos de dioses se construían templos?**
>
> _____
>
> _____
>
> _____

para honrar a los dioses romanos. Esas estructuras se llamaban panteones. Los romanos también construyeron templos en honor a los dioses de las nuevas religiones, de modo que el conocimiento religioso se expandió por todo el imperio.

## JEWS AND ROMANS CLASH/ENFRENTAMIENTOS ENTRE JUDÍOS Y ROMANOS

Roman leaders thought Judaism was a problem for both religious and political reasons. The Jews only worshipped one god and thought their God was the only god. Some Romans thought these ideas insulted their own religious beliefs./Los líderes romanos sostenían que el judaísmo representaba un problema por motivos religiosos y políticos. Los judíos solo adoraban a un dios y creían que era el único Dios. Algunos romanos creían que esas ideas eran incompatibles con sus creencias religiosas.

> **Why did some Romans think Judaism insulted their own religious beliefs?/**
> **¿Por qué algunos romanos pensaban que el judaísmo era incompatible con sus creencias religiosas?**
> _____
> _____
> _____
> _____

Many Jews were unhappy about the way Rome ruled Judea, a Jewish territory. The Jews wanted their rulers to be Jewish and follow their beliefs. Some Jews rebelled several times. In the 100s, the Roman emperor Hadrian banned Jews from practicing some Jewish rituals./Muchos judíos estaban descontentos con la forma en que Roma gobernaba Judea, un territorio judío. Querían que sus gobernantes fueran judíos y que respaldaran sus creencias. En varias ocasiones, algunos judíos se rebelaron. En el siglo 2, el emperador romano Adriano les prohibió a los judíos que practicaran ciertos rituales.

This meant that Jews could not do certain things that were part of their religion. Hadrian thought this would make the Jews give up and follow Roman religion, rules, and laws./

Esto implicaba que los judíos no podían hacer algunas cosas que eran parte de su religión. Adriano creía que los judíos se darían por vencidos y adoptarían la religión, las reglas y las leyes romanas.

He was wrong. Hadrian's actions upset the Jews even more, and they rebelled again. After the last revolt, the Romans destroyed Jerusalem and forced all Jews out of the city. Jews moved throughout the Roman world./Pero estaba equivocado. Las acciones de Adriano disgustaron aún más a los judíos, que volvieron a rebelarse. Después de la última revuelta, los romanos destruyeron Jerusalén y expulsaron a todos los judíos de la ciudad. Como consecuencia, los judíos migraron a otras regiones del mundo romano.

## THE ROOTS OF CHRISTIANITY/LAS RAÍCES DEL CRISTIANISMO

At the start of the first century AD, a new religion appeared. **Christianity** had roots in Judaism, but it was based on the life and teachings of **Jesus of Nazareth.** During this time, many Jews were waiting for the **Messiah** (muh-sy-uh)./A comienzos del siglo 1 d. C., surgió una nueva religión: el **cristianismo.** El cristianismo tenía sus raíces en el judaísmo, pero se basaba en la vida y las enseñanzas de **Jesús de Nazaret.** En esa época, muchos judíos estaban esperando al **Mesías.**

The Messiah was a savior chosen by God that had been foretold by Jewish prophets. One of the most famous prophets was **John the Baptist.** He traveled throughout Judea to announce the Messiah was coming. Jews believed the Messiah would lead their people. He would be a descendent of King David and would restore

> **Underline two ideas that Jews believed about the Messiah./**Subraya dos de las creencias que tenían los judíos sobre el Mesías.

> **What did the Romans do after the last Jewish revolt?/**¿Qué hicieron los romanos después de la última revuelta de los judíos?
>
> _____
>
> _____
>
> _____

the greatness of the ancient kingdom of Israel./
Según las predicciones de los profetas judíos, el
Mesías era un salvador elegido por Dios. Uno
de los profetas más famosos fue **Juan el Bautista,**
que viajó por toda Judea para anunciar la llegada
del Mesías. Los judíos creían que el Mesías
guiaría a su pueblo, que sería un descendiente
del rey David y que restituiría la grandeza del
antiguo reino de Israel.

No one knew when the Messiah would come.
To encourage him to appear, some Jews followed
strict religious rules that Moses had given them.
When the Romans took over Judea in 63 BC,
many Jews hoped the Messiah would arrive
soon./Nadie sabía cuándo llegaría el Mesías. Para
alentar su aparición, algunos judíos respetaban al
pie de la letra las estrictas tradiciones religiosas
de Moisés. Cuando los romanos se apoderaron
de Judea en el año 63 a. C., muchos judíos
creyeron que el Mesías llegaría pronto.

> **Why did some Jews follow strict religious rules that Moses had given them?/**
> **¿Por qué algunos judíos seguían las estrictas tradiciones religiosas de Moisés?**
>
> _____
>
> _____
>
> _____

## CHALLENGE ACTIVITY/ACTIVIDAD AVANZADA

**Critical Thinking: Summarize/Pensamiento crítico:**
**Resumir** Jews who follow the strict religious rules
of Moses are called Orthodox Jews. Use print or
digital resources to research two rules of this type
of Judaism. Write a short summary that explains
each rule and tells what makes it strict./Los judíos
que siguen al pie de la letra las estrictas tradiciones
religiosas de Moisés se llaman judíos ortodoxos.
Usa recursos impresos o digitales para investigar
dos de los principios de este tipo de judaísmo.
Escribe un resumen breve en el que expliques
cada principio e indiques por qué es estricto.

**DIRECTIONS/INSTRUCCIONES** Read each sentence and fill in the blank with the word in the word pair that best completes the sentence./Lee cada oración y escribe en el espacio en blanco la palabra del par de palabras que mejor la completa.

1. A savior chosen by God that had been foretold by Jewish prophets was _____. **(John the Baptist/Messiah)**/Según las predicciones de los profetas judíos, _____ era un salvador elegido por Dios. **(Juan el Bautista/el Mesías)**

2. _____ founded a religion based on his life and teachings. **(John the Baptist/Jesus of Nazareth)**/_____ fundó una religión basada en su vida y sus enseñanzas. **(Juan el Bautista/Jesús de Nazaret)**

3. The religion of _____ had roots in Judaism. **(Messiah/Christianity)**/El _____ era una religión cuyas raíces estaban basadas en el judaísmo. **(Mesías/cristianismo)**

4. _____ was a famous prophet who traveled throughout Judea to announce the Jewish leader was coming. **(John the Baptist/Jesus of Nazareth)**/_____ fue un famoso profeta que viajó por toda Judea para anunciar la llegada del líder judío. **(Juan el Bautista/Jesús de Nazaret)**

# The Growth of Christianity/La expansión del cristianismo

## Lesson/Lección 2

 **MAIN IDEAS/IDEAS PRINCIPALES**
1. In Christian belief, Jesus was the Messiah and the son of God./Según la fe cristiana, Jesús era el Mesías y el hijo de Dios.
2. Jesus taught about salvation, love for God, and kindness./Jesús predicaba sobre la salvación, el amor a Dios y la bondad.
3. Jesus' followers spread his teachings after his death./Los seguidores de Jesús difundieron sus enseñanzas después de su muerte.

# Key Terms and People/Personas y palabras clave

**Bible/Biblia** the holy book of Christianity/el libro sagrado del cristianismo

**crucifixion/crucifixión** a type of execution that involved being nailed to a cross/ tipo de ejecución en la que se clavaba a una persona a una cruz

**Resurrection/resurrección** Christian belief that Jesus rose from the dead after his death/creencia cristiana de que Jesús volvió a la vida de entre los muertos después de su muerte

**disciples/discípulos** followers/seguidores

**Apostles/apóstoles** the 12 disciples whom Jesus chose to receive special teaching/ los 12 discípulos que eligió Jesús para que recibieran enseñanzas especiales

# Lesson Summary/Resumen de la lección

**THE LIFE AND DEATH OF JESUS OF NAZARETH/
VIDA Y MUERTE DE JESÚS DE NAZARET**

Jesus of Nazareth was born at the end of the first century BC. Much of what we know about Jesus is from the **Bible,** the holy book of Christianity. This book has two parts. The Old Testament tells the history and ideas of the Hebrew people. The New Testament is the second part of the Bible. It is about the life and teachings of Jesus and the early history of Christianity./Jesús de Nazaret nació a fines del siglo 1 a. C. Gran parte de lo que sabemos sobre Jesús se encuentra en la **Biblia,** el libro sagrado del cristianismo. La Biblia se divide en dos partes: el Antiguo Testamento, que cuenta la historia y las ideas del pueblo hebreo, y el Nuevo Testamento, que trata sobre la vida y las enseñanzas de Jesús y los comienzos del cristianismo.

The Bible states that Jesus was born in a small town called Bethlehem (BETH-li-hem). His birth marked the shift from BC to AD in our dating system. Jesus' mother, Mary, was married to a carpenter named Joseph. But Christians believe God, not Joseph, was the father of Jesus./Según la Biblia, Jesús nació en un pueblo pequeño llamado Belén. Su nacimiento marca el cambio de a. C. a d. C. en nuestro calendario. La madre de Jesús, María, estaba casada con un carpintero llamado José. Sin embargo, los cristianos creen que el padre de Jesús no era José, sino Dios.

Roman leaders thought Jesus' teachings challenged their authority. He was arrested and executed by **crucifixion.** Christians believe Jesus rose from the dead in an event called the **Resurrection.** Many of Jesus' **disciples** claimed to see him again./Los líderes romanos pensaban que las enseñanzas de Jesús desafiaban su autoridad. Por eso, Jesús fue arrestado y ejecutado mediante el método de **crucifixión.** Los cristianos creen que Jesús volvió a la vida en un suceso llamado **resurrección,** y muchos de sus **discípulos** aseguraron que volvieron a verlo.

| How did Jesus' birth affect our dating system?/¿De qué manera el nacimiento de Jesús afectó nuestro calendario? |
| --- |
| _____ |
| _____ |

| What did many disciples claim after the Resurrection?/¿Qué aseguraron muchos discípulos después de la resurrección? |
| --- |
| _____ |
| _____ |

## ACTS AND TEACHINGS/ACCIONES Y ENSEÑANZAS

Jesus spread his message among the Jewish people. People who liked what he did and said became the first Christians./Jesús difundió su mensaje entre los judíos. Los primeros cristianos fueron las personas a las que les gustaba lo que él hacía y decía.

Many acts that Jesus performed were miracles. These events cannot normally be performed by a human. The New Testament describes a miracle where Jesus fed an entire crowd with just a small amount of bread and fish./Muchas de las acciones que realizó Jesús eran milagros. Los milagros son sucesos que no puede hacer comúnmente ningún ser humano. El Nuevo Testamento describe un milagro en el que Jesús alimentó a una multitud entera con una pequeña cantidad de panes y peces.

Jesus told stories known as parables to give lessons about his teachings. There are many parables in the New Testament. Parables helped Jesus explain complicated ideas by connecting them to people's daily lives. Then people could understand the lessons./Para transmitir sus enseñanzas, Jesús contaba historias conocidas como parábolas. En el Nuevo Testamento hay muchas parábolas, que ayudaban a Jesús a explicar ideas complicadas estableciendo una relación entre esas ideas y la vida cotidiana de las personas. Así se comprendían mejor los mensajes.

The main message Jesus talked about was that people should love God and each other. He also taught about salvation./El mensaje principal de Jesús era que las personas deben amar a Dios y a sus semejantes. Jesús también enseñaba sobre la salvación.

## JESUS'S FOLLOWERS/LOS SEGUIDORES DE JESÚS

Jesus chose 12 of his disciples, the **Apostles,** to spread his teachings. Peter brought Christianity to the people of Rome after Jesus died. Matthew, Mark, Luke, and John wrote the four Gospels of the New Testament. The tradition of baptism came from the Gospel account of John the

> **How did Jesus perform a miracle with bread and fish?/¿Qué milagro hizo Jesús con panes y peces?**
> _____
> _____
> _____
> _____

> **What did parables allow Jesus to do?/¿Cómo ayudaban las parábolas a Jesús?**
> _____
> _____
> _____
> _____
> _____
> _____
> _____
> _____

> **Circle the names of the people who wrote the four Gospels./Encierra en un círculo los nombres de los discípulos que escribieron los cuatro Evangelios.**

Baptist immersing Jesus in water to clean him of sin./Jesús eligió a 12 de sus discípulos, los **apóstoles,** para que difundieran sus enseñanzas. Pedro llevó el cristianismo a los romanos después de la muerte de Jesús. Mateo, Marcos, Lucas y Juan escribieron los cuatro Evangelios del Nuevo Testamento. La tradición del bautismo proviene de la versión del Evangelio en la que se narra cómo Juan el Bautista sumerge a Jesús en agua para limpiar sus pecados.

The Apostles also shared a special prayer with others. It was one that Jesus had taught them. The Lord's Prayer is now a common prayer for many Christians, and the act of saying prayers is an important tradition in the Christian faith./Los apóstoles también compartieron una plegaria especial con los demás. Era una oración que Jesús les había enseñado. En la actualidad, el Padrenuestro es una oración común para muchos cristianos, y rezar es una tradición importante de la fe cristiana.

## CHALLENGE ACTIVITY/ACTIVIDAD AVANZADA

**Critical Thinking: Analyze/Pensamiento crítico: Analizar** Find and read an example of a parable in the New Testament. Then write a short essay that explains the lesson the parable teaches./Busca y lee un ejemplo de una parábola del Nuevo Testamento. Luego, escribe un ensayo breve en el que expliques la lección que enseña esa parábola.

| Bible/Biblia | crucifixion/crucifixión | Resurrection/resurrección |
| disciples/discípulos | Apostles/apóstoles | |

**DIRECTIONS/INSTRUCCIONES** Answer each question by writing
a sentence that contains at least one word from the word bank./
Responde cada pregunta con una oración que contenga al menos
una palabra del banco de palabras.

1. Who were the 12 people whom Jesus chose to receive special teaching?/
   ¿Quiénes eran las 12 personas elegidas por Jesús para que recibieran
   enseñanzas especiales?

   _____

   _____

2. Which Christian belief states that Jesus rose from the dead after his death?/
   ¿Qué creencia cristiana sostiene que Jesús volvió a la vida después de su
   muerte?

   _____

   _____

3. What is the name of the holy book of Christianity?/¿Cómo se llama el libro
   sagrado del cristianismo?

   _____

   _____

4. Who were followers of Jesus?/¿Quiénes eran los seguidores de Jesús?

   _____

   _____

5. What type of execution involves being nailed to a cross?/¿Qué tipo de
   ejecución implica clavar a una persona a una cruz?

   _____

   _____

# The Growth of Christianity/La expansión del cristianismo

**MAIN IDEAS/IDEAS PRINCIPALES**

**1.** Paul, one of Jesus' followers, spread his teachings after his death./Pablo, uno de los seguidores de Jesús, difundió sus enseñanzas después de su muerte.

**2.** Christianity spread quickly in Rome, but its growing strength worried some emperors./El cristianismo se difundió rápidamente en Roma, pero su creciente popularidad inquietaba a algunos emperadores.

# Key Terms and People/Personas y palabras clave

**Paul/Pablo** follower whose letters defined Christianity as separate from Judaism/discípulo cuyas cartas definían el cristianismo como una religión distinta del judaísmo

**saint/santo** a person known and admired for his or her holiness/persona conocida y admirada por su espiritualidad

**monotheism/monoteísmo** belief in the existence of only one god; central feature of Christianity/creencia en la existencia de un solo dios; característica central del cristianismo

**martyrs/mártires** people who die for their religious beliefs/personas que mueren por sus creencias religiosas

**persecution/persecución** punishing people for their beliefs/acción de castigar a las personas por sus creencias

# Lesson Summary/Resumen de la lección

## PAUL OF TARSUS/PABLO DE TARSO

**Paul** of Tarsus was most important in spreading Christianity. Even though he had never met Jesus, Paul traveled and wrote letters explaining Christian ideals. Many Christians think of Paul as another Apostle, and he was named a **saint** after he died. Paul helped Christianity break away from Judaism./**Pablo** de Tarso fue una figura muy importante en la difusión del cristianismo. A pesar de que nunca había conocido a Jesús, Pablo viajó mucho y escribió cartas que explicaban los ideales cristianos. Muchos cristianos lo consideran

> Underline two details that show that Paul was an important person in the Christian Church./Subraya dos detalles que muestren que Pablo fue una figura importante para la Iglesia cristiana.

otro apóstol. Pablo fue declarado **santo** después de
su muerte. Contribuyó a separar el cristianismo
del judaísmo.

At first, Paul did not like Christianity. He was
born Jewish and thought Jesus' ideas would
threaten Judaism. Paul tried to stop the Christian
message from spreading. The Bible states that Paul
then saw a blinding light while he was traveling
one day. Jesus' voice called out to him. After that,
Paul became a Christian./Al principio, a Pablo no
le gustaba el cristianismo. Era judío de nacimiento
y creía que las ideas de Jesús pondrían en peligro
al judaísmo. Por eso, intentó detener la expansión
del mensaje cristiano. Según la Biblia, un día
Pablo vio una luz muy brillante durante uno de
sus viajes y escuchó la voz de Jesús que lo llamaba.
A raíz de eso, se convirtió al cristianismo.

> **While he was traveling, what happened to Paul that caused him to become a Christian?**/¿Qué le pasó a Pablo en uno de sus viajes que lo llevó a convertirse al cristianismo?
>
> _____
> _____
> _____

He traveled to many major Mediterranean cities
so that he could share Christian teachings with
others. Paul also wrote long letters and sent them
to communities throughout the Roman world.
These letters helped to explain Jesus' teachings
and give more details about them./Pablo viajó a
muchas ciudades importantes del Mediterráneo
para compartir las enseñanzas cristianas con otras
personas. También escribió cartas extensas y las
envió a comunidades de todo el mundo romano.
Esas cartas ayudaban a explicar las enseñanzas de
Jesús y daban más detalles sobre ellas.

Paul mentioned the Trinity in his letters.
Christians believe that three persons—God the
Father, Jesus the Son, and the Holy Spirit—all
make up one God. **Monotheism** is the belief
that only one god exists./En sus cartas, Pablo
mencionaba la Trinidad. Los cristianos creen
que en Dios existen tres personas: Dios, el Padre;
Jesús, el Hijo; y el Espíritu Santo. El **monoteísmo**
es la creencia de que solo existe un dios.

> **In Christianity, who are the three persons who make up the Trinity?**/En el cristianismo, ¿quiénes son las tres personas que constituyen la Trinidad?
>
> _____
> _____
> _____

## CHRISTIANITY SPREADS QUICKLY IN ROME/ EL CRISTIANISMO SE DIFUNDE RÁPIDAMENTE EN ROMA

People like Paul wanted to share Christian teachings with as many people as possible, not just with people who were Jewish. Christians began to write down the Gospels and other writings about their religion. This information helped Christians strengthen their faith, and Christianity spread throughout the Roman Empire./Aquellos que pensaban como Pablo querían compartir las enseñanzas cristianas con la mayor cantidad de personas posible, no solo con los judíos. Los cristianos comenzaron a escribir los Evangelios y otros escritos sobre su religión. Esa información les ayudó a fortalecer su fe, y el cristianismo se difundió en todo el Imperio romano.

As this religion became more popular, Roman leaders began to worry. Some local leaders arrested and killed Christians. These **martyrs** died for their religious beliefs. Some Roman emperors outlawed Christianity and **persecuted** Christians. This did not stop followers from practicing their faith. Christians began to hold secret meetings. They used secret symbols so they could identify other Christians and gather together safely. One of the most common symbols was a fish, and this image is still used as a Christian symbol today./A medida que el cristianismo cobraba mayor popularidad, los líderes romanos comenzaron a preocuparse. Algunos líderes locales arrestaron y mataron a cristianos. Estos **mártires** murieron por sus creencias religiosas. Algunos emperadores romanos prohibieron el cristianismo y ordenaron la **persecución** de los cristianos. Pero esto no impidió que los seguidores continuaran profesando su fe. Los cristianos comenzaron a reunirse en secreto. Usaban símbolos secretos para poder identificar a otros cristianos y reunirse sin

> **What risks did early Christians face in spreading their religion?/**¿Qué riesgos corrieron los primeros cristianos al difundir su religión?
>
> _____
>
> _____

corer ningún peligro. Uno de los símbolos más comunes era un pez, y esta imagen todavía se usa como símbolo cristiano en la actualidad.

## CHALLENGE ACTIVITY/ACTIVIDAD AVANZADA

**Critical Thinking: Make Judgments/Pensamiento crítico: Dar opiniones** Paul of Tarsus has been called the most influential person in the history of Christianity besides Jesus. Do you agree with this statement? Why or why not?/Hay quienes afirman que Pablo de Tarso es la persona más influyente en la historia del cristianismo además de Jesús. ¿Estás de acuerdo con esa afirmación? ¿Por qué?

## DIRECTIONS/INSTRUCCIONES Use at least three of the vocabulary words **Paul, saint, monotheism, martyrs,** and **persecution** to write a letter that relates to the lesson./Usa por lo menos tres de las palabras de vocabulario **Pablo, santo, monoteísmo, mártires** y **persecución** para escribir una carta que se relacione con el contenido de la lección.

_____

_____

_____

_____

_____

_____

_____

_____

_____

_____

_____

_____

_____

_____

_____

_____

_____

_____

_____

_____

_____

_____

# The Growth of Christianity/La expansión del cristianismo

 **MAIN IDEAS/IDEAS PRINCIPALES**
1. The Pope influenced the growth of the early Christian Church./El papa influyó en la expansión de la Iglesia cristiana en sus comienzos.
2. As the church grew, new leaders and ideas appeared and Christianity's status in the empire changed./A medida que la Iglesia iba creciendo, surgieron nuevos líderes y nuevas ideas, y el estatus del cristianismo en el imperio cambió.

# Key Terms and People/Personas y palabras clave

**bishops/obispos** local leaders in Christian communities/líderes locales de las comunidades cristianas

**Eucharist/Eucaristía** central Christian ceremony that honors the last supper Jesus shared with his Apostles/principal ceremonia cristiana en la que se honra la última cena que Jesús compartió con sus apóstoles

**pope/papa** the head of the whole Christian Church; comes from the Greek word for "father"/jefe de toda la Iglesia cristiana; proviene de la palabra griega que significa "padre"

**Augustine of Hippo/Agustín de Hipona** writer who linked the ideas of classical philosophers with Christian beliefs/escritor que vinculó las ideas de los filósofos clásicos con las creencias cristianas

**Constantine/Constantino** Roman emperor who became a Christian/emperador romano que se convirtió al cristianismo

# Lesson Summary/Resumen de la lección

## THE CHURCH GROWS/EL CRECIMIENTO DE LA IGLESIA

Early Christians had to meet in secret, so the church did not have a single leader. Each Christian community had a **bishop,** or local leader. Most bishops lived in cities. Bishops helped people understand Christian teachings and live by them. One of their most important duties was to lead Christians during the celebration of the **Eucharist** (yoo-kuh-ruhst)./Los primeros cristianos tenían que reunirse en secreto, por lo que la Iglesia no tenía un único líder. Cada una de las comunidades cristianas

> **Where did most bishops live?/¿Dónde vivía la mayoría de los obispos?**
> _____
> _____

tenía un **obispo,** es decir, un líder local. La mayoría de los obispos vivía en las ciudades. Los obispos ayudaban a que las personas comprendieran las enseñanzas cristianas y se guiaran por ellas. Uno de sus deberes más importantes era guiar a los cristianos durante la celebración de la **Eucaristía.**

The Eucharist was the central ceremony of the Christian Church. It honored the last supper Jesus shared with his Apostles. Christians ate bread and drank wine in memory of Jesus' death. This is still how the Eucharist is celebrated in Christian churches today./La Eucaristía era la ceremonia principal de la Iglesia cristiana. En ella se honraba la última cena que Jesús compartió con sus apóstoles. Los cristianos comían pan y bebían vino en conmemoración de la muerte de Jesús. Así es como todavía se celebra la Eucaristía en las iglesias cristianas en la actualidad.

> **What did Christians do during the Eucharist?/¿Qué hacían los cristianos durante la Eucaristía?**
>
> _____
> _____
> _____

By the late 100s, the bishops in large cities had become very powerful. They had great influence over Christians and other bishops. The Apostle Peter had been the first bishop of Rome. He was an important leader in the early church. Christians considered anyone who was the bishop of Rome to be the most honored bishop of all. This church leader became known as the **pope,** a word that means "father" in Greek./Hacia fines del siglo 2, los obispos de las grandes ciudades habían adquirido mucho poder y ejercían gran influencia sobre los cristianos y sobre otros obispos. El apóstol Pedro había sido el primer obispo de Roma. Era un líder importante de la Iglesia en sus comienzos. Los cristianos consideraban que el obispo de Roma era el obispo más respetado de todos. El líder de

> **Why did Christians consider the bishop of Rome the most honored bishop of all?/¿Por qué los cristianos consideraban que el obispo de Roma era el obispo más respetado de todos?**
>
> _____
> _____

esa iglesia comenzó a conocerse como **papa,**
una palabra que en griego significa "padre".

## NEW TEACHINGS AND EMPERORS/NUEVAS ENSEÑANZAS Y NUEVOS EMPERADORES

As Christianity spread through the Roman
world, Christian teachings began to mix with the
works of classical philosophers like Plato. In the
late 300s and early 400s, Christian writers like
**Augustine** (AW-guhs-teen) **of Hippo** had begun
to read classical works. After studying Plato's
writings, Augustine felt that Christians should
focus on God's plan for the world instead of on
material goods. Augustine's ideas helped shape
Christian beliefs for hundreds of years./A medida
que el cristianismo se expandía por el mundo
romano, las enseñanzas cristianas comenzaron
a mezclarse con las obras de filósofos clásicos
como Platón. A fines del siglo 4 y principios del
siglo 5, escritores cristianos como **Agustín de
Hipona** habían comenzado a leer obras clásicas.
Después de estudiar las obras de Platón, Agustín
consideró que los cristianos debían enfocarse
en el plan de Dios para el mundo, en lugar de
centrarse en los bienes materiales. Las ideas de
Agustín ayudaron a desarrollar las creencias
cristianas durante cientos de años.

In the early 300s, emperor **Constantine** (KAHN-
stuhn-teen) became a Christian and removed
the bans on Christians. He created a council
of Christian leaders, and his government had a
close relationship with the church. Constantine
had several great Christian churches built in the
empire. He believed that God had helped him have
a successful life. Later, Emperor Theodosius I
(theeuh-DOH-shuhs) made Christianity the official
religion of Rome./A principios del siglo 4, el
emperador **Constantino** se convirtió al cristianismo

> What did Augustine of Hippo think Christians should focus on?/¿En qué pensaba Agustín de Hipona que debían enfocarse los cristianos?
> _____
> _____

> Circle the name of the emperor who made Christianity the official religion of Rome./Encierra en un círculo el nombre del emperador que adoptó el cristianismo como la religión oficial de Roma.

y levantó las prohibiciones a los cristianos. Creó
un concilio de líderes cristianos y su gobierno
pasó a tener una relación estrecha con la Iglesia.
Constantino mandó a construir varias iglesias
cristianas importantes en el imperio. Estaba
convencido de que Dios lo había ayudado a tener
una vida exitosa. Más adelante, el emperador
Teodosio I adoptó el cristianismo como la
religión oficial de Roma.

## CHALLENGE ACTIVITY/ACTIVIDAD AVANZADA

**Critical Thinking: Elaborate/Pensamiento crítico:
Profundizar** Sometimes popes choose names
that are different from the ones their parents
gave them. Use an encyclopedia or other
reference source to do research on some of
the popes of the early church. Write three
facts that you think are interesting or unusual
about their names./A veces, los papas escogen
nombres que son diferentes de los que les
pusieron sus padres. Usa una enciclopedia
u otra fuente de referencia para investigar
sobre algunos de los primeros papas de la
Iglesia. Escribe tres hechos que te parezcan
interesantes o inusuales sobre sus nombres.

**DIRECTIONS/INSTRUCCIONES** Match the terms in the first column with their correct definition from the second column by placing the letter of the correct definition in the space provided before each term./Une los términos de la primera columna con su definición correcta en la segunda columna. Escribe la letra de la definición correcta en el espacio que precede a cada término.

_____ 1. pope/papa

a. local leaders in Christian communities/ líderes locales de las comunidades cristianas

_____ 2. Augustine of Hippo/ Agustín de Hipona

b. Roman emperor who became a Christian/emperador romano que se convirtió al cristianismo

_____ 3. bishops/obispos

c. Christian ceremony that honors the last supper Jesus had with the Apostles/ceremonia cristiana en la que se honra la última cena que Jesús compartió con los apóstoles

_____ 4. Constantine/Constantino

d. writer who linked classical philosophy with Christian beliefs/escritor que vinculó la filosofía clásica con las creencias cristianas

_____ 5. Eucharist/Eucaristía

e. Greek word for "father"/palabra que significa "padre" en griego

## Civilizations of Eastern Europe/Civilizaciones de Europa oriental

### Lesson/Lección 1

**MAIN IDEAS/IDEAS PRINCIPALES**

1. The physical geography of eastern Europe varies widely from place to place./La geografía física de Europa oriental varía ampliamente de un lugar a otro.

2. The climate and vegetation of eastern Europe also vary greatly from place to place./El clima y la vegetación de Europa oriental también varían ampliamente de un lugar a otro.

3. The early history of eastern Europe was shaped by the movement of different groups of people into the region from other areas./Las migraciones de diferentes pueblos desde otras áreas hacia Europa oriental moldeó la historia de la región desde sus inicios.

## Key Terms and People/Personas y palabras clave

**Ural Mountains/montes Urales** used by most modern geographers as the solid eastern boundary between Asia and Europe/utilizados por la mayoría de los geógrafos modernos para marcar la frontera oriental natural entre Asia y Europa

**Carpathians/Cárpatos** low, rugged mountains that are an extension of the Alps/montañas bajas y escarpadas que son una extensión de los Alpes

**Balkan Peninsula/península balcánica** one of the largest peninsulas in Europe; extends south into the Mediterranean Sea/una de las grandes penínsulas de Europa; se extiende hacia el sur hasta el mar Mediterráneo

**Danube/Danubio** river that begins in Germany and flows east/río que nace en Alemania y fluye hacia el este

**Volga/Volga** river that flows south through western Russia to the Caspian Sea/río que fluye hacia el sur a través del oeste de Rusia hasta el mar Caspio

**taiga/taiga** huge forest of evergreen trees that covers about half of Russia/extenso bosque de árboles de hoja perenne que ocupa aproximadamente la mitad de Rusia

**Rus/rus** Vikings from Scandinavia/vikingos de Escandinavia

## Lesson Summary/Resumen de la lección

### PHYSICAL FEATURES/CARACTERÍSTICAS FÍSICAS

Eastern Europe is a region with a variety of landforms, water features, and climates. Geographically, eastern Europe's boundary with Asia are the **Ural Mountains,** in western

Russia./Europa oriental es una región con
una amplia variedad de accidentes geográficos,
masas de agua y climas. Desde el punto de
vista geográfico, la frontera oriental de Europa
con Asia son los **montes Urales**, que están
ubicados en el oeste de Rusia.

Several other mountain ranges are also in
the eastern Europe. The **Carpathians** are a low
mountain range that stretch in a long arc from
the Alps of west-central Europe to the Black
Sea. East of the Black Sea are the Caucasus
Mountains. Two more mountain ranges, the
Dinaric Alps and Balkan Mountains, cover most
of the **Balkan Peninsula.** This landform is one of
Europe's largest peninsulas. It extends south into
the Mediterranean Sea./En Europa oriental, hay
varias otras cordilleras. Los **Cárpatos** son una
cadena de montañas bajas que forman un arco
largo desde los Alpes en el área central oeste de
Europa hasta el mar Negro. Al este del mar
Negro, se alzan las montañas del Cáucaso. Otras
dos cadenas montañosas, los Alpes Dináricos y
los montes Balcanes, cubren la mayor parte de
la **península balcánica**, una de las penínsulas
más grandes de Europa, que se extiende hacia
el sur hasta el mar Mediterráneo.

Eastern Europe has many seas and rivers. Many
rivers are vital to trade and transportation. The
**Danube** begins in Germany and flows east through
nine countries before flowing into the Black Sea.
The **Volga** is Europe's longest river and flows south
through western Russia. It forms the center of
Russia's river network. Canals connect the Volga
to the Don River and the Baltic Sea./En Europa
oriental hay muchos mares y ríos. Muchos de los
ríos son fundamentales para el comercio y el
transporte. El **Danubio** nace en Alemania y fluye
hacia el este a través de nueve países antes

**Underline the name of the landform that is eastern Europe's boundary with Asia.**/Subraya el nombre del accidente geográfico que constituye la frontera oriental de Europa con Asia.

**The Carpathians stretch to what body of water?/** ¿Hasta qué masa de agua llegan los Cárpatos?

_____

_____

**Why is the Volga an important river in Europe?/** ¿Por qué el Volga es un río importante de Europa?

_____

_____

_____

_____

_____

_____

de desembocar en el mar Negro. El **Volga** es el río más largo de Europa y fluye hacia el sur por el oeste de Rusia. Es, además, el centro de la red fluvial de Rusia. Una serie de canales conectan el Volga con el río Don y el mar Báltico.

## CLIMATE AND VEGETATION/CLIMA Y VEGETACIÓN

The climate is cold and harsh in the far north of eastern Europe. Winters are long. There is less rain than in other parts of the region and not that much sun. Huge forests of evergreen trees are able to grow, including **taiga** in Russia. Frozen soil, or tundra, is also found here./En el extremo norte de Europa oriental, el clima es frío y severo. Los inviernos son largos, llueve menos que en otras partes de la región y no hay tanto sol. En esta región, crecen extensos bosques de árboles de hoja perenne, entre los que se encuentra la **taiga** rusa. Allí también se puede encontrar suelo congelado, o tundra.

Winter is still cold in the interior plains, but the summers are pleasant. The grassland of the steppe is Russia's most important farming area./En las llanuras interiores, el invierno también es frío, pero los veranos son agradables. Las praderas de la estepa constituyen la zona agrícola más importante de Rusia.

Temperatures are warm in the Mediterranean climate along the Balkan coast. Hardy trees and shrubs grow in this area that gets little rain./A lo largo de la costa balcánica, el clima mediterráneo ofrece temperaturas cálidas. En esta área, que recibe poca lluvia, crecen árboles y arbustos resistentes a las sequías.

> **What are the climate and vegetation like along the Balkan coast?/¿Cómo son el clima y la vegetación a lo largo de la costa balcánica?**
>
> _____
> _____
> _____
> _____
> _____

## EASTERN EUROPEAN PEOPLES/PUEBLOS DE EUROPA ORIENTAL

Throughout history, many different peoples have moved into eastern Europe. They all brought their customs and cultures. For example, the word *Russia* probably comes from the name of the **Rus.** These Vikings were from Scandinavia./ A lo largo de la historia, muchos grupos distintos han llegado a Europa oriental. Todos ellos han traído consigo sus costumbres y su cultura. Por ejemplo, la palabra *Rusia* probablemente viene del nombre de los **rus,** que eran vikingos de Escandinavia.

The Slavs created kingdoms and traded. The Balts farmed land and raised cattle. One people, the Magyars, even helped establish the Hungarian language. By the 600s BC, areas of eastern Europe would become colonies of ancient Greece and later be part of the Roman Empire./Los eslavos crearon reinos y comerciaron con otros pueblos. Los bálticos cultivaron la tierra y criaron ganado. Un pueblo, los magiares, ayudó a establecer la lengua húngara. En el siglo 7 a. C., algunas áreas de Europa oriental pasaron a ser colonias de la antigua Grecia y, posteriormente, fueron parte del Imperio romano.

> **Circle the name of the language that the Magyars helped establish in eastern Europe./Encierra en un círculo el nombre de la lengua que los magiares ayudaron a establecer en Europa oriental.**

## CHALLENGE ACTIVITY/ACTIVIDAD AVANZADA

**Critical Thinking: Rank/Pensamiento crítico: Ordenar** Use an almanac, atlas, or other source to research the mountains, rivers, or seas of eastern Europe. Choose a category (like length, depth, or height), and rank five examples. List them by least to most or most to least. Use at least one example not found in the text./Usa un almanaque, un atlas u otra fuente para investigar sobre las montañas, los ríos o los mares de Europa oriental. Escoge una categoría (como longitud, profundidad o altura) y ordena cinco ejemplos de menor a mayor o de mayor a menor. Utiliza al menos un ejemplo que no esté en el texto.

**DIRECTIONS/INSTRUCCIONES** Read each sentence and fill
in the blank with the word in the word pair that best completes
the sentence./Lee cada oración y escribe en el espacio en blanco
la palabra del par de palabras que mejor la completa.

1. The _____ forms the center of Russia's river network.
   **(Danube/Volga)**/El _____ es el centro de la red fluvial
   de Rusia. **(Danubio/Volga)**

2. The _____ is one of the largest of these landforms in
   Europe. **(Ural Mountains/Balkan Peninsula)**/_____ es
   uno de los accidentes geográficos más grandes de su tipo en Europa. **(Los
   montes Urales/La península balcánica)**

3. Vikings named the _____ came to eastern
   Europe from Scandinavia. **(Carpathians/Rus)**/Los vikingos llamados
   _____ llegaron a Europa oriental desde Escandinavia.
   **(Cárpatos/rus)**

4. Evergreen trees of the _____ cover about half
   of Russia. **(taiga/Volga)**/Los árboles de hoja perenne que crecen en
   _____ cubren aproximadamente la mitad de
   Rusia. **(la taiga/el Volga)**

5. Flowing east, the _____ goes through nine
   countries before flowing into the Black Sea. **(Rus/Danube)**/El
   _____, que fluye hacia el este, atraviesa nueve
   países antes de desembocar en el mar Negro. **(rus/Danubio)**

6. Most modern geographers use the _____ as the
   solid eastern boundary between Asia and Europe. **(Ural Mountains/
   Balkan Peninsula)**/La mayoría de los geógrafos modernos utilizan
   _____ como la frontera natural oriental entre Asia
   y Europa. **(los montes Urales/la península balcánica)**

7. The _____ are low, rugged mountains that are an
   extension of the Alps. **(Danube/Carpathians)**/_____
   son montañas bajas y escarpadas que constituyen una extensión de los
   Alpes. **(El Danubio/Los Cárpatos)**

# Civilizations of Eastern Europe/Civilizaciones de Europa oriental

**MAIN IDEAS/IDEAS PRINCIPALES**

1. Eastern emperors ruled from Constantinople and tried but failed to reunite the whole Roman Empire./Los emperadores de Oriente gobernaron desde Constantinopla y trataron de reunificar el Imperio romano, pero fracasaron.

2. The people of the eastern empire created a new society that was different from society in the west./Los habitantes del Imperio de Oriente desarrollaron una nueva sociedad que era distinta de la sociedad de Occidente.

3. Byzantine Christianity was different from religion in the west./El cristianismo bizantino era diferente del que se practicaba en Occidente.

## Key Terms and People/Personas y palabras clave

**Justinian/Justiniano** last ruler of the Roman Empire/el último emperador del Imperio romano

**Theodora/Teodora** Justinian's wife, a wise woman who advised her husband during his reign/esposa de Justiniano; una mujer sabia que aconsejó a su esposo durante su reinado

**Byzantine Empire/Imperio bizantino** civilization that developed in the eastern Roman Empire/civilización que se desarrolló en el Imperio romano de Oriente

**mosaics/mosaicos** pictures made with pieces of colored glass and stone/ imágenes realizadas con pedazos de vidrio y piedras de colores

## Lesson Summary/Resumen de la lección

### EMPERORS RULE FROM CONSTANTINOPLE/ EMPERADORES GOBIERNAN DESDE CONSTANTINOPLA

After Diocletian divided the Roman Empire into east and west, Constantinople became its center. Located on a peninsula between the Black and Mediterranean Seas, it was protected from attack. The city had a natural harbor, and it was located along major trade routes, such as the Silk Road. So Constantinople controlled trade between Europe and Asia./Después de que Diocleciano dividió el Imperio romano en el Imperío de Oriente y el de Occidente, Constantinopla se convirtió en el centro del

> **Why was Constantinople an important center?/¿Por qué Constantinopla fue un centro importante?**
>
> _____
> _____
> _____
> _____

imperio. Como estaba ubicada en una península entre los mares Negro y Mediterráneo, estaba protegida contra los ataques. La ciudad tenía un puerto natural y estaba ubicada en el camino de las principales rutas comerciales, como la Ruta de la Seda. Por lo tanto, Constantinopla controlaba el comercio entre Europa y Asia.

After Rome fell in AD 476, the emperor **Justinian,** who ruled in the 500s, wanted to reunite the Roman Empire. His armies recaptured Italy. He was respected for making laws fairer. But he made enemies who tried to overthrow him. Groups led riots and set fire to buildings. Justinian feared for his life and planned to leave Constantinople. He was stopped by his wife, **Theodora.** She persuaded him to stay and helped him rule successfully. Together, they ended the riots. Justinian was able to keep his throne. Despite Justinian's success, later emperors could not fight off attacks or hold onto the land./ Después de la caída de Roma en el año 476 a. C., el emperador **Justiniano,** que gobernó en el siglo 6, se propuso reunificar el Imperio romano. Sus ejércitos recuperaron Italia. Justiniano fue respetado por hacer leyes más justas. Sin embargo, también tuvo enemigos que trataron de derrocarlo. Algunos grupos crearon disturbios e incendiaron edificios. Justiniano temía por su vida y planificó abandonar Constantinopla. Sin embargo, su esposa, **Teodora,** impidió que huyera: lo convenció de que se quedara y lo ayudó a gobernar con éxito. Juntos, Justiniano y Teodora acabaron con los disturbios. Justiniano pudo conservar su trono. A pesar del éxito de Justiniano, los emperadores posteriores no pudieron combatir los ataques ni conservar las tierras.

The eastern empire lasted for several hundred years, but it never regained its former strength. After Justinian's death, Constantinople was defeated by the Ottoman Turks in 1453./

| Who was Justinian's most trusted advisor?/¿Quién fue la consejera más confiable de Justiniano? |
| --- |
| _____ |

El Imperio romano de Oriente duró varios
cientos de años, pero nunca pudo recuperar la
fortaleza que había tenido anteriormente. Tras
la muerte de Justiniano, Constantinopla fue
derrotada por los turcos otomanos en 1453.

## A NEW SOCIETY/UNA SOCIEDAD NUEVA

People began to follow Greek culture instead
of Roman culture. The cultural ties to Rome
were slowly lost./El pueblo empezó a adoptar
la cultura griega en lugar de la cultura romana.
Poco a poco, se perdieron los lazos culturales
con Roma.

Constantinople was a major trade route among
Europeans, Africans, and Asians. Because of this,
the people were exposed to new ideas from other
cultures. They blended those ideas with their own
Roman and Greek roots. Historians call the new
society that developed in the east the **Byzantine
Empire.** Byzantine culture developed its own
distinct features. An eastern emperor, for example,
was head of both the church and the government.
In the west, popes and bishops ruled the church,
but the emperor held political power./
Constantinopla era una de las principales rutas
comerciales entre europeos, africanos y asiáticos.
Por eso, sus pobladores estaban expuestos a ideas
nuevas de otras culturas, y mezclaron esas ideas
con sus propias raíces romanas y griegas. Los
historiadores llaman **Imperio bizantino** a esta
nueva sociedad que surgió en Oriente. La cultura
bizantina desarrolló características propias. El
emperador de Oriente, por ejemplo, era jefe tanto
de la Iglesia como del gobierno. En Occidente, los
papas y los obispos dirigían la Iglesia, mientras
que el emperador tenía el poder político.

> **What name was given to
> the society that developed
> out of the eastern Roman
> Empire?/¿Qué nombre
> recibió la sociedad que
> surgió del Imperio romano
> de Oriente?**
>
> _____

## BYZANTINE CHRISTIANITY/CRISTIANISMO BIZANTINO

Christianity was central to the Byzantine Empire. Byzantine artists showed their devotion to God and the Christian church by creating religious art. **Mosaics,** pictures made with pieces of colored stone or glass, were grand. The Byzantine churches were magnificent./El cristianismo fue fundamental para el Imperio bizantino. Los artistas bizantinos demostraron su devoción a Dios y a la Iglesia cristiana mediante el arte religioso. Los **mosaicos,** imágenes realizadas con pedazos de piedras o vidrios de colores, eran majestuosos. Las iglesias bizantinas eran magníficas.

For hundreds of years, church leaders of the east and west worked together. In the 1000s, the church split in two. Christians in the east formed the Eastern Orthodox Church. As a result, eastern and western Europe were divided by religion./Los líderes religiosos de Oriente y Occidente trabajaron juntos durante cientos de años. Sin embargo, en el siglo 11, la Iglesia se dividió en dos. Los cristianos de Oriente formaron la Iglesia ortodoxa oriental. Como resultado, la religión dividió a Europa oriental y occidental.

> **Underline the way in which Byzantine artists showed their devotion to Christianity./Subraya la manera en que los artistas bizantinos mostraron su devoción al cristianismo.**

## CHALLENGE ACTIVITY/ACTIVIDAD AVANZADA

**Critical Thinking: Explain/Pensamiento crítico: Explicar** Imagine that you are Theodora, the wife of Roman Emperor Justinian. Your husband wants to leave his kingdom because his enemies have started a riot and threaten to kill him. You think he is wrong. Write a short speech that you would make to Justinian to persuade him to stay and solve his problems./Imagina que eres Teodora, la esposa del emperador romano

Justiniano. Tu esposo quiere abandonar el reino porque sus enemigos han comenzado un disturbio y amenazan con asesinarlo. Tú no estás de acuerdo con su decisión. Escribe un breve discurso en el que trates de convencer a Justiniano de quedarse para resolver sus problemas.

| | |
|---|---|
| Byzantine Empire/Imperio bizantino | Justinian/Justiniano |
| mosaics/mosaicos | Theodora/Teodora |

**DIRECTIONS/INSTRUCCIONES** Answer each question by writing a sentence that contains at least one word from the word bank./ Responde cada pregunta con una oración que contenga al menos una palabra del banco de palabras.

1. Who was the emperor who wanted to reunite the Roman Empire?/¿Quién fue el emperador que se propuso reunificar el Imperio romano?

   _____

   _____

2. What are pictures made with pieces of colored stone or glass known as?/ ¿Cómo se denominan las imágenes realizadas con pedazos de piedras o vidrios de colores?

   _____

   _____

3. Who advised Justinian to solve his problems rather than give up the throne?/ ¿Quién le aconsejó a Justiniano que resolviera sus problemas en lugar de abandonar el trono?

   _____

   _____

4. What do historians call the society that developed in the eastern Roman Empire?/¿Cómo llaman los historiadores a la sociedad que se desarrolló en el Imperio romano de Oriente?

   _____

   _____

# Civilizations of Eastern Europe/Civilizaciones de Europa oriental

## Lesson/Lección 3

**MAIN IDEAS/IDEAS PRINCIPALES**

1. Russia was invaded by Mongol armies and later freed by Prince Ivan III./Rusia fue invadida por los mongoles y posteriormente fue liberada por el príncipe Iván III.

2. Trade played an important part in Russian daily life./El comercio tuvo un papel importante en la vida cotidiana rusa.

3. Orthodox Christianity greatly influenced Russian culture./El cristianismo ortodoxo tuvo gran influencia en la cultura rusa.

## Key Terms and People/Personas y palabras clave

**Ivan III/Iván III** prince of Muscovy who broke away from the Mongol Empire/ príncipe de Moscovia que se separó del Imperio mongol

**czar/zar** title of Russian emperors/título que reciben los emperadores rusos

**principalities/principados** small states ruled by princes/pequeños estados gobernados por príncipes

**icons/iconos** religious images painted on wood/imágenes religiosas pintadas sobre madera

## Lesson Summary/Resumen de la lección

### EARLY RUSSIAN HISTORY/COMIENZOS DE LA HISTORIA RUSA

As Christianity spread throughout eastern Europe, a people called the Rus formed the kingdom that would become Russia. The Rus were Vikings. They set up a capital near Kiev, which formed part of a trade route that stretched from Scandinavia to the Byzantine Empire. Kiev became powerful, and the rulers formed alliances with other kingdoms. However, after the death of powerful ruler Yaroslav, Kiev was invaded by the Mongols. For 200 years, Russia was under Mongol rule. Then in Muscovy, which is now Moscow, **Ivan III** began to strengthen his rule. He worked with the Mongols and gained additional power. In 1480, Prince Ivan broke away from the Mongol Empire and made himself **czar,** or emperor of Russia. He successfully fought the Mongols for Russia's

> Which group ruled Russia for 200 years?/¿Qué grupo gobernó Rusia durante 200 años?
>
> _____
>
> _____

> Underline the title Prince Ivan gave himself after freeing Russia./Subraya el título que el príncipe Iván se dio a sí mismo después de liberar a Rusia.

independence./A medida que el cristianismo se
extendía por Europa oriental, un pueblo llamado
rus formó el reino que se convertiría en Rusia. Los
rus eran vikingos. Establecieron su capital cerca de
Kiev, que formaba parte de la ruta comercial que
se extendía desde Escandinavia hasta el Imperio
bizantino. Kiev se hizo poderosa y sus gobernantes
formaron alianzas con otros reinos. No obstante,
tras la muerte del poderoso gobernante Yaroslav,
Kiev fue invadida por los mongoles. Durante
200 años, Rusia estuvo bajo el dominio mongol.
Entonces, en Moscovia, que actualmente es
Moscú, **Iván III** comenzó a fortalecer su gobierno.
Trabajó con los mongoles y acumuló más poder.
En 1480, el príncipe Iván se separó del Imperio
mongol y se autoproclamó **zar,** o emperador de
Rusia. Derrotó a los mongoles y declaró la
independencia de Rusia.

## RUSSIAN SOCIETY AND DAILY LIFE/SOCIEDAD RUSA Y VIDA COTIDIANA

During its early history, Russia was a cluster of
**principalities,** small states ruled by princes. These
princes had great power. Even when the Mongols
invaded, the princes remained in power if they
swore allegiance to the Mongols. After Ivan III
won Russia's independence, he was the most
powerful Russian prince. He launched a series
of wars to conquer other Russian states. He was
able to unify much of Russia into a single state./
En los comienzos de su historia, Rusia era un
cúmulo de **principados,** o pequeños estados
gobernados por príncipes. Los príncipes tenían
mucho poder. Aun cuando los mongoles invadían
los principados, los príncipes permanecían en el
poder si juraban lealtad a los mongoles. Después
de que Iván III logró la independencia de Rusia,
se convirtió en el príncipe ruso más poderoso.
Dirigió una serie de guerras para conquistar

otros estados rusos y logró unificar gran parte
de Rusia en un solo estado.

Russian culture remained the same even with
government changes. For example, Christianity
stayed Russia's official religion. Russia had close
ties to the Byzantine Empire. As a result, when
the Roman Catholic and Eastern Orthodox
churches split, Russia became part of the Eastern
Orthodox Church./La cultura rusa permaneció
intacta a pesar de los cambios de gobierno. Por
ejemplo, el cristianismo siguió siendo la religión
oficial. Rusia mantuvo lazos estrechos con el
Imperio bizantino. Como resultado, formó
parte de la Iglesia ortodoxa oriental cuando
se dividieron las Iglesias católica romana y
ortodoxa oriental.

Russia's economy was based on trade, and
its most important trading partner was the
Byzantine Empire. Trade goods from Russia were
fur, wax, and honey. In return, Russians received
wine, silk, art objects, and spices. Trade brought
wealth to Russia. In fact, traders were ranked
just below princes and nobles. Clergy were also
respected./La economía de Rusia se basaba en el
comercio, y su socio comercial más importante
era el Imperio bizantino. Los productos
comerciales de Rusia eran las pieles, la cera y
la miel. A cambio, los rusos recibían vino, seda,
piezas de arte y especias. El comercio trajo
riqueza a Rusia. De hecho, los comerciantes
se encontraban justo debajo de los príncipes
y los nobles en la jerarquía social. El clero
también era respetado.

| Why was Russia part of the Eastern Orthodox Church?/ ¿Por qué Rusia fue parte de la Iglesia ortodoxa oriental? |
| --- |
| _____ |
| _____ |
| _____ |
| _____ |
| _____ |
| _____ |

## RUSSIAN CULTURE AND ACHIEVEMENTS/
## LA CULTURA RUSA Y SUS LOGROS

Most of Russia's culture reflects a religious
influence. Early Russians designed churches
with multiple domes. Inside Russian churches

were mosaics and paintings. **Icons,** religious images on wood, showed figures from the Bible so that people could focus on their prayers./ La mayor parte de la cultura rusa refleja su influencia religiosa. Los primeros rusos diseñaron iglesias con múltiples bóvedas. Dentro de las iglesias rusas, había mosaicos y pinturas. Los **iconos,** imágenes religiosas pintadas sobre madera, mostraban figuras de la Biblia de manera que las personas pudieran enfocarse en sus rezos.

> **What is an icon?/¿Qué es un icono?**
>
> _____
>
> _____

Music was important in Russian church celebrations. Choirs from later periods sang in complex harmonies. Russian music and religious texts were created in Slavonic. At first, it could not be written down. Then missionaries developed a Slavonic alphabet called Cyrillic. It is still used to write Russian and other related languages, but its characters are not familiar to English or Spanish speakers./La música era importante en las celebraciones de la Iglesia rusa. Los coros de períodos posteriores entonaron armonías complejas. La música rusa y los textos religiosos se creaban en eslavo. En un principio, no podían escribirse. Después, los misioneros desarrollaron un alfabeto eslavo que se llamó cirílico. Ese alfabeto todavía se utiliza para escribir en ruso y otros idiomas relacionados, pero sus caracteres no son familiares para quienes hablan inglés o español.

> **Underline the sentence that explains the reason for the Slavonic language in Russia./Subraya la oración que explica por qué existe la lengua eslava en Rusia.**

## CHALLENGE ACTIVITY/ACTIVIDAD AVANZADA

**Critical Thinking: Summarize/Pensamiento crítico: Resumir** Use the Internet or other resources to gather information about Prince Ivan III. Write a biography about how he became prince, his role in Russia's independence, and his importance to the country's growth./Utiliza la Internet u otros recursos para recopilar información sobre el

príncipe Iván III. Escribe una biografía en la que
cuentes cómo se convirtió en príncipe, cuál fue su
papel en la independencia de Rusia y cuál fue su
importancia para el crecimiento de ese país.

**DIRECTIONS/INSTRUCCIONES** Write a word or descriptive
phrase to describe each term./Escribe una palabra o frase
descriptiva para describir cada término.

1. Ivan III/Iván III _____

_____

2. czar/zar _____

_____

3. principalities/principados _____

_____

4. icon/icono _____

_____

**DIRECTIONS/INSTRUCCIONES** Write a vocabulary term that has
a *similar* meaning to the word or words given./Escribe un término
de vocabulario que tenga un significado *similar* a la palabra o las
palabras dadas.

5. strong ruler/gobernante fuerte _____

6. religious symbol/símbolo religioso _____

7. small, independent area/área pequeña e independiente _____

# The Rise of Islam/El surgimiento del islam

## Lesson/Lección 1

 **MAIN IDEAS/IDEAS PRINCIPALES**
1. Arabia is a mostly a desert land./Arabia es, en su mayor parte, una tierra desértica.
2. Two ways of life—nomadic and sedentary—developed in the desert./Dos formas de vida, la nómada y la sedentaria, se desarrollaron en el desierto.

## Key Terms and People/Personas y palabras clave

**sand dunes/dunas** hills of sand shaped by the wind/colinas de arena formadas por el viento

**oasis/oasis** a wet, fertile area in the desert/zona húmeda y fértil en el desierto

**sedentary/sedentario** settled/asentado

**caravan/caravana** a group of traders that travels together/grupo de comerciantes que viajan juntos

**souk/souk** a market or bazaar/mercado o bazar

## Lesson Summary/Resumen de la lección

### A DESERT LAND/UNA TIERRA DESÉRTICA

The Arabian Peninsula is a mostly hot and dry desert of scorching temperatures and little water. Yet people have lived there for thousands of years./La península arábiga es un desierto caluroso y seco con temperaturas muy altas y poca agua. Sin embargo, es una zona habitada desde hace miles de años.

Arabia, located in the southwest corner of Asia, is the crossroads for three continents—Africa, Europe, and Asia. Trade routes cross the region by both land and sea. These routes have brought many different people and customs through Arabia, influencing the people who live there./En Arabia, ubicada en el extremo suroeste de Asia, se cruzan los caminos de tres continentes: África, Europa y Asia. Las rutas comerciales atraviesan la región por tierra y por mar. Estas rutas han llevado personas y costumbres a Arabia y han influido en la vida de las personas que viven allí.

> Arabia was the trading crossroads for what three continents?/¿Las rutas comerciales de qué tres continentes se cruzaban en Arabia?
>
> _____
> _____

The world's largest sand desert, the Rub'al-Khali, which means "Empty Quarter," lies in Arabia. There is little life there. **Sand dunes,** or hills of sand shaped by the wind, can rise to 800 feet and stretch for hundreds of miles. Water is scarce and exists mainly in oases throughout the desert. An **oasis** is a wet, fertile area in the desert. Oases have always been key stops along Arabia's trade routes./El desierto más grande del mundo, el Rub'al-Khali, que significa "cuarto vacío", está en Arabia. Hay poca vida allí. Las **dunas,** o colinas de arena formadas por el viento, pueden elevarse hasta 800 pies y extenderse por cientos de millas. El agua es escasa y se encuentra principalmente en los oasis. Un **oasis** es una zona húmeda y fértil en el desierto. Los oasis siempre han sido paradas clave a lo largo de las rutas comerciales de Arabia.

Deserts cover much of Arabia's interior, but other landforms are along its edges. Mountains border the southern and western coasts, and marshy land is near the Persian Gulf. Most people have settled in the milder coastal regions./Los desiertos cubren gran parte del interior de Arabia, pero existen otros accidentes geográficos en sus fronteras. Las montañas bordean las costas sur y oeste, y hay terrenos pantanosos cerca del Golfo Pérsico. La mayoría de las personas se asentaron en las templadas zonas costeras.

> **Why would oases be important to people traveling along trade routes?/¿Por qué los oasis eran importantes para las personas que viajaban por las rutas comerciales?**
>
> _____
> _____
> _____

## TWO WAYS OF LIFE/DOS FORMAS DE VIDA

People developed two main ways to live in the desert: nomadic and **sedentary,** or settled. Nomads moved from place to place. They lived in tents and raised goats, sheep, and camels. They traveled with their herds across the desert, moving along regular routes as seasons changed. They depended on camels for transportation and milk. Nomads traveled in tribes, or groups of people.

Tribe membership was important to nomads. It offered protection from desert dangers and reduced competition for grazing lands./En el desierto, se desarrollaron dos formas de vida: la nómada y la **sedentaria,** o asentada. Los nómadas se trasladaban constantemente de un lugar a otro. Vivían en tiendas y criaban cabras, ovejas y camellos. Viajaban por el desierto con sus rebaños, siguiendo rutas regulares según las estaciones. Los camellos servían como medio de transporte y proveían leche. Los nómadas viajaban en tribus, o grupos de personas. La pertenencia a una tribu era importante para ellos, ya que las tribus brindaban protección contra los peligros del desierto y reducían la competencia por las tierras de pastoreo.

> **Why did nomads want to travel in a tribe?/¿Por qué los nómadas viajaban en tribus?**
> _____
> _____
> _____

Other people settled in oases and farmed. Settlements in oases along the trade routes became towns, where most people in Arabia lived. Merchants and craftspeople lived there too and worked with people in caravans. A **caravan** is a group of traders that travel together. Most town centers featured a **souk,** which is a market or bazaar. Both nomads and caravans used these centers of trade. Nomads traded animal products and desert herbs for cooking supplies and clothing. Merchants sold spices, gold, leather, and other goods brought by the caravans./Otros grupos se asentaron en los oasis y se dedicaron a la agricultura. Los asentamientos de los oasis que se encontraban cerca de las rutas comerciales se convirtieron en pueblos, donde vivía la mayoría de los árabes. Los comerciantes y los artesanos también vivían allí y comerciaban con la gente de las caravanas. Una **caravana** es un grupo de comerciantes que viajan juntos. La mayoría de los pueblos tenían un **souk,** un mercado o bazar, donde comerciaban tanto los nómadas como las caravanas. Los nómadas intercambiaban productos animales

> **Underline the sentence that tells where most people in Arabia lived./Subraya la oración que indica dónde vivía la mayoría de los árabes.**

> **What are some things that could be found at a souk?/¿Qué productos se podrían encontrar en un souk?**
> _____
> _____
> _____

y hierbas del desierto por utensilios de cocina y
ropa. Los comerciantes vendían especias, oro,
cuero y otros productos que traían las caravanas.

Arabian towns were important places
along the trade routes. They linked India
with Northeast Africa and the Mediterranean.
Trade made it possible for Arabs to come in
contact with people and ideas from different
cultures around the world./Los pueblos árabes
eran puntos importantes en las rutas comerciales.
Conectaban India con el noreste de África y
el Mediterráneo. El comercio hizo posible que
los árabes entraran en contacto con personas
e ideas de diferentes culturas del mundo.

## CHALLENGE ACTIVITY/ACTIVIDAD AVANZADA

**Critical Thinking: Elaborate/Pensamiento crítico:
Profundizar** If you lived in Arabia, would you
choose a nomadic or sedentary life? Write a one-
page description of what your life would be like
based on the lifestyle you would prefer to live./Si
vivieras en Arabia, ¿elegirías una vida nómada
o sedentaria? Escribe una descripción de una
página sobre cómo sería tu vida según el estilo
de vida que prefieras.

**DIRECTIONS/INSTRUCCIONES** Write a descriptive phrase to describe each term./Escribe una frase descriptiva para describir cada término.

1. sand dunes/dunas _____

_____

2. souk/souk _____

_____

3. caravan/caravana _____

_____

4. oasis/oasis _____

_____

5. sedentary/sedentario _____

_____

**DIRECTIONS/INSTRUCCIONES** Look at each set of vocabulary terms. On the line provided, write the letter of the term that does not relate to the others./Observa cada conjunto de términos de vocabulario. En el espacio en blanco, escribe la letra del término que no tiene relación con los demás.

_____ 6. a. sand dunes/dunas
        b. souk/souk
        c. oasis/oasis

_____ 7. a. souk/souk
        b. sedentary/sedentario
        c. sand dunes/dunas

# The Rise of Islam/El surgimiento del islam

## Lesson/Lección 2

**MAIN IDEAS/IDEAS PRINCIPALES**

1. Muhammad became a prophet and introduced a religion called Islam in Arabia./Mahoma se convirtió en profeta y llevó a Arabia una religión llamada islam.

2. Muhammad's teachings had similarities to Judaism and Christianity, but they also presented new ideas./Las enseñanzas de Mahoma tenían semejanzas con el judaísmo y el cristianismo, pero también presentaban ideas nuevas.

3. Islam spread in Arabia after being rejected at first./Al principio, el islam fue rechazado, pero luego se expandió por toda Arabia.

4. The Qur'an is the holy book of Islam./El Corán es el libro sagrado del islam.

5. Along with the Qur'an, the Sunnah guide Muslims' lives./Junto con el Corán, la Sunna guía la vida de los musulmanes.

6. Islamic law is based on the Qur'an and the Sunnah./La ley islámica se basa en el Corán y la Sunna.

# Key Terms and People/Personas y palabras clave

**Muhammad/Mahoma** an Arabian man whose teachings became the basis for a new religion/hombre árabe cuyas enseñanzas formaron la base de una nueva religión

**Islam/islam** religion based on messages Muhammad received from God/ religión basada en mensajes que Mahoma recibió de Dios

**Muslim/musulmán** a person who follows Islam/seguidor del islam

**Qur'an/Corán** the holy book of Islam/el libro sagrado del islam

**shrine/santuario** a place where people worship a saint or god/lugar donde se alaba a un santo o dios

**pilgrimage/peregrinación** journey to a sacred place/viaje a un lugar sagrado

**mosque/mezquita** a building for Muslim prayer/edificio musulmán para la oración

**jihad/yihad** literally means "to make an effort" or "to struggle"/literalmente, significa "esforzarse" o "luchar"

**Sunnah/Sunna** a collection of actions or sayings by Muhammad/recopilación de las acciones y palabras de Mahoma

**Five Pillars of Islam/los cinco pilares del islam** the five acts of worship required of all Muslims/las cinco prácticas religiosas que todos los musulmanes tienen que cumplir

# Lesson Summary/Resumen de la lección

## MUHAMMAD BECOMES A PROPHET/MAHOMA SE CONVIERTE EN PROFETA

**Muhammad** brought a new religion to Arabia. What is known about him is from religious writings. He was born in the city of Mecca around 570./**Mahoma** llevó a Arabia una religión nueva. Lo que se sabe de él proviene de escritos religiosos. Mahoma nació en la ciudad de La Meca, alrededor del año 570.

Muhammad became upset that Mecca's rich people did not help the poor. According to Islamic teachings, when he was 40, an angel revealed God's messages to him. These form the basis of **Islam.** A follower of Islam is a **Muslim.** Islam's messages were written in the **Qur'an,** the holy book of Islam./A Mahoma le molestaba ver que las personas adineradas de La Meca no ayudaban a los pobres. Según las creencias islámicas, cuando Mahoma tenía 40 años de edad, un ángel le transmitió los mensajes de Dios que formaron la base del **islam.** Las personas que practican el islam se llaman **musulmanes.** Los mensajes del islam se escribieron en el **Corán,** el libro sagrado del islam.

> Underline the name of Islam's founder./Subraya el nombre del fundador del islam.

> What did the messages Muhammad received from God form?/¿Qué formaron los mensajes que Mahoma recibió de Dios?
>
> _____

## MUHAMMAD'S TEACHINGS/ENSEÑANZAS DE MAHOMA

Some of Muhammad's ideas came from Judaism and Christianity, including monotheism, or belief in one god. This was a new idea for many Arabs who prayed to gods at a **shrine.** The most important shrine was in Mecca. People traveled there on a **pilgrimage.**/Algunas de las ideas de Mahoma provenían del judaísmo y el cristianismo, incluido el monoteísmo, o la creencia en un solo dios. Esta era una idea nueva para muchos árabes, que rendían culto a muchos dioses en los **santuarios.** El santuario más importante estaba en La Meca. Muchos iban en **peregrinación** hasta allí.

> Why did people travel to Mecca on a pilgrimage?/¿Por qué las personas peregrinaban a La Meca?
>
> _____
> _____
> _____
> _____

Lesson/Lección 2, *continued*/*continuación*

## ISLAM SPREADS IN ARABIA/EL ISLAM SE EXTIENDE EN ARABIA

Mecca's rulers felt threatened by Muhammad. So he left and went to Medina. His house became the first **mosque,** or Muslim prayer building. Many Arab tribes accepted Islam. After years of fighting, Meccans welcomed back Muhammad and accepted Islam./Los gobernantes de La Meca se sintieron amenazados por Mahoma. Por eso, Mahoma se fue a Medina. Su casa en esa ciudad se convirtió en la primera **mezquita,** o edificio musulmán para la oración. Muchas tribus árabes aceptaron el islam. Después de muchos años de conflicto, los habitantes de La Meca aceptaron a Mahoma y al islam.

> Underline the name for a Muslim prayer building./Subraya el nombre de un edificio musulmán para la oración.

## THE QUR'AN/EL CORÁN

Muslims believe that the Qur'an is the word of God as told to Muhammad. Muslims believe that God wishes them to follow rules. These rules affect Muslims' everyday life./Los musulmanes creen que el Corán es la palabra de Dios, tal como le fue dada a Mahoma, y que Dios desea que sigan sus normas. Estas normas afectan la vida cotidiana de los musulmanes.

> Why is the Qur'an so important?/¿Por qué es tan importante el Corán?
>
> _____
> _____
> _____
> _____

**Jihad** is an important Islamic concept, which means "to make an effort" or "to struggle." It refers to the internal struggle of a Muslim trying to follow Islamic beliefs. It can also mean the struggle to defend the Muslim community or convert people. The word has also been translated as "holy war."/La **yihad** representa un importante concepto islámico. Literalmente, yihad significa "esforzarse" o "luchar". Se refiere a la lucha interior de un musulmán que trata de seguir las creencias islámicas. Además, puede referirse a la lucha para defender a la comunidad musulmana o para convertir personas al islam. Esta palabra también se ha traducido como "guerra santa".

> What two struggles does jihad refer to?/¿A qué dos luchas hace referencia la yihad?
>
> _____
> _____
> _____
> _____
> _____

## THE SUNNAH/LA SUNNA

Another important Islamic holy book is the **Sunnah,** a written record of Muhammad's words and actions. It spells out the five acts of worship required of Muslims—the **Five Pillars of Islam.**/ Otro libro sagrado importante para el islam es la **Sunna,** un conjunto de escritos sobre las palabras y las acciones de Mahoma. La Sunna explica en detalle los cinco actos de alabanza que deben respetar los musulmanes, es decir, **los cinco pilares del islam.**

## ISLAMIC LAW/LEY ISLÁMICA

The Qur'an and the Sunnah form the basis of Islamic law, or Shariah. This sets punishments or rewards. It makes no distinction between religious and secular life. Most Islamic countries today blend Islamic law with a legal system like that in the United States./El Corán y la Sunna son la base de la ley islámica, o Sharia. La Sharia establece castigos y recompensas, y no hace distinciones entre la vida secular y la vida religiosa. Hoy en día, la mayoría de los países islámicos combinan la ley islámica con un sistema jurídico parecido al de los Estados Unidos.

> **How is Shariah law used in Islamic countries today?**/ **¿Cómo se aplica la Sharia en los países islámicos hoy en día?**
>
> _____
> _____
> _____

## CHALLENGE ACTIVITY/ACTIVIDAD AVANZADA

**Critical Thinking: Summarize/Pensamiento crítico: Resumir** Suppose you had to explain Islam to someone who knew nothing about it. Write a one-page paper that includes important information about the religion./Imagina que debes explicar el islam a alguien que no sabe nada sobre él. Escribe un texto de una página en el que incluyas información importante sobre esta religión.

| Five Pillars of Islam/los cinco pilares del islam | Islam/el islam | jihad/la yihad |
|---|---|---|
| Mosque/mezquita | Muhammad/Mahoma | Muslim/un musulmán |
| pilgrimage/peregrinación | Qur'an/Corán | shrine/santuario |
| Sunnah/la Sunna | | |

**DIRECTIONS/INSTRUCCIONES** Read each sentence and fill in the blank with a word from the word bank that best completes the sentence./Lee cada oración y escribe en el espacio en blanco la palabra del banco de palabras que mejor la completa.

1. The first acts of worship required of all Muslims are known as the _____ ./
   Los primeros actos de alabanza que deben respetar los musulmanes se conocen como_____ .

2. The inner struggle people go through in their effort to obey God or to convert others to Islam is known as _____ . /
   La lucha interior de las personas para obedecer a Dios o para convertir a otras personas al islam se conoce como_____ .

3. The religion based on messages sent by God through an angel to an Arabian man is _____ ./
   La religión que se basa en los mensajes enviados por Dios a un hombre árabe mediante un ángel se conoce como_____ .

4. A collection of actions or sayings by an Arabian man who founded a religion is the _____ ./
   La recopilación de las acciones y palabras del hombre árabe que fundó una religión se llama _____ .

5. A person who follows Islam is a(n) _____ ./
   Un seguidor del islam es _____ .

6. A building for Muslim prayer is known as a(n) _____ ./
   Se denomina _____ al edificio musulmán para la oración.

7. The holy book of Islam is the _____ ./
   El libro sagrado del islam se llama _____ .

8. A place where people worship a saint or god is a(n) _____ ./
   Se denomina _____ al lugar donde las personas alaban a un santo o dios.

9. A journey to a sacred place is a(n) _____ ./
   Un viaje a un lugar sagrado se denomina _____ .

10. The Arabian man whose teachings became the basis for a new religion
    was _____ ./
    El hombre árabe cuyas enseñanzas formaron la base de una nueva religión se
    llamaba _____ .

# The Rise of Islam/El surgimiento del islam

## Lesson/Lección 3

**MAIN IDEAS/IDEAS PRINCIPALES**

1. Muslim armies conquered many lands into which Islam slowly spread./Los ejércitos musulmanes conquistaron muchas tierras, donde lentamente se difundió el islam.

2. Trade helped Islam spread into new areas./El comercio contribuyó a que el islam se difundiera en nuevas regiones.

3. A mix of cultures was one result of Islam's spread./La expansión del islam tuvo como resultado una mezcla de culturas.

4. Islamic influence encouraged the growth of cities./La influencia islámica fomentó el desarrollo de ciudades.

## Key Terms and People/Personas y palabras clave

**Abu Bakr/Abu Bakr** one of Islam's first converts, appointed caliph after Muhammad's death/uno de los primeros conversos al islam; fue nombrado califa después de la muerte de Mahoma

**caliph/califa** title of the highest Islamic leader/título que los musulmanes le dan al líder supremo del islam

**tolerance/tolerancia** acceptance/aceptación

## Lesson Summary/Resumen de la lección

### MUSLIMS ARMIES CONQUER MANY LANDS/EJÉRCITOS MUSULMANES CONQUISTAN MUCHAS TIERRAS

After Muhammad's death, his followers chose **Abu Bakr** to be the next leader of Islam. He was one of Muhammad's first converts. Abu Bakr became the first **caliph,** a title that Muslims use for the highest Islamic leader./Después de la muerte de Mahoma, sus seguidores eligieron a **Abu Bakr** como líder del islam. Abu Bakr fue uno de los primeros conversos de Mahoma. También fue el primer **califa,** un título que los musulmanes le dan al líder supremo del islam.

Abu Bakr directed battles against Arab tribes who did not follow Muhammad's teachings. He unified Arabia as a Muslim state. Muslim leaders who followed Abu Bakr conquered the Persian and Byzantine empires. Muslim leaders made

> Who was the first caliph?/
> ¿Quién fue el primer califa?
>
> _____

> Underline the sentence that describes Abu Bakr's major contribution as a caliph./Subraya la oración que describe la principal contribución de Abu Bakr como califa.

treaties with non-Muslims that listed rules conquered people had to follow. For example, non-Muslims could not build places of worship in Muslim cities. In return, Muslims would not attack them./Abu Bakr luchó contra las tribus árabes que no respetaban las enseñanzas de Mahoma y unificó Arabia como estado islámico. Los líderes musulmanes que seguían a Abu Bakr conquistaron los Imperios persa y bizantino y, junto con los líderes de otras religiones, firmaron tratados que enumeraban normas que los pueblos conquistados debían respetar. Por ejemplo, las personas que no eran musulmanas no podían construir lugares de alabanza en ciudades musulmanas. A cambio de esto, los musulmanes no los atacarían.

During this time, the conflict between different groups of Muslims led to the Shia-Sunni split. The conflict stemmed from a disagreement about who should be caliph. Shias said caliphs should be descended from Muhammad's family. Sunnis believed that religious leaders should elect caliphs. Today, most Muslims are Sunni. Shia Muslims live in Iran, Iraq, Pakistan, and India./Durante esta época, el conflicto entre distintos grupos de musulmanes produjo la división entre sunitas y chiitas. Este conflicto surgió a partir de un desacuerdo acerca de quién debía ser califa. Los chiitas decían que los califas debían descender de la familia de Mahoma. Los sunitas consideraban que los líderes religiosos debían elegir a los califas. En la actualidad, la mayoría de los musulmanes son sunitas. Los chiitas viven en Irán, Irak, Pakistán y la India.

Many caliphs came from the Umayyad family. They conquered lands in Central Asia, northern India, and North Africa. They controlled eastern Mediterranean trade routes. After many years of fighting, the Berbers of North Africa converted

> **What was the source of the conflict between different groups of Muslims?/¿Cuál fue el origen del conflicto entre los diferentes grupos de musulmanes?**
>
> _____
>
> _____
>
> _____

to Islam. A combined Arab and Berber army conquered Spain and ruled for 700 years./ Muchos califas provenían de la familia Omeya. Conquistaron territorios en Asia Central, en el norte de la India y en el norte de África. Pronto controlaron las rutas comerciales del este del Mediterráneo. Después de muchos años de guerra, los bereberes del norte de África se convirtieron al islam. Un ejército conjunto de árabes y bereberes conquistó España y gobernó la región durante 700 años.

> **How were the Arabs able to conquer Spain?/¿Cómo lograron conquistar España los árabes?**
>
> _____
> _____
> _____
> _____

## TRADE HELPS ISLAM SPREAD/EL COMERCIO CONTRIBUYE A LA DIFUSIÓN DEL ISLAM

Arab merchants took Islamic beliefs and practices with them to new lands. They brought back products such as cotton and rice. They learned of inventions such as paper and gunpowder. Coastal trading cities grew into large Muslim communities./Los comerciantes árabes llevaban las costumbres y creencias islámicas a nuevas tierras. A su vez, traían productos como el algodón y el arroz, y conocieron inventos como el papel y la pólvora. Las ciudades comerciales costeras se convirtieron en grandes comunidades musulmanas.

> **Why do you think trade flourishes in coastal cities?/ ¿Por qué crees que el comercio prospera en las ciudades costeras?**
>
> _____
> _____
> _____

## A MIX OF CULTURES/UNA MEZCLA DE CULTURAS

Muslims generally practiced religious **tolerance,** or acceptance. More people began speaking Arabic and practicing Islam. The Arabs also took on non-Muslim customs. Cultural blending changed Islam from a mostly Arab religion into a religion of many different cultures./En general, los musulmanes practicaban la **tolerancia,** o aceptación. Más personas comenzaron a hablar árabe y a practicar el islam. Los árabes, a su vez, adoptaron costumbres que no eran musulmanas. La mezcla cultural hizo que el islam pasara de

> **Underline the sentence that explains how cultural blending affected Islam./ Subraya la oración que explica de qué manera la mezcla de culturas afectó el islam.**

ser una religión principalmente árabe a ser una
religión de varias culturas diferentes.

## THE GROWTH OF CITIES/DESARROLLO DE CIUDADES

The growing Muslim cities reflected this blending
of cultures. For example, the wealthy city of
Baghdad was a major trading center. It attracted
artists and writers. Córdoba, in Spain, was the
largest, most advanced European city during the
early 900s. It was a center of learning. People
from across the Muslim world came there to
study. It was also a center of Jewish culture.
Jewish poets, philosophers, and scientists made
contributions to Córdoba's growth./El desarrollo
de las ciudades musulmanas reflejó esta mezcla
de culturas. Por ejemplo, la opulenta ciudad de
Bagdad era un importante centro comercial que
atraía a artistas y escritores. Córdoba, en España,
era la ciudad europea más avanzada a principios
del siglo 10 y se convirtió en un centro de
aprendizaje: gente de todo el mundo musulmán
iba allí a estudiar. También fue un centro para
la cultura judía; poetas, filósofos y científicos
judíos contribuyeron al crecimiento de Córdoba.

> In addition to Muslims,
> what other religious group
> had a thriving culture in
> Islamic Spain?/Además de
> los musulmanes, ¿qué otro
> grupo religioso tuvo una
> cultura pujante en la
> España islámica?
>
> _____
> _____

## CHALLENGE ACTIVITY/ACTIVIDAD AVANZADA

**Critical Thinking: Draw Conclusions/Pensamiento
crítico: Sacar conclusiones** Consider the benefits
to Islam from cultural blending. Write a one-page
paper that demonstrates how this practice helped
Islam become a more universal faith./Piensa en
cómo la mezcla de culturas benefició al islam.
Escribe un texto de una página en el que
demuestres de qué manera esta práctica ayudó al
islam a convertirse en una religión más universal.

**DIRECTIONS/INSTRUCCIONES** Write a word or phrase that defines or describes the name or term given./Escribe una palabra o frase que defina o describa el nombre o término dado.

1. Abu Bakr/Abu Bakr _____

2. caliph/califa _____

3. tolerance/tolerancia _____

**DIRECTIONS/INSTRUCCIONES** Use the two vocabulary words **caliph** and **tolerance** and the name **Abu Bakr** to write a short summary that relates to the lesson./Usa las palabras de vocabulario **califa** y **tolerancia** y el nombre **Abu Bakr** para escribir un breve resumen que se relacione con la lección.

_____

_____

_____

_____

_____

_____

_____

_____

_____

_____

_____

_____

_____

_____

# The Rise of Islam/El surgimiento del islam

**Lesson/Lección 4**

**MAIN IDEAS/IDEAS PRINCIPALES**
1. Muslim scholars made advances in various fields of science and philosophy./Los estudiosos musulmanes hicieron avances en la ciencia y la filosofía.
2. Islam influenced styles of literature and the arts./El islam influyó en diferentes estilos de literatura y en las artes.

## Key Terms and People/Personas y palabras clave

**Ibn Battutah/Ibn Battuta** Muslim explorer and geographer/geógrafo y explorador musulmán

**Sufism/sufismo** a movement of Islam, based on the belief that one must have a personal relationship with God/movimiento perteneciente al islam, basado en la creencia de que las personas deben establecer una relación personal con Dios

**Omar Khayyám/Omar Kayam** famous Sufi poet who wrote *The Rubáiyát*/famoso poeta sufista que escribió *Las Rubaiyat*

**patrons/mecenas** sponsors/patrocinadores

**minaret/minarete** a narrow tower on a mosque from which Muslims are called to pray/torre angosta de las mezquitas, desde donde se convoca a los musulmanes a rezar

**calligraphy/caligrafía** decorative writing/escritura decorativa

## Lesson Summary/Resumen de la lección
### SCIENCE AND PHILOSOPHY/CIENCIA Y FILOSOFÍA

Islamic scholars made great advances in many fields. These included astronomy, geography, math, and science. At Baghdad and Córdoba, Greek and other writings were translated into Arabic. A common language helped scholars share research./Los estudiosos musulmanes hicieron grandes avances en diversos campos, como la astronomía, la geografía, las matemáticas y la ciencia. En Bagdad y Córdoba, se tradujeron escritos del griego y de otros idiomas al árabe. El hecho de tener un idioma común ayudaba a los estudiosos a compartir las investigaciones.

Muslim scientists built observatories to study the sun, the moon, and stars. They also improved

> **In which two cities were scholarly writings translated into Arabic?/**¿En qué dos ciudades se tradujeron escritos al árabe?
>
> _____
> _____

the astrolabe. The Greeks had invented this tool
to chart the position of the stars. The astrolabe
would later be used in sea exploration. Also, it
helped Muslim explorers spread Islam to different
parts of the globe, which expanded the Islamic
world./Los científicos musulmanes construyeron
observatorios para estudiar el sol, la luna y las
estrellas. Además, realizaron mejoras al astrolabio,
un instrumento que los griegos habían inventado
para trazar mapas de las estrellas. Más adelante,
el astrolabio sería utilizado en las exploraciones
marítimas y ayudaría a los exploradores
musulmanes a difundir el islam en distintas
regiones del mundo, lo que expandió el
mundo islámico.

It was a Muslim mathematician who invented
algebra. Muslims found better ways to calculate
distance and make precise maps. They also used
the stars to navigate. Muslim merchants and
explorers traveled wide and far. One great
explorer was **Ibn Battutah.** He traveled to
Africa, India, China, and Spain in the 1320s./
Un matemático musulmán fue el que inventó
el álgebra. Los musulmanes hallaron mejores
maneras de calcular distancias y trazaron mapas
más exactos. También usaban las estrellas para
navegar. Los exploradores y comerciantes
musulmanes viajaron a lugares remotos. Un gran
explorador fue **Ibn Battuta,** quien viajó a África,
la India, China y España en la década de 1320.

Muslims were also known in medicine. They
added to Greek and Indian medicine. Muslim
doctors created tests for doctors to pass before
they could treat people. They wrote descriptions
of diseases, started the first school of pharmacy,
and built public hospitals. A Baghdad doctor
found out how to detect and treat smallpox.
Another doctor, known in the West as Avicenna,
wrote a medical encyclopedia widely used in
Europe for centuries./En el campo de la medicina,

> **Why do you think the astrolabe would be useful in sea exploration?/¿Por qué crees que podría ser útil el astrolabio en la exploración de los mares?**
>
> _____
> _____
> _____
> _____

> **Underline advances in medicine made by Muslims./Subraya los avances en medicina que hicieron los médicos musulmanes.**

los musulmanes hicieron grandes aportes a las investigaciones de los indios y los griegos. Los médicos musulmanes idearon exámenes que los médicos debían aprobar antes de tratar a sus pacientes. Comenzaron a escribir descripciones de las enfermedades, fundaron la primera escuela de farmacia y construyeron hospitales públicos. Un médico de Bagdad descubrió cómo detectar y tratar la viruela. Otro médico, conocido en Occidente como Avicena, escribió una enciclopedia médica que fue muy utilizada en toda Europa durante siglos.

Some Muslims developed a new philosophy called **Sufism.** People who practice Sufism are Sufis. Sufis seek a personal relationship with God. Sufism has brought many followers to Islam./ Algunos musulmanes desarrollaron una nueva filosofía llamada **sufismo.** Las personas que practican esta filosofía, conocidas como sufistas, buscan establecer una relación personal con Dios. El sufismo ha atraído a muchas personas al islam.

## LITERATURE AND THE ARTS/LITERATURA Y ARTE

Poetry and short stories were popular among Muslims. The collection of stories called *The Thousand and One Nights* includes tales about legendary heroes and characters. The most famous Sufi poet was **Omar Khayyám.** He wrote about faith, hope, and other emotions in *The Rubáiyát.*/La poesía y los cuentos eran populares entre los musulmanes. La colección de relatos conocida como *Las mil y una noches* incluye relatos sobre héroes y personajes legendarios. El poeta sufista más famoso fue **Omar Kayam,** quien escribió sobre la fe, la esperanza y otras emociones en *Las Rubaiyat*.

> **What is the name of Islam's great collection of stories?/**
> ¿Cómo se llama la gran colección de relatos del islam?
> 
> _____
> _____

There were many achievements in architecture. Rulers liked to be **patrons.** Patrons helped fund the design and construction of mosques. The main

part of a mosque is a huge hall where thousands
of people gather to pray. Often mosques have
a large dome and a **minaret,** or narrow tower
from which Muslims are called to prayer./Los
musulmantes también tuvieron muchos logros
arquitectónicos. A los gobernantes les gustaba
ser **mecenas** y ayudar a financiar el diseño y la
construcción de mezquitas. El área principal de
una mezquita es una sala enorme donde miles
de personas se reúnen para rezar. Las mezquitas
suelen tener una cúpula grande y un **minarete,**
o torre angosta, desde donde se convoca a los
musulmanes a rezar.

Muslims believe only Allah (God) can create
humans and animals or their images, so artists
did not show them in religious art. In part for
this reason, Muslim artists turned to **calligraphy.**
This decorative writing became an art form./Los
musulmanes creen que solamente Alá (Dios)
puede crear seres humanos y animales, o sus
imágenes, por lo que no son representados en
las obras de arte de carácter religioso. En parte
por este motivo, los artistas musulmanes se
dedicaron a la **caligrafía,** la escritura decorativa
que se volvió una forma de arte.

> **Underline the sentence that helps to explain why Muslim artists developed calligraphy as an art form./** Subraya la oración que explica por qué los artistas musulmanes desarrollaron la calgrafía como una forma de arte.

## CHALLENGE ACTIVITY/ACTIVIDAD AVANZADA

**Critical Thinking: Explain/Pensamiento crítico:
Explicar** Islamic culture made many advances
in science, medicine, and art that people still use
today. Choose the advancement that you think is
the most important to our modern society. Then
write a one-page paper explaining your position./
La cultura islámica hizo muchos avances en las
ciencias, la medicina y el arte que siguen vigentes
en la actualidad. Elige el avance que consideras
más importante para la sociedad moderna.
Luego, escribe un texto de una página en el
que expliques tu elección.

**DIRECTIONS/INSTRUCCIONES** Read each sentence and fill in the blank with the word in the word pair that best completes the sentence./Lee cada oración y escribe en el espacio en blanco la palabra del par de palabras que mejor la completa.

1. Decorative writing that became a Muslim art form is known as
   _____. **(minaret/calligraphy)**/La escritura decorativa
   que se convirtió en una forma de arte musulmán se conoce como
   _____. **(minarete/caligrafía)**

2. The famous Sufi poet who wrote *The Rubáiyát* was
   _____. **(Ibn Battutah/Omar Khayyám)**/El famoso poeta
   sufista que escribió *Las Rubaiyat* se llamaba _____.
   **(Ibn Battuta/Omar Kayam)**

3. People who helped sponsor the design and construction of mosques in the
   Muslim Empire were known as _____. **(patrons/Sufis)**/
   Las personas que ayudaban a patrocinar el diseño y la construcción de
   mezquitas en el Imperio musulmán eran conocidas como
   _____. **(mecenas/sufistas)**

4. A narrow tower on a mosque from which Muslims are called to pray is called
   a(n) _____. **(patron/minaret)**/Una torre angosta en una
   mezquita, desde donde se convoca a los musulmanes a rezar, se llama
   _____. **(mecenas/minarete)**

5. The great explorer who traveled to Africa, India, China, and Spain in the
   1320s was _____. **(Omar Khayyám/Ibn Battutah)**/El
   gran explorador que viajó a África, la India, China y España en la década
   de 1320 se llamaba _____. **(Omar Kayam/Ibn Battuta)**

6. A movement of Islam that is based on the belief that one must have a
   personal relationship with God is known as _____.
   **(Sufism/Calligraphy)**/El movimiento perteneciente al islam basado en la
   creencia de que las personas deben establecer una relación personal con
   Dios se llama _____. **(sufismo/caligrafía)**

# Early African Civilizations/Primeras civilizaciones de África

## Lesson/Lección 1

**MAIN IDEAS/IDEAS PRINCIPALES**

1. The landforms, water, climate, and plant life affected history in West Africa./Los accidentes geográficos, el agua, el clima y la vegetación influyeron en la historia de África occidental.

2. West Africa's resources included farmland, gold, and salt./Los recursos naturales de África occidental son las tierras de cultivo, el oro y la sal.

3. Family and religion influenced daily life in early West African society./La familia y la religión influyeron en la vida cotidiana de las primeras sociedades de África occidental.

4. Iron technology changed life in West Africa./La tecnología del hierro cambió la vida en África occidental.

# Key Terms and People/Personas y palabras clave

**rifts/fisuras** long, deep valleys formed by the movement of the earth's crust/valles extensos y profundos formados por el movimiento de la corteza terrestre

**sub-Saharan Africa/África subsahariana** Africa south of the Sahara/la parte de África ubicada al sur del Sahara

**Sahel/Sahel** a strip of land in West Africa that divides the desert from wetter areas/franja de tierra ubicada en África occidental que divide el desierto de las zonas más húmedas

**savannah/sabana** open grassland with scattered trees/pradera abierta con árboles dispersos

**rain forests/bosque tropical** moist, densely wooded areas near the equator/zonas húmedas y muy arboladas cercanas al ecuador

**kinship system/sistema de parentesco** a system of social organization based on family ties/sistema de organización social que se basa en los lazos familiares

**extended family/familia extendida** a father, mother, children, and close relatives/el padre, la madre, los hijos y los parientes cercanos

**patrilineal/patrilineal** leadership passed down from the father's family/liderazgo que se hereda de la familia del padre

**matrilineal/matrilineal** leadership passed down from the mother's family/liderazgo que se hereda de la familia de la madre

**animism/animismo** the belief that bodies of water, animals, trees, and other natural objects have spirits/creencia de que las masas de agua, los animales, los árboles y otros elementos de la naturaleza tienen espíritu

# Lesson Summary/Resumen de la lección

## LANDFORMS, WATER, CLIMATE, AND PLANT LIFE/ACCIDENTES GEOGRÁFICOS, AGUA, CLIMA Y VEGETACIÓN

Africa is the world's second-largest continent. The Sahara, a desert, stretches across North Africa. In eastern Africa, mountains extend along **rifts.** These are long, deep valleys formed by movements of the earth's crust. Large rivers cross the plains of **sub-Saharan Africa,** or Africa south of the Sahara./África es el segundo continente más grande del mundo. El Sahara, un desierto, se extiende a lo ancho del norte de África. En África oriental, las montañas se extienden a lo largo de **fisuras,** valles extensos y profundos formados por los movimientos de la corteza terrestre. Grandes ríos atraviesan las planicies del **África subsahariana,** o la parte de África ubicada al sur del Sahara.

Great civilizations grew up near the Niger River. Its regions are warm and rainfall varies, which has an impact on plant life. The southern Sahara is hot and dry. The **Sahel** divides the desert from wetter areas and has grazing animals. So does the **savannah,** or open grasslands. Near the equator are **rain forests.** These are moist, densely wooded areas with many plants and animals./Cerca del río Níger, surgieron grandes civilizaciones. Las regiones que atraviesa el río son cálidas y las precipitaciones varían, lo que afecta la vegetación. El Sahara meridional es cálido y seco. El **Sahel** divide el desierto de las zonas más húmedas; en él se pueden encontrar animales de pastoreo. Lo mismo sucede en la **sabana,** o pradera abierta. Cerca del ecuador, hay **bosques tropicales,** que son zonas húmedas y muy arboladas, con muchas plantas y animales.

> **What caused the great rift valleys of eastern Africa?/ ¿Cómo se formaron las grandes fisuras de África oriental?**
>
> _____
>
> _____

> **How has rainfall impacted plant life in the Sahel, savannah, and rain forests?/ ¿Cómo influyeron las precipitaciones en la vegetación del Sahel, la sabana y los bosques tropicales?**
>
> _____
>
> _____
>
> _____
>
> _____

## WEST AFRICA'S RESOURCES/RECURSOS DE ÁFRICA OCCIDENTAL

West Africa's farmland is a major resource. Its different climates help grow many traditional crops such as dates and medicinal kola nuts. Minerals such as gold and salt are also important resources./Uno de los principales recursos de África occidental son sus tierras de cultivo. Los diferentes climas de la zona permiten sembrar cultivos tradicionales, como los dátiles y las nueces de cola medicinales. Los minerales, como el oro y la sal, también son recursos importantes.

## FAMILIES, RELIGION, AND DAILY LIFE/ FAMILIA, RELIGIÓN Y VIDA COTIDIANA

People once were organized according to a **kinship system,** which is based on family ties. An **extended family**—a father, mother, children, and close relatives—lived in villages. Usually, leadership was hereditary. It could be **patrilineal,** or passed through the father's family. It could be **matrilineal,** or passed through the mother's family. Within the community, men hunted and farmed. Women took care of the children, farmed, and did other chores./En el pasado, las personas se organizaban según el **sistema de parentesco,** que se basa en los lazos familiares. La **familia extendida** (el padre, la madre, los hijos y los parientes cercanos) vivía en aldeas. Por lo general, el liderazgo era hereditario. Podía ser **patrilineal,** heredado de la familia del padre, o **matrilineal,** heredado de la familia de la madre. Dentro de la comunidad, los hombres cazaban y trabajaban la tierra. Las mujeres cuidaban a los hijos, trabajaban la tierra y realizaban otras tareas domésticas en el hogar.

> Underline the sentences that tell the differences between patrilineal and matrilineal./Subraya la oración que indica las diferencias entre la sociedad patrilineal y la sociedad matrilineal.

Religion was central to West African life. People believed their ancestors' spirits stayed nearby. They believed in **animism,** or that animals, trees, bodies of water, and other natural objects have spirits./La religión era un aspecto fundamental de la vida en África occidental. Las personas creían que los espíritus de sus ancestros permanecían a su alrededor. También creían en el **animismo,** o la creencia de que los animales, los árboles, las masas de agua y otros elementos de la naturaleza tienen espíritu.

> **Explain how religion was central to West African life./Explica por qué la religión era un aspecto fundamental de la vida en África occidental.**
>
> _____
> _____
> _____
> _____

## TECHNOLOGY AND CHANGE/TECNOLOGÍA Y CAMBIO

Around 500 BC, West Africans learned how to make iron tools. These tools meant they could clear land more quickly and grow more food. They had better weapons for hunting and defense. They could live in more places so the population grew./Alrededor del año 500 a. C., los habitantes de África occidental aprendieron a hacer herramientas de hierro. Con esas herramientas, podían preparar la tierra más rápido y cultivar más alimentos. Contaban con mejores armas para cazar y defenderse. Tenían la posibilidad de vivir en más lugares, por lo que la población creció.

> **Underline three effects of iron tools./Subraya tres consecuencias del desarrollo de herramientas de hierro.**

## CHALLENGE ACTIVITY/ACTIVIDAD AVANZADA

**Critical Thinking: Compare and Contrast/**
**Pensamiento crítico: Comparar y contrastar**
Write a one-page essay explaining any similarities and differences between the ways the early West Africans lived and the way you live./Escribe un ensayo de una página en el que expliques las similitudes y las diferencias entre cómo vivían los primeros habitantes de África occidental y cómo vives tú.

**DIRECTIONS/INSTRUCCIONES** Write a word that has the same meaning as the term given or a definition of the term./Escribe una palabra que tenga el mismo significado que el término dado o la definición del término.

1. animism/animismo _____

_____

2. extended family/familia extendida _____

_____

3. rain forests/bosques tropicales _____

_____

4. rifts/fisuras _____

_____

5. Sahel/Sahel _____

_____

6. savannah/sabana _____

_____

7. sub-Saharan Africa/África subsahariana _____

_____

8. kinship system/sistema de parentesco _____

_____

9. matrilineal/matrilineal _____

_____

10. patrilineal/patrilineal _____

_____

# Early African Civilizations/Primeras civilizaciones de África

**MAIN IDEAS/IDEAS PRINCIPALES**

1. Ghana grew as larger populations settled on desert trade routes./Ghana creció a medida que poblaciones cada vez mayores se asentaron en las rutas comerciales del desierto.

2. Ghana controlled trade and became wealthy./Ghana controlaba el comercio y así prosperó.

3. Through its control of trade, Ghana built an empire./Mediante su control del comercio, Ghana levantó un imperio.

4. Ghana's decline was caused by attacking invaders, overgrazing, and the loss of trade./La decadencia de Ghana se produjo por el ataque de pueblos invasores, el exceso de pastoreo y la pérdida del comercio.

# Key Terms and People/Personas y palabras clave

**silent barter/trueque silencioso** a process in which people exchange goods without ever contacting each other directly/proceso por el cual las personas intercambian bienes sin entrar en contacto directo

**income/ingreso** taxes, tributes, and gold/impuestos, tributos y oro

**Tunka Manin/Tunka Manin** Ghana's king who ruled the empire at the height of its power/rey de Ghana que gobernó el imperio en la época de su máximo esplendor

# Lesson Summary/Resumen de la lección

## AN EMPIRE AT THE DESERT'S EDGE/UN IMPERIO A ORILLAS DEL DESIERTO

Ghana (GAH-nuh), a West African empire, profited from Saharan trade because it gained control of the trade routes. This made it a powerful state./Ghana, un imperio de África occidental, se enriqueció con el comercio sahariano debido a que logró el control de las rutas comerciales. Así se convirtió en un estado poderoso.

Ghana lay between the Niger and Senegal rivers in sub-Saharan Africa, northwest of the nation now called Ghana. Historians think the first people were farmers. Starting around 300, these farmers were threatened by nomadic herders. The herders wanted the water and pastures. For protection, small groups banded together. These

> **How did Ghana become powerful?/¿Cómo obtuvo Ghana su poder?**
>
> _____
> _____
> _____
> _____

groups grew stronger with the introduction of
farming tools and weapons made of iron./Ghana
estaba situada entre los ríos Níger y Senegal en el
África subsahariana, al noroeste del país que hoy
en día se llama Ghana. Los historiadores creen
que los primeros habitantes eran agricultores.
A partir del año 300 aproximadamente, los
agricultores se vieron amenazados por pastores
nómadas que querían adueñarse del agua y las
pasturas. Para protegerse, los agricultores se
unieron en grupos pequeños. Estos grupos se
volvieron más fuertes con la introducción de
herramientas agrícolas y armas de hierro.

## TRADE IN GHANA AND WEST AFRICA/COMERCIO EN GHANA Y ÁFRICA OCCIDENTAL

Ghana lay between the desert and the forests.
These were areas rich with gold and salt. The
gold and salt trade sometimes followed a **silent
barter** process. In this process, people exchange
goods without contacting each other directly.
This kept business peaceful and the location
of gold mines secret. As gold and salt trade
increased, Ghana's rulers gained power.
Their armies took control of the trade routes./
Ghana se encontraba entre el desierto y las selvas.
Estas zonas eran ricas en oro y sal. El comercio
de oro y sal a veces se realizaba mediante un
proceso de **trueque silencioso** en el cual las
personas intercambian bienes sin entrar en
contacto directo. De este modo, el comercio era
pacífico y la ubicación de las minas de oro se
mantenía en secreto. A medida que el comercio
de oro y sal creció, los gobernantes de Ghana se
volvieron más poderosos. Sus ejércitos tomaron
el control de las rutas comerciales.

> Underline the sentence that describes what was found in the desert and forest areas./Subraya la oración que describe lo que había en el desierto y las selvas.

Ghana was influenced by Islam in its written language, currency, architecture, and business practices. Muslims were government officials too./Ghana recibió la influencia del islam en el lenguaje escrito, la moneda, la arquitectura y las prácticas comerciales. Los musulmanes también eran funcionarios del gobierno.

> **How was Ghana influenced by Islam?/¿Qué influencia tuvo el Islam en Ghana?**
>
> _____
>
> _____
>
> _____

## GHANA BUILDS AN EMPIRE/GHANA LEVANTA UN IMPERIO

By 800, Ghana was firmly in control of West Africa's trade routes. As a result, trade became safer and Ghana's influence increased. Traders and Ghana's people were charged a tax. Conquered tribes paid tribute. The kings made gold their property. Taxes, tributes, and gold were **income.**/Para el año 800, Ghana tenía el control absoluto de las rutas comerciales de África occidental. En consecuencia, el comercio se volvió más seguro y la influencia de Ghana creció. A los comerciantes y los habitantes de Ghana se les cobraba un impuesto. Las tribus conquistadas pagaban un tributo. Los reyes se apropiaron del oro. Los impuestos, los tributos y el oro eran **ingresos.**

The kings built a powerful army and conquered other tribes. However, Ghana's kings allowed former rulers to keep their own power. They acted as governors of their territories. Ghana reached its peak under **Tunka Manin** (TOOHN-kah MAH-nin). He had a splendid court with many luxuries./Los reyes de Ghana formaron un ejército poderoso y conquistaron otras tribus. No obstante, permitían a los gobernantes vencidos conservar su poder regional. Estos actuaban como gobernadores de sus territorios. Ghana alcanzó su máximo esplendor durante el gobierno de **Tunka Manin,** quien tenía una corte majestuosa repleta de lujos.

## GHANA'S DECLINE/DECADENCIA DE GHANA

By the end of the 1200s, Ghana had collapsed. Three major factors contributed to its decline. A Muslim group called the Almoravids attacked and tried to force Ghana's leaders to convert to Islam. The attacks weakened the empire. Also, the Almoravids brought herds of animals with them. Their animals overgrazed and ruined the farmland. Many farmers left. At around the same time, internal rebellion occurred. People took over trade routes. However, they could not keep order. Ghana was attacked and defeated by a neighbor. The empire fell apart./Hacia finales del siglo 13, Ghana colapsó. Fueron tres los factores principales que contribuyeron a su decadencia. Un grupo de musulmanes llamados almorávides atacaron Ghana e intentaron convertir a sus gobernantes al islam. Los ataques debilitaron el imperio. Además, los almorávides llevaban manadas de animales con ellos. El exceso de pastoreo arruinó las tierras de cultivo. Muchos agricultores se marcharon. En la misma época, se produjeron rebeliones internas. Los pueblos se apropiaron de las rutas comerciales, pero no pudieron mantener el orden. Ghana fue atacada y derrotada por un pueblo vecino, y el imperio se derrumbó.

> **Who owned gold in Ghana?/¿Quiénes eran los dueños del oro en Ghana?**
> _____

> **List two reasons for the decline of Ghana's empire./Enumera dos motivos que provocaron la decadencia del Imperio de Ghana.**
> _____
> _____
> _____
> _____
> _____
> _____
> _____
> _____
> _____
> _____

## CHALLENGE ACTIVITY/ACTIVIDAD AVANZADA

**Critical Thinking: Analyze/Pensamiento crítico: Analizar** Imagine that you are a gold or salt trader. Work with your classmates to recreate the silent barter system. Then write a one-page paper detailing the advantages and disadvantages of silent barter./Imagina que eres comerciante de oro o sal. Trabaja con tus compañeros para recrear el sistema de trueque silencioso. Luego, escribe un ensayo de una página en el que detalles las ventajas y desventajas del trueque silencioso.

**DIRECTIONS/INSTRUCCIONES** Use the vocabulary words **silent barter, income,** and **Tunka Manin** to write a letter that relates to the section./Usa las palabras de vocabulario **trueque silencioso, ingreso** y **Tunka Manin** para escribir una carta relacionada con esta lección.

_____

_____

_____

_____

_____

_____

_____

_____

_____

_____

_____

_____

_____

_____

_____

_____

_____

# Early African Civilizations/Primeras civilizaciones de África

## Lesson/Lección 3

**MAIN IDEAS/IDEAS PRINCIPALES**
1. A ruler named Sundiata made Mali into an empire./Un gobernante llamado Sundiata convirtió a Malí en imperio.
2. Mali reached its height under the ruler Mansa Musa./Malí alcanzó su máximo esplendor durante el gobierno de Mansa Musa.
3. Mali fell to invaders in the late 1,400s./Malí sucumbió a los invasores a finales del siglo 15.
4. Songhai regained power from Mali./Songhai recuperó el control de Malí.
5. Askia the Great ruled Songhai as an Islamic empire./Askia el Grande gobernó Songhai como un imperio islámico.
6. Songhai fell to Moroccan invaders, ending the great era of West African empires./Songhai sucumbió a invasores marroquíes, lo que puso fin a la era de los grandes imperios de África occidental.

# Key Terms and People/Personas y palabras clave

**Sundiata/Sundiata** ruler that led the Mali Empire's rise to power/gobernante que logró el ascenso al poder del Imperio de Malí

**Mansa Musa/Mansa Musa** Muslim king who ruled the Mali Empire at the height of its power and spread Islam through a large part of Africa/rey musulmán que gobernó el Imperio de Malí en su época de máximo esplendor y difundió el islam por gran parte de África

**Sunni Ali/Sonni Alí** first leader of Songhai, the last of the great West African empires/primer líder de Songhai, el último de los grandes imperios de África occidental

**Askia the Great/Askia el Grande** Muslim ruler who led Songhai to the height of its power/gobernante musulmán que llevó a Songhai a su máximo poderío

# Lesson Summary/Resumen de la lección

### SUNDIATA MAKES MALI AN EMPIRE/SUNDIATA CONVIERTE A MALÍ EN UN IMPERIO

Like Ghana, Mali lay along the upper Niger River. Mali's location on the Niger allowed its people to control trade on the river. Mali's rise to power began under its first strong leader, **Sundiata.**/Al igual que Ghana, Malí estaba ubicado a orillas del alto Níger. Esto permitía a sus habitantes

> **What river flowed through both Ghana and Mali?/**
> **¿Qué río atravesaba Ghana y Malí?**
>
> _____
> _____

mantener el control comercial del río. El ascenso al poder de Malí comenzó durante el gobierno de su primer líder fuerte, **Sundiata.**

A cruel ruler conquered Mali when Sundiata was a boy. When Sundiata grew older, he built an army and won Mali's independence. He conquered nearby kingdoms, including Ghana. He took over the salt and gold trades and religious and political authority held by local leaders./Un gobernante despiadado conquistó Malí cuando Sundiata era niño. Cuando creció, Sundiata formó un ejército y logró la independencia de Malí. Conquistó reinos cercanos (incluido el de Ghana) y se apropió del comercio de la sal y el oro, y de la autoridad política y religiosa de los líderes locales.

## MANSA MUSA/MANSA MUSA

Mali's most famous ruler was a Muslim named **Mansa Musa.** He made Mali wealthy and powerful and ruled for about 25 years. He captured trading cities, including Timbuktu, and made the Islamic world aware of Mali on his pilgrimage to Mecca./El gobernante más famoso de Malí fue un musulmán llamado **Mansa Musa.** Convirtió a Malí en un imperio rico y poderoso y gobernó por unos 25 años. Capturó ciudades comerciales, como Tombuctú, y advirtió al mundo islámico sobre la existencia de Malí durante su peregrinación a La Meca.

Mansa Musa stressed the importance of learning Arabic in order to read the Qur'an. He spread Islam through West Africa by building mosques in cities./Mansa Musa enfatizó la importancia de aprender árabe para leer el Corán. Difundió el islam en África occidental mediante la construcción de mezquitas en las ciudades.

> **Why did Mansa Musa stress the importance of learning Arabic?/¿Por qué Mansa Musa enfatizó la importancia de aprender árabe?**
>
> _____
>
> _____
>
> _____

## THE FALL OF MALI/LA CAÍDA DE MALÍ

Mali's success depended on strong leaders, but after he died, poor leadership weakened the empire. Invaders destroyed Timbuktu's schools and mosques. Rebel groups seized the city. By 1500, nearly all of the empire's lands were lost./ El éxito de Malí dependía de los líderes fuertes, pero tras la muerte de Mansa Musa, la falta de liderazgo debilitó el imperio. Los invasores destruyeron las escuelas y mezquitas de Tombuctú. Grupos rebeldes tomaron la ciudad. Hacia el siglo 16, casi todas las tierras del imperio se habían perdido.

## THE SONGHAI BUILD AN EMPIRE/LOS SONGHAI LEVANTAN UN IMPERIO

During the 1300s, Songhai lands were part of the Mali Empire. As Mali weakened, the Songhai leader, **Sunni Ali,** worked to unify, strengthen, and enlarge the empire. He took part in both Muslim and local religions to build peace between religions./Durante el siglo 14, las tierras songhai formaban parte del Imperio de Malí. A medida que Malí se debilitaba, el líder songhai **Sonni Alí** trabajaba para unificar, fortalecer y expandir el imperio. Profesaba tanto el islam como las religiones locales para fomentar la paz entre las religiones.

## ASKIA THE GREAT/ASKIA EL GRANDE

After Sunni Ali's death, Sunni Baru became ruler. Unlike his father and most of the people, he was not Muslim. Fearing that if Sunni Baru did not support Islam they would lose trade and power, the people rebelled. The leader of the rebellion became known as **Askia the Great.** During his reign, Muslim culture and education thrived./Tras la muerte de Sonni Alí, Sonni Baro

> **Why was Sunni Baru overthrown?/¿Por qué fue derrocado Sonni Baro?**
>
> _____
> _____
> _____
> _____
> _____
> _____

asumió el poder. A diferencia de su padre y de la mayoría del pueblo, no era musulmán. Por temor a perder el comercio y el poder si Sonni Baru no apoyaba el islam, el pueblo se rebeló. El líder de la rebelión fue conocido como **Askia el Grande.** Durante su reinado, prosperaron la cultura y la educación musulmanas.

## SONGHAI FALLS TO MOROCCO/SONGHAI SUCUMBE ANTE MARRUECOS

Morocco invaded Songhai so it could control the salt mines and gold trade. It used a weapon that was an early form of a gun and destroyed Timbuktu and other cities. Other fighters carried various other weapons, too. Songhai never recovered from losing its cities and its overland trade declined. The period of great West African empires ended./Marruecos invadió Songhai para obtener el control de las minas de sal y el comercio del oro. Utilizó una versión primitiva de un arma de fuego y destruyó Tombuctú y otras ciudades. Otros guerreros también llevaban otros tipos de armas. Songhai nunca se recuperó de la pérdida de sus ciudades, y su comercio terrestre decayó. Así finalizó el período de los grandes imperios de África occidental.

> Underline the sentence that explains why Morocco was successful in it invasion of Songhai./Subraya las oraciones que explican por qué Marruecos logró derrotar a Songhai.

## CHALLENGE ACTIVITY/ACTIVIDAD AVANZADA
**Critical Thinking: Summarize/Pensamiento crítico: Resumir** You are a reporter who is unfamiliar with Africa. You meet a Mali or Songhai ruler. Write an article about this person./Eres un periodista que no sabe mucho sobre África y te presentan a un gobernante de Malí o Songhai. Escribe un artículo sobre esta persona.

| Askia the Great/Askia el Grande | Mansa Musa/ Mansa Musa | Sundiata/Sundiata |
|---|---|---|
| Sunni Ali/Sonni Alí | | |

**DIRECTIONS/INSTRUCCIONES** Answer each question by writing a sentence that contains at least one name from the word bank./ Responde cada pregunta con una oración que contenga al menos un nombre del banco de palabras.

1. Who was the leader of the Songhai people that rebelled against the king because the people feared that if the king did not support Islam they would lose their trade with Muslim lands?/¿Quién fue el líder del pueblo songhai que se rebeló contra el rey porque el pueblo temía que si el rey no apoyaba el islam, perderían el comercio con las tierras musulmanas?

   _____

   _____

2. Mali's rise to power began under what ruler?/¿Bajo el mando de qué gobernante se produjo el ascenso al poder de Malí?

   _____

   _____

3. As the Songhai gained in wealth, the Songhai people expanded their territory and built an empire under which ruler?/A medida que los songhai aumentaban su riqueza, el pueblo songhai expandió su territorio y construyó un imperio. ¿Bajo el mando de qué gobernante ocurrió esto?

   _____

   _____

   _____

4. Who was Mali's most famous ruler?/¿Quién fue el gobernante más famoso de Malí?

   _____

   _____

   _____

# Early African Civilizations/Primeras civilizaciones de África

## Lesson/Lección 4

**MAIN IDEAS/IDEAS PRINCIPALES**

1. Storytellers helped maintain the oral history of the cultures of West Africa./Los narradores ayudaron a preservar la historia oral de las culturas de África occidental.

2. Visitors to West Africa from other lands wrote histories and descriptions of what they saw there./Los viajeros que llegaron a África occidental desde otras tierras escribieron historias y descripciones de lo que vieron allí.

3. Traditionally, West Africans have valued the arts./Por tradición, los habitantes de África occidental valoran las artes.

## Key Terms and People/Personas y palabras clave

**oral history/historia oral** a spoken record of past events/registro hablado de sucesos ocurridos en el pasado

**griots/griots** West African storytellers/narradores de África occidental

**proverbs/proverbios** short sayings of wisdom or truth/refranes breves que expresan sabiduría o una verdad

**kente/kente** a hand-woven, brightly colored fabric/tela muy colorida tejida a mano

## Lesson Summary/Resumen de la lección

### STORYTELLERS MAINTAIN ORAL HISTORY/
### NARRADORES PRESERVAN LA HISTORIA ORAL

Although cities like Timbuktu and Djenné were known for their universities and libraries, writing was not common in West Africa. None of the major early West African civilizations developed a written language. Arabic was the only written language used. However, West Africans passed along information about their civilization through **oral history,** a spoken record of past events./Aunque las ciudades de Tombuctú y Djenné eran famosas por sus universidades y bibliotecas, la escritura no era común en África occidental. Ninguna de las primeras civilizaciones importantes de esa región desarrolló un lenguaje escrito. El árabe era el

> Underline the sentence that tells about a similarity among major early West African civilizations./Subraya la oración que menciona una similitud entre las primeras civilizaciones importantes de África occidental.

único idioma escrito que usaban. Sin embargo,
los habitantes de África occidental transmitían
información sobre su civilización a través de la
**historia oral,** un registro hablado de los sucesos
ocurridos en el pasado.

West Africa's history was entrusted to
storytellers called **griots.** Griots' stories were
entertaining and informative. Some acted out
past events like scenes in a play. Griots also told
**proverbs,** or short sayings of wisdom or truth.
Griots had to memorize hundreds of names and
events. However, some griots confused names
and events in their heads, so some stories became
distorted. Still, the griots' stories tell a lot about
life in West African empires./La historia de
África occidental estuvo a cargo de narradores
llamados **griots.** Las historias que contaban los
griots eran entretenidas e informativas. Algunos
griots actuaban los sucesos del pasado como si
fueran escenas de una obra de teatro. También
decían **proverbios,** o refranes breves que expresan
sabiduría o una verdad. Sin embargo, como
debían memorizar cientos de nombres y sucesos,
a veces confundían nombres o fechas, por lo que
algunos relatos se distorsionaron. De todos
modos, las historias de los griots aportan mucha
información sobre la vida en los imperios de
África occidental.

Some griot poems are epics, long poems about
kingdoms and heroes. Many of these poems
were collected in the *Dausi* and the *Sundiata.*
The *Dausi* tells the history of Ghana, but it also
includes myths and legends. The *Sundiata* tells
the story of Mali's first ruler. A conqueror killed
his family, but the boy was spared because he
was sick. He grew up to be a great warrior who
overthrew the conqueror./Algunos de los poemas
de los griots son epopeyas, poemas extensos

> **Why might the history of the griots not be perfectly accurate?/¿Por qué es posible que las historias de los griots no sean del todo precisas?**
>
> _____
>
> _____
>
> _____

sobre reinos y héroes. Muchos de estos poemas fueron recopilados en el *Dausi* y el *Sundiata*. El *Dausi* narra la historia de Ghana, pero también contiene mitos y leyendas. El *Sundiata* narra la historia del primer gobernante de Malí: un conquistador asesinó a su familia, pero él se salvó porque era un niño enfermo. De grande, se convirtió en un gran guerrero que derrocó al conquistador.

## VISITORS WRITE HISTORIES/VIAJEROS ESCRIBEN HISTORIAS

Although the West Africans left no written histories, visitors from other parts of the world wrote about the region. Much of what we know about early West Africa comes from the writings of travelers and scholars from Muslim lands such as Spain and Arabia. Arab scholar al-Masudi described West Africa's geography, customs, history, and scientific achievements. Ibn Battutah was the most famous visitor to write about West Africa. He described the political and cultural lives of West Africans./A pesar de que los habitantes de África occidental no dejaron una historia escrita, viajeros de otras partes del mundo escribieron sobre la región. Gran parte de lo que sabemos sobre las primeras civilizaciones de África occidental proviene de escritos de viajeros y eruditos que llegaban de tierras musulmanas como España y Arabia. El erudito árabe al-Masudi describió la geografía, las costumbres, la historia y los avances científicos de África occidental. Ibn Battutah fue el viajero más famoso que escribió sobre África occidental. Describió la vida política y cultural del pueblo de esta región.

> **What role did some visitors play in educating the world about early West Africa?/** ¿Qué rol tuvieron los viajeros en el conocimiento que se tiene de las primeras civilizaciones de África occidental en el resto del mundo?
>
> _____
> _____
> _____
> _____
> _____
> _____

## WEST AFRICANS VALUE ARTS/LOS HABITANTES DE ÁFRICA OCCIDENTAL VALORAN LAS ARTES

West Africans valued the arts, including sculpture, mask making, cloth making, music, and dance. West African artists made statues and carvings from wood, brass, clay, ivory, stone, and other materials. Some West African sculpture inspired European artists such as Henri Matisse and Pablo Picasso./Los habitantes de África occidental valoraban las artes, entre ellas la escultura, la fabricación de máscaras, la confección de telas, la música y la danza. Los artistas de África occidental hacían estatuas y esculturas en madera, latón, arcilla, marfil, piedra y otros materiales. Parte de la escultura de África occidental sirvió de inspiración a artistas europeos, como Henri Matisse y Pablo Picasso.

> **Underline the names of European artists inspired by West African sculptors./** Subraya los nombres de artistas europeos que se inspiraron en los escultores de África occidental.

West Africans carved elaborate masks of wood. They show the faces of animals and were worn during rituals. Also, African societies were famous for the cloth they wore. The most famous is **kente,** a hand-woven, brightly colored fabric. Kings and queens wore kente garments for special occasions./ Los habitantes de África occidental tallaban elaboradas máscaras de madera que mostraban caras de animales y se usaban durante rituales. Además, las sociedades africanas eran famosas por las telas que vestían. La más famosa es el **kente,** una tela muy colorida tejida a mano que los reyes y las reinas vestían en ocasiones especiales.

> **List three ways in which music and dance had a place in West African culture./**Enumera tres maneras en que la música y la danza cumplieron un papel importante en la cultura de África occidental.
>
> _____
> _____
> _____

In many West African societies, music and dance were important too. Singing and dancing entertained, but they also helped people honor their history and were central to many celebrations./En muchas sociedades de África occidental, la música y la danza también eran muy importantes. El canto y la danza, además de entretener, permitían al pueblo celebrar su historia y eran parte fundamental de muchas celebraciones.

## CHALLENGE ACTIVITY/ACTIVIDAD AVANZADA
### Critical Thinking: Compare and Contrast/
**Pensamiento crítico: Comparar y contrastar** People know about West Africa from oral histories or visitors' written accounts. Write a one-page paper that compares and contrasts the accuracy of these resources./Lo que sabemos sobre África occidental proviene de historias orales y de registros escritos de viajeros. Escribe un ensayo de una página en el que compares y contrastes la precisión de estas fuentes.

**DIRECTIONS/INSTRUCCIONES** Read each sentence and fill in the blank with the word in the word pair that best completes the sentence./Lee cada oración y escribe en el espacio en blanco la palabra del par de palabras que mejor la completa.

1. West African storytellers are known as _____.
   **(griots/proverbs)**/Los narradores de África occidental se conocen como _____. **(griots/proverbios)**

2. A hand-woven, brightly colored fabric is _____.
   **(griot/kente)**/El _____ es una tela colorida tejida a mano. **(griot/kente)**

3. A spoken record of past events is a(n) _____.
   **(kente/oral history)**/El registro hablado de un suceso ocurrido en el pasado se denomina _____. **(kente/historia oral)**

4. A short saying of wisdom or truth is a(n) _____.
   **(proverb/oral history)**/Un refrán breve que expresa sabiduría o una verdad es _____. **(un proverbio/una historia oral)**

**DIRECTIONS/INSTRUCCIONES** Look at each set of four vocabulary terms. On the line provided, write the letter of the term that does not relate to the others./Observa cada conjunto de cuatro términos de vocabulario. En el espacio en blanco, escribe la letra del término que no tiene relación con los demás.

_____ 5. a. spoken record/registro hablado
           b. oral history/historia oral
           c. griots/griots
           d. kente/kente

_____ 6. a. kente/kente
           b. proverbs/proverbios
           c. hand-woven/tejido a mano
           d. bright colors/colorido

# Early African Civilizations/Primeras civilizaciones de África

## Lesson/Lección 5

**MAIN IDEAS/IDEAS PRINCIPALES**

1. African customs blended with Christian religious beliefs to create a new form of Christianity in Ethiopia./Las costumbres africanas se mezclaron con las creencias religiosas cristianas y dieron lugar a una nueva forma de cristianismo en Etiopía.

2. Some historians think the migration of the Bantu caused one of the most significant cultural transformations in African history./Algunos historiadores sostienen que la migración de los bantú provocó una de las transformaciones culturales más importantes de la historia africana.

3. Sub-Saharan Africans and Muslim merchants, among others, traded precious metals and cattle./Los africanos subsaharianos y los comerciantes musulmanes, entre otros, comerciaban metales preciosos y ganado.

# Key Terms and People/Personas y palabras clave

**Ethiopia/Etiopía** powerful East African kingdom formed by the descendants of Aksum/reino poderoso de África oriental formado por los descendientes de Aksum

**Coptic Christianity/cristianismo copto** form of Christianity that blends Christian teaching with African customs; name comes from Arabic word for "Egyptian"/ forma de cristianismo que combina las enseñanzas cristianas con las costumbres africanas; el nombre proviene de la palabra árabe que significa "egipcio"

**Bantu/bantú** name for 400 ethnic groups that come from the eastern, central, and southern regions of Africa; means "people" in many native languages/nombre que designa 400 grupos étnicos de las regiones este, central y sur de África; significa "pueblo" en muchos idiomas nativos

**Great Zimbabwe/Gran Zimbabue** a Bantu kingdom founded by the Shona in about AD 1000; name means "stone houses"/reino bantú fundado por los shonas alrededor del año 1000 d. C.; el nombre significa "casas de piedra"

**Swahili/suajili** blended African-Arab culture common in East Africa/cultura que combina las culturas africana y árabe, común en África oriental

# Lesson Summary/Resumen de la lección

## THE ETHIOPIAN KINGDOM/EL REINO DE ETIOPÍA

**Ethiopia** was an East African kingdom that formed at the same time that Ghana declined and Mali began growing in importance. The descendants of Aksum created Ethiopia. By 1150, it had become one of Africa's most powerful kingdoms./**Etiopía** fue un reino de África oriental que se formó al mismo tiempo que ocurría la decadencia de Ghana y el crecimiento de Malí. Fue fundado por los descendientes de Aksum. Hacia 1150, se había convertido en uno de los reinos más importantes de África.

> **By 1150, what had happened to Ethiopia?/ Para 1150, ¿qué había sucedido con Etiopía?**
> _____
> _____
> _____

King Lalibela was Ethiopia's most famous ruler. He ruled in the 1200s and had 11 Christian churches built during that time. They were carved into solid rock, and many still stand today./El gobernante más reconocido de Etiopía fue el rey Lalibela, quien gobernó en el siglo 13. Mandó a construir 11 iglesias cristianas que fueron talladas en piedra maciza; muchas siguen en pie hoy día.

Most Ethiopians believed in Christian teachings and African customs. These two things blended together to form **Coptic Christianity.** Christianity made Ethiopia different from its neighbors because most of them were Muslim./La mayoría de los etíopes seguían las enseñanzas cristianas y las costumbres africanas. Esta combinación dio origen al **cristianismo copto.** El cristianismo diferenció a Etiopía de sus vecinos, pues la mayoría de ellos eran musulmanes.

> **What made Ethiopia different from its neighbors?/¿Qué diferenciaba a Etiopía de sus vecinos?**
> _____

## THE BANTU MIGRATION AND GREAT ZIMBABWE/ LA MIGRACIÓN BANTÚ Y EL GRAN ZIMBABUE

No one is certain why the **Bantu** migrated. It might have been because the Sahara was becoming a desert. Maybe the Bantu needed new crops for food. Historians think the way these ethnic groups moved caused a great cultural change in Africa./ Nadie sabe con certeza por qué migraron los pueblos de origen **bantú.** Quizás haya sido porque el Sahara se estaba convirtiendo en un desierto

> **Underline two reasons that might explain why the Bantu migrated./Subraya dos motivos que puedan explicar por qué migraron los bantúes.**

o porque necesitaban nuevos cultivos para
alimentarse. Los historiadores piensan que el
modo en que se desplazaron estos grupos étnicos
provocó un gran cambio cultural en África.

Most Bantu were farmers or herders who
raised cattle. They needed pasture where they
could raise animals and fields for their crops. By
about AD 300, the Bantu had settled much of
Africa that was south of the Sahara./La mayoría
de los bantúes eran agricultores o pastores que
criaban ganado. Necesitaban pasturas para el
ganado y campos para los cultivos. Alrededor del
año 300 d. C., los bantúes ya habían poblado
gran parte del África subsahariana.

One Bantu ethnic group called the Shona
founded the kingdom of **Great Zimbabwe.** No
written records exist about it, but archeologists
have found three sets of ruins that are the
remains of granite structures. There are many
theories about how the structures were used
and why they might have been built. However,
scholars and experts disagree on these ideas./Los
shonas, un grupo étnico bantú, fundaron el reino
de **Gran Zimbabue.** No hay registros escritos de
este reino, pero los arqueólogos han hallado tres
conjuntos de ruinas formadas por estructuras de
granito. Existen muchas teorías sobre cómo se
usaban las estructuras y por qué se construyeron,
pero los académicos y los expertos no han
llegado a un consenso.

> Why do scholars and experts only have ideas and theories about Great Zimbabwe?/¿Por qué los académicos y los expertos apenas tienen ideas y teorías sobre Gran Zimbabue?
>
> _____
>
> _____

## SUB-SAHARAN TRADE/COMERCIO SUBSAHARIANO

Trade was important to the Bantu. They traded
iron tips for weapons to get plants or wild game
from hunter-gatherers. Based on artifacts they
have found, archaeologists know that Great
Zimbabwe was also a trading city./El comercio
era importante para los bantúes. Intercambiaban

puntas de hierro para las armas por plantas o presas de los cazadores y recolectores. Gracias a los artefactos encontrados, los arqueólogos saben que Gran Zimbabue fue también una ciudad comercial.

Cities in East Africa became trading centers for resources like copper and goods like coffee. Muslim traders lived in this area because it was an easy place to do their work, and they made lots of money. Muslim communities grew. **Swahili,** a culture that blended elements of African and Arab life, also developed in East Africa./Las ciudades de África oriental se convirtieron en centros comerciales donde circulaban recursos como el cobre y bienes como el café. Los comerciantes musulmanes vivían en esta región porque era un lugar donde se les hacía fácil realizar su trabajo y ganaban mucho dinero. Las comunidades musulmanas crecieron. El **suajili,** una cultura que combina elementos de la vida africana y la vida árabe, también se desarrolló en África oriental.

> **Who lived in East Africa because it was an easy place to do work and make money?/¿Quiénes vivían en África oriental porque les resultaba fácil trabajar allí y ganar dinero?**
>
> _____
>
> _____

## CHALLENGE ACTIVITY/ACTIVIDAD AVANZADA

**Critical Thinking: Analyze/Pensamiento crítico: Analizar**
Use the library or Internet to research a tradition in Swahili life or Coptic Christianity. Then write a short essay that explains how the tradition shows that different cultures or ideas have blended./Usa la biblioteca o la Internet para investigar una tradición de la vida suajili o del cristianismo copto. Luego escribe un ensayo breve en el que expliques de qué manera la tradición demuestra la combinación de diferentes culturas o ideas.

**DIRECTIONS/INSTRUCCIONES** On the line before each statement, write **T** if the statement is true and **F** if the statement is false. If the statement is false, change the underlined term to make the sentence true. Then write the correct term on the line after the sentence./En la línea que precede a cada enunciado, escribe **V** si el enunciado es verdadero y **F** si es falso. Si el enunciado es falso, cambia el término subrayado para que el enunciado sea verdadero. Luego escribe el término correcto en la línea que sigue al enunciado.

_____ 1. <u>Bantu</u> was an East African kingdom created by the descendants of Aksum./<u>Bantú</u> fue un reino de África oriental fundado por los descendientes de Aksum.

_____

_____ 2. The name of <u>Coptic Christianity</u> comes from the Arabic word for "Egyptian."/El nombre <u>cristianismo copto</u> proviene de la palabra árabe que significa "egipcio".

_____

_____ 3. The Shona founded a kingdom called <u>Ethiopia</u> in about AD 1000./ Los shonas fundaron un reino llamado <u>Etiopía</u> alrededor del año 1000 d. C.

_____

_____ 4. <u>Great Zimbabwe</u> is the name for 400 ethnic groups that come from the eastern, central, and southern regions of Africa./<u>Gran Zimbabue</u> es el nombre que denomina a 400 grupos étnicos que provienen de las regiones este, central y sur de África.

_____

_____ 5. Elements of African and Arab culture are blended together in <u>Swahili</u>./ <u>El suajili</u> combina elementos de las culturas africana y árabe.

_____

**DIRECTIONS/INSTRUCCIONES** Look at each set of vocabulary terms. On the line provided, write the letter of the term that does not relate to the others./Observa cada conjunto de términos de vocabulario. En el espacio en blanco, escribe la letra del término que no tiene relación con los demás.

_____ 6. a. Ethiopia/Etiopía
        b. Swahili/suajili
        c. Coptic Christianity/cristianismo copto

_____ 7. a. Aksum/Aksum
        b. Bantu/bantú
        c. Great Zimbabwe/Gran Zimbabue

## Later Chinese Dynasties/Las últimas dinastías chinas

**MAIN IDEAS/IDEAS PRINCIPALES**

1. The Period of Disunion was a time of war and disorder that followed the end of the Han dynasty./El Período de Desunión fue una época de guerras y desorden tras la caída de la dinastía Han.

2. China was reunified under the Sui, Tang, and Song dynasties./China fue reunificada bajo las dinastías Sui, Tang y Song.

3. The Age of Buddhism saw major religious changes in China./Durante la era del budismo se produjeron importantes cambios religiosos en China.

## Key Terms and People/Personas y palabras clave

**Period of Disunion/Período de Desunión** era following the fall of the Han dynasty during which China was split into several competing kingdoms/período en el que China quedó dividida en varios reinos que competían entre sí, tras la caída de la dinastía Han

**Grand Canal/Gran Canal** waterway begun by the Sui dynasty that linked northern and southern China/vía acuática que comenzó a construir la dinastía Sui para conectar el norte y el sur de China

**Empress Wu/emperatriz Wu** Tang ruler whose methods were sometimes vicious, but whose reign was stable and prosperous/gobernante de la dinastía Tang; sus métodos a veces eran despiadados, pero su reinado fue estable y próspero

## Lesson Summary/Resumen de la lección

### THE PERIOD OF DISUNION/PERÍODO DE DESUNIÓN

After the Han dynasty collapsed in 220, China was split into several competing kingdoms, each ruled by military leaders. This time is called the **Period of Disunion.** The era lasted for more than 350 years, from 220 to 589. During this period, nomadic tribes settled in northern China, and many northern Chinese moved south. These movements resulted in blended cultures in both north and south China./Tras la caída de la dinastía Han en 220, China quedó dividida en varios reinos que competían entre sí y estaban gobernados por líderes militares. Esa época se conoce como **Período de Desunión** y duró más de 350 años, desde 220 hasta 589. Durante ese

> **What was the Period of Disunion?/¿Qué fue el Período de Desunión?**
>
> _____
>
> _____
>
> _____
>
> _____

período, hubo tribus nómadas que se establecieron en el norte de China, y muchos chinos del norte se trasladaron al sur. A raíz de esos movimientos, se produjo una mezcla de culturas tanto en el norte como en el sur de China.

## THE SUI, TANG, AND SONG/DINASTÍAS SUI, TANG Y SONG

China then reunified. Under the Sui, Tang, and Song dynasties, China remained a unified nation for almost 700 years./Luego, China se reunificó. Bajo las dinastías Sui, Tang y Song, China permaneció unificada durante casi 700 años.

> Who was the first Sui ruler?/ ¿Quién fue el primer gobernante de la dinastía Sui?
> _____

The Sui (SWAY) dynasty was established by a northern leader called Yang Jian (YANG jee-en). In 589, he led his army to conquer the south and reunified China. The Sui began the **Grand Canal** to link northern and southern China. In 618, the Tang dynasty replaced the Sui. The Tang ruled China for nearly 300 years. During this period, Chinese power and influence reached most of eastern Asia, as well as much of Central Asia./ La dinastía Sui fue instaurada por un líder del norte llamado Yang Jiang, que en 589 dirigió a su ejército para conquistar el sur y reunificar China. Durante la dinastía Sui se comenzó a construir el **Gran Canal** para conectar el norte y el sur de China. En 618, la dinastía Tang sucedió a la Sui. La dinastía Tang gobernó China durante casi 300 años. Durante ese período, el poder y la influencia de China alcanzaron la mayor parte del este de Asia, así como gran parte de Asia central.

> How many years did the Sui dynasty last?/¿Cuántos años duró la dinastía Sui?
> _____

Historians view the Tang dynasty as a golden age of Chinese civilization. One Tang leader named Taizong (TY-tzoong) conquered most of Central Asia, reformed the military, and created law codes. In the reign of Xuanzong (SHOO-an-tzoong), culture flourished and many of China's finest poets wrote. **Empress Wu,** the only woman

> Circle the names of three important Tang rulers./ Encierra en un círculo los nombres de tres gobernantes importantes de la dinastía Tang.

to rule China, ruled with an iron first, but
she kept China stable and prosperous./Los
historiadores consideran a la dinastía Tang como
la época de oro de la civilización china. Un líder
de la dinastía Tang llamado Taizong conquistó
la mayor parte de Asia central, reformó el ejército
y creó códigos de derecho. Durante el reinado de
Xuanzong floreció la cultura y surgieron muchos
de los mejores poetas de China. La **emperatriz
Wu,** la única mujer que gobernó China, lo
hizo con mano de hierro, pero mantuvo la
estabilidad y la prosperidad en China.

After the Tang dynasty fell, China became
divided again and entered a period known as
Five Dynasties and Ten Kingdoms. This lasted
53 years. Then, in 960, China was again unified
under the Song dynasty, and another great period
of accomplishment began that lasted for about
300 years, until 1279./Tras la caída de la dinastía
Tang, China quedó dividida nuevamente y
comenzó un período de 53 años conocido como
las Cinco Dinastías y los Diez Reinos. Luego,
en 960, China se reunificó bajo la dinastía Song
y comenzó otro gran período de logros que
duró aproximadamente 300 años, hasta 1279.

## THE AGE OF BUDDHISM/LA ERA DEL BUDISMO

During the troubled Period of Disunion, many
Chinese people turned to Buddhism. They took
comfort in the Buddhist teaching that people
can escape suffering and achieve a state of peace.
During the Sui and Tang dynasties, Buddhism
became well established throughout China and
Buddhist temples arose across the land./Durante
el difícil Período de Desunión, muchos chinos se
volcaron al budismo. Encontraron consuelo en
las enseñanzas budistas que afirman que las
personas pueden librarse del sufrimiento y
alcanzar un estado de paz. Durante las dinastías
Sui y Tang, el budismo se estableció ampliamente

> Why did many people
> convert to Buddhism
> during the Period of
> Disunion?/¿Por qué
> muchas personas se
> convirtieron al budismo
> durante el Período de
> Desunión?
>
> _____
> _____
> _____

en China y se construyeron templos budistas en todo el territorio.

Buddhism influenced many aspects of Chinese culture, including art, literature, and architecture. Chinese Buddhist missionaries brought the religion to Japan, Korea, and other Asian lands. Despite a Tang emperor's campaign against the religion, Buddhism remained a vital part of Chinese culture./El budismo ejerció su influencia sobre varios aspectos de la cultura china, entre ellos el arte, la literatura y la arquitectura. Los misioneros budistas chinos llevaron la religión a Japón, Corea y otras tierras de Asia. A pesar de las campañas que realizó un emperador de la dinastía Tang contra la religión, el budismo continuó siendo una parte fundamental de la cultura china.

## CHALLENGE ACTIVITY/ACTIVIDAD AVANZADA

**Critical Thinking: Sequence/Pensamiento crítico:**

**Hacer una secuencia** Research the development of Buddhism in China during the Period of Disunion. Create an illustrated and annotated timeline showing key events and people in the religion's history./Investiga el desarrollo del budismo en China durante el Período de Desunión. Crea una línea cronológica ilustrada y anotada en la que muestres los sucesos y personas clave en la historia de la religión.

**DIRECTIONS/INSTRUCCIONES** Read each sentence and fill in the blank with the word in the word pair that best completes the sentence./Lee cada oración y escribe en el espacio en blanco la palabra del par de palabras que mejor la completa.

1. The _____ was a time when China was split into several competing kingdoms that were ruled by military leaders.
   **(Age of Buddhism/Period of Disunion)**/_____
   fue una época en la que China estaba dividida en varios reinos que competían entre sí y que estaban gobernados por líderes militares.
   **(La era del budismo/El Período de Desunión)**

2. The only woman to rule China, _____
   was a ruthless ruler, but under her reign China was stable and prosperous.
   **(Empress Wu/Yang Jian)**/La única mujer que gobernó China,
   _____, era despiadada pero bajo su
   reinado China llegó a ser una nación estable y próspera. **(la emperatriz
   Wu/Yang Jian)**

3. Yang Jian established the _____, during
   which the _____ began to link China and
   the Period of Disunion ended. **(Sui dynasty/missionaries) (Grand Canal/Age
   of Buddhism)**/Yang Jian estableció _____,
   período durante el cual _____ comenzó
   a conectar el norte y el sur de China y terminó el Período de Desunión.
   **(la dinastía Sui/los misioneros) (el Gran Canal/la Era del Budismo)**

4. After the Tang dynasty fell, China was divided into separate kingdoms
   competing for power in a period known as the
   _____. **(Age of Buddhism/Five Dynasties
   and Ten Kingdoms)**/Tras la caída de la dinastía Tang, China quedó dividida
   en varios reinos que competían por el poder en un período que se conoce
   como _____. **(la era del budismo/las
   Cinco Dinastías y los Diez Reinos)**

5. The period from 400 to 845 can be called the _____
   because of the influence Buddhism had on Chinese culture. **(Age of
   Buddhism/Period of Disunion)**/El período que abarca los años 400 a 845
   puede denominarse _____ debido a la
   influencia que tuvo el budismo en la cultura China. **(la era del budismo/
   el Período de Desunión)**

6. In 960 China was reunified under the _____,
   which, like the Tang dynasty, was a period of great accomplishments. **(Song
   dynasty/Period of Disunion)**/En el año 960, China fue reunificada bajo
   _____, que al igual que la dinastía Tang,
   fue un período de grandes logros. **(la dinastía Song/el Período de Desunión)**

7. During the _____, Chinese power
   and influence reached much of eastern Asia, as well as large parts
   of Central Asia. **(Tang dynasty/Period of Disunion)**/Durante
   _____, el poder y la influencia chinas
   alcanzaron la mayor parte del este de Asia, así como gran parte de
   Asia central. **(la dinastía Tang/el Período de Desunión)**

# Later Chinese Dynasties/Las últimas dinastías chinas

**Lesson/Lección 2**

### MAIN IDEAS/IDEAS PRINCIPALES

1. Advances in agriculture led to increased trade and population growth./Los adelantos en la agricultura dieron como resultado un aumento en el comercio y el crecimiento de la población.
2. Cities and trade grew during the Tang and Song dynasties./Las ciudades y el comercio crecieron durante las dinastías Tang y Song.
3. The Tang and Song dynasties produced fine arts and inventions./Durante las dinastías Tang y Song se desarrollaron las bellas artes y se produjeron importantes inventos.

## Key Terms and People/Personas y palabras clave

**porcelain/porcelana** a thin, beautiful pottery invented by the Chinese/cerámica bella y delicada inventada por los chinos

**celadon/celadón** a pale green glaze that covers porcelain items/esmalte de color verde pálido con que se cubren las piezas de porcelana

**gunpowder/pólvora** a mixture of powders used in guns and explosives/mezcla de polvos utilizada en armas de fuego y explosivos

**compass/brújula** an instrument that uses the earth's magnetic field to indicate direction/instrumento que utiliza el campo magnético de la Tierra para indicar una dirección

**woodblock printing/xilografía** a form of printing in which an entire page is carved into a block of wood, which is covered with ink and then pressed against paper to make a copy of the page/forma de impresión en la que una página completa se talla en una plancha de madera, que se cubre con tinta y luego se presiona sobre un papel para crear una copia de la página

## Lesson Summary/Resumen de la lección

### ADVANCES IN AGRICULTURE/ADELANTOS EN LA AGRICULTURA

Under the Song dynasty, Chinese agriculture reached new heights. Farmers created elaborate irrigation systems based on new techniques and devices. The amount of land under cultivation increased. Farmers developed a new type of fast-ripening rice that enabled them to grow two or even three crops in the time it used to take to grow just one. They also learned to grow cotton efficiently and processed the fiber to make clothes

> **What was the advantage of fast-ripening rice?/¿Qué ventaja ofrecía el arroz que maduraba rápidamente?**
>
> _____
> _____
> _____
> _____

and other goods./Durante la dinastía Song, la agricultura en China alcanzó nuevos horizontes. Los agricultores crearon sistemas elaborados de irrigación basados en nuevos dispositivos y técnicas. Se incrementó la cantidad de tierra cultivada. Los agricultores desarrollaron un nuevo tipo de arroz que maduraba rápidamente y que les permitía recoger dos o hasta tres cosechas en el mismo tiempo que antes les llevaba realizar una sola. También aprendieron a cultivar algodón de manera eficiente y a procesar la fibra para fabricar ropa y otros productos.

Merchants traded food crops, so food was abundant not just in the countryside but in the cities, too. The population grew to more than 100 million people, making China the most populous country in the world./Los mercaderes compraban y vendían las cosechas; por lo tanto, había abundancia de alimentos no solo en el campo sino también en las ciudades. La población aumentó hasta alcanzar los 100 millones de habitantes, con lo que China pasó a ser el país más poblado del mundo.

> How were the abundance of food and the growth of cities connected?/¿Cómo se relacionó la abundancia de alimentos con el crecimiento de las ciudades?
>
> _____
> _____
> _____

## CITIES AND TRADE/CIUDADES Y COMERCIO

Chinese cities grew and flourished as the trade centers of the Tang and Song dynasties. Chang'an (chahng-AHN), with a population of more than a million people, was by far the largest city in the world at the time. Traders used the Grand Canal to ship goods and agricultural products throughout China./Las ciudades chinas crecieron y se transformaron en los centros de comercio de las dinastías Tang y Song. Chang'an, que tenía más de un millón de habitantes, era sin lugar a dudas la ciudad más poblada del mundo en ese momento. Los comerciantes usaban el Gran Canal para transportar mercaderías y productos agrícolas por toda China.

Foreign trade used both land routes and sea routes. China's Pacific ports were open to foreign traders. A bustling trade was carried on with India, Africa, and Southwest Asia. Chinese exports included tea, rice, spices, and jade. Especially prized by foreigners, however, were silk and **porcelain.** The methods of making these Chinese inventions were kept secret for centuries./Para el comercio exterior se utilizaban tanto rutas terrestres como marítimas. Los puertos de China sobre el Pacífico estaban abiertos a los comerciantes extranjeros. Se generó una importante actividad comercial con la India, África y el sudoeste asiático. China exportaba, entre otros productos, té, arroz, especias y jade. Sin embargo, lo que más apreciaban los extranjeros era la seda y la **porcelana.** Los métodos que se usaban para fabricar esos inventos chinos se mantuvieron en secreto durante varios siglos.

> **Why might foreigners prize Chinese silk and porcelain?/** ¿Por qué crees que los extranjeros apreciaban la seda y la porcelana chinas?
> _____
> _____
> _____

## ARTS AND INVENTIONS/ARTES E INVENTOS

The Tang dynasty produced some of China's greatest artists and writers, including Li Bo and Du Fu—the most famous of all Chinese poets— and the Buddhist painter Wu Daozi (DOW-tzee). The Song dynasty produced Li Qingzhao (ching-ZHOW), perhaps China's greatest female poet. Artists of both dynasties created exquisite objects in clay, particularly porcelain items with a pale green glaze called **celadon** (SEL-uh-duhn)./ Durante la dinastía Tang, surgieron algunos de los artistas y escritores más importantes de China, tales como Li Bo y Du Fu (los poetas chinos más famosos) y el pintor budista Wu Daozi. Durante la dinastía Song surgió Li Qingzhao, quizás la poetisa más importante de China. Los artistas de ambas dinastías crearon objetos exquisitos en arcilla, especialmente artículos de porcelana con un esmalte verde pálido llamado **celadón.**

> **Underline three famous Chinese poets. Circle a famous Chinese artist./** Subraya los nombres de tres poetas chinos famosos. Encierra en un círculo el nombre de un pintor chino famoso.

The Tang and Song dynasties produced some of the most remarkable—and important—inventions in human history, including **gunpowder** and the **compass.**/Durante las dinastías Tang y Song se produjeron algunos de los inventos más extraordinarios e importantes en la historia de la humanidad, como la **pólvora** y la **brújula.**

The world's oldest known printed book, using **woodblock printing,** was printed in China in 868. Later, during the Song dynasty, the Chinese invented movable type for printing. The Song dynasty also introduced the concept of paper money./El libro más antiguo del mundo, impreso por medio de la **xilografía,** se imprimió en China en 868. Luego, durante la dinastía Song, los chinos inventaron la imprenta de tipos móviles. La dinastía Song también introdujo el concepto del papel moneda.

> **What printing technology was developed after woodblock printing?**/¿Qué tecnología de impresión se desarrolló después de la xilografía?
>
> _____
>
> _____

## CHALLENGE ACTIVITY/ACTIVIDAD AVANZADA

**Critical Thinking: Describe/Pensamiento crítico: Describir** Write a paragraph describing an exchange of goods that could have taken place between a Song dynasty Chinese trader and a foreign merchant./Escribe un párrafo en el que describas un intercambio comercial que pudo haberse realizado entre un comerciante chino de la dinastía Song y un mercader extranjero.

## DIRECTIONS/INSTRUCCIONES Write a word or phrase that has the same meaning as the term given./Escribe una palabra o frase breve que tenga el mismo significado que el término dado.

1. compass/brújula _____

   _____

2. gunpowder/pólvora _____

   _____

3. porcelain/porcelana _____

_____

4. woodblock printing/xilografía _____

_____

5. movable type/tipos móviles _____

_____

6. celadon/celadón _____

_____

7. merchants/mercaderes _____

_____

8. Li Qingzhao/Li Qingzhao _____

_____

**DIRECTIONS/INSTRUCCIONES** Look at each set of four vocabulary
terms. On the line provided, write the letter of the term that does not
relate to the others./Observa cada conjunto de cuatro términos de
vocabulario. En el espacio en blanco, escribe la letra del término que
no tiene relación con los demás.

| | | | |
|---|---|---|---|
| _____ 9. a. compass/ brújula | b. Li Bo/ Li Bo | c. gunpowder/ pólvora | d. movable type/ tipos móviles |
| _____ 10. a. tea/té | b. porcelain/ porcelana | c. silk/seda | d. Li Qingzhao/ Li Qingzhao |
| _____ 11. a. porcelain/ porcelana | b. paper money/ papel moneda | c. movable type/ tipos móviles | d. block printing/ xilografía |

## Later Chinese Dynasties/Las últimas dinastías chinas

### Lesson/Lección 3

**MAIN IDEAS/IDEAS PRINCIPALES**

1. Confucianism underwent changes and influenced Chinese government./El confucianismo sufrió cambios y ejerció una gran influencia en el gobierno chino.

2. Scholar-officials ran China's government during the Song dynasty./Durante la dinastía Song, funcionarios eruditos dirigían el gobierno de China.

## Key Terms and People/Personas y palabras clave

**bureaucracy/burocracia** body of unelected government officials/cuerpo de empleados no electos del gobierno

**civil service/administración pública** service as a government official/personas que prestan servicios como empleados del gobierno

**scholar-official/funcionario erudito** an educated member of the government/miembro culto del gobierno

## Lesson Summary/Resumen de la lección

### DEVELOPMENT OF CONFUCIANISM/DESARROLLO DEL CONFUCIANISMO

Confucianism is the name given to the ideas of the Chinese philosopher Confucius. Confucius's teachings focused on ethics, or proper behavior, of individuals and governments. He argued that society would function best if everyone followed two principles, *ren* and *li*. *Ren* means concern for others, and *li* means practicing appropriate behavior. Order in society is maintained when people know their place and behave appropriately. Confucius said that order happened when young people obeyed their elders and subjects obeyed their rulers./El confucianismo es el nombre que se da a las ideas del filósofo chino Confucio. Sus enseñanzas se basaban en la ética, o el comportamiento apropiado, de las personas y los gobiernos. Confucio sostenía que la sociedad funcionaría mejor si todos seguían dos principios: *ren* y *li*. *Ren* significa la preocupación por los demás y *li* significa tener un comportamiento adecuado. La sociedad puede mantener el orden

> **What is the meaning of *ren* and *li*?/¿Qué significan los términos *ren* y *li*?**
>
> _____
> _____
> _____
> _____

> **According to Confucius, when is order in society maintained?/Según Confucio, ¿cuándo se mantiene el orden en la sociedad?**
>
> _____
> _____
> _____
> _____

cuando las personas conocen el lugar que les corresponde y se comportan de manera apropiada. Confucio afirmaba que el orden se logra cuando los jóvenes obedecen a sus mayores y los súbditos obedecen a sus gobernantes.

During the thousand years after his death, Confucius's ideas went in and out of favor several times. The Period of Disunion was a time when Buddhism became more popular than Confucianism. Buddhism also greatly influenced Chinese society during the Sui and early Tang dynasties./Durante los primeros mil años después de su muerte, las ideas de Confucio ganaron y perdieron popularidad varias veces. El Período de Desunión fue una época en la que el budismo era más popular que el confucianismo. El budismo también tuvo gran influencia en la sociedad china durante la dinastía Sui y al comienzo de la dinastía Tang.

Early in the Song dynasty, however, a new version of Confucianism, known as neo-Confucianism, was adopted as official government policy. In addition to teaching proper behavior, neo-Confucian scholars and officials discussed such spiritual questions as what made human beings do bad things even if their basic nature was good./Sin embargo, a comienzos de la dinastía Song se adoptó como política oficial del gobierno una nueva versión del confucianismo conocida como neoconfucianismo. Además de enseñar a las personas a comportarse adecuadamente, los eruditos y los funcionarios neoconfucianistas debatían sobre cuestiones espirituales, como por ejemplo, por qué los seres humanos hacen cosas malas aunque sean buenos por naturaleza.

> **Under which dynasty did neo-Confucianism take hold in China?/¿Durante qué dinastía se extendió el neoconfucianismo en China?**
>
> _____
>
> _____

## SCHOLAR-OFFICIALS/FUNCIONARIOS ERUDITOS

The Song dynasty took another major step that would affect China for centuries to come. The

Song established a system by which people went to work for the government. These workers formed a large **bureaucracy** by passing a series of written **civil service** examinations./La dinastía Song tomó otra medida importante que afectaría a China durante siglos: estableció un sistema de personas que trabajaban para el gobierno. Estos trabajadores formaban una enorme **burocracia** después de aprobar una serie de exámenes escritos para unirse a la **administración pública.**

The tests covered both the traditional teachings of Confucius and spiritual questions. Because the tests were extremely difficult, students spent years preparing for them. Often only very few students passed the exam./Las pruebas incluían tanto las enseñanzas tradicionales de Confucio como cuestiones espirituales. Como las pruebas eran sumamente difíciles, los estudiantes dedicaban años enteros a prepararse. Generalmente, muy pocos aprobaban el examen.

Candidates had a good reason to study hard. Passing the tests meant life as a **scholar-official,** whose benefits included considerable respect and reduced penalties for breaking the law. Scholar-officials were admired for their knowledge and ethics. Many became wealthy because they received gifts from people who wanted their help./Los candidatos tenían una buena razón para estudiar tanto. Aprobar los exámenes significaba llevar la vida de un **funcionario erudito,** cuyos beneficios incluían un gran respeto y penas reducidas por violar la ley. Los funcionarios eruditos eran admirados por sus conocimientos y su ética. Muchos de ellos se enriquecían al recibir regalos de personas que necesitaban su ayuda.

The civil service examination system helped ensure that talented, intelligent people became scholar-officials. This system was a major factor in the stability of the Song government./El sistema de exámenes para formar parte de la

> **How did people get government jobs under the Song dynasty?**/¿Cuál era la manera de conseguir un empleo en el gobierno durante la dinastía Song?
>
> _____
>
> _____

> **Underline three benefits enjoyed by scholar-officials.**/Subraya tres beneficios que tenían los funcionarios eruditos.

administración pública ayudaba a garantizar
que los funcionarios eruditos fueran personas
talentosas e inteligentes. Este sistema fue un
factor fundamental en la estabilidad del
gobierno de la dinastía Song.

## CHALLENGE ACTIVITY/ACTIVIDAD AVANZADA

**Critical Thinking: Elaborate/Pensamiento crítico:
Profundizar** Write a short essay on the
relationship between the Confucian ideals of
*ren* and *li* and the Chinese development of civil
service examinations. Explain why you think
that Confucian ethics were valued in government
employees./Escribe un ensayo breve acerca de
la relación entre los ideales del *ren* y el *li* del
confucianismo y el desarrollo del sistema de
exámenes para formar parte de la administración
pública china. Explica por qué crees que se
valoraba que los empleados del gobierno
siguieran la ética del confucianismo.

**DIRECTIONS/INSTRUCCIONES** Read each sentence and fill in
the blank with the word in the word pair that best completes
the sentence./Lee cada oración y escribe en el espacio en blanco
la palabra del par de palabras que mejor la completa.

1. _____ means service as a
   government official. **(Bureaucracy/Civil service)**/Formar parte de la
   _____ significa prestar servicios como
   empleado del gobierno. **(burocracia/administración pública)**

2. A _____ was an elite member of society
   who was admired for his knowledge and ethics. **(scholar-official/bureaucracy)**/
   _____ era un miembro de la élite admirado
   por sus conocimientos y su ética. **(Un funcionario erudito/La burocracia)**

3. People who went to work for the government formed a large
   _____, a body of unelected government
   officials. **(bureaucracy/scholar-official)**/Las personas que trabajaban para
   el gobierno formaban _____, un cuerpo
   de empleados no electos del gobierno. **(una enorme burocracia/los
   funcionarios eruditos)**

4. _____ followed the teachings of Confucius
but also emphasized spiritual matters. **(Civil service/Neo-Confucianism)/**
_____ seguía las enseñanzas de Confucio,
pero también hacía hincapié en cuestiones espirituales. **(La administración
pública/El neoconfucianismo)**

5. Confucius's teachings focused on _____,
or proper behavior, instead of religious beliefs. **(civil service/ethics)/**
Las enseñanzas de Confucio se centraban en la
_____, o el comportamiento adecuado,
en lugar de las creencias religiosas. **(administración pública/ética)**

6. In order to become a government official, a person had to pass a series of
exams based on the teachings of _____
and spiritual questions. **(bureaucracy/Confucius)/**Para ser empleado
del gobierno, había que aprobar una serie de exámenes basados en las
enseñanzas de _____ y en cuestiones
espirituales. **(la burocracia/Confucio)**

**DIRECTIONS/INSTRUCCIONES** On the line provided before each
statement, write **T** if a statement is true and **F** if a statement is false.
If the statement is false, write the correct term on the line after each
sentence that makes the sentence a true statement./En la línea que
precede a cada enunciado, escribe **V** si el enunciado es verdadero y
**F** si es falso. Si el enunciado es falso, escribe en la línea que sigue
a la oración el término correcto que lo hace verdadero.

_____ 7. Bureaucracy taught that people should conduct their lives according to
two basic principles, *ren* and *li*./La burocracia enseñaba a las personas
a guiarse por dos principios básicos en su vida: *ren* y *li*.

_____

_____ 8. Often, only a small fraction of students passed the civil service
examinations./Generalmente, un pequeño porcentaje de los estudiantes
aprobaba los exámenes para formar parte de la administración pública.

_____

# Later Chinese Dynasties/Las últimas dinastías chinas

## Lesson/Lección 4

**MAIN IDEAS/IDEAS PRINCIPALES**
1. The Mongol Empire included China, and the Mongols ruled China as the Yuan dynasty./China pasó a formar parte del Imperio mongol. Los mongoles gobernaron China durante la dinastía Yuan.
2. China under the Ming saw great changes in its government and relations with other countries./Durante la dinastía Ming, China experimentó grandes cambios en su gobierno y en las relaciones con otros países.

## Key Terms and People/Personas y palabras clave

**Genghis Khan/Gengis Kan** powerful leader who united the Mongols/poderoso líder que unió a los mongoles

**Kublai Khan/Kublai Kan** Genghis Khan's grandson, who completed the conquest of China/nieto de Gengis Kan; completó la conquista de China

**Zheng He/Zheng He** famous seafaring voyager of the Ming dynasty/famoso navegante de la dinastía Ming

**isolationism/aislacionismo** a policy of avoiding contact with other countries/política que consiste en evitar el contacto con otros países

## Lesson Summary/Resumen de la lección

**THE MONGOL EMPIRE/EL IMPERIO MONGOL**

In 1206, a powerful leader known as **Genghis Khan** (JENG-giz KAHN) united the nomadic Mongol tribes. He led huge armies on bloody expeditions of conquest throughout much of Asia and Eastern Europe. Many men, women, and children were killed, and the Mongols caused terrible destruction. By the time of Genghis Khan's death in 1227, all of northern China was under Mongol control./En 1206, un poderoso líder conocido como **Gengis Kan** unió a las tribus nómadas mongoles. Dirigió enormes ejércitos en expediciones sangrientas dedicadas a la conquista de gran parte de Asia y Europa oriental. Muchos hombres, mujeres y niños fueron asesinados, y los mongoles causaron

> **What were two effects of the Mongol conquest of Asia and Eastern Europe?/** ¿Cuáles fueron dos de los efectos de la conquista de Asia y Europa oriental por parte de los mongoles?
>
> _____
> _____
> _____
> _____
> _____

una terrible destrucción. En 1227, cuando murió Gengis Kan, todo el norte de China estaba bajo el control de los mongoles.

**Kublai Khan** (KOO-bluh KAHN), Genghis Khan's grandson, declared himself emperor of China in 1279. He named his new dynasty the Yuan dynasty. This empire, which stretched all the way to Eastern Europe, covered more land than any other empire in world history. Kublai Khan's regime preserved much of the structure of the Song dynasty, including the civil service and trade routes./**Kublai Kan,** el nieto de Gengis Kan, se declaró emperador de China en 1279. Dio a su nueva dinastía el nombre de dinastía Yuan. El imperio de Kublai Kan, que se extendía hasta Europa oriental, abarcaba más territorios que ningún otro imperio en la historia del mundo. El régimen de Kublai Kan conservó muchas de las estructuras de la dinastía Song, entre ellas la administración pública y las rutas comerciales.

The Italian merchant Marco Polo, who traveled in China, wrote about generous leaders and beautiful buildings. This sparked Europeans' interest in China. However, the Chinese actually thought the Mongols were rude and uncivilized./El mercader italiano Marco Polo viajó a China y escribió en sus crónicas acerca de los generosos líderes y los hermosos edificios de ese país. Eso despertó el interés de los europeos. Sin embargo, los chinos pensaban que los mongoles eran toscos y poco civilizados.

Two failed campaigns against Japan and expensive public works projects gradually weakened the Yuan dynasty. Many Chinese groups rebelled. Finally, in 1368, Chu

---

**Name two Mongol leaders involved in the conquest of China.**/Menciona dos líderes mongoles que participaron en la conquista de China.

_____

_____

---

**How was Marco Polo's view of the Mongols different from the way the Chinese viewed them?**/¿Qué diferencias había entre el concepto que tenía Marco Polo de los mongoles y la visión de ese pueblo que tenían los chinos?

_____

_____

_____

_____

_____

Yuan-Chang (JOO yoo-ahn-JAHNG) took control and founded the Ming dynasty./Dos campañas fallidas contra Japón y una serie de costosos proyectos de obras públicas debilitaron lentamente a la dinastía Yuan. Muchos grupos chinos se rebelaron. Finalmente, en 1368, Zhu Yuanzhang tomó el control del gobierno y fundó la dinastía Ming.

**THE MING DYNASTY/LA DINASTÍA MING**

The Ming dynasty lasted nearly 300 years, from 1368 to 1644. Ming China proved to be one of the most stable and prosperous times in Chinese history. Great Ming achievements include the fabulous ships and goodwill voyages of **Zheng He** (juhng HUH), the famous Forbidden City at the center of Beijing, and the Great Wall of China./ La dinastía Ming duró aproximadamente 300 años, desde 1368 hasta 1644. La era Ming fue una de las épocas más estables y prósperas de la historia china. Algunos de los grandes logros de esta dinastía son los fabulosos barcos y los viajes marítimos de **Zheng He,** la famosa Ciudad Prohibida que se construyó en el centro de Beijing y la Gran Muralla china.

> **Underline three achievements that happened during the Ming dynasty./Subraya tres logros que ocurrieron durante la dinastía Ming.**

The Forbidden City is a huge complex of palaces, temples, and government buildings in the middle of Beijing. Ming emperors built it as a symbol of China's glory, but the Forbidden City was only for the emperor, his family and servants, and the emperor's court. Ordinary people were forbidden, or not allowed to enter, the area./La Ciudad Prohibida es un inmenso complejo de palacios, templos y edificios gubernamentales ubicado en el centro de Beijing. Los emperadores de la dinastía Ming la construyeron como símbolo de la gloria de China, pero la Ciudad

Prohibida era para uso exclusivo del emperador, su familia, sus sirvientes y la corte imperial. La gente común tenía prohibido entrar en la ciudad.

## CHINA UNDER THE MING/CHINA BAJO LA DINASTÍA MING

Around 1400 China's emperor and scholar-officials began to react against the influence of foreign goods, beliefs, and customs, and the increasing wealth and power of merchants. China entered a period of **isolationism.** However, this led to weakness that allowed Westerners to seize considerable power in some parts of China. China's imperial glory faded./Alrededor de 1400, el emperador y los funcionarios eruditos de China comenzaron a reaccionar contra la influencia que ejercían las mercancías, las creencias y las costumbres extranjeras, y contra las riquezas y el poder que acumulaban los mercaderes. China instauró un período de **aislacionismo.** Sin embargo, esa política generó una debilidad que permitió a los occidentales acumular un poder considerable en algunas partes de China, a medida que la gloria imperial se desvanecía.

> What did China's isolationism allow Westerners to do?/
> ¿Qué les permitió hacer a los occidentales el aislacionismo de China?
>
> _____
> _____
> _____

## CHALLENGE ACTIVITY/ACTIVIDAD AVANZADA

**Critical Thinking: Make Judgments/Pensamiento crítico: Dar opiniones** Why did Ming rulers prohibit common people from entering the Forbidden City? Imagine that you had lived during the period and write a response to this exclusionary policy./¿Por qué los gobernantes de la dinastía Ming no dejaban que la gente común entrara en la Ciudad Prohibida? Imagina que vives durante ese período y escribe una respuesta a esa política de exclusión.

| Genghis Khan/ | Kublai Khan/ | isolationism/ |
|---|---|---|
| Gengis Kan | Kublai Kan | aislacionismo |
| Ming dynasty/ | Zheng He/ | |
| dinastía Ming | Zheng He | |

**DIRECTIONS/INSTRUCCIONES** Answer each question by writing a sentence that contains at least one word from the word bank./Responde cada pregunta con una oración que contenga al menos una palabra del banco de palabras.

1. Who was considered one of the greatest sailors during the history of early China?/¿Quién es considerado uno de los principales navegantes de la historia de la antigua China?

   _____

   _____

2. Who was the powerful leader that first united the Mongols?/¿Quién fue el líder poderoso que unió a los mongoles por primera vez?

   _____

   _____

3. In the 1430s, what policy did China follow in terms of contact with other countries?/¿Qué política adoptó China en la década de 1430 respecto del contacto con otros países?

   _____

   _____

4. Which ruler of the Mongol Empire completed his grandfather's conquest of China?/¿Qué líder del Imperio mongol completó la conquista de China que había iniciado su abuelo?

   _____

   _____

5. What was the name of the prosperous and stable dynasty that rose after the defeat of the Mongols?/¿Cuál fue el nombre de la dinastía próspera y estable que surgió tras la derrota de los mongoles?

_____

_____

# Later Chinese Dynasties/Las últimas dinastías chinas

## Lesson/Lección 5

**MAIN IDEAS/IDEAS PRINCIPALES**

1. Ideas and philosophies central to life in China spread to other nearby states and took root./Las ideas y filosofías que regían la vida en China se expandieron a otros estados cercanos, que las incorporaron como propias.

2. The Koryo dynasty of Korea adopted several elements of Chinese culture, including the civil service system./La dinastía Koryo de Corea adoptó varios elementos de la cultura china, entre ellos el sistema de administración pública.

3. Under Chinese rule, the Vietnamese absorbed many features of Chinese civilization./Mientras estaban gobernados por los chinos, los vietnamitas absorbieron muchas de las características de la civilización china.

## Key Terms and People/Personas y palabras clave

**cultural diffusion/difusión cultural** the spread of cultural traits from one region to another/la difusión de los rasgos culturales de una región a otra

**Trung sisters/hermanas Trung** Vietnamese sisters who raised an army and briefly drove the Chinese out of Vietnam in AD 39; regarded as heroes in Vietnam today/hermanas vietnamitas que reclutaron un ejército que expulsó a los chinos de Vietnam por un breve período en el año 39 d. C.; hoy en día se las considera heroínas en Vietnam

## Lesson Summary/Resumen de la lección

### NEIGHBORS TO THE NORTH, EAST, AND SOUTH/
### VECINOS DEL NORTE, ESTE Y SUR

Beginning with the Sui dynasty, the Chinese forced civilizations in East Asia to live the way people did in China. Chinese traders brought their cultural ideas and philosophies with them as they traveled widely throughout Asia. This **cultural diffusion** allowed China to become a major influence in the region./A partir de la dinastía Sui, los chinos obligaron a las civilizaciones del este asiático a adoptar sus costumbres. En sus viajes por toda Asia, los comerciantes chinos llevaron sus ideas culturales y su filosofía a otros países. Esta **difusión cultural** permitió que China se proyectara como uno de los países más influyentes de la región.

Name/Nombre_____ Class/Clase _____ Date/Fecha_____

Lesson/Lección 5, *continued*/*continuación*

During this period, the Chinese tried to invade and conquer Korea more than once. Most times they were unsuccessful. Traders and missionaries brought elements of Chinese culture such as Buddhism into Korea./Durante este período, los chinos trataron de invadir y conquistar Corea más de una vez. Sin embargo, la mayoría de las veces fracasaron. Los comerciantes y misioneros introdujeron en Corea algunos elementos de la cultura china, como el budismo.

Chinese missionaries brought Buddhism to Japan, too. Several Japanese rulers invited officials and scholars from China to visit them. The rulers wanted the Chinese to share their ideas. Vietnam was one place in Southeast Asia where Chinese culture influenced life for centuries./Los misioneros chinos también llevaron el budismo a Japón. Varios gobernantes japoneses invitaron a funcionarios y eruditos chinos a visitar su país, ya que querían que los chinos compartieran sus ideas con ellos. Uno de los países del sudeste asiático que se vio influenciado por la cultura china durante siglos fue Vietnam.

**CHINESE INFLUENCE IN KOREA/INFLUENCIA CHINA EN COREA**

China's Han dynasty colonized part of Korea in 108 BC. In addition to practicing Buddhism, Koreans began to use Chinese writing, political systems, and farming methods./La dinastía china Han colonizó parte de Corea en 108 a. C. Además de convertirse al budismo, los coreanos adoptaron la escritura, los sistemas políticos y los métodos agrícolas chinos.

By 668, the Silla had become a powerful Korean kingdom. First, it was China's ally, but then the Silla drove the Chinese out of Korea. Eventually, rebels overthrew the Silla and formed the Koryo dynasty. During the time of the Koryo, Korean

> Which two groups of people helped spread Chinese influence in East Asia?/¿Cuáles son los dos grupos que ayudaron a esparcir la influencia china en el este asiático?
>
> _____
> _____

> Why did Japanese rulers invite officials and scholars from China to visit them?/¿Por qué los gobernantes japoneses invitaron a funcionarios y eruditos de China a visitarlos?
>
> _____
> _____
> _____

artisans created beautiful pottery. Printers created metal moveable type. The Koryo did not want Korea to be exactly the same as China. It encouraged people to practice a religion that blended Buddhism with traditional Korean beliefs in nature spirits./Hacia el año 668, Silla se había convertido en un reino poderoso en Corea. Al principio, la dinastía Silla era aliada de China, pero luego expulsó a los chinos de Corea. Con el tiempo, el reino Silla fue derrocado por rebeldes que formaron la dinastía Koryo. Durante la dinastía Koryo, los artesanos coreanos crearon hermosos objetos de cerámica y los imprenteros crearon tipos móviles de metal. Los gobernantes de la dinastía Koryo no querían que Corea fuera exactamente igual que China. Por eso, alentaron a la población a practicar una religión que combinaba el budismo con la creencia en los espíritus naturales, que era una tradición coreana.

> **Describe the religion that the Koryo encouraged people to practice./**Describe la religión que se fomentó durante la dinastía Koryo.
>
> _____
> _____
> _____
> _____

## VIETNAM SEEKS INDEPENDENCE/VIETNAM LUCHA POR SU INDEPENDENCIA

For about 800 years, northern Vietnam was also ruled by China. The Vietnamese were forced to use the Chinese system of government and wear Chinese clothing styles. Buddhist art and architecture became common in Vietnam./ Durante aproximadamente 800 años, Vietnam del Norte también estuvo dominado por China. Los vietnamitas fueron obligados a adoptar el sistema de gobierno chino y a usar vestimentas de estilo chino. El arte y la arquitectura budistas se hicieron comunes en Vietnam.

In AD 39, the **Trung sisters** raised an army. They briefly drove the Chinese out of Vietnam, but China regained its control. In 939, the independent Vietnamese kingdom of Dai Viet was finally established. There was chaos for about 60 years./En el año 39 d. C., las **hermanas Trung** reclutaron un ejército que expulsó a los

> **What were the Trung sisters able to do in AD 39?/**¿Qué lograron hacer las hermanas Trung en el año 39 d. C.?
>
> _____
> _____
> _____

chinos de Vietnam por un período breve, pero luego China volvió a tomar el control de ese país. Finalmente, en el año 939 se creó el reino vietnamita independiente de Dai Viet, pero reinó el caos durante aproximadamente 60 años más.

The Ly dynasty created the first university in Vietnam. Many great works of Vietnamese literature were written during the reign of the Tran dynasty. In 1400, the Tran dynasty fell, and China took control of Vietnam again./La dinastía Ly creó la primera universidad de Vietnam. Durante el reinado de la dinastía Tran, se escribieron muchas de las obras maestras de la literatura vietnamita. Sin embargo, en 1400 esa dinastía cayó y China recuperó el control de Vietnam.

> **What two things happened when the Ly and Tran dynasties ruled Dai Viet?/** Menciona dos sucesos que ocurrieron en Vietnam durante el reinado de las dinastías Ly y Tran.
>
> _____
> _____
> _____
> _____
> _____

## CHALLENGE ACTIVITY/ACTIVIDAD AVANZADA

**Critical Thinking: Categorize/Pensamiento crítico: Categorizar** Create a chart with the categories Japan, Korea, and Vietnam. Find images of ancient or present-day examples of Buddhist influence in these three nations, such as art, temples, or people worshipping. Write a caption for each image that tells what it is and how it is an example of Buddhist influence./Crea un cuadro con las siguientes categorías: Japón, Corea y Vietnam. Busca imágenes que muestren ejemplos antiguos o actuales de la influencia budista en esas tres naciones, como obras de arte, templos o personas practicando la religión. Escribe una leyenda que describa cada imagen y explique por qué es un ejemplo de la influencia budista.

**DIRECTIONS/INSTRUCCIONES** Write a word or descriptive phrase to describe each term./Escribe una palabra o frase descriptiva para describir cada término.

1. cultural diffusion/difusión cultural _____

_____

_____

2. Trung sisters/hermanas Trung _____

_____

_____

# Japan/Japón

**MAIN IDEAS/IDEAS PRINCIPALES**
1. Geography shaped life in Japan./La geografía influyó en la vida en Japón.
2. Early Japanese society was organized in clans, which came to be ruled by an emperor./La antigua sociedad japonesa estaba organizada en clanes, que luego pasaron a ser gobernados por un emperador.
3. Japan learned about language, society, and government from China and Korea./Japón aprendió sobre el lenguaje, la sociedad y el gobierno de China y Corea.
4. During the Nara period, Buddhism became the official religion of Japan./Durante el período Nara, el budismo se convirtió en la religión oficial de Japón.

## Key Terms and People/Personas y palabras clave

**clans/clanes** extended families/familias extendidas

**Shinto/shintoísmo** the traditional religion of Japan, based on the belief that everything in nature has a spirit/religión tradicional de Japón, basada en la creencia de que todo lo que existe en la naturaleza tiene un espíritu

**Prince Shotoku/príncipe Shotoku** popular Japanese ruler who brought many Chinese ideas to Japan/popular gobernante japonés que introdujo numerosas ideas chinas en Japón

**regent/regente** someone who rules a country for someone who is unable to rule alone/persona que gobierna un país en nombre de alguien que no puede gobernar solo

## Lesson Summary/Resumen de la lección

### GEOGRAPHY SHAPES LIFE IN JAPAN/LA GEOGRAFÍA INFLUYE EN LA VIDA EN JAPÓN

The islands of Japan are the tops of undersea mountains and volcanoes. Since it is difficult to live and farm on mountain slopes, most Japanese people lived in the coastal plains because they are flat./Las islas que conforman Japón son las cimas de montañas y volcanes submarinos. Puesto que es difícil vivir y cultivar en las laderas de las montañas, la mayoría de los japoneses vivían en las llanuras costeras, que son tierras planas.

Living on islands near the sea affected Japanese life and culture. Seafood has been a key part of the

> **What landforms make up most of Japan's islands?/**¿Qué accidentes geográficos constituyen la mayor parte de las islas de Japón?
>
> _____
> _____

Japanese diet for thousands of years. They created
their own religion and social structure. With Korea
and China nearby, Japan isn't totally isolated
and those cultures influenced the new culture
of Japan./Vivir en islas cercanas al mar afectó la
vida y la cultura de Japón. Los mariscos han sido
parte esencial de la dieta japonesa durante miles
de años. Los japoneses crearon su propia religión
y estructura social. Sin embargo, Japón no se
encuentra completamente aislado: debido a
su cercanía, las culturas de Corea y China
influyeron sobre la nueva cultura japonesa.

## EARLY JAPANESE SOCIETY/ANTIGUA SOCIEDAD JAPONESA

Early Japan was home to two different cultures,
neither of which had any contact with the rest of
Asia. The Ainu (EYE-noo) had a different look and
language from the rest of Asia. They were eventually
driven back onto the northern island of Hokkaido.
Over time, the Ainu culture almost disappeared./En
sus comienzos, en Japón habitaban dos culturas,
ninguna de las cuales mantenía contacto con el resto
de Asia. Los ainu tenían una apariencia y un idioma
propios. En cierto momento, debieron replegarse
hacia el norte, a la isla de Hokkaido. Con el tiempo,
su cultura prácticamente desapareció.

The people living to the south of the Ainu
eventually became the Japanese. Most lived
in small farming villages. **Clans,** or extended
families, ruled these villages. They practiced
rituals that became **Shinto,** the traditional
religion of Japan, which teaches that everything
in nature has a spirit—*kami.*/Las personas que
habitaban al sur de los ainu se convirtieron
finalmente en los japoneses. La mayoría de ellos
vivían en pequeñas aldeas rurales gobernadas
por **clanes,** o familias extendidas. Practicaban
rituales religiosos que devinieron en el **shintoísmo,**
la religión tradicional de Japón que enseña que

> What family groups
> controlled life in early
> Japanese villages?/
> ¿Qué grupos familiares
> controlaban la vida en las
> antiguas aldeas japonesas?
>
> _____

todo lo que existe en la naturaleza tiene un
espíritu, o *kami*.

Some clans became so powerful that they took
over much of Japan. The Yamato rulers were the
first clan to call themselves emperors of Japan./
Algunos clanes se volvieron tan poderosos que
tomaron control de gran parte de Japón. Los
gobernantes del clan Yamato fueron los primeros
en otorgarse el título de emperadores de Japón.

## JAPAN LEARNS FROM CHINA AND KOREA/ JAPÓN APRENDE DE CHINA Y COREA

By the mid-500s, Japanese rulers sent emissaries
to Korea and China to learn about their cultures.
The Japanese had no written language, so they
used Chinese characters to spell out Japanese
sounds and words. Chinese was actually Japan's
official language from about 500 to about
1100./A mediados del siglo 6, los gobernantes
japoneses enviaron emisarios a Corea y China
para aprender sobre sus culturas. Dado que los
japoneses no poseían una escritura propia,
utilizaban los caracteres chinos para representar
los sonidos y palabras de su idioma. De hecho,
el chino fue la lengua oficial de Japón entre los
años 500 y 1100, aproximadamente.

**Prince Shotoku** (shoh-TOH-koo) served as
**regent** for his aunt, the empress. Shotoku had
advisors introduce the Chinese philosophy of
Confucianism to Japan. He also encouraged the
spread of Buddhism. Shotoku's attempt to bring
a more absolute, Chinese-style of rule to Japan
was not as successful. Clan leaders, fearful of
giving up power, fought against Shotoku's ideas.
So the emperors gained little real power./El
**príncipe Shotoku** gobernó como **regente** en lugar
de su tía, la emperatriz. Shotoku hizo que sus
consejeros introdujeran en Japón la filosofía
china del confucianismo. También fomentó la

> For about how many years
> was Chinese the official
> language of Japan?/
> ¿Durante cuántos años,
> aproximadamente, fue
> el chino la lengua oficial
> de Japón?
>
> _____

> Underline the sentence
> that explains why the clan
> leaders did not want a
> Chinese-style rule./Subraya
> la oración que explica por
> qué los líderes de los
> clanes no querían una
> forma de gobierno similar
> a la de China.

difusión del budismo. El intento de Shotoku
de instaurar en Japón una forma de gobierno
similar a la de China, más absolutista, no tuvo el
mismo éxito. Los líderes de los clanes temían
perder su poder y se opusieron a sus ideas. Así, el
poder real de los emperadores aumentó poco.

## THE NARA PERIOD/PERÍODO NARA

Yamato rulers had capitals on their own estates.
The capital moved with each new ruler.
Eventually, the Japanese followed the Chinese
practice of setting up a permanent capital. Nara,
in 710, became the permanent governing city.
This began the 84 years known as the Nara
Period in which Nara grew, built roads, and
the emperor collected taxes./Los gobernantes
del clan Yamato establecían las capitales dentro
de sus dominios. Por ello, la capital se mudaba
con cada nuevo gobernante. Con el tiempo, los
japoneses adoptaron la práctica china de fundar
una capital permanente. En el año 710, Nara se
convirtió en la ciudad principal permanente,
dando comienzo a los 84 años conocidos como
el período Nara. Durante este período, Nara
creció, se construyeron rutas y el emperador
recaudó impuestos.

> **Underline what Chinese practice the Japanese adopted in 710./Subraya la práctica china que adoptaron los japoneses en el año 710.**

## CHALLENGE ACTIVITY/ACTIVIDAD AVANZADA

**Critical Thinking: Make Inferences/Pensamiento
crítico: Hacer inferencias** Japanese rulers wanted
to learn from the Chinese and Koreans. Write
a paragraph to explain why./Los gobernantes
japoneses querían aprender de los chinos y
los coreanos. Escribe un párrafo que explique
por qué.

| Buddhism/el budismo | China/China | clans/clanes | Confucianism/el confucianismo |
| Korea/Corea | Prince Shotoku/el príncipe Shotoku | regent/un regente | Shinto/el shintoísmo |
| | structure/una estructura | | |

**DIRECTIONS/INSTRUCCIONES** Read each sentence and fill in the blank with the word from the word bank that best completes the sentence./Lee cada oración y escribe en el espacio en blanco la palabra del banco de palabras que mejor la completa.

1. The Japanese adopted many ideas about language, society, religion, philosophy, and government from China and_____./Los japoneses adoptaron muchas ideas sobre el lenguaje, la sociedad, la religión, la filosofía y el gobierno de China y _____.

2. The first Japanese lived mostly in small farming villages that were ruled by _____, or extended families./Los primeros japoneses vivían principalmente en pequeñas aldeas rurales que eran gobernadas por _____, o familias extendidas.

3. A _____ is a person who rules a country for someone who is unable to rule alone./_____ es una persona que gobierna un país en lugar de alguien que es incapaz de gobernar solo.

4. _____ is the traditional religion of Japan./_____ es la religión tradicional de Japón.

5. One of the people most influential in bringing Chinese ideas to Japan was _____./Una de las personas más influyentes en cuanto a la introducción de ideas chinas en Japón fue

_____.

6. Among the ideas that the scholars brought back from China was _____, which helped shape family life in Japan for centuries./Entre las ideas que los estudiosos introdujeron de China se encontraba _____, que ayudó a modelar la vida familiar en Japón durante siglos.

7. Prince Shotoku worked to spread the religion of _____ across Japan./El príncipe Shotoku impulsó la difusión de la religión de _____ en Japón.

8. The early Japanese created a religion and social _____ very different from those in other parts of Asia./Los primeros japoneses crearon una religión y _____ social muy diferentes a las de otras partes de Asia.

9. One of the first things the Japanese learned from _____ was their written language./Una de las primeras cosas que los japoneses aprendieron de _____ fue su lengua escrita.

## Japan/Japón

**MAIN IDEAS/IDEAS PRINCIPALES**
1. Japanese nobles created great art in their court at Heian./Los nobles japoneses crearon grandes obras de arte en su corte de Heian.
2. Buddhism changed in Japan during the Heian period./El budismo experimentó cambios en Japón durante el período heian.

## Key Terms and People/Personas y palabras clave

**court/corte** group of nobles who live near and serve or advise a ruler/grupo de nobles que vive cerca de un gobernante y lo sirve o aconseja

**Lady Murasaki Shikibu/dama Murasaki Shikibu** Japanese writer credited with writing the world's first novel/escritora japonesa considerada la autora de la primera novela del mundo

**Zen/zen** form of Buddhism involving quiet, thoughtful meditation/forma del budismo que supone la meditación silenciosa y reflexiva

## Lesson Summary/Resumen de la lección

### JAPANESE NOBLES CREATE GREAT ART/NOBLES JAPONESES CREAN GRANDES OBRAS DE ARTE

In 794, the emperor and empress of Japan moved to Heian (HAY-ahn), a city now called Kyoto. The nobles who followed created an imperial **court.** These nobles had little to do with the common people of Heian. They lived apart from poorer citizens and seldom left the city. The nobles had easy lives and more free time than poorer citizens. They loved beauty and made the court at Heian the center of a golden age of art and learning between 794 and 1185./En 794, el emperador y la emperatriz de Japón se trasladaron a Heian, una ciudad que en la actualidad se llama Kioto. Los nobles que los siguieron crearon una **corte** imperial. Estos nobles tenían poco que ver con la gente común de Heian. Vivían separados de los ciudadanos más pobres y raras veces salían de la ciudad. Los nobles llevaban una vida fácil y tenían más

> **Why do you think the nobles of Heian devoted so much time to the promotion of the arts?/** ¿Por qué piensas que los nobles de Heian dedicaban tanto tiempo a la promoción de las artes?
>
> _____
> _____
> _____

tiempo libre que los pobres. Les encantaban
las cosas bellas y, entre 794 y 1185, convirtieron
la corte de Heian en el centro de una época de
oro para el arte y el saber.

These nobles dressed in beautiful silk robes
and carried decorative fans. They were also lovers
of the written and spoken word, and spent many
hours writing in journals. Men usually wrote in
Chinese, but many women wrote in Japanese.
Thus women wrote most of the major works of
early Japanese literature. Both men and women
did write poetry./Estos nobles vestían hermosas
túnicas de seda y llevaban abanicos decorativos.
Además, eran amantes de la palabra escrita y
oral, y pasaban muchas horas escribiendo en
diarios. Los hombres generalmente escribían en
chino, pero muchas mujeres escribían en japonés.
Por lo tanto, las mujeres escribieron la mayor
parte de las obras más importantes de la
literatura japonesa de los primeros tiempos.
Tanto hombres como mujeres escribieron poesía.

Probably the greatest of these early writers was
**Lady Murasaki Shikibu** (moohr-ah-SAHK-ee
shee-KEE-boo). Around 1000, she wrote *The Tale
of Genji,* often considered the world's first full-
length novel. It is the story of a prince named
Genji and his long quest for love. During his
search he meets women from many different social
classes./La más sobresaliente de los primeros
escritores probablemente fue la **dama Murasaki
Shikibu.** Alrededor del año 1000, escribió *La
historia de Genji,* que suele considerarse la primera
novela completa del mundo. Es la historia de un
príncipe llamado Genji y de su larga búsqueda
del amor. Durante su búsqueda conoce mujeres
de muchas clases sociales distintas.

> **Underline the title of what
> is considered to be the
> world's first novel.**/Subraya
> el título de lo que se
> considera la primera
> novela del mundo.

Visual arts were also popular, particularly painting, calligraphy, and architecture. The paintings were made in bright, bold colors. Most Heian architecture was based on that of the Chinese capital, Chang'an. Other architectural styles were simple and airy. Wood houses with tiled roofs featured large open spaces surrounded by elegant gardens. Performing arts also flourished at the Heian court. Eventually a form of drama called Noh developed, which combined music, dance and speaking parts. Noh plays often presented the feats of great Japanese heroes./Las artes visuales también gozaban de popularidad, en especial la pintura, la caligrafía y la arquitectura. Las pinturas eran de colores vivos y brillantes. La mayor parte de la arquitectura heian se basaba en la de la capital china, Chang'an. Otros estilos arquitectónicos eran sencillos y espaciosos. Las casas de madera con techos de tejas tenían grandes espacios abiertos rodeados de jardines elegantes. Las artes escénicas también florecieron en la corte de Heian. Con el tiempo se creó un género teatral llamado noh, que combinaba música, danza y partes habladas. Las obras de teatro noh solían representar las hazañas de los grandes héroes japoneses.

> **What were some of the art forms popular among the nobles of Heian?**/¿Cuáles son algunas de las expresiones artísticas que gozaban de popularidad entre los nobles de Heian?
>
> _____
> _____
> _____
> _____

## BUDDHISM CHANGES/CAMBIOS EN EL BUDISMO

Common Japanese people had no time for the long, elaborate rituals practiced by the court. Both groups were deeply religious, however. The Japanese introduced important changes to the Buddhism that had arrived from China. One very popular Japanese form, called Pure Land Buddhism, did not require any special rituals. Instead, Pure Land Buddhists chanted the Buddha's name over and over again to find enlightenment./La gente común de Japón no tenía tiempo para los rituales largos y

> **What did Pure Land Buddhism require of its followers?**/¿Qué requería de sus seguidores el budismo de la tierra pura?
>
> _____
> _____
> _____
> _____

elaborados que se practicaban en la corte. Sin embargo, ambos grupos eran profundamente religiosos. Los japoneses introdujeron cambios importantes en el budismo, que había llegado de China. Una forma japonesa muy popular, llamada budismo de la tierra pura, no requería rituales especiales. En cambio, los budistas de la tierra pura recitaban el nombre de Buda una y otra vez para alcanzar la iluminación.

In the 1100s, a new form of Buddhism called **Zen** developed. Zen Buddhists believed that neither faith nor good behavior led to wisdom. Instead, people should practice self-discipline and meditation, or quiet thinking. These ideas appealed to many Japanese, especially warriors. As these warriors gained more influence in Japan, so did Zen Buddhism./En el siglo 12, se desarrolló una nueva forma de budismo llamado **zen.** Los budistas zen no creían que la fe ni el buen comportamiento llevaran a la sabiduría. En cambio, las personas debían practicar la autodisciplina y la meditación, o reflexión silenciosa. Estas ideas atrajeron a muchos japoneses, en especial a los guerreros. A medida que estos guerreros lograron ejercer mayor influencia en Japón, también lo hizo el budismo zen.

> **Underline the phrase that defines the central practices of Zen Buddhism./** Subraya la frase que define las prácticas centrales del budismo zen.

## CHALLENGE ACTIVITY/ACTIVIDAD AVANZADA

**Critical Thinking: Make Inferences/Pensamiento crítico: Hacer inferencias** If you were a noble in the Heian court who did not have to work, what would you do all day? Pretend you're a Japanese noble and write a journal entry describing a typical day./Si fueras un noble de la corte de Heian y no tuvieras que trabajar, ¿qué harías durante todo el día? Simula que eres un noble japonés y escribe una entrada de diario en la que describas un día normal.

**DIRECTIONS/INSTRUCCIONES** On the line provided before each statement, write **T** if a statement is true and **F** if a statement is false. If the statement is false, write the correct term on the line after each sentence that makes the sentence a true statement./En la línea que precede a cada enunciado, escribe **V** si el enunciado es verdadero y **F** si es falso. Si el enunciado es falso, escribe en la línea que sigue a la oración el término correcto que lo hace verdadero.

_____ 1. <u>Noh</u> is a form of drama that combines music, speaking, and dance. Its plays tell about great heroes or figures from Japan's past./<u>Noh</u> es un género teatral que combina música, diálogos y danza. Sus obras tratan sobre los grandes héroes o figuras del pasado de Japón.

_____

_____ 2. <u>Lady Murasaki Shikibu</u> wrote *The Tale of Genji* and is probably the greatest writer in early Japanese history./<u>La dama Murasaki Shikibu</u> escribió *La historia de Genji* y probablemente sea la escritora más importante de los primeros tiempos de Japón.

_____

_____ 3. <u>Calligraphy</u> is a form of Buddhism that teaches self-discipline and meditation as the keys to wisdom./<u>La caligrafía</u> es una forma de budismo que enseña la autodisciplina y la meditación como las llaves para alcanzar la sabiduría.

_____

_____ 4. A group of nobles that served and advised a ruler was called a <u>court</u>./Se llamaba <u>corte</u> a un grupo de nobles que servía a un gobernante y lo aconsejaba.

_____

_____ 5. <u>Chang'an</u> is most famous for writing *The Tale of Genji*./<u>Chang'an</u> es famoso por haber escrito *La historia de Genji*.

_____

_____ 6. <u>Heian</u>, the city now called Kyoto, was the site of the imperial court and was a great center of the arts./<u>Heian</u>, la ciudad que hoy se conoce como Kioto, fue la sede de la corte imperial y un gran centro de las artes.

_____

_____ 7. A popular form of art in Heian was <u>Zen</u>, which is a style of decorative writing./Una forma popular de arte en Heian fue <u>el zen</u>, que es un estilo de escritura decorativa.

_____

## Japan/Japón

**MAIN IDEAS/IDEAS PRINCIPALES**

1. Samurai and shoguns took over Japan as emperors lost influence./Los samuráis y shogúns se apoderaron de Japón a medida que los emperadores fueron perdiendo su influencia.

2. Samurai warriors lived honorably./Los guerreros samuráis vivían de manera honorable.

3. Order broke down when the power of the shoguns was challenged by invaders and rebellions./El orden colapsó cuando invasores y rebeliones desafiaron el poder de los shogúns.

4. Strong leaders took over and reunified Japan./Líderes fuertes se apoderaron de Japón y lograron su reunificación.

## Key Terms and People/Personas y palabras clave

**daimyo/daimyos** large landowners in early Japan/grandes terratenientes en el antiguo Japón

**samurai/samuráis** trained professional warriors in early Japan/guerreros profesionales entrenados en el antiguo Japón

**figurehead/gobernante decorativo** a person who appears to rule though real power rests with someone else/persona que aparenta gobernar, aunque el poder real lo tiene otra persona

**shogun/shogún** a general who ruled Japan in the emperor's name/general que gobernaba Japón en nombre del emperador

**Bushido/Bushido** the strict samurai code of rules/código estricto de reglas de los samuráis

## Lesson Summary/Resumen de la lección

### SAMURAI AND SHOGUNS TAKE OVER JAPAN/ SAMURÁIS Y SHOGÚNS TOMAN EL CONTROL DE JAPÓN

While the Heian court flourished, order was breaking down in Japanese society. By the late 1100s, powerful nobles were openly at war. Rebels fought against imperial officials. Japan's rulers did not notice the problems growing in their country./ Mientras la corte de Heian florecía, el orden en la sociedad japonesa colapsaba. Para fines del siglo 12, los nobles poderosos se encontraban abiertamente en guerra. Los rebeldes luchaban

contra los funcionarios del imperio. Los
gobernantes de Japón no se daban cuenta
de los crecientes problemas en el país.

Japan's large landowners, or **daimyo** (DY-mee-oh), decided they could not rely on the emperor
to protect them. They hired **samurai** (SA-muh-ry), trained professional warriors, to defend
their property. Several noble clans decided to
seize power themselves./Los grandes
terratenientes de Japón, o **daimyos,** decidieron
que no podían contar con el emperador para
protegerse. Contrataron **samuráis,** guerreros
profesionales entrenados, para que defendieran
sus propiedades. Varios clanes de nobles
decidieron tomar el poder en sus propias manos.

> **Underline the phrase that explains why the daimyo hired their own protection in the late 1100s./**Subraya la frase que explica por qué los daimyos contrataban su propia protección a fines del siglo 12.

Two of these clans fought each other fiercely
for 30 years. Finally, the head of the Minamoto
clan declared himself Japan's new ruler. The
Minamoto leader kept the emperor on as a
**figurehead.** The Minamoto leader took the title
**shogun.** He ruled in the emperor's name. When
he died, he passed his title and power on to one
of his children. For about the next 700 years,
Japan was ruled by shoguns./Dos de esos clanes
combatieron ferozmente entre sí durante
30 años. Finalmente, el jefe del clan Minamoto
se declaró el nuevo gobernante de Japón. El
líder minamoto mantuvo al emperador como
**gobernante decorativo** y tomó el título de **shogún.**
Gobernó en nombre del emperador y cuando
murió, traspasó su título y su poder a uno de
sus hijos. Durante los siguientes 700 años
aproximadamente, Japón fue gobernado
por shogúns.

> **To what clan did Japan's first shogun belong?/**¿A qué clan pertenecían los primeros shogúns de Japón?
> _____

> **Underline how many years the shoguns ruled Japan./**Subraya la cantidad de años que los shogúns gobernaron Japón.

## SAMURAI LIVE HONORABLY/LOS SAMURÁIS VIVEN DE MANERA HONORABLE

The samurai enjoyed many privileges, but they
also had to follow a strict code of rules called
**Bushido** (BOOH-shi-doh). Loyalty and honor

were central to this code. Both men and women of samurai families learned to fight. Most importantly, Bushido required a samurai be loyal to his lord. The values of loyalty and honor remain very important in modern Japan./Los samuráis gozaban de muchos privilegios, pero también tenían que seguir un estricto código de reglas llamado **Bushido.** La lealtad y el honor eran elementos fundamentales de este código. Tanto los hombres como las mujeres de las familias samuráis aprendían a luchar. El requisito más importante del Bushido era que el samurái fuese leal a su señor. Los valores de la lealtad y el honor continúan siendo de gran importancia en Japón en la actualidad.

> **To whom were samurai loyal?/¿A quién eran leales los samuráis?**
>
> _____
>
> _____
>
> _____

## ORDER BREAKS DOWN/SE QUIEBRA EL ORDEN

The shoguns, with the help of the samurai, kept order in Japan for about a century, but that order broke down. Two foreign invasions by the Mongols were stopped. A storm helped stop the second invasion. The Japanese called it kamikaze (kah-mi-KAH-zee), or "divine wind." After the invasions, the authority of the shoguns weakened. Nobles began to resent the shoguns' power over them. The daimyo fought to limit the power of the shogun./Con la ayuda de los samuráis, los shogúns mantuvieron el orden en Japón durante casi un siglo, pero ese orden se vino abajo. Lograron detener dos invasiones extranjeras de los mongoles. Una tormenta ayudó a detener la segunda invasión. Los japoneses la llamaban kamikaze, o "viento divino". Tras las invasiones, se debilitó la autoridad de los shogúns. A los nobles comenzó a molestarles el poder que tenían los shogúns sobre ellos. Los daimyos lucharon para limitar el poder del shogún.

> **What challenges did the shoguns face to their authority?/¿Qué cuestionamientos a su autoridad enfrentaban los shogúns?**
>
> _____
>
> _____
>
> _____
>
> _____
>
> _____

## STRONG LEADERS TAKE OVER/LÍDERES FUERTES TOMAN EL CONTROL

Eventually, new leaders rose to power. Each fought to unify all of Japan under his control. The first to restore the power of the shogun was Oda Nobunaga (OHD-ah noh-booh-NAH-gah). Later shoguns unified Japanese rule. In 1603, the emperor made Tokugawa Ieyasu (toh-koohg-AH-wuhee e-YAHS-ooh) the shogun. He opened trade with other countries. Others, however, feared the intrusion of foreigners. In 1630, the ruling shogun closed off Japan and the samurai period lasted until the 1800s./Con el tiempo, nuevos líderes subieron al poder. Todos lucharon para unificar a Japón bajo su dominio. El primero en restaurar el poder de los shogúns fue Oda Nobunaga. Los shogúns que le siguieron lograron unificar el gobierno japonés. En 1603, el emperador nombró shogún a Tokugawa Ieyasu. Este estableció el comercio con otros países. Sin embargo, otros temían la intromisión extranjera. En 1630, el shogún que gobernaba cerró por completo las puertas de Japón, y el período samurái duró hasta el siglo 19.

> **Which shogun opened Japan up the world?/¿Qué shogún abrió las puertas de Japón al mundo?**
>
> _____
>
> _____

## CHALLENGE ACTIVITY/ACTIVIDAD AVANZADA

**Critical Thinking: Make Inferences/Pensamiento crítico: Hacer inferencias** You are an ordinary Japanese citizen living in the early 1200s. To whom do you pledge the highest allegiance—the emperor, the shogun, or the samurai who work for them? Explain your reasoning in a one-page essay./Imagina que eres un ciudadano japonés común a principios del siglo 13. ¿A quién le prometes mayor lealtad: al emperador, al shogún o a los samuráis que trabajan para ellos? Explica tu razonamiento en un ensayo de una página.

**DIRECTIONS/INSTRUCCIONES** Match the terms in the first column
with their correct definition from the second column by placing the
letter of the correct definition in the space provided before each
term./Une los términos de la primera columna con su definición
correcta en la segunda columna. Escribe la letra de la definición
correcta en el espacio que precede a cada término.

_____ 1. samurai/samurái

_____ 2. daimyo/daimyo

_____ 3. shogun/shogún

_____ 4. figurehead/gobernante
decorativo

_____ 5. kamikaze/kamikaze

_____ 6. emperor/emperador

_____ 7. Bushido/Bushido

a. person who appears to rule even though
the real power rests with someone else/
persona que aparenta gobernar, aunque
el poder real lo tiene otra persona

b. samurai code that means "the way of
the warrior"/código samurái que
significa "el camino del guerrero"

c. powerful landowners who held great
power in Japan/terratenientes que
tenían mucho poder en Japón

d. the title of a general who ruled Japan in
the emperor's name/título de un general
que gobernaba Japón en nombre del
emperador

e. trained professional warriors that
defended the large landowners and
protected their property/guerreros
profesionales entrenados que defendían
a los grandes terratenientes y protegían
su propiedad

f. the head of Japan's government, often
with little real power/líder del gobierno
japonés, a menudo con muy poco
poder real

g. name given to the storm that helped
the Japanese soldiers defeat the second
Mongol invasion/nombre que se le dio
a la tormenta que ayudó a los soldados
japoneses a derrotar la segunda invasión
de los mongoles

## Cultures of South and Southwest Asia/Culturas del sur y suroeste asiático

**MAIN IDEAS/IDEAS PRINCIPALES**

**1.** The Ottoman Empire covered a large area in eastern Europe and was a large commercial center./El Imperio otomano abarcó una amplia región de Europa oriental y constituyó un gran centro comercial.

**2.** Ottoman society produced lasting scientific and cultural contributions./La sociedad otomana hizo contribuciones científicas y culturales duraderas.

## Key Terms and People/Personas y palabras clave

**Janissaries/jenízaros** enslaved youths converted to Islam and trained as soldiers/ jóvenes esclavizados, convertidos al islam y entrenados para ser soldados

**Mehmed II/Mehmet II** Ottoman ruler who defeated the Byzantine Empire/ gobernante otomano que derrotó al Imperio bizantino

**sultan/sultán** Ottoman ruler/gobernante otomano

**Suleyman I/Solimán I** Ottoman ruler who led the empire to its heights/gobernante otomano que llevó al imperio a su mayor esplendor

**harem/harén** separate area of a household where women lived away from men/ área que se encontraba aislada dentro del hogar y donde las mujeres vivían separadas de los hombres

## Lesson Summary/Resumen de la lección

### THE RISE OF THE OTOMAN EMPIRE/ASCENSO DEL IMPERIO OTOMANO

Centuries after the early Arab Muslim conquests, Muslims ruled several powerful empires. One of these empires was the Ottoman Empire. This empire controlled much of Europe, Asia, and Africa. Built on conquest, the Ottoman Empire was a political and cultural force for centuries./ Siglos después de las primeras conquistas de los musulmanes árabes, los musulmanes gobernaron varios imperios muy poderosos. Uno de ellos fue el Imperio otomano. Este imperio controló gran parte de Europa, Asia y África. Conformado mediante la conquista, el Imperio otomano fue una potencia política y cultural durante siglos.

In the mid-1200s, Muslim Turkish warriors took land from the Christian Byzantine Empire. The

Ottomans eventually ruled lands from eastern Europe to North Africa and Arabia. **Janissaries,** enslaved youths taken from conquered towns and converted to Islam, were fierce fighters for the Ottomans. The Byzantine Empire came to an end in 1453 when Ottomans led by **Mehmed II** captured Constantinople. The Ottomans named it Istanbul./Hacia mediados del siglo 13, los soldados turcos musulmanes ocuparon tierras del Imperio cristiano bizantino. Con el tiempo, los otomanos gobernaron tierras desde Europa oriental hasta el norte de África y Arabia. Los **jenízaros,** jóvenes capturados de entre los pueblos conquistados, y luego esclavizados y convertidos al islam, eran guerreros feroces que luchaban a favor de los otomanos. El Imperio bizantino llegó a su fin en 1453, cuando los otomanos, liderados por **Mehmet II,** conquistaron Constantinopla. Los otomanos la llamaron Estambul.

Istanbul became the capital and a commercial and cultural center. A later **sultan,** or Ottoman ruler, continued Mehmed's conquests. The Ottoman Empire reached its height under **Suleyman I.** By 1566, the Ottomans took control of the eastern Mediterranean and pushed farther into Europe./Estambul se convirtió en la capital y en un foco comercial y cultural. Un **sultán,** o gobernante otomano, posterior continuó con las conquistas de Mehmet. El Imperio otomano alcanzó su máximo esplendor durante el gobierno de **Solimán I.** Hacia 1566, los otomanos tomaron control de la región este del Mediterráneo y siguieron desplazándose más hacia Europa.

Ottoman society was divided into two classes. Judges and others who advised the sultan were part of the ruling class. They had to be loyal to the sultan, practice Islam, and understand Ottoman customs. The other class included Christians and Jews from lands the Ottomans had conquered. Ottoman society limited the

---

| Underline the phrase that tells where the Ottomans found fierce soldiers./ Subraya la frase que menciona dónde los otomanos conseguían guerreros feroces. |

| What year signifies the final end of the Byzantine Empire?/¿Qué año representa el final absoluto del Imperio bizantino? _____ |

| Which groups were part of the ruling class in Ottoman society?/¿Qué grupos eran parte de la clase gobernante de la sociedad otomana? _____ _____ _____ |

freedom of women, especially those in the ruling class. Women had to live apart from men in an area called a **harem.**/La sociedad otomana se dividía en dos clases. Los jueces y otros funcionarios que aconsejaban al sultán pertenecían a la clase gobernante. Debían ser fieles al sultán, practicar el islam y respetar las costumbres otomanas. La otra clase estaba formada por los cristianos y judíos de las tierras conquistadas por los otomanos. La sociedad otomana limitaba la libertad de las mujeres, especialmente de aquellas que pertenecían a la clase gobernante. Las mujeres tenían que vivir aisladas de los hombres en un área conocida como **harén.**

## SCIENTIFIC AND CULTURAL ADVANCES/
### AVANCES CIENTÍFICOS Y CULTURALES

The Ottoman Empire is well known for its many scientific advancements. Taqi al-Din was an Ottoman astronomer and mathematician who founded the Istanbul Observatory. He wrote books on astronomy, medicine, and physics. He used mechanical-automatic clocks to make his astronomical observations./Al Imperio otomano se lo reconoce por sus múltiples avances científicos. Taqi al-Din fue el astrónomo y matemático otomano que fundó el Observatorio de Estambul. Escribió libros sobre astronomía, medicina y física. Además, utilizó relojes mecánicos automáticos para realizar sus observaciones astronómicas.

Since the Ottoman Empire controlled parts of different continents, people from many cultures lived under its rule. Parts of these cultures are seen in its art and architecture. Previous buildings in the region influenced Ottoman architecture. For example, the Hagia Sophia was once a Byzantine church from the fourth and fifth centuries. The

> **Underline the sentence that explains why elements of many cultures are found in Ottoman art and architecture.**/Subraya la oración que explica por qué los elementos de muchas culturas se encuentran en el arte y la arquitectura otomanas.

Ottomans converted it to a mosque. Other mosques share its features, such as large domes. Also, the designs of exteriors, windows, and gates of mosques have features found in Italian buildings./Como el Imperio otomano controlaba partes de diferentes continentes, bajo su dominio vivían pueblos de distintas culturas. Algunos rasgos de estas culturas pueden descubrirse en el arte y la arquitectura otomanos. Los edificios que ya se encontraban en la región influyeron en la arquitectura. Por ejemplo, la catedral de Santa Sofía solía ser una iglesia bizantina de los siglos 4 y 5. Los otomanos la convirtieron en mezquita. Otras mezquitas comparten características con ella, como las enormes cúpulas. Además, los diseños de los exteriores, las ventanas y las puertas de las mezquitas presentan características que pueden encontrarse en las construcciones italianas.

Literature and poetry were popular too. Yunus Emre introduced a form of mythical poetry. Some later poets imitated his style. Different forms of theater were popular, including mime shows and comedies./La literatura y la poesía también gozaron de popularidad. Yunus Emre introdujo una forma de poesía mítica. Otros poetas posteriores imitaron su estilo. También eran populares distintos géneros dramáticos, como los espectáculos de mimos y las comedias.

> **What forms of poetry and theater were found throughout the Ottoman Empire?/¿Qué formas de poesía y teatro estuvieron presentes en todo el Imperio otomano?**
>
> _____
>
> _____

## CHALLENGE ACTIVITY/ACTIVIDAD AVANZADA

**Critical Thinking: Make Inferences/Pensamiento crítico: Hacer inferencias** Suppose you are a visitor to the Ottoman Empire. Write two or three journal entries about what you might see there and your impressions of Ottoman society./Imagina que visitas el Imperio otomano. Escribe dos o tres entradas de diario sobre lo que podrías observar allí y qué impresiones te genera la sociedad otomana.

**DIRECTIONS/INSTRUCCIONES** Read each sentence and fill in
the blank with the word in the word pair that best completes
the sentence./Lee cada oración y escribe en el espacio en blanco
la palabra del par de palabras que mejor la completa.

1. The Ottoman used fierce fighters called _____·_____, enslaved
   youths that converted to Islam. **(harem /Janissaries)**/Los otomanos contaban
   con guerreros feroces llamados _____, que
   eran jóvenes esclavizados y convertidos al islam. **(harén/jenízaros)**

2. The Ottoman ruler who was responsible for leading the empire to its greatest
   heights was _____. **(Suleyman I/Mehmed II)**/El
   gobernante otomano responsable de llevar el imperio a su máximo esplendor
   fue _____. **(Solimán I/Mehmet II)**

3. The title given to an Ottoman ruler was _____.
   **(harem/sultan)**/El título otorgado a un gobernante otomano era
   _____. **(harén/sultán)**

4. The separate area of a household where women lived away from men was
   known as a _____. **(sultan/harem)**/El área que estaba
   aislada dentro del hogar y donde las mujeres vivían separadas de los hombres
   era conocida como _____. **(sultán/harén)**

5. The Ottoman ruler who was responsible for defeating the Byzantine Empire
   was _____·_____. **(Suleyman I/Mehmed II)**/El gobernante
   otomano responsable de derrotar al Imperio bizantino fue
   _____. **(Solimán I/Mehmet II)**

# Cultures of South and Southwest Asia/Culturas del sur y suroeste asiático

**MAIN IDEAS/IDEAS PRINCIPALES**
1. The Safavid Empire blended Persian cultural traditions with Shia Islam./El Imperio safávida mezcló las tradiciones culturales persas con el islam chiita.
2. The Safavids supported trade networks throughout the region./Los safávidas fortalecieron las redes comerciales en toda la región.

## Key Terms and People/Personas y palabras clave

**Shia/chiita** Muslims who thought that only members of Muhammad's family could become caliphs/musulmanes que pensaban que solo los parientes de Mahoma podían ser califas

**Sunni/sunita** Muslims who believed caliphs did not have to be related to Muhammad as long as they were good Muslims and strong leaders/musulmanes que creían que los califas no necesitaban ser parientes de Mahoma, siempre y cuando fueran buenos musulmanes y líderes fuertes

## Lesson Summary/Resumen de la lección
### THE SAFAVID EMPIRE/IMPERIO SAFÁVIDA

To the east of the Ottoman Empire, the Safavids, a group of Persian Muslims, started gaining power. They came into conflict with the Ottomans and other Muslims. The conflict was about the old disagreement among Muslims over who should be caliph. Since a caliph is someone who leads all Muslims, he is viewed as Muhammad's successor. During the mid-600s, Islam had split into two groups over this issue. The **Shia** were Muslims who thought that only members of Muhammad's family could become caliph. In contrast, the **Sunni** did not think caliphs had to be related to Muhammad as long as they were good Muslims and strong leaders. While the two groups both believed in daily prayer and fasting during Ramadan, some religious differences developed between them./Al este del Imperio otomano, los safávidas, un grupo persa musulmán, comenzaron a ganar poder. Entraron en conflicto con los otomanos y otros musulmanes. El

> What was the basis for the split between the Sunnis and the Shias?/¿Cuál fue la causa de la división entre sunitas y chiitas?
> _____
> _____

conflicto se trataba de un antiguo desacuerdo entre los musulmanes acerca de quién debía ser califa. Como el califa es quien dirige a todos los musulmanes, se lo considera el sucesor de Mahoma. Hacia mediados del siglo 7, el islam se dividió en dos grupos en torno a este conflicto. Los **chiitas** eran los musulmanes que pensaban que solo los parientes de Mahoma podían ser califas. En cambio, los **sunitas** consideraban que los califas no necesitaban estar relacionados con Mahoma, siempre y cuando fueran buenos musulmanes y líderes fuertes. A pesar de que ambos grupos creían en el rezo diario y en el ayuno durante el Ramadán, surgieron algunas diferencias entre ellos.

The Safavid leader Esma'il conquered Persia in 1501 and became shah, or king. He made Shiism, the beliefs of the Shia, the official religion of the empire. However, most people in the empire were Sunnis. Esma'il was committed to conquering other Muslim territories and converting all Muslims to Shiism. After his death, his successors struggled to keep the empire together. In 1588, 'Abbas, the greatest Safavid leader, became shah. He strengthened the military and had his soldiers use gunpowder weapons. Similar to the Ottomans, 'Abbas trained foreign enslaved boys to be soldiers. Under his rule, the Safavids defeated the Uzbeks and took back land that had been lost to the Ottomans. 'Abbas also made many contributions to Safavid culture and economy./El líder safávida Esma'il conquistó Persia en 1501 y se convirtió en Shah, o rey. Hizo del chiismo, el conjunto de creencias de los chiitas, la religión oficial del imperio. Sin embargo, la mayoría de los habitantes del imperio eran sunitas. Esma'il se dedicó a conquistar otros territorios musulmanes y convertir a todos los musulmanes al chiismo. Tras su muerte, sus sucesores tuvieron dificultades

> **Underline the sentence that tells what Esma'il did after he became shah./** Subraya la oración que dice lo que hizo Esma'il tras convertirse en Shah.

> **What made 'Abbas the greatest Safavid leader?/** ¿Qué hizo que 'Abbas fuera el más grande de los líderes safávidas?
>
> _____
> _____
> _____
> _____
> _____
> _____

Lesson/Lección 2, *continued*/*continuación*

---

para mantener unido el imperio. En 1588, 'Abbas,
el más grande de los líderes safávidas, se convirtió
en Shah, fortaleció el ejército e hizo que sus
soldados emplearan armas que usaban pólvora.
De manera similar a lo que hicieron los otomanos,
'Abbas entrenó a niños extranjeros esclavizados
para que fueran soldados. Durante su reinado, los
safávidas derrotaron a los uzbekos y recuperaron
tierras que habían perdido a manos de los
otomanos. 'Abbas también contribuyó mucho a la
cultura y la economía safávida.

## SAFAVID CULTURE AND ECONOMY/CULTURA Y ECONOMÍA SAFÁVIDAS

The Safavids blended Persian and Muslim
traditions. They built beautiful mosques in their
capital city of Esfahan. The Shah's mosque, built
for 'Abbas, was admired for its colorful tiles and
large dome. In the 1600s, Esfahan was considered
one of the world's most magnificent cities. It
was said to have 162 mosques and more than
1,800 commercial buildings. It had rugs and
objects made in silver, gold, and enamel.
Poetry, painting, and drawing were popular./
Los safávidas combinaron tradiciones persas y
musulmanas. Construyeron mezquitas hermosas
en la ciudad capital, Isfahán. La mezquita del
Shah, construida para 'Abbas, era admirada
por sus coloridos azulejos y su gran cúpula.
En el siglo 17, Isfahán era consideraba una de
las ciudades más imponentes del mundo. Se
decía que contaba con 162 mezquitas y más de
1,800 edificios comerciales. Tenía alfombras y
objetos de plata, oro y esmalte. La poesía, la
pintura y el dibujo gozaban de popularidad.

Safavid culture was important to the empire's
economy because 'Abbas encouraged the
manufacturing of traditional products. Major
exports included handwoven carpets, silk, and

> **Why was Esfahan thought of as a magnificent city?/**
> ¿Por qué Isfahán era considerada una ciudad imponente?
>
> _____
> _____
> _____
> _____
> _____
> _____

velvet. Also, the Safavids were admired for
their skills in making ceramic and metal goods,
especially goods made from steel./La cultura
safávida era importante para la economía
del imperio, ya que 'Abbas fomentaba la
fabricación de productos tradicionales. Entre
las exportaciones principales del imperio se
encontraban las alfombras tejidas a mano, la
seda y el terciopelo. Además, los safávidas eran
admirados por su destreza para hacer cerámica
y para fabricar objetos metálicos, especialmente
artículos de acero.

The Safavids also built roads and bridges,
which made it possible for merchants to come
from as far away as Europe to trade. This led
to wealth for the Safavid Empire and helped
establish it as a major Islamic civilization.
It lasted until the mid-1700s./Los safávidas
también construyeron caminos y puentes, lo
que permitió que llegaran comerciantes
provenientes desde lugares tan lejanos como
Europa. Esto generó riqueza para el Imperio
safávida y ayudó a establecerlo como una de
las principales civilizaciones islámicas. Duró
hasta mediados del siglo 18.

> **Underline the sentence that explains why the Safavid Empire became wealthy and a major Islamic civilization./Subraya la oración que explica por qué el Imperio safávida se enriqueció y se convirtió en una civilización islámica importante.**

## CHALLENGE ACTIVITY/ACTIVIDAD AVANZADA

**Critical Thinking: Make Judgements/Pensamiento crítico: Dar opiniones** The Safavid shah made Shiism the official religion of the empire. Do you think he should have done this? Write a one-page paper about his action, how it most likely affected people of other religions, and your opinion of this kind of rule./El Shah safávida convirtió el chiismo en la religión oficial del imperio. ¿Piensas que hizo lo correcto? Escribe un ensayo de una página sobre esta medida y sobre cómo debió afectar a las personas de otras religiones. Opina sobre este tipo de mandato.

**DIRECTIONS/INSTRUCCIONES** Use the vocabulary words **Shia** and
**Sunni** to write a letter that relates to the lesson./Usa las palabras de
vocabulario **chiita** y **sunita** para escribir una carta que se relacione
con la lección.

_____

_____

_____

_____

_____

_____

_____

_____

_____

_____

_____

_____

_____

_____

_____

_____

# Cultures of South and Southwest Asia/Culturas del sur y suroeste asiático

## Lesson/Lección 3

**MAIN IDEAS/IDEAS PRINCIPALES**

1. Sikhs believe in equality and generally reject the Hindu caste system./Los sijes creen en la igualdad y, en términos generales, rechazan el sistema de castas hindú.

2. Sikhs have responded to historical and modern-day challenges./Los sijes han respondido a los retos históricos y actuales.

## Key Terms and People/Personas y palabras clave

**langar/langar** kitchen/cocina

**gurdwara/gurdwara** places of worship/lugares de culto

## Lesson Summary/Resumen de la lección

### SIKH RELIGIOUS PHILOSOPHIES/FILOSOFÍAS RELIGIOSAS DE LOS SIJES

Sikhism began in the Punjab in the late 15th century and was started by Guru Nanak. People who follow the religion are Sikhs. Guru Nanak was raised a Hindu, but he did not believe some Hindu teachings. For example, he thought people from different social classes should be treated fairly. People liked his ideas about equality. After his death, there were nine other gurus. The teachings of the ten gurus form the essential beliefs of Sikhism./El sijismo comenzó en el Punjab hacia fines del siglo 15 y fue impulsado por Gurú Nanak. Quienes adhieren a esta religión se llaman sijes. Gurú Nanak fue criado como hindú, pero no creía en algunas de las enseñanzas hindúes. Por ejemplo, él pensaba que debía tratarse con equidad a personas pertenecientes a clases sociales diferentes. Sus ideas sobre la igualdad encontraban aceptación entre la gente. Tras su muerte, hubo otros nueve gurús. Las enseñanzas de los diez gurús componen las creencias básicas del sijismo.

> **What did Guru Nanak believe about the Hindu social classes?/¿Qué pensaba Gurú Nanak sobre las clases sociales hindúes?**
>
> _____
> _____
> _____
> _____

Sikhs believe that the gurus were inhabited by a single spirit. When one guru died, the spirit, or eternal Guru, transferred to the next human guru through reincarnation. After the tenth guru died in 1708, Sikhs believe the spirit transferred itself to the sacred scripture called Guru Granth Sahib. It has the actual words spoken by the gurus. Sikhs believe these words are the word of God, or Wahegure./Los sijes creen que los gurús compartían un mismo espíritu. Cuando un gurú moría, su espíritu, o Gurú eterno, se transfería al próximo gurú humano a través de la reencarnación. Los sijes consideran que con la muerte del décimo gurú, en 1708, el espíritu se transfirió a las sagradas escrituras llamadas Gurú Granth Sahib, que, según esta creencia, contiene las palabras exactas que pronunciaron los gurús. Los sijes creen que estas palabras son la palabra de Dios, o Wahegure.

Sikhs believe that there is only one God. They believe that everyone has equal access to God and is equal before God. Like Hindus, they believe that humans cycle through life, death, and reincarnation, and they believe in karma./Los sijes creen que solo existe un Dios. Piensan que todos tenemos el mismo acceso a Dios y que todos somos iguales frente a él. Como los hindúes, ellos también creen que los humanos transitan un ciclo de vida, muerte y reencarnación, y además creen en el karma.

Sikhs believe in equality between social classes, so they do not agree with most of the Hindu caste system. In places of worship, food is served without charge in the kitchen, or **langar**./Los sijes creen en la igualdad entre las clases sociales, así que no están de acuerdo con gran parte del sistema de castas hindú. En los lugares de culto, la comida se sirve sin costo en la cocina, o **langar.**

**Underline the phrase that tells what the Sikhs believe about the ten gurus./**
Subraya la frase que dice qué creen los sijes sobre los diez gurús.

**What beliefs do Sikhs and Hindus have in common?/**
¿Qué creencias tienen en común los sijes y los hindúes?

_____
_____
_____

Two areas of the caste system Sikhs observe are related to marriage and **gurdwaras,** or places of worship. It is expected that Sikhs will marry someone of their own caste./Dos aspectos del sistema de castas que siguen los sijes están relacionados con el matrimonio y los **gurdwaras,** o lugares de culto. Se espera que los sijes se casen con alguien de su misma casta.

> Underline the sentence that tells something Sikhs observe that is part of the caste system./Subraya la oración que menciona algo que hacen los sijes y que es parte del sistema de castas.

## SIKH HISTORY/HISTORIA DE LOS SIJES

During the 1600s, many Sikhs lived in India's Punjab region, which was controlled by the Mughal Empire. The Sikhs protested unfair taxes and other mistreatment. To stop the protests, the Mughals used war elephants. Violent revolts occurred throughout the region during the 1600s and 1700s./Durante el siglo 17, muchos sijes vivían en la región del Punjab, en la India, que estaba controlada por el Imperio mogol. Los sijes protestaron a causa de los impuestos injustos y otros maltratos. Para detener las protestas, los mogoles utilizaron elefantes de guerra. Durante los siglos 17 y 18, se produjeron revueltas violentas por toda la región.

> How did the Mughal stop Sikh protests?/¿Cómo detuvieron los mogoles las protestas de los sijes?
>
> _____
>
> _____

As the Mughal Empire began to weaken, Sikh resistance got stronger. By the late 1700s, Sikhs controlled much of the Punjab. In 1799, Ranjit Singh declared himself maharaja, or ruler of the Punjab. The Sikh Empire had finally begun./A medida que el Imperio mogol empezó a debilitarse, la resistencia sij se consolidó. Hacia fines del siglo 18, los sijes controlaban gran parte del Punjab. En 1799, Ranjit Singh se autoproclamó marajá, o gobernante del Punjab. El Imperio sij finalmente había nacido.

During this time, a gurdwara was rebuilt using marble and gold. It became a symbol of Sikh power. It was called the Golden Temple. Singh was a strong ruler and the empire thrived.

However, Singh died in 1839, and the empire began to weaken. Then after conflict with the British, the Punjab became part of British India in 1849./En estos años, se reconstruyó un gurdwara utilizando mármol y oro, y se convirtió en un símbolo del poder de los sijes. Se lo llamó el Templo Dorado. Singh fue un gobernante poderoso, y el imperio prosperó bajo su mando. No obstante, Singh murió en 1839, y el imperio comenzó a debilitarse. Luego, en 1849, tras un conflicto con los británicos, el Punjab pasó a formar parte de la India británica.

| Who was Ranjit Singh?/ ¿Quién fue Ranjit Singh? |
| --- |
| _____ |
| _____ |
| _____ |
| _____ |
| _____ |

Today, there are about 25 million Sikhs worldwide. At first, most migrant Sikhs settled in India close to the Punjab. When the British took control of India in 1858, Sikhs became soldiers and were sent to the British colonies of Malaya and Hong Kong. So Sikh migration expanded to Asia, Australia, and North America. Many live in the United Kingdom, Canada, and the United States./Actualmente, hay alrededor de 25 millones de sijes en el mundo. En un principio, la mayoría de los migrantes sijes se establecieron en la India, cerca del Punjab. Cuando los británicos tomaron el control de la India en 1858, los sijes se convirtieron en soldados y fueron enviados a las colonias británicas de Malaya y Hong Kong. De esta manera, la migración sij se expandió por Asia, Australia y América del Norte. Muchos de ellos viven en el Reino Unido, Canadá y los Estados Unidos.

## CHALLENGE ACTIVITY/ACTIVIDAD AVANZADA

**Critical Thinking: Draw Conclusions/Pensamiento crítico: Sacar conclusiones** Think about what you know about Sikhism. Write a one-page paper telling why you think Sikhism developed and spread./Piensa en lo que sabes sobre el sijismo. Escribe un ensayo de una página para expresar por qué crees que surgió y se expandió el sijismo.

**DIRECTIONS/INSTRUCCIONES** Look up the vocabulary terms
**langar** and **gurdwara** on the Internet or another resource. Write a
description of each word that is closest to the definition used in
your textbook./Busca en Internet o en otras fuentes los términos
de vocabulario **langar** y **gurdwara.** Escribe una descripción para
cada palabra que sea lo más parecida posible a la definición que
figura en tu libro de texto.

1. langar/langar_____

_____

2. gurdwara/gurdwara _____

_____

# Cultures of South and Southwest Asia/Culturas del sur y suroeste asiático

**MAIN IDEAS/IDEAS PRINCIPALES**

1. Akbar was able to unify the Mughal Empire through his tolerant religious and political policies./Akbar logró unificar el Imperio mogol gracias a medidas respetuosas de cuestiones religiosas y políticas.

2. Many cultures blended together to create a society unique to the Mughal Empire./Muchas culturas se mezclaron para crear una sociedad que solo existió en el Imperio mogol.

## Key Terms and People/Personas y palabras clave

**Babur/Babur** founder of the Mughal Empire; the name means "tiger"/fundador del Imperio mogol; su nombre significa "tigre"

**Akbar/Akbar** emperor who helped the Mughal Empire to grow/emperador que contribuyó al crecimiento del Imperio mogol

## Lesson Summary/Resumen de la lección

### THE HISTORY OF THE MUGHAL EMPIRE/ HISTORIA DEL IMPERIO MOGOL

The Mughal Empire was to the east of the Safavid Empire in India. The Mughals were Turkish Muslims from Central Asia. **Babur,** or "tiger," was the founder of the Mughal Empire. He established it in 1526. During the mid-1500s, the empire grew under **Akbar.** He conquered new lands. He created a government with four departments and provincial governments. Akbar also had a tolerant religious policy. He stopped the tax on non-Muslims, and he included Hindus in the Mughal governments. These policies helped unite the empire./El Imperio mogol se situaba en la India, al este del Imperio safávida. Los mogoles eran musulmanes turcos de Asia central. **Babur,** o "tigre", fue el fundador del Imperio mogol. Lo estableció en 1526. A mediados del siglo 16, el imperio creció bajo el mando de **Akbar,** que conquistó nuevas tierras y creó un gobierno con cuatro departamentos y gobiernos provinciales. Akbar también impulsó una política religiosa tolerante. Detuvo el cobro de impuestos a

> **Who was the founder of the Mughal empire?/¿Quién fue el fundador del Imperio mogol?**
>
> _____

> **How did Akbar's tolerant religious policies help the Mughal empire?/¿Cómo ayudaron las políticas religiosas tolerantes de Akbar al Imperio mogol?**
>
> _____
> _____

quienes no eran musulmanes y permitió que los hindúes formaran parte de los gobiernos mogoles. Estas políticas ayudaron a unificar el imperio.

The Mughal Empire was located along the center of trade routes that stretched across Asia. This contributed to its growth. It produced quality textiles and became a commercial center./ El Imperio mogol se ubicaba en la zona central de las rutas comerciales que atravesaban Asia. Esto contribuyó a su crecimiento. El Imperio mogol producía tejidos de calidad y constituyó un centro comercial.

During the 1600s, Mughal emperors took control of almost all of India. Then a new emperor, Aurangzeb, came to power. He ordered people to obey strict religious laws and destroyed Hindu temples. He ended Akbar's tolerant policies by persecuting non-Muslims and reinstituting the tax./Durante el siglo 17, los emperadores mogoles tomaron el control de casi toda la India. Luego, un nuevo emperador, Aurangzeb, llegó al poder. Ordenó a los habitantes obedecer leyes religiosas estrictas y destruyó templos hindúes. Acabó con las políticas tolerantes de Akbar, dado que persiguió a quienes no eran musulmanes y restituyó el cobro de impuestos.

Aurangzeb's political and religious intolerance caused problems for the empire. Hindus could not have their own customs, and the entire empire was under Islamic law. Hindus and others revolted, and over time the government declined. The economy weakened and soon the empire fell apart./La intolerancia política y religiosa de Aurangzeb causó problemas al imperio. Los hindúes no podían practicar sus propias costumbres y el imperio entero se encontraba bajo la ley islámica. Los hindúes y otros grupos se rebelaron y con el tiempo el gobierno entró en decadencia. La economía se debilitó y pronto el imperio se vino abajo.

> **How was Aurangzeb different from Akbar?/ ¿En qué se diferenciaba Aurangzeb de Akbar?**
>
> _____
> _____
> _____
> _____
> _____

The British began to take greater control over political and economic life in India. Great Britain replaced Indian leaders with British officials. Indians were unhappy and in 1857, people in different cities throughout India began a mutiny. However, the British military was strong. It had rifles and cannons, which gave the British an advantage over Indian troops. The mutiny was ended in 1858, and the last Mughal shah had to leave the region. The British had control of India./Los británicos empezaron a ejercer mayor control sobre la vida política y económica de la India. Gran Bretaña reemplazó a los líderes indios con oficiales británicos. Los indios no estaban contentos y, en 1857, los habitantes de diferentes ciudades de toda la India comenzaron un motín. Sin embargo, el ejército británico era poderoso, ya que contaba con rifles y cañones, y esto le daba una ventaja sobre las tropas indias. El motín fue neutralizado en 1858, y el último Shah mogol tuvo que abandonar la región. Los británicos tomaron el control de la India.

> **Underline the sentence that tells why the British were able to end the mutiny in India./**Subraya la oración que explica por qué los británicos pudieron terminar con el motín de la India.

## CULTURAL ACHIEVEMENTS/LOGROS CULTURALES

When Akbar had been ruler, he welcomed different forms of Hindu culture. Persians and Indians lived and worked in the same areas. So elements of their cultures blended together and formed a culture unique to the Mughal Empire./Cuando Akbar fue gobernante, acogió las diferentes expresiones de la cultura hindú. Los persas y los indios vivían y trabajaban en las mismas zonas. Así, algunos elementos de sus culturas se mezclaron y crearon una cultura que solo existió en el Imperio mogol.

Also during Akbar's rule, the Persian language and Persian clothing styles were popular. He also encouraged people to write in Hindi and Urdu. Education was reformed and many buildings blended Persian, Islamic, and Hindu styles./

> **What languages were part of the Mughal Empire?/**¿Qué lenguas formaron parte del Imperio mogol?
>
> _____

Lesson/Lección 4, *continued*/*continuación*

Además, durante el reinado de Akbar, la lengua y los estilos de vestimenta persas eran populares. Él también fomentó que las personas escribieran en hindi y urdu. Hubo una reforma en la educación y, en cuanto a la arquitectura, muchos edificios combinaron los estilos persa, islámico e hindú.

The Mughal Empire is famous for its architecture, especially the Taj Mahal. Built by Akbar's grandson as a tomb for his wife, it brought workers and materials from all over India and Central Asia. The palace buildings include a main gateway and a mosque. Its many gardens with pathways and fountains make the palace beautiful./El Imperio mogol es famoso por su arquitectura, especialmente por el Taj Mahal. Construido por el nieto de Akbar como tumba para su esposa, su edificación trajo trabajadores y materiales de toda la India y Asia central. Los edificios del palacio incluyen una puerta de entrada principal y una mezquita. Contiene muchos jardines con veredas y fuentes que embellecen el palacio.

> **What is the most famous architectural achievement of the Mughal Empire?/**
> **¿Cuál es el logro arquitectónico más famoso del Imperio mogol?**
> _____

## CHALLENGE ACTIVITY/ACTIVIDAD AVANZADA

**Critical Thinking: Make Inferences/Pensamiento crítico: Hacer inferencias** Akbar encouraged diversity. The United States is a diverse society, too. Should a nation encourage diversity? What can a lack of diversity cause? Write a one-page paper explaining how diversity affects you./Akbar fomentó la diversidad. Los Estados Unidos también son una sociedad diversa. ¿Una nación debe fomentar la diversidad? ¿Qué podría provocar la falta de diversidad? Escribe un ensayo de una página para explicar qué consecuencias genera en tu vida la diversidad.

**DIRECTIONS/INSTRUCCIONES** Write a word or descriptive phrase to describe each person./Escribe una palabra o frase descriptiva que describa a cada persona.

1. Babur/Babur_____

_____

2. Akbar/Akbar_____

_____

3. Aurangzeb/Aurangzeb_____

_____

Name/Nombre_____ Class/Clase _____ Date/Fecha_____

# The Early Americas/El continente americano en sus inicios

Lesson/Lección 1

**MAIN IDEAS/IDEAS PRINCIPALES**

1. The geography of the Americas is varied, with a wide range of landforms./La geografía del continente americano es variada e incluye una amplia variedad de accidentes geográficos.

2. The first people to arrive in the Americas were hunter-gatherers./Las primeras personas en llegar al continente americano eran cazadores y recolectores.

3. The development of farming led to early settlements in the Americas./El desarrollo de la agricultura permitió los primeros asentamientos en el continente americano.

## Key Terms and People/Personas y palabras clave

**Mesoamerica/Mesoamérica** region that includes the southern part of what is now Mexico and parts of the northern countries of Central America/región que incluye la parte sur de lo que hoy es México y partes de los países del norte de América Central

**maize/maíz** corn/cereal también conocido como elote o choclo

## Lesson Summary/Resumen de la lección
### GEOGRAPHY OF THE AMERICAS/GEOGRAFÍA DEL CONTINENTE AMERICANO

The Americas are made up of two continents, North America and South America. These continents have a wide range of landforms. North America has high mountains, desert plateaus, grassy plains, and forests./El continente americano está dividido en dos subcontinentes: América del Norte y América del Sur. Estos subcontinentes poseen una amplia variedad de accidentes geográficos. América del Norte tiene montañas altas, mesetas desérticas, llanuras con pastizales y bosques.

Historians call the cultural region in the southern part of North America **Mesoamerica.** Mesoamerica reached from the middle of modern-day Mexico south into Central America. The region's many rain forests and rivers created fertile farmland. The first farmers in the

**Where was the region of Mesoamerica located?/ ¿Dónde se ubicaba la región de Mesoamérica?**

_____
_____
_____
_____

Americas domesticated plants there./Los historiadores llaman **Mesoamérica** a la región cultural de la parte sur de América del Norte. Mesoamérica se extendía desde el centro de la zona sur del México actual hasta América Central. La gran cantidad de bosques tropicales y ríos de la región crearon tierras fértiles para la agricultura. Los primeros agricultores del continente americano domesticaron las plantas de ese lugar.

The Andes Mountains run along the western side of South America. Narrow desert runs along the edge of fishing waters in the Pacific Ocean. East of the Andes lies a region with a hot rain forest and a mighty river. The region, the river, and the rain forest all share the same name—Amazon./ La cordillera de los Andes se extiende a lo largo del lado oeste de América del Sur. A orillas del océano Pacífico, cuyas aguas son aptas para la pesca, se extiende un desierto angosto. Al este de los Andes se encuentra una región que posee un bosque tropical caluroso y un río caudaloso. Tanto la región como el río y el bosque tropical llevan el mismo nombre: Amazonas.

> **What three geographic elements share the name Amazon?/¿Cuáles son los tres elementos geográficos que llevan el nombre de Amazonas?**
>
> _____
> _____
> _____

## THE FIRST PEOPLE ARRIVE/LLEGADA DE LOS PRIMEROS HABITANTES

No one is sure how people first arrived in the Americas. Some scientists believe they came from Asia up to 15,000 years ago by walking over a land bridge that crossed the Bering Strait. Other historians think the first Americans arrived by sea./No se sabe con certeza cuándo llegaron las primeras personas al continente americano. Algunos científicos creen que llegaron desde Asia hace no más de 15,000 años, después de cruzar un puente de tierra que atravesaba el estrecho de Bering. Otros historiadores piensan que los primeros habitantes del continente americano llegaron por mar.

> **Underline two ways that scientists think people might have come to the Americas./Subraya dos maneras en que los científicos creen que las personas pueden haber llegado al continente americano.**

The earliest people were hunter-gatherers. These people survived on wild buffalo and other animals, as well as fruits, nuts, and wild grains. They moved often, going where food was most plentiful. Some people eventually settled along the coastal areas. They fished and planted different types of seeds./Los primeros habitantes eran cazadores y recolectores. Sobrevivían cazando búfalos salvajes y otros animales y recolectando frutas, frutos secos y granos silvestres. Se trasladaban con frecuencia hacia los lugares donde el alimento era más abundante. Con el tiempo, algunas personas se asentaron a lo largo de las zonas costeras. Pescaban y sembraban distintos tipos de semillas.

## FARMING AND SETTLEMENT/AGRICULTURA Y ASENTAMIENTOS

The experiments with seeds led to farming. This allowed people to live in one place permanently. The first farming settlements were in Mesoamerica. By 3500 BC, Mesoamericans were growing **maize,** or corn. Later they learned to grow squash and beans. South Americans in the Andes started growing potatoes. By about 2000 BC, they were also growing maize and beans. Once people settled, the population grew. Societies began to develop religion, art, and trade opportunities./Los experimentos con semillas llevaron al desarrollo de la agricultura. Esto permitió que las personas vivieran en un lugar de manera permanente. Los primeros asentamientos agrícolas ocurrieron en Mesoamérica. Hacia el año 3500 a. C., los mesoamericanos cultivaban **maíz,** o elote. Luego aprendieron a cultivar calabacines y frijoles. Los sudamericanos de los Andes comenzaron a cultivar patatas. Hacia el 2000 a. C., también cultivaban maíz y frijoles. Una vez que se asentaron las personas, la población creció.

> When did the South Americans start growing maize and beans?/
> ¿Cuándo comenzaron los sudamericanos a cultivar maíz y frijoles?
>
> _____

Las sociedades comenzaron a desarrollar la religión, el arte y las oportunidades comerciales.

Historians believe that the Olmec (OHL-mek) were the first Mesoamericans to live in villages. Some Olmec lived in bigger towns, which were the centers of government and religion. They developed a large trading network. Archaeological evidence suggests the Olmec may have created the first written language in the Americas and designed a calendar. The Chavín was the first major civilization in South America. Its city was also a center for areas of life like religion and trade. The Chavín wove textiles, carved monuments, and created pottery shaped like animals./Los historiadores creen que los olmecas fueron los primeros mesoamericanos que vivieron en aldeas. Algunos olmecas vivían en ciudades grandes, que eran los centros del gobierno y la religión. Los olmecas desarrollaron una amplia red comercial. La evidencia arqueológica sugiere que es posible que hayan creado la primera lengua escrita del continente americano y que hayan diseñado un calendario. La cultura chavín fue la primera de las grandes civilizaciones de América del Sur. Su ciudad también fue un centro para áreas de la vida cotidiana, como la religión y el comercio. Los chavines tejían productos textiles, tallaban monumentos y creaban obras de alfarería con forma de animales.

> **What were some accomplishments of the Olmec and the Chavin?/ ¿Cuáles fueron algunos logros de los olmecas y los chavines?**
>
> _____
> _____
> _____
> _____
> _____
> _____
> _____
> _____

## CHALLENGE ACTIVITY/ACTIVIDAD AVANZADA

**Critical Thinking: Sequence/Pensamiento crítico: Hacer una secuencia** Draw a series of sketches showing how the first human civilization developed in the Americas. Start with the two theories of how humans first arrived to the Americas, and end with the establishment of the Olmec and Chavín civilizations./Haz una serie de

bosquejos que muestren cómo se desarrollaron
las primeras civilizaciones humanas en el
continente americano. Comienza tus bosquejos
con las dos teorías de cómo llegaron los primeros
seres humanos al continente americano, y finaliza
con el surgimiento de las civilizaciones olmeca
y chavín.

**DIRECTIONS/INSTRUCCIONES** Write a word or descriptive phrase
to describe each term./Escribe una palabra o frase descriptiva para
describir cada término.

1. Mesoamerica/Mesoamérica _____

_____

_____

2. maize/maíz _____

_____

_____

| | | | |
|---|---|---|---|
| Amazon/ Amazonas | Chavín/chavines | Mesoamerica/ Mesoamérica | North America/ América del Norte |
| Olmec/ olmecas | pottery pottery/ alfarería | South America/ América del Sur | textiles/productos textiles |

**DIRECTIONS/INSTRUCCIONES** Answer each question by writing a
sentence that contains at least one word from the word bank. Not all
words are used./Responde cada pregunta con una oración que
contenga al menos una palabra del banco de palabras. No se usan
todas las palabras.

1. Where are the Amazon region, river, and rain forest all located?/¿Dónde se
   ubican la región, el río y la selva tropical que llevan el nombre de Amazonas?

_____

_____

2. Which civilization lived in villages or bigger towns that were centers of government and religion?/¿Qué civilización vivió en aldeas o en pueblos más grandes que eran centros del gobierno y la religión?

_____

_____

3. What did the Chavín create that was shaped like animals?/¿Qué crearon los chavines que tenía forma de animales?

_____

_____

# The Early Americas/El continente americano en sus inicios

**MAIN IDEAS/IDEAS PRINCIPALES**

1. Geography affected early Maya civilization./La geografía afectó a la civilización maya en sus inicios.

2. The Maya Classic Age was characterized by great cities, trade, and warfare./La Era Clásica de los mayas se caracterizó por las grandes ciudades, el comercio y las guerras.

3. A complex class structure shaped roles in Maya society./Los roles de la sociedad maya estaban determinados por una compleja estructura de clases.

4. The Maya worshipped many gods and believed their kings communicated with them./Los mayas adoraban a muchos dioses y creían que sus reyes se comunicaban con ellos.

5. The Maya culture made great achievements in art, science, math, and writing./La cultura maya realizó grandes avances en las artes, las ciencias, las matemáticas y la escritura.

6. Maya civilization declined, and historians have several theories about why./Los historiadores tienen varias teorías sobre por qué la civilización maya entró en decadencia.

## Key Terms and People/Personas y palabras clave

**obsidian/obsidiana** a sharp, glasslike volcanic rock found in Mesoamerica/roca volcánica filosa, semejante al vidrio, que se encuentra en Mesoamérica

**Pacal/Pacal** Maya king who dedicated a temple to record his achievements as ruler/rey maya que dedicó un templo a documentar sus logros como gobernante

**observatories/observatorios** buildings designed to study astronomy and view the stars/edificios diseñados para realizar estudios de astronomía y observar las estrellas

**Popol Vuh/Popol Vuh** a book containing legends and some history of the Maya civilization/libro que contiene leyendas y parte de la historia de la civilización maya

## Lesson Summary/Resumen de la lección

**GEOGRAPHY AFFECTS EARLY MAYA/LA GEOGRAFÍA AFECTA A LOS PRIMEROS MAYAS**

The Maya (MY-uh) civilization developed in the lowlands of Mesoamerica around 1000 BC. Forests were a source of many resources for the Maya. They lived in villages and traded such items as woven cloth and **obsidian.** By AD 200, the Maya were building the first large cities in the Americas./La civilización maya se desarrolló en las tierras bajas de Mesoamérica alrededor del año 1000 a. C. Los bosques eran fuente de muchos recursos para los mayas, que vivían en pueblos y comerciaban con productos como telas tejidas y obsidiana. Hacia el 200 d. C., los mayas construyeron las primeras grandes ciudades del continente americano.

> **What were the Maya doing by AD 200?/¿Qué hacían los mayas hacia el año 200 d. C.?**
>
> _____
>
> _____
>
> _____

## MAYA CLASSIC AGE/ERA CLÁSICA DE LOS MAYAS

Maya civilization reached its height between AD 250 and 900, a period called the Classic Age. Large stone pyramids, temples, and palaces were built to honor local kings like **Pacal** (puh-KAHL). The Maya also built canals to bring water to the cities. Hillsides were shaped into flat terraces so crops could be grown on them. The Maya did not have a central government. Cities often fought each other over territory and resources. This warfare was violent and destructive./La civilización maya alcanzó su máximo esplendor entre el 250 y el 900 d. C., un período conocido como la Era Clásica. Se construyeron grandes templos, palacios y pirámides de piedra para honrar a reyes locales como **Pacal.** Los mayas también construyeron canales para transportar agua a las ciudades y transformaron las laderas de las colinas en terrazas planas para poder cultivar en ellas. Los mayas no tenían un gobierno central. Las ciudades a menudo luchaban entre sí por el territorio y los recursos. Esas guerras eran violentas y destructivas.

> **Underline two sentences that tell how the Maya was affected by having no central government./ Subraya dos oraciones que indican cómo afectó a los mayas la falta de un gobierno central.**

## ROLES IN MAYA SOCIETY/ROLES DE LA SOCIEDAD MAYA

Kings held the highest position in Maya social structure. Priests, warriors, and merchants made up the upper class. The Maya believed that their

> **Who made up the upper class in Maya society?/ ¿Quiénes formaban parte de la clase alta de la sociedad maya?**
>
> _____

rulers were related to the gods. Most Maya belonged to lower-class farming families. Slaves held the lowest position in Maya society./Los reyes ocupaban el lugar más alto de la estructura social de los mayas. La clase alta estaba compuesta por los sacerdotes, los guerreros y los comerciantes. Los mayas creían que sus gobernantes estaban emparentados con los dioses. La mayoría de los mayas pertenecían a familias de agricultores de clase baja. Los esclavos estaban en el escalón más bajo de la sociedad maya.

## RELIGIOUS TRADITIONS/TRADICIONES RELIGIOSAS

The Maya believed that their kings spoke with the gods. Each god represented a different area of life. The Maya believed the gods could either help them or hurt them, and the gods needed blood. Special rituals of blood giving were held at births, weddings, and funerals. The Maya made human sacrifices to the gods as well./Los mayas creían que sus reyes hablaban con los dioses. Cada dios representaba un área diferente de la vida. Los mayas creían que los dioses podían ayudarlos o perjudicarlos, y que los dioses necesitaban sangre. Se realizaban rituales especiales con derramamiento de sangre en los nacimientos, las bodas y los funerales. Los mayas también ofrecían sacrificios humanos a los dioses.

> **What did the Maya believe their gods needed?/¿Qué creían los mayas que necesitaban sus dioses?**
>
> _____

## CULTURAL ACHIEVEMENTS/LOGROS CULTURALES

The Maya built **observatories** for their priests to study the stars. They learned that the year had about 365 days. They developed a number system and a calendar to record important events. Maya legends and history were written in a book called the **Popol Vuh** (poh-pohl VOO)./Los mayas construyeron **observatorios** para que sus sacerdotes estudiaran las estrellas. Descubrieron que el año tenía aproximadamente 365 días. Crearon un sistema numérico y un calendario para registrar los acontecimientos importantes. Las leyendas mayas y parte de su historia se escribieron en un libro llamado **Popol Vuh.**

## MAYA CIVILIZATION DECLINES/DECADENCIA DE LA CIVILIZACIÓN MAYA

Maya civilization began to collapse in the 900s. Historians are not sure why. Some believe that fewer crops grew because of weakened soil and drought. Others think that the Maya people got tired of working for the kings and rebelled./La civilización maya comenzó a decaer en el siglo 10. Los historiadores no saben con certeza cuál fue la causa. Algunos creen que crecían menos cultivos como consecuencia de los suelos debilitados y las sequías. Otros piensan que el pueblo maya se cansó de trabajar para los reyes y se rebeló.

> **What are two reasons why historians think Maya civilization might have collapsed?/¿Cuáles son dos razones por las que, según los historiadores, puede haber decaído la civilización maya?**
>
> _____
> _____
> _____
> _____

## CHALLENGE ACTIVITY/ACTIVIDAD AVANZADA

**Critical Thinking: Evaluate/Pensamiento crítico: Evaluar** Which of the Maya's achievements do you think has had the greatest influence on history? Write a paragraph to explain your answer./¿Cuál de los logros de los mayas crees que tuvo la mayor influencia en la historia? Escribe un párrafo para explicar tu respuesta.

**DIRECTIONS/INSTRUCCIONES** Read each sentence and circle the term in the word pair that best completes each sentence./Lee cada oración y encierra en un círculo la palabra del par de palabras que mejor la completa.

1. _____ is a book containing legends and some history of the Maya civilization. **(Pacal/Popol Vuh)**/El _____ es un libro que contiene leyendas y parte de la historia de la civilización maya. **(Pacal/Popol Vuh)**

2. Priests studied the stars in buildings called _____.
   **(obsidian/observatories)/** Los sacerdotes estudiaban las estrellas en edificios
   llamados _____. **(obsidianas/observatorios)**

3. A Maya king named _____ dedicated a temple to
   record his achievements as ruler. **(Pacal/Popol Vuh)/** Un rey maya llamado
   _____ dedicó un templo a documentar
   sus logros como gobernante. **(Pacal/Popol Vuh)**

4. The Maya traded _____, which are sharp, glasslike
   volcanic rocks. **(obsidian/observatories)/** Los mayas comerciaron con
   _____, que son rocas volcánicas filosas
   semejantes al vidrio. **(obsidianas/observatorios)**

# The Early Americas/El continente americano en sus inicios

**MAIN IDEAS/IDEAS PRINCIPALES**

1. The Aztecs built an empire through warfare and trade, and created an impressive capital city in Mesoamerica./Los aztecas construyeron un imperio mediante la guerra y el comercio, y crearon una ciudad capital impresionante en Mesoamérica.

2. Aztec society was divided by social roles and by class./La sociedad azteca estaba dividida por roles sociales y por clases.

3. Aztec religion required human sacrifice for keeping the gods happy./La religión azteca exigía sacrificios humanos para complacer a los dioses.

4. The Aztecs had many achievements in science, art, and language./Los aztecas realizaron muchos avances en las ciencias, el arte y el lenguaje.

5. Hernán Cortés conquered the Aztec Empire./Hernán Cortés conquistó el Imperio azteca.

## Key Terms and People/Personas y palabras clave

**causeways/carreteras elevadas** raised roads across water or wet ground/ carreteras construidas sobre el agua o sobre suelo húmedo

**conquistadors/conquistadores** Spanish soldiers and explorers/exploradores y soldados españoles

**Hernán Cortés/Hernán Cortés** Spanish conquistador leader who conquered the Aztec Empire/líder y conquistador español que conquistó el Imperio azteca

**Moctezuma II/Moctezuma II** Aztec ruler who mistook Cortés for a god, leading to the Aztec's downfall/gobernante azteca que confundió a Cortés con un dios, lo que llevó a la caída de los aztecas

**codex/códice** a written historical record/registro histórico escrito

## Lesson Summary/Resumen de la lección

### THE AZTECS BUILD AN EMPIRE/LOS AZTECAS CONSTRUYEN UN IMPERIO

By the early 1500s, the Aztecs ruled the most powerful empire in Mesoamerica. War was key to the Aztecs. They also controlled a huge trade network. The capital city Tenochtitlán (tay-NAWCH-teet-LAHN) featured a stunning array of Aztec power and wealth. It had temples, palaces, and a busy market. Three wide **causeways** connected Tenochtitlán's island location to the shore./Hacia principios del siglo 16, los aztecas gobernaban el

> **Where was Tenochtitlán located?/¿Dónde se ubicaba Tenochtitlán?**
> _____

imperio más poderoso de Mesoamérica. La guerra era fundamental para los aztecas. Ellos también controlaban una enorme red comercial. La ciudad capital de Tenochtitlán era un imponente despliegue del poder y la riqueza de los aztecas. Tenía templos, palacios y un mercado muy activo. Tres amplias **carreteras elevadas** conectaban la isla donde estaba ubicada Tenochtitlán con la costa.

## AZTEC SOCIETY/SOCIEDAD AZTECA

The king was the most important person in Aztec society. He was in charge of law, trade and tribute, and warfare. Young nobles learned to be government officials, military leaders, or priests. Just below the king and his nobles were priests and warriors. Merchants and artisans were just below them. Farmers, pawns, slaves, and captives were in the lower class. Most slaves were sold as laborers. Captives were often sacrificed to the Aztec gods./ El rey era la persona más importante de la sociedad azteca. Estaba a cargo de las leyes, del comercio y los tributos, y de la guerra. Los jóvenes nobles aprendían a ser funcionarios del gobierno, líderes militares o sacerdotes. Justo debajo del rey y de sus nobles se encontraban los sacerdotes y los guerreros. Los comerciantes y los artesanos se encontraban por debajo de ellos. Los agricultores, los peones, los esclavos y los cautivos formaban el nivel social más bajo. La mayoría de los esclavos eran vendidos como mano de obra. Los cautivos a menudo eran sacrificados para complacer a los dioses aztecas.

> In Aztec society, what did young nobles learn to be?/ En la sociedad azteca, ¿qué ocupaciones aprendían los jóvenes nobles?
>
> _____
> _____
> _____

> What often happened to captives?/¿Qué ocurría generalmente con los cautivos?
>
> _____
> _____
> _____

## AZTEC RELIGION/RELIGIÓN AZTECA

Like other Mesoamericans, the Aztecs always tried to please their gods. They believed sacrifice was necessary to keep the gods happy, and that the gods literally fed on human blood. Aztec priests led bloody ceremonies and sacrificed

nearly 10,000 human victims a year./Al igual
que otros mesoamericanos, los aztecas siempre
intentaban complacer a sus dioses. Creían que
los sacrificios eran necesarios para que sus
dioses estuvieran contentos, y que los dioses
literalmente se alimentaban con sangre humana.
Los sacerdotes aztecas conducían ceremonias
sangrientas y sacrificaban casi 10,000 víctimas
humanas al año.

## SCIENCE, ART, AND LANGUAGE/CIENCIA, ARTE Y LENGUAJE

The Aztecs sometimes borrowed scientific
advances from the tribes they conquered. They
also studied astronomy and created a calendar
much like the Maya calendar. The Aztecs kept
written history records in a kind of book called
a **codex.** They also had strong oral and artistic
traditions./Algunas veces los aztecas adoptaban
los avances científicos de las tribus que
conquistaban. También tenían conocimientos
de astronomía, y crearon un calendario muy
parecido al calendario maya. Los aztecas
llevaban registros escritos de su historia en una
especie de libro llamado **códice.** También tenían
fuertes tradiciones orales y artísticas.

> From whom did the Aztecs sometimes borrow scientific advances?/¿De quiénes tomaban avances científicos los aztecas, en ocasiones?
>
> _____
> _____

## CORTÉS CONQUERS THE AZTECS/CORTÉS CONQUISTA A LOS AZTECAS

**Hernán Cortés** (er-NAHN kawr-TAYS) led
**conquistadors** into Mexico in 1519. The ruler of
the Aztecs, **Moctezuma II** (MAWK-tay-SOO-
mah), thought Cortés was a god. Moctezuma's
motive was to welcome him, but Cortés took the
emperor prisoner. Enraged, the Aztecs attacked
the Spanish, and Moctezuma was killed. The
conquistadors used guns and rode horses. Their
attack terrified the Aztecs. The Spanish also
carried diseases like smallpox that weakened

> How did Cortés respond to Moctezuma's welcome?/ ¿Cuál fue la respuesta de Cortés ante la bienvenida de Moctezuma?
>
> _____
> _____

and killed many Aztecs./**Hernán Cortés** dirigió a los **conquistadores** que ingresaron a México en 1519. El gobernante azteca, **Moctezuma II,** creyó que Cortés era un dios. Moctezuma se proponía darle la bienvenida, pero Cortés tomó prisionero al emperador. Enfurecidos, los aztecas atacaron a los españoles y Moctezuma fue asesinado. Los conquistadores usaban armas de fuego y andaban a caballo. Su ataque aterrorizó a los aztecas. Los españoles también trajeron enfermedades, como la viruela, que debilitaron a muchos aztecas y les causaron la muerte.

> Circle the name of a disease that weakened and killed many Aztecs./Encierra en un círculo el nombre de una enfermedad que debilitó a muchos aztecas y les causó la muerte.

## CHALLENGE ACTIVITY/ACTIVIDAD AVANZADA

**Critical Thinking: Form Opinions/Pensamiento crítico: Formarse opiniones** What do you think about Hernán Cortés and his actions? Write a one-page opinion paper defending your point of view. Give at least three examples to support your opinion./¿Qué piensas de Hernán Cortés y sus acciones? Escribe un ensayo de opinión de una página en el que defiendas tu punto de vista. Da al menos tres ejemplos que respalden tu opinión.

**DIRECTIONS/INSTRUCCIONES** On the line before each statement, write **T** if the statement is true and **F** if the statement is false. If the statement is false, change the underlined term to make the sentence true. Then write the correct term on the line after the sentence./En la línea que precede a cada enunciado, escribe **V** si el enunciado es verdadero y **F** si es falso. Si el enunciado es falso, cambia el término subrayado para que el enunciado sea verdadero. Luego escribe el término correcto en la línea que sigue al enunciado.

_____ 1. Conquistadors are raised roads across water or wet ground./Los conquistadores son carreteras construidas sobre el agua o sobre suelo húmedo.

_____

_____ 2. The Spanish leader who conquered the Aztec Empire was <u>Hernán Cortés</u>./El líder español que conquistó al Imperio azteca fue <u>Hernán Cortés</u>.

_____

_____ 3. The Aztecs kept their written history in a book called a <u>codex</u>./Los aztecas llevaban registro escrito de su historia en un libro llamado <u>códice</u>.

_____

_____ 4. Spanish <u>causeways</u> used guns and rode horses when they attacked the Aztecs./<u>Las carreteras elevadas de los españoles</u> usaban armas de fuego y montaban a caballo cuando atacaron a los aztecas.

_____

_____ 5. <u>Moctezuma II</u> was the Aztec ruler who thought a Spanish explorer was a god./<u>Moctezuma II</u> fue el gobernante azteca que creyó que un explorador español era un dios.

_____

# The Early Americas/El continente americano en sus inicios

## Lesson/Lección 4

**MAIN IDEAS/IDEAS PRINCIPALES**

1. The rise of the Inca Empire was due to conquest and the achievements of the Inca people./El surgimiento del Imperio inca se debió a las conquistas y los logros del pueblo inca.

2. For the Incas, position in society affected daily life./Para los incas, la posición social afectaba la vida diaria.

3. The Incas made great achievements in building, art, and in oral literature./Los incas lograron grandes avances en la arquitectura, el arte y la literatura oral.

4. Pizarro conquered the Incas and took control of the region./Pizarro conquistó a los incas y tomó el control de la región.

## Key Terms and People/Personas y palabras clave

**Pachacuti/Pachacuti** ruler who expanded the Inca Empire in the mid-1400s/ gobernante que expandió el Imperio inca a mediados del siglo 15

**Quechua/quechua** the official language of the Incas/idioma oficial de los incas

**llamas/llamas** animals related to camels but native to South America/animales que están relacionados con los camellos, pero son nativos de América del Sur

**Atahualpa/Atahualpa** the last Inca ruler/el último gobernante inca

**Francisco Pizarro/Francisco Pizarro** Spanish conquistador leader who conquered the Incas/líder y conquistador español que conquistó a los incas

## Lesson Summary/Resumen de la lección

### THE RISE OF THE INCA EMPIRE/SURGIMIENTO DEL IMPERIO INCA

The Chavín, Nazca, Moche, and Chimú cultures influenced the development of the Inca civilization. In the mid-1400s, the ruler **Pachacuti** (pah-chah-KOO-tee) led the Incas to expand their territory. The Incas formed a strong central government and established an official language, **Quechua** (KE-chuh-wuh)./Las culturas chavín, nazca, moche y chimú influyeron en el desarrollo de la civilización inca. A mediados del siglo 15, el gobernante **Pachacuti** dirigió a los incas en la expansión de su territorio. Los incas formaron un gobierno central fuerte y establecieron un idioma oficial, el **quechua.**

> **What four cultures influenced the development of the Inca?/¿Cuáles son las cuatro culturas que influyeron en el desarrollo de la cultura inca?**
>
> _____
> _____
> _____
> _____

Instead of taxes, Incas had to "pay" their government in a labor tax system called the *mita* (MEE-tah). Most Incas raised **llamas,** provided grain for the army, or worked on government-owned farms and mines. There were no merchants or markets. Government officials distributed goods collected through the *mita.*/En lugar de pagar impuestos, los incas tenían que "pagarle" a su gobierno con un sistema de trabajo llamado *mita.* La mayoría de los incas criaban **llamas,** le proveían granos al ejército o trabajaban en granjas y minas que pertenecían al gobierno. No había comerciantes ni mercados. Los funcionarios del gobierno distribuían los artículos recolectados por medio de la *mita.*

> **What was the name of the Inca labor tax system?/**
> ¿Cómo se llamaba el sistema de trabajo que usaban los incas en lugar de recaudar impuestos?
> _____

## SOCIETY AND DAILY LIFE/SOCIEDAD Y VIDA COTIDIANA

The king, priests, and government officials were the upper class in Inca society. Most Incas belonged to the lower class. This included farmers, artisans, and servants. There were no slaves in Inca society. Most children worked and did not go to school. People from conquered lands were part of the lower class./La clase alta de la sociedad inca estaba compuesta por el rey, los sacerdotes y los funcionarios del gobierno. La mayoría de los incas pertenecían a la clase baja, que incluía a agricultores, artesanos y sirvientes. En la sociedad inca no había esclavos. La mayoría de los niños trabajaban y no iban a la escuela. Las personas provenientes de las tierras conquistadas formaban parte de la clase baja.

> **Circle the group that was not part of Inca society./**
> Encierra en un círculo el grupo que no formaba parte de la sociedad inca.

Incas believed that Inca rulers were related to the sun god and never really died. Inca religious ceremonies often included sacrifice, but humans were rarely harmed./Los incas creían que los gobernantes incas eran parientes del dios Sol y que nunca morían realmente. Las ceremonias religiosas incas a menudo incluían sacrificios, pero rara vez se hacía daño a los seres humanos.

## BUILDING, ART, AND ORAL LITERATURE/ ARQUITECTURA, ARTE Y LITERATURA ORAL

Inca workers built massive buildings and forts of huge stone blocks. The blocks were cut so precisely that no cement was needed to hold them together. The Incas also built a good system of roads. Artisans did beautiful metalwork and produced brightly colored textiles./Los trabajadores incas construyeron imponentes edificios y fortalezas con enormes bloques de piedra. Los bloques estaban cortados con tanta precisión que no hacía falta usar cemento para unirlos. Los incas también construyeron un buen sistema de caminos. Los artesanos realizaban hermosas obras en metal y productos textiles de colores vivos.

The Incas had no written language. Instead, they passed down stories and songs orally. After the conquistadors came, some Incas learned Spanish and wrote about Inca legends./Los incas no tenían un idioma escrito. En cambio, transmitían los relatos y las canciones oralmente. Después de la llegada de los conquistadores, algunos incas aprendieron español y escribieron sobre las leyendas incas.

> **Why did the Inca not use cement to build buildings and forts?/¿Por qué los incas no usaron cemento para construir edificios y fortalezas?**
>
> _____
>
> _____
>
> _____

## PIZARRO CONQUERS THE INCAS/PIZARRO CONQUISTA A LOS INCAS

On his way to be crowned king after a civil war, **Atahualpa** (ah-tah-WAHL-pah) heard that conquistadors led by **Francisco Pizarro** were in Peru. He agreed to meet with them. The Spanish tried to convert Atahualpa to Christianity, but he refused. He was captured, and the Spanish killed thousands of Inca soldiers. The Incas brought gold and silver for Atahualpa's return, but the Spanish killed him, too. They ruled the Inca

> **What caused the Spanish to capture Atahualpa and kill Inca soldiers?/¿Qué provocó que los españoles capturaran a Atahualpa y mataran a los soldados incas?**
>
> _____
>
> _____
>
> _____

lands for the next 300 years./Mientras iba en camino a ser coronado rey luego de una guerra civil, **Atahualpa** se enteró de que unos conquistadores liderados por **Francisco Pizarro** estaban en Perú y aceptó reunirse con ellos. Los españoles intentaron convertir a Atahualpa al cristianismo, pero él se negó. Entonces, lo capturaron y mataron a miles de soldados incas. Los incas les llevaron oro y plata para que les devolvieran a Atahualpa, pero los españoles lo mataron. Los españoles gobernaron las tierras incas durante los próximos 300 años.

## CHALLENGE ACTIVITY/ACTIVIDAD AVANZADA

**Critical Thinking: Evaluate/Pensamiento crítico: Evaluar**  The Inca used labor as a form of currency instead of money or trading markets. What are the advantages and disadvantages of this type of economic system? Write a brief essay explaining your answer./Los incas usaron el trabajo como moneda en lugar del dinero o los mercados comerciales. ¿Cuáles son las ventajas y desventajas de este tipo de sistema económico? Escribe un ensayo breve en el que expliques tu respuesta.

**DIRECTIONS/INSTRUCCIONES**  Write two descriptive phrases that describe the term given./Escribe dos frases descriptivas que describan el término dado.

1. Quechua/quechua_____

_____

2. llamas/llamas_____

_____

3. Francisco Pizarro/Francisco Pizarro _____

_____

**DIRECTIONS/INSTRUCCIONES** Read each sentence and fill in the blank with the word in the word pair that best completes the sentence./Lee cada oración y escribe en el espacio en blanco la palabra del par de palabras que mejor la completa.

4. The Incas brought gold and silver because _____ had been captured, but the Spanish killed him. **(Pachacuti/Atahualpa)/**Los incas llevaron oro y plata a los españoles porque habían capturado a _____, pero los españoles lo mataron. **(Pachacuti/Atahualpa)**

5. _____ was the leader who expanded Inca territory. **(Francisco Pizarro/Pachacuti)/**_____ fue el líder que expandió el territorio inca. **(Francisco Pizarro/Pachacuti)**

**MAIN IDEAS/IDEAS PRINCIPALES**

1. The earliest North American cultures developed in the Southwest and eastern woodlands./Las primeras culturas de América del Norte se desarrollaron en el Suroeste y en los bosques del este.

2. North America's different geographical features led to the development of varied cultures./Las distintas características geográficas de América del Norte llevaron al desarrollo de culturas diversas.

## Key Terms and People/Personas y palabras clave

**adobe/adobe** clay that the Anasazi used to make roofs for houses/arcilla que usaban los anasazi para hacer los techos de las casas

**potlatch/potlatch** social event and feast of the Northwestern Native American peoples; used to increase trade or improve relationships with others/evento y festividad social de los pueblos amerindios del Noroeste; se utilizaba para fomentar el comercio o mejorar las relaciones con otros pueblos

**wampum/wampum** strings of beads that many Native American groups used as currency/collares de cuentas que muchos grupos amerindios usaban como moneda

**Iroquois Confederacy/Confederación Iroquesa** powerful alliance of the Cayuga, Mohawk, Oneida, Onondaga, and Seneca Native American peoples/poderosa alianza formada por los pueblos amerindios cayuga, mohawk, oneida, onondaga y seneca

## Lesson Summary/Resumen de la lección

### THE EARLIEST NORTH AMERICAN CULTURES/
### PRIMERAS CULTURAS NORTEAMERICANAS

The Anasazi were a society that thrived in what is now the southwestern United States. They survived because they adapted to the dry environment and harsh desert conditions. For example, they built irrigation canals to bring water to their fields and villages. The Anasazi also dug pit houses into the ground. These houses had **adobe** roofs that were made of clay. A new form of architecture developed called pueblo. Pueblo structures were like modern apartment buildings. They were several stories tall and had

> Why were the Anasazi able to survive and thrive in the Southwest?/¿Por qué los anasazi pudieron sobrevivir y prosperar en el Suroeste?
>
> _____
>
> _____
>
> _____

many rooms./Los anasazi fueron una sociedad que prosperó en lo que actualmente es el suroeste de los Estados Unidos. Sobrevivieron porque se adaptaron al ambiente seco y a las duras condiciones del desierto. Por ejemplo, construyeron canales de irrigación para transportar agua hasta sus campos y aldeas. Los anasazi también construyeron casas semienterradas en el suelo. Esas casas tenían techos de **adobe,** un tipo de arcilla. La cultura anazasi desarrolló una nueva forma de arquitectura llamada pueblo. Las estructuras de este tipo de arquitectura eran como los edificios de apartamentos modernos. Tenían varios pisos y muchas habitaciones.

Historians are not sure why, but the Anasazi began to abandon their villages after AD 1300. Drought, disease, or attacks might have caused them to leave the area. Descendants of the Anasazi still live in the Southwest./Los historiadores no saben con certeza por qué, pero los anasazi comenzaron a abandonar sus aldeas después de 1300 d. C. Quizás las sequías, las enfermedades o los ataques hayan provocado que se fueran de la zona. Los descendientes de los anasazi todavía viven en el Suroeste.

> **What three reasons might have caused the Anasazi to abandon their villages?/** ¿Cuáles son tres razones que podrían haber provocado que los anasazi abandonaran sus aldeas?
>
> _____
> _____
> _____

A different culture developed in the woodlands along the Mississippi and Ohio rivers. The two rivers provided large amounts of fish to eat and fertile land to use. People also had access to transportation routes. Societies in this region were known for building huge earthen mounds. Historians call them the mound-building cultures. The Hopewell built their mounds as burial sites. Later, a more advanced culture named the Mississippians built mounds for religious ceremonies./En los bosques ubicados a lo largo de los ríos Mississippi y Ohio, se desarrolló una cultura diferente. Los dos ríos

> **How were the mounds built by the Mississippians different from the mounds built by the Hopewell?/**¿En qué se diferenciaban los túmulos construidos por los misisipienses de los túmulos construidos por los hopewell?
>
> _____
> _____
> _____
> _____
> _____

ofrecían gran cantidad de peces para comer y
tierra fértil. También había fácil acceso a caminos
para el transporte. Las sociedades de esta región
son conocidas por construir enormes túmulos
de tierra. Los historiadores las llaman culturas
constructoras de túmulos. Los hopewell
utilizaron sus túmulos como lugares de sepultura.
Posteriormente, una cultura más avanzada
llamada misisipiense construyó túmulos para
realizar ceremonias religiosas.

## LATER CULTURES/CULTURAS POSTERIORES

By the 1500s, there were thousands of Native
American groups in North America. The
environment in each region affected how people
lived and culture developed. Many Northwestern
cultures depended on fish like salmon for food.
In these communities, **potlatches** were social
events that encouraged trade and good relations.
Objects like totem poles were important religious
symbols./Hacia el siglo 16, había miles de grupos
indígenas en América del Norte. El medio
ambiente de cada región influyó en el estilo de
vida de las personas y el desarrollo de su cultura.
Muchas culturas del Noroeste dependían de
peces como el salmón para su alimentación. En
esas comunidades, se organizaban **potlatches,**
eventos sociales que fomentaban el comercio y
las buenas relaciones. Algunos objetos, como los
tótems, eran símbolos religiosos importantes.

Cultures that lived on the Great Plains were
nomadic peoples. The region had few trees, so
hunters used bows and arrows to provide buffalo
hides for shelter and meat for food./Las culturas
que vivían en las Grandes Llanuras eran pueblos
nómadas. Como había pocos árboles en la
región, los cazadores usaban arcos y flechas
para conseguir pieles de búfalo, que utilizaban
como refugio, y carne para comer.

> **Why did Great Plains
> hunters provide buffalo
> hides for shelter?/¿Por
> qué los cazadores de las
> Grandes Llanuras usaban
> las pieles de búfalo como
> refugio?**
>
> _____
>
> _____

Southeastern groups like the Cherokee and the Seminole used **wampum** as currency. People in this region farmed, hunted, gathered plants, and fished. Villages were governed by councils./ Los grupos del Sureste, como los cherokee y los seminolas, usaban el **wampum** como moneda. Los pueblos de esta región se dedicaban a la agricultura, cazaban, recolectaban plantas y pescaban. Las aldeas estaban gobernadas por consejos.

In the Northeast, family and social life was based on the clan. Clans were responsible for the well-being of their members. Five Native American peoples formed the **Iroquois Confederacy.** This strong alliance waged war or made peace with peoples who were not part of the group./En el Noreste, la familia y la vida social se basaban en el clan. Los clanes se ocupaban del bienestar de sus miembros. Cinco pueblos amerindios formaron la **Confederación Iroquesa.** Esta fuerte alianza hacía la guerra o la paz con los pueblos que no formaban parte del grupo.

> **What were the clans responsible for in Northeastern groups?/¿De qué se encargaban los clanes en los grupos del Noreste?**
>
> _____
>
> _____

## CHALLENGE ACTIVITY/ACTIVIDAD AVANZADA

**Critical Thinking: Compare and Contrast/Pensamiento crítico: Comparar y contrastar** Use print or digital resources to research the Iroquois Confederacy and a modern-day alliance like NATO. Write a short summary that gives examples of how the organizations are the same and different from each other./Usa recursos impresos o digitales para investigar sobre la Confederación Iroquesa y una alianza contemporánea como la OTAN. Escribe un breve resumen en el que des ejemplos de semejanzas y diferencias entre las organizaciones.

Name/Nombre_____ Class/Clase _____ Date/Fecha_____

**DIRECTIONS/INSTRUCCIONES** Look at each set of four terms. On the line provided, write the letter of the term that does not relate to the others./Observa cada conjunto de cuatro términos. En el espacio en blanco, escribe la letra del término que no tiene relación con los demás.

_____ 1. a. strings of beads/collares de cuentas
        b. the Anasazi/los anasazi
        c. Cherokee and Seminole/cherokee y seminola
        d. currency/moneda

_____ 2. a. clay/arcilla
        b. pueblo/pueblo
        c. form of architecture/forma de arquitectura
        d. village council/consejo de la aldea

_____ 3. a. feast/festividad
        b. increase trade/fomentar el comercio
        c. clan/clan
        d. social event/evento social

_____ 4. a. Great Plains/Grandes Llanuras
        b. powerful alliance/alianza poderosa
        c. Mohawk and Seneca/mohawk y seneca
        d. war and peace/guerra y paz

**MAIN IDEAS/IDEAS PRINCIPALES**

1. Geography has shaped life in Europe, including where and how people live./La geografía ha influido en la vida en Europa, por ejemplo, en dónde y cómo viven sus habitantes.

2. Christianity spread to northern Europe through the work of missionaries and monks./El cristianismo se expandió hacia el norte de Europa mediante el trabajo de los misioneros y los monjes.

3. The Franks, led by Charlemagne, created a huge Christian empire and brought together scholars from around Europe./Los francos, liderados por Carlomagno, crearon un inmenso imperio cristiano y reunieron estudiosos de todas partes de Europa.

4. Invaders threatened much of Europe in the 700s and 800s./Los invasores amenazaron gran parte de Europa durante los siglos 8 y 9.

# Key Terms and People/Personas y palabras clave

**Eurasia/Eurasia** the large landmass that includes Europe and Asia/gran masa de tierra que incluye Europa y Asia

**Middle Ages/Edad Media** the period lasting from about 500 to about 1500/período que abarca aproximadamente desde el año 500 hasta el 1500

**medieval/medieval** another name for the Middle Ages/otra manera de referirse a la Edad Media

**Patrick/Patricio** Christian missionary credited with converting Ireland to Christianity/misionero cristiano al que se le atribuye la conversión de Irlanda al cristianismo

**monks/monjes** religious men who lived apart from society in isolated communities/religiosos que vivían apartados de la sociedad en comunidades aisladas

**monasteries/monasterios** communities of monks/comunidades de monjes

**Benedict/Benito** monk responsible for creating the Benedictine Rule, a set of rules for monks/monje que creó la Regla de San Benito, un conjunto de reglas que los monjes deben seguir

**Charlemagne/Carlomagno** warrior and king who led the Franks in building a huge empire/guerrero y rey que guio a los francos en la construcción de un inmenso imperio

## Lesson Summary/Resumen de la lección

### GEOGRAPHY SHAPES LIFE IN EUROPE/LA GEOGRAFÍA INFLUYE EN LA VIDA EN EUROPA

Europe is a small but diverse continent with different landforms, water features, and climates. We call Europe a continent, but it is part of **Eurasia,** a large landmass that includes both Europe and Asia. The climates and vegetation vary widely from region to region. Its geography influenced where and how people lived. In southern Europe, most people lived on coastal plains or river valleys and farmed. Those near the sea became traders and seafarers. In northern Europe, the rivers provided transportation and towns grew along them. Farmers grew all sorts of crops on the excellent farmland near the cities. The flat land, however, made it easy for invaders to enter. These invasions changed Europe./Europa es un continente pequeño pero con mucha diversidad: tiene diversos accidentes geográficos, masas de agua y climas. Decimos que Europa es un continente, pero en realidad es parte de **Eurasia,** una gran masa de tierra que incluye Europa y Asia. El clima y la vegetación varían mucho de una región a la otra. La geografía influyó en dónde y cómo vivían los habitantes. En el sur de Europa, la mayoría de las personas vivían en llanuras costeras o en los valles de los ríos y se dedicaban a la agricultura. Quienes se encontraban cerca del mar se dedicaban al comercio y a la navegación. En el norte de Europa, los ríos servían como medio de transporte y permitieron el desarrollo de ciudades a sus orillas. En las excelentes tierras de labranza que rodeaban a las ciudades, los agricultores sembraban todo tipo de cultivos. Sin embargo, debido a que el terreno era llano, era muy fácil invadir la zona. Esas invasiones cambiaron Europa.

> **Why is Europe considered to be part of Eurasia?**/¿Por qué se considera que Europa es parte de Eurasia?
>
> _____
>
> _____
>
> _____

## CHRISTIANITY SPREADS TO NORTHERN EUROPE/EL CRISTIANISMO SE EXPANDE HACIA EL NORTE DE EUROPA

As the Roman Empire fell, various groups from the north and east moved into former Roman lands, creating their own states and making their own kings. These kings often fought among themselves, dividing Europe into many small kingdoms. This marked the beginning of the **Middle Ages,** or **medieval** period./Con la caída del Imperio romano, diferentes grupos del norte y del este invadieron tierras que habían pertenecido al Imperio, crearon sus propios estados y nombraron a sus propios reyes. A menudo, esos reyes luchaban entre sí, y así Europa quedó dividida en muchos reinos pequeños. Estos hechos marcaron el comienzo de la **Edad Media,** o el período **medieval.**

In the early Middle Ages, most kingdoms of northern Europe were not Christian. The pope sent missionaries and converted much of Britain, then Germany, and France. One early missionary, **Patrick,** was an English Christian who took it upon himself to convert Ireland. Unlike missionaries, **monks** lived apart from society in isolated communities, where they prayed, worked, and meditated. Communities of monks, or **monasteries,** were built all over Europe in the Middle Ages. Most monks followed a strict set of rules created in the early 500s by **Benedict.**/A principios de la Edad Media, la mayoría de los reinos del norte de Europa no eran cristianos. El papa envió misioneros y convirtió a una gran parte de Britania y luego a Alemania y Francia. Uno de los primeros misioneros, **Patricio,** era un cristiano inglés que se dedicó a convertir Irlanda. A diferencia de los misioneros, los **monjes** vivían apartados de la sociedad en

> **How was Europe ruled at the beginning of the Middle Ages?/¿Cómo estaba gobernada Europa a principios de la Edad Media?**
>
> _____
> _____
> _____

> **Why did Patrick go to Ireland?/¿Para qué fue Patricio a Irlanda?**
>
> _____
> _____
> _____

comunidades aisladas, donde pasaban el tiempo rezando, trabajando o meditando. Durante la Edad Media se formaron comunidades de monjes, o **monasterios,** por toda Europa. La mayoría de los monjes seguían un estricto conjunto de reglas creadas a principios del siglo 6 por **Benito.**

## THE FRANKS BUILD AN EMPIRE/LOS FRANCOS CONSTRUYEN UN IMPERIO

In the 500s, a powerful Germanic tribe called the Franks conquered Gaul, the region we now call France. The Franks became Christian and created one of the strongest kingdoms in Europe. The Franks reached their greatest power during the 700s under **Charlemagne** (SHARH-luh-mayn). Religious scholarship flourished in Charlemagne's time./En el siglo 6, los francos, una tribu germánica poderosa, conquistaron Galia, la región que actualmente llamamos Francia. Los francos se convirtieron al cristianismo y crearon uno de los reinos más fuertes de Europa. Los francos alcanzaron su apogeo durante el siglo 8, bajo el reinado de **Carlomagno.** En la época de Carlomagno, florecieron los estudios religiosos.

> Underline the name of the most powerful leader of the Franks./Subraya el nombre del líder más poderoso de los francos.

## INVADERS THREATEN EUROPE/LOS INVASORES AMENAZAN EUROPA

While Charlemagne was building his empire, Europe was being attacked on all sides by invaders. The most fearsome invaders were the Vikings from Scandinavia./Mientras Carlomagno construía su imperio, Europa recibía ataques de invasores por todas partes. Los invasores más temidos eran los vikingos de Escandinavia.

> Who were the most fearsome invaders during Charlemagne's reign?/ Durante el reinado de Carlomagno, ¿quiénes eran los invasores más temidos?
>
> _____
>
> _____

## CHALLENGE ACTIVITY/ACTIVIDAD AVANZADA

**Critical Thinking: Make Inferences/Pensamiento crítico: Hacer inferencias** The life of a monk was strict. Write a letter from the point of view of someone who wishes to join a monastery. Explain why you want to live the life of a monk./La vida de los monjes era estricta. Escribe una carta desde el punto de vista de alguien que quiere entrar en un monasterio. Explica por qué quieres vivir como un monje.

**DIRECTIONS/INSTRUCCIONES** Read each sentence and fill in the blank with the word in the word pair that best completes the sentence./Lee cada oración y escribe en el espacio en blanco la palabra del par de palabras que mejor la completa.

1. The large landmass that includes both Europe and Asia is called _____. **(Eurasia/Northern Europe)**/_____ es el nombre de la gran masa de tierra que incluye Europa y Asia. **(Eurasia/Europa del Norte)**

2. _____ were religious men who lived apart from society in isolated communities. **(Charlemagne/Monks)**/Los hombres religiosos que vivían apartados de la sociedad en comunidades aisladas se llamaban _____. **(carlomagnos/monjes)**

3. The _____ fall between ancient times and modern times. **(medieval/Middle Ages)**/_____ es el período que se encuentra entre la Antigüedad y la Edad Moderna. **(Medieval/La Edad Media)**

4. One of the first missionaries to travel to northern Europe was _____, who took it upon himself to teach people about Christianity. **(Benedict/Patrick)**/Uno de los primeros misioneros en viajar al norte de Europa se llamaba _____. Él se dedicó a enseñar a las personas sobre el cristianismo. **(Benito/Patricio)**

5. _____ was a brilliant warrior and a strong king who led the Franks in building a huge empire. **(Patrick/Charlemagne)**/_____ fue un brillante guerrero y un rey poderoso que guio a los francos en la construcción de un inmenso imperio. **(Patricio/Carlomagno)**

6. Monks live in communities called _____.
   **(monasteries/medieval)**/Los monjes viven en comunidades llamadas
   _____. **(monasterios/medievales)**

7. An Italian monk by the name of _____ created a
   set of rules that most European monasteries followed. **(Patrick/Benedict)**/
   _____ fue un monje italiano que creó un conjunto de
   reglas posteriormente adoptado por la mayoría de los monasterios europeos.
   **(Patricio/Benito)**

8. Another name for the Middle Ages is the _____
   period. **(monasteries/medieval)**/Otro nombre que se da a la Edad Media es
   el período _____. **(monasterial/medieval)**

## The Middle Ages/La Edad Media

### Lesson/Lección 2

**MAIN IDEAS/IDEAS PRINCIPALES**
1. Feudalism governed how knights and nobles dealt with each other./El feudalismo regía las relaciones entre los caballeros y los nobles.
2. Feudalism spread through much of Europe./El feudalismo se propagó por gran parte de Europa.
3. The manor system dominated Europe's economy./El sistema de señorío dominaba la economía de Europa.
4. Towns and trade grew and helped end the feudal system./El crecimiento de las ciudades y el comercio ayudó a poner fin al sistema feudal.

## Key Terms and People/Personas y palabras clave

**knights/caballeros** warriors who fought on horseback/guerreros que luchaban a caballo

**vassal/vasallo** a knight who promised to support a lord in exchange for land/ caballero que prometía apoyar a un señor feudal a cambio de tierras

**feudalism/feudalismo** the system that governs the relationship between lords and vassals/sistema que rige las relaciones entre los señores feudales y los vasallos

**William the Conqueror/Guillermo el Conquistador** French noble who conquered England and spread feudalism/noble francés que conquistó Inglaterra y propagó el feudalismo

**manor/señorío** large estate owned by a knight or lord/gran finca perteneciente a un caballero o a un señor feudal

**serfs/siervos** workers who were tied to the land on which they lived/ trabajadores que estaban atados a la tierra en la que vivían

**Eleanor of Aquitaine/Leonor de Aquitania** powerful French noblewoman who became queen of France and England/poderosa mujer noble francesa que se convirtió en reina de Francia e Inglaterra

## Lesson Summary/Resumen de la lección

### FEUDALISM GOVERNS KNIGHTS AND NOBLES/ EL FEUDALISMO GOBIERNA A CABALLEROS Y NOBLES

When the Vikings, Magyars, and Muslims began their raids in the 800s, the Frankish kings were unable to defend their empire. Nobles had to defend their own lands. Many nobles began to rule their lands as independent territories. These nobles needed soldiers. They gave **knights,** warriors who fought on horseback, land in exchange for military service. A noble who gave land to a knight was called a lord, while the knight was called a **vassal.** The system that governed the promises between lords and vassals is called **feudalism.**/Cuando los vikingos, los magiares y los musulmanes empezaron a atacar Europa en el siglo 9, los reyes francos no podían defender su imperio. Los nobles tuvieron que defender sus propias tierras. Muchos nobles comenzaron a gobernar sus tierras como territorios independientes. Como necesitaban soldados, otorgaban tierras a los **caballeros,** guerreros que luchaban a caballo, a cambio de su servicio militar. El noble que otorgaba tierras a un caballero se llamaba señor feudal, mientras que el caballero recibía el nombre de **vasallo.** El sistema que regía las promesas entre los señores feudales y los vasallos se llamaba **feudalismo.**

| Why did many nobles become rulers of their own lands?/¿Por qué muchos nobles empezaron a gobernar sus propias tierras? |
| --- |
| _____ |
| _____ |
| _____ |

Lords and vassals had responsibilities to each other. A lord had to send help if an enemy attacked a vassal. A lord had to be fair or vassals could break all ties with him. Vassals had to fight at a lord's command. They also had to house and feed a lord if he visited and sometimes pay him money./Los señores feudales y los vasallos tenían responsabilidades mutuas. Los señores feudales debían enviar ayuda si los enemigos atacaban a un vasallo. Además, tenían que ser justos porque, de lo contrario, los vasallos podían romper lazos con ellos. Los vasallos tenían que luchar si el señor feudal se lo ordenaba. También debían hospedarlo y alimentarlo si los visitaba y, a veces, pagarle dinero.

| List two responsibilities of a vassal toward a lord./Enumera dos responsabilidades que tenían los vasallos hacia su señor feudal. |
| --- |
| _____ |
| _____ |
| _____ |
| _____ |

## FEUDALISM SPREADS/EL FEUDALISMO SE PROPAGA

Frankish knights introduced feudalism into northern Italy, Spain, and Germany. From Germany, knights carried feudalism into eastern Europe. Feudalism reached Britain when **William the Conqueror** invaded and made himself king of England./Los caballeros francos introdujeron el feudalismo en el norte de Italia, en España y en Alemania. Desde Alemania, los caballeros llevaron el feudalismo a Europa oriental. El feudalismo llegó a Britania cuando **Guillermo el Conquistador** la invadió y se autoproclamó rey de Inglaterra.

> **Who brought feudalism to Britain?/¿Quién llevó el feudalismo a Britania?**
>
> _____
>
> _____

## THE MANOR SYSTEM/SISTEMA DE SEÑORÍOS

An estate owned by a knight or lord was called a **manor.** As fighters, knights had no time to work in the fields. Most peasants, or small farmers, owned no land but needed to grow food to live. Knights let them live and farm land on their estates. In return, the peasants gave them food or other payment. **Serfs,** workers who were tied to the land on which they lived, were not allowed to leave without their lord's permission. Skilled workers also lived and worked on the manor. They traded goods and services to the peasants in exchange for food./Un **señorío** era una finca perteneciente a un caballero o a un señor feudal. Los caballeros eran guerreros y, por lo tanto, no tenían tiempo para trabajar la tierra. Como la mayoría de los campesinos, es decir, los pequeños agricultores, no tenían tierra pero necesitaban cultivar alimentos para poder vivir, los caballeros les permitían vivir en las tierras de su finca y cultivarlas. A cambio, los campesinos les pagaban con alimento o con otro tipo de pago. Los **siervos** eran trabajadores que estaban atados a la tierra en la que vivían y no podían irse sin el permiso del señor feudal. En el señorío también vivían y

> **What did knights and peasants provide each other under feudalism?/ Durante el feudalismo, ¿qué intercambiaban los caballeros y los campesinos?**
>
> _____
>
> _____
>
> _____
>
> _____

trabajaban trabajadores especializados que intercambiaban bienes y servicios por alimentos con los campesinos.

Women in the Middle Ages had fewer rights than men, but they still played important roles in society. Some women, like the French woman **Eleanor of Aquitaine,** even became politically powerful./En la Edad Media, las mujeres tenían menos derechos que los hombres, pero aun así desempeñaron roles importantes en la sociedad. Algunas mujeres, como **Leonor de Aquitania,** incluso llegaron a tener poder político.

## TOWNS AND TRADE GROW/CRECIMIENTO DE LAS CIUDADES Y EL COMERCIO

Most people lived in manors or small farms during the Middle Ages. However, as Europe's population grew, more people began living in towns and cities. The invention of a horse collar and a heavier plow made more food available. Increased trade eventually led to the decline of feudalism because people could make a living by making or selling particular types of goods./En la Edad Media, la mayoría de las personas vivían en los señoríos o en pequeñas granjas. Sin embargo, cuando la población de Europa comenzó a crecer, más personas se mudaron a los pueblos y las ciudades. Gracias a la invención de la collera y los arados más pesados, había más alimentos. El crecimiento del comercio provocó la decadencia del feudalismo porque las personas podían vivir de la confección o la venta de ciertos bienes.

> **What changes helped lead to a decline in feudalism?/¿Qué cambios provocaron la decadencia del feudalismo?**
>
> _____
> _____
> _____
> _____
> _____
> _____

## CHALLENGE ACTIVITY/ACTIVIDAD AVANZADA

**Critical Thinking: Summarize/Pensamiento crítico: Resumir** During the Middle Ages, the ability for people to improve their lives depended upon where they started out in life. Research the options for advancement for one of the following people: the lord of a manor, lady of a manor, a vassal, or a peasant. Then write a short summary describing any options this person had./En la Edad Media, la capacidad de progreso de las personas dependía de su punto de partida en la vida. Investiga las opciones de progreso de una de las siguientes personas: el señor de un señorío, la señora de un señorío, un vasallo y un campesino. Luego, escribe un resumen que describa las opciones que tenía esa persona.

**DIRECTIONS/INSTRUCCIONES** On the line provided before each statement, write **T** if a statement is true and **F** if a statement is false. If the statement is false, write the correct term on the line after each sentence that makes the sentence a true statement./En la línea que precede a cada enunciado, escribe **V** si el enunciado es verdadero y **F** si es falso. Si el enunciado es falso, escribe en la línea que sigue a la oración el término correcto que lo hace verdadero.

_____ 1. <u>William the Conqueror</u> declared himself king of England after defeating the English king near the town of Hastings./<u>Guillermo el Conquistador</u> se autoproclamó rey de Inglaterra después de derrotar al rey inglés cerca de la ciudad de Hastings.

_____

_____ 2. <u>Eleanor of Aquitaine</u> was a French woman who had great political power./<u>Leonor de Aquitania</u> era una mujer francesa que tenía mucho poder político.

_____

_____ 3. A knight who promised to support a lord in exchange for money was called a <u>serf</u>./<u>Un siervo</u> era un caballero que prometía apoyar a un señor feudal a cambio de dinero.

_____

_____ 4. <u>Vassals</u> were tied to the land on which they lived and could not leave their land without permission from the lord./<u>Los vasallos</u> estaban atados a la tierra en la que vivían y no podían irse sin el permiso del señor feudal.

_____

_____ 5. The best soldiers were <u>manors</u>, or warriors who fought on horseback./
Los mejores soldados eran <u>los señoríos</u>, es decir, guerreros que
luchaban a caballo.

_____

_____ 6. The large estate owned by a knight or a lord was called a <u>manor</u>./<u>Un
señorío</u> era una gran finca perteneciente a un caballero o señor feudal.

_____

_____ 7. <u>Fiefs</u> were parcels of land that nobles gave knights for their military
service./<u>Los feudós</u> eran parcelas de tierra que los nobles otorgaban
a los caballeros a cambio de sus servicios militares.

_____

# The Middle Ages/La Edad Media

## Lesson/Lección 3

**MAIN IDEAS/IDEAS PRINCIPALES**
1. Popes and kings ruled Europe as spiritual and political leaders./Los papas y los reyes gobernaban Europa como líderes espirituales y políticos.
2. Popes fought for power, leading to a permanent split within the church./La lucha de los papas por el poder provocó una división permanente dentro de la Iglesia.
3. Kings and popes clashed over some issues./Los reyes y los papas estaban en desacuerdo con respecto a algunas cuestiones.

## Key Terms and People/Personas y palabras clave

**excommunicate/excomulgar** casting an offender out of the church/expulsar de la Iglesia a alguien que ha cometido una ofensa grave

**Pope Gregory VII/papa Gregorio VII** pope who excommunicated Emperor Henry IV/papa que excomulgó al emperador Enrique IV

**Emperor Henry IV/emperador Enrique IV** Holy Roman ruler who challenged Pope Gregory VII/gobernante del Sacro Imperio Romano que desafió al papa Gregorio VII

## Lesson Summary/Resumen de la lección

### POPES AND KINGS RULE EUROPE/PAPAS Y REYES GOBIERNAN EUROPA

In the early Middle Ages, great nobles and their knights held most of the political power. As time passed this power began to shift to two types of leaders, popes and kings. Popes had great spiritual power. The kings had political power. Together, popes and kings controlled most of European society./A principios de la Edad Media, los grandes nobles y sus caballeros tenían la mayor parte del poder político. Con el paso del tiempo, ese poder comenzó a traspasarse a dos tipos de líderes: los papas y los reyes. Los papas tenían un gran poder espiritual. Los reyes tenían el poder político. Juntos, los papas y los reyes controlaban la mayoría de los aspectos de la sociedad europea.

Lesson/Lección 3, *continued/continuación*

---

The pope was the head of the Christian Church in Western Europe. Since nearly everyone in the Middle Ages belonged to this church, the pope had great power. Christians believed that the pope was God's representative on Earth. Because the pope was seen as God's representative, it was his duty to decide what the church would teach. From time to time, a pope would write a letter called a bull to explain a religious teaching or outline a church policy./El papa era el líder de la Iglesia cristiana en Europa occidental. En la Edad Media, casi todos pertenecían a esta iglesia, así que el papa tenía mucho poder. Los cristianos creían que el papa era el representante de Dios en la Tierra y que, por lo tanto, era su deber decidir cuáles serían las enseñanzas de la Iglesia. De vez en cuando, los papas escribían cartas llamadas bulas, que explicaban una enseñanza religiosa o informaban sobre una política de la Iglesia.

It was also the pope's duty to decide when someone was acting against the church. For the most serious offenses, the pope could choose to **excommunicate,** or cast out, an offender from the church. The offender, upon death, would not get into heaven. This much power often put the pope in direct conflict with the kings./Otro deber del papa era decidir en qué casos las personas actuaban en contra de la Iglesia. El papa podía **excomulgar,** o expulsar de la Iglesia, a una persona que cometiera una ofensa grave. Cuando moría, la persona que había sido excomulgada no podía entrar al cielo. Este poder tan grande provocó muchos conflictos entre el papa y los reyes.

In 1000 Europe was divided into many small states that were ruled by kings. Many of the kings did not have much power. But the kings of England, France, and the Holy Roman Empire held a lot of power. In France and England, kings inherited the throne through their fathers. The Holy Roman Empire got its name because

---

**Name two of the pope's responsibilities as leader of the Christian Church./Menciona dos responsabilidades del papa como líder de la Iglesia cristiana.**

_____

_____

_____

_____

**Why do you think people feared the pope's ability to excommunicate them?/¿Por qué crees que las personas tenían miedo de ser excomulgadas por el papa?**

_____

_____

_____

**Underline how kings were selected in France and England. Then, circle how an emperor was selected in the Holy Roman Empire./Subraya cómo se elegía a los reyes de Francia e Inglaterra. Luego, encierra en un círculo cómo se elegía al emperador del Sacro Imperio Romano.**

---

the empire existed with the pope's approval. In the Holy Roman Empire, the nobles elected the emperor. The pope settled any disagreements among the nobles./Hacia el año 1000, Europa estaba dividida en muchos estados pequeños gobernados por reyes. Muchos de los reyes no tenían tanto poder, pero los reyes de Inglaterra, Francia y el Sacro Imperio Romano sí eran muy poderosos. En Francia e Inglaterra, el trono se heredaba de padre a hijo. El Sacro Imperio Romano obtuvo ese nombre porque el imperio existía con la aprobación del papa. En el Sacro Imperio Romano, los nobles elegían al emperador y el papa resolvía los desacuerdos entre los nobles.

## POPES FIGHT FOR POWER/LOS PAPAS LUCHAN POR EL PODER

The bishops of eastern Europe, unlike those in western Europe, did not consider the pope the head of the church. Pope Leo IX excommunicated the bishop of Constantinople when the bishop would not recognize the pope's authority. This caused a permanent split, called a schism, in the church. The bishop's supporters formed the Orthodox Church. The pope headed the Roman Catholic Church from Rome./Los obispos de Europa oriental, a diferencia de los de Europa occidental, no consideraban que el papa fuera el líder de la Iglesia. El papa León IX excomulgó al obispo de Constantinopla cuando este se negó a reconocer la autoridad papal. Eso provocó una división permanente, o cisma, en la Iglesia. Los seguidores del obispo formaron la Iglesia ortodoxa. El papa encabezaba la Iglesia católica romana desde Roma.

> **What event caused a permanent split in the church?/¿Qué suceso provocó una división permanente en la Iglesia?**
>
> _____
> _____
> _____
> _____
> _____

## KINGS AND POPES CLASH/LOS REYES Y LOS PAPAS SE ENFRENTAN

Popes also argued with kings, particularly over the king's right to select bishops. A dispute arose when **Pope Gregory VII** did not like a bishop chosen by the Holy Roman **Emperor Henry IV.** Henry tried to remove the pope from office. The pope excommunicated Henry. Henry had to beg for the pope's forgiveness to remain in power. After their deaths, a compromise was reached. From then on, the pope would select religious officials, but religious officials would have to obey the emperor./Los papas también tenían desacuerdos con los reyes, especialmente sobre el derecho de los reyes de elegir a los obispos. Surgió una gran disputa cuando el **papa Gregorio VII** no aceptó a un obispo elegido por el **emperador Enrique IV** del Sacro Imperio Romano. Enrique trató de apartar al papa de su cargo. El papa excomulgó a Enrique, quien tuvo que rogar por el perdón del papa para seguir en el poder. Tras la muerte de ambos, se llegó a un acuerdo: desde ese momento, el papa elegiría a los funcionarios religiosos, pero estos debían obedecer al emperador.

> **How did Pope Gregory respond to Henry IV's attempt to remove him from power?/¿Cómo respondió el papa Gregorio al intento de Enrique IV de removerlo de su cargo?**
>
> _____
>
> _____
>
> _____

## CHALLENGE ACTIVITY/ACTIVIDAD AVANZADA

**Critical Thinking: Contrast/Pensamiento crítico: Contrastar** Popes and kings both had power during the Middle Ages. Write two paragraphs to show how their powers were different using examples from the text./Durante la Edad Media, tanto los papas como los reyes tenían mucho poder. Usando ejemplos del texto, escribe dos párrafos en los que expliques las diferencias entre el poder de cada uno.

**DIRECTIONS/INSTRUCCIONES** Match the terms in the first column with the correct definition from the second column by placing the letter of the correct definition in the space provided before each term./Une los términos de la primera columna con su definición correcta en la segunda columna. Escribe la letra de la definición correcta en el espacio que precede a cada término.

_____ 1. excommunicate/
excomulgar

_____ 2. Pope Gregory VII/
papa Gregorio VII

_____ 3. Henry IV/Enrique IV

_____ 4. Roman Catholic Church/
Iglesia católica romana

_____ 5. kings/reyes

_____ 6. Holy Roman Empire/
Sacro Imperio Romano

_____ 7. popes/papas

a. Holy Roman Emperor in 1073/
emperador del Sacro Imperio
Romano en el año 1073

b. their power was inherited from their
fathers/heredaban el poder de
su padre

c. excommunicated Emperor Henry IV/
excomulgó al emperador Enrique IV

d. powerful spiritual leaders/líderes
espirituales poderosos

e. to cast out from the church/expulsar
de la Iglesia

f. state that existed with the pope's
approval/estado que existía con
la aprobación del papa

g. led by a pope/encabezada por
un papa

**DIRECTIONS/INSTRUCCIONES** Read each sentence and circle the term in the word pair that best completes each sentence./Lee cada oración y encierra en un círculo el término del par de palabras que mejor la completa.

8. After a disagreement over who could select bishops,
_____ was excommunicated from the church. (**Henry
IV/Pope Gregory VII**)/Después de un desacuerdo sobre quién debía elegir a los
obispos, _____ fue excomulgado de la Iglesia. (**Enrique
IV/el papa Gregorio VII**)

9. People feared being _____ because they would not
go to heaven when they died. (**evicted/excommunicated**)/Las personas temían
ser _____ porque cuando murieran no iban a poder
entrar al cielo. (**desalojadas/excomulgadas**)

10. Because the _____ was seen as God's representative, it was his duty to decide what the church would teach. **(pope/king)**/Como se creía que el _____ era el representante de Dios, era su deber decidir cuáles serían las enseñanzas de la Iglesia. **(papa/rey)**

11. The _____, ruled by an emperor, got its name because the pope approved of it. **(Roman Catholic Church/Holy Roman Empire)**/ _____, que tenía un emperador, obtuvo ese nombre porque contaba con la aprobación del papa. **(La Iglesia católica romana/El Sacro Imperio Romano)**

# The Middle Ages/La Edad Media

## Lesson/Lección 4

**MAIN IDEAS/IDEAS PRINCIPALES**

1. The pope called on Crusaders to invade the Holy Land./El papa hizo un llamamiento a los cruzados para que invadieran Tierra Santa.

2. Despite some initial success, the later Crusades failed./A pesar del relativo éxito inicial, las Cruzadas posteriores fracasaron.

3. The Crusades changed Europe forever./Las Cruzadas cambiaron Europa para siempre.

# Key Terms and People/Personas y palabras clave

**Crusades/Cruzadas** a long series of wars fought between Christians and Muslims over control of Palestine/larga serie de guerras entre cristianos y musulmanes por el control de Palestina

**Holy Land/Tierra Santa** the European name for Palestine, the region where Jesus had lived, preached, and died/nombre europeo de Palestina, la región donde vivió, predicó y murió Jesús

**Pope Urban II/papa Urbano II** head of the Roman Catholic Church who started the Crusades/líder de la Iglesia católica romana que dio inicio a las Cruzadas

**King Richard I/rey Ricardo I** English king who led the third, ill-fated Crusade to seize Palestine/rey inglés que dirigió la tercera y fatídica Cruzada para tomar Palestina

**Saladin/Saladino** Turkish leader of the Muslim forces that prevented England from taking Palestine/líder turco de las fuerzas musulmanas que impidió a Inglaterra tomar el control de Palestina

# Lesson Summary/Resumen de la lección

### CRUSADERS INVADE THE HOLY LAND/LOS CRUZADOS INVADEN TIERRA SANTA

The **Crusades** were a long series of wars between Christians and Muslims in Southwest Asia. The Europeans fought the Muslims to retake Palestine. Christians call the region the **Holy Land** because it was where Jesus had lived, preached, and died./Las **Cruzadas** fueron una larga serie de guerras entre cristianos y musulmanes en el suroeste asiático. Los europeos querían recuperar Palestina de manos de los musulmanes. Los cristianos llaman

> **Why did Christians call Palestine the "Holy Land"?/¿Por qué los cristianos llamaban "Tierra Santa" a Palestina?**
>
> _____
> _____
> _____

a esta región **Tierra Santa** porque allí fue donde
vivió, predicó y murió Jesús.

For many years, Palestine had been ruled by
Muslims. In general, the Muslims did not bother
Christians who visited the region. In the late
1000s, however, a new group of Turkish Muslims
captured the city of Jerusalem. Pilgrims returning
to Europe said that these Turks had attacked
them./Durante muchos años, Palestina había
sido gobernada por los musulmanes. En general,
los musulmanes no interferían con los cristianos
que visitaban la región. Sin embargo, a fines del
siglo 11, un nuevo grupo de musulmanes turcos
capturó la ciudad de Jerusalén. Los peregrinos
que regresaban a Europa dijeron que los turcos
los habían atacado.

Before long the Turks began to raid the
Byzantine Empire. The Byzantine emperor asked
**Pope Urban II** of the Roman Catholic Church
for help. Although the Byzantines were Eastern
Orthodox Christians and not Roman Catholic,
the pope agreed to help./Poco tiempo después,
los turcos empezaron a atacar el Imperio
bizantino. El emperador bizantino le pidió
ayuda al **papa Urbano II** de la Iglesia católica
romana. Aunque los bizantinos eran cristianos
ortodoxos de oriente y no católicos romanos,
el papa accedió a ayudarlos.

> **Underline the name of the person who made the call to arms that led to the Crusades./**Subraya el nombre de la persona que hizo el llamado a las armas que dio inicio a las Cruzadas.

Pope Urban called on Christians to retake the
Holy Land from the Muslim Turks. Crusaders
from all over Europe flocked to France to prepare
to fight. About 5,000 Crusaders left Europe for
the Holy Land in 1096. Many were peasants,
not soldiers. On their way to the Holy Land, the
peasant Crusaders attacked Jews in Germany.
They blamed the Jews for Jesus's death. Turkish
troops killed most of these untrained peasants
before they even reached the Holy Land. However,

> **What happened to the peasant Crusaders?/**¿Qué pasó con los cruzados campesinos?
>
> _____
> _____
> _____
> _____

the nobles and knights, in 1099, were able take Jerusalem and set up four kingdoms there./El papa Urbano hizo un llamamiento a los cristianos para que recuperaran Tierra Santa de manos de los turcos musulmanes. Los cruzados de toda Europa acudieron a Francia para prepararse para la lucha. Aproximadamente 5,000 cruzados partieron de Europa con rumbo a Tierra Santa en 1096. Muchos eran campesinos, no soldados. Camino a Palestina, los cruzados campesinos atacaron a los judíos en Alemania porque los culpaban por la muerte de Jesús. Las tropas turcas mataron a la mayoría de esos campesinos, que no tenían entrenamiento, antes de que pudieran llegar a Tierra Santa. Sin embargo, en 1099, los nobles y los caballeros tomaron Jerusalén y establecieron allí cuatro reinos.

## LATER CRUSADES FAIL/LAS CRUZADAS POSTERIORES FRACASAN

Within 50 years the Muslims had started taking land back from the Christians. The Europeans launched more Crusades, but these invasions ended in defeat for the Christians. The Third Crusade started as a group effort between the German, French, and English kings. But only **King Richard I** of England stayed on to fight. His opponent was the brilliant Muslim leader **Saladin,** known for his kindness toward fallen enemies. Eventually, King Richard left the Holy Land, which was still under Muslim control. By 1291, Muslim armies had taken back all of the Holy Land. The Crusades were over./En menos de 50 años, los musulmanes habían comenzado a recuperar las tierras tomadas por los cristianos. Los europeos emprendieron más cruzadas, pero estas invasiones terminaron en derrota para los cristianos. La Tercera Cruzada comenzó como una campaña conjunta de los reyes de Alemania, Francia e Inglaterra, pero solamente el **rey**

> Underline the name of the English and Muslim leaders fighting in the Third Crusade./Subraya los nombres del líder inglés y del líder musulmán que lucharon en la Tercera Cruzada.

**Ricardo I** de Inglaterra se quedó a luchar. Su oponente era el brillante líder musulmán **Saladino,** quien era conocido por su clemencia con los enemigos derrotados. Finalmente, el rey Ricardo se retiró de Tierra Santa, que seguía bajo control musulmán. Para 1291, los ejércitos musulmanes habían recuperado toda Tierra Santa. Las cruzadas habían llegado a su fin.

## CRUSADES CHANGE EUROPE/LAS CRUZADAS CAMBIAN EUROPA

The Crusades increased trade between Europe and Asia. In some cases, the Crusades increased the power of the European kings. But the main impact of the wars was divisive. The Crusades hurt the trust European Jews had developed with Christians. The Crusades also caused distrust between Muslims and Christians. Those tensions are still felt today./Las Cruzadas produjeron un aumento en el comercio entre Europa y Asia. En algunos casos, aumentaron el poder de los reyes europeos. Sin embargo, el impacto principal de las guerras fue causar divisiones. Las Cruzadas dañaron la confianza que los judíos europeos habían depositado en los cristianos y también provocaron desconfianza entre musulmanes y cristianos. Esas tensiones aún se sienten hoy en día.

> **How did the Crusades affect relations between Europe and Asia?/¿De qué manera las cruzadas afectaron las relaciones entre Europa y Asia?**
>
> _____
> _____
> _____
> _____
> _____
> _____

## CHALLENGE ACTIVITY/ACTIVIDAD AVANZADA

**Critical Thinking: Make Judgments/Pensamiento crítico: Dar opiniones** Using what you know, write a brief paper describing how the Crusades continue to have an impact on our society today./Usa lo que sabes para escribir un artículo breve en el que describas cómo las Cruzadas siguen teniendo un impacto en la sociedad actual.

Lesson/Lección 4, *continued*/ *continuación*

---

| | | | |
|---|---|---|---|
| Crusades/las Cruzadas | Holy Land/Tierra Santa | King Richard I/el rey Ricardo I | Muslims/ musulmanes |
| Palestine/ Palestina | Pope Urban II/el papa Urbano II | Saladin/Saladino | |

---

**DIRECTIONS/INSTRUCCIONES** Read each sentence and fill in the blank with the word from the word bank that best completes the sentence./Lee cada oración y escribe en el espacio en blanco la palabra del banco de palabras que mejor la completa.

1. _____ agreed to help the Byzantines who were attacked by Muslim Turks in the Holy Land./_____ accedió a ayudar a los bizantinos cuando los turcos musulmanes los estaban atacando en Tierra Santa.

2. The leader of the Muslim forces who was respected for his kindness toward fallen enemies was _____./El líder de las fuerzas musulmanas que era muy respetado por su clemencia hacia los enemigos derrotados se llamaba _____.

3. The _____ were a long series of wars between Christians and Muslims in Southwest Asia./_____ fueron una larga serie de guerras entre cristianos y musulmanes en el suroeste asiático.

4. Though the rulers of England, France, and the Holy Roman Empire led armies during the Third Crusade, only _____ of England stayed in the Holy Land to fight./A pesar de que los gobernantes de Inglaterra, Francia y el Sacro Imperio Romano condujeron tropas durante la Tercera Cruzada, solo _____ de Inglaterra se quedó a luchar en Tierra Santa.

5. Palestine is called the _____ because it was the region where Jesus had lived, preached, and died./Palestina también recibe el nombre de _____ porque es la región donde vivió, predicó y murió Jesús.

6. The goal of the Crusades was to take the control of _____ away from the Muslim Turks./El objetivo de las Cruzadas era tomar el control de _____, que estaba en manos de los turcos musulmanes.

Lesson/Lección 4, *continued*/*continuación*

7. The English leader _____ returned home with Jerusalem still in Muslim hands./El líder inglés _____ regresó a su tierra mientras Jerusalén seguía bajo dominio musulmán.

8. Following the Crusades, tension between Christians and Jews and _____ grew./Después de las cruzadas, crecieron las tensiones entre cristianos, judíos y _____.

# The Middle Ages/La Edad Media

**MAIN IDEAS/IDEAS PRINCIPALES**

1. The Christian Church shaped both society and politics in medieval Europe./ La Iglesia cristiana influyó en la sociedad y la política de la Europa medieval.

2. Orders of monks and friars did not like the church's political nature./Las órdenes de monjes y frailes no estaban de acuerdo con el carácter político de la Iglesia.

3. Church leaders helped build the first universities in Europe./Los líderes de la Iglesia ayudaron a construir las primeras universidades de Europa.

4. The church influenced the arts in medieval Europe./La Iglesia influyó en las artes en la Europa medieval.

# Key Terms and People/Personas y palabras clave

**clergy/clero** church officials/funcionarios de la Iglesia

**religious order/orden religiosa** group of people who dedicate their lives to religion and follow common rules/grupo de personas que dedican su vida a la religión y que siguen una serie de normas comunes

**Francis of Assisi/Francisco de Asís** founder of the Franciscan order/fundador de la orden de los franciscanos

**friars/frailes** members of religious orders who lived and worked among the general public/miembros de una orden religiosa que vivían y trabajaban entre la gente

**Thomas Aquinas/Tomás de Aquino** philosopher who showed how religious faith and reason could coexist/filósofo que demostró que la razón y la fe religiosa podían coexistir

**natural law/ley natural** Thomas Aquinas's concept that God created a law that governed how the world operated/concepto de Tomás de Aquino; indica que Dios creó una ley que gobierna el funcionamiento del mundo

# Lesson Summary/Resumen de la lección

**THE CHURCH SHAPES SOCIETY AND POLITICS/LA IGLESIA INFLUYE EN LA SOCIEDAD Y LA POLÍTICA**

The **clergy,** church officials, were very influential in medieval European culture and politics. For many people in the European Middle Ages, life revolved around the local church. Markets, festivals, and religious ceremonies all took

place there. Some people made pilgrimages, or
journeys to religious locations./El **clero,** es decir,
el conjunto de funcionarios de la Iglesia, ejercía
una gran influencia en la cultura y la política
de la Europa medieval. Para muchas personas
que vivían en Europa en la Edad Media, la
vida giraba en torno a la iglesia local. Allí
funcionaban los mercados y se llevaban a cabo
festivales y ceremonias religiosas. Algunas
personas participaban en peregrinaciones,
o viajes a lugares sagrados.

The church owned a lot of land in Europe
because many people left their property to the
church when they died. In this way the church
became a major feudal lord. Of all the clergy,
bishops and abbots were most involved in
political matters. They often advised local rulers./
La Iglesia poseía una gran cantidad de tierras
en Europa porque muchas personas dejaban sus
propiedades a la Iglesia cuando morían. De esta
manera, la Iglesia se convirtió en un gran señor
feudal. De todos los miembros del clero, los
obispos y los abades eran los que estaban más
involucrados en los asuntos políticos. Muchas
veces aconsejaban a los gobernantes locales.

> **How did the church become a feudal lord during the Middle Ages?/**
> **¿Cómo se convirtió la Iglesia en un señor feudal durante la Edad Media?**
>
> _____
> _____
> _____

## MONKS AND FRIARS/MONJES Y FRAILES

Some people thought that the church was
becoming too involved with politics. The French
monks of Cluny established a new **religious order.**
They dedicated their lives to religion and followed
a strict schedule of worship. Other new orders
followed. Women created religious communities
in convents. Most monks lived apart from society,
but two new religious orders developed for those
who wanted to live, work, and teach among
people. These were the Dominicans, started by
Dominic de Guzmán, and the Franciscans,

> **Underline the sentence that explains why the monks of Cluny established a new religious order./Subraya la oración que explica por qué los monjes de Cluny fundaron una nueva orden religiosa.**

started by **Francis of Assisi.** The members of
these orders were called **friars.**/Algunas personas
pensaban que la Iglesia se estaba involucrando
demasiado en la política. Los monjes de Cluny,
en Francia, crearon una nueva **orden religiosa.**
Dedicaban sus vidas a la religión y tenían un
estricto cronograma de oración. Más tarde se
crearon otras órdenes. Las mujeres crearon
comunidades religiosas dentro de los conventos.
La mayoría de los monjes vivían apartados de
la sociedad, pero se crearon dos nuevas órdenes
religiosas para quienes querían vivir, trabajar
y enseñar entre la gente: los dominicos, una
orden fundada por Domingo de Guzmán, y
los franciscanos, una orden fundada por
**Francisco de Asís.** Los miembros de estas
órdenes se llamaban **frailes.**

> **How were the Dominicans and Franciscans different from the orders who lived in monasteries?**/¿En qué se diferenciaban los franciscanos y los dominicos de las órdenes que vivían en monasterios?
> _____
> _____
> _____

## UNIVERSITIES ARE BUILT/SE CONSTRUYEN UNIVERSIDADES

Europe's first universities were built by the
church. Religion, law, medicine, and philosophy
were taught. Scholars wanted to establish a
connection between religious faith and human
reason. The Dominican friar **Thomas Aquinas**
wrote a reasoned argument for the existence of
God. He also developed a philosophical system
called **natural law** to show how God had ordered
the world./Las primeras universidades de Europa
fueron construidas por la Iglesia. En ellas se
enseñaba religión, derecho, medicina y filosofía.
Los estudiosos querían establecer una conexión
entre la fe religiosa y la razón humana. El fraile
dominico **Tomás de Aquino** escribió un
argumento racional en favor de la existencia de
Dios. También desarrolló un sistema filosófico
denominado **ley natural** para demostrar cómo
Dios había ordenado el mundo.

> **Why did Thomas Aquinas write about the existence of God?**/¿Por qué Tomás de Aquino escribió sobre la existencia de Dios?
> _____
> _____
> _____
> _____

## THE CHURCH AND THE ARTS/LA IGLESIA Y LAS ARTES

In the 1100s Europeans built great Gothic cathedrals that are beautiful architectural achievements. They were symbols of people's faith. Everything, including the high ceilings and stained glass windows, were designed to show respect for God. Everything inside the church, from the clergy's robes to the books used, were works of art./En el siglo 12, se construyeron en Europa grandes catedrales góticas que son hermosos logros arquitectónicos. Esas catedrales eran un símbolo de la fe cristiana. Todo, incluidos los altos techos y los vitrales, estaba diseñado para mostrar respeto hacia Dios. Todos los objetos que estaban en el interior de la iglesia, desde los hábitos del clero hasta los libros que se usaban, eran obras de arte.

> Why do you think so much medieval European art was made for the church?/¿Por qué crees que en la Edad Media se hicieron tantas obras de arte para la Iglesia?
>
> _____
> _____
> _____
> _____
> _____

## CHALLENGE ACTIVITY/ACTIVIDAD AVANZADA

**Critical Thinking: Draw Conclusions/Pensamiento crítico: Sacar conclusiones** Which medieval religious people do you agree with the most— those involved in politics, the monks who left society, or the friars who believed in working among the people? Write a one-page paper defending your views./¿Cón qué grupo religioso medieval estás más de acuerdo: con los que se involucraban en la política, con los monjes que vivían apartados de la sociedad o con los frailes que trabajaban entre la gente? Escribe un ensayo de una página en el que defiendas tu punto de vista.

**DIRECTIONS/INSTRUCCIONES** Read each sentence and fill in
the blank with the word in the word pair that best completes the
sentence./Lee cada oración y escribe en el espacio en blanco la
palabra del par de palabras que mejor la completa.

1. As a young man, _____ gave all of his possessions
   away and began preaching and tending to people who were poor or ill.
   **(Francis of Assisi/Thomas Aquinas)**/De joven, _____
   donó todas sus posesiones y se dedicó a predicar y a ayudar a los pobres y
   a los enfermos. **(Francisco de Asís/Tomás de Aquino)**

2. _____, according to Thomas Aquinas, is created by
   God and governs how the world operates. **(Natural law/Religious order)**/
   Según Tomás de Aquino, la _____ fue creada por
   Dios para controlar el funcionamiento del mundo. **(ley natural/orden
   religiosa)**

3. Journeys to religious locations are also referred to as
   _____. **(friars/pilgrimages)**/_____
   son viajes a lugares sagrados. **(Los frailes/Las peregrinaciones)**

4. Dominican philosopher _____ believed reason and
   faith could work together. **(Francis of Assisi/Thomas Aquinas)**/El filósofo
   dominico _____ creía que la razón y la fe podían
   trabajar en conjunto. **(Francisco de Asís/Tomás de Aquino)**

5. The _____, or church officials, and their teachings
   were very influential in European culture and politics. **(friars/clergy)**/
   _____, es decir, los funcionarios de la iglesia,
   influyeron mucho en la cultura y la política europeas con sus enseñanzas.
   **(Los frailes/El clero)**

6. A group of people who dedicate their lives to religion and follow
   common rules is a _____. **(clergy/religious order)**/
   _____ es un grupo de personas que dedican sus vidas
   a la religión y que siguen normas comunes. **(El clero/Una orden religiosa)**

7. _____ were people who belonged to religious
   orders but lived and worked among the general public. **(Friars/Clergy)**/
   _____ eran personas que pertenecían a órdenes
   religiosas pero que vivían y trabajaban entre la gente. **(Los frailes/El clero)**

# The Middle Ages/La Edad Media

**MAIN IDEAS/IDEAS PRINCIPALES**

1. Magna Carta caused changes in England's government and legal system./La Carta Magna provocó cambios en el gobierno y el sistema legal de Inglaterra.

2. The Hundred Years' War led to political changes in England and France./La Guerra de los Cien Años produjo cambios políticos en Inglaterra y Francia.

3. The Black Death led to social changes./La peste negra produjo cambios sociales.

4. The church reacted to challengers by punishing people who opposed its teachings./Al ser cuestionada, la Iglesia comenzó a castigar a las personas que se oponían a sus enseñanzas.

5. Christians fought Moors in Spain and Portugal in an effort to drive all Muslims out of Europe./En un intento por expulsar a todos los musulmanes de Europa, los cristianos lucharon contra los moros en España y Portugal.

6. Jews faced discrimination across Europe in the Middle Ages./Durante la Edad Media, los judíos eran discriminados en toda Europa.

## Key Terms and People/Personas y palabras clave

**Magna Carta/Carta Magna** document written by English nobles and signed by King John listing rights the king could not ignore/documento escrito por nobles ingleses y firmado por el rey Juan que enumeraba los derechos que el rey no podía pasar por alto

**Parliament/Parlamento** lawmaking body that governs England/órgano legislativo que gobierna Inglaterra

**Hundred Years' War/Guerra de los Cien Años** long conflict between England and France during the 1300s and 1400s/largo conflicto entre Inglaterra y Francia que tuvo lugar durante los siglos 14 y 15

**Joan of Arc/Juana de Arco** teenage peasant girl who rallied the French troops during the Hundred Years' War/campesina adolescente que reunió a las tropas francesas durante la Guerra de los Cien Años

**Black Death/peste negra** deadly plague that killed millions of Europeans between 1347 and 1351/plaga mortal que mató a millones de europeos entre 1347 y 1351

**heresy/herejía** religious ideas that oppose accepted church teachings/ideas religiosas que se oponen a las enseñanzas oficiales de la Iglesia

**Reconquista/Reconquista** Christian efforts to retake Spain from the Muslim Moors/intento de los cristianos de recuperar España de manos de los moros musulmanes

**King Ferdinand/rey Fernando** Aragon prince who married Isabella of Castile to rule a united Spain/príncipe de Aragón que se casó con Isabel de Castilla para gobernar una España unida

**Queen Isabella/reina Isabel** Castilian princess who ruled Spain with her husband, Ferdinand of Aragon/princesa de Castilla que gobernó España junto con su esposo, Fernando de Aragón

**Spanish Inquisition/Inquisición española** organization of priests charged with seeking out and punishing non-Christians/organización de sacerdotes que tenía encomendada la tarea de perseguir y castigar a las personas que no eran cristianas

# Lesson Summary/Resumen de la lección

**MAGNA CARTA CAUSES CHANGE IN ENGLAND/**
**LA CARTA MAGNA PROVOCA CAMBIOS EN**
**INGLATERRA**

In 1215, a group of English nobles decided to force the king to respect their rights. They made King John approve a document listing 63 rights the king had to follow. This document was called **Magna Carta,** or "Great Charter." This charter became a key principle of English government and an important step in the development of democracy./En 1215, un grupo de nobles ingleses decidió obligar al rey a respetar sus derechos. Le exigieron al rey Juan que aprobara un documento en el que se enumeraban 63 derechos que el rey tenía que respetar. Ese documento se denominó **Carta Magna,** o "Gran Carta". La Carta Magna se convirtió en un principio clave del gobierno inglés y significó un paso importante en el desarrollo de la democracia.

> **What was Magna Carta?/**
> **¿Qué era la Carta Magna?**
> _____
> _____
> _____
> _____

The kings soon turned to a council of nobles for advice and money. This council developed into **Parliament,** the lawmaking body that still governs England today./Pronto, los reyes recurrieron a un consejo de nobles para que les proporcionaran dinero y asesoramiento. Este consejo se convirtió en el **Parlamento,** el órgano legislativo que todavía gobierna Inglaterra hoy en día.

> **Who made up the original**
> **British Parliament?/**
> **Originalmente, ¿quiénes**
> **constituían el Parlamento**
> **británico?**
> _____
> _____

## THE HUNDRED YEARS' WAR/LA GUERRA DE LOS CIEN AÑOS

In Europe, kings were not giving up their power, but other events forced changes. The **Hundred Years' War,** a long conflict between England and France, started when the English king invaded France. Nearly 100 years later **Joan of Arc,** a teenage peasant girl, rallied the French troops. The English killed Joan, but the French won the war./En Europa los reyes no querían ceder el poder, pero otros sucesos provocaron cambios políticos. La **Guerra de los Cien Años,** un largo conflicto entre Inglaterra y Francia, comenzó cuando el rey inglés invadió Francia. Casi 100 años después, **Juana de Arco,** una campesina adolescente, reunió a las tropas francesas para la lucha. Los ingleses mataron a Juana, pero los franceses ganaron la guerra.

> Why was Joan of Arc's feat truly remarkable?/¿Por qué fue tan notable la hazaña de Juana de Arco?
>
> _____
> _____
> _____
> _____
> _____

## THE BLACK DEATH/LA PESTE NEGRA

During the Hundred Years' War an even greater crisis arose. This crisis was the **Black Death,** a deadly plague that swept through Europe between 1347 and 1351. The plague originally came from infected rats from central and eastern Asia./Durante la Guerra de los Cien Años, hubo una crisis aún mayor. Se trataba de la **peste negra,** una plaga mortal que arrasó Europa entre los años 1347 y 1351. La plaga provenía de ratas infectadas del centro y el este de Asia.

Some historians think the Black Death killed a third of Europe's population—perhaps 25 million people. This caused sweeping changes all over Europe. The old manor system, already weakened by the growth of cities, fell apart. Plague survivors found their skills in high demand. They could demand wages for their labor. Many fled their manors, moving to Europe's growing cities. The power of the church also began to decline./Algunos historiadores

> Underline the estimated number of victims of the Black Death./Subraya el número estimado de víctimas de la peste negra.

creen que la peste negra mató a la tercera parte de la población europea (aproximadamente 25 millones de personas). Este suceso provocó cambios radicales en toda Europa. El antiguo sistema de señoríos, que ya se encontraba debilitado por el crecimiento de las ciudades, terminó de desmoronarse. Los sobrevivientes de la plaga se dieron cuenta de que se necesitaban sus habilidades y que podían pedir mejores sueldos por su trabajo. Muchos se fueron de los señoríos y se mudaron a las ciudades de Europa, que estaban en plena expansión. El poder de la Iglesia también empezó a decaer.

> **How did the Black Death change Europe?/¿De qué manera la peste negra cambió Europa?**
>
> _____
> _____
> _____
> _____
> _____

## THE CHURCH REACTS TO CHALLENGERS/ LA IGLESIA REACCIONA A LOS OPOSITORES

Around 1100, some Christians felt that the clergy were more concerned with money and land than with God. Others did not agree with the church's ideas and preached their own ideas about religion. Religious ideas that oppose church teachings are called **heresy.** Church officials sent priests and friars throughout Europe to find heretics./Hacia el siglo 12 aproximadamente, algunos cristianos pensaban que el clero les daba más importancia al dinero y a las tierras que a Dios. Otros no compartían las ideas de la Iglesia y comenzaron a predicar sus propias ideas acerca de la religión. Las ideas religiosas que se oponen a las enseñanzas de la Iglesia se conocen como **herejía.** Los funcionarios de la Iglesia enviaban a sacerdotes y frailes de toda Europa a buscar a los herejes.

> **What two things did some Christians feel that the clergy was more concerned with than God?/ Según algunos cristianos, ¿a qué dos cosas les daba el clero más importancia que a Dios?**
>
> _____
> _____

In the early 1200s, Pope Innocent III called for a crusade against heretics in southern France. The result was a bloody struggle that lasted about 20 years, destroying towns and cities and costing thousands of lives./A principios del siglo 13, el papa Inocencio III pidió que se iniciara una cruzada contra los herejes en el sur de Francia. El resultado fue una lucha sangrienta que duró

aproximadamente 20 años. Ciudades y pueblos
enteros fueron destruidos y miles de personas
perdieron la vida.

## CHRISTIANS FIGHT THE MOORS/LOS CRISTIANOS LUCHAN CONTRA LOS MOROS

In Spain, the reign of the Muslim Moors collapsed
in the 1000s. Christian kingdoms in Spain started
a war to drive them out. They called their war
**Reconquista** (reh-kahn-KEES-tuh), or reconquest.
The kingdom of Castile freed itself of Muslim
rule. Portugal and Aragon soon followed. Castile
and Aragon became united by the marriage of
two royals, **King Ferdinand** of Aragon and **Queen
Isabella** of Castile. Spain became a nation-state. In
addition to banning Islam, the royals required all
Jews to convert to Christianity or leave./En
España, el reinado de los moros musulmanes se
desmoronó en el siglo 11. Los reinos cristianos
de España iniciaron una guerra para expulsar
a los musulmanes. Llamaron a esta guerra la
**Reconquista.** El reino de Castilla fue el primero en
liberarse del gobierno musulmán. Poco después,
Portugal y Aragón también lo lograron. Castilla
y Aragón se unieron con el matrimonio de dos
miembros de la familia real, el **rey Fernando** de
Aragón y la **reina Isabel** de Castilla. España se
convirtió en una nación estado. Además de
prohibir el Islam, España exigió que todos los
judíos se convirtieran al cristianismo o se fueran.

Ferdinand and Isabella created the **Spanish
Inquisition,** an organization of priests that found
and punished non-Christians. The inquisition
executed about 2,000 people in Spain and almost
1,400 more in Portugal./Fernando e Isabel crearon
la **Inquisición española,** una organización de
sacerdotes que perseguía y castigaba a quienes
no eran cristianos. La Inquisición ejecutó a casi
2,000 personas en España y a casi 1,400 más
en Portugal.

> **What was the Reconquista?/**
> ¿Qué fue la Reconquista?
>
> _____
> _____
> _____

> **How many people in both
> Portugal and Spain died at
> the hands of the Spanish
> Inquisition?/**¿Cuántas
> personas murieron a
> manos de la Inquisición
> española en Portugal y
> España?
>
> _____
> _____

## JEWS FACE DISCRIMINATION/DISCRIMINACIÓN CONTRA LOS JUDÍOS

Jews were persecuted all over Europe. Many Christians blamed all Jews for the persecution and death of Jesus. Some people even blamed the Jews for the Black Death. In many kingdoms, Jews were driven out by angry mobs, and sometimes by the kings themselves. They had to flee from their homes or die./Los judíos eran perseguidos en toda Europa. Muchos cristianos culpaban a todos los judíos por la persecución y la muerte de Jesús. Algunos incluso culpaban a los judíos por la peste negra. En muchos reinos, los judíos eran expulsados por muchedumbres furiosas y, a veces, por los mismos reyes. La opción que enfrentaban era huir de sus casas o morir.

> **Name two things that some medieval Europeans blamed on the Jews./ Menciona dos cosas de las que se acusaba a los judíos en Europa durante la Edad Media.**
>
> _____
> _____
> _____

## CHALLENGE ACTIVITY/ACTIVIDAD AVANZADA

**Critical Thinking: Make Inferences/Pensamiento crítico: Hacer inferencias** Write a one-page paper explaining how our lives might be different if the Magna Carta had *not* been created./Escribe un ensayo de una página en el que expliques de qué manera nuestras vidas serían diferentes si *no* se hubiera creado la Carta Magna.

**DIRECTIONS/INSTRUCCIONES** Match the terms in the first column with their correct definition from the second column by placing the letter of the correct definition in the space provided before each term./Une los términos de la primera columna con su definición correcta en la segunda columna. Escribe la letra de la definición correcta en el espacio que precede a cada término.

_____ 1. Magna Carta/
Carta Magna

_____ 2. Parliament/
Parlamento

_____ 3. Hundred Years' War/
Guerra de los Cien Años

_____ 4. Joan of Arc/
Juana de Arco

_____ 5. Black Death/
peste negra

a. teenage peasant girl that rallied the French troops/campesina adolescente que reunió a las tropas francesas

b. long conflict between England and France/largo conflicto entre Inglaterra y Francia

c. a document listing rights that the king could not ignore/documento en el que se enumeraban los derechos que el rey no podía pasar por alto

d. a deadly plague that swept through Europe between 1347 and 1351/plaga mortal que arrasó Europa entre los años 1347 y 1351

e. the lawmaking body that governs England today/el órgano legislativo que gobierna Inglaterra hoy en día

**DIRECTIONS/INSTRUCCIONES** Read each sentence and fill in the blank with the word in the word pair that best completes the sentence./Lee cada oración y escribe en el espacio en blanco la palabra del par de palabras que mejor la completa.

6. King _____ was a prince from Aragon, one of the largest Spanish kingdoms. **(John/Ferdinand)**/El rey _____ era el príncipe de Aragón, uno de los reinos más grandes de España. **(Juan/Fernando)**

7. The _____ was the effort to retake Spain from the Moors. **(Reconquista/Hundred Years War)**/La _____ fue un intento de recuperar España de las manos de los moros. **(Reconquista/ Guerra de los Cien Años)**

8. The _____ was an organization of priests that looked for and punished non-Christians in Spain. **(Reconquista/Spanish Inquisition)**/ La _____ era una organización de sacerdotes que buscaba y castigaba a las personas que no eran cristianas en España. **(Reconquista/Inquisición española)**

9. _____ was married to King Ferdinand and together they ruled all of Spain. **(Queen Isabella/Joan of Arc)**/ _____ se casó con el rey Fernando y juntos gobernaron toda España. **(La reina Isabel/Juana de Arco)**

10. Religious ideas that disagree with church teachings are called _____. **(Black Death/heresy)**/Las ideas religiosas que se oponen a las enseñanzas de la Iglesia se llaman _____. **(peste negra/herejías)**

## The Renaissance/El Renacimiento

**Lesson/Lección 1**

---

**MAIN IDEAS/IDEAS PRINCIPALES**

1. European trade with Asia increased in the 1300s./El comercio entre Europa y Asia aumentó en el siglo 14.

2. Trade cities in Italy grew wealthy and competed against each other./Las ciudades comerciales de Italia se enriquecieron y compitieron entre sí.

3. As Florence became a center for arts and learning, the Renaissance began./Con la constitución de Florencia como centro de las artes y el aprendizaje, comenzó el Renacimiento.

## Key Terms and People/Personas y palabras clave

**Marco Polo/Marco Polo**  European explorer who traveled through Asia in the 1200s/explorador europeo que viajó por Asia en el siglo 13

**interest/interés**  a fee that borrowers pay for the use of someone else's money/ cuota que los prestatarios pagan por el uso del dinero de otra persona

**Cosimo de' Medici/Cosme de Médici**  wealthy banker who turned Florence into a center of arts, culture, and education/banquero acaudalado que convirtió a Florencia en un centro para las artes, la cultura y la educación

**Renaissance/Renacimiento**  period following the Middle Ages, characterized by renewed interest in Greek and Roman culture and an emphasis on people as individuals/período que sigue a la Edad Media, caracterizado por un renovado interés por las culturas griega y romana, y por un énfasis en la visión de las personas como individuos

## Lesson Summary/Resumen de la lección

### TRADE WITH ASIA/COMERCIO CON ASIA

Despite the Black Death's terrible death toll, the disease did not harm farmland, buildings, ships, machines, or gold. Survivors used these things to raise more food or make new products. Europe's economy began to grow. Some new products from the east appeared in markets. Traders brought these new goods across the Silk Road, a caravan route from Europe to China that had fallen into disuse. In the 1200s, the Mongols reopened the Silk Road./A pesar de que la peste negra dejó un terrible saldo de muertes, la enfermedad no afectó las tierras de cultivo, los edificios, los barcos, las máquinas ni el oro.

> List two consequences of the Black Death./Enumera dos consecuencias de la peste negra.
>
> _____
> _____
> _____
> _____
> _____
> _____
> _____
> _____
> _____
> _____

Los sobrevivientes usaron estos elementos para producir más alimentos o fabricar nuevos productos. La economía de Europa comenzó a crecer. Aparecieron en los mercados algunos productos provenientes del este. Los comerciantes trajeron estos productos nuevos a través de la Ruta de la Seda, una ruta de caravanas que se extendía desde Europa hasta China y que había caído en desuso. En el siglo 13, los mongoles reabrieron la Ruta de la Seda.

A traveler named **Marco Polo** journeyed along the Silk Road. When he and his family arrived in China, they met the Mongol emperor Kublai Khan. He made Marco Polo a government official./Un viajero llamado **Marco Polo** recorrió la Ruta de la Seda. Cuando él y su familia llegaron a China, se encontraron con el emperador mongol Kublai Kan, quien nombró a Marco Polo funcionario del gobierno.

Marco Polo visited India and Southeast Asia as a messenger for the emperor. He spent 20 years in Asia. When he returned to Venice, a writer helped him record his journey. His descriptions made Europeans curious about Asia. People began to demand goods from Asia. Trade between Europe and Asia increased./Marco Polo visitó la India y el sureste asiático como mensajero del emperador. Pasó 20 años en Asia. Cuando regresó a Venecia, un escritor lo ayudó a documentar su viaje. Sus descripciones despertaron la curiosidad de los europeos por Asia, que comenzaron a pedir productos de ese continente. El comercio entre Europa y Asia aumentó.

> **Who recorded information about his journey that made Europeans curious about Asia?**/¿Quién documentó información sobre sus viajes y despertó la curiosidad de los europeos por Asia?
>
> _____

## TRADE CITIES IN ITALY/CIUDADES COMERCIALES DE ITALIA

By the 1300s, Florence, Genoa, Milan, and Venice had become major trading centers in Italy. Venice and Genoa were port cities. Huge ships brought goods from Asia into their harbors. From there,

> **Underline the names of the major trading cities in Italy during the 1300s.**/Subraya los nombres de las principales ciudades comerciales de Italia durante el siglo 14.

Lesson/Lección 1, *continued*/*continuación*

merchants shipped the goods across Europe. However, more than goods were exchanged in these cities. People from many cultures interacted. Ideas began to spread throughout Europe and other places./Para el siglo 14, Florencia, Génova, Milán y Venecia se habían convertido en los centros comerciales más importantes de Italia. Venecia y Génova eran ciudades portuarias. Unos barcos enormes traían productos de Asia hasta sus puertos. Desde allí, los comerciantes enviaban los productos por barco a toda Europa. Sin embargo, no solo había intercambio de productos en esas ciudades. También se produjo una interacción entre visitantes provenientes de distintas culturas. Las ideas comenzaron a difundirse por toda Europa y hacia otros lugares.

Italian cities also were manufacturing centers. They made many specialized products. Venice produced glass. Milan was known for weapons and silk. Florence was a center for weaving wool into cloth. Economic activity made Italy's merchant families wealthy./Las ciudades italianas también se dedicaban a la manufactura. Fabricaban diversos productos especializados. Venecia fabricaba vidrio. A Milán se le conocía por fabricar armas y producir seda. Florencia se dedicaba a tejer telas a partir de la lana. La actividad económica enriqueció a las familias de comerciantes de Italia.

| How did ideas begin to spread throughout Europe?/ ¿Cómo comenzaron a difundirse las ideas a través de toda Europa? |
|---|
| _____ _____ _____ |

## FLORENCE/FLORENCIA

Florence developed a banking system used all over Europe. Bankers made money by charging **interest,** which is a fee that borrowers pay for the use of someone else's money. The greatest bankers were the Medici family, who were also the richest family in Florence. In Italian cities, rich families controlled the government. By 1434, **Cosimo de' Medici** ruled Florence. He wanted to make Florence the most beautiful city in the world.

| Who usually controlled the Italian cities during this time period?/¿Quiénes solían controlar las ciudades italianas durante este período? |
|---|
| _____ |

**Lesson/Lección 1**, *continued/continuación*

He hired artists to decorate his palace and architects to redesign many buildings. He valued education and Florence became a center of art, literature, and culture. This love of art and education was key to the **Renaissance,** which means "rebirth." It followed the Middle Ages, but its ideas were different from that period. It saw an interest in Greek and Roman writings and emphasized people as individuals./Florencia desarrolló un sistema bancario que se usó en toda Europa. Los banqueros ganaban dinero cobrando **intereses,** la cuota que se paga por usar el dinero de otra persona. Los banqueros más importantes eran la familia Médici, que también era la familia más acaudalada de Florencia. En las ciudades italianas, las familias ricas controlaban el gobierno. Para 1434, **Cosme de Médici** gobernaba Florencia. Él quería convertir a Florencia en la ciudad más hermosa del mundo. Contrató a artistas para decorar su palacio y a arquitectos para rediseñar muchos edificios. Valoraba la educación, y así Florencia se convirtió en un centro para el arte, la literatura y la cultura. Este amor por el arte y la educación fue clave para el **Renacimiento.** Este período siguió a la Edad Media, pero sus ideas eran distintas: surgió un interés por los escritos griegos y romanos y se hizo hincapié en la visión de las personas como individuos.

| **How did the Renaissance come about?/¿Cómo surgió el Renacimiento?** |
|---|
| _____ |
| _____ |
| _____ |
| _____ |
| _____ |
| _____ |
| _____ |

**CHALLENGE ACTIVITY/ACTIVIDAD AVANZADA**

**Critical Thinking: Make Inferences/Pensamiento crítico: Hacer inferencias** Why do you think beauty and education were so important to the Medici family of Florence? Write a short paper explaining your answer./¿Por qué crees que la belleza y la educación eran tan importantes para la familia Médici de Florencia? Escribe un ensayo breve en el que expliques tu respuesta.

| | |
|---|---|
| Cosimo de' Medici/Cosme de Médici | interest/interés |
| Marco Polo/Marco Polo | Renaissance/Renacimiento |

**DIRECTIONS/INSTRUCCIONES** Read each sentence and fill in the blank with a word from the word bank that best completes the sentence./Lee cada oración y escribe en el espacio en blanco la palabra del banco de palabras que mejor la completa.

1. A fee that borrowers pay for the use of someone else's money is called _____./El precio que se paga por pedir en préstamo el dinero de otra persona se llama _____.

2. The period that followed the Middle Ages during which interest in Greek and Roman writings was revived was the _____./El período que siguió a la Edad Media y durante el cual resurgió el interés por los escritos griegos y romanos fue el _____.

3. The European explorer from Venice who spent 20 years traveling in Asia and then wrote about his journey was _____./El explorador europeo oriundo de Venecia que dedicó 20 años a viajar por Asia y luego escribió acerca de sus viajes fue _____.

4. A wealthy banker who turned Florence into a center of arts, culture, and education was _____./El banquero acaudalado que convirtió a Florencia en un centro para las artes, la cultura y la educación fue _____.

**MAIN IDEAS/IDEAS PRINCIPALES**

1. During the Italian Renaissance, people found new ways to see the world./ Durante el Renacimiento italiano, se descubrieron nuevas formas de ver el mundo.

2. Italian writers contributed great works of literature./Los escritores italianos produjeron grandes obras literarias.

3. Italian art and artists were among the finest in the world./El arte y los artistas italianos estuvieron entre los mejores del mundo.

4. Science and education made advances during this time./Se produjeron avances en la ciencia y la educación durante esta época.

# Key Terms and People/Personas y palabras clave

**humanism/humanismo** emphasis on human value and achievement/énfasis en el valor que se atribuye al ser humano y sus logros

**Dante Alighieri/Dante Alighieri** Italian poet who wrote *The Divine Comedy*/poeta italiano que escribió *La divina comedia*

**Niccolo Machiavelli/Nicolás Maquiavelo** political writer who wrote *The Prince*/ escritor político que escribió *El príncipe*

**Petrarch/Petrarca** Renaissance poet and scholar who helped change education/ poeta y erudito del Renacimiento que ayudó a reformar la educación

**perspective/perspectiva** technique in art to represent a three-dimensional scene on a flat space so that it looks real/técnica artística usada para representar una escena tridimensional sobre una superficie plana para que se vea real

**Michelangelo/Miguel Ángel** master artist who painted the ceiling of the Vatican's Sistine Chapel/artista maestro que pintó la bóveda de la Capilla Sixtina del Vaticano

**Leonardo da Vinci/Leonardo da Vinci** master inventor, engineer, and artist who painted the *Mona Lisa*/maestro inventor, ingeniero y artista que pintó la *Mona Lisa*

# Lesson Summary/Resumen de la lección

## NEW WAYS TO SEE THE WORLD/NUEVAS FORMAS DE VER EL MUNDO

During the Middle Ages, most people in Europe were devoted to Christianity. The same was true during the Renaissance. However, Renaissance people were interested in ideas and in the positive qualities that make us human. This new emphasis on human value and achievement was called **humanism.** There was a revived interest in history, ancient Greek and Roman writings, and the humanities. Artists and architects were inspired by these writings, Roman ruins, and classical statues./Durante la Edad Media, la mayoría de las personas en Europa profesaba el cristianismo. Lo mismo sucedió durante el Renacimiento. Sin embargo, los renacentistas estaban interesados en las ideas y las cualidades positivas que nos hacen humanos. Este nuevo énfasis en el valor que se atribuye al ser humano y a sus logros se llamó **humanismo.** Se generó un renovado interés por la historia, los antiguos escritos griegos y romanos y las humanidades. Los artistas y arquitectos se inspiraron en estos escritos, las ruinas romanas y las estatuas clásicas.

> **How were the humanists of the Renaissance different from the people of the Middle ages?/¿En qué se diferenciaban los humanistas del Renacimiento de las personas de la Edad Media?**
>
> _____
> _____
> _____

## ITALIAN WRITERS/ESCRITORES ITALIANOS

The poet **Dante Alighieri** wrote in Italian, the language of the common people, rather than in Latin. His major work was *The Divine Comedy*. A later politician and writer, **Niccolo Machiavelli,** advised leaders on how they should rule in his book *The Prince*. A poet and scholar, **Petrarch,** explored classical thought and Christian teachings. Some historians believe that humanism would not have developed without Petrarch's ideas./En lugar de escribir en latín, el poeta **Dante Alighieri** escribió en italiano, la lengua de la gente común. Su obra principal fue *La divina comedia*. Un político y escritor posterior, **Nicolás Maquiavelo,** escribió el libro *El príncipe,* que instruía a los líderes acerca de cómo gobernar. **Petrarca,** poeta y erudito, estudió el pensamiento clásico y las enseñanzas del cristianismo. Algunos historiadores

> **How might Machiavelli's experience as a politician have helped him write *The Prince*?/¿Cómo pudo la experiencia de Maquiavelo como político haberlo ayudado a escribir *El príncipe*?**
>
> _____
> _____
> _____
> _____

consideran que el humanismo no se habría
desarrollado sin las ideas de Petrarca.

## ITALIAN ART AND MUSIC/ARTE Y MÚSICA ITALIANOS

Italian artists used new techniques such as
perspective. **Perspective** shows a three-dimensional
scene on a flat surface so that it looks real. Italian
artists showed people as individuals by giving
them clear personalities./Los artistas italianos
usaron nuevas técnicas, como la perspectiva. La
**perspectiva** muestra una escena tridimensional
sobre una superficie plana de manera tal que
parece real. Los artistas italianos representaban
a las personas como individuos al darles
personalidades definidas.

A Renaissance person is someone who does
everything well. Two men best fit this name.
**Michelangelo** had many talents. He designed
buildings, wrote poetry, made sculptures, and was
a master painter. One of his most famous works is
the painting on the ceiling of the Sistine Chapel
in the Vatican. Another master in the arts was
**Leonardo da Vinci.** Some say he was the greatest
genius who ever lived. He was a sculptor, painter,
architect, inventor, engineer, and map maker. He
also studied anatomy. Like Michelangelo's works,
many of his works had religious themes, but not
all. Two of his famous works are *The Last Supper*
and the *Mona Lisa.*/Un renacentista es aquel que
hace todo bien. Dos hombres son los más dignos
de ser llamados así. **Miguel Ángel** tenía muchos
talentos. Diseñaba edificios, escribía poesía, hacía
esculturas y era un pintor maestro. Una de sus
obras más famosas es la que pintó en la bóveda de
la Capilla Sixtina que se encuentra en el Vaticano.
Otro maestro de las artes fue **Leonardo da Vinci.**
Algunos dicen que fue el mayor genio de todos

> Underline the sentence that explains how perspective helped Renaissance artists draw more realistically./Subraya la oración que explica cómo la perspectiva ayudó a los artistas renacentistas a crear dibujos más realistas.

> Why was Leonardo da Vinci considered a Renaissance man?/¿Por qué Leonardo da Vinci es considerado un renacentista?
>
> _____
> _____
> _____
> _____
> _____

los tiempos. Era escultor, pintor, arquitecto, inventor, ingeniero y cartógrafo. También estudió anatomía. Como la obra de Miguel Ángel, muchos de sus trabajos eran de temática religiosa, pero no todos. Dos de sus obras más famosas son *La última cena* y la *Mona Lisa*.

## SCIENCE AND EDUCATION/CIENCIA Y EDUCACIÓN

Scholars in Italy and other parts of Europe read Greek and Roman texts on scientific subjects and then made their own scientific advances. Engineers and architects used new mathematical formulas to strengthen buildings. Renaissance scientists studied astronomy. Some wrote almanacs based on the idea that Earth was round. Other scholars made more accurate maps. The changes that occurred in the arts and sciences spread beyond Italy, which led to changes in education. Petrarch wrote about the importance of knowing history. His ideas would affect education for many years./ Los eruditos de Italia y de otras partes de Europa leían textos griegos y romanos sobre temas científicos y luego hacían sus propios avances científicos. Los ingenieros y arquitectos usaron nuevas fórmulas matemáticas para reforzar los edificios. Los científicos renacentistas estudiaron astronomía. Algunos escribieron almanaques basados en la idea de que la Tierra era redonda. Otros eruditos elaboraron mapas más exactos. Los cambios que se produjeron en las artes y las ciencias se extendieron más allá de Italia, y esto condujo a reformas en la educación. Petrarca escribió acerca de la importancia de saber historia. Sus ideas influirían en la educación durante muchos años.

> **Why might Petrarch have thought it was important to know history?/¿Por qué Petrarca pudo haber considerado que era importante saber historia?**
>
> _____
> _____
> _____
> _____
> _____
> _____

## CHALLENGE ACTIVITY/ACTIVIDAD AVANZADA

**Critical Thinking: Elaborate/Pensamiento crítico: Profundizar** Now is the time to stop and think big, like the Renaissance humanists did. Write for five minutes, listing every great thing you ever might want to do in your life./Es hora de detenerse y pensar a lo grande, como lo hicieron los humanistas del Renacimiento. Escribe durante cinco minutos sobre cada logro grandioso que quisieras alcanzar en la vida.

**DIRECTIONS/INSTRUCCIONES** On the line provided before each statement, write **T** if a statement is true and **F** if a statement is false. If the statement is false, write the correct term on the line after each sentence that makes the sentence a true statement./En la línea que precede a cada enunciado, escribe **V** si el enunciado es verdadero y **F** si es falso. Si el enunciado es falso, escribe en la línea que sigue a la oración el término correcto que lo hace verdadero.

_____ 1. <u>Michelangelo</u>, whose work included the famous portrait *Mona Lisa*, was an expert painter./<u>Miguel Ángel</u>, cuyas obras incluyen el famoso retrato la *Mona Lisa*, fue un pintor excelso.

_____

_____ 2. A technique in art that was used to make a three-dimensional scene on a flat space appear real was known as <u>humanism</u>./La técnica del arte usada para lograr que una escena tridimensional sobre una superficie plana pareciera real era conocida como <u>humanismo</u>.

_____

_____ 3. An Italian writer who contributed great works of literature to the Renaissance and wrote in Italian instead of Latin was <u>Dante Alighieri</u>./Un escritor italiano que contribuyó al Renacimiento con grandes obras literarias y escribió en italiano en lugar de latín fue <u>Dante Alighieri</u>.

_____

_____ 4. The painting that covers the ceiling of the Sistine Chapel in the Vatican was painted by <u>Leonardo da Vinci</u>./La obra que cubre la bóveda de la Capilla Sixtina del Vaticano fue pintada por <u>Leonardo da Vinci</u>.

_____

_____ 5. <u>Renaissance</u> is way of thinking and learning that stresses the importance of human abilities and actions./<u>El Renacimiento</u> es una manera de pensar y aprender que destaca la importancia de las habilidades y acciones humanas.

_____

_____ 6. *The Prince*, written by an Italian writer and politician <u>Niccolo Machiavelli</u>, gave leaders advice on how they should rule./*El príncipe*, obra del escritor y político italiano <u>Nicolás Maquiavelo</u>, instruía a los líderes sobre cómo debían gobernar.

_____

_____ 7. The Renaissance poet and scholar who had strong ideas about humanism and wrote about the importance of history was <u>Petrarch</u>./<u>Petrarca</u> fue el poeta y erudito que tenía ideas firmes sobre el humanismo y escribió acerca de la importancia de la historia.

_____

# The Renaissance/El Renacimiento

**MAIN IDEAS/IDEAS PRINCIPALES**

1. Paper, printing, and new inventions led to the spread of new ideas/El papel, la imprenta y otros nuevos inventos permitieron la difusión de nuevas ideas.

2. The ideas of the Northern Renaissance differed from those of the Italian Renaissance./Las ideas del Renacimiento nórdico fueron diferentes a las del Renacimiento italiano.

3. Literature beyond Italy also thrived in the Renaissance./La literatura fuera de Italia también prosperó durante el Renacimiento.

## Key Terms and People/Personas y palabras clave

**Johannes Gutenberg/Johannes Gutenberg** German inventor of a printing press with movable type/inventor alemán de la imprenta de tipos móviles

**Christian humanism/humanismo cristiano** combination of humanism and Christianity/combinación del humanismo con el cristianismo

**Desiderius Erasmus/Desiderio Erasmo** priest and Christian humanist who critiqued corrupt clergy/sacerdote y humanista cristiano que criticó la corrupción del clero

**Albrecht Dürer/Alberto Durero** German painter who is also known for his block printing/pintor alemán también conocido por sus grabados con bloques de madera

**Miguel de Cervantes/Miguel de Cervantes** Spanish writer of *Don Quixote*, a novel that mocked medieval habits and customs/autor español del *Don Quijote*, novela que parodia los hábitos y costumbres medievales

**William Shakespeare/William Shakespeare** English dramatist and poet inspired by the Renaissance/dramaturgo y poeta inglés inspirado por el Renacimiento

## Lesson Summary/Resumen de la lección

### SPREAD OF NEW IDEAS/DIFUSIÓN DE NUEVAS IDEAS

Travelers and artists helped spread Renaissance ideas throughout Europe. The development of printing, however, was a major step in spreading ideas. For the first time, thousands of people could read books and share ideas about them./Los viajeros y artistas ayudaron a difundir las ideas del Renacimiento por toda Europa. Sin

> **What development contributed to the spread of ideas?/¿Qué invento contribuyó a la difusión de las ideas?**
>
> _____
>
> _____

embargo, un paso primordial en la difusión de las ideas fue la invención de la imprenta. Por primera vez, miles de personas pudieron leer libros y compartir ideas sobre ellos.

Papermaking came from China to the Middle East and from there to Europe. European factories were making paper by the 1300s. Then in the mid-1400s, a German named **Johannes Gutenberg** developed a printing press that used movable type. Using this method, an entire page could be printed at once. The first printed book was a Bible printed in Latin. Soon it was translated into common languages and printed. People wanted to learn to read, which made them want more education./La fabricación del papel llegó desde China hasta Medio Oriente y desde allí se extendió a Europa. Para el siglo 14, las fábricas europeas ya fabricaban papel. Luego, a mediados del siglo 15, un alemán llamado **Johannes Gutenberg** inventó una imprenta que usaba tipos móviles. Mediante este método, se podía imprimir una página entera de una sola vez. El primer libro impreso fue una Biblia en latín. Pronto se tradujo a las lenguas comunes y se volvió a imprimir. Las personas querían aprender a leer, y esto las incentivaba a querer recibir más educación.

Scholars from around Europe came to Italy to study. Universities opened throughout Europe and most teachers were humanists. Only men could attend universities, but women helped spread Renaissance ideas. They were educated at home, and some became powerful political figures when they married European nobles. They encouraged the spread of ideas in their husbands' lands./Los eruditos de distintas partes de Europa vinieron a Italia para estudiar. Se abrieron universidades en toda Europa, y la mayoría de los profesores eran humanistas. Solo

> The Bible was the first book printed using Gutenberg's movable type. Why do you think that is?/ La Biblia fue el primer libro que se imprimió usando los tipos móviles de Gutenberg. ¿A qué crees que se debió esto?
>
> _____
> _____

los hombres podían asistir a la universidad, pero las mujeres ayudaron a difundir las ideas renacentistas. Recibían educación en sus casas, y algunas se convirtieron en figuras políticas poderosas al casarse con nobles europeos. Incentivaban la difusión de las ideas en las tierras de sus esposos.

## THE NORTHERN RENAISSANCE/EL RENACIMIENTO NÓRDICO

Northern European scholars changed some Renaissance concepts because they related humanism to religious topics. This combination of humanism with religion is called **Christian humanism.** These scholars believed the church was corrupt and called for church reform. A Dutch priest, **Desiderius Erasmus,** was one of these scholars. He believed in the idea that humans had free will. He criticized corrupt clergy and wanted to get rid of some church rituals./Los eruditos del norte de Europa modificaron algunos conceptos del Renacimiento al vincular el humanismo con temas religiosos. Esta combinación de humanismo con religión se llama **humanismo cristiano.** Estos eruditos creían que la iglesia era corrupta y que era necesaria una reforma eclesiástica. Un sacerdote holandés, **Desiderio Erasmo,** fue uno de estos eruditos. Creía en la idea de que los seres humanos poseían libre albedrío. Criticó la corrupción del clero y quería deshacerse de algunos rituales religiosos.

> How did northern European scholars change some Renaissance concepts?/¿Cómo lograron los eruditos del norte de Europa cambiar algunos conceptos renacentistas?
>
> _____
> _____
> _____
> _____

Northern Europeans also changed some Renaissance ideas about art. Northern artists created paintings that were realistic, showing humans' physical flaws. German artist **Albrecht Dürer** painted objects in great detail. He is known for his prints./Los europeos del norte también modificaron algunas ideas renacentistas acerca del arte. Los artistas nórdicos crearon pinturas

> Underline the name of a famous northern Renaissance painter who drew in a realistic style./ Subraya el nombre de un famoso pintor del Renacimiento nórdico que dibujaba con estilo realista.

que eran realistas y representaban los defectos
físicos del ser humano. El artista alemán **Alberto
Durero** pintaba objetos con mucho detalle. Es
famoso por sus grabados.

## LITERATURE BEYOND ITALY/LA LITERATURA FUERA DE ITALIA

Writers from countries other than Italy also
included Renaissance ideas in their works. Many
were inspired by how different life had become
since the Middle Ages. In Spain, **Miguel de
Cervantes** wrote *Don Quixote*. Cervantes poked
fun at the romantic tales of the Middle Ages.
The Renaissance also inspired the great English
playwright and poet **William Shakespeare.** He
wrote more than 30 comedies, tragedies, and
histories. London audiences of the late 1500s
and 1600s packed the theatre to see Shakespeare's
plays./Los escritores de otros países además de
Italia también incluyeron ideas renacentistas en
sus obras. Muchos se inspiraron en lo diferente
que se había vuelto la vida desde la Edad Media.
En España, **Miguel de Cervantes** escribió *Don
Quijote*. Cervantes parodió los romances de la
Edad Media. El Renacimiento también inspiró
al gran dramaturgo y poeta inglés **William
Shakespeare**, que escribió más de 30 comedias,
tragedias y dramas históricos. Los teatros de
Londres de fines del siglo 16 y del siglo 17
estaban abarrotados de gente que deseaba
ver las obras de Shakespeare.

> **In what book did Cervantes make fun of the Middle Ages?/¿En qué libro Cervantes parodia la Edad Media?**
>
> _____

## CHALLENGE ACTIVITY/ACTIVIDAD AVANZADA

**Critical Thinking: Explain/Pensamiento crítico:
Explicar**  How did the northern Europeans build
upon Renaissance ideas? Write a paragraph using
specific examples./¿Cómo desarrollaron los
europeos del norte las ideas del Renacimiento?
Escribe un párrafo en el que uses ejemplos
específicos.

**DIRECTIONS/INSTRUCCIONES** Read each sentence and fill in the blank with the word in the word pair that best completes the sentence./Lee cada oración y escribe en el espacio en blanco la palabra del par de palabras que mejor la completa.

1. _____ is a blend of humanist and religious ideas. **(Miguel de Cervantes /Christian humanism)**/_____ es una mezcla de ideas humanistas y religiosas. **(Miguel de Cervantes/El humanismo cristiano)**

2. A printing press that used movable type was developed in the 1400s by the German _____. **(Albrecht Dürer/Johannes Gutenberg)**/ Una imprenta que usaba tipos móviles fue inventada en el siglo 15 por el alemán _____. **(Alberto Durero/Johannes Gutenberg)**

3. The English dramatist and poet who wrote more than 30 comedies, tragedies, and histories was _____. **(William Shakespeare/Miguel de Cervantes)**/El dramaturgo y poeta inglés que escribió más de 30 comedias, tragedias y dramas históricos fue _____. **(William Shakespeare/Miguel de Cervantes)**

4. _____, a Dutch priest, criticized corrupt clergy and wanted to get rid of some church rituals that he considered meaningless. **(Albrecht Dürer/Desiderius Erasmus)**/_____, un sacerdote holandés, criticó la corrupción del clero y quiso deshacerse de algunos rituales religiosos que consideraba carentes de sentido. **(Alberto Durero/Desiderio Erasmo)**

5. _____ wrote *Don Quixote*, which poked fun at the romantic tales of the Middle Ages. **(William Shakespeare/Miguel de Cervantes)**/_____ escribió *Don Quijote,* que es una parodia de los romances de la Edad Media. **(William Shakespeare/Miguel de Cervantes)**

6. One of the most famous artists of the northern Renaissance was a German, _____. **(Albrecht Dürer/Johannes Gutenberg)**/Uno de los artistas más famosos del Renacimiento nórdico fue un alemán, _____. **(Alberto Durero/Johannes Gutenberg)**

# The Reformation/La Reforma

**MAIN IDEAS/IDEAS PRINCIPALES**

1. The Catholic Church faced challengers who were upset with the behavior of Catholic clergy and with church practices./La Iglesia católica se enfrentó a opositores que no estaban conformes con las conductas del clero católico y con las prácticas de la Iglesia.

2. Martin Luther urged reform in the Catholic Church, but he eventually broke away from the church./Martín Lutero exigió una reforma en la Iglesia católica, pero finalmente se separó de ella.

3. Other reformers built on the ideas of early reformers to create their own churches./Otros reformadores se basaron en las ideas de los primeros reformadores para crear sus propias iglesias.

## Key Terms and People/Personas y palabras clave

**Reformation/Reforma** reform movement of Western Christianity/movimiento de reforma del cristianismo occidental

**indulgence/indulgencia** a relaxation of penalties for sins people had committed sold by the church/relajación de las penas aplicadas por los pecados cometidos, vendida por la Iglesia

**purgatory/purgatorio** in Catholic theology, a place where souls went before they went to heaven/según la teología católica, lugar al que iban las almas antes de ir al cielo

**Martin Luther/Martín Lutero** priest who criticized the church abuses and started the Reformation/sacerdote que criticó los abusos de la Iglesia e inició la Reforma

**Protestants/protestantes** those who protested against the Catholic Church/ personas que protestaban en contra de la Iglesia católica

**John Calvin/Juan Calvino** reformer who believed in the idea of predestination/ reformador que creía en la idea de la predestinación

**King Henry VIII/rey Enrique VIII** English king who started the Church of England/rey inglés que fundó la Iglesia de Inglaterra

## Lesson Summary/Resumen de la lección

### THE CATHOLIC CHURCH FACES CHALLENGERS/ LA IGLESIA CATÓLICA ENFRENTA OPOSICIÓN

By the late Renaissance people began complaining about the Catholic Church. They wanted church leaders to rid the church of corruption and focus on religion. Their calls led to a reform movement of Western Christianity called the **Reformation.**/En las últimas etapas del Renacimiento, algunas personas comenzaron a criticar a la Iglesia católica. Querían que los líderes de la Iglesia erradicaran la corrupción de la Iglesia y se centraran en la religión. Sus pedidos llevaron a un movimiento de reforma del cristianismo occidental, llamado **Reforma.**

Some reformers thought that the clergy were not very religious anymore. Others thought that the pope was too involved in politics. Others thought the church had grown too rich. The sale of indulgences was a serious problem. An **indulgence** was a relaxation of penalties for sins people had committed. The church claimed it reduced the punishment that a person would receive in purgatory for sins they had committed while they were alive. **Purgatory** was the place where souls went before going to heaven. Many Christians thought the church was letting people buy their way into heaven. The church's unpopular practices weakened its influence./Algunos reformadores consideraban que el clero ya no era tan religioso. Otros pensaban que el papa estaba muy involucrado en la política. Y otras personas opinaban que la Iglesia se había enriquecido demasiado. La venta de indulgencias era un problema grave. Una **indulgencia** era una relajación de las penas aplicadas por los pecados cometidos. La Iglesia sostenía que una indulgencia reducía la pena que se aplicaba a una persona en el purgatorio por los pecados que había cometido durante su vida. El **purgatorio** era el lugar al que iban las almas antes de ir al cielo. Muchos cristianos creían que la Iglesia permitía que las personas compraran su ingreso al cielo. Estas prácticas poco populares de la Iglesia debilitaron su influencia.

> **List four reasons for the Reformation./**Enumera cuatro motivos que llevaron a la Reforma.
>
> _____
> _____
> _____
> _____
> _____

## MARTIN LUTHER URGES REFORM/MARTÍN LUTERO DEMANDA REFORMAS

In 1517, a priest named **Martin Luther** called for reform. He nailed a list of complaints to a church door in Germany. Luther criticized the church's practices. He outlined many of his own beliefs. They included that people could have a direct relationship with God and that as long as people believed in God and lived by the Bible, their souls would be saved. Luther was excommunicated and ordered to leave the empire. His ideas led to a split in the church. Those who protested against the Catholic Church were known as **Protestants.** Some of his followers became known as Lutherans. Many German nobles liked Luther's ideas. This led to Lutheranism becoming the dominant church in northern Germany./En 1517, un sacerdote llamado **Martín Lutero** demandó una reforma. Clavó una lista de quejas en la puerta de una iglesia en Alemania. Lutero criticaba las prácticas de la Iglesia. Resumió muchas de sus propias creencias, entre ellas la idea de que las personas podían tener una relación directa con Dios y que, siempre que creyeran en Dios y vivieran de acuerdo con los preceptos de la Biblia, sus almas serían salvadas. Lutero fue excomulgado y obligado a abandonar el imperio. Sus ideas provocaron una ruptura en la Iglesia. Aquellos que protestaban contra la Iglesia católica recibieron el nombre de **protestantes.** Algunos de sus seguidores fueron conocidos como luteranos. A muchos nobles alemanes les gustaban las ideas de Lutero, por lo que el luteranismo se convirtió en la iglesia predominante en el norte de Alemania.

> Which man's ideas led to a split in the Catholic Church?/¿Las ideas de quién llevaron a una ruptura en la Iglesia católica?
>
> _____

> Underline the name of the group who protested against the Catholic Church./Subraya el nombre del grupo que protestaba contra la Iglesia católica.

## OTHER REFORMERS/OTROS REFORMADORES

Another influential reformer was **John Calvin.** His teachings included predestination—the idea that

God knew who would be saved even before they were born. **King Henry VIII** was a major figure in the Reformation in England. After the pope refused to officially end Henry's marriage, Henry made himself the head of a new church, the Church of England. He broke from the Catholic Church for personal reasons and did not change many church practices. However, his break from the church opened the door for other Protestant beliefs to take hold in England./**Juan Calvino** fue otro reformador influyente. Entre sus enseñanzas se encuentra el concepto de predestinación: la idea de que Dios sabe quiénes se salvarán, aun antes de que nazcan. El **rey Enrique VIII** fue una figura importante de la Reforma en Inglaterra. Cuando el papa se negó a anular oficialmente el matrimonio del rey, Enrique VIII se autoproclamó líder de una iglesia nueva: la Iglesia de Inglaterra. Se separó de la Iglesia católica por razones personales y no cambió muchas de sus prácticas. Sin embargo, su separación de la Iglesia abrió la puerta a la adopción de otras creencias protestantes en Inglaterra.

> **What role did King Henry VIII play in the Reformation?/**
> **¿Qué papel tuvo el rey Enrique VIII en la Reforma?**
>
> _____
> _____
> _____
> _____
> _____
> _____

## CHALLENGE ACTIVITY/ACTIVIDAD AVANZADA

**Critical Thinking: Describe/Pensamiento crítico: Describir** Imagine how you might feel if you were Martin Luther, pinning his complaints to the church door. Think of something you personally care about and write a list of things that need to change. Your list should have at least 10 items./Imagina cómo te sentirías si fueras Martín Lutero cuando clavó la lista de quejas en la puerta de la iglesia. Piensa en un tema que te interese y escribe una lista de aspectos que te gustaría cambiar. La lista debería tener al menos 10 puntos.

**DIRECTIONS/INSTRUCCIONES** Write two descriptive phrases
that describe the term./Escribe dos frases descriptivas que
describan el término.

1. Reformation/Reforma _____

   _____

2. Protestants/protestantes_____

   _____

3. indulgence/indulgencia _____

   _____

**DIRECTIONS/INSTRUCCIONES** On the line provided before each
statement, write **T** if a statement is true and **F** if a statement is false.
If the statement is false, write the correct term on the line after each
sentence that makes the sentence a true statement./En la línea que
precede a cada enunciado, escribe **V** si el enunciado es verdadero
y **F** si es falso. Si el enunciado es falso, escribe en la línea que
sigue a la oración el término correcto que lo hace verdadero.

_____ 4. <u>Martin Luther</u> was an influential reformer who mainly taught
predestination, or the idea that God knew who would be saved even
before they were born./<u>Martín Lutero</u> fue un reformador influyente
que principalmente enseñó la predestinación, o la idea de que Dios
sabe quiénes se salvarán, aun antes de que nazcan.

   _____

_____ 5. <u>Henry VIII</u> was the English king who started the Church of England./
<u>Enrique VIII</u> fue el rey inglés que fundó la Iglesia de Inglaterra.

   _____

_____ 6. <u>John Calvin</u> was a priest who criticized the Catholic Church and
started the Reformation./<u>Juan Calvino</u> fue un sacerdote que criticó la
Iglesia católica e inició la Reforma.

   _____

_____ 7. <u>Indulgences</u>, a part of Catholic theology, was a place where souls went
before going to heaven./<u>Las indulgencias</u>, parte de la teología católica,
eran el lugar al que iban las almas antes de ir al cielo.

   _____

# The Reformation/La Reforma

## Lesson/Lección 2

| **MAIN IDEAS/IDEAS PRINCIPALES** |
| --- |
| **1.** The influence of the church created a Catholic culture in Spain./La influencia de la Iglesia generó una cultura católica en España. |
| **2.** Catholic reforms emerged in response to the Reformation./Las reformas católicas surgieron como respuesta a la Reforma. |
| **3.** Missionaries worked to spread Catholic teachings./Los misioneros trabajaron para difundir las enseñanzas católicas. |

# Key Terms and People/Personas y palabras clave

**Catholic Reformation/Reforma católica** the effort to reform the Catholic Church from within/iniciativa para reformar la Iglesia católica desde adentro

**Ignatius of Loyola/Ignacio de Loyola** man responsible for founding the Jesuit order/responsable de fundar la orden jesuita

**Jesuits/jesuitas** religious order founded to serve the pope and spread Catholic teachings/orden religiosa fundada para servir al papa y difundir las enseñanzas de la Iglesia católica

**Francis Xavier/Francisco Javier** Jesuit missionary who went to Asia and brought Catholicism to parts of India and Japan/misionero jesuita que viajó a Asia y difundió el catolicismo en algunas regiones de la India y Japón

# Lesson Summary/Resumen de la lección

## CATHOLIC CULTURE IN SPAIN/CULTURA CATÓLICA EN ESPAÑA

The effort to reform the Catholic Church from within is called the **Catholic Reformation.** Throughout the late 1500s and 1600s, Catholic leaders worked to strengthen the church and stop the spread of Protestantism. Many leaders came from southern Europe, especially Spain./La iniciativa para reformar la Iglesia católica desde adentro se conoce como **Reforma católica.** Hacia fines del siglo 16 y durante el siglo 17, los líderes católicos trabajaron para fortalecer la Iglesia y detener la difusión del protestantismo. Muchos líderes provenían del sur de Europa; en especial, de España.

> Underline the name for efforts to reform the Catholic Church from within./Subraya el nombre de la iniciativa para reformar la Iglesia católica desde adentro.

For centuries, what is now Spain had three religions. Muslims, Christians, and Jews lived and worked together. Eventually, the Catholic rulers decided to force Muslims and Jews out of Spain. To enforce their decision, Spanish monarchs ordered the Spanish Inquisition to find and punish any Muslims or Jews left in Spain. The Inquisition hunted down and punished converted Muslims and Jews who were suspected of keeping their old beliefs. Then the Inquisition also started seeking out Protestants. By the late 1400s and 1500s, the Spanish church had no opposition./ Durante siglos, el territorio que hoy es España tuvo tres religiones: musulmanes, cristianos y judíos vivían y trabajaban en comunidad. Con el tiempo, los líderes católicos decidieron expulsar a musulmanes y judíos de España. Para imponer su decisión, los monarcas españoles ordenaron la Inquisición española para que buscara y castigara a los musulmanes y judíos que quedaban en España. La Inquisición persiguió y castigó a los musulmanes y judíos convertidos sospechados de aferrarse a sus antiguas creencias. Luego, la Inquisición comenzó a perseguir a los protestantes. Hacia fines del siglo 15 y durante el siglo 16, la Iglesia española no tenía oposición.

> The followers of which three religious groups were found in Spain?/ ¿Los seguidores de qué tres grupos religiosos se encontraban en España?
>
> _____
>
> _____

## CATHOLIC REFORMS/REFORMAS CATÓLICAS

In an attempt to win back support for the church, Catholic reformers created many new religious orders in southern Europe in the 1500s. **Ignatius Loyola** founded the Society of Jesus, or the Jesuits. The **Jesuits** were a religious order created to serve the pope and the church. One of the Jesuits' goals was to teach people about Catholic ideas. They hoped that a strong Catholic education would turn people away from Protestant ideas./En un intento por recuperar el apoyo a la Iglesia, los reformadores católicos crearon varias órdenes

> How did the Jesuits hope to bring people to the Catholic Church?/¿De qué manera los jesuitas esperaban llevar fieles a la Iglesia católica?
>
> _____
>
> _____
>
> _____
>
> _____
>
> _____

Lesson/Lección 2, *continued/continuación*

religiosas nuevas en el sur de Europa en el siglo 16.
**Ignacio de Loyola** fundó la Compañía de Jesús, o
los jesuitas. La orden de los jesuitas fue una orden
religiosa creada para servir al papa y a la Iglesia.
Uno de los objetivos de los **jesuitas** era predicar
las ideas católicas. Tenían la esperanza de que una
sólida educación católica alejaría a las personas
de las ideas protestantes.

Many Catholic leaders thought greater change
was needed. They assembled at the Council of
Trent to discuss church reforms. This council
met three times between 1545 and 1563. The
council restated the importance of the clergy
in interpreting the Bible, but created new rules
for the clergy. The council endorsed Catholic
teachings and instituted reforms. Now there
was a clear distinction between Catholic and
Protestant beliefs and practices. The pope created
religious courts to punish any Protestants found
in Italy. He also threatened excommunication
for those who read Protestant books./Muchos
líderes católicos pensaban que era necesario
implementar cambios más profundos. Se
reunieron en el Concilio de Trento para hablar
de las reformas de la Iglesia. El Concilio se
reunió tres veces entre 1545 y 1563. Replanteó
la importancia del clero en la interpretación de
la Biblia, pero creó leyes nuevas para el clero. El
Concilio respaldaba las enseñanzas católicas e
instauró reformas. En ese momento, se marcó
una distinción clara entre las creencias y las
prácticas católicas y protestantes. El papa
creó cortes religiosas para castigar a todos
los protestantes que encontraran en Italia.
También amenazó con excomulgar a
quienes leyeran libros protestantes.

> **Underline the name of the group assembled to discuss church reforms./** Subraya el nombre del grupo que se reunió para analizar las reformas de la Iglesia.

## MISSIONARIES SPREAD CATHOLIC TEACHINGS/ LOS MISIONEROS DIFUNDEN LAS ENSEÑANZAS CATÓLICAS

Rather than change the church, many Catholics decided to help it grow by becoming missionaries. Their goal was to take Catholic teachings to people around the world. Many missionaries were Jesuits, including the most important, the priest **Francis Xavier.** He traveled throughout Asia in the mid-1500s, bringing Catholicism to parts of India and Japan. As a result of his efforts, many people in those regions became Catholics. Catholic missionaries baptized millions of people around the world. Through their efforts the effects of the Catholic Reformation reached far beyond Europe./ En lugar de cambiar la Iglesia, muchos católicos decidieron convertirse en misioneros para ayudarla a crecer. Su objetivo era difundir las enseñanzas católicas en el mundo. Muchos misioneros eran jesuitas, entre ellos el más importante, el sacerdote **Francisco Javier.** Viajó por Asia a mediados del siglo 16 y llevó el catolicismo a algunas regiones de India y Japón. Como resultado de sus esfuerzos, muchas personas en esas regiones se convirtieron al catolicismo. Los misioneros católicos bautizaron a millones de personas en todo el mundo. A través de sus esfuerzos, los efectos de la Reforma católica se extendieron mucho más allá de Europa.

**What was the goal of missionaries?/¿Cuál era el objetivo de los misioneros?**

_____
_____
_____
_____
_____

**Where did Francis Xavier go to convert people to Catholicism?/¿Adónde fue Francisco Javier para convertir fieles al catolicismo?**

_____
_____

## CHALLENGE ACTIVITY/ACTIVIDAD AVANZADA

**Critical Thinking: Make Judgments/Pensamiento crítico: Dar opiniones** Think about what happened during the Catholic Reformation. Write a paragraph on your view of the Catholic Reformation. Include whether you think the reforms were effective and why./Piensa en lo que ocurrió durante la Reforma católica. Escribe un párrafo para expresar tu opinión sobre la Reforma católica. Explica si piensas que las reformas fueron eficaces y por qué.

**DIRECTIONS/INSTRUCCIONES** Read each sentence and fill in the blank with the word in the word pair that best completes the sentence./Lee cada oración y escribe en el espacio en blanco la palabra del par de palabras que mejor la completa.

1. The Jesuit missionary who went to Asia and brought Catholicism to parts of Japan and India was _____. **(Francis Xavier/Ignatius of Loyola)**/El misionero jesuita que viajó a Asia y difundió el catolicismo en algunas regiones de Japón y la India fue _____. **(Francisco Javier/Ignacio de Loyola)**

2. The _____ was the effort made by the Catholic Church to reform its practices. **(Jesuits/Catholic Reformation)**/ _____ fue la iniciativa de la Iglesia católica para reformar sus prácticas. **(Los jesuitas/La Reforma católica)**

3. The _____ were a religious order founded to serve the pope and spread Catholic teachings. **(Spanish Inquisition/Jesuits)**/ _____ fue una orden religiosa fundada para servir al papa y difundir las enseñanzas católicas. **(La Inquisición española/Los jesuitas)**

4. The man who founded the Jesuit order was _____. **(Ignatius of Loyola/Francis Xavier)**/El hombre que fundó la orden jesuita fue _____. **(Ignacio de Loyola/Francisco Javier)**

5. The _____ endorsed Catholic teachings and instituted reforms. **(Catholic Reformation/Council of Trent)**/_____ respaldaba las enseñanzas católicas e instauró reformas. **(La Reforma católica/El Concilio de Trento)**

6. The purpose of the _____ was to find and punish any Muslims or Jews left in Spain during the late 1400s and 1500s. **(Spanish Inquisition/Council of Trent)**/El propósito de _____ era buscar y castigar a los musulmanes y judíos que quedaban en España a fines del siglo 15 y durante el siglo 16. **(la Inquisición española/el Concilio de Trento)**

# The Reformation/La Reforma

**MAIN IDEAS/IDEAS PRINCIPALES**

1. Religious division occurred within Europe and the Americas./Se produjo una división religiosa entre Europa y América.

2. Religious wars broke out between Protestants and Catholics./Se desataron guerras religiosas entre protestantes y católicos.

3. Social changes were a result of the Reformation./La Reforma provocó cambios sociales.

## Key Terms and People/Personas y palabras clave

**Huguenots/hugonotes** French Protestants/protestantes franceses

**Edict of Nantes/Edicto de Nantes** law granting religious freedom in most of France/ley que concedió libertad religiosa a la mayor parte de Francia

**Thirty Years' War/Guerra de los Treinta Años** long series of wars between Catholics and Protestants involving much of Europe/larga serie de guerras entre católicos y protestantes que involucró gran parte de Europa

**congregation/congregación** church assembly/asamblea de la iglesia

**federalism/federalismo** sharing of power between national and local governments/sistema de distribución del poder entre el gobierno nacional y los gobiernos locales

## Lesson Summary/Resumen de la lección

### RELIGIOUS DIVISION/DIVISIÓN RELIGIOSA

At the beginning of the 1500s, nearly all of Europe was Catholic. But the situation had changed dramatically 100 years later. In many southern European countries, such as Spain, most people remained Catholic. However, in the northern countries such as England, Scotland, and the Scandinavian countries, most people were Protestant. The emperor of the Holy Roman Empire allowed each prince to choose the religion for his territory. As a result, the empire became a patchwork of small kingdoms, some Catholic and some Protestant. Keeping peace was often difficult./A principios del siglo 16, casi la totalidad de Europa era católica.

> Which part of Europe became mainly Protestant in the span of only 100 years?/¿Qué parte de Europa se hizo principalmente protestante en un lapso de apenas 100 años?

Pero 100 años después, la situación había cambiado drásticamente. En muchos países del sur de Europa, como España, la mayor parte de la población seguía siendo católica. Sin embargo, en los países del norte, como Inglaterra, Escocia y los países escandinavos, la mayoría de las personas era protestante. El emperador del Sacro Imperio Romano permitió que cada príncipe eligiera una religión para su territorio. Como resultado, el imperio se convirtió en una mezcla de pequeños reinos, algunos católicos y algunos protestantes. Con frecuencia, mantener la paz se tornaba difícil.

The explorers and missionaries who went to other parts of the world took their religions with them. This influenced the distribution of religions around the world. For example, parts of Canada and most of Mexico, Central and South America were settled by people from Catholic countries./Los exploradores y misioneros que viajaron a otras partes del mundo llevaron su religión con ellos. Esto influyó en la distribución de las religiones en el mundo. Por ejemplo, partes de Canadá y la mayor parte de México, América Central y América del Sur fueron pobladas por personas provenientes de países católicos.

> **Underline the regions settled by people from Catholic countries./** Subraya las regiones pobladas por personas de países católicos.

The 13 colonies that became the United States were settled by Protestants from England and so became mostly Protestant./Las 13 colonias que se convirtieron en Estados Unidos fueron pobladas por protestantes de Inglaterra; por lo tanto, los Estados Unidos pasaron a ser un país en el que predominó el protestantismo.

> **Circle the region settled by Protestants./**Encierra en un círculo la región poblada por protestantes.

## RELIGIOUS WARS/GUERRAS RELIGIOSAS

Disagreements about religion and violence often went hand in hand. Although most people in France stayed Catholic, some became Protestants. French Protestants were called **Huguenots.** But the

king of France outlawed the Huguenots. So
a series of conflicts between Catholics and
Huguenots began that led to years of bloody war.
The worst incident was the St. Bartholomew's Day
Massacre in 1572. In one night, Catholic rioters
killed about 3,000 Protestants in Paris. The war in
France ended in 1598 with the **Edict of Nantes.** It
granted religious freedom to most of France./Los
desacuerdos en materia religiosa y la violencia a
menudo iban de la mano. Si bien en Francia la
mayoría de las personas continuaron siendo
católicas, algunas se volcaron al protestantismo. El
rey de Francia declaró ilegales a los protestantes,
llamados **hugonotes.** Así fue que comenzó una
serie de conflictos entre católicos y hugonotes,
que llevó a años de guerras sangrientas. El peor
incidente fue la Matanza de San Bartolomé, en
1572. En una noche, amotinados católicos
mataron a 3,000 protestantes en París. La guerra
en Francia terminó en 1598, con el **Edicto de
Nantes,** que concedió la libertad religiosa a la
mayor parte de Francia.

> **Why do you think the Huguenots chose to fight?/¿Por qué piensas que los hugonotes optaron por luchar?**
>
> _____
> _____
> _____
> _____

The Holy Roman Empire also had wars.
Starting in Prague with Protestants overthrowing
their Catholic leader, the revolt evolved into the
**Thirty Years' War.** This was a long series of wars
that involved many European countries. After
30 years of fighting, peace was reached. Rulers
then determined the religion for their countries,
but the Holy Roman Empire ceased to exist./El
Sacro Imperio Romano también tuvo guerras.
La primera fue en Praga, cuando los protestantes
derrocaron al líder católico, y la revuelta se
transformó en la **Guerra de los Treinta Años.**
Esta fue una extensa serie de guerras en la que
participaron muchos países europeos. Después
de 30 años de guerra, se firmó la paz. Los
gobernantes eligieron la religión de su país,
pero el Sacro Imperio Romano dejó de existir.

> **Underline the place where the Thirty Years' War started./Subraya el lugar en el que comenzó la Guerra de los Treinta Años.**

## SOCIAL CHANGES/CAMBIOS SOCIALES

Before the Reformation, most Europeans had no voice in governing the Catholic Church. But most Protestant churches did not have clergy. Instead, each **congregation,** or church assembly, made its own rules. People began to think that their own ideas were important. This led to demands for more political power, which led to **federalism,** the sharing of power between national and local governments. People became willing to question authority and figure out things on their own. This desire people had to investigate led them to turn increasingly to science./Antes de la Reforma, la mayoría de los europeos no tenía ni voz ni voto en la dirección de la Iglesia católica, pero gran parte de las iglesias protestantes no tenía clero. En cambio, cada **congregación,** o asamblea de la iglesia, establecía sus propias reglas. La gente comenzó a pensar que sus propias ideas eran importantes. Esto llevó a reclamos de mayor poder político, lo que dio lugar al **federalismo,** un sistema de distribución del poder entre el gobierno nacional y los gobiernos locales. Como consecuencia, las personas comenzaron a cuestionar a las autoridades y a entender las cosas por sus propios medios. Este deseo de las personas por investigar los llevó a volcarse cada vez más a las ciencias.

> Underline the sentence that explains how religious reform led to political reform./Subraya la oración que explica de qué manera la reforma religiosa llevó a la reforma política.

## CHALLENGE ACTIVITY/ACTIVIDAD AVANZADA

**Critical Thinking: Explain/Pensamiento crítico: Explicar** You have been reading a lot about the Reformation period. What is the most important thing that has come out of the Reformation that still impacts society today? Write a one-page essay explaining you answer./Has leído mucho sobre la Reforma. ¿Cuál fue la consecuencia más importante de la Reforma que todavía afecta a la sociedad actual? Escribe un ensayo de una página en el que expliques tu respuesta.

**DIRECTIONS/INSTRUCCIONES** Match the terms in the first column with their correct definition from the second column by placing the letter of the correct definition in the space provided before each term./Une los términos de la primera columna con su definición correcta en la segunda columna. Escribe la letra de la definición correcta en el espacio que precede a cada término.

_____ 1. Edict of Nantes/Edicto de Nantes

_____ 2. congregation/congregación

_____ 3. huguenots/hugonotes

_____ 4. federalism/federalismo

_____ 5. Thirty Years' War/Guerra de los Treinta Años

a. church assembly/asamblea de la iglesia

b. law granting religious freedom in most of France/ley que concedió libertad religiosa a la mayor parte de Francia

c. sharing of power between national and local governments/sistema de distribución del poder entre el gobierno nacional y los gobiernos locales

d. long series of wars between Catholics and Protestants involving much of Europe/larga serie de guerras entre católicos y protestantes que involucró a gran parte de Europa

e. French Protestants/protestantes franceses

# The Scientific Revolution/La Revolución Científica

## Lesson/Lección 1

**MAIN IDEAS/IDEAS PRINCIPALES**
1. The Scientific Revolution marked the birth of modern science./La Revolución Científica marcó el nacimiento de la ciencia moderna.
2. The roots of the Scientific Revolution can be traced to ancient Greece, the Muslim world, and Europe./Los orígenes de la Revolución Científica pueden hallarse en la antigua Grecia, el mundo musulmán y Europa.

## Key Terms and People/Personas y palabras clave

**Scientific Revolution/Revolución científica** series of events that led to the birth of modern science/serie de sucesos que produjeron el nacimiento de la ciencia moderna

**science/ciencia** a particular way of gaining knowledge about the world/manera específica de adquirir conocimientos sobre el mundo

**theories/teorías** explanations developed by scientists to explain observable facts/explicaciones que desarrollan los científicos para describir hechos observables

**Ptolemy/Ptolomeo** Greek astronomer whose work was based on observation and logic/astrónomo griego cuyo trabajo se basó en la observación y la lógica

**rationalists/racionalistas** people who looked at the world in a rational, reasonable, and logical way/personas que observaban el mundo de manera racional, razonable y lógica

**alchemy/alquimia** the study of different natural substances, such as metals/estudio de diferentes sustancias naturales, como los metales

## Lesson Summary/Resumen de la lección

### THE BIRTH OF MODERN SCIENCE/NACIMIENTO DE LA CIENCIA MODERNA

The series of events that led to the birth of modern science is called the **Scientific Revolution.** It occurred between 1540 and 1700. Science was a radical new idea as it was a completely different way of looking at the world. Before this time, educated people relied on authorities—the ancient Greek writers or Catholic Church officials—for explanations about the world. Afterward, people

> **What was so revolutionary about the Scientific Revolution?/¿Por qué fue tan innovadora la Revolución Científica?**
>
> _____
> _____
> _____
> _____

gained knowledge by observing the world around them and forming logical conclusions./La serie de sucesos que produjeron el nacimiento de la ciencia moderna se conoce como **Revolución Científica.** Tuvo lugar en Europa entre 1540 y 1700, aproximadamente. La ciencia era una idea completamente innovadora y revolucionaria, ya que consistía en una manera totalmente nueva de ver el mundo. Antes de la revolución, la mayoría de las personas cultas dependían de las explicaciones sobre el mundo que daban las autoridades, como los antiguos griegos o la Iglesia católica. Después de la revolución, comenzaron a observar el mundo a su alrededor y a sacar conclusiones lógicas para adquirir conocimientos.

**Science** is a particular way of gaining knowledge. Scientists identify facts by observation and then develop **theories,** which are explanations based on the facts. Theories must be tested to see if they are true. Before the Scientific Revolution, this way of learning about the world did not exist./ La **ciencia** es una manera específica de adquirir conocimientos. Los científicos identifican los hechos por medio de la observación y luego desarrollan **teorías** para explicar esos hechos. Las teorías deben ponerse a prueba para saber si son verdaderas. Antes de la Revolución Científica, esta manera de aprender sobre el mundo no existía.

## ROOTS OF THE REVOLUTION/RAÍCES DE LA REVOLUCIÓN

Some of the basic ideas of science are ancient. The Greek philosopher Aristotle's greatest contribution to science was the idea that people should observe the world carefully and draw logical conclusions about what they see. The Greek thinker **Ptolemy** studied and wrote about astronomy, logic, and geography. Aristotle, Ptolemy and other Greek thinkers were **rationalists,** people who looked at the world in a rational, or reasonable and logical, way. Europeans studied their works and began to view the world in a rational way. They began to think like scientists./Algunas de las ideas básicas de la ciencia son antiguas. La principal contribución del filósofo griego Aristóteles a la ciencia fue la idea de que las personas deben observar el mundo atentamente y sacar conclusiones lógicas sobre lo que ven. El pensador griego **Ptolomeo** estudió y escribió sobre astronomía, lógica y geografía. Aristóteles, Ptolomeo y otros pensadores griegos eran **racionalistas,** personas que observaban el mundo de manera racional, o razonable y lógica. Los europeos estudiaron sus obras y comenzaron a ver el mundo de manera racional. Empezaron a pensar como científicos.

Europeans could study ancient Greek writings because Muslim scholars had translated them into Arabic. Later, Arabic versions were translated into Latin, which was read in Europe. This work preserved ancient knowledge and spread interest in science to Europe./Los europeos pudieron estudiar los escritos de la antigua Grecia gracias a que los estudiosos musulmanes los habían traducido al árabe. Posteriormente, las versiones árabes se tradujeron al latín, lo que permitió leerlas en Europa. Ese trabajo preservó los conocimientos de la antigüedad y divulgó el interés en la ciencia por toda Europa.

Religious scholars also played a role in preserving Greek ideas. The Jewish scholar Maimonides wrote to unite Aristotle's work with Jewish ideas. The scholar Thomas Aquinas did the same with Christian ideas. The Catholic Church

> **What roots did science have in ancient Greece?/**
> ¿Qué raíces de la antigua Grecia tomó la ciencia moderna?
>
> _____
> _____
> _____
> _____
> _____
> _____

helped pay for scientific research and sent priests to universities. The Church supported the teaching of math and science./Los estudiosos religiosos también tuvieron un papel fundamental en la preservación de las ideas griegas. El estudioso judío Maimónides escribió una obra que combinaba el trabajo de Aristóteles con las ideas judías. El estudioso Tomás de Aquino hizo lo mismo con las ideas cristianas. La Iglesia católica ayudó a financiar investigaciones científicas y envió sacerdotes a las universidades. La Iglesia apoyaba la enseñanza de matemáticas y ciencias.

> **Name two scholars who united Greek ideas with religion./**Nombra dos estudiosos que combinaron ideas griegas con la religión.
>
> _____
>
> _____
>
> _____

Other developments in Europe helped bring about the Scientific Revolution. Humanist artists and writers spent their time studying the natural world. Another development was a growing interest in **alchemy** (AL-kuh-mee), a forerunner of chemistry. Alchemists are best known for trying, and failing, to change other metals into gold. They experimented with natural substances to learn more about nature./Otros desarrollos en Europa contribuyeron con la Revolución Científica. Los artistas y escritores humanistas empezaron a dedicar su tiempo a estudiar el mundo natural. Otro desarrollo fue el creciente interés en la **alquimia,** una disciplina que se considera predecesora de la química. Los alquimistas se destacaron por intentar, sin éxito, convertir metales en oro. Experimentaban con sustancias naturales para aprender más sobre la naturaleza.

## CHALLENGE ACTIVITY/ACTIVIDAD AVANZADA

**Critical Thinking: Make Inferences**/**Pensamiento crítico: Hacer inferencias** Write a one-page creative essay describing a world without any rationalist ideas. How would people understand their world without reason and logic?/Escribe un ensayo creativo de una página en el que describas un mundo sin ideas racionalistas. ¿De qué manera las personas comprenderían el mundo si no usaran la razón ni la lógica?

**DIRECTIONS/INSTRUCCIONES** On the line provided before each statement, write **T** if a statement is true and **F** if a statement is false. If the statement is false, write the correct term on the line after each sentence that makes the sentence a true statement./En la línea que precede a cada enunciado, escribe **V** si el enunciado es verdadero y **F** si es falso. Si el enunciado es falso, escribe en la línea que sigue a la oración el término correcto que lo hace verdadero.

_____ 1. The <u>Renaissance</u> looked at the world in a reasonable and logical way./<u>El Renacimiento</u> observaba el mundo de manera razonable y lógica.

_____

_____ 2. The series of events that led to the birth of modern science is called the <u>rationalists</u>./La serie de sucesos que produjeron el nacimiento de la ciencia moderna se denomina <u>racionalistas</u>.

_____

_____ 3. <u>Theories</u> are explanations scientists develop to explain observed facts./<u>Las teorías</u> son explicaciones que desarrollan los científicos para describir hechos observables.

_____

_____ 4. <u>Ptolemy</u> wrote about astronomy, geography, and logic./<u>Ptolomeo</u> escribió sobre astronomía, geografía y lógica.

_____

**DIRECTIONS/INSTRUCCIONES** Write three adjectives or a descriptive phrase that describes the term or person given./Escribe tres adjetivos o una frase descriptiva que describan la persona o el término dado.

5. Aristotle/Aristóteles _____

_____

6. science/ciencia _____

_____

7. rationalists/racionalistas _____

_____

8. theories/teorías _____

_____

9. alchemy/alquimia _____

_____

# The Scientific Revolution/La Revolución Científica

## Lesson/Lección 2

---

**MAIN IDEAS/IDEAS PRINCIPALES**

1. The discovery of the Americas led scholars to doubt ancient Greek ideas./El descubrimiento de América hizo que los estudiosos dudaran de las ideas de la antigua Grecia.

2. Advances in astronomy were key events of the Scientific Revolution./Los avances en astronomía fueron sucesos clave de la Revolución Científica.

3. Sir Isaac Newton developed laws that explained much of the natural world./Sir Isaac Newton desarrolló leyes que explicaban gran parte del mundo natural.

4. New inventions helped scientists study the natural world./Los nuevos inventos permitieron a los científicos estudiar el mundo natural.

---

# Key Terms and People/Personas y palabras clave

**Nicolaus Copernicus/Nicolás Copérnico** Polish astronomer who theorized that the planets orbit the sun/astrónomo polaco que desarrolló la teoría de que los planetas giran en órbita alrededor del Sol

**Tycho Brahe/Tycho Brahe** Danish astronomer who made detailed charts of the stars' movements/astrónomo danés que hizo gráficos detallados del movimiento de las estrellas

**Johannes Kepler/Johannes Kepler** German astronomer who proved that planets' orbits are elliptical/astrónomo alemán que demostró que los planetas tienen órbitas elípticas

**Galileo Galilei/Galileo Galilei** Italian scientist and astronomer who tested his theories in experiments/científico y astrónomo italiano que puso a prueba sus teorías por medio de experimentos

**Sir Isaac Newton/Sir Isaac Newton** English scientist who discovered laws of motion and of gravity/científico inglés que descubrió las leyes del movimiento y de la gravedad

**barometer/barómetro** scientific instrument that measures air pressure/instrumento científico que mide la presión atmosférica

# Lesson Summary/Resumen de la lección

## DISCOVERY LEADS TO DOUBT/EL DESCUBRIMIENTO GENERA DUDAS

In 1492, Columbus found a new continent. The world map of the ancient Greek scholar, Ptolemy, did not show this entire continent. Scholars began to question the accuracy of all of the ancient authorities for the first time. More and more, observations the Europeans made did not fit with what the authorities had described. Such observations helped lead to the Scientific Revolution./En 1492, Colón descubrió un nuevo continente. El mapamundi de Ptolomeo, estudioso de la antigua Grecia, no mostraba este continente completo. Por primera vez, los estudiosos comenzaron a cuestionar la exactitud de todas las autoridades de la antigüedad. Las observaciones que hacían los europeos cada vez cuadraban menos con lo que las autoridades habían descrito. Esas observaciones llevaron a la Revolución Científica.

> **Why do you think Columbus's discovery of a continent cast doubt on the writings of ancient authorities?/¿Por qué crees que el hecho de que Colón descubriera un continente generó dudas sobre los escritos de las autoridades de la antigüedad?**
>
> _____
> _____
> _____
> _____
> _____
> _____

## ADVANCES IN ASTRONOMY/AVANCES EN ASTRONOMÍA

Ptolemy thought that the planets moved around the earth. For 1,400 years, people accepted this belief as fact. Polish astronomer **Nicolaus Copernicus** disagreed with him. Copernicus thought the planets orbited the sun. His 1543 book, *On the Revolution of Celestial Spheres*, explained his theory based on what he observed in the sky./Ptolomeo pensaba que los planetas giraban alrededor de la Tierra. Durante 1,400 años, las personas aceptaron esta creencia como un hecho. Sin embargo, el astrónomo polaco **Nicolás Copérnico** no estaba de acuerdo. Copérnico pensaba que los planetas giraban alrededor del Sol. Su libro del año 1543, *Las revoluciones de las esferas celestes*, explicaba su teoría sobre la base de lo que observó en el cielo.

> **Underline the name of the astronomer that Copernicus proved wrong./Subraya el nombre del astrónomo cuyo trabajo fue refutado por Copérnico.**

An important Danish astronomer was **Tycho Brahe** (TYOO-koh BRAH-huh). He spent most of his life observing the stars. In the late 1500s, Brahe charted the positions of more than

750 stars through careful observation and detailed accurate records. Careful recording of information allows other scientists to use what has been previously learned./**Tycho Brahe** fue un importante astrónomo danés que dedicó la mayor parte de su vida a observar las estrellas. A fines del siglo 16, Brahe graficó la ubicación de más de 750 estrellas mediante la observación detallada y registros precisos. Documentar información minuciosamente permite a otros científicos utilizar conocimientos previos.

The German astronomer **Johannes Kepler** proved that the planets orbit the sun in oval-shaped orbits. **Galileo Galilei** was the first person to study the sky with a telescope. He was also interested in mechanics—the study of objects and motion. He was the first to use experiments to test his theories./El astrónomo alemán **Johannes Kepler** demostró que los planetas se mueven en órbitas ovaladas alrededor del Sol. **Galileo Galilei** fue la primera persona en estudiar el cielo con un telescopio. También estaba interesado en la mecánica: el estudio de los objetos y el movimiento. Fue el primero en usar experimentos para poner a prueba sus teorías.

> **Name two astronomers who studied after Copernicus./**Menciona dos astrónomos que estudiaron el cielo después de Copérnico.
>
> _____
>
> _____

## SIR ISAAC NEWTON/SIR ISAAC NEWTON

With his book *Principia Mathematica* published in 1687, **Sir Isaac Newton** became one of the most important scientists of all time. He reviewed and evaluated all previous scientific work, coupled it with his own observations, and developed four theories about how the natural world worked. He also developed mathematical calculus./Con su libro *Principia Mathematica*, publicado en 1687, **Sir Isaac Newton** se convirtió en uno de los científicos más importantes de todos los tiempos. Newton revisó y evaluó todos

> **What book established Isaac Newton as an important scientist?/**¿Qué libro consagró a Isaac Newton como científico destacado?
>
> _____

los trabajos científicos previos y los sumó a sus propias observaciones, y así desarrolló cuatro teorías sobre cómo funcionaba el mundo natural. También desarrolló el cálculo matemático.

## NEW INVENTIONS/NUEVOS INVENTOS

Scientists invented new and better tools to study the natural world. The **barometer,** invented in 1643, is an instrument that measures air pressure. It is used to help forecast the weather. Other inventions included the microscope, telescope, and the thermometer. They all allowed scientists to make more accurate observations of the world and to conduct experiments./Los científicos inventaron nuevas y mejores herramientas para estudiar el mundo natural. El **barómetro,** inventado en 1643, es un instrumento que mide la presión atmosférica. Se utiliza para predecir las condiciones del tiempo. Otros inventos fueron el microscopio, el telescopio y el termómetro, que permitieron a los científicos hacer observaciones del mundo con mayor precisión y llevar a cabo experimentos.

> **List three inventions that helped the development of science./Enumera tres inventos que contribuyeron al desarrollo de la ciencia.**
>
> _____
>
> _____
>
> _____

## CHALLENGE ACTIVITY/ACTIVIDAD AVANZADA

**Critical Thinking: Make Judgments/Pensamiento crítico: Dar opiniones** Consider the accomplishments of the scientists who lived during the Scientific Revolution. Which scientist do you think made the largest contributions to science? Write a one-page essay that explains your choice./Considera los logros de los científicos que vivieron durante la Revolución Científica. ¿Qué científico crees que hizo el mayor aporte a la ciencia? Escribe un ensayo de una página en el que expliques tu elección.

**DIRECTIONS/INSTRUCCIONES** On the line provided before each statement, write **T** if a statement is true and **F** if a statement is false. If the statement is false, write the correct term on the line after each sentence that makes the sentence a true statement./En la línea que precede a cada enunciado, escribe **V** si el enunciado es verdadero y **F** si es falso. Si el enunciado es falso, escribe en la línea que sigue a la oración el término correcto que lo hace verdadero.

_____ 1. The series of events that led to the birth of modern science is called the Scientific Revolution./La serie de sucesos que marcó el nacimiento de la ciencia moderna se denomina Revolución Científica.

_____

_____ 2. The Italian scientist Tycho Brahe regularly used experiments to test his theories./El científico italiano Tycho Brahe utilizaba experimentos con regularidad para poner a prueba sus teorías.

_____

_____ 3. Tycho Brahe was a Danish astronomer who kept detailed records of his observations of the stars./Tycho Brahe fue un astrónomo danés que llevó registros detallados de sus observaciones de las estrellas.

_____

_____ 4. English scientist Galileo Galilei made observations about gravity and the behavior of objects in motion./El científico inglés Galileo Galilei hizo observaciones sobre la gravedad y el comportamiento de los objetos en movimiento.

_____

_____ 5. The thermometer is a scientific instrument that measures air pressure./El termómetro es un instrumento científico que mide la presión atmosférica.

_____

_____ 6. Nicolaus Copernicus was a German astronomer who tried to map the orbits of the planets./Nicolás Copérnico fue un astrónomo alemán que intentó trazar un mapa de la órbita de los planetas.

_____

_____ 7. <u>Nicolaus Copernicus</u> was a Polish astronomer who wrote *On the Revolution of the Celestial Spheres.*/<u>Nicolás Copérnico</u> fue un astrónomo polaco que escribió *Las revoluciones de las esferas celestes.*

_____

_____ 8. <u>Sir Isaac Newton</u> invented calculus, an advanced form of mathematics that scientists use to solve complex problems./<u>Sir Isaac Newton</u> inventó el cálculo, una forma avanzada de matemáticas que los científicos usan para resolver problemas complejos.

_____

# The Scientific Revolution/La Revolución Científica

**MAIN IDEAS/IDEAS PRINCIPALES**

1. The ideas of Francis Bacon and René Descartes helped clarify the scientific method./Las ideas de Francis Bacon y René Descartes ayudaron a aclarar el método científico.

2. Science influenced new ideas about government./La ciencia influyó en las ideas nuevas sobre el gobierno.

3. Medical treatments changed as scientists better understood the human body./Los tratamientos médicos cambiaron a medida que los científicos comenzaron a comprender mejor el cuerpo humano.

4. Science and religion developed a sometimes uneasy relationship./Entre la ciencia y la religión se desarrolló una relación a veces difícil.

## Key Terms and People/Personas y palabras clave

**Francis Bacon/Francis Bacon** English philosopher who argued for systematic scientific research/filósofo inglés que defendió la investigación científica sistemática

**René Descartes/René Descartes** French philosopher who argued for clear thinking and reason to establish proof/filósofo francés que defendió el pensamiento claro y la razón para establecer pruebas

**scientific method/método científico** step-by-step procedure for performing experiments or research/procedimiento paso a paso para realizar experimentos o investigaciones

**hypothesis/hipótesis** a solution that the scientist proposes to solve a problem/solución que un científico propone para resolver un problema

## Lesson Summary/Resumen de la lección

**BACON, DESCARTES, AND THE SCIENTIFIC METHOD/**
**BACON, DESCARTES Y EL MÉTODO CIENTÍFICO**

The Scientific Revolution led to a dramatic change in the way people learned about the world. The new, scientific way of gaining knowledge had far-reaching effects. Science became the most effective way to learn about the natural world./La Revolución Científica provocó un cambio drástico en la manera de observar el mundo. Esta nueva manera científica de adquirir conocimientos tuvo efectos de amplio

> Underline the sentence that explains how science changed people during the Scientific Revolution./Subraya la oración que explica de qué manera la ciencia cambió a las personas durante la Revolución Científica.

alcance. La ciencia pasó a ser la manera más eficaz para aprender sobre el mundo natural.

Two important philosophers played a leading role in supporting science. **Francis Bacon** from England and **René Descartes** (ruh-NAY day-CART) from France encouraged the use of orderly experiments and clear reasoning. Descartes believed that nothing should be accepted as true if it could not be proven to be true. Their ideas led to the development of the **scientific method,** a step-by-step procedure for doing scientific research through observation and experimentation. These are the main principles of modern science. There are six basic steps in the scientific method, starting with stating the problem and gathering information. The third step is forming a hypothesis. A **hypothesis** is a solution that the scientist proposes to solve the problem. Fourth is testing the hypothesis by performing experiments. The fifth step is recording and analyzing the data gathered from the experiments. The final step is drawing conclusions from the data./Dos filósofos importantes tuvieron un papel principal en el apoyo a la ciencia. **Francis Bacon,** inglés, y **René Descartes,** francés, fomentaron el uso de experimentos ordenados y razonamientos claros. Descartes sostenía que nada debía aceptarse como verdad si no se podía demostrar. Sus ideas llevaron al desarrollo del **método científico,** un procedimiento paso a paso para llevar a cabo investigaciones científicas mediante la observación y la experimentación. Esos son los principios fundamentales de la ciencia moderna. Existen seis pasos básicos en el método científico: primero se plantea el problema y luego se reúne información. El tercer paso es formular una hipótesis. Una **hipótesis** es una solución

> **What are the main principles of modern science?/¿Cuáles son los principios fundamentales de la ciencia moderna?**
>
> _____
>
> _____
>
> _____
>
> _____

propuesta por un científico para resolver un problema. El cuarto paso es poner a prueba la hipótesis mediante experimentos. El quinto paso es registrar y analizar los datos obtenidos a partir de los experimentos. El último paso es sacar conclusiones acerca de los datos.

## SCIENCE AND GOVERNMENT/CIENCIA Y GOBIERNO

Science had a great impact on society and politics. Human reason, or logical thought, was a powerful tool. Philosophers thought they could use reason to improve society. If laws governed nature, laws could govern human behavior as well. Scientists' use of reason and logic helped pave the way for new democratic ideas in Europe, such as personal freedom, individual rights, and equality./ La ciencia tuvo un profundo impacto social y político. La razón humana, o el pensamiento lógico, era una herramienta poderosa. Los filósofos pensaban que podían usar la razón para mejorar la sociedad. Si las leyes gobernaban la naturaleza, también podían gobernar el comportamiento humano. El uso de la razón y la lógica por parte de los científicos ayudó a preparar el camino para el surgimiento de nuevas ideas democráticas en Europa, como la libertad personal, los derechos individuales y la igualdad.

> Underline three democratic ideas new to Europe./ Subraya tres ideas democráticas nuevas que surgieron en Europa.

## ADVANCES IN MEDICINE/AVANCES EN MEDICINA

The field of medicine changed thanks to the scientific methods. Doctors' observations and experiments led to changes in the way they treated sick patients. The invention of the microscope allowed scientists to see things not visible to the human eye./El campo de la medicina cambió gracias a los métodos científicos. Las observaciones y los experimentos de los médicos produjeron cambios en la manera de tratar a los

> What was one effect of the Scientific Revolution in the field of medicine?/¿Cuál fue uno de los efectos de la Revolución Científica en el campo de la medicina?
>
> _____
>
> _____
>
> _____

pacientes enfermos. La invención del microscopio permitió a los científicos ver elementos que no pueden observarse a simple vista.

## SCIENCE AND RELIGION/CIENCIA Y RELIGIÓN

The advances of science also brought conflict. The Roman Catholic Church leaders tried to force scientists to reject findings that opposed the Church's teachings. Galileo was put on trial for saying that the planets orbit the sun. The Church taught that the earth was the center of the universe and did not move. Galileo was threatened with torture unless he agreed with the church./Los avances científicos también causaron conflictos. Los líderes de la Iglesia católica romana trataron de obligar a los científicos a rechazar los descubrimientos que se oponían a las enseñanzas de la Iglesia. Galileo fue llevado a juicio por afirmar que los planetas giraban alrededor del Sol. La Iglesia sostenía que la Tierra era el centro del universo y no se movía. Galileo recibió amenazas: si no estaba de acuerdo con la Iglesia, lo torturarían.

Interestingly, Galileo and other scientists did not think science went against religion. They believed it helped people understand that these natural laws were God's creation./Curiosamente, Galileo y otros científicos no pensaban que la ciencia se oponía a la religión, sino que creían que ayudaba a comprender que las leyes naturales eran parte de la creación de Dios.

> **Why was Galileo put on trial?/¿Por qué Galileo fue llevado a juicio?**
>
> _____
>
> _____
>
> _____
>
> _____
>
> _____
>
> _____

## CHALLENGE ACTIVITY/ACTIVIDAD AVANZADA

**Critical Thinking: Summarize/Pensamiento crítico: Resumir** Write an essay describing the significance of the scientific method in modern science./Escribe un ensayo en el que describas la importancia del método científico en la ciencia moderna.

**DIRECTIONS/INSTRUCCIONES** Match the terms in the first column
with their correct definition from the second column by placing the
letter of the correct definition in the space provided before each
term./Une los términos de la primera columna con su definición
correcta en la segunda columna. Escribe la letra de la definición
correcta en el espacio que precede a cada término.

_____ 1. scientific method/
　　　　　 método científico

_____ 2. Galileo Galilei/
　　　　　 Galileo Galilei

_____ 3. microscope/
　　　　　 microscopio

_____ 4. René Descartes/
　　　　　 René Descartes

_____ 5. Scientific Revolution/
　　　　　 Revolución Científica

_____ 6. hypothesis/hipótesis

a. a solution that the scientist proposes to
solve a problem/solución propuesta por
un científico para resolver un problema

b. French philosopher who believed that
nothing should be accepted as true if it
could not be proven to be true/filósofo
francés que sostenía que nada debía
aceptarse como verdad si no se podía
demostrar

c. step-by-step process for performing
experiments and other scientific research/
proceso paso a paso para realizar
experimentos u otras investigaciones
científicas

d. invention that helped doctors see things
too small for the human eye alone/invento
que ayudó a los médicos a ver elementos
que eran demasiado pequeños para
observarlos a simple vista

e. Italian scientist put on trial by the Roman
Catholic Church for publicly saying that
the planets orbit the sun and not the
earth/científico italiano que fue llevado a
juicio por la Iglesia católica romana por
afirmar públicamente que los planetas
giraban alrededor del Sol y no de la Tierra

f. time when people began to question the
accepted wisdom about medicine and
the human body/momento en que las
personas comenzaron a cuestionar los
conocimientos previos sobre medicina
y el cuerpo humano

# The Age of Exploration/La era de las exploraciones

 **MAIN IDEAS/IDEAS PRINCIPALES**
1. Europeans had a desire and opportunity to explore./Los europeos tuvieron el deseo y la oportunidad de explorar.
2. Portuguese and Spanish explorations led to discoveries of new trade routes, lands, and people./Las exploraciones portuguesas y españolas llevaron al descubrimiento de nuevas rutas comerciales, tierras y pueblos.
3. English and French explorers found land in North America./Los exploradores ingleses y franceses hallaron tierras en América del Norte.
4. A new European worldview developed because of the discoveries./Los europeos se formaron una nueva visión del mundo a raíz de los descubrimientos.

## Key Terms and People/Personas y palabras clave

**Henry the Navigator/Enrique el Navegante** Portuguese prince who started a sailing school and funded many expeditions/príncipe portugués que fundó una escuela de navegación y financió múltiples expediciones

**Vasco da Gama/Vasco da Gama** first explorer to sail safely around Africa to India/ primer explorador que navegó con éxito hasta la India bordeando la costa de África

**Christopher Columbus/Cristóbal Colón** Italian explorer who accidentally discovered the Americas/explorador italiano que descubrió América por casualidad

**Ferdinand Magellan/Fernando de Magallanes** Portuguese navigator who first circumnavigated the globe/navegante portugués que fue el primero en circunnavegar el mundo

**circumnavigate/circunnavegar** to go all the way around/rodear por completo

**Francis Drake/Francis Drake** famous English pirate who robbed Spanish ships in the Americas/famoso pirata inglés que asaltaba naves españolas en América

**Spanish Armada/Armada española** huge fleet of Spanish ships defeated during an attack on England in 1588/inmensa flota de naves españolas que fue derrotada durante un ataque a Inglaterra en 1588

## Lesson Summary/Resumen de la lección

### DESIRE AND OPPORTUNITY TO EXPLORE/ DESEO Y OPORTUNIDAD DE EXPLORAR

During the 1400s, technology like the astrolabe and the sextant helped European sailors reach faraway places and return home safely. More accurate maps and ships called caravels encouraged explorers to set off to search for new trade routes to Asia and find rare spices. They also wanted to spread Christianity and discover new lands and people./Durante el siglo 15, algunos avances tecnológicos como el astrolabio y el sextante ayudaron a los marineros europeos a llegar a lugares remotos y regresar a sus hogares sanos y salvos. Los mapas trazados con mayor precisión y una clase de barcos llamados carabelas incentivaron a los exploradores a partir en busca de nuevas rutas comerciales hasta Asia y a encontrar especias raras. También buscaban difundir el cristianismo y descubrir tierras y pueblos nuevos.

> **Underline four motivations that encouraged European explorers during the 1400s./**Subraya cuatro motivaciones que animaron a los exploradores europeos durante el siglo 15.

## PORTUGUESE AND SPANISH EXPLORATIONS/
## EXPLORACIONES PORTUGUESAS Y ESPAÑOLAS

**Henry the Navigator** built an observatory and started a sailing school. Sailors often paid attention to the earlier voyages of others. **Vasco da Gama** used information that another sailor had learned to help him became the first person to sail safely around Africa to India./**Enrique el Navegante** construyó un observatorio y fundó una escuela de navegación. Los marineros a menudo tomaban en cuenta los viajes en barco que otros marineros habían hecho antes. Con ayuda de cierta información que otro marinero había obtenido, **Vasco da Gama** logró convertirse en el primero en navegar con éxito hasta la India bordeando la costa de África.

> **What did Vasco da Gama and other sailors do to help them sail?/**¿Qué hicieron Vasco da Gama y otros marineros para mejorar sus viajes por mar?
>
> _____
> _____
> _____
> _____

   **Christopher Columbus** was an Italian who worked for Spain. Knowing the world was round, he headed west to reach Asia but accidentally discovered the Americas instead. It was **Ferdinand Magellan,** a Portuguese navigator sailing for Spain, who first **circumnavigated** the globe.

Unfortunately, he was killed before the end of the journey. Following Columbus's path, the Spanish conquistadors sailed to the Americas in the early 1500s and conquered the Inca and Aztec civilizations./**Cristóbal Colón** era un italiano al servicio de España. Sabía que el mundo era redondo y se dirigió hacia el oeste pensando que se toparía con Asia, pero terminó descubriendo América por casualidad. Fue **Fernando de Magallanes,** navegante portugués al servicio de España, el primero en **circunnavegar** el mundo. Lamentablemente, lo mataron antes de que el viaje terminara. Siguiendo la ruta de Colón, los conquistadores españoles navegaron hasta América a principios del siglo 16 y conquistaron las civilizaciones inca y azteca.

> **What happened to Ferdinand Magellan when he circumnavigated the globe?/**¿Qué le sucedió a Fernando de Magallanes mientras navegaba alrededor del mundo?
>
> _____
>
> _____

## EUROPEANS IN AMERICA/EUROPEOS EN AMÉRICA

Portugal and Spain controlled southern trade routes, so French and English explorers went north. These early journeys again confused North America with Asia, but France and England claimed the land. The famous pirate **Francis Drake,** who worked for England, raided Spanish ships for their treasures. Spain responded by sending the **Spanish Armada** to attack England in 1588. The English navy defeated the Armada with the help of a great storm at sea. Spanish sea power never recovered./Dado que Portugal y España controlaban las rutas comerciales del sur, los exploradores ingleses y franceses se dirigieron al norte. En estos primeros viajes, se volvió a confundir América del Norte con Asia, pero Francia e Inglaterra reclamaron las tierras. El famoso pirata **Francis Drake,** al servicio de Inglaterra, asaltaba naves españolas para apoderarse de sus tesoros. En respuesta, España envió la **Armada española** a atacar Inglaterra, en

> **What happened to Spanish sea power after the English navy defeated the Spanish Armada?/**¿Qué sucedió con el poderío naval español después de que la marina inglesa derrotó a la Armada española?
>
> _____
>
> _____

1588. La marina inglesa derrotó a la Armada con ayuda de una gran tormenta que se desató en el mar. El poderío naval de España nunca logró recuperarse.

## A NEW EUROPEAN WORLDVIEW/UNA NUEVA VISIÓN EUROPEA DEL MUNDO

After the voyages of the 1400s and 1500s, Europeans learned that some of their geographic knowledge had been wrong. They created new maps that helped spread European influence around the world./Tras los viajes marítimos de los siglos 15 y 16, los europeos se dieron cuenta de que algunos aspectos de su conocimiento geográfico habían sido incorrectos. En consecuencia, elaboraron nuevos mapas que contribuyeron a extender la influencia europea alrededor del mundo.

> **What did Europeans learn after the voyages of the 1400s and 1500s?/¿Qué aprendieron los europeos tras los viajes marítimos de los siglos 15 y 16?**
>
> _____
> _____
> _____

## CHALLENGE ACTIVITY/ACTIVIDAD AVANZADA

**Critical Thinking: Elaborate/Pensamiento crítico: Profundizar** Assume that you are an explorer living in Spain, Portugal, France, or England during the 1400s. You need to persuade a rich patron to pay for a sailing expedition. Write a proposal in which you explain the purpose for your trip and list several reasons for taking it./Imagina que eres un explorador que vive en España, Portugal, Francia o Inglaterra en el siglo 15. Necesitas convencer a un patrocinador adinerado para que financie tu expedición marítima. Escribe una propuesta en la que expliques el objetivo del viaje y menciones distintas razones por las que deseas hacerlo.

**DIRECTIONS/INSTRUCCIONES** Write a word or descriptive phrase to describe each term./Escribe una palabra o frase descriptiva para describir cada término.

1. Christopher Columbus/Cristóbal Colón _____

   _____

2. circumnavigate/circunnavegar _____

   _____

3. Ferdinand Magellan/Fernando de Magallanes _____

   _____

4. Henry the Navigator/Enrique el Navegante _____

   _____

5. Sir Frances Drake/Sir Francis Drake _____

   _____

6. Spanish Armada/Armada española _____

   _____

7. Vasco da Gama/Vasco da Gama _____

   _____

# The Age of Exploration/La era de las exploraciones

## Lesson/Lección 2

**MAIN IDEAS/IDEAS PRINCIPALES**

1. Plants and animals were exchanged among Europe, Asia, Africa, and the Americas./Se estableció un intercambio de plantas y animales entre Europa, Asia, África y América.

2. Culture and technology changed as ideas were exchanged between Europe and the Americas./La cultura y la tecnología fueron cambiando a medida que se intercambiaban ideas entre Europa y América.

3. Society and the economy changed in Europe and the Americas./La sociedad y la economía de Europa y América cambiaron.

## Key Terms and People/Personas y palabras clave

**Columbian Exchange/Intercambio colombino** exchange of plants, animals and ideas between the New World (the Americas) and the Old World (Europe)/ intercambio de plantas, animales e ideas entre el Nuevo Mundo (América) y el Viejo Mundo (Europa)

**plantations/plantaciones** large farms/haciendas de gran extensión

**Bartolomé de las Casas/Bartolomé de las Casas** Spanish priest who opposed harsh treatment of the Indians and wanted to bring slaves from Africa to work the plantations/sacerdote español que se opuso al trato cruel que recibían los indígenas y que quería traer esclavos de África para que trabajaran en las plantaciones

**racism/racismo** belief that some people are better than others because of racial traits/creencia de que algunas personas son mejores que otras debido a sus rasgos raciales

## Lesson Summary/Resumen de la lección

### PLANTS AND ANIMALS/PLANTAS Y ANIMALES

One primary effect of European sea explorations was the exchange of plants, animals, and ideas between the New World (the Americas) and the Old World (Europe). This is called the **Columbian Exchange.**/Una consecuencia importante de las exploraciones marítimas de los europeos fue el intercambio de plantas, animales e ideas entre el Nuevo Mundo (América) y el Viejo Mundo (Europa). Esto se denominó **Intercambio colombino.**

> **Which two places were connected by the Columbian Exchange?/ ¿Qué dos lugares conectó el Intercambio colombino?**
> _____
> _____
> _____
> _____

Europeans brought crops such as bananas
and sugarcane from Asia to Central and South
America. They also planted oranges, onions,
and lettuce. Cows, goats, sheep, horses, pigs, and
chickens were also brought to the New World.
Europeans took home tomatoes, potatoes, beans,
squash, avocados, pineapples, tobacco, and chili
peppers. This exchange changed the eating habits
of the entire world, not just Europe and the
Americas. Sweet potatoes and peanuts became
popular in Africa. In China, peanuts and maize
became major crops./Los europeos trajeron
a América Central y América del Sur ciertos
cultivos de Asia, como el plátano y la caña de
azúcar. También plantaron naranjas, cebollas
y lechuga. Además, trajeron al Nuevo Mundo
vacas, cabras, ovejas, caballos, cerdos y pollos.
A su vez, los europeos llevaron a sus países
tomates, papas, frijoles, calabazas, aguacates,
piñas, tabaco y chile. Este intercambio modificó
los hábitos alimentarios de todo el mundo, no
solo de Europa y América. La batata y el maní
se volvieron populares en África. En China, el
maní y el maíz se convirtieron en dos de los
principales cultivos.

> **Underline the crops that
> the Europeans brought to
> the New World. Circle the
> crops that they took home
> to Europe./Subraya los
> cultivos que los europeos
> trajeron al Nuevo Mundo.
> Encierra en un círculo
> los cultivos que llevaron
> a Europa.**

## CULTURE AND TECHNOLOGY/CULTURA Y TECNOLOGÍA

Besides food and animals, religion and language
were probably the biggest changes Europeans
brought to the New World. Both Protestant and
Catholic missionaries traveled to the Americas.
They set up schools to convert people to
Christianity and teach them European languages.
In some places, Christianity blended with local
customs to create new religious practices./
Además de los alimentos y los animales,
probablemente la religión y el idioma fueron los
principales cambios que los europeos trajeron
al Nuevo Mundo. Muchos misioneros, tanto

> **Why did missionaries
> set up schools in the
> New World?/¿Por qué los
> misioneros establecieron
> escuelas en el Nuevo
> Mundo?**
>
> _____
> _____
> _____
> _____

protestantes como católicos, viajaron a América, donde establecieron escuelas para convertir a los pueblos al cristianismo y enseñarles idiomas europeos. En algunos lugares, el cristianismo se fusionó con ciertas costumbres locales, lo que dio origen a nuevas prácticas religiosas.

The Europeans also introduced technologies and animals that made life and work easier to do. Horses were used for transportation and oxen and the plough for farming. Guns, steel, and the wheel also came to the New World. **Plantations** and mining developed from these innovations. These new industries were mostly run by the Europeans./Los europeos también introdujeron innovaciones tecnológicas y animales que facilitaron la vida y el trabajo. Los caballos se usaban como medio de transporte, y los bueyes y el arado se usaban para las tareas agrícolas. También llegaron al Nuevo Mundo la pistola, el acero y la rueda. A partir de estas innovaciones, surgieron las **plantaciones** y la minería. Estas industrias eran administradas principalmente por europeos.

> **What two factors allowed plantations and mining to begin in the Americas?/**
> **¿Qué dos factores permitieron el surgimiento de la minería y del sistema de plantaciones en América?**
>
> _____
>
> _____

## SOCIETY AND THE ECONOMY/SOCIEDAD Y ECONOMÍA

Sugarcane plantations and mines made a lot of money for Spain and Portugal. But American Indians were forced into slave labor to work in these industries. Many Native Americans died as a result of harsh treatment and new diseases./ Las plantaciones de caña de azúcar y las minas generaban grandes sumas de dinero para España y Portugal. Sin embargo, los indígenas de América eran obligados a trabajar como esclavos en estas industrias. Muchos amerindios murieron como resultado del trato cruel que recibieron y debido a nuevas enfermedades.

Spanish priest **Bartolomé de las Casas** did not like the way the Indians were treated on the plantations. Unfortunately, his solution to the problem was to use Africans as slaves instead of American Indians. This created a new society based on **racism.** The white Europeans thought they were superior to the darker-skinned Indians and Africans, as well as those of mixed blood./ El sacerdote español **Bartolomé de las Casas** no estaba de acuerdo con el trato que recibían los indígenas que trabajaban en las plantaciones. Lamentablemente, la solución que buscó a este problema fue utilizar esclavos africanos en vez de amerindios. Esta situación dio lugar a una nueva sociedad basada en el **racismo.** Los europeos blancos se creían superiores a los indígenas y los africanos de tez oscura, y también a los mestizos.

> **Why did Bartolomé de las Casas suggest to use Africans as slaves?/¿Por qué Bartolomé de las Casas sugirió usar a los africanos como esclavos?**
>
> _____
> _____
> _____
> _____

## CHALLENGE ACTIVITY/ACTIVIDAD AVANZADA

**Critical Thinking: Analyze Effects/Pensamiento crítico: Analizar efectos** Write a short paragraph that identifies and explains the effects of the plantation system on the Americas./Escribe un párrafo corto en el que identifiques y expliques los efectos que generó en América el sistema de plantaciones.

| | | |
|---|---|---|
| Bartolomé de las Casas/<br>Bartolomé de las Casas | Columbian Exchange/el<br>Intercambio colombino | oxen/los bueyes |
| plantations/plantaciones | Protestant/protestantes | racism/el racismo |
| Spain/España | | |

**DIRECTIONS/INSTRUCCIONES** Read each sentence and fill in
the blank with a word from the word bank that best completes
the sentence./Lee cada oración y escribe en el espacio en blanco
la palabra del banco de palabras que mejor la completa.

1. Due to _____, white Europeans thought they were
   superior to darker-skinned Indians and Africans, and those of mixed blood./
   Por _____, los europeos blancos se creían superiores a
   los indígenas y los africanos de tez oscura, y también a los mestizos.

2. Catholic and _____ missionaries from Europe
   brought religion and language to the New World./Los misioneros católicos
   y _____ provenientes de Europa trajeron nuevas religiones
   e idiomas al Nuevo Mundo.

3. Animals and technologies like _____ and the plough
   made farming easier to do./Los animales y las innovaciones tecnológicas
   como _____ y el arado facilitaron las tareas agrícolas.

4. Through the _____, crops, animals, and ideas went back
   and forth between Europe and the Americas./Con _____,
   diferentes cultivos, animales e ideas llegaron hasta América desde Europa
   y viceversa.

5. The sugarcane crop made a lot of money for _____ and
   Portugal./El cultivo de caña de azúcar generó grandes sumas de dinero para
   _____ y Portugal.

6. Large farms called _____ were mostly run by the
   Europeans./Las grandes haciendas llamadas _____ eran
   administradas principalmente por europeos.

7. _____ was the name of the Spanish priest who wanted to
   use Africans as slaves instead of American Indians./_____
   era el nombre del sacerdote español que quiso utilizar a los africanos como
   esclavos en vez de usar a los amerindios.

## The Age of Exploration/La era de las exploraciones

### Lesson/Lección 3

**MAIN IDEAS/IDEAS PRINCIPALES**

1. A new economic system called mercantilism emerged./Surgió un nuevo sistema económico llamado mercantilismo.

2. New trading patterns developed in the 1600s and 1700s./Se desarrollaron nuevas prácticas comerciales en los siglos 17 y 18.

3. Power in Europe shifted as a result of new trade routes, banking, and increased manufacturing./El poder en Europa cambió debido a las nuevas rutas comerciales, al sistema bancario y al aumento de la manufacturación.

4. Market economies changed business in Europe./Las economías de mercado cambiaron la actividad comercial en Europa.

## Key Terms and People/Personas y palabras clave

**mercantilism/mercantilismo** trading system.in which the government controls all economic activity/sistema de comercio en el que el gobierno controla toda la actividad económica

**balance of trade/balanza comercial** relationship between imported goods and exported goods/relación que existe entre los bienes importados y los bienes exportados

**cottage industry/industria artesanal** home-based manufacturing businesses run by families/sistema de fabricación administrado por los miembros de una familia en su propia casa

**atlas/atlas** collection of maps/colección de mapas

**capitalism/capitalismo** system in which individuals and private businesses run most industries/sistema en el que los individuos y las empresas privadas administran la mayoría de las industrias

**market economy/economía de mercado** system in which individuals decide what goods and services to buy/sistema en el que los individuos deciden qué bienes y servicios desean adquirir

## Lesson Summary/Resumen de la lección

### A NEW ECONOMY/UNA NUEVA ECONOMÍA

**Mercantilism** was the main economic policy in Europe between 1500 and 1800. In this system, the government controls all economic activity in a country and its colonies. The government becomes stronger and richer./El **mercantilismo** fue la principal política económica de Europa entre los años 1500 y 1800. En este sistema, el gobierno controla toda la actividad económica de un país y sus colonias. El mercantilismo fortalece y enriquece al gobierno.

To stay rich, countries tried to maintain a **balance of trade.** They exported more goods than they imported. Each colony only traded with its home country. Colonies were places to acquire raw materials like wood, cotton, and dyes. When the time came to sell finished manufactured products, they were sold in the colonies. These products were made by an increasing number of European families who ran businesses called **cottage industries.**/Para conservar sus riquezas, los países intentaban mantener una **balanza comercial.** Exportaban más bienes de los que importaban. Cada colonia comerciaba solamente con el país del que dependía. En las colonias, se podían conseguir materias primas, como madera, algodón y tintes. Cuando llegaba el momento de vender los bienes manufacturados terminados, la venta se llevaba a cabo en las colonias. Estos productos eran fabricados por un creciente número de familias europeas que administraban un sistema comercial llamado **industria artesanal.**

> What effect does mercantilism have on government?/¿Qué efecto tiene el mercantilismo sobre el gobierno?
>
> _____
> _____
> _____

> Where was the only place where a colony could trade raw materials and manufactured products?/ ¿Cuál era el único lugar donde una colonia podía intercambiar materias primas y bienes manufacturados?
>
> _____
> _____

## NEW TRADING PATTERNS/NUEVOS PATRONES DE COMERCIO

The triangular trade network sent raw materials, manufactured products, and slaves back and forth to Europe, Africa, and the Americas. Portuguese, English, and Dutch traders increased the new Atlantic slave trade by cramming Africans into ships without food or water. People got sick, and many died./Se inició una red comercial triangular mediante la cual se intercambiaban materias primas, bienes manufacturados y esclavos entre Europa, África y América. Los comerciantes portugueses, ingleses y holandeses aumentaron el nuevo comercio de esclavos que se realizaba

> Underline the three things that were sent back and forth in the triangular trade network. Circle the three places that were part of the triangular trade network./ Subraya las tres cosas que se intercambiaban mediante la red comercial triangular. Encierra en un círculo los lugares que conformaban esa red.

a través del Atlántico. Los africanos viajaban
apretujados en los barcos sin recibir comida ni
agua, por lo que se enfermaban y muchos morían.

## POWER SHIFTS IN EUROPE/EL PODER CAMBIA EN EUROPA

Mercantilism was most successful in Portugal
and Spain, but the English and French discovered
new northern trade routes. They also established
a banking system that helped shift economic
power in their favor. A new book of much better
maps, called an **atlas,** helped improve northern
trading expeditions. The Dutch were the first to
form a company to deal directly with trade from
Africa and Asia. This helped Dutch merchants
control many trading posts in these regions and
in India and Japan./El mercantilismo tuvo mucho
éxito en Portugal y España, pero los ingleses y los
franceses descubrieron nuevas rutas comerciales
en el norte. También establecieron un sistema
bancario que contribuyó a inclinar el poder
económico a su favor. Un nuevo libro de mapas
mucho mejor elaborados, llamado **atlas,** optimizó
las expediciones comerciales que se desarrollaban
en el norte. Los holandeses fueron los primeros
en crear una compañía para manejar de manera
directa el comercio proveniente de África y Asia.
Esto ayudó a los comerciantes holandeses a
controlar muchos puntos de comercio ubicados
en estas regiones y también en la India y Japón.

> How were Dutch merchants able to control trading posts in Asia and Africa?/ ¿Cómo hicieron los comerciantes holandeses para controlar los puntos de comercio de Asia y África?
>
> _____
> _____
> _____
> _____

## MARKET ECONOMIES/ECONOMÍAS DE MERCADO

Increased wealth in Europe led to an increased
demand for manufactured goods. People came
up with ways to increase the supply to meet the
demand for goods. This created the basis of
**capitalism.** Capitalism encourages competition
among manufacturers and creates a **market
economy.** Individuals decide what goods and

> What does capitalism encourage among manufacturers?/¿Qué es lo que estimula el capitalismo entre los fabricantes?
>
> _____

services they want to buy./El aumento de las riquezas en Europa produjo un aumento de la demanda de bienes manufacturados. Surgieron nuevas formas de incrementar la oferta para satisfacer la demanda de estos productos. Esto creó las bases del **capitalismo,** que estimula la competencia entre los fabricantes y crea una **economía de mercado.** En este sistema, los individuos deciden qué bienes y servicios desean adquirir.

## CHALLENGE ACTIVITY/ACTIVIDAD AVANZADA

**Critical Thinking: Develop/Pensamiento crítico: Desarrollar** You are a shoemaker in England during the 1700s. You hear that the American colonies are in desperate need of shoes. A trader asks you if you can fill an order for 5,000 pairs of shoes—by next week! You say yes. Develop a plan to fill the order./Eres fabricante de zapatos en Inglaterra durante el siglo 18. Te enteras de que las colonias americanas necesitan zapatos con urgencia. Un comerciante te pregunta si puedes enviarle un pedido de 5,000 pares de zapatos... ¡para la próxima semana! Aceptas. Desarrolla un plan para cumplir con el pedido.

**DIRECTIONS/INSTRUCCIONES** On the line before each statement, write **T** if the statement is true and **F** if the statement is false. If the statement is false, change the underlined term to make the sentence true. Then write the correct term on the line after the sentence./En la línea que precede a cada enunciado, escribe **V** si el enunciado es verdadero y **F** si es falso. Si el enunciado es falso, cambia el término subrayado para que el enunciado sea verdadero. Luego escribe el término correcto en la línea que sigue al enunciado.

_____ 1. An <u>atlas</u> is a collection of maps that helped improve northern trading expeditions./<u>Un atlas</u> es una colección de mapas que ayudó a optimizar las expediciones comerciales del norte.

_____

_____ 2. In a <u>cottage industry</u>, individuals decide what goods and services they want to buy./En <u>una industria artesanal</u>, los individuos deciden qué bienes y servicios desean adquirir.

_____

_____ 3. The government controls all economic activity in the trading system called <u>capitalism</u>./El gobierno controla toda la actividad económica en el sistema comercial llamado <u>capitalismo</u>.

_____

_____ 4. Countries tried to maintain a <u>balance of trade</u> so they could stay rich./Los países intentaban mantener <u>una balanza comercial</u> para conservar sus riquezas.

_____

_____ 5. Private businesses and individuals run most industries in the system of <u>mercantilism</u>./Las empresas privadas y los individuos controlan la mayoría de las industrias en el sistema llamado <u>mercantilismo</u>.

_____

_____ 6. A home based manufacturing business run by families is a <u>market economy</u>./Una actividad comercial desarrollada por las familias en sus propias casas se denomina <u>economía de mercado</u>.

_____

# Enlightenment and Revolution/La Ilustración y la Revolución

## Lesson/Lección 1

> **MAIN IDEAS/IDEAS PRINCIPALES**
> 1. The Enlightenment was also called the Age of Reason./La Ilustración también fue conocida como la Edad de la Razón.
> 2. The Enlightenment's roots can be traced back to earlier ideas./Los orígenes de la Ilustración se remontan a ideas de épocas anteriores.
> 3. New ideas came mainly from French and British thinkers./Las nuevas ideas provinieron principalmente de pensadores ingleses y franceses.

# Key Terms and People/Personas y palabras clave

**Enlightenment/Ilustración** period in which people valued the use of reason as a guide to improving society/período en el que las personas valoraban el uso de la razón como guía para mejorar la sociedad

**Voltaire/Voltaire** French philosopher and writer who mocked government and religion/filósofo y escritor francés que se burlaba del gobierno y de la religión

**salon/salón** social gathering in which people discuss ideas/reunión social para discutir ideas

**Mary Wollstonecraft/Mary Wollstonecraft** British writer who believed women should have the same rights as men/escritora inglesa que creía que las mujeres debían tener los mismos derechos que los hombres

# Lesson Summary/Resumen de la lección

## THE AGE OF REASON/LA EDAD DE LA RAZÓN

Discoveries made during the Scientific Revolution and explorers led to changes in Europe. Many scholars challenged long-held beliefs about science, religion, and government. They relied on reason, or logical thought, to explain how the world worked. They believed human reason could be used to reach three great goals—knowledge, freedom, and happiness. This time period is called the **Enlightenment.** It is also known as the Age of Reason./Los descubrimientos realizados durante la Revolución Científica y también los exploradores provocaron cambios en Europa. Muchos estudiosos cuestionaban ciertas creencias muy arraigadas sobre la ciencia, la religión y el

> Underline the three goals that scholars believed humans could achieve through the use of reason./Subraya los tres objetivos que los estudiosos creían que los seres humanos podían alcanzar mediante el uso de la razón.

gobierno. Comenzaron a basarse en la razón,
o el pensamiento lógico, para explicar el
funcionamiento del mundo. Creían que la razón
humana se podía utilizar para alcanzar tres
grandes objetivos: el conocimiento, la libertad y
la felicidad. Este período se conoce como la
**Ilustración.** También se conoce como la Edad
de la Razón.

## THE ENLIGHTENMENT'S ROOTS/ORÍGENES DE LA ILUSTRACIÓN

The main ideas of the Enlightenment came from
earlier eras. Enlightenment thinkers looked to the
Greeks, Romans and the history of Christianity.
They also got ideas from the Renaissance, the
Reformation, and the Scientific Revolution. For
example, the ancient Greeks observed the order
in the natural world, and Roman thinkers had
the idea that natural law governed how the world
worked. Enlightenment thinkers applied these
beliefs of natural laws to the human world of
society and government. They questioned the
Christian Church's religious beliefs and power.
They learned from the Renaissance thinkers who
believed that humans had value and the scientists
from the Scientific Revolution who used the
scientific method./Las principales ideas de la
Ilustración provenían de épocas anteriores. Los
pensadores de la Ilustración se basaron en ideas
de los griegos, los romanos y la historia del
cristianismo. También tomaron ideas del
Renacimiento, la Reforma y la Revolución
Científica. Por ejemplo, los antiguos griegos
observaban el orden del mundo natural y los
pensadores romanos sostenían que la ley natural
gobernaba el funcionamiento del mundo. Los
pensadores de la Ilustración aplicaron esa creencia
en las leyes naturales al mundo humano de la

> **Where did Enlightenment scholars get their ideas?/**
> **¿De dónde provenían las ideas de los estudiosos de la Ilustración?**
>
> _____
> _____
> _____
> _____

sociedad y el gobierno. Cuestionaban las creencias religiosas y el poder de la Iglesia cristiana. Seguían las enseñanzas de los pensadores del Renacimiento, quienes sostenían que los seres humanos tenían valor, y de los científicos de la Revolución Científica, quienes utilizaban el método científico.

## NEW IDEAS/NUEVAS IDEAS

Enlightenment thinkers expanded on ideas from history to think about the world in a new way. They believed the use of reason could improve society. To do so, they had to share their ideas with others./Los pensadores de la Ilustración tomaron ideas históricas y las ampliaron en busca de una nueva manera de considerar el mundo. Creían que el uso de la razón podía mejorar la sociedad. Para ello, debían compartir sus ideas con los demás.

French philosophers made many of the ideas of the Enlightenment popular. The philosopher **Voltaire** (vohl-TAYR) believed humans could improve their lives and poked fun at government and religion in his writings. When he was censored for his writings, Voltaire spoke out. He said, "I [may] disapprove of what you say, but I will defend to the death your right to say it." This is the Enlightenment goal of freedom of thought./Los filósofos franceses popularizaron muchas de las ideas de la Ilustración. El filósofo **Voltaire** creía que los seres humanos podían progresar hacia una vida mejor y, en sus escritos, se burlaba del gobierno y la religión. Cuando lo censuraron debido a lo que escribía, Voltaire manifestó su posición y dijo: "[Puedo] estar en desacuerdo con lo que usted diga, pero defenderé hasta la muerte su derecho a decirlo". Esto refleja la lucha por la libertad de pensamiento, una meta fundamental de la Ilustración.

> **Why do you think Voltaire's writings were censored?/**
> **¿Por qué crees que censuraron los escritos de Voltaire?**
>
> _____
> _____
> _____
> _____
> _____

Enlightenment ideas spread. An important place for the exchange of ideas was the salon. The **salon** was a social gathering held to discuss ideas. Some British men and women also began to publish their ideas in books, pamphlets, and newspaper articles. The British writer **Mary Wollstonecraft** wrote that women should have the same rights as men. The British writer Adam Smith believed economics was governed by natural laws and should not be controlled by governments./Las ideas de la Ilustración se difundieron. Un lugar importante para el intercambio de ideas fueron los salones. El **salón** era una reunión social organizada para discutir ideas. Algunos hombres y mujeres ingleses también comenzaron a publicar sus ideas en libros, panfletos y artículos periodísticos. La escritora inglesa **Mary Wollstonecraft** escribió que las mujeres debían tener los mismos derechos que los hombres. El escritor inglés Adam Smith creía que la economía se regía por leyes naturales y debía estar libre del control de los gobiernos.

> **What did Enlightenment thinkers do to spread their ideas?/¿Qué hicieron los pensadores de la Ilustración para difundir sus ideas?**
>
> _____
>
> _____
>
> _____

## CHALLENGE ACTIVITY/ACTIVIDAD AVANZADA

**Critical Thinking: Develop/Pensamiento crítico: Desarrollar** If you were to hold a salon today, what would the topics of discussion include? List three important topics you would discuss and your ideas on how to resolve these issues./Si organizaras una reunión social, o salón, en la actualidad, ¿qué temas incluirías en la discusión? Menciona tres temas importantes que discutirías y tus ideas sobre cómo resolver esas cuestiones.

Lesson/Lección 1, *continued*/*continuación*

| Enlightenment/<br>Ilustración | Mary Wollstonecraft/<br>Mary Wollstonecraft | Voltaire/Voltaire | salon/salón |
|---|---|---|---|

**DIRECTIONS/INSTRUCCIONES** Use the vocabulary terms in the word bank to write a summary of how the thinkers of the Enlightenment developed their ideas./Usa el vocabulario del banco de palabras para escribir un resumen de cómo desarrollaron sus ideas los pensadores de la Ilustración.

_____

_____

_____

_____

_____

_____

_____

_____

_____

_____

_____

_____

_____

_____

_____

_____

_____

_____

# Enlightenment and Revolution/La Ilustración y la Revolución

## Lesson/Lección 2

**MAIN IDEAS/IDEAS PRINCIPALES**

1. The Enlightenment influenced some monarchies./La Ilustración tuvo influencia en algunas monarquías.
2. Enlightenment thinkers helped the growth of democratic ideas./Los pensadores de la Ilustración contribuyeron al desarrollo de las ideas democráticas.
3. In the Americas, the Enlightenment inspired a struggle for independence./En América, la Ilustración inspiró la lucha por la independencia.

# Key Terms and People/Personas y palabras clave

**unlimited government/gobierno ilimitado** where one person or group holds all the power/gobierno en el que una persona o grupo tiene todo el poder

**limited government/gobierno limitado** state in which power is checked by laws and institutions/estado en el que el poder está regulado por leyes e instituciones

**John Locke/John Locke** English philosopher who said government is a contract between the ruler and the people/filósofo inglés que sostenía que el gobierno es un contrato entre el gobernante y el pueblo

**natural rights/derechos naturales** Locke's idea that every person has the right to life, liberty, and property/idea enunciada por Locke de que cada persona tiene derecho a la vida, a la libertad y a la propiedad

**majority rule/gobierno de la mayoría** system in which ideas and decisions supported by the most people are followed/sistema en el que se adoptan las ideas y las decisiones apoyadas por la mayoría

**Charles-Louis Montesquieu/Charles-Louis Montesquieu** French philosopher who said government should be divided into separate branches, each branch limiting the power of the other branch/filósofo francés que sostenía que el gobierno debía dividirse en poderes separados y que cada poder debía limitar la autoridad de los otros poderes

**Jean-Jacques Rousseau/Jean-Jacques Rousseau** French writer who proposed the idea of popular sovereignty/escritor francés que propuso la idea de la soberanía popular

**popular sovereignty/soberanía popular** government that expresses the will of the people/gobierno que expresa la voluntad del pueblo

# Lesson Summary/Resumen de la lección
## ENLIGHTENMENT INFLUENCE ON MONARCHIES/ INFLUENCIA DE LA ILUSTRACIÓN EN LAS MONARQUÍAS

In the 1600s and 1700s, kings, queens, and emperors ruled Europe. People believed God had given them the right to rule as they chose. This is **unlimited government** in which one person or group holds all power. **Limited government** is one that is not all-powerful and is checked by laws and institutions that represent the will of the people. The spread of Enlightenment ideas pushed some monarchs to make life better for commoners. They made laws they thought would make people happier. Empress Catherine the Great of Russia increased the number of schools for the people./ Durante los siglos 17 y 18, Europa estuvo gobernada por reyes, reinas y emperadores a quienes el pueblo creía que Dios les había otorgado el derecho de gobernar como quisieran. Se trataba de un **gobierno ilimitado,** en el que una persona o grupo tenía todo el poder. Un **gobierno limitado,** en cambio, es aquel que no es omnipotente y está regulado por leyes e instituciones que representan la voluntad del pueblo. La difusión de las ideas de la Ilustración incentivó a algunos monarcas a mejorar la vida de los plebeyos. Crearon leyes creyendo que estas contribuirían a la felicidad del pueblo. La emperatriz rusa Catalina la Grande aumentó el número de escuelas.

> In Europe in the 1700s, what was the type of government in most countries?/¿Qué tipo de gobierno existía en la mayoría de los países de Europa en el siglo 18?
>
> _____
>
> _____

## DEMOCRATIC IDEAS/IDEAS DEMOCRÁTICAS

Enlightenment thinkers challenged rule by divine right. English philosopher **John Locke** wrote that government should be a contract between the ruler and the people that limits the ruler's power. Locke said that all people had **natural rights,** which included the rights to life, liberty, and property. He believed in **majority rule,** a system in which the

ideas and decisions supported by the most people
are followed. Government should be for the
common good of the people. Frenchman **Charles-
Louis Montesquieu** (mohn-te-SKYOO) said that
government should be divided into separate
branches to protect people's freedom. Each branch
is limited by the others. French thinker **Jean-
Jacques Rousseau** (roo-SOH) believed in **popular
sovereignty,** the idea that governments should
express the will of the people./Los pensadores
de la Ilustración cuestionaban el gobierno por
derecho divino. El filósofo inglés **John Locke**
escribió que el gobierno debía ser un contrato
entre el gobernante y el pueblo que limitara la
autoridad del gobernante. Locke afirmaba que
todas las personas tenían **derechos naturales,** como
el derecho a la vida, a la libertad y a la propiedad.
Creía en **el gobierno de la mayoría,** sistema en el
que se adoptan las ideas y las decisiones apoyadas
por la mayoría. El gobierno debía procurar el
bien común del pueblo. El francés **Charles-Louis
Montesquieu** sostenía que el gobierno debía
dividirse en poderes separados para proteger la
libertad de las personas y que cada poder debía
limitar la autoridad de los otros poderes. El
pensador francés **Jean-Jacques Rousseau** creía en
la **soberanía popular,** la idea de que los gobiernos
deben expresar la voluntad del pueblo.

| **What is majority rule?/ ¿Qué es el gobierno de la mayoría?** |
| --- |
| _____ |
| _____ |
| _____ |

## THE ENLIGHTENMENT IN THE AMERICAS/ LA ILUSTRACIÓN EN AMÉRICA

The philosophers' ideas spread from Europe to
the British colonists in North America. The
British government created new taxes to raise
funds to fight the French, who also controlled
land in North America. The colonists thought
the taxes were unfair. Two leaders, Benjamin
Franklin and Thomas Jefferson, applied the
ideas of the Enlightenment to the colonists'

| **Why were the colonists upset with the British government?/¿Por qué los colonos estaban molestos con el gobierno británico?** |
| --- |
| _____ |
| _____ |
| _____ |

complaints. They wanted independence for the
colonies. Jefferson supported the separation
of religion and political power./Las ideas de los
filósofos se difundieron desde Europa hasta las
colonias británicas en América del Norte. El
gobierno británico creó nuevos impuestos para
recaudar fondos para luchar contra los franceses,
que también controlaban tierras en América
del Norte. Los colonos consideraban que los
impuestos eran injustos. Dos líderes, Benjamin
Franklin y Thomas Jefferson, aplicaron las ideas
de la Ilustración a los reclamos de los colonos.
Querían la independencia de las colonias.
Jefferson apoyaba la separación entre el
poder religioso y el poder político.

## CHALLENGE ACTIVITY/ACTIVIDAD AVANZADA

**Critical Thinking: Compare/Pensamiento crítico:**
**Comparar** Imagine living today under a king who
could rule as he pleased. Compare this to your life
now in which you live with limited government.
Write a one-page essay explaining what would be
different and what would be the same./Imagina
que vives en la actualidad bajo el gobierno de un
rey que puede mandar a voluntad. Compara este
estilo de vida con tu vida actual, que se rige por
un gobierno limitado. Escribe un ensayo de una
página en el que expliques las diferencias y las
similitudes entre estos dos estilos de vida.

| Charles-Louis Montesquieu/ Charles-Louis Montesquieu | Jean-Jacques Rousseau/ Jean-Jacques Rousseau | John Locke/ John Locke |
|---|---|---|
| limited government/un gobierno limitado | majority rule/el gobierno de la mayoría | natural rights/ derechos naturales |
| popular sovereignty/la soberanía popular | unlimited government/un gobierno ilimitado | |

**DIRECTIONS/INSTRUCCIONES** Read each sentence and fill in the blank with a word from the word bank that best completes the sentence./Lee cada oración y escribe en el espacio en blanco la palabra del banco de palabras que mejor la completa.

1. French thinker _____ believed that governments should express the will of the people./El pensador francés _____ consideraba que los gobiernos debían expresar la voluntad del pueblo.

2. Frenchman _____ claimed that a government should be divided into separate branches to protect people's freedom./ El francés _____ sostenía que el gobierno debía dividirse en poderes separados para proteger la libertad del pueblo.

3. John Locke wrote that all people had _____, which include the rights to life, liberty, and property./John Locke escribió que todas las personas tenían _____, como el derecho a la vida, a la libertad y a la propiedad.

4. _____ is a system where one person, or a small group, holds all of the power./_____ es un sistema en el que una persona o grupo pequeño tiene todo el poder.

5. _____ is not all powerful and is checked by laws that were created by the will of the people./_____ no es omnipotente y está regido por leyes creadas por la voluntad del pueblo.

6. The British philosopher and writer _____
   wrote that government should be a contract between the ruler and
   the people that limits the ruler's power./El filósofo y escritor británico
   _____ escribió que el gobierno debía ser un
   contrato entre el gobernante y el pueblo que limitara la autoridad
   del gobernante.

7. _____ is the principle that governments should
   express the will of the people./_____ es el principio
   que establece que los gobiernos deben expresar la voluntad del pueblo.

# Enlightenment and Revolution/La Ilustración y la Revolución

## Lesson/Lección 3

**MAIN IDEAS/IDEAS PRINCIPALES**

1. Revolution and reform changed the government of England./La revolución y las reformas produjeron cambios en el gobierno de Inglaterra.
2. Enlightenment ideas led to democracy in North America./Las ideas de la Ilustración llevaron al establecimiento de la democracia en América del Norte.
3. The French Revolution caused major changes in France's government./La Revolución francesa provocó grandes cambios en el gobierno de Francia.

## Key Terms and People/Personas y palabras clave

**English Bill of Rights/Declaración de Derechos inglesa** document that listed the rights of the British people, passed in 1689/documento aprobado en 1689 que detallaba los derechos del pueblo británico

**rule of law/imperio de la ley** principle that everyone, including monarchs, is subject to the laws of the land/principio que establecía que todos, incluidos los monarcas, estaban sujetos a las leyes de la tierra

**Declaration of Independence/Declaración de Independencia** document declaring the American colonies' independence from British rule in 1776/documento aprobado en 1776 que declaró la independencia de las colonias de América del Norte respecto del dominio británico

**Declaration of the Rights of Man and of the Citizen/Declaración de los Derechos del Hombre y del Ciudadano** document issued during the French Revolution granting freedom of speech, the press, and religion for the French/documento redactado durante la Revolución francesa que otorgaba a los franceses libertad de expresión, de prensa y de religión

## Lesson Summary/Resumen de la lección

### REVOLUTION AND REFORM IN ENGLAND/ REVOLUCIÓN Y REFORMA EN INGLATERRA

In England, the uneasy relationship been Parliament and the monarchy exploded into a civil war in 1642. A series of rulers took power before Parliament invited William of Orange to invade and become king in 1688. William took power, but only after agreeing to sign an **English Bill of Rights** for Parliament and the English people in 1689. William became king, but shared power with Parliament. The monarchs had to follow the laws of the land like everyone else. This principle is known as the **rule of law.**/En Inglaterra, la complicada relación entre el Parlamento y la monarquía desató una guerra civil en 1642. Una serie de gobernantes estuvo en el poder hasta que el Parlamento le pidió a Guillermo de Orange que invadiera el país y se convirtiera en rey en 1688. Guillermo asumió el poder, pero solo después de que acordara firmar, en 1689, la **Declaración de Derechos inglesa,** que detallaba los derechos del Parlamento y del pueblo inglés. Guillermo se convirtió en rey, pero compartía el poder con el Parlamento. Los monarcas debían respetar las leyes de la tierra, como cualquier otra persona. Este principio se conoce como el **imperio de la ley.**

**DEMOCRACY IN AMERICA/DEMOCRACIA EN AMÉRICA**

The English Bill of Rights did not apply to the American colonies. The colonies developed their own governing bodies, but were still subject to taxes and laws they considered to be unfair. When their protests were put down by British troops, the colonists organized militias, groups of armed men, to protect themselves. In 1776, the colonial leaders met and Thomas Jefferson drafted the **Declaration of Independence,** announcing the colonies' independence from British rule./La Declaración de Derechos inglesa no se aplicaba a las colonias de América del Norte. Las colonias desarrollaron sus propios órganos de gobierno, pero seguían estando sujetas a impuestos y leyes que consideraban injustos. Cuando las tropas británicas sofocaron sus protestas, los colonos organizaron milicias (grupos de hombres armados) para protegerse.

> When was the English Bill of Rights signed?/¿Cuándo se firmó la Declaración de Derechos inglesa?
> _____

> Underline the phrase that shows the main American grievances against English rule./Subraya la frase que menciona los principales reclamos de los colonos al gobierno inglés.

> Why did American colonists organize militias?/¿Por qué organizaron milicias los colonos de América del Norte?
> _____

En 1776, los líderes de las colonias se reunieron, y Thomas Jefferson redactó la **Declaración de Independencia,** que anunciaba la independencia de las colonias respecto del dominio británico.

The Declaration clearly expresses Enlightenment ideals. When its army was defeated by the colonial army, Britain was forced to recognize the independence of the colonies. A new government plan for the United States, the U.S. Constitution, was developed by James Madison and others. It reflected Montesquieu's idea about separate branches./En la Declaración se expresan claramente los ideales de la Ilustración. Cuando el ejército de las colonias venció al ejército inglés, Gran Bretaña se vio obligada a reconocer la independencia de las colonias. James Madison, entre otros, desarrolló un nuevo plan de gobierno para los Estados Unidos: la Constitución de los EE. UU., que incorporaba la idea de Montesquieu sobre la separación de poderes.

> **Circle the name of the person who wrote the document announcing the colonies' independence from British rule./Encierra en un círculo el nombre de la persona que escribió el documento que anunciaba la independencia de las colonias respecto del dominio británico.**

## THE FRENCH REVOLUTION/LA REVOLUCIÓN FRANCESA

The American Revolution inspired the French to rebel against their own king. Most commoners in France had no say in government at all, paid high taxes, and had very few rights. A National Assembly was formed to demand rights from King Louis XVI, but he refused to listen./La Guerra de Independencia de los Estados Unidos inspiró a los franceses a rebelarse contra su propio rey. La mayoría de los plebeyos de Francia no tenían voz en el gobierno, pagaban impuestos elevados y casi no tenían derechos. Se constituyó una Asamblea Nacional para exigirle derechos al rey Luis XVI, pero este se negó a escuchar.

The French Revolution began in 1789. The revolution's leaders issued a document similar

> **Why were the commoners of France angry at the king?/¿Por qué los plebeyos franceses estaban enojados con el rey?**
>
> _____
> _____
> _____

to the English Bill of Rights and the American Declaration of Independence, called the **Declaration of the Rights of Man and the Citizen,** During the revolution, King Louis XVI was tried and executed. It took the French several years to develop a stable new government, but they created a democracy./La Revolución francesa comenzó en 1789. Los líderes de la revolución redactaron un documento similar a la Declaración de Derechos inglesa y la Declaración de Independencia de los Estados Unidos: la **Declaración de los Derechos del Hombre y del Ciudadano.** Durante la revolución, el rey Luis XVI fue juzgado y ejecutado. Los franceses tardaron varios años en desarrollar un nuevo gobierno estable, pero lograron establecer un sistema democrático de gobierno.

> **What happened to Louis XVI during the revolution?/ ¿Qué sucedió con Luis XVI durante la revolución?**
>
> _____
>
> _____

## CHALLENGE ACTIVITY/ACTIVIDAD AVANZADA

**Critical Thinking: Make Inferences/Pensamiento crítico: Hacer inferencias** You are a revolutionary agitator in England, in the British colonies in America, or in France. How would you inspire your neighbors and friends to join you in the fight? Develop a character and write a persuasive speech that is historically appropriate to the period./Eres un agitador revolucionario de Inglaterra, de las colonias británicas de América del Norte o de Francia. ¿Cómo inspirarías a tus vecinos y amigos para que se unan a la lucha? Crea un personaje y escribe un discurso persuasivo que sea adecuado para este período desde el punto de vista histórico.

**DIRECTIONS/INSTRUCCIONES** Read each sentence and fill in the blank with the word in the word pair that best completes the sentence./Lee cada oración y escribe en el espacio en blanco la palabra del par de palabras que mejor la completa.

1. The _____ was signed by William of Orange before he became king. **(English Bill of Rights/Declaration of the Rights of Man and of the Citizen)**/La _____
_____ fue firmada por Guillermo de Orange antes de proclamarse rey. **(Declaración de Derechos inglesa/Declaración de los Derechos del Hombre y del Ciudadano)**

2. Before William became king he agreed to share power with Parliament and follow the principle of the _____
_____. **(Declaration of Independence/rule of law)**/Antes de convertirse en rey, Guillermo aceptó compartir el poder con el Parlamento y adoptar el principio _____. **(de la Declaración de Independencia/del imperio de la ley)**

3. The _____, which came out of the French Revolution, was similar to the English Bill of Rights. **(Declaration of Independence/Declaration of the Rights of Man and of the Citizen)**/La _____, que surgió como resultado de la Revolución francesa, era similar a la Declaración de Derechos inglesa. **(Declaración de Independencia/Declaración de los Derechos del Hombre y del Ciudadano)**

4. Thomas Jefferson wrote the _____, which declared the colonies' independence from British rule. **(Declaration of Independence/Declaration of the Rights of Man and of the Citizen)**/Thomas Jefferson escribió la _____, que declaraba la independencia de las colonias respecto del dominio británico. **(Declaración de Independencia/Declaración de los Derechos del Hombre y del Ciudadano)**

5. James Madison was a main author of the _____, which adopted Montesquieu's idea of dividing power among separate branches of government. **(U.S. Constitution/rule of law)**/James Madison fue uno de los principales autores _____
_____, que adoptó la idea de Montesquieu de que el gobierno debía estar separado en distintos poderes. **(de la Constitución de los EE. UU./del imperio de la ley)**

# Enlightenment and Revolution/La Ilustración y la Revolución

## Lesson/Lección 4

**MAIN IDEAS/IDEAS PRINCIPALES**

1. During the Napoleonic Era, Napoleon conquered vast territories in Europe and spread reforms across the continent./Durante la era napoleónica, Napoléon conquistó grandes territorios de Europa y estableció reformas en todo el continente.

2. At the Congress of Vienna, European leaders tried to restore the old monarchies and ensure peace./Durante el Congreso de Viena, los líderes europeos intentaron restaurar las antiguas monarquías y garantizar la paz.

3. Inspired by revolutionary ideals in Europe, Latin American colonies began to win their independence./Inspiradas por los ideales revolucionarios de Europa, las colonias latinoamericanas comenzaron a independizarse.

# Key Terms and People/Personas y palabras clave

**Napoleon Bonaparte/Napoleón Bonaparte** French general who became emperor/general francés que se convirtió en emperador

**coup d'état/golpe de estado** forceful overthrow of a government/derrocamiento de un gobierno por medio de la fuerza

**Klemens von Metternich/Klemens von Metternich** Austrian prince who led the Congress of Vienna/príncipe austriaco que presidió el Congreso de Viena

**conservatism/conservadurismo** movement to preserve the old social order and governments/movimiento que busca preservar el orden social y los gobiernos antiguos

**liberalism/liberalismo** movement for individual rights and liberties/movimiento a favor de los derechos y las libertades individuales

**Simon Bolívar/Simón Bolívar** a leader of South American independence movements/líder de los movimientos independentistas de América del Sur

# Lesson Summary/Resumen de la lección

## THE NAPOLEONIC ERA/LA ERA NAPOLEÓNICA

**Napoleon Bonaparte** became a hero in France after the French Revolution. In 1799, he took power in a **coup d'état,** the forceful overthrow of the government. While he was emperor, France controlled much of Europe. He improved the education and banking systems. Napoleon issued a new set of laws, called the Napoleonic Code, that brought new freedoms to the French people. But he did not allow opposition to his rule, and he

> Why do you think the new set of laws was known as the Napoleonic Code?/¿Por qué crees que el nuevo conjunto de leyes se llamó Código Napoleónico?
>
> _____
>
> _____

punished those who opposed him./**Napoleón Bonaparte** se convirtió en héroe de Francia después de la Revolución francesa. En 1799, asumió el poder mediante un **golpe de estado,** es decir, el derrocamiento de un gobierno por medio de la fuerza. Mientras Napoleón fue emperador, Francia controló gran parte de Europa. Napoleón mejoró los sistemas educativo y bancario, y redactó un nuevo conjunto de leyes, llamado Código Napoleónico, que otorgó nuevas libertades al pueblo francés. Sin embargo, no permitía la oposición a su gobierno y castigaba a quienes se oponían a él.

Napoleon's rule ended after the British defeated his navy and Russia defeated his armies. European nations worked together to remove him from power. They forced him to leave France. A year later, he returned and raised a new army. Napoleon was defeated by British and Russian forces at the Battle of Waterloo in Belgium in June 1815./El gobierno de Napoleón terminó cuando Inglaterra derrotó a su armada y Rusia venció a su ejército. Las naciones europeas se unieron para destituirlo y lo obligaron a abandonar Francia. Un año más tarde, Napoleón regresó y formó un nuevo ejército, pero fue derrotado por las fuerzas británicas y rusas en la Batalla de Waterloo, que tuvo lugar en Bélgica en junio de 1815.

## THE CONGRESS OF VIENNA/EL CONGRESO DE VIENA

At the Congress of Vienna, European leaders met to write a peace settlement. Prince **Klemens von Metternich** (MEH-tuhr-nik) of Austria led the meetings. France was forced to give back territories conquered by Napoleon. The shapes of the countries near France were changed to balance power in Europe. These changes were to ensure that no one power could threaten the rest of

> **What was the goal of the Congress of Vienna?/ ¿Cuál fue el objetivo del Congreso de Viena?**
>
> _____
>
> _____

Lesson/Lección 4, *continued*/*continuación*

Europe./Los líderes europeos se reunieron en el Congreso de Viena para redactar un acuerdo de paz. El príncipe austriaco **Klemens von Metternich** presidió estas reuniones. Francia se vio obligada a devolver territorios conquistados por Napoléon. Se modificaron las fronteras de los países que rodeaban Francia para equilibrar el poder en Europa. Estos cambios tenían como objetivo garantizar que ninguna potencia pudiera amenazar al resto de Europa.

These leaders opposed the ideals of the French Revolution. They preferred **conservatism** and the way things had been. They wanted the old system and old rulers to continue. **Liberalism,** which was built on individual rights, gained strength in the next few decades. Conservatives remained in control, but things had begun to change./Estos líderes se oponían a los ideales de la Revolución francesa. Preferían el **conservadurismo** y la manera en que las cosas habían sido en el pasado. Querían que continuaran los antiguos sistemas y gobernantes. El **liberalismo,** que se basaba en los derechos individuales, cobró fuerza en las décadas siguientes. Los conservadores permanecieron en el poder, pero las cosas habían empezado a cambiar.

> **Why did European leaders oppose the ideals of the French Revolution?/¿Por qué los líderes europeos se oponían a los ideales de la Revolución francesa?**
>
> _____
> _____
> _____
> _____

## LATIN AMERICAN INDEPENDENCE/ INDEPENDENCIA LATINOAMERICANA

The ideals of the French Revolution spread through the Caribbean and South America. Many colonies fought for their independence. In the French colony of Haiti, Toussaint L'Ouverture led a slave rebellion. The result was Haiti's independence. **Simon Bolívar** led the fight for independence across South America. By 1831, a dozen Latin American nations had won their freedom./Los ideales de la Revolución francesa se diseminaron por el Caribe y América del Sur. Muchas colonias lucharon por su independencia.

Lesson/Lección 4, *continued*/*continuación*

En la colonia francesa de Haití, Toussaint L'Ouverture lideró una rebelión de esclavos que culminó con la independencia de Haití. **Simón Bolívar** lideró la lucha por la independencia en América del Sur. Hacia 1831, una docena de naciones latinoamericanas habían obtenido su libertad.

Bolívar tried to build peace on the continent. But the new nations fought over borders. There was also conflict between conservatives and liberals. Conservatives wanted the rich to control the new governments. Liberals wanted the people to vote for leaders. These conflicts caused many governments to be unstable. There were many changes of leaders as the governments rose and fell./Bolívar intentó fomentar la paz en el continente, pero las nuevas naciones comenzaron a luchar por sus fronteras. También surgió un conflicto entre conservadores y liberales. Los conservadores querían que los ricos tuvieran el control de los nuevos gobiernos. Los liberales, en cambio, querían que el pueblo votara para elegir a sus líderes. Estos conflictos generaron inestabilidad en muchos gobiernos. Se produjeron muchos cambios de líderes a medida que los gobiernos ascendían y caían.

> **List one reason that the new governments in Latin America became unstable./**
> Menciona un motivo por el cual los gobiernos de Latinoamérica se volvieron inestables.
>
> _____
> _____
> _____
> _____

## CHALLENGE ACTIVITY/ACTIVIDAD AVANZADA

**Critical Thinking: Explain/Pensamiento crítico:**
**Explicar** Write a paragraph explaining why changes in government often occur as a result of conflict./Escribe un párrafo en el que expliques por qué los cambios de gobierno suelen ser producto de conflictos.

Lesson/Lección 4, *continued*/*continuación*

**DIRECTIONS/INSTRUCCIONES** Look at each set of four vocabulary terms. On the line provided, write the letter of the term that does not relate to the others./Observa cada conjunto de cuatro términos de vocabulario. En el espacio en blanco, escribe la letra del término que no tiene relación con los demás.

_____ 1. a. overthrow of government/derrocamiento de un gobierno
      b. coup d'état/golpe de estado
      c. conservatism/conservadurismo
      d. Napoleon Bonaparte/Napoleón Bonaparte

_____ 2. a. Klemens von Metternich/Klemens von Metternich
      b. Simon Bolívar/Simón Bolívar
      c. South America/América del Sur
      d. revolutionary/revolucionario

_____ 3. a. Klemens von Metternich/Klemens von Metternich
      b. prince of Austria/príncipe de Austria
      c. conservatism/conservadurismo
      d. liberalism/liberalismo

_____ 4. a. Latin America/Latinoamérica
      b. Napoleon Bonaparte/Napoleón Bonaparte
      c. South America/América del Sur
      d. Haiti/Haití

_____ 5. a. Enlightenment/Ilustración
      b. Simon Bolívar/Simón Bolívar
      c. Klemens von Metternich/Klemens von Metternich
      d. liberalism/liberalismo

# Industry and Imperialism/Industria e imperialismo

**MAIN IDEAS/IDEAS PRINCIPALES**

1. During the Industrial Revolution, new machines and methods dramatically changed the way goods were produced./Durante la Revolución Industrial, las nuevas máquinas y los nuevos métodos cambiaron drásticamente la forma en que se producían los bienes.

2. Industrialization and the factory system brought a new way of life to Europe and America./La industrialización y el sistema de fábrica llevaron a un nuevo estilo de vida en Europa y América del Norte.

## Key Terms and People/Personas y palabras clave

**factory system/sistema de fábrica** a production system in which machines rapidly produce goods/sistema de producción en el que las máquinas producen bienes rápidamente

**laissez-faire/laissez-faire** an attitude that government should stay out of business matters/postura que sostiene que el gobierno debe mantenerse al margen de los asuntos de negocios

**socialism/socialismo** a system in which businesses are owned by workers or the government/sistema en el que las empresas son propiedad de los trabajadores o del gobierno

**Karl Marx/Karl Marx** German philosopher who called for workers to unite against the capitalist system/filósofo alemán que alentó a los trabajadores a unirse en contra del sistema capitalista

## Lesson Summary/Resumen de la lección

**NEW MACHINES AND METHODS/NUEVAS MÁQUINAS Y NUEVOS MÉTODOS**

In the 1700s and 1800s, there were many new inventions and scientific discoveries. This period was called the Industrial Revolution. It changed the way people lived and worked. Factories grew. Great strides in communication and transportation made it easier for people to send messages and travel./En los siglos 18 y 19, surgieron muchos inventos nuevos y descubrimientos científicos. Este período fue denominado Revolución Industrial. La Revolución Industrial cambió el modo en

que la gente vivía y trabajaba. Las fábricas
crecieron. Grandes avances en la comunicación
y el transporte permitieron que las personas
pudieran enviar mensajes y viajar más fácilmente.

Machines like the cotton gin and the flying
shuttle sped up the weaving process for textiles.
The **factory system** made it possible to rapidly
produce large quantities of goods. The invention
of the steam engine provided power for the
machines and for trains and ships. Goods could
be delivered to faraway markets faster than
ever before./Máquinas como la desmotadora
de algodón y la lanzadera volante aceleraron el
proceso de fabricación de los productos textiles.
El **sistema de fábrica** permitió producir
rápidamente grandes cantidades de bienes. La
invención del motor a vapor suministró energía
para hacer funcionar las máquinas, los trenes y
los barcos. Los bienes podían ser entregados en
mercados lejanos más rápido que nunca.

> **How did development
> of the steam engine help
> business?**/¿De qué manera
> el desarrollo del motor de
> vapor ayudó a fomentar
> los negocios?
>
> _____
> _____
> _____
> _____

Factories grew in the United States and
Western Europe in the 1800s. The factory system
was funded by capitalists. These were bankers
and merchants who invested capital, or money.
Because they provided the money, they did not
want the government to control business. They
favored a **laissez-faire** (leh-say-FAR) approach
to the economy, in which the government leaves
business alone./En el siglo 19, aumentó la
cantidad de fábricas en los Estados Unidos y
Europa occidental. El sistema de fábrica estaba
financiado por capitalistas. Estos eran banqueros
y comerciantes que invertían capital, o dinero.
Como ellos proporcionaban el dinero, no
querían que el gobierno controlara los negocios.
Favorecían un enfoque **laissez-faire** de la
economía, en el cual el gobierno no interviene
en los negocios.

> **Underline the sentence that
> explains why capitalists did
> not want the government to
> control business.**/Subraya
> la oración que explica por
> qué los capitalistas no
> querían que el gobierno
> controlara los negocios.

Scientists found ways to kill germs and prevent diseases like smallpox. Chemists and physicists made discoveries about the structure of atoms, the particles that make up everything. Other fields of science, such as geology and psychology, advanced as well./Los científicos encontraron maneras de eliminar los gérmenes y prevenir enfermedades como la viruela. Los químicos y los físicos realizaron descubrimientos en relación con la estructura de los átomos, las partículas que componen todo. Otros campos de la ciencia, como la geología y la psicología, también avanzaron.

> **In what two ways did scientific research lead to medical advances?/ Menciona dos avances médicos que se lograron gracias a la investigación científica.**
>
> _____
> _____
> _____

## A NEW WAY OF LIFE/UN NUEVO ESTILO DE VIDA

Europeans began to move to other countries. Some farmers came to the United States because they received land. Many immigrants moved to cities in Europe and America and took new jobs in factories./Los europeos comenzaron a trasladarse a otros países. Algunos agricultores llegaron a los Estados Unidos porque recibieron tierras. Muchos inmigrantes se mudaron a ciudades de Europa y América, y ocuparon nuevos puestos de trabajo en fábricas.

Factory workers worked long hours in dangerous and tiring jobs for low wages. Even children worked in the factories. In addition to the hard work, people in the cities had to endure crowding, crime, and pollution./Los trabajadores de las fábricas trabajaban muchas horas en tareas peligrosas y agotadoras a cambio de salarios bajos. Incluso los niños trabajaban en las fábricas. Además del duro trabajo, los habitantes de las ciudades debían soportar el hacinamiento, la delincuencia y la contaminación.

Some people wanted to replace the capitalist system. They hoped workers would be treated better in a socialist system. **Socialism** is a system in which the government or the workers own the businesses. German philosopher **Karl Marx** called for workers to unite and bring down capitalism. Reform led child labor to be banned in the United States. Workers created labor unions./Algunas personas querían reemplazar el sistema capitalista. Creían que los trabajadores recibirían un mejor trato en un sistema socialista. El **socialismo** es un sistema en el que el gobierno o los trabajadores son los dueños de las empresas. El filósofo alemán **Karl Marx** alentó a los trabajadores a unirse para derrocar el capitalismo. Un movimiento de reforma llevó a la prohibición del trabajo infantil en los Estados Unidos. Los trabajadores crearon sindicatos.

> **Why did some people want to replace the capitalist system?/¿Por qué algunas personas querían reemplazar el sistema capitalista?**
>
> _____
>
> _____
>
> _____

A middle class grew. It included factory managers, clerks, merchants, engineers, doctors, and other well-educated people that had good incomes. Both the upper and middle classes had time for the arts. There were two major trends in the arts. Romanticism stressed beauty, nature, emotions, and simpler times. Realism tried to show everyday life as it really was./Surgió una clase media formada por gerentes de fábricas, empleados administrativos, comerciantes, ingenieros, médicos y otras personas que tenían una buena educación y buenos ingresos. Tanto la clase alta como la clase media tenían tiempo para las artes. Existían dos tendencias artísticas principales: el romanticismo, que enfatizaba la belleza, la naturaleza, las emociones y las épocas en las que la vida era más simple; y el realismo, que buscaba mostrar la vida cotidiana como realmente era.

> **Underline the sentence that lists different jobs in the middle class./Subraya la oración que menciona diferentes puestos de trabajo de la clase media.**

## CHALLENGE ACTIVITY/ACTIVIDAD AVANZADA

**Critical Thinking: Make Judgments/Pensamiento crítico: Dar opiniones** Do you think that a socialist system would have cured all of the problems caused by the Industrial Revolution? Write a one-page paper defending your opinion./¿Crees que un sistema socialista habría remediado todos los problemas causados por la Revolución Industrial? Escribe un ensayo de una página en el que defiendas tu opinión.

**DIRECTIONS/INSTRUCCIONES** Read each sentence and fill in the blank with the word in the word pair that best completes the sentence./Lee cada oración y escribe en el espacio en blanco la palabra del par de palabras que mejor la completa.

1. _____ means government should stay out of business matters. **(Laissez-faire/Socialism)**/El _____ significa que el gobierno debe mantenerse al margen de los asuntos de negocios. **(laissez-faire/socialismo)**

2. A system in which businesses are either owned by the workers or controlled by the government is called _____. **(socialism/factory system)**/Un sistema en el que las empresas son propiedad de los trabajadores o están controladas por el gobierno se llama _____. **(socialismo/sistema de fábrica)**

3. In the _____, machines rapidly produce large quantities of goods. **(laissez-faire/factory system)**/En el _____, las máquinas producen rápidamente grandes cantidades de bienes. **(laissez-faire/ sistema de fábrica)**

4. German philosopher _____ called for workers to unite in a revolution to bring down the capitalist system. **(laissez-faire/Karl Marx)**/El filósofo alemán _____ alentó a los trabajadores a unirse en una revolución para derrocar el sistema capitalista. **(laissez-faire/Karl Marx)**

# Industry and Imperialism/Industria e imperialismo

**MAIN IDEAS/IDEAS PRINCIPALES**

1. The search for raw materials led to a new wave of European involvement in Africa./La búsqueda de materias primas llevó a una nueva oleada de intervención europea en África.

2. The Scramble for Africa was a race by Europeans to form colonies there./El reparto de África fue una carrera llevada a cabo por los europeos para establecer colonias allí.

3. Some Africans resisted rule by Europeans./Algunos africanos se resistieron a ser gobernados por los europeos.

## Key Terms and People/Personas y palabras clave

**entrepreneurs/empresarios** independent businesspeople/gente de negocios independiente

**imperialism/imperialismo** attempts to dominate a country's government, trade, or culture/acciones para dominar el gobierno, el comercio o la cultura de un país

**Suez Canal/canal de Suez** a waterway built in Egypt in the 1860s to connect the Mediterranean and Red Seas/una vía de agua construida en Egipto en la década de 1860 para conectar los mares Mediterráneo y Rojo

**Berlin Conference/Conferencia de Berlín** series of meetings of European leaders, begun in 1884, intended to maintain order in Africa by dividing it among various European powers/una serie de reuniones de líderes europeos que se inició en 1884 para mantener el orden en África dividiéndola entre las diversas potencias europeas

**Boers/bóers** Dutch farmers who moved to South Africa in the 1600s/agricultores holandeses que llegaron a Sudáfrica en el siglo 17

## Lesson Summary/Resumen de la lección

### NEW INVOLVEMENT IN AFRICA/NUEVA INTERVENCIÓN EN ÁFRICA

By the 1880s, Europe's industrial growth led to a second rush to Africa. European **entrepreneurs** established colonies so they could have access to raw materials that were not available in Europe, such as minerals and woods. Colonists also became involved in local affairs and tried to force European values on the local people. Many entrepreneurs such as Cecil Rhodes felt it was

> **Why did European entrepreneurs establish colonies in Africa?/¿Por qué algunos empresarios europeos establecieron colonias en África?**
>
> _____
>
> _____
>
> _____
>
> _____

their duty to share their superior culture with the people of Africa. They demanded that Africans become Christian and speak European languages./En la década de 1880, el crecimiento industrial de Europa llevó a una segunda carrera por África. Algunos **empresarios** europeos establecieron colonias para tener acceso a materias primas, como minerales y maderas, que no estaban disponibles en Europa. Los colonos también se involucraron en los asuntos locales e intentaron imponer los valores europeos a la población local. Muchos empresarios, como Cecil Rhodes, sentían que debían compartir su cultura superior con los pueblos de África. Exigían que los africanos se convirtieran al cristianismo y hablaran los idiomas europeos.

African colonies began to produce cash crops for the Europeans instead of growing food for the people of Africa to eat. This kind of attempt to dominate a country's government, trade, or culture is called **imperialism.** Famines got worse, there were food shortages, and thousands of Africans died./Las colonias africanas comenzaron a producir cultivos comerciales para los europeos en lugar de cultivar alimentos para que los pueblos de África pudieran comer. Este tipo de acciones para dominar el gobierno, el comercio o la cultura de un país se denomina **imperialismo.** Las hambrunas empeoraron, hubo escasez de alimentos y miles de africanos murieron.

The English government got involved in Africa to guard their access to the **Suez Canal,** a fast route to their colonies in India. In the 1880s, they invaded and took partial control of Egypt./ El gobierno inglés intervino en África para custodiar su acceso al **canal de Suez,** una ruta de acceso rápido a sus colonias en la India. En la década de 1880, invadieron y tomaron control parcial de Egipto.

> **What two things did many Europeans in Africa believe about European culture?/ ¿Qué dos cosas sobre la cultura europea sostenían muchos europeos en África?**
>
> _____
> _____
> _____
> _____

> **Why was the Suez Canal important to the English government?/¿Por qué el canal de Suez era importante para el gobierno inglés?**
>
> _____
> _____
> _____

## THE SCRAMBLE FOR AFRICA/EL REPARTO DE ÁFRICA

Leaders of Europe met at the **Berlin Conference** in 1884 and agreed on how to divide Africa among themselves. The conference paid little attention to the African people. It divided kingdoms, clans, and families, and forced rivals and enemies to live together./En 1884, los líderes de Europa se reunieron en la **Conferencia de Berlín** y acordaron el modo en que se repartirían África entre ellos. La conferencia prácticamente no tuvo en cuenta a los pueblos africanos. Dividió reinos, clanes y familias, y obligó a rivales y enemigos a vivir juntos.

> Underline the sentence that describes the effect of the Berlin Conference on African people./Subraya la oración que describe el efecto de la Conferencia de Berlín sobre los pueblos de África.

Despite the Berlin Conference, war broke out in the late 1890s between British and Dutch settlers. Dutch farmers called **Boers** had lived in South Africa since the 1600s. After gold was discovered there, the British conquered the Boers and took South Africa as a colony./A pesar de la Conferencia de Berlín, a fines de la década de 1890 estalló la guerra entre los colonos británicos y holandeses. Los agricultores holandeses llamados **bóers** habían vivido en Sudáfrica desde el siglo 17. Cuando se descubrió que había oro allí, los británicos conquistaron a los bóers y tomaron Sudáfrica como colonia.

## AFRICAN RESISTANCE/RESISTENCIA AFRICANA

Like the Boers, native Africans did not want to be ruled by others or to give up their own cultures. Europeans crushed most resistance quickly, but it was not always easy. The fierce Zulu army fought off the British for more than 50 years. In the end, however, the Zulu were defeated./Al igual que los bóers, los pueblos originarios de África no querían ser gobernados por otros ni renunciar a sus propias culturas. Los europeos doblegaron la mayor parte de la resistencia rápidamente, pero no siempre fue fácil. El feroz ejército zulú repelió a los británicos por más de 50 años. Sin embargo, al final los zulúes fueron derrotados.

Ethiopia did avoid European control. Emperor Menelik II created a powerful army by buying modern weapons from Europe. In 1895, Ethiopia fought off an Italian invasion at the Battle of Adwa. This victory is celebrated as a high point in Ethiopian history./Etiopía logró evitar el control europeo. El emperador Menelik II formó un ejército poderoso mediante la compra de armas modernas a Europa. En 1895, Etiopía repelió la invasión italiana en la Batalla de Adwa. Esta victoria se celebra como un hito en la historia de Etiopía.

> **Which African nation avoided European control?/¿Qué nación africana evitó el control europeo?**
> _____

> **Underline the name of this nation's emperor. Circle the name of the battle his country won in 1895./Subraya el nombre del emperador de esta nación. Encierra en un círculo el nombre de la batalla que ganó este país en 1895.**

## CHALLENGE ACTIVITY/ACTIVIDAD AVANZADA

**Critical Thinking: Analyze Cause and Effect/Pensamiento crítico: Analizar causa y efecto** Write a short essay about the problems that European imperialism caused in Africa and the effects these problems had on the African population./Escribe un ensayo breve acerca de los problemas que causó el imperialismo europeo en África y los efectos que estos problemas tuvieron sobre la población africana.

## DIRECTIONS/INSTRUCCIONES Write a word or descriptive phrase to describe each term./Escribe una palabra o frase descriptiva para describir cada término.

1. imperialism/imperialismo _____

_____

2. entrepreneurs/empresarios _____

_____

3. Europeans/europeos _____

_____

**DIRECTIONS/INSTRUCCIONES** Look at each set of four vocabulary terms. On the line provided, write the letter of the term that does not relate to the others./Observa cada conjunto de cuatro términos de vocabulario. En el espacio en blanco, escribe la letra del término que no tiene relación con los demás.

_____ 4. a. Great Britain/Gran Bretaña
　　　　　b. the Boer War/la Guerra de los bóers
　　　　　c. Dutch farmers/agricultores holandeses
　　　　　d. Indian colonies/colonias en la India

_____ 5. a. Egypt/Egipto
　　　　　b. Ethiopia/Etiopía
　　　　　c. Red Sea/mar Rojo
　　　　　d. Mediterranean Sea/mar Mediterráneo

_____ 6. a. Zulu army/ejército zulú
　　　　　b. European leaders/líderes europeos
　　　　　c. series of meetings/serie de reuniones
　　　　　d. forced enemies together/obligaron a los
　　　　　　 enemigos a vivir juntos

## Industry and Imperialism/Industria e imperialismo

**MAIN IDEAS/IDEAS PRINCIPALES**

1. The British made India into a colony in the 1700s and 1800s./Los británicos colonizaron la India en los siglos 18 y 19.

2. European countries used force to make China open its ports to trade./Los países europeos se valieron de la fuerza para lograr que China abriera sus puertos al comercio.

3. Led by the United States, the West began to trade in Japan./Liderado por los Estados Unidos, Occidente comenzó a comerciar con Japón.

4. Britain colonized and allowed self-rule in Australia and New Zealand./Gran Bretaña colonizó Australia y Nueva Zelanda, y permitió el autogobierno en esos dos países.

## Key Terms and People/Personas y palabras clave

**British East India Company/Compañía Británica de las Indias Orientales** a British company created to control trade with India and East Asia/empresa británica creada para controlar el comercio con la India y Asia oriental

**Raj/Raj** the period of British control in India, from the Hindi word for "rule"/ el período de control británico en la India; su nombre proviene de la palabra "ley" en hindi

**Guangzhou/Guangzhou** Chinese port city, known to the British as Canton/ ciudad portuaria china, conocida por los británicos como Cantón

**spheres of influence/esferas de influencia** areas of China over which other countries had economic power/áreas de China sobre las cuales otros países tenían poder económico

**Boxer Rebellion/Levantamiento de los bóxers** an attempt in 1899 to drive all Westerners out of China/un intento, iniciado en 1899, por sacar a todos los occidentales de China

**Aborigines/aborígenes** native people of Australia; the longest ongoing culture in the world/los pueblos originarios de Australia; la cultura más antigua del mundo en la actualidad

**Maori/maorí** people who settled New Zealand between AD 950 and 1300; accepted British rule in exchange for land rights/pueblo que se asentó en Nueva Zelanda entre 950 y 1300 d. C.; los maoríes aceptaron el gobierno británico a cambio de derechos sobre las tierras

## Lesson Summary/Resumen de la lección

### THE BRITISH IN INDIA/LOS BRITÁNICOS EN LA INDIA

In the late 1700s, the **British East India Company** became involved in Indian politics. Before long, it controlled nearly all of India. In 1857 sepoys—Indian soldiers who fought in the British army—staged the Sepoy Rebellion to oppose the British East India Company's policies. Brutal fighting lasted for more than two years./A fines del siglo 18, la **Compañía Británica de las Indias Orientales** se involucró en la política india. En poco tiempo, llegó a controlar casi toda la India. En 1857, los cipayos (soldados indios que luchaban para el ejército británico) organizaron la Rebelión de los cipayos para oponerse a las políticas de la Compañía Británica de las Indias Orientales. La lucha brutal duró más de dos años.

> **Who were the sepoys?/ ¿Quiénes eran los cipayos?**
> _____
> _____
> _____

Then the British government began to directly control India in a period called the **Raj** (RAHZH). During this time, the British forced Indian children in schools to learn English. They tried to spread Christianity and banned some Indian customs. Soon, many Indian people staged protests and boycotted British goods./Luego, el gobierno británico comenzó a controlar la India directamente en un período denominado **Raj.** Durante ese tiempo, los británicos obligaron a los niños indios a aprender inglés en las escuelas. Intentaron difundir el cristianismo y prohibieron algunas costumbres indias. Pronto, muchas personas de la India organizaron protestas y organizaron boicots contra los bienes británicos.

> **Underline three things the British did in India during the Raj./Subraya tres cosas que los británicos hicieron en la India durante el Raj.**

### EUROPEANS IN CHINA/LOS EUROPEOS EN CHINA

Through the 1700s, China's rulers allowed European traders to live in only a single city, **Guangzhou** (gwang-JOH). In 1839, the British navy forced the Chinese to open other ports to trade. Then the Chinese also had to make more such deals with other countries. Europeans divided China into many **spheres of influence.** In 1899, some Chinese rose up violently in the **Boxer Rebellion.** The Western powers easily put down the fighting./Durante el siglo 18, los gobernantes de China solamente permitieron a los comerciantes europeos vivir en una ciudad, **Guangzhou.** En 1839, la armada británica obligó a los chinos a abrir otros puertos al comercio. Luego, los chinos también tuvieron que hacer más tratos de este tipo con otros países. Los europeos dividieron China en varias **esferas de influencia.** En 1899, algunos chinos se rebelaron violentamente en el **Levantamiento de los bóxers.** Sin embargo, las potencias europeas sofocaron el levantamiento con facilidad.

> **How did the Western powers respond to the Boxer Rebellion?/¿Cómo respondieron las potencias europeas a la Rebelión de los Bóxers?**
> _____
> _____

## THE WEST IN JAPAN/OCCIDENTE EN JAPÓN

Japan had been able to remain isolated until 1852. American naval commander Matthew Perry then forced the Japanese to open trade directly with him. Japan's new rulers decided their best plan was to modernize. They studied Western military tactics and economic practices and copied them./Japón había logrado mantenerse aislado hasta 1852. Entonces, el comandante de la armada estadounidense Matthew Perry obligó a los japoneses a abrir el comercio directamente con él. Los nuevos gobernantes de Japón decidieron que la mejor estrategia sería modernizarse. Estudiaron las tácticas militares y las prácticas económicas occidentales y las copiaron.

> **What did Japanese rulers do to modernize Japan?/ ¿Qué hicieron los gobernantes japoneses para modernizar Japón?**
> _____
> _____
> _____
> _____

## AUSTRALIA AND NEW ZEALAND/ AUSTRALIA Y NUEVA ZELANDA

British criminals who settled in Australia discovered that the **Aborigines** inhabited the continent. The **Maori** people had lived in New Zealand for hundreds of years. Australia and New Zealand became self-governing British colonies./Los ex convictos británicos que se establecieron en Australia descubrieron que el continente estaba habitado por **aborígenes.** El pueblo **maorí** había vivido en Nueva Zelanda por cientos de años. Australia y Nueva Zelanda se convirtieron en colonias británicas autónomas.

As Australia's population grew, colonists killed Aborigines or moved them off of their land. Eventually, disease and several wars against powerful British weapons forced the Maori to move to a remote part of New Zealand./A medida que la población de Australia creció, los colonos asesinaron a los aborígenes o los obligaron a abandonar sus tierras. Finalmente, las enfermedades y varias guerras contra las poderosas armas británicas forzaron al pueblo maorí a trasladarse a una zona remota de Nueva Zelanda.

> **What two words describe the kind of colonies that Australia and New Zealand became?/Menciona dos palabras que describan el tipo de colonia en que se convirtieron Australia y Nueva Zelanda.**
>
> _____
>
> _____

## CHALLENGE ACTIVITY/ACTIVIDAD AVANZADA

**Critical Thinking: Describe/Pensamiento crítico: Describir** Suppose it is the 1800s. You have lived in India, China, Japan, Australia, or New Zealand for your entire life. Write a journal entry telling about how the Europeans have affected daily life in your country./Imagina que es el siglo 19. Has vivido toda tu vida en la India, China, Japón, Australia o Nueva Zelanda. Escribe una entrada de diario en la que cuentes cómo los europeos han influido en la vida cotidiana de tu país.

**DIRECTIONS/INSTRUCCIONES** Match the terms in the first column with their correct definition from the second column by placing the letter of the correct definition in the space provided before each term./Une los términos de la primera columna con su definición correcta en la segunda columna. Escribe la letra de la definición correcta en el espacio que precede a cada término.

_____ 1. Guangzhou/Guangzhou

    a. Australians who are the longest ongoing culture in the world/ australianos que pertenecen a la cultura más antigua del mundo en la actualidad

_____ 2. spheres of influence/ esferas de influencia

    b. British business created to control trade with India and East Asia/ empresa británica creada para controlar el comercio con la India y Asia oriental

_____ 3. Raj/Raj

    c. Chinese port city known to the British as Canton/ciudad portuaria china conocida por los británicos como Cantón

_____ 4. Maori/maorí

    d. 1899 attempt to drive all Westerners out of China/intento por expulsar a todos los occidentales de China en 1899

_____ 5. Boxer Rebellion/ Levantamiento de los bóxers

    e. from the Hindi word for "rule"/ proveniente de la palabra "ley" en hindi

_____ 6. Aborigines/aborígenes

    f. areas of China where other countries had economic power/ áreas de China donde otros países tenían poder económico

_____ 7. British East India Company/ Compañía Británica de las Indias Orientales

    g. New Zealand people who accepted British rule for land rights/pueblo de Nueva Zelanda que aceptó el gobierno británico a cambio de derechos sobre las tierras

# Industry and Imperialism/Industria e imperialismo

## Lesson/Lección 4

**MAIN IDEAS/IDEAS PRINCIPALES**

1. Many people living in Spain's colonies in both the Caribbean and the Pacific wanted independence./Muchas de las personas que vivían en las colonias españolas del Caribe y el Pacífico querían la independencia.

2. In 1898, the United States went to war with Spain in the Spanish-American War./En 1898, los Estados Unidos entraron en guerra con España en la Guerra Hispano-Americana.

3. The United States gained territories in the Caribbean and Pacific./Los Estados Unidos obtuvieron territorios en el Caribe y el Pacífico.

## Key Terms and People/Personas y palabras clave

**Emilio Aguinaldo/Emilio Aguinaldo** Filipino revolutionary who fought for independence from Spain/revolucionario filipino que luchó por la independencia respecto de España

**José Martí/José Martí** Cuban revolutionary who spoke out for independence from Spain/revolucionario cubano que se pronunció a favor de la independencia respecto de España

**yellow journalism/prensa amarilla** newspapers that exaggerate the facts to attract readers/periódicos que exageran los hechos para atraer a los lectores

**Anti-Imperialist League/Liga antiimperialista** group opposed to creating an American colonial empire/grupo que se opuso a la creación de un imperio colonial estadounidense

**Platt Amendment/Enmienda Platt** part of the 1902 Cuban constitution that limited Cuba's right to make treaties and allowed the United States to be involved in Cuban affairs/parte de la Constitución de Cuba de 1902 que limitó el derecho de Cuba a hacer tratados y permitió a los Estados Unidos intervenir en los asuntos cubanos

## Lesson Summary/Resumen de la lección

### SPAIN'S COLONIES IN THE CARIBBEAN AND THE PACIFIC/ COLONIAS ESPAÑOLAS EN EL CARIBE Y EL PACÍFICO

At the end of the 1800s, Spain controlled Puerto Rico and Cuba in the Carribean. In the Pacific, Spain controlled the Philippines and Guam. Spain's control of its colonies weakened as revolutions broke out in the Philippines and Cuba. **Emilio Aguinaldo** was a leader of the rebellion in the Philippines. Spain agreed to change the government. Aguinaldo was exiled. In 1868, Cuba fought an unsuccessful war for independence against Spain. **José Martí** was banished from Cuba for speaking out for Cuban independence. In 1895, Martí returned to launch a second war against Spain, but he was killed early in the fighting./A fines del siglo 19, España controlaba Puerto Rico y Cuba en el Caribe, y las Filipinas y Guam en el Pacífico. El control que ejercía España sobre sus colonias se debilitó a medida que estallaron revoluciones en Filipinas y Cuba. Uno de los líderes del levantamiento en Filipinas fue **Emilio Aguinaldo.** España aceptó cambiar el gobierno, y Aguinaldo fue exiliado. En 1868, Cuba libró una guerra contra España por la independencia, pero no tuvo éxito. **José Martí** fue expulsado de Cuba por pronunciarse a favor de la independencia cubana. En 1895, Martí regresó para emprender una segunda guerra contra España, pero fue asesinado poco después de empezar la lucha.

The United States was interested in the revolutions in the Philippines and Cuba. Americans came to believe that the United States should protect its trade with a modern navy. Newspapers in the United States printed sensational news stories to sell their papers. This technique, where facts are exaggerated, is called **yellow journalism.** Many Americans were angered by stories about the Spanish brutality in Cuba. They wanted the U.S. military to support the Cuban rebels./Los Estados Unidos mostraron interés por las revoluciones en Filipinas y Cuba. El pueblo estadounidense llegó a creer que debían proteger su comercio con una armada moderna. La prensa estadounidense imprimió noticias sensacionalistas para vender sus periódicos. Esta técnica, que consiste en exagerar

**Circle the countries in the Pacific. Underline the Caribbean colonies under Spanish control in the 1800s.**/Encierra en un círculo los países del Pacífico. Subraya las colonias del Caribe que estaban bajo control español en el siglo 19.

**How did Spain handle rebels in their colonies?**/¿Cómo manejó España a los rebeldes en sus colonias?

_____
_____
_____

los hechos, se denomina **prensa amarilla.** Muchos estadounidenses se enfadaron por las historias acerca de la brutalidad española en Cuba. Querían que el ejército de los Estados Unidos apoyara a los rebeldes cubanos.

## WAR ERUPTS/ESTALLA LA GUERRA

In 1898, President McKinley sent a battleship, the USS *Maine*, to Cuba. The ship exploded and 266 men died. The American press blamed Spain. "Remember the *Maine*!" was the rallying cry for angry Americans. The United States declared war against Spain. U.S. troops, aided by Cuban rebels, defeated the Spanish. They also successfully invaded Spanish-held Puerto Rico. American warships also attacked the Spanish fleet in the Philippines. With help from Filipino rebels, the Americans took control of Manila, the capital city./En 1898, el presidente McKinley envió a Cuba un buque de guerra, el *USS Maine*. La nave explotó y murieron 266 hombres. La prensa estadounidense culpó a España. "¡Recuerden al *Maine*!" fue el grito de guerra para los enfadados estadounidenses. Los Estados Unidos le declararon la guerra a España. Las tropas estadounidenses, ayudadas por los rebeldes cubanos, derrotaron a los españoles. También invadieron con éxito Puerto Rico, que aún se encontraba bajo dominio español. Los buques de guerra estadounidenses también atacaron la flota española en Filipinas. Con la ayuda de los rebeldes filipinos, los estadounidenses tomaron el control de Manila, la capital.

> **How did Cuban and Filipino rebels help U.S. interests?/¿Cómo colaboraron los rebeldes cubanos y filipinos con los intereses de los E.E. U.U.?**
>
> _____
>
> _____
>
> _____

## THE UNITED STATES GAINS TERRITORIES/ LOS ESTADOS UNIDOS AMPLÍAN SU TERRITORIO

A peace treaty between Spain and the United States was signed in 1899. The treaty placed Cuba, Guam, Puerto Rico, and the Philippines under

U.S. control. The **Anti-Imperialist League** was formed by some Americans who opposed the treaty and the creation of an American colonial empire. They believed people in those territories did not have self-government. In Cuba, the United States helped write the Cuban constitution. This included the **Platt Amendment,** which allowed for U.S. involvement in Cuban affairs./En 1899, se firmó un tratado de paz entre España y los Estados Unidos. El tratado colocaba a Cuba, Guam, Puerto Rico y las Filipinas bajo el control de los EE. UU. Algunos estadounidenses que se oponían al tratado y a la creación de un imperio colonial estadounidense formaron la **Liga antiimperialista.** Sostenían que las personas de esos territorios no tenían un gobierno propio. En Cuba, los Estados Unidos ayudaron a redactar la constitución cubana. Esta incluía la **Enmienda Platt,** que permitió a los EE. UU. involucrarse en los asuntos cubanos.

In 1903 Panama declared its independence from Colombia. Panama's signed a treaty that gave the United States a strip of land where the Panama Canal was built./En 1903, Panamá declaró su independencia respecto de Colombia. Panamá firmó un tratado que otorgó a los Estados Unidos una franja de tierra donde se construyó el canal de Panamá.

> Underline what the peace treaty between Spain and the United States did./ Subraya lo que estableció el tratado de paz entre España y los Estados Unidos.

## CHALLENGE ACTIVITY/ACTIVIDAD AVANZADA
**Critical Thinking: Summarize/Pensamiento crítico: Resumir** Write a short essay that describes how Spain's colonies became U.S. territories in 1899. Include information that led to the signing of a peace treaty between the United States and Spain./ Escribe un ensayo breve en el que describas cómo las colonias de España se convirtieron en territorios de los EE. UU. en 1899. Incluye información que llevó a la firma de un tratado de paz entre los Estados Unidos y España.

Lesson/Lección 4, *continued/continuación*

| Anti-Imperialist League/Liga antiimperialista | Emilio Aguinaldo/ Emilio Aguinaldo | José Martí/ José Martí |
| Platt Amendment/Enmienda Platt | yellow journalism/ prensa amarilla | |

**DIRECTIONS/INSTRUCCIONES** Answer each question by writing a sentence that contains at least one term from the word bank. Not all terms are used./Responde cada pregunta con una oración que contenga al menos una palabra del banco de palabras. No se usan todos los términos.

1. How did newspapers affect U.S. support for military action in Cuba?/¿Cómo influyó la prensa en el apoyo estadounidense a la acción militar en Cuba?

_____

_____

_____

2. What happened to Cuban rebels who spoke out for independence from Spain?/¿Qué les pasó a los rebeldes cubanos que se pronunciaron a favor de la independencia respecto de España?

_____

_____

_____

3. Why weren't all Americans pleased with the peace treaty signed with Spain in 1899?/¿Por qué no todos los estadounidenses estaban satisfechos con el tratado de paz que se firmó con España en 1899?

_____

_____

_____

4. How did the United States give itself power to control Cuban affairs?/¿Cómo lograron los Estados Unidos obtener poder para controlar los asuntos cubanos?

_____

_____

_____

# Nationalism and World War I/Nacionalismo y Primera Guerra Mundial

## Lesson/Lección 1

**MAIN IDEAS/IDEAS PRINCIPALES**

1. Nationalism sparked independence movements in Europe./El nacionalismo desencadenó movimientos a favor de la independencia en Europa.

2. Newly created nations in Europe sought to expand their influence./Las nuevas naciones surgidas en Europa buscaban expandir su influencia.

## Key Terms and People/Personas y palabras clave

**nationalism/nacionalismo** devotion and loyalty to one's country/devoción y lealtad hacia el país propio

**nation-states/naciones Estado** self-governing countries made up of people with a common culture/países autónomos cuyos habitantes tienen una cultura común

**Giuseppe Garibaldi/Giuseppe Garibaldi** Sicilian leader who helped unite Italy into a single country/líder siciliano que ayudó a unificar Italia en un solo país

**Otto von Bismarck/Otto von Bismark** Prussian leader who developed a plan to unify Germany/líder prusiano que ideó un plan para unificar Alemania

## Lesson Summary/Resumen de la lección

### NATIONALIST UPRISINGS/
### REBELIONES NACIONALISTAS

**Nationalism** is devotion and loyalty to one's country. It usually comes about among people who share a common language and religion and who believe that they share a common culture. During the 1800s, nationalism was a powerful force. It led to independence movements in Latin America. It also led some groups in Europe to create their own nations, which changed the map of Europe./El **nacionalismo** es la devoción y la lealtad hacia el país propio. Generalmente, surge entre personas que comparten idioma y religión, y que piensan que comparten una misma cultura. En el siglo 19, el nacionalismo fue una fuerza poderosa que desencadenó los movimientos de independencia en América Latina. También llevó a varios grupos en Europa a·crear sus propias naciones, lo que cambió el mapa de Europa.

> What factors help feelings of nationalism to develop?/¿Qué factores contribuyeron a crear el sentimiento nacionalista?
> _____
> _____
> _____

In the early 1800s, many people who had been conquered by Napoleon wanted to rule themselves. They began to unite with others who shared their cultures. They supported the idea of **nation-states,** self-governing countries of people with a common cultural background./A principios del siglo 19, muchos de los pueblos que habían sido conquistados por Napoleón querían gobernarse a sí mismos. Empezaron a unirse con otros pueblos que tenían la misma cultura. Apoyaban la idea de las **naciones Estado,** países autónomos cuyos habitantes comparten un trasfondo cultural común.

> **Underline the definition of nation-states./Subraya la definición de naciones Estado.**

After Napoleon was defeated, some groups in Europe rebelled against foreign control. Some succeeded such as Greece, which won independence from the Ottoman Empire. But some revolutions failed. Hungarian and Czech nationalists in the Austrian Empire were defeated. Italians and Germans failed to form their own countries at that time too./Después de que Napoleón fue derrotado, algunos grupos en Europa se rebelaron contra el control extranjero. Algunos tuvieron éxito, como Grecia, que se independizó del Imperio otomano. Sin embargo, otras revoluciones fracasaron. Por ejemplo, los nacionalistas húngaros y checos del Imperio austriaco fueron derrotados. En esa misma época, los italianos y los alemanes también fracasaron en su intento de formar países propios.

> **Which groups failed to gain independence the first time they tried?/¿Qué grupos fracasaron en su primer intento de obtener la independencia?**
>
> _____
> _____
> _____

## NEW COUNTRIES ARE FORMED/SURGEN NUEVAS NACIONES

In the early 1800s, what is now Italy was divided into many states. Each had a different ruler. As nationalism grew, many people in Italy wanted to unite into one country. Efforts to unite the country failed at first. Then Camillo di Cavour became prime minister of Sardinia and formed alliances. After driving the Austrians from the north out of the area, other Italian states united with Sardinia. Also, **Giuseppe Garibaldi** overthrew the government in Sicily. He and Camillo di Cavour joined their lands together into one kingdom./A principios del siglo 19, el territorio que actualmente es Italia estaba dividido en muchos estados. Cada uno de ellos tenía un gobernante distinto. A medida que se extendió el nacionalismo, muchas personas en Italia querían unirse para formar un solo país. En un primer momento, los esfuerzos de unir el país fracasaron. Entonces, Camillo di Cavour se convirtió en el primer ministro de Cerdeña y formó alianzas. Después de expulsar del área a los austriacos del norte, otros estados italianos se unieron a Cerdeña. Además, **Giuseppe Garibaldi** derrocó el gobierno de Sicilia. Él y Camillo di Cavour unieron sus territorios en un solo reino.

> **Who were the men responsible for the unification of Italy?/¿Quiénes fueron los responsables de la unificación de Italia?**
> _____
> _____

Germany was also made of many small states in the 1800s. German nationalists grew stronger as Italy became united. Prussia was the largest of the German states and Austria was its closest rival. **Otto von Bismarck** was the prime minister of Prussia. He came up with a plan to unite Germany. He built a strong army and won wars against Denmark and Austria. Prussia's victories gave it more territory and made it leader of the northern German states. Then Bismarck waged war against France. Feelings of nationalism in the southern German states caused them to side with Prussia. They won and agreed to unite. Bismarck's plan had succeeded, and the German Empire was proclaimed in 1871. King Wilhelm of Prussia became emperor, ruling over all of Germany except Austria./En el siglo 19, Alemania también estaba formada por muchos estados pequeños. Los nacionalistas alemanes se fortalecieron

> **How did Otto von Bismarck get smaller states to join Prussia without attacking them?/¿Cómo logró Otto von Bismark que los estados más pequeños se unieran a Prusia sin atacarlos?**
> _____
> _____

después de la unificación de Italia. Prusia era el estado alemán más grande y Austria era su rival más cercano. **Otto von Bismark** era el primer ministro de Prusia. Ideó un plan para unificar Alemania. Formó un poderoso ejército y ganó guerras contra Dinamarca y Austria. Estas victorias le añadieron más territorios a Prusia y la convirtieron en líder de los estados alemanes del norte. Entonces, Bismark le declaró la guerra a Francia. El sentimiento nacionalista en los estados alemanes del sur los llevó a aliarse con Prusia. Ganaron y acordaron unirse. El plan de Bismark tuvo éxito y, en 1871, se proclamó el Imperio alemán. El rey Guillermo de Prusia se convirtió en emperador y gobernó toda Alemania, excepto Austria.

Then Germany concentrated on building its economy and military. It joined other European countries in competition for colonies. European imperialism, or control of a region or country by another country, strengthened during this time. By controlling other regions of the world, Europeans gained raw materials for industry./Entonces, Alemania se concentró en desarrollar su economía y su ejército. Además, se unió a otros países europeos en la competencia por las colonias. El imperialismo europeo, o el control de una región o país por parte de otro país, se fortaleció durante este período. Al controlar otras regiones del mundo, los europeos obtenían materias primas para sus industrias.

## CHALLENGE ACTIVITY/ACTIVIDAD AVANZADA
### Critical Thinking: Evaluate/Pensamiento crítico:
Evaluar Write an explanation for how nationalism contributed to the unification of Italy and the unification of Germany./Explica cómo el nacionalismo contribuyó a la unificación de Italia y a la unificación de Alemania.

**DIRECTIONS/INSTRUCCIONES** Match the terms or description in the first column with their correct definition from the second column by placing the letter of the correct definition in the space provided before each term or description./Une los términos o descripciones de la primera columna con su definición correcta en la segunda columna. Escribe la letra de la definición correcta en el espacio que precede a cada término o descripción.

_____ 1. Self-governing countries made up of people with a common background/ Países autónomos cuyos habitantes comparten un trasfondo común

a. Giuseppe Garibaldi/ Giuseppe Garibaldi

_____ 2. Devotion and loyalty to one's country/ Devoción y lealtad hacia el país propio

b. Otto von Bismarck/ Otto von Bismark

_____ 3. Leader who overthrew the government of Sicily/Líder que derrocó el gobierno de Sicilia

c. nation-states/ naciones Estado

_____ 4. Prussian prime minister who unified Germany/Primer ministro de Prusia que unificó Alemania

d. nationalism/ nacionalismo

# Nationalism and World War I/Nacionalismo y Primera Guerra Mundial

---

**MAIN IDEAS/IDEAS PRINCIPALES**

1. The onset of World War I can be traced to nationalism, imperialism, and the buildup of military forces in Europe./El origen de la Primera Guerra Mundial puede encontrarse en el nacionalismo, el imperialismo y el aumento de las fuerzas militares en Europa.

2. World War I was notable for new forms of warfare and fighting on several continents./La Primera Guerra Mundial se caracterizó por las nuevas formas de combate y por los enfrentamientos en distintos continentes.

3. The Allies' victory over the Central Powers came soon after the United States entered the war./La victoria de los Aliados sobre las Potencias Centrales se produjo poco después de que los Estados Unidos entraran en la guerra.

---

## Key Terms and People/Personas y palabras clave

**militarism/militarismo** the idea that a country should use a strong military to defend its interests/la idea de que un país debe usar un ejército poderoso para defender sus intereses

**genocide/genocidio** a deliberate killing of a large group of people/exterminio deliberado de un grupo grande de personas

## Lesson Summary/Resumen de la lección

### THE ONSET OF WAR/ORIGEN DE LA GUERRA

In 1914, war broke out in Europe. Factors that led to this conflict included nationalism, imperialism, and militarism./En 1914, estalló la guerra en Europa. Entre los factores que llevaron a este conflicto se incluyen el nacionalismo, el imperialismo y el militarismo.

Nationalism caused strong rivalries among Europe's nations. People were willing to go to war to prove their nation's superiority. Imperialism also caused rivalries. Many people believed that if their country had an empire, it was great. Nations needed raw materials from the colonies for their industries too. So the race to get these territories caused crises. Also, the idea that a country should use a strong military to defend its interest, or **militarism,** grew. European nations built large armies, and then they began to fear one another.

> **What caused strong rivalries among European nations?/¿Qué causó fuertes rivalidades entre las naciones europeas?**
>
> _____
>
> _____

> **Underline the sentence that explains why European alliances formed./Subraya la oración que explica por qué se formaron las alianzas europeas.**

Nations formed alliances and promised to defend their allies if attacked./El nacionalismo provocó grandes rivalidades entre las naciones de Europa. Las personas estaban dispuestas a ir a la guerra para demostrar la superioridad de su nación. El imperialismo también generó rivalidades. Muchas personas pensaban que era estupendo que su país se convirtiera en imperio. Además, las naciones necesitaban materias primas de las colonias para sus industrias. De esta manera, la competencia por esos territorios generó crisis. También aumentó el **militarismo,** o la idea de que un país debe usar un ejército poderoso para defender sus intereses. Las naciones europeas formaron grandes ejércitos y, entonces, empezaron a temerse. También formaron alianzas y prometieron defender a sus aliados en caso de ataque.

In 1914, a Serbian nationalist killed Archduke Francis Ferdinand, the heir to the throne of Austria-Hungary. Austria-Hungary then declared war on Serbia. The alliances caused Europe to split into two warring sides. The Central Powers were led by Austria-Hungary and Germany. The Allies were led by Great Britain, France, and Russia./En 1914, un nacionalista serbio asesinó al archiduque Francisco Fernando, heredero del trono de Austria-Hungría. Entonces, los austrohúngaros le declararon la guerra a Serbia. Las alianzas hicieron que Europa se dividiera en dos bandos en guerra. Las Potencias Centrales estaban encabezadas por Austria-Hungría y Alemania. Los Aliados estaban liderados por Gran Bretaña, Francia y Rusia.

> **Why did Austria-Hungary declare war on Serbia?/ ¿Por qué Austria-Hungría le declaró la guerra a Serbia?**
>
> _____
> _____
> _____
> _____

## THE GREAT WAR ESCALATES/SE INTENSIFICA LA GRAN GUERRA

When Germany attacked France and Belgium, French and British troops stopped them near Paris./Cuando Alemania atacó Francia

Lesson/Lección 2, *continued*/*continuación*

y Bélgica, las tropas de Francia y Gran Bretaña detuvieron al ejército alemán cerca de París.

Neither side gained an advantage for three years. Powerful weapons such as machine guns and poison gas killed millions of people. Then Germany started using submarines to attack supply ships headed for Britain./Durante tres años, ningún país fue superior al otro. Millones de personas murieron como consecuencia del uso de armas poderosas, como metralletas y gases venenosos. Entonces, Alemania comenzó a usar submarinos para atacar a los barcos con provisiones que se dirigían a Gran Bretaña.

Near the end of 1914, the Ottoman Empire joined the Central Powers. Before the war, the Turks and Armenians in the Ottoman Empire had an uneasy relationship. As World War I began, some Armenians fought for Russia rather than for the Ottoman Empire. So the Ottomans began to commit **genocide,** a deliberate killing of a large group of people, against the Armenians within its borders./Hacia fines de 1914, el Imperio otomano se unió a las Potencias Centrales. Antes de la guerra, los turcos y los armenios del Imperio otomano tenían una relación difícil. Al comienzo de la Primera Guerra Mundial, algunos armenios pelearon por Rusia en lugar de luchar por el Imperio otomano. Por eso, los otomanos empezaron a cometer **genocidio,** o el exterminio deliberado de un grupo grande de personas, en contra de los armenios que vivían en su territorio.

Fighting took place not only in Europe but Asia and Africa as well. Japan fought against Germany, so battles took place around the Pacific. Soldiers also came from British Empire colonies such as India, Canada, and Australia./Los combates no solo se produjeron en Europa, sino también en Asia y África. Japón luchó contra Alemania, por lo que algunas batallas ocurrieron en el Pacífico.

| |
|---|
| **Why did the Ottoman Empire commit genocide against Armenians within its borders?**/¿Por qué el Imperio otomano cometió genocidio contra los armenios que vivían en su territorio? |
| _____ |
| _____ |
| _____ |
| _____ |

Además, también venían soldados de las colonias
del Imperio británico, como India, Canadá
y Australia.

## THE ALLIES' VICTORY/VICTORIA DE LOS ALIADOS

The U.S. had vowed to remain neutral. But when
Germany began using submarines to sink ships
headed for Britain, the U.S. warned against
attacking unarmed ships. Germany ignored the
warning, and the U.S. joined the Allies. American
troops gave the Allies an advantage./Los EE. UU.
habían prometido permanecer neutrales, pero
cuando Alemania comenzó a usar submarinos
para hundir barcos que se dirigían a Gran Bretaña,
los EE. UU. le advirtieron de que no atacara a
barcos desarmados. Alemania ignoró la
advertencia, y los EE. UU. se unieron a los
Aliados. Las tropas estadounidenses les dieron
ventaja a los Aliados.

> Underline the sentences
> that explain why the United
> States became involved in
> a war in Europe./Subraya
> las oraciones que explican
> por qué los Estados
> Unidos participaron en
> una guerra en Europa.

Germany knew that American troops would shift
the balance of power to the Allies. It launched a
new attack on France, but eventually the American
troops stopped them. By November of 1918, the
Central Powers were defeated./Alemania sabía que
las tropas estadounidenses alterarían el equilibrio
de poder a favor de los Aliados. Alemania lanzó un
nuevo ataque contra Francia, pero finalmente las
tropas estadounidenses lo detuvieron. Para
noviembre de 1918, las Potencias Centrales
habían sido derrotadas.

## CHALLENGE ACTIVITY/ACTIVIDAD AVANZADA

**Critical Thinking: Explain/Pensamiento crítico:**
**Explicar** Write a paragraph explaining how the
alliance system in Europe made it easier for
nations to go to war./Escribe un párrafo en el que
expliques cómo el sistema de alianzas en Europa
les facilitó a las naciones la entrada en la guerra.

**DIRECTIONS/INSTRUCCIONES** Use the two vocabulary words
from the lesson, **militarism** and **genocide,** to write a summary of
what you learned in the lesson./Usa los dos términos de vocabulario
de la lección, **militarismo** y **genocidio,** para escribir un resumen de
lo que aprendiste en la lección.

_____

_____

_____

_____

_____

_____

_____

_____

_____

_____

_____

_____

_____

_____

_____

_____

_____

_____

_____

_____

## Nationalism and World War I/Nacionalismo y Primera Guerra Mundial

### MAIN IDEAS/IDEAS PRINCIPALES

1. The League of Nations was formed, but it had mixed success./Se creó la Liga de las Naciones, pero tuvo un éxito relativo.

2. The Treaty of Versailles changed the map of Europe./El Tratado de Versalles cambió el mapa de Europa.

3. Resentment and economic problems developed in Germany after World War I./Después de la Primera Guerra Mundial, surgieron problemas económicos y resentimientos en Alemania.

## Key Terms and People/Personas y palabras clave

**Treaty of Versailles/Tratado de Versalles**  peace treaty signed near Paris in 1919 that ended World War I/tratado de paz firmado cerca de París en 1919, que puso fin a la Primera Guerra Mundial

**League of Nations/Liga de las Naciones**  organization created after World War I so that countries could try to solve problems peacefully/organización creada después de la Primera Guerra Mundial con el fin de que los países trataran de resolver sus problemas de forma pacífica

**reparations/indemnización**  money that nations have to pay for causing damage during war/dinero que las naciones deben pagar por los daños causados durante la guerra

## Lesson Summary/Resumen de la lección

### LEAGUE OF NATIONS/LIGA DE LAS NACIONES

When the **Treaty of Versailles** was signed, U.S. President Woodrow Wilson hoped an organization would promote democracy and prevent future wars. He called this group the **League of Nations.** President Wilson thought member countries could combine their economic and military power together to maintain peace./Cuando se firmó el **Tratado de Versalles,** el presidente de los EE. UU. Woodrow Wilson tenía la esperanza de que una organización fomentara la democracia y evitara guerras futuras. Llamó a este grupo la **Liga de las Naciones.** El presidente Wilson pensaba que los países miembro podrían combinar sus poderes militares y económicos para mantener la paz.

> What were two reasons some members of Congress did not agree with President Wilson?/¿Cuáles eran dos de las razones por las que algunos miembros del Congreso no estaban de acuerdo con el presidente Wilson?
>
> _____
> _____
> _____
> _____
> _____
> _____
> _____

**Lesson/Lección 3,** *continued/continuación*

Some members of Congress did not agree with President Wilson about the League of Nations. They thought the United States should make its own decisions. They also did not want to become involved in European politics. President Wilson could not convince Congress to change its mind, so the United States never joined the group./Algunos miembros del Congreso no estaban de acuerdo con el presidente Wilson acerca de la Liga de las Naciones. Pensaban que los Estados Unidos deberían tomar sus propias decisiones. Tampoco querían involucrarse en la política europea. El presidente Wilson no pudo convencer al Congreso de que cambiara de opinión, por lo que los Estados Unidos nunca se unieron al grupo.

The League of Nations could not stop nations from doing what they wanted. Japan and Italy both invaded other countries, but they did not allow the League of Nations to help settle those disputes. Germany began to gather military resources again even though The Treaty of Versailles stated that was not allowed./La Liga de las Naciones no pudo impedir a las naciones que hicieran lo que quisieran. Tanto Japón como Italia invadieron otros países, pero no le permitieron a la Liga de las Naciones ayudar a resolver esas disputas. Alemania comenzó otra vez a reunir recursos militares, a pesar de que el Tratado de Versalles establecía que eso no estaba permitido.

> **What action showed that the League of Nations could not stop Germany from doing what it wanted?/¿Qué acción demostró que la Liga de las Naciones no podía impedir a Alemania que hiciera lo que quisiera?**
>
> _____
>
> _____

## NEW NATIONAL BORDERS/NUEVAS FRONTERAS NACIONALES

The Allies redrew the map of Europe after World War I. Estonia, Latvia, and Lithuania were created from areas that Germany had controlled. Czechoslovakia and Yugoslavia came from part of Austria-Hungary. Russia gave up some territory to create Finland, and the borders of Poland were redrawn, too. Some countries increased in size, while others lost land. One small piece of the Ottoman Empire became the nation of Turkey./ Después de la Primera Guerra Mundial, los Aliados modificaron el mapa de Europa. Estonia, Letonia y Lituania surgieron de zonas que Alemania había controlado. Checoslovaquia y Yugoslavia provenían de una parte de Austria-Hungría. Rusia renunció a algunos de sus territorios para crear Finlandia, y las fronteras de Polonia también se modificaron. Algunos países aumentaron de tamaño, mientras que otros perdieron tierras. Una pequeña parte del Imperio otomano se convirtió en la nación de Turquía.

> Circle three countries that were created from German areas. Underline two countries that came from part of Austria-Hungary./ Encierra en un círculo los tres países que se crearon a partir de zonas alemanas. Subraya dos países que surgieron a partir de Austria-Hungría.

People had fled or settled into new places during and after the war. New nations and movement from place to place meant that different ethnic groups were now living together in the same country./Durante la guerra y después de ella, muchas personas huyeron o se asentaron en nuevos lugares. La creación de nuevas naciones y el movimiento de un lugar a otro provocó que distintos grupos étnicos ahora vivieran juntos en el mismo país.

> Why were different ethnic groups living together in the same countries?/ ¿Por qué distintos grupos étnicos convivían en un mismo país?
>
> _____
> _____
> _____

## ECONOMIC PENALTIES/SANCIONES ECONÓMICAS

A clause in the Treaty of Versailles forced Germany to pay large amounts of **reparations** for World War I. Germany thought this was unfair, but France believed the payments should be high. The French did not want the Germans to become powerful again. Germany also had to reduce the size of its army and navy./Una cláusula del Tratado de Versalles obligaba a Alemania a pagar una gran **indemnización** por la Primera Guerra Mundial. Alemania pensaba que esto era injusto, mientras que Francia creía que los pagos debían ser elevados. Los franceses no querían que los alemanes volvieran a ser poderosos. Alemania

> Why did France believe in high reparations payments for Germany?/¿Por qué Francia pensaba que Alemania debía pagar elevadas indemnizaciones?
>
> _____
> _____
> _____

también tuvo que reducir el tamaño de su ejército y su armada.

Resentment began to build in Germany. It had borrowed lots of money to pay for weapons and war expenses. Germany could not pay those debts and the reparations that it owed. Many Germans believed that the terms of the Treaty of Versailles were too harsh. The economic problems and geographic changes in Europe caused tension that led to future conflict./En Alemania, el resentimiento comenzó a crecer. El país había tenido que pedir prestada una gran cantidad de dinero para pagar las armas y otros gastos de la guerra. Alemania no podía pagar esas deudas ni las indemnizaciones que debía. Muchos alemanes pensaban que los términos del Tratado de Versalles eran demasiado duros. Los problemas económicos y los cambios geográficos en Europa causaron una tensión que llevó a futuros conflictos.

## CHALLENGE ACTIVITY/ACTIVIDAD AVANZADA

**Critical Thinking: Persuade/Pensamiento crítico: Persuadir** Write an essay that supports either President Wilson's view of the League of Nations or the opinion of some members of Congress. Use research to help explain why readers should agree with your point of view./Escribe un ensayo en el que apoyes la visión del presidente Wilson sobre la Liga de las Naciones o bien la opinión de algunos de los miembros del Congreso. Investiga para explicar por qué los lectores deberían estar de acuerdo con tu punto de vista.

| Finland/Finlandia | Germany/ Alemania | League of Nations/la Liga de las Naciones |
| President Woodrow Wilson/el presidente Woodrow Wilson | reparations/las indemnizaciones | Treaty of Versailles/el Tratado de Versalles |

**DIRECTIONS/INSTRUCCIONES** Read each sentence and fill in the blank(s) with the term(s) from the word bank that best complete the sentence./Lee cada oración y escribe en el/los espacio(s) en blanco la palabra del banco de palabras que mejor la completa.

1. After World War I, Russia gave up some territory to create the nation of _____./Después de la Primera Guerra Mundial, Rusia renunció a algunos de sus territorios para crear la nación de

   _____.

2. The _____ was signed near Paris in 1919./_____
   _____ se firmó cerca de París en 1919.

3. _____ could not pay for its debts and for _____
   _____./_____ no podía pagar la deuda ni _____ que debía.

4. _____ could not convince Congress to allow the United States to join the _____./
   _____ no pudo convencer al Congreso de que permitiera a los Estados Unidos unirse a _____.

# Nationalism and World War I/Nacionalismo y Primera Guerra Mundial

**Lesson/Lección 4**

---

**MAIN IDEAS/IDEAS PRINCIPALES**

1. Population growth, wars, and limited food production caused unrest in Russia./El crecimiento de la población, las guerras y la producción limitada de alimentos causaron malestar en Rusia.

2. Communism is a political system in which the government controls much of the economy./El comunismo es un sistema político en el que el gobierno controla gran parte de la economía.

3. The Soviet Union was formed after revolution and civil war in Russia./ Después de la revolución y la guerra civil en Rusia, se formó la Unión Soviética.

---

## Key Terms and People/Personas y palabras clave

**Nicholas II/Nicolás II** czar of Russia who was forced to give up power in 1917/ zar de Rusia que se vio forzado a renunciar al poder en 1917

**Karl Marx/Karl Marx** newspaper editor who supported rights for working class people/editor de periódico que apoyó los derechos de las personas de la clase trabajadora

**marxism/marxismo** the idea that social change is based on the struggle of the oppressed working classes/la idea de que el cambio social se basa en la lucha de las clases trabajadoras oprimidas

**Vladimir Lenin/Vladimir Lenin** Russian leader of the Bolsheviks who became leader of the Soviet Union in 1922/líder ruso de los bolcheviques que en 1922 se convirtió en el líder de la Unión Soviética

**communism/comunismo** economic and political system in which there is no privately owned property/sistema político y económico en el que no existen los bienes de propiedad privada

## Lesson Summary/Resumen de la lección

### RUSSIA FACES CHALLENGES/RUSIA ENFRENTA DESAFÍOS

In the 1800s, many Russians lived in rural areas. Farmers grew food to feed their local communities. The population doubled in the last half of the 1800s. Russia's government also wanted to sell crops to other countries. Farmers struggled to produce enough food, and there

> **What event in 1891 caused half a million people to starve in Russia?/¿Qué suceso causó en 1891 que medio millón de personas murieran de hambre en Rusia?**
>
> _____
>
> _____

was a great famine in 1891. Half a million people starved./En el siglo 19, muchos rusos vivían en áreas rurales. Los agricultores cultivaban alimentos para las comunidades locales. En la segunda mitad del siglo 19, la población se duplicó. Además, el gobierno de Rusia quería vender su cosecha a otros países. Los agricultores se esforzaron por producir suficientes alimentos, pero en 1891 hubo una gran hambruna. Medio millón de personas murieron de hambre.

Russia fought a war with Japan in the early 1900s. Japan wanted Russian troops to leave Manchuria in East Asia. Russia wanted to stay to protect its railroads in the region. The Japanese had better technology and skilled commanders. Russia lost the conflict and had to give land to Japan./Rusia libró una guerra contra Japón a principios del siglo 20. Japón deseaba que las tropas rusas se fueran de Manchuria, en el este asiático. Rusia quería permanecer en la región para proteger sus ferrocarriles. Los japoneses tenían mejor tecnología y comandantes diestros. Rusia perdió este conflicto y tuvo que cederle territorios a Japón.

> **Why did Russia want its troops to stay in Manchuria?/¿Por qué Rusia quería que sus tropas permanecieran en Manchuria?**
>
> _____
>
> _____

Groups of people had been protesting against the Russian government for years. **Nicholas II** ordered his guards to shoot at protestors in 1905. The Bloody Sunday Massacre led to a revolution. The czar promised to create a legislature and a constitution for Russia./Algunos grupos de personas habían protestado durante años en contra del gobierno ruso. En 1905, **Nicolás II** ordenó a sus guardias disparar contra los manifestantes. La masacre del Domingo Sangriento desató una revolución. El zar prometió crear una asamblea legislativa y una constitución para Rusia.

> **What did the czar promise to create for Russia after the revolution in 1905?/¿Qué prometió crear el zar para Rusia después de la revolución de 1905?**
>
> _____
>
> _____

## NEW IDEAS ABOUT GOVERNMENT/
## NUEVAS IDEAS SOBRE EL GOBIERNO

**Karl Marx** believed many workers should have
more rights because they were oppressed by
their employers. He wrote that the struggles
of the workers should cause social change. His
ideas became known as **Marxism./Karl Marx**
pensaba que muchos trabajadores debían tener
más derechos porque estaban oprimidos por sus
empleadores. Escribió que las luchas de los
trabajadores debían provocar el cambio social.
Sus ideas se conocen como **marxismo.**

**Vladimir Lenin** led the Bolsheviks in Russia. He
agreed with most of Karl Marx's ideas. However,
Marx believed in giving more people voting rights.
Then social change could happen peacefully. Lenin
believed in violent revolution and **communism.** He
wanted the government to control a nation's
economy and how it produced goods./**Vladimir
Lenin** lideró a los bolcheviques en Rusia. Estaba
de acuerdo con la mayoría de las ideas de Karl
Marx. Sin embargo, Marx creía en conceder el
derecho al voto a más personas. De esta manera,
el cambio social se produciría pacíficamente.
Lenin, en cambio, creía en la revolución violenta
y en el **comunismo.** Deseaba que el gobierno
controlara la economía de la nación y el modo
en que esta producía bienes.

> **Describe the different ways that Karl Marx and Vladimir Lenin thought social change should happen./ Describe las distintas maneras en que Karl Marx y Vladimir Lenin pensaban que debía ocurrir el cambio social.**
>
> _____
> _____
> _____
> _____

## THE SOVIET UNION/LA UNIÓN SOVIÉTICA

Nicholas II did create a new legislature in Russia,
but it could not keep order. In 1917, Lenin and
the Bolsheviks permanently forced the czar out
of power. Then civil war broke out between the
Reds and the Whites. The Reds supported Lenin
and the Bolsheviks, and the Whites still wanted
a czar to rule Russia./Nicolás II creó una nueva
asamblea legislativa en Rusia, pero esta no pudo
mantener el orden. En 1917, Lenin y los

bolcheviques obligaron al zar a abandonar
permanentemente el poder. Se desató una guerra
civil entre los Rojos y los Blancos. Los Rojos
apoyaban a Lenin y a los bolcheviques, mientras
que los Blancos todavía querían que el zar
gobernara en Rusia.

The Whites received money and troops from the
Allied nations, but the Reds won the civil war. In
1922, Russia was renamed the Union of Soviet
Socialist Republics, or the Soviet Union. Vladimir
Lenin became the leader of this new communist
nation./Los Blancos recibieron dinero y tropas
de los Aliados, pero los Rojos ganaron la guerra
civil. En 1922, Rusia pasó a llamarse Unión de
Repúblicas Socialistas Soviéticas, o Unión
Soviética. Vladimir Lenin se convirtió en el
líder de esta nueva nación comunista.

> **Underline the two names that Russia had after 1922./** Subraya los dos nombres que tuvo Rusia después de 1922.

## CHALLENGE ACTIVITY/ACTIVIDAD AVANZADA

**Critical Thinking: Predict/Pensamiento crítico:**
**Predecir** Write a response that explains how you
think Russia's history might have changed if the
government and Nicholas II had made different
choices before 1917. Describe some changes that
you might have made if you had been the Russian
leader./Escribe una respuesta en la que expliques
cómo piensas que habría sido distinta la historia
de Rusia si Nicolás II y el gobierno hubieran
tomado otras decisiones antes de 1917. Describe
algunos cambios que tú habrías realizado si
hubieses sido el líder de Rusia.

Lesson/Lección 4, *continued/ continuación*

**DIRECTIONS/INSTRUCCIONES** On the line before each statement, write **T** if the statement is true and **F** if the statement is false. If the statement is false, change the underlined term to make the sentence true. Then write the correct term on the line after the sentence./En la línea que precede a cada enunciado, escribe **V** si el enunciado es verdadero y **F** si es falso. Si el enunciado es falso, cambia el término subrayado para que el enunciado sea verdadero. Luego escribe el término correcto en la línea que sigue al enunciado.

_____ 1. <u>Vladimir Lenin</u> was a newspaper editor who supported rights for working class people./<u>Vladimir Lenin</u> fue un editor de periódico que apoyó los derechos de las personas de la clase trabajadora.

_____

_____ 2. In 1905, <u>Nicholas II</u> caused the Bloody Sunday Massacre when he ordered his guards to shoot at protestors./En 1905, <u>Nicolás II</u> provocó la masacre del Domingo Sangriento al ordenar a sus guardias disparar contra los manifestantes.

_____

_____ 3. Some supporters of <u>Marxism</u> believed in violent revolution./Algunos partidarios del <u>marxismo</u> creían en la revolución violenta.

_____

_____ 4. <u>Karl Marx</u> was both the leader of the Bolsheviks and of the Union of Soviet Socialist Republics./<u>Karl Marx</u> fue el líder de los bolcheviques y de la Unión de Repúblicas Socialistas Soviéticas.

_____

_____ 5. The idea that social change is based on the struggle of the oppressed working classes is known as <u>communism</u>./La idea de que el cambio social se basa en la lucha de las clases trabajadoras oprimidas se llama <u>comunismo</u>.

_____

## Nationalism and World War I/Nacionalismo y Primera Guerra Mundial

**MAIN IDEAS/IDEAS PRINCIPALES**

1. The stock market crash and bank failures led to the Great Depression./ La crisis del mercado de valores y las quiebras bancarias provocaron la Gran Depresión.

2. The Great Depression challenged people and nations around the world./ La Gran Depresión fue un reto para las personas y las naciones de todo el mundo.

3. Nations responded to the Great Depression in different ways./Las naciones respondieron a la Gran Depresión de diferentes maneras.

## Key Terms and People/Personas y palabras clave

**Great Depression/Gran Depresión** period in the late 1920s and 1930s when the value of money was extremely low and unemployment increased throughout the world/período que abarca desde fines de la década de 1920 hasta la década de 1930 en el que se produjo una disminución extrema del valor del dinero y un aumento del desempleo en todo el mundo

**stocks/acciones** pieces of a company that are bought, sold, or traded on the stock market/porciones de una compañía que se pueden comprar, vender o intercambiar en el mercado de valores

**Franklin Delano Roosevelt/Franklin Delano Roosevelt** U.S. president whose goal was to improve the American economy and end the Great Depression in the United States/presidente de los EE. UU. cuya meta fue mejorar la economía estadounidense y poner fin a la Gran Depresión en los Estados Unidos

**New Deal/Nuevo Trato** group of U.S. government programs developed to fix American business practices and cause positive economic changes during the Great Depression/grupo de programas del gobierno de los EE. UU. desarrollados durante la Gran Depresión para corregir las prácticas comerciales estadounidenses y provocar cambios económicos positivos

## Lesson Summary/Resumen de la lección

### CAUSES OF THE GREAT DEPRESSION/ CAUSAS DE LA GRAN DEPRESIÓN

After World War I, Americans began to buy, sell, or trade **stocks** on the stock market. Stocks can gain or lose value based on how well companies do in business./Después de la Primera Guerra Mundial, los estadounidenses empezaron a

comprar, vender o intercambiar **acciones** en el
mercado de valores. Las acciones pueden ganar
o perder valor según cómo les va a las compañías
en sus negocios.

In October 1929, the stock market crashed.
Many people lost all the money they had invested.
Companies laid off workers, which caused many
to lose their savings and homes as well./En
octubre de 1929, el mercado de valores entró en
crisis. Muchas personas perdieron todo el dinero
que habían invertido. Las compañías despidieron
a sus empleados, lo que provocó que muchos de
ellos también perdieran sus ahorros y hogares.

The crash happened because investors liked to
try to guess what a stock's price would be before
it was bought or sold. Speculating about stocks
was risky, but most people had not thought about
what might happen. Banks also failed. Many had
borrowed money from banks but now could not
afford to pay back their loans./La crisis se
produjo porque los inversionistas solían tratar
de adivinar cuál sería el valor de una acción
antes de que fuera comprada o vendida.
Especular sobre las acciones era una práctica
muy arriesgada, pero la mayoría de las personas
no pensaron en lo que podría ocurrir. Los bancos
también quebraron. Muchas personas que
habían tomado dinero prestado de los bancos
ahora no podían pagar sus deudas.

> **How can a company's business affect its stock?/¿Cómo pueden los negocios de una compañía afectar sus acciones?**
>
> _____
>
> _____
>
> _____

> **What did investors do when they speculated about stocks?/¿Qué hacían los inversionistas cuando especulaban sobre las acciones?**
>
> _____
>
> _____
>
> _____
>
> _____

## EFFECTS OF THE GREAT DEPRESSION/ EFECTOS DE LA GRAN DEPRESIÓN

The **Great Depression** affected countries around
the world in different ways. American workers
had stopped producing goods, so the economic
problems were severe in the United States.
Germany and other European countries tried to
solve their financial problems by printing more
money. This made the value of their currency

fall./La **Gran Depresión** afectó a países de todo
el mundo de diferentes maneras. Los trabajadores
estadounidenses dejaron de producir bienes, por
eso los problemas económicos fueron muy graves
en los Estados Unidos. Alemania y otros países
europeos trataron de resolver sus problemas
financieros imprimiendo más dinero, lo que
hizo caer el valor de sus monedas.

Countries in Latin America suffered because
they could not trade as many goods with the
United States. African sellers and Japanese
exporters also found fewer buyers for their goods.
In contrast, the Nordic countries continued to
produce and export goods. Their national
economies did not collapse./Los países de
Latinoamérica sufrieron porque no podían
comerciar con los Estados Unidos en la
medida en que lo hacían antes. Los vendedores
africanos y los exportadores japoneses tampoco
encontraban tantos compradores para sus
productos. En cambio, los países nórdicos
siguieron produciendo y exportando bienes, y
sus economías nacionales no entraron en crisis.

> **Which nations continued
> to produce and export
> goods during the Great
> Depression?/¿Qué
> naciones continuaron
> produciendo y exportando
> bienes durante la Gran
> Depresión?**
>
> _____
>
> _____

## RESPONSES TO THE GREAT DEPRESSION/
## RESPUESTAS A LA GRAN DEPRESIÓN

In the United States, **Franklin Delano Roosevelt**
developed the **New Deal** to create jobs and offer
financial help to those who needed it. Great
Britain used a policy called retrenchment. Wages
and spending were kept low. People received
only small amounts of money if they did not
have a job./En los Estados Unidos, **Franklin
Delano Roosevelt** desarrolló el **Nuevo Trato**
para crear empleos y ofrecer ayuda financiera
a quienes lo necesitaban. Gran Bretaña puso en
práctica una política llamada racionalización.
Los salarios y el gasto se mantuvieron bajos. Las
personas solo recibían pequeñas cantidades de
dinero si no tenían trabajo.

> **Circle the name of the
> policy that Great Britain
> used during the Great
> Depression./Encierra en
> un círculo el nombre de
> la política que aplicó
> Gran Bretaña durante
> la Gran Depresión.**

Adolf Hitler began to rise to power in Germany. German money was almost worthless, people were hungry and unemployed, and other countries refused to lend money to the Germans. Hitler thought Germany should build its military again and not pay reparations. Many agreed with him. They thought he was a strong leader who could fix the economy. Hitler's government spent money to build a highway. He helped farmers, and the economy improved. But Hitler was a dictator, and democracy soon ended in Germany./En Alemania, Adolf Hitler empezó a acumular poder. El dinero alemán casi no tenía valor, el pueblo estaba hambriento y desempleado, y otros países se negaban a prestar dinero a los alemanes. Hitler pensaba que Alemania debía construir nuevamente su ejército y no pagar las indemnizaciones. Muchas personas estaban de acuerdo con él. Pensaban que Hitler era un líder fuerte que podría arreglar la economía. El gobierno de Hitler gastó dinero para construir carreteras. Ayudó a los agricultores, y la economía mejoró. Pero Hitler era un dictador, y pronto terminó la democracia en Alemania.

> **Describe conditions in Germany when Adolf Hitler rose to power./Describe la situación en Alemania cuando Hitler llegó al poder.**
>
> _____
> _____
> _____
> _____
> _____
> _____
> _____

## CHALLENGE ACTIVITY/ACTIVIDAD AVANZADA

**Critical Thinking: Summarize/Pensamiento crítico: Resumir**  Use the Library of Congress or other online resources to find interviews with people who lived during the Great Depression. Read 2–3 interviews and write a summary of each one. Include details about the events, experiences, and thoughts that people had about their lives at that time./Consulta la Biblioteca del Congreso o recursos en línea para buscar entrevistas a personas que vivieron durante la Gran Depresión. Lee dos o tres entrevistas y escribe un resumen de cada una. Incluye detalles sobre los sucesos y las experiencias que vivieron esas personas en aquel momento y los pensamientos que tuvieron.

**DIRECTIONS/INSTRUCCIONES** Write a word or descriptive phrase to describe each term./Escribe una palabra o una frase descriptiva para describir cada término.

1. Great Depression/Gran Depresión _____

_____

2. stocks/acciones _____

_____

3. Franklin Delano Roosevelt/Franklin Delano Roosevelt _____

_____

4. New Deal/Nuevo Trato _____

_____

5. retrenchment/racionalización _____

_____

6. Adolf Hitler/Adolf Hitler _____

_____

# World War II/Segunda Guerra Mundial

**MAIN IDEAS/IDEAS PRINCIPALES**

1. The devastation of World War I and economic hardship pushed many Europeans to look for stronger leadership./La devastación de la Primera Guerra Mundial y las dificultades económicas llevaron a muchos europeos a buscar liderazgos más fuertes.

2. After Vladimir Lenin's death, totalitarian dictator Joseph Stalin took control of the Soviet Union./Tras la muerte de Vladimir Lenin, el dictador totalitario José Stalin tomó el control de la Unión Soviética.

3. Beginning in the early 1900s, nationalistic military leaders played an increasingly dominant role in the Japanese government./A principios del siglo 20, los líderes militares nacionalistas desemperañon un papel cada vez más dominante en el gobierno japonés.

# Key Terms and People/Personas y palabras clave

**fascism/fascismo** political system based on extreme nationalism and a strong military/sistema político basado en un nacionalismo extremo y un ejército fuerte

**Benito Mussolini/Benito Mussolini** Italy's dictator who founded the Fascist Party/dictador de Italia que fundó el Partido Fascista

**Adolf Hitler/Adolf Hitler** Germany's dictator who led the Nazi Party/dictador de Alemania que dirigió el Partido Nazi

**Nazi Party/Partido Nazi** political party that believed Germans were superior to all other races/partido político que creía que los alemanes eran superiores a las demás razas

**Gestapo/Gestapo** German secret police force created by Adolf Hitler/fuerza policial secreta alemana creada por Adolf Hitler

**totalitarianism/totalitarismo** system where government controls all aspects of people's lives/sistema en el que el gobierno controla todos los aspectos de la vida de las personas

**Joseph Stalin/José Stalin** Soviet dictator who came to power after Vladimir Lenin died/dictador soviético que llegó al poder tras la muerte de Vladimir Lenin

**collectivization/colectivización** process of taking private resources and using them for large groups/proceso de tomar los recursos privados y usarlos para grupos grandes

**Emperor Hirohito/emperador Hirohito** Japan's leader who could not control Japanese military officers/líder japonés que no pudo controlar a los oficiales militares japoneses

# Lesson Summary/Resumen de la lección

## FASCISM IN EUROPE/FASCISMO EN EUROPA

**Benito Mussolini** and **Adolf Hitler** came to power because their nations were looking for strong leaders who could fix problems. Mussolini used his powerful personality to encourage people to support **fascism** and restore Italy to greatness. To help accomplish that goal and create an empire, the Italian army invaded Ethiopia in 1935./**Benito Mussolini** y **Adolf Hitler** llegaron al poder porque sus naciones buscaban líderes fuertes que pudieran resolver los problemas que enfrentaban. Mussolini usó su potente personalidad para alentar a las personas a apoyar el **fascismo** y restaurar la grandeza de Italia. Para alcanzar dicho objetivo y crear un imperio, el ejército italiano invadió Etiopía en 1935.

> **Why did Benito Mussolini and Adolf Hitler come to power?/¿Por qué Benito Mussolini y Adolf Hitler llegaron al poder?**
>
> _____
> _____
> _____
> _____

Hitler was a forceful speaker who believed that Germany had to become a world power again. The **Nazi Party** gained followers because it promised a better life for Germans. Hitler also believed in **totalitarianism** and created the **Gestapo** to deal harshly with anyone who opposed him. He disliked groups like communists and democrats, but he particularly blamed Jews for Germany's problems./Hitler era un enérgico orador que creía que Alemania tenía que convertirse nuevamente en una potencia mundial. El **Partido Nazi** ganó seguidores porque prometía una vida mejor para los alemanes. Hitler también creía en el **totalitarismo** y creó la **Gestapo** para tratar con rigor a quienes se le opusieran. Le desagradaban algunos grupos, como los comunistas y los demócratas, pero culpaba particularmente a los judíos de los problemas de Alemania.

> **What was the Gestapo's purpose?/¿Cuál era el propósito de la Gestapo?**
>
> _____
> _____
> _____

## STALIN'S SOVIET UNION/LA UNIÓN SOVIÉTICA DE STALIN

When Vladimir Lenin died in 1924, **Joseph Stalin** used brutal terror to keep control of the Soviet

Union. The people had no rights. Stalin also had his rivals and some military leaders executed./
Tras las muerte de Vladimir Lenin en 1924, **José Stalin** usó una violencia brutal para mantener el control sobre la Unión Soviética. El pueblo no tenía derechos. Stalin también mandó a ejecutar a sus enemigos y a algunos líderes militares.

The Soviet leader started a series of Five-Year Plans so his nation would catch up with the advanced world. Stalin wanted to increase heavy industry, reform agriculture, and build up the military. **Collectivization** was one part of these plans. Peasants were arrested or killed if they did not agree to give up their farms./El líder soviético implementó una serie de Planes de Cinco Años con el objetivo de que su nación se pusiera al nivel del mundo desarrollado. Stalin quería aumentar la industria pesada, reformar la agricultura y fortalecer el ejército. La **colectivización** fue parte de esos planes. Si los campesinos se negaban a ceder sus granjas, eran arrestados o asesinados.

> **Underline three things Stalin wanted to do to make the Soviet Union part of the advanced world./**
> **Subraya tres cosas que Stalin quería hacer para lograr que la Unión Soviética formara parte del mundo desarrollado.**

## MILITARY DOMINANCE IN JAPAN/DOMINIO MILITAR EN JAPÓN

After two wars in the early 1900s, Japan had more influence in territories like Korea and Taiwan. Military leaders had slowly gained complete control of Japan's government. **Emperor Hirohito** could not stop Japanese troops from taking over in Manchuria in 1931. By the mid-1930s, even the prime minister was a military official./Después de dos guerras a principios del siglo 20, Japón tenía más influencia en territorios como Corea y Taiwán. Los líderes militares habían ganado de a poco el control total del gobierno japonés. El **emperador Hirohito** no pudo evitar que las tropas japonesas tomaran el control de Manchuria en 1931. Para mediados de la década de 1930, incluso el primer ministro era un oficial militar.

> **What evidence shows that the military had taken control of Japan's government?/¿Cuál es la prueba de que los militares habían tomado el control del gobierno japonés?**
>
> _____
> _____
> _____
> _____
> _____

Japan's military forces then moved into China. In 1937, they took over the coast and put troops in many Chinese cities. When soldiers arrived in Nanking, they destroyed more than a third of the buildings in the city. Tens of thousands of Chinese were massacred. Japan had a firm grip on most of the lands that surrounded it./Luego, las fuerzas militares de Japón se establecieron en China. En 1937, tomaron el control de la costa e introdujeron sus tropas en numerosas ciudades chinas. Cuando los soldados llegaron a Nankín, destruyeron más de un tercio de los edificios de la ciudad. Decenas de miles de chinos fueron masacrados. Japón tenía un fuerte control en la mayoría de los territorios que lo rodeaban.

> **Circle the name of the city where Japanese soldiers destroyed buildings and massacred tens of thousands of Chinese./** **Encierra en un círculo el nombre de la ciudad donde los soldados japoneses destruyeron edificios y masacraron a decenas de miles de chinos.**

## CHALLENGE ACTIVITY/ACTIVIDAD AVANZADA

**Critical Thinking: Develop Historical Perspective/**
**Pensamiento crítico: Desarrollar perspectiva histórica** Research what life was like in the Japanese-controlled parts of China or Manchuria in the 1930s. Write a fictional narrative of a person who might have lived in the area or a Japanese soldier who might have been stationed there./ Investiga cómo era la vida en la década de 1930 en las partes de China controladas por Japón o en Manchuria. Escribe una ficción narrativa sobre una persona que podría haber vivido en esa zona o sobre un soldado japonés destinado allí.

**DIRECTIONS/INSTRUCCIONES** Read each sentence and circle the term in the word pair that best completes each sentence./Lee cada oración y encierra en un círculo el término del par de palabras que mejor la completa.

1. The name of the German secret police force was the _____.
   **(Gestapo/Nazi Party)**/El nombre de la fuerza policial secreta alemana era _____. **(Gestapo/Partido Nazi)**

2. He wanted to create an empire, so _____ had the Italian army invade Ethiopia in 1935. **(Benito Mussolini/Adolf Hitler)/**Quería crear un imperio, por lo que _____ hizo que el ejército italiano invadiera Etiopía en 1935. **(Benito Mussolini/Adolf Hitler)**

3. Governments that control all aspects of people's lives are using a system of _____. **(fascism/totalitarianism)/**Los gobiernos que controlan todos los aspectos de la vida de las personas emplean un sistema conocido como _____. **(fascismo/totalitarismo)**

4. The Five-Year Plans were started by _____ so the Soviet Union would become a more advanced nation. **(Emperor Hirohito/ Joseph Stalin)/**Los Planes de Cinco Años fueron implementados por _____ para que la Unión Soviética se convirtiera en una nación más desarrollada. **(el emperador Hirohito/José Stalin)**

5. People who believed in _____ thought Germans were superior to all other races. **(the Nazi Party/totalitarianism)/**Las personas que apoyaban _____ pensaban que los alemanes eran superiores a las demás razas. **(al Partido Nazi/el totalitarismo)**

6. Peasants in the Soviet Union were arrested or killed if they did not agree to give up their farms as part of the _____ process. **(totalitarianism/collectivization)/**Los campesinos de la Unión Soviética eran arrestados o asesinados si se negaban a ceder sus granjas como parte del proceso de _____. **(totalitarismo/colectivización)**

7. A forceful speaker named _____ particularly blamed Jews for Germany's problems. **(Benito Mussolini/Adolf Hitler)/**Un orador enérgico llamado _____ culpaba particularmente a los judíos de los problemas de Alemania. **(Benito Mussolini/Adolf Hitler)**

8. _____ is a political system based on extreme nationalism and a strong military. **(Fascism/Collectivization)/**_____ es un sistema político que se basa en el nacionalismo extremo y en un fuerte ejército. **(El fascismo/La colectivización)**

9. _____ could not control Japanese military forces. **(Emperor Hirohito/Joseph Stalin)/**_____ no pudo controlar las fuerzas militares japonesas. **(El emperador Hirohito/José Stalin)**

# World War II/Segunda Guerra Mundial

## Lesson/Lección 2

**MAIN IDEAS/IDEAS PRINCIPALES**

1. The war in Europe began with Germany's invasion of Poland, and the war in the Pacific began with Japan's attack on Pearl Harbor./La guerra en Europa comenzó con la invasión de Polonia por parte de Alemania; la guerra en el Pacífico comenzó con el ataque a Pearl Harbor por parte de Japón.

2. The Germans controlled much of Europe before the Allies invaded on D-Day./Los alemanes controlaban gran parte de Europa antes de la invasión de los Aliados en el Día D.

3. The Japanese controlled much of Asia and the Pacific until the Allies defeated Japanese naval forces at the Battle of Midway./Los japoneses controlaron gran parte de Asia y del Pacífico hasta que sus fuerzas navales fueron derrotadas por los Aliados en la Batalla de Midway.

## Key Terms and People/Personas y palabras clave

**Axis Powers/Potencias del Eje** Germany, Italy, and Japan during World War II/ Alemania, Italia y Japón durante la Segunda Guerra Mundial

**Allied Powers/Potencias aliadas** Great Britain, France, the Soviet Union, and eventually, the United States/Gran Bretaña, Francia, la Unión Soviética y, más tarde, los Estados Unidos

**blitzkrieg/blitzkrieg** a "lightning war" in which tanks, trucks, and bombers quickly strike the enemy/"guerra relámpago" en la que tanques, camiones y bombarderos atacan rápidamente al enemigo

**Winston Churchill/Winston Churchill** prime minister of Great Britain from 1940 to 1945 and from 1951 to 1954/primer ministro de Gran Bretaña de 1940 a 1945 y de 1951 a 1954

**Dwight D. Eisenhower/Dwight D. Eisenhower** U.S. general who was Supreme Allied Commander in charge of planning the Allied invasion/general estadounidense que fue el comandante supremo de las fuerzas aliadas y el encargado de planificar la invasión de los Aliados

## Lesson Summary/Resumen de la lección

### THE WAR BEGINS/COMIENZA LA GUERRA

After Adolf Hitler became ruler of Germany, he formed an alliance with Italy and Japan in 1936. This group became known as the **Axis Powers.** Hitler wanted to expand Germany and unite all people of German heritage. He easily took over Austria and part of Czechoslovakia. Using tanks and trucks and bomber planes, Germany quickly

> Underline what Hitler wanted to do as leader of Germany./Subraya lo que Hitler quería lograr como líder de Alemania.

defeated Poland in what the Germans called a **blitzkrieg,** or "lightning war." When Germany attacked Poland, the **Allied Powers**—Great Britain and France—declared war on Germany. France fell to the German army in 1940. British Prime Minister **Winston Churchill** inspired his people with well-known speeches to fight against the Germans./Después de convertirse en gobernante de Alemania, Adolf Hitler creó una alianza con Italia y Japón en 1936. Este grupo fue conocido como las **Potencias del Eje.** Hitler quería que Alemania se expandiera y que todas las personas de ascendencia alemana se unieran. Tomó el control de Austria y de parte de Checoslovaquia con facilidad. Con tanques, camiones y bombarderos, Alemania derrotó rápidamente a Polonia en lo que los alemanes llamaban **blitzkrieg,** o "guerra relámpago". Fue entonces cuando las **Potencias aliadas,** Gran Bretaña y Francia, le declararon la guerra a Alemania. Francia cayó frente al ejército alemán en 1940. El primer ministro británico, **Winston Churchill,** motivó a su pueblo a luchar contra los alemanes mediante sus famosos discursos.

> **What action caused the Allies to declare war on Germany?/¿Qué acción hizo que los Aliados le declararan la guerra a Alemania?**
>
> _____
>
> _____

The United States wanted to avoid becoming involved in other nations' affairs. But on December 7, 1941, Japan attacked the U.S. naval base at Pearl Harbor, Hawaii. With fighter planes and bombers, the Japanese killed more than 2,000 American soldiers. The United States declared war against the Axis Powers and joined the Allies./Los Estados Unidos querían evitar involucrarse en los asuntos de otras naciones. Sin embargo, el 7 de diciembre de 1941, Japón atacó la base naval de los Estados Unidos en Pearl Harbor, Hawái. Con aviones de combate y bombarderos, los japoneses mataron a más de 2,000 soldados estadounidenses. Entonces, los Estados Unidos declararon la guerra a las Potencias del Eje y se unieron a los Aliados.

> **Why did the United States join the Allied Powers in World War II?/¿Por qué los Estados Unidos se unieron a las Potencias aliadas durante la Segunda Guerra Mundial?**
>
> _____
>
> _____
>
> _____
>
> _____

## FINAL YEARS OF THE WAR IN EUROPE/ ÚLTIMOS AÑOS DE LA GUERRA EN EUROPA

The Axis Powers controlled much of Europe at the beginning of the war. In 1941, Hitler's troops invaded the Soviet Union. The German troops were not prepared for the harsh Russian winter. The Soviet army was able to push the Germans back. The British air force and American bombers began to bomb Germany. In 1943, Allied forces defeated Axis troops in Africa and then invaded Italy./Al comienzo de la guerra, las Potencias del Eje controlaban gran parte de Europa. En 1941, las tropas de Hitler invadieron la Unión Soviética, pero no estaban preparadas para el crudo invierno ruso. El ejército soviético logró hacer retroceder a los alemanes. Las fuerzas aéreas británicas y los bombarderos estadounidenses comenzaron a bombardear Alemania. En 1943, los Aliados derrotaron a las tropas del Eje en África y luego invadieron Italia.

U.S. general **Dwight D. Eisenhower,** the Supreme Allied Commander, led the planning of an allied invasion of Europe from the west. On June 6, 1944, called D-Day, over 156,000 Allied troops landed on Normandy's beaches in France. It was the largest invasion by sea in history. The German forces were waiting and a huge number of soldiers died. Two months later, Allied forces entered Paris. Germans fought hard through April of 1945, until the Soviets made it to Berlin, Germany's capital./El general estadounidense **Dwight D. Eisenhower,** comandante supremo de las fuerzas aliadas, dirigió la planificación de la invasión de Europa desde el oeste por parte de los Aliados. El 6 de junio de 1944, conocido como el Día D, más de 156,000 soldados aliados desembarcaron en las playas de Normandía, en Francia. Fue la invasión por mar más grande de la historia. Las fuerzas alemanas estaban

> **What happened on D-Day?/ ¿Qué sucedió en el Día D?**
> _____
> _____
> _____

Lesson/Lección 2, *continued*/*continuación*

a la espera y una enorme cantidad de soldados murieron. Dos meses más tarde, las fuerzas aliadas entraron en París. Los alemanes lucharon arduamente durante el mes de abril de 1945, hasta que los soviéticos llegaron a Berlín, la capital de Alemania.

## WAR IN ASIA AND THE PACIFIC/GUERRA EN ASIA Y EL PACÍFICO

For several months after Pearl Harbor, Japan controlled the Pacific. In mid-1942, American bombers sank four Japanese carriers at the Battle of Midway. From that point on, the Allies began to attack and take control of Japanese-held islands. By the fall of 1944, U.S. forces regained control of the Philippines and Burma and started bombing targets in Japan. The defeat of Japan was near./Después del ataque a Pearl Harbor, durante varios meses Japón controló el Pacífico. A mediados de 1942, los bombarderos estadounidenses hundieron cuatro portaaviones japoneses en la Batalla de Midway. A partir de ese momento, los Aliados comenzaron a atacar y tomar el control de las islas que se encontraban bajo dominio japonés. Para el otoño de 1944, las fuerzas de los EE. UU. habían recuperado el control de Filipinas y Birmania, y comenzaron a bombardear blancos en Japón. La derrota de Japón estaba próxima.

> **What was the turning point of the war in Asia and the Pacific?/¿Cuál fue el momento decisivo de la guerra en Asia y el Pacífico?**
>
> _____
>
> _____
>
> _____

## CHALLENGE ACTIVITY/ACTIVIDAD AVANZADA

**Critical Thinking: Predict/Pensamiento crítico: Predecir** How might World War II have been different if Japan had not decided to bomb the U.S. forces at Pearl Harbor? Write a short paper to explain your answer./¿De qué manera habría sido distinta la Segunda Guerra Mundial si Japón no hubiera decidido bombardear a las fuerzas estadounidenses en Pearl Harbor? Escribe un texto breve en el que expliques tu respuesta.

| Allied Powers/ Potencias aliadas | Axis Powers/Potencias del Eje | blitzkrieg/blitzkrieg |
| D-Day/Día D | Dwight D. Eisenhower/ Dwight D. Eisenhower | Winston Churchill/ Winston Churchill |

**DIRECTIONS/INSTRUCCIONES** Use the words in the word bank to write a summary of what you have learned./Usa las palabras del banco de palabras para escribir un resumen de lo que aprendiste.

_____

_____

_____

_____

_____

_____

_____

_____

_____

_____

_____

_____

_____

_____

_____

_____

_____

_____

_____

_____

_____

# World War II/Segunda Guerra Mundial

## Lesson/Lección 3

---

**MAIN IDEAS/IDEAS PRINCIPALES**

1. The Nazis launched a campaign to terrorize and kill European Jews and other groups shortly after Hitler gained power./Poco después de la llegada de Hitler al poder, los nazis iniciaron una campaña para aterrorizar y matar a los judíos europeos y a otros grupos.

2. The Final Solution was the Nazi plan to ship Jews to extermination camps in Poland./La Solución final fue el plan nazi que consistía en enviar a los judíos a campos de exterminio en Polonia.

3. Allied armies liberated the Nazi camps in 1944 and 1945./En 1944 y 1945, las tropas aliadas liberaron los campos nazis.

---

# Key Terms and People/Personas y palabras clave

**anti-Semitism/antisemitismo** hostility and discrimination toward Jewish people/ hostilidad y discriminación contra los judíos

**Holocaust/Holocausto** the Nazi murder of millions of Jewish men, women, and children during World War II/matanza por parte de los nazis de millones de hombres, mujeres y niños judíos durante la Segunda Guerra Mundial

**genocide/genocidio** the deliberate destruction of a group of people because of their race, politics, or culture/destrucción deliberada de un grupo de personas debido a su raza, sus ideas políticas o su cultura

**Kristallnacht/Kristallnacht** night of November 9, 1938, when the Nazis carried out violent attacks against Jews in Germany, Austria, and German-controlled Czechoslovakia/la noche del 9 de noviembre de 1938, en la que los nazis emprendieron violentos ataques contra los judíos en Alemania, Austria y la Checoslovaquia controlada por Alemania

**concentration camp/campo de concentración** prison camp where political prisoners and other enemies of the state are confined/campo de prisioneros donde están confinados los presos políticos y otros enemigos del estado

**ghetto/gueto** area of a city or town where Jews were confined by walls, fences, and gates/área de una ciudad o un pueblo en la que los judíos eran confinados mediante muros, cercas y puertas

**Final Solution/Solución final** Nazi plan to ship European Jews to killing centers in Poland/plan nazi que consistía en enviar a los judíos europeos a centros de exterminio en Polonia

# Lesson Summary/Resumen de la lección

## NAZI ANTI-SEMITISM/ANTISEMITISMO NAZI

Jews had lived in Europe for centuries. They had faced **anti-Semitism** before because of their religion, but the Nazis believed that the German race was superior to all others. The Nazis decided to commit **genocide** against the Jews in an act called the **Holocaust.**/Los judíos habían vivido en Europa por siglos. Habían sufrido anteriormente el **antisemitismo** debido a su religión, pero los nazis creían que los alemanes eran una raza superior a las demás. Los nazis decidieron cometer un **genocidio** contra los judíos en un acto conocido como el **Holocausto.**

When Adolf Hitler first came to power, the Nazis passed the Nuremberg Laws. Jews were no longer considered to be German citizens. They could also only marry other Jews. The Nazis did not want to mix races. There was also violence against the Jews, such as on the "Night of Broken Glass," or *Kristallnacht.* Soon Jews and "undesirables," like gypsies and people with disabilities, were sent to **concentration camps.** Once there, the SS killed them or forced them to work./Cuando Adolf Hitler llegó al poder, los nazis aprobaron las Leyes de Núremberg, según las cuales los judíos ya no eran considerados ciudadanos alemanes. Solo podían casarse con otros judíos, ya que los nazis no querían mezclar las razas. También hubo violencia contra los judíos, como en la "Noche de los cristales rotos", o *Kristallnacht.* Pronto, los judíos y otros "indeseables", como los gitanos y las personas con discapacidades, fueron enviados a **campos de concentración.** Una vez allí, las SS los mataban o los obligaban a trabajar.

> **What were two ways that the Nuremberg Laws affected Jews in Germany?/** ¿De qué dos maneras las Leyes de Núremberg afectaron a los judíos en Alemania?
>
> _____
> _____
> _____
> _____

> **What is another name for** *Kristallnacht*?/¿De qué otra forma se conoce a la *Kristallnacht*?
>
> _____
> _____

## THE FINAL SOLUTION/LA SOLUCIÓN FINAL

Beginning in 1940, the Nazis decided to separate
and isolate Polish Jews. The largest **ghetto** in
Poland was in the city of Warsaw. The Germans
also set up many ghettos in the Soviet Union.
Food was scarce in these enclosed spaces, and
many people died from starvation or disease./
A partir de 1940, los nazis decidieron separar y
aislar a los judíos polacos. El **gueto** más grande
de Polonia se encontraba en la ciudad de
Varsovia. Los alemanes también establecieron
muchos guetos en la Unión Soviética. La comida
era escasa en estos espacios cerrados, y muchas
personas morían de hambre o por enfermedades.

   The Nazis built killing centers in Poland
so they could massacre the Jews quickly. This
was the **Final Solution.** The largest camp was
at Auschwitz-Birkenau. Some Jews went into
hiding, while others fought to resist the Nazi
plan. Some people who were not Jewish helped
Jews to fight or hide./Los nazis construyeron
centros de exterminio en Polonia con el objetivo
de aniquilar rápidamente a los judíos. Esto fue
conocido como la **Solución final.** El campo más
grande se encontraba en Auschwitz-Birkenau.
Algunos judíos se escondieron, mientras que
otros lucharon para resistir al plan nazi. Algunas
personas que no eran judías ayudaron a los
judíos a luchar o a esconderse.

> **Circle the name of a concentration camp./**
> Encierra en un círculo el nombre de un campo de concentración.

## AFTERMATH OF THE HOLOCAUST/SECUELAS DEL HOLOCAUSTO

At the end of the war, SS officers began to force
concentration camp prisoners to walk on "death
marches" to Germany. The Nazis did not want
anyone to be able to tell how badly they were
treated. Hundreds of prisoners were shot if they
could not keep up. Allied forces liberated the
camps in 1944 and 1945. They found piles of

> **What was the purpose of the "death marches"?/**
> ¿Cuál era el objetivo de las "marchas de la muerte"?
> _____
> _____
> _____
> _____

dead bodies and other signs of cruelty and horror./Al final de la guerra, los oficiales de las SS obligaron a los prisioneros de los campos de concentración a emprender las "marchas de la muerte" hacia Alemania. Los nazis no querían que nadie pudiera notar lo mal que habían tratado a los judíos. Cientos de prisioneros fueron fusilados por no poder seguir el ritmo de la caminata. Las fuerzas aliadas liberaron los campos en 1944 y 1945. Allí encontraron montones de cadáveres y otros indicios de crueldad y horror.

Israel was founded in 1948 as a nation where Jews could live. Many feared returning to their homes in Europe. Other Jews moved to places like the United States, Canada, and South America./En 1948, se fundó Israel como una nación en la que los judíos podían vivir. Muchos de ellos temían regresar a sus hogares en Europa. Otros se mudaron a lugares como los Estados Unidos, Canadá y América del Sur.

> After the war, why did Jews go to live in places like Israel, the United States, Canada, and South America?/Después de la guerra, ¿por qué los judíos se fueron a vivir a lugares como Israel, los Estados Unidos, Canadá y América del Sur?
>
> _____
>
> _____
>
> _____

## CHALLENGE ACTIVITY/ACTIVIDAD AVANZADA

**Critical Thinking: Summarize/Pensamiento crítico: Resumir**  Research someone like Raoul Wallenberg, Oskar Schindler, Sir Nicholas Winton, or the fishermen of Denmark. Write a summary that tells details about what they did to help Jews during World War II. Include any dangers they faced./Investiga la vida de personas como Raoul Wallenberg, Oskar Schindler, Sir Nicholas Winton o los pescadores de Dinamarca. Escribe un resumen en el que cuentes detalles de lo que hicieron para ayudar a los judíos durante la Segunda Guerra Mundial. Incluye los peligros a los que se enfrentaron.

Lesson/Lección 3, *continued*/*continuación*

| anti-Semitism/ antisemitismo | concentration camp/ campo de concentración | Final Solution/ Solución final | genocide/ genocidio |
| ghetto/gueto | Holocaust/Holocausto | *Kristallnacht*/ *Kristallnacht* | |

**DIRECTIONS/INSTRUCCIONES** Answer each question by writing
a sentence that contains at least one word from the word bank./
Responde cada pregunta con una oración que contenga al menos
una palabra del banco de palabras.

1. What happened on the night of November 9, 1938?/¿Qué ocurrió la noche
del 9 de noviembre de 1938?

_____

_____

2. In Poland, where was the largest area of a city or town that confined Jews?/
En Polonia, ¿cuál era el área de mayor tamaño destinada al confinamiento
de judíos?

_____

_____

3. What is the name of the Nazi murder of millions of Jewish men, women,
and children during World War II?/¿Cómo se llamó la matanza por parte
de los nazis de millones de hombres, mujeres y niños judíos durante la
Segunda Guerra Mundial?

_____

_____

4. What is it called when Jewish people face hostility and discrimination?/
¿Cómo se denomina el padecimiento de hostilidades y discriminación
que enfrentan los judíos?

_____

_____

5. Why did the Nazis think of a plan to ship European Jews to killing centers?/
¿Por qué los nazis idearon un plan para enviar a los judíos europeos a centros de exterminio?

_____

_____

6. What were the Nazis doing when they deliberately tried to destroy the Jews?/
¿Qué cometían los nazis cuando deliberadamente intentaban destruir a los judíos?

_____

_____

7. In what place did the SS kill Jews and "undesirables" or force them to work?/
¿En qué lugares las SS asesinaban u obligaban a trabajar a los judíos y a los "indeseables"?

_____

_____

# World War II/Segunda Guerra Mundial

## Lesson/Lección 4

**MAIN IDEAS/IDEAS PRINCIPALES**

1. World War II ended in 1945 with the defeat of the Axis Powers by the Allies./La Segunda Guerra Mundial terminó en 1945 con la derrota de las Potencias del Eje frente a los Aliados.

2. After the war, Japan adopted a new constitution that lessened the influence of the military and established a democratic government./Tras la guerra, Japón adoptó una nueva constitución que reducía la influencia del ejército y establecía un gobierno democrático.

3. Europe was divided into communist-controlled Eastern Europe and democratic Western Europe after the war ended./Cuando terminó la guerra, Europa se dividió en Europa oriental, controlada por los comunistas, y Europa occidental, que era democrática.

## Key Terms and People/Personas y palabras clave

**atomic bomb/bomba atómica** a nuclear weapon that splits atoms to cause a powerful explosion/arma nuclear que divide átomos para causar una potente explosión

**United Nations/Naciones Unidas** a group of countries that aims to maintain world peace and security/grupo de países que procura mantener la paz y la seguridad mundiales

**Douglas MacArthur/Douglas MacArthur** U.S. general who was the Supreme Commander for Allied Powers in Japan/general estadounidense que fue el comandante supremo de las Potencias aliadas en Japón

**war crime/crimen de guerra** a violation of the defined laws of war/violación de las leyes de guerra establecidas

**Nuremberg Trials/Juicios de Núremberg** court proceedings in Germany that were about war crimes committed by Nazi leaders/procedimientos judiciales en Alemania que trataron los crímenes de guerra cometidos por los líderes nazis

## Lesson Summary/Resumen de la lección

### WAR ENDS/FIN DE LA GUERRA

V-E Day marked the end of World War II in Europe. Allied military leaders warned that invading Japan would cause the death of over a million Allied troops. An **atomic bomb** was dropped on the Japanese city of Hiroshima. Days later, another one fell on Nagasaki. Over

> **Where did the Allies use the atomic bomb in Japan?/¿En qué lugares de Japón lanzaron bombas atómicas los Aliados?**
>
> _____
>
> _____

100,000 people were killed. Japan surrendered, and V-J Day was declared. World War II was over./El Día de la Victoria en Europa marcó el fin de la Segunda Guerra Mundial en Europa. Los líderes militares aliados advirtieron que invadir Japón causaría la muerte de más de un millón de soldados aliados. Entonces, lanzaron una **bomba atómica** en la ciudad japonesa de Hiroshima. Días después, otra bomba cayó sobre Nagasaki. Más de 100,000 personas fueron asesinadas. Japón se rindió, y se declaró el Día de la Victoria sobre Japón. La Segunda Guerra Mundial había terminado.

The war had weakened many economies and governments in the world. The United States and the Soviet Union also began to distrust each other. One positive event during this time was the creation of the **United Nations.**/La guerra había debilitado muchas economías y muchos gobiernos del mundo. Los Estados Unidos y la Unión Soviética comenzaron a desconfiar el uno del otro. Un suceso positivo que tuvo lugar durante este período fue la creación de las **Naciones Unidas.**

> **How did the relationship between the United States and the Soviet Union change after the war?/** ¿De qué manera cambió la relación entre los Estados Unidos y la Unión Soviética después de la guerra?
>
> _____
> _____

## POSTWAR JAPAN/JAPÓN EN LA POSGUERRA

Japan had little industry left after the war, and its cities had been bombed and burned. **Douglas MacArthur** was in charge of the Allied forces that occupied Japan until 1952. The United States helped the Japanese write a new constitution that reduced the power of the emperor and the military. The document also increased the authority of the Japanese legislature and gave men and women the right to vote./Tras la guerra, a Japón le quedaba poco de su industria, y sus ciudades habían sido bombardeadas e incendiadas. **Douglas MacArthur** estuvo a cargo de las fuerzas

> **Underline three ways that Japan's new constitution changed Japanese government./**Subraya tres maneras en las que la nueva constitución de Japón cambió el gobierno japonés.

aliadas que ocuparon Japón hasta el año 1952.
Los Estados Unidos ayudaron a los japoneses a
redactar una nueva constitución que reducía el
poder del emperador y del ejército. Asimismo,
el documento aumentaba la autoridad de la
asamblea legislativa japonesa y otorgaba a
hombres y mujeres el derecho al voto.

The Allies also held trials of Japanese officials
who had committed **war crimes** in China. Most
of the defendants were convicted and sentenced
to prison. Seven were put to death./Los Aliados
también celebraron juicios contra los oficiales
japoneses que habían cometido **crímenes de
guerra** en China. La mayoría de los acusados
fueron declarados culpables y condenados a
prisión. Siete de ellos fueron ejecutados.

## POSTWAR EUROPE/EUROPA EN LA POSGUERRA

Nazi leaders also had to face justice in court. The
**Nuremberg Trials** included many major Nazi
officials but not Adolf Hitler or his top leaders.
All of those people were either dead or missing.
As in Japan, most of the defendants were
convicted. Some were sent to prison, but many
were given death sentences and hanged./Los
líderes nazis también tuvieron que rendir cuentas
ante la justicia. En los **Juicios de Núremberg,**
fueron juzgados muchos de los principales
oficiales nazis, pero no Adolf Hitler ni sus más
altos dirigentes, dado que todos estaban muertos
o desaparecidos. Al igual que en Japón, la
mayoría de los acusados fueron declarados
culpables. Algunos fueron enviados a prisión,
pero muchos fueron condenados a la pena
de muerte y fueron ahorcados.

Allied leaders held a conference at Potsdam to
discuss the future of Europe. The Soviet Union
occupied the nations between it and Germany.

> **Why did the Nuremberg Trials not include Adolf Hitler or his top leaders?/¿Por qué los Juicios de Núremberg no incluyeron a Adolf Hitler ni a sus más altos dirigentes?**
>
> _____
> _____
> _____

No one agreed on how to handle these lands. The Soviets placed communist governments in these countries and controlled the new nation of East Germany as well. The remaining German territory became the democratic country of West Germany. Europe was now divided into East and West, and this separation would last for decades./Los líderes de los Aliados celebraron una conferencia en Potsdam para debatir el futuro de Europa. La Unión Soviética ocupaba las naciones que se encontraban entre su territorio y Alemania. No se llegó a un acuerdo con respecto a cómo manejar esas tierras. Los soviéticos establecieron gobiernos comunistas en esos países y también mantuvieron el control de la nueva nación de Alemania Oriental. El resto del territorio alemán se convirtió en la nación democrática de Alemania Occidental. Así, Europa quedó dividida en oriente y occidente, y esta separación duraría décadas.

> **Which parts of postwar Europe were occupied or controlled by the Soviet Union?/**¿Qué partes de la Europa de posguerra estaban ocupadas o controladas por la Unión Soviética?
>
> _____
>
> _____
>
> _____

## CHALLENGE ACTIVITY/ACTIVIDAD AVANZADA

**Critical Thinking: Elaborate/Pensamiento crítico: Profundizar** Write a response to these questions: Do you agree or disagree with the decision to drop the atomic bomb on Japan? Why? If not, would you have supported an invasion? Why? If you would not have supported an invasion or an atomic bomb, what would you have supported instead? Why?/Escribe una respuesta para las siguientes preguntas: ¿Estás de acuerdo con la decisión de lanzar las bombas atómicas en Japón? ¿Por qué? Si no estás de acuerdo, ¿habrías apoyado una invasión? ¿Por qué? Si no hubieras apoyado la invasión ni el lanzamiento de las bombas atómicas, ¿qué otra medida habrías apoyado? ¿Por qué?

**DIRECTIONS/INSTRUCCIONES** Look at each set of four vocabulary terms. On the line provided, write the letter of the term that does not relate to the others./Observa cada conjunto de cuatro términos de vocabulario. En el espacio en blanco, escribe la letra del término que no tiene relación con los demás.

_____ 1. a. justice/justicia
         b. Nazi leaders/líderes nazis
         c. court proceedings/procedimientos judiciales
         d. Hiroshima/Hiroshima

_____ 2. a. Japan/Japón
         b. Germany/Alemania
         c. United States/los Estados Unidos
         d. Supreme Commander/comandante supremo

_____ 3. a. constitution/constitución
         b. violation/violación
         c. laws/leyes
         d. trials/juicios

_____ 4. a. peace/paz
         b. group/grupo
         c. distrust/desconfianza
         d. security/seguridad

_____ 5. a. explosion/explosión
         b. Nuremberg/Núremberg
         c. weapon/arma
         d. Nagasaki/Nagasaki

# The Cold War Years/Los años de la Guerra Fría

## Lesson/Lección 1

### MAIN IDEAS/IDEAS PRINCIPALES

1. After World War II, the Soviet Union and the other Allied powers became enemies./Después de la Segunda Guerra Mundial, la Unión Soviética y las demás Potencias aliadas quedaron enfrentadas.

2. Communism expanded as the Soviet Union took control of Eastern European countries./El comunismo se expandió a medida que la Unión Soviética tomó el control de varios países de Europa oriental.

3. The United States took several steps to stop the expansion of communism./ Los Estados Unidos tomaron distintas medidas para detener la expansión del comunismo.

4. As the Cold War heated up, tensions between communist and capitalist countries increased./Con el avance de la Guerra Fría, las tensiones entre los países comunistas y capitalistas aumentaron.

## Key Terms and People/Personas y palabras clave

**Cold War/Guerra Fría** nonmilitary conflict between the Soviet Union and the United States/conflicto no militar entre la Unión Soviética y los Estados Unidos

**containment/contención** goal of preventing the Soviet Union from expanding its influence/objetivo de impedir la expansión de la influencia de la Unión Soviética

**Truman Doctrine/Doctrina Truman** policy of providing aid to help foreign countries fight communism/política de proporcionar ayuda a los países extranjeros para luchar contra el comunismo

**Marshall Plan/Plan Marshall** program under which the U.S. gave aid to Western European countries to rebuild and stabilize their economies/programa bajo el cual los EE. UU. ayudaron a países de Europa occidental a reconstruir y estabilizar sus economías

**North Atlantic Treaty Organization (NATO)/Organización del Tratado del Atlántico Norte (OTAN)** defensive military alliance of the U.S., Canada, and ten Western European nations/alianza militar defensiva formada por los EE. UU., Canadá y diez naciones de Europa occidental

**Warsaw Pact/Pacto de Varsovia** alliance between Soviet Union and Eastern European countries/alianza entre la Unión Soviética y los países de Europa oriental

**arms race/carrera armamentista** competition between U.S. and Soviet Union for greater military might/competencia entre los EE. UU. y la Unión Soviética por una mayor potencia militar

# Lesson Summary/Resumen de la lección

## ALLIES BECOME ENEMIES/LOS ALIADOS SE ENFRENTAN

Allied leaders divided Germany and its capital into four parts after World War II. They were occupied by Britain, France, the U.S., and the Soviet Union./Después de la Segunda Guerra Mundial, los líderes Aliados dividieron Alemania y su capital en cuatro partes, que fueron ocupadas por Gran Bretaña, Francia, los EE. UU. y la Unión Soviética.

In 1945, the U.S. and the Soviet Union were the most powerful nations. The Soviet Union wanted to spread communism around the world. The U.S. was committed to democracy. These differences led to the **Cold War,** a conflict in which no weapons were fired that lasted for about 50 years./ En 1945, los EE. UU. y la Unión Soviética eran las naciones más poderosas. La Unión Soviética quería propagar el comunismo por todo el mundo. Los EE. UU., por su parte, estaban comprometidos con la democracia. Estas diferencias desencadenaron la **Guerra Fría,** un conflicto que duró cerca de 50 años y durante el cual no se disparó ningún arma.

> **What happened to Germany after World War II?/¿Qué sucedió con Alemania después de la Segunda Guerra Mundial?**
> _____
> _____
> _____

> **Underline the phrase that describes how the Cold War was different from other wars./Subraya la frase que describe en qué sentido la Guerra Fría fue diferente a otras guerras.**

## BUILDING AN IRON CURTAIN/LA CONSTRUCCIÓN DE UNA CORTINA DE HIERRO

The Soviet Union occupied its western border and made Poland a communist government. It expanded to Eastern Europe and the Balkan countries. These countries became "satellite states." They were cut off from contact with the rest of Europe. Winston Churchill described this division as "an iron curtain."/La Unión Soviética extendió su frontera occidental y estableció un gobierno comunista en Polonia. También se expandió hacia Europa oriental y los países balcánicos. Esos países se convirtieron en

> **What term did Winston Churchill use to describe how some countries were cut off from the rest of Europe?/¿Qué término utilizó Winston Churchill para describir cómo algunos países estaban aislados del resto de Europa?**

"estados satélite" soviéticos y perdieron contacto con el resto de Europa. Winston Churchill describió esta división como "una cortina de hierro".

## EFFORTS TO HALT COMMUNIST EXPANSION/ ESFUERZOS POR DETENER LA EXPANSIÓN COMUNISTA

To try to prevent the spread of communism, the U.S. developed the policy of **containment.** This did not stop the Soviet Union, so Congress provided aid to help foreign countries fight communism. This policy was the **Truman Doctrine.** Also, under the **Marshall Plan,** help was provided to Western European countries to rebuild and stabilize their economies./Con el objetivo de impedir la expansión del comunismo, los EE. UU. desarrollaron la política de **contención.** Como esa política no detuvo a la Unión Soviética, el Congreso brindó ayuda a los países extranjeros para luchar contra el comunismo a través de otra política, conocida como la **Doctrina Truman.** Asimismo, bajo el **Plan Marshall,** los Estados Unidos ayudaron a los países de Europa occidental a reconstruir y estabilizar sus economías.

> Underline the phrase that explains the purpose of containment./Subraya la frase que explica el objetivo de la contención.

## COLD WAR HEATS UP/AUMENTA LA TEMPERATURA DE LA GUERRA FRÍA

The U.S., France, and Britain withdrew their forces from Germany and West Berlin in 1948 so their areas could be reunified. This created a problem for West Berlin because East Berlin was held by the Soviets. They created a blockade to cut off West Berlin so the city had no way of getting supplies. Stalin thought the Allies would give up West Berlin. Instead, British and U.S. officials flew supplies into West Berlin in what was called the Berlin Airlift. The Soviets

> Why did the Soviet Union blockade West Berlin?/ ¿Por qué la Unión Soviética impuso un bloqueo a Berlín Occidental?
>
> _____
>
> _____
>
> _____
>
> _____

eventually ended the blockade./En 1948, los
EE. UU., Francia y Gran Bretaña retiraron sus
fuerzas de Alemania y Berlín Occidental para que
pudieran reunificarse. Esto generó un problema,
dado que Berlín Oriental estaba bajo el control
de los soviéticos. Ellos impusieron un bloqueo
a Berlín Occidental para que la ciudad no
pudiese obtener provisiones. Stalin pensó que
los Aliados abandonarían Berlín Occidental,
pero los oficiales británicos y estadounidenses
aprovisionaron la ciudad por medio de aviones
en lo que se llamó "el puente aéreo de Berlín".
Finalmente, los soviéticos levantaron el bloqueo.

However, Soviet aggression worried Western
Europeans. In 1949, ten Western European nations
joined with the U.S. and Canada to form a
military alliance called the **North Atlantic Treaty
Organization (NATO).** An attack on any NATO
member would be met with armed force by all
member nations. The Soviet Union saw NATO
as a threat and formed its own alliance. It was
the **Warsaw Pact.** Then in 1961, East Germans
built the Berlin Wall. It separated East and
West Berlin./Sin embargo, la agresión soviética
preocupaba a Europa occidental. En 1949, diez
naciones de Europa occidental se unieron con
los EE. UU. y Canadá para formar una alianza
militar llamada **Organización del Tratado del
Atlántico Norte (OTAN).** Un ataque a cualquiera
de los miembros de la OTAN sería respondido
por las fuerzas armadas de todas las naciones
miembro. La Unión Soviética percibió a la OTAN
como una amenaza y formó su propia alianza, el
**Pacto de Varsovia.** Luego, en 1961, los alemanes
orientales construyeron el Muro de·Berlín, que
separaba Berlín Oriental de Berlín Occidental.

> **Why do you think the
> Soviet Union was
> threatened by NATO?/¿Por
> qué piensas que la Unión
> Soviética se sintió
> amenazada por la OTAN?**
>
> _____
> _____
> _____
> _____
> _____

The U.S. and the Soviet Union had atomic weapons. Both feared each side could to destroy the other. So they entered into the **arms race,** a competition for greater military strength./Tanto los EE. UU. como la Unión Soviética tenían armas nucleares. Ambos temían que el otro pudiera destruirlos. Así, iniciaron la **carrera armamentista,** una competencia por lograr una mayor potencia militar.

## CHALLENGE ACTIVITY/ACTIVIDAD AVANZADA

**Critical Thinking: Describe/Pensamiento crítico: Describir**  Imagine that you were living behind the Iron Curtain. Write a short paper describing what your life is like./Imagina que vives detrás de la cortina de hierro. Escribe un ensayo breve en el que describas cómo es tu vida.

| arms race/la carrera armamentista | Cold War/la Guerra Fría | containment/contención |
|---|---|---|
| Marshall Plan/el Plan Marshall | North Atlantic Treaty Organization/la Organización del Tratado del Atlántico Norte | Truman Doctrine/la Doctrina Truman |
| Warsaw Pact/el Pacto de Varsovia | | |

**DIRECTIONS/INSTRUCCIONES**  Read each sentence and fill in the blank with a term from the word bank that best completes the sentence./Lee cada oración y escribe en el espacio en blanco la palabra del banco de palabras que mejor la completa.

1. The alliance between the Soviet Union and Eastern European countries was called the _____./La alianza entre la Unión Soviética y los países de Europa oriental se llamó _____ _____.

2. The program under which the United States gave aid to Western European countries to help rebuild and stabilize their economies was the _____ _____./El programa bajo el cual los Estados Unidos ayudaron a los países de Europa occidental a reconstruir y estabilizar sus economías era _____.

3. The competition between the United States and the Soviet Union for greater military strength was the _____./La competencia entre los Estados Unidos y la Unión Soviética por una mayor potencia militar fue _____.

4. The nonmilitary conflict between the Soviet Union and the United States that lasted for almost 50 years was the _____./El conflicto no militar entre la Unión Soviética y los Estados Unidos que duró casi 50 años fue _____.

5. The _____ is the defensive military alliance among the U.S., Canada, and ten European nations./_____ es la alianza militar defensiva entre los EE. UU., Canadá y diez naciones europeas.

6. The goal of preventing the Soviet Union from expanding its influence around the world was called _____./El objetivo de impedir que la Unión Soviética expandiera su influencia en todo el mundo se llamó _____.

7. The _____ was the policy of providing aid to help foreign countries fight communism./_____ fue la política de proporcionar ayuda a los países extranjeros para luchar contra el comunismo.

# The Cold War Years/Los años de la Guerra Fría

**MAIN IDEAS/IDEAS PRINCIPALES**

1. Following a civil war in China, Communists took control of the country./Tras una guerra civil, los comunistas tomaron el control de China.

2. A war was fought between anti-Communist and pro-Communist forces in Korea./En Corea se desató una guerra entre las fuerzas anticomunistas y procomunistas.

3. A war was fought between anti-Communist and pro-Communist forces in Vietnam./En Vietnam se desató una guerra entre las fuerzas anticomunistas y procomunistas.

4. Differences led to violent and nonviolent conflicts in Cuba, Africa, and the Middle East./Los desacuerdos llevaron a conflictos violentos y no violentos en Cuba, África y Oriente Medio.

# Key Terms and People/Personas y palabras clave

**Mao Zedong/Mao Zedong** leader of the Communist army in China/líder del ejército comunista en China

**communes/comunas** large collective farms/grandes granjas colectivas

**Ho Chi Minh/Ho Chi Minh** head of Communist Party in Vietnam and later North Vietnam/líder del Partido Comunista en Vietnam y, posteriormente, Vietnam del Norte

**domino theory/teoría del dominó** belief that if one Southeast Asian country fell to communism, it would lead to the fall of its neighbors/creencia de que, si un país del sureste asiático caía bajo el dominio comunista, los países vecinos también lo harían

**Vietcong/Viet Cong** Communist fighters in South Vietnam/combatientes comunistas en Vietnam del Sur

**Fidel Castro/Fidel Castro** dictator of Cuba/dictador de Cuba

**Anwar Sadat/Anwar Sadat** Egyptian president; first Arab leader to make peace with Israel/presidente egipcio; primer líder árabe en hacer las paces con Israel

# Lesson Summary/Resumen de la lección

## COMMUNISM IN CHINA/COMUNISMO EN CHINA

In 1949 after years of civil war, **Mao Zedong** led the Communist army and became leader of the People's Republic of China. Mao forced peasants to join large collective farms called **communes.** The people did all the work, but only the government profited. This plan failed. Then in 1966, Mao urged China's young people to form militia units called Red Guards. They led an uprising, the Cultural Revolution. Schools were closed, and writers, teachers, and others were imprisoned or executed. Life became harder for the people. By 1968, the revolution ended, leaving China unstable./En 1949, tras años de guerra civil, **Mao Zedong** dirigió el ejército comunista y se convirtió en el líder de la República Popular China. Mao obligó a los campesinos a formar grandes granjas colectivas llamadas **comunas,** donde los pobladores realizaban todo el trabajo, pero únicamente el gobierno se beneficiaba. Ese plan fracasó. Luego, en 1966, Mao instó a los jóvenes chinos a formar unidades de milicianos llamadas Guardias Rojos. Los Guardias Rojos encabezaron un levantamiento, la Revolución Cultural, durante el cual se cerraron escuelas y escritores y maestros, entre otros, fueron tomados prisioneros o ejecutados. La vida se volvió cada vez más difícil para la gente. En 1968, la revolución finalizó, pero China quedó inestable.

> **What actions did Mao Zedong take and how did they affect China?/¿Qué medidas tomó Mao Zedong y cómo afectaron a China?**
> _____
> _____
> _____
> _____
> _____
> _____

## THE KOREAN WAR/LA GUERRA DE COREA

Korea was divided in two after World War II. The Soviet Union controlled the north. The U.S. occupied the south. In 1950, North Korean troops invaded the south. The U.S. and the United Nations decided to fight back. Fighting lasted for several years before a cease-fire agreement was signed in 1953. The 38th parallel became the border between the two Koreas. A demilitarized zone separates the countries. Today, North Korea is a totalitarian dictatorship. South Korea is a democratic nation./Corea fue dividida en dos después de la Segunda Guerra Mundial. La Unión Soviética controlaba el norte;

> **Underline the sentences that tell how Korea was divided after World War II./Subraya las oraciones que explican cómo se dividió Corea después de la Segunda Guerra Mundial.**

> **Underline the sentences that tell how Korea is divided today./Subraya las oraciones que explican cómo está dividida Corea actualmente.**

los EE. UU. ocupaban el sur. En 1950, tropas norcoreanas invadieron el sur. Los EE. UU. y las Naciones Unidas decidieron contraatacar. El enfrentamiento duró varios años, hasta que finalmente se firmó un acuerdo de cese al fuego en 1953. El paralelo 38 se convirtió en la frontera entre las dos Coreas. Una zona desmilitarizada separa ambos países. Actualmente, Corea del Norte es una dictadura totalitaria. Corea del Sur, por su parte, es una nación democrática.

## WAR IN VIETNAM/GUERRA EN VIETNAM

In the early 1900s, France controlled Vietnam. **Ho Chi Minh** fought against the French and won control with the help of Communists. Since the U.S. believed in the **domino theory,** it was afraid other countries would fall to communism too. Vietnam was already divided; the U.S. and France had an anti-Communist government in the south, while Communist forces controlled the north. Communist fighters in the south called the **Vietcong** were against the south's government. They took control of large areas. So the U.S. sent soldiers to fight them. Fighting was difficult for soldiers, and it continued for years. The war became unpopular. By 1973, all U.S. troops were withdrawn, and the U.S. had been defeated./A principios del siglo 20, Vietnam se encontraba bajo el poder de Francia. **Ho Chi Minh** luchó contra los franceses y tomó el poder con la ayuda de los comunistas. Puesto que los EE. UU. creían en la **teoría del dominó,** temían que otros países del sureste asiático cayeran bajo el dominio comunista. Vietnam se encontraba dividido: en el sur, había un gobierno anticomunista respaldado por Francia y los EE. UU., mientras que las fuerzas comunistas dominaban el norte. Los combatientes comunistas, denominados **Viet Cong,** estaban en contra del

> Why did Ho Chi Minh and his forces fight against the French?/¿Por qué Ho Chi Minh y sus fuerzas lucharon contra los franceses?
>
> _____

> Why might the Vietcong have had an advantage over U.S. soldiers?/¿Qué ventaja puede haber tenido el Viet Cong sobre los soldados estadounidenses?
>
> _____
> _____
> _____

gobierno del sur. Puesto que los comunistas comenzaron a tomar el control de grandes zonas, los EE. UU. enviaron soldados para que los combatieran. La lucha era complicada para los soldados y se prolongó durante años. La guerra se volvió impopular. En 1973, todas las tropas estadounidenses fueron retiradas: los EE. UU. habían sido derrotados.

## COLD WAR FLARES IN THE THIRD WORLD/ LA GUERRA FRÍA ESTALLA EN EL TERCER MUNDO

In 1959, **Fidel Castro** overthrew a Cuban dictator and became a dictator himself. He asked the Soviets for economic and military aid. Cuba became a communist country./En 1959, **Fidel Castro** derrocó al dictador cubano que estaba en el gobierno y se convirtió él mismo en un dictador. Castro pidió a los soviéticos ayuda económica y militar. Así, Cuba pasó a ser un país comunista.

Egyptian president **Anwar Sadat** broke his ties with the Soviets during the 1970s. This led to a 1979 peace treaty between Egypt and Israel./El presidente egipcio **Anwar Sadat** disolvió sus vínculos con los soviéticos durante la década de 1970. Eso condujo a la firma de un tratado de paz entre Egipto e Israel en 1979.

The Soviet Union gained influence in Afghanistan, Nicaragua, and parts of Africa. This led the U.S. to continue its containment policy until the end of the Cold War./La Unión Soviética ganó influencia en Afganistán, Nicaragua y parte de África. Eso llevó a los Estados Unidos a continuar su política de contención hasta el final de la Guerra Fría.

> **Cuba is located close to the United States. Why might U.S. officials have been worried when Cuba became communist?/Cuba está situada cerca de los Estados Unidos. ¿Por qué podrían haberse preocupado los oficiales estadounidenses cuando Cuba se volvió comunista?**
>
> _____
> _____
> _____
> _____

## CHALLENGE ACTIVITY/ACTIVIDAD AVANZADA

**Critical Thinking: Predict/Pensamiento crítico: Predecir**

Think about how the history of Korea might have been affected if the UN and the U.S. had not become involved after North Korea attacked South Korea. Write a short essay in which you predict the consequences./Piensa cómo podría haber cambiado la historia de Corea si las Naciones Unidas y los EE. UU. no se hubieran involucrado después del ataque de Corea del Norte a Corea del Sur. Escribe un ensayo breve en el que predigas las consecuencias.

**DIRECTIONS/INSTRUCCIONES** Read each sentence and fill in the blank with the term in the word pair that best completes the sentence./Lee cada oración y escribe en el espacio en blanco la palabra del par de palabras que mejor la completa.

1. Communist fighters in South Vietnam who took control of the south's countryside were called _____. **(Vietcong/communes)**/Los combatientes comunistas de Vietnam del Sur, que tomaron el control de los campos del sur, se llamaban _____. **(Viet Cong/comunas)**

2. The dictator of Cuba beginning in 1959 was _____. **(Anwar Sadat/Fidel Castro)**/El dictador que tomó el poder en Cuba en 1959 fue _____. **(Anwar Sadat/Fidel Castro)**

3. The Communist leader in China who urged the Cultural Revolution was _____. **(Ho Chi Minh/Mao Zedong)**/El líder comunista chino que alentó la Revolución Cultural fue _____. **(Ho Chi Minh/Mao Zedong)**

4. Large collective farms in China were known as _____. **(communes/domino theory)**/Las grandes granjas colectivas de China eran conocidas como _____. **(comunas/teoría del dominó)**

5. The Egyptian president who signed a peace treaty with Israel was _____. **(Mao Zedong/Anwar Sadat)**/El presidente egipcio que firmó el tratado de paz con Israel fue _____. **(Mao Zedong/Anwar Sadat)**

6. The belief that if one Southeast Asian country fell to communism its neighbors would fall too is the _____.
   **(domino theory/commune)**/La creencia de que, si un país del sureste asiático caía bajo el dominio comunista, los países vecinos también lo harían es la _____. **(teoría del dominó/comuna)**

7. The leader of the Communist Party in Vietnam and later North Vietnam was _____. **(Ho Cho Minh/Mao Zedong)**/El líder del Partido Comunista en Vietnam y, posteriormente, Vietnam del Norte fue _____. **(Ho Chi Minh/Mao Zedong)**

## The Cold War Years/Los años de la Guerra Fría

### Lesson/Lección 3

**MAIN IDEAS/IDEAS PRINCIPALES**

1. The Soviet Union maintained firm control over Eastern European communist countries but had disagreements with the Chinese./La Unión Soviética mantenía un control firme sobre los países comunistas de Europa oriental, pero tenía desacuerdos con los chinos.

2. In the 1970s, Cold War tensions eased, but they reemerged by the end of the decade./En la década de 1970, las tensiones de la Guerra Fría se redujeron, pero volvieron a surgir hacia fines de la década.

## Key Terms and People

**Nikita Khrushchev/Nikita Khrushchev** Communist party leader of the Soviet Union/líder del Partido Comunista de la Unión Soviética

**de-Stalinization/desestalinización** reforming the Soviet Union to ease Stalin's repressive policies/cambios que se realizaron en la Unión Soviética para aliviar las políticas represivas estalinistas

**Imre Nagy/Imre Nagy** popular Hungarian Communist leader/popular líder comunista húngaro

**Alexander Dubček/Alexander Dubček** Czech Communist leader/líder comunista checoslovaco

**détente/Détente** U.S. policy of easing Cold War tensions/política de los EE. UU. de aliviar las tensiones de la Guerra Fría

## Lesson Summary/Resumen de la lección

### POLICY CHANGES IN THE COMMUNIST WORLD/
### CAMBIOS DE POLÍTICA EN EL MUNDO COMUNISTA

With Joseph Stalin's death in 1953, more moderate Soviet leaders came to power. They allowed satellite countries more independence as long as they continued to be allied with the Soviet Union. **Nikita Khrushchev** became the Communist Party leader in 1956. He rejected Stalin's policies and started **de-Stalinization.** He wanted to reform the country to ease Stalin's repressive policies./Tras la muerte de Stalin en 1953, llegaron al poder líderes soviéticos menos radicales. Se dio a los estados satélite una mayor independencia, siempre y cuando continuaran siendo aliados de la Unión

> **How was Khrushchev different from Stalin?/**
> **¿En qué se diferenciaba Khrushchev de Stalin?**
>
> _____
> _____
> _____
> _____

Soviética. En 1956, **Nikita Khrushchev** se convirtió en el líder del Partido Comunista. Rechazó las políticas de Stalin y comenzó un proceso de **desestalinización** que buscaba transformar el país para aliviar las políticas represivas estalinistas.

However, these policies did not help people living in Soviet satellite countries. In Hungary, people protested their lack of freedom. They overthrew Hungary's Soviet-controlled government. **Imre Nagy,** a popular Hungarian Communist leader, formed a new government. He demanded that Soviet troops leave, but they entered the capital. Hungarian freedom fighters fought against the Soviet troops, but they were no match. A new Soviet-friendly government took over./Sin embargo, estas nuevas políticas no beneficiaban a quienes habitaban en los estados satélite soviéticos. En Hungría, la gente empezó a protestar por su falta de libertad. El gobierno húngaro, controlado por los soviéticos, fue derrocado. **Imre Nagy,** un popular líder comunista húngaro, formó un nuevo gobierno y exigió que se retiraran las tropas soviéticas. Estas, sin embargo, tomaron la capital. Los luchadores por la libertad húngaros se enfrentaron a las tropas soviéticas, pero era un combate desigual. Finalmente, se estableció un nuevo gobierno de orientación soviética.

In 1964, Khrushchev was replaced by Leonid Brezhnev, who adopted harsh policies. He punished opposition in Eastern Europe beginning in 1968 in Czechoslovakia. Czech Communist leader **Alexander Dubček** began reforms. However, armed forces from the Warsaw Pact nations invaded the country. Dubček's policies were ended./En 1964, Khrushchev fue sucedido por Leonid Brezhnev, quien adoptó políticas severas. Brezhnev castigó a la oposición que se había originado en Europa oriental,

> **What effect did de-Stalinization have on Hungary and other satellite countries?**/¿Qué efectos tuvo la desestalinización en Hungría y en otros estados satélite?
> _____
> _____
> _____
> _____
> _____
> _____

> **Underline the sentence that describes what happened after Dubček began reforms in Czechoslovakia./**
> Subraya la oración que explica qué sucedió después de que Dubček comenzara reformas en Checoslovaquia.

**Lesson/Lección 3, *continued/*continuación**

especificamente en Checoslovaquia, en 1968. Allí, el líder comunista checoslovaco **Alexander Dubček** había iniciado reformas. Sin embargo, fuerzas armadas de las naciones miembro del Pacto de Varsovia invadieron el país y acabaron con las nuevas políticas.

China was committed to communism, but it did not like being in the shadow of the Soviet Union. So China began spreading its own form of communism in Africa and other parts of Asia. The Soviets did not like this, so they refused to share Soviet nuclear technology. This led to fighting along their border./China estaba comprometida con el comunismo, pero no aceptaba estar a la sombra de la Unión Soviética. Por eso, empezó a difundir su propia forma de comunismo en África y otras partes de Asia. A los soviéticos no les gustó eso y se negaron a compartir su tecnología nuclear. Esto llevó a una lucha en la frontera entre ambos países.

## THE UNITED STATES SEEKS PEACE/LOS ESTADOS UNIDOS BUSCAN LA PAZ

The policies followed by Presidents Eisenhower, Kennedy, and Johnson had led to many crises. In 1960, a spy plane was shot down in Soviet airspace. In 1962, the Cuban Missile Crisis made the superpowers' use of nuclear weapons a possibility. Then in the 1970s under President Nixon, the U.S. followed a policy of easing Cold War tensions called **détente.** It involved following national interests while still dealing with other nations in a realistic way. So the U.S. continued to try to contain communism, but both countries agreed to pursue détente and reduce tensions. They slowed the arms race and signed the Strategic Arms Limitation Treaty to put limits on the number of missiles each country could have./Las políticas de los presidentes Eisenhower,

> **What policy did the United States follow during the 1970s?/¿Qué política adoptaron los Estados Unidos en la década de 1970?**
>
> _____
>
> _____
>
> _____

Kennedy y Johnson habían provocado numerosas crisis. En 1960, un avión espía fue derribado en el espacio aéreo soviético. En 1962, la Crisis de los misiles en Cuba hizo que el uso de armas nucleares por parte de las superpotencias fuera una posibilidad real. Entonces, en la década de 1970, bajo el mandato del presidente Nixon, los EE. UU. adoptaron una política de alivio de las tensiones de la Guerra Fría llamada **Détente.** Esta política se basaba en perseguir los intereses nacionales lidiando con las otras naciones de una forma realista. Por lo tanto, los EE. UU. siguieron intentando contener la expansión del comunismo, pero la Unión Soviética y los EE. UU. acordaron promover la Détente y reducir las tensiones. La carrera armamentista se hizo más lenta y se firmó el Tratado de Limitación de Armas Estratégicas con el objetivo de poner límites a la cantidad de misiles que cada país podía poseer.

During the 1970s, relations seemed to be improving. However, actions such as Soviet treatment of protesters and its invasion of Afghanistan changed this. Also, more nations started to build nuclear arsenals. President Reagan changed to a policy of military readiness. The arms race was reinstated and détente was over./ Durante la década de 1970, las relaciones exteriores parecían estar mejorando. Sin embargo, diversos hechos, como el trato por parte de los soviéticos hacia los disidentes y su invasión a Afganistán, modificaron esta situación. Asimismo, otras naciones empezaron a desarrollar arsenales nucleares. El presidente Reagan cambió el rumbo de la política exterior y adoptó una política de disposición militar. La carrera armamentista se restableció, y se puso fin a la Détente.

> **What led to a reinstatement of the arms race?/¿Qué llevó al restablecimiento de la carrera armamentista?**
>
> _____
> _____
> _____
> _____

## CHALLENGE ACTIVITY/ACTIVIDAD AVANZADA
**Critical Thinking: Draw Conclusions/Pensamiento crítico: Sacar conclusiones** Although Khrushchev claimed to want to change Soviet repressive policies, he continued to repress people in Soviet satellites such as Hungary. Write an essay attempting to explain these contradictions./A pesar de que Khrushchev afirmaba que quería modificar las políticas represivas soviéticas, continuó reprimiendo a los habitantes de los estados satélite, como Hungría. Escribe un ensayo en el que intentes explicar esas contradicciones.

**DIRECTIONS/INSTRUCCIONES** On the line before each statement, write **T** if the statement is true and **F** if the statement is false. If the statement is false, change the underlined term to make the sentence true. Then write the correct term on the line after the sentence./En la línea que precede a cada enunciado, escribe **V** si el enunciado es verdadero y **F** si es falso. Si el enunciado es falso, cambia el término subrayado para que el enunciado sea verdadero. Luego escribe el término correcto en la línea que sigue al enunciado.

_____ 1. The U.S. policy of easing Cold War tensions was known as <u>de-Stalinization</u>./La política de los EE. UU. de aliviar las tensiones de la Guerra Fría se llamó <u>desestalinización</u>.

_____

_____ 2. The Communist party leader of the Soviet Union from 1956 to 1964 was <u>Nikita Khrushchev</u>./El líder del Partido Comunista de la Unión Soviética de 1956 a 1964 era <u>Nikita Khrushchev</u>.

_____

_____ 3. The Czech Communist leader was <u>Imre Nagy</u>./El líder comunista checoslovaco era <u>Imre Nagy</u>.

_____

_____ 4. The policy related to reforming the Soviet Union to ease Stalin's repressive policies was called <u>de-Stalinization</u>./La política de reforma de la Unión Soviética para aliviar las políticas represivas estalinistas se llamó <u>desestalinización</u>.

_____

_____ 5. The popular Hungarian Communist leader who tried to form a new government was <u>Nikita Khrushchev</u>./El popular líder comunista húngaro que intentó formar un nuevo gobierno era <u>Nikita Khrushchev</u>.

_____

# The Cold War Years/Los años de la Guerra Fría

## MAIN IDEAS/IDEAS PRINCIPALES
1. Mikhail Gorbachev's reforms led to the collapse of the Soviet Union./Las reformas efectuadas por Mijaíl Gorbachov provocaron el colapso de la Unión Soviética.
2. The fall of the Berlin Wall marked the beginning of the end of communism in Europe./La caída del Muro de Berlín marcó el comienzo del final del comunismo en Europa.

## Key Terms and People/Personas y palabras clave

**Mikhail Gorbachev/Mijaíl Gorbachov** last leader of the Soviet Union/último líder de la Unión Soviética

**glasnost/glásnost** policy of openness/política de apertura

**perestroika/perestroika** economic restructuring/política de reestructuración económica

**Ronald Reagan/Ronald Reagan** 40th president of the United States, elected in 1981/cuadragésimo presidente de los Estados Unidos, elegido en 1981

**Margaret Thatcher/Margaret Thatcher** British prime minister/primera ministra británica

**Václav Havel/Václav Havel** Czechoslovakian playwright who was elected president/dramaturgo checoslovaco que fue elegido presidente

**European Union/Unión Europea** an economic and political union among the nations of Europe/unión económica y política entre las naciones de Europa

## Lesson Summary/Resumen de la lección

### SOVIET UNION COLLAPSES/COLAPSO DE LA UNIÓN SOVIÉTICA

During the 1980s, **Mikhail Gorbachev** became the Soviet Union leader. He began **glasnost,** a policy of openness. Soviet citizens had more freedoms. Soon they began complaining about the economy./Durante la década de 1980, **Mijaíl Gorbachov** se convirtió en el líder de la Unión Soviética e instauró la **glásnost,** una política de apertura. Los ciudadanos soviéticos obtuvieron mayores libertades. Pronto, comenzaron a quejarse de la economía.

> How did glasnost change the Soviet Union?/¿De qué manera la glásnost cambió la Unión Soviética?
>
> _____
> _____

U.S. president **Ronald Reagan** took a tough stand against the Soviet Union and expanded the military. He had support from the British prime minister, **Margaret Thatcher.** When the Soviet Union tried to match American spending in the arms race, its economy suffered. So in 1984 Gorbachev introduced **perestroika,** or economic restructuring. He wanted to revive the Soviet economy. Because of glasnost and perestroika, Reagan believed Gorbachev wanted to change. The two leaders signed a treaty eliminating all medium-range nuclear weapons in Europe./El presidente de los EE. UU., **Ronald Reagan,** se posicionó fuertemente en contra de la Unión Soviética y aumentó el presupuesto militar. Contaba con el apoyo de la primera ministra británica, **Margaret Thatcher.** Cuando la Unión Soviética intentó igualar el gasto de los Estados Unidos en la carrera armamentista, su economía sufrió las consecuencias. Entonces, en 1984, Gorbachov introdujo la **perestroika,** una política de reestructuración económica que buscaba reactivar la economía soviética. Reagan, al observar la glásnost y la perestroika, interpretó que Gorbachov deseaba un cambio. Ambos líderes firmaron un tratado para eliminar todas las armas nucleares de alcance medio en Europa.

Gorbachev did not oppose reform. Lithuania declared its independence in 1990, and Estonia and Latvia followed. Then Boris Yeltsin was elected president of the newly named Russian Federation in 1991. Russia was still part of the Soviet Union under Gorbachev. Yeltsin put more reforms in place. Communist Party officials tried to overthrow Gorbachev and undo all the reforms. They failed, and Russia's Communist Party collapsed. By the end of 1991, all 15 Soviet republics had declared independence. The Soviet Union no longer existed./Gorbachov no se resistía

> Underline the sentence that tells why President Reagan signed a treaty eliminating all medium-range nuclear weapons in Europe./Subraya la oración que explica por qué el presidente Reagan firmó un tratado para eliminar todas las armas nucleares de alcance medio en Europa.

> What happened to the Soviet Union by the end of 1991?/¿Qué sucedió con la Unión Soviética hacia fines del año 1991?
>
> _____
> _____
> _____
> _____

a las reformas. Lituania declaró su independencia en 1990; pronto, Estonia y Letonia hicieron lo mismo. En 1991, Boris Yeltsin fue elegido presidente de la ahora llamada Federación Rusa, que aún formaba parte de la Unión Soviética, gobernada por Gorbachov. Yeltsin efectuó nuevas reformas. Oficiales del Partido Comunista intentaron derrocar a Gorbachov y revertir las reformas más recientes, pero fracasaron, y el Partido Comunista ruso colapsó. Hacia fines de 1991, las 15 repúblicas soviéticas habían declarado su independencia: la Unión Soviética ya no existía.

## EUROPE AFTER COMMUNISM/EUROPA DESPUÉS DEL COMUNISMO

East Germany fought reforms in the late 1980s, but East Germans wanted freedom. In 1989, Hungary allowed East German tourists to cross the border into Austria. From there, they entered West Germany. So the East German government closed its borders. People protested. Eventually, the Berlin wall was opened and torn down. This was a symbol of the fall of the Iron Curtain. By the end of 1989, the East German Communist Party was no more./Alemania Oriental se resistió a las reformas a fines de la década de 1980, pero sus ciudadanos querían mayor libertad. En 1989, Hungría permitió que turistas de Alemania Oriental cruzaran la frontera hacia Austria, desde donde pudieron ingresar a Alemania Occidental. En consecuencia, el gobierno de Alemania Oriental cerró sus fronteras. La gente salió a manifestarse. Finalmente, el Muro de Berlín fue abierto y derribado. La caída del Muro de Berlín fue un símbolo de la caída de la cortina de hierro. Para fines del año 1989, el Partido Comunista de Alemania Oriental ya no existía.

---

**Which country's actions may have led to the opening of the Berlin wall? Why?/¿Las acciones de qué país pudieron conducir a la apertura del Muro de Berlín? ¿Por qué?**

_____

_____

_____

_____

---

After communism fell in East Germany, Germany became one country again. Communist governments fell in Poland, Czechoslovakia, and Romania. **Václav Havel,** a playwright, was elected the president of Czechoslovakia. Eventually, it split into the Czech Republic and Slovakia./Tras la caída del comunismo en Alemania Oriental, Alemania volvió a ser un solo país. Los gobiernos comunistas de Polonia, Checoslovaquia y Rumania cayeron. **Václav Havel,** un dramaturgo, fue elegido presidente de Checoslovaquia, que finalmente se dividió en la República Checa y Eslovaquia.

Some countries in Eastern Europe saw economic improvement, while others had high unemployment and other economic problems. Many people left Eastern Europe and moved to Western Europe. The **European Union** (EU) was established in 1992 to build an economic and political union among Europe's nations. Many Eastern European nations and former Soviet republics joined, but many were poorer than Western European members. As a result, some people in wealthier nations began to worry that their own economies would suffer./Algunos países de Europa oriental experimentaron una mejoría económica, pero otros tenían altas tasas de desempleo y otros problemas económicos. Muchas personas dejaron Europa oriental y se instalaron en Europa occidental. En 1992, se formó la **Unión Europea** (UE) con el objetivo de construir una unión económica y política entre las naciones de Europa. Muchas naciones de Europa oriental y antiguas repúblicas soviéticas se sumaron a la unión, pero varias de ellas eran más pobres que los miembros de Europa occidental. Esto hizo que algunas personas pertenecientes a los países más ricos comenzaran a temer por sus propias economías.

> Underline the sentence that tells the purpose of the European Union./Subraya la oración que explica el propósito de la Unión Europea.

## CHALLENGE ACTIVITY/ACTIVIDAD AVANZADA
### Critical Thinking: Identify Cause and Effect/
### Pensamiento crítico: Identificar causa y efecto

The collapse of the Soviet Union ended its days as a superpower. Write a one-page paper on how this affected the power of other countries worldwide./ La caída de la Unión Soviética significó el fin de sus días como superpotencia. Escribe un ensayo de una página en el que expliques cómo esto afectó el poder de otros países en todo el mundo.

**DIRECTIONS/INSTRUCCIONES** Match the terms in the first column with their correct definition from the second column by placing the letter of the correct definition in the space provided before each term./Une los términos de la primera columna con su definición correcta en la segunda columna. Escribe la letra de la definición correcta en el espacio que precede a cada término.

_____ 1. Margaret Thatcher/ Margaret Thatcher

_____ 2. perestroika/ perestroika

_____ 3. European Union/ Unión Europea

_____ 4. Václav Havel/ Václav Havel

_____ 5. Ronald Reagan/ Ronald Reagan

_____ 6. Mikhail Gorbachev/ Mijaíl Gorbachov

_____ 7. glasnost/glásnost

a. 40th president of the U.S., elected in 1981/cuadragésimo presidente de los EE. UU., elegido en 1981

b. last leader of the Soviet Union/último líder de la Unión Soviética

c. economic restructuring/política de reestructuración económica

d. British prime minister/primera ministra británica

e. policy of openness/política de apertura

f. an economic and political union among Europe's nations/unión económica y política entre las naciones de Europa

g. Czechoslovakian playwright who was elected president/dramaturgo checoslovaco que fue elegido presidente

# The Postwar World/El mundo de la posguerra

## Lesson/Lección 1

**MAIN IDEAS/IDEAS PRINCIPALES**

1. The call for Indian independence was accompanied by nonviolent protests./ El reclamo por la independencia de la India estuvo acompañado de protestas no violentas.

2. The early 1900s saw the end of China's imperial period and the beginning of communism in the country./A principios del siglo 20, finalizó el período imperial de China y comenzó el comunismo en el país.

3. Changes in Japan's government led to the formation of a new empire./ Los cambios en el gobierno de Japón llevaron a la formación de un nuevo imperio.

## Key Terms and People/Personas y palabras clave

**nonviolence/no violencia** the avoidance of violent actions/evitar acciones violentas

**civil disobedience/desobediencia civil** refusing to obey unjust laws in order to bring about change/desobedecer las leyes injustas con el fin de lograr cambios

**partition/partición** division into separate parts/división en partes independientes

**Pakistan/Pakistán** an independent country created after the partition of India in 1947/país independiente creado después de la partición de la India en 1947

**Diet/Dieta** the elected legislature that still governs Japan/asamblea legislativa elegida que aún gobierna en Japón

## Lesson Summary/Resumen de la lección

### THE CALL FOR INDIAN INDEPENDENCE/RECLAMO DE LA INDEPENDENCIA DE LA INDIA

British officials in India dealt harshly with protests against their rule. In one incident at Amritsar (uhm-RIT-suhr), British troops killed more than 400 people. Then a new leader arose in the Indian resistance. Mohandas Gandhi based his strategy on two key beliefs: **nonviolence** (the avoidance of violent actions) and **civil disobedience** (the refusal to obey laws in order to bring about change). Gandhi told people to avoid paying taxes and to boycott British products. In steps, the British government gave up power to the Indian people./ Los funcionarios británicos de la India controlaban con dureza las protestas contra el

> **What did Mohandas Gandhi accomplish?/¿Qué logró Mahatma Gandhi?**
>
> _____
> _____
> _____

gobierno. En un incidente en Amritsar, las tropas británicas mataron a más de 400 personas. Entonces, surgió un nuevo líder en la resistencia india. Mahatma Gandhi basó su estrategia en dos creencias clave: la **no violencia** (evitar acciones violentas) y la **desobediencia civil** (desobedecer las leyes injustas con el fin de lograr cambios). Gandhi pidió a la población que dejara de pagar los impuestos y que boicoteara los productos británicos. Gradualmente, el gobierno británico cedió poder al pueblo indio.

Tensions between the Hindu and Muslim people led Great Britain to the **partition,** or division, of India. In 1947, two countries were formed. India was mostly Hindu and **Pakistan** was mostly Muslim. Millions of people rushed to cross these new borders. Many Muslims and Hindus wanted to live in a country in which they would be the majority./Las tensiones entre hindúes y musulmanes hicieron que Gran Bretaña llevara a cabo la **partición,** o división, de la India. En 1947, se formaron dos países. La India era predominantemente hindú y **Pakistán,** musulmán. Millones de personas se apresuraron a cruzar las nuevas fronteras. Muchos musulmanes e hindúes querían vivir en un país donde fueran mayoría.

> Underline the sentence that explains why India was partitioned./Subraya la oración que explica por qué se dividió la India.

## THE END OF IMPERIAL CHINA/FIN DE LA CHINA IMPERIAL

Chinese rebels forced the Qing emperor out of power in 1911. One of the rebel leaders was Sun Yixian (SUN YEE-SHAHN). Two groups—the Communists and the Nationalists—fought a civil war for control of the new government. By 1949 the Communists, now led by Mao Zedong (MOW ZUH-DOOHNG) had won. They declared the People's Republic of China. The surviving Nationalists fled to the island of Taiwan, where they founded the Republic of China./Rebeldes chinos expulsaron al emperador Qing del poder

> What two groups fought for control of China's government?/¿Qué dos grupos luchaban por el control del gobierno de China?
>
> _____
>
> _____

en 1911. Uno de los líderes rebeldes fue Sun Yixian. Dos grupos, los comunistas y los nacionalistas, se enfrentaron en una guerra civil por el control del nuevo gobierno. En 1949, los comunistas, dirigidos por Mao Zedong, ganaron y declararon la República Popular de China. Los nacionalistas sobrevivientes huyeron a la isla de Taiwán, donde fundaron la República de China.

China's new Communist government took over all private farms, businesses, and factories. Women gained more equality. Millions of people were imprisoned or killed for criticizing the government. Many economic programs were unsuccessful, and famines killed millions./El nuevo gobierno comunista de China quedó a cargo de todas las granjas, empresas y fábricas privadas. Las mujeres lograron mayor igualdad. Millones de personas fueron encarceladas o asesinadas por criticar al gobierno. Muchos programas económicos fracasaron, y la hambruna mató a millones de personas.

Today there is no freedom of the press or freedom of speech in modern China. Citizens may be jailed if they disagree with government policies./En la actualidad, no existe libertad de prensa ni libertad de expresión en la China moderna. Los ciudadanos pueden ser penados con encarcelamiento si no están de acuerdo con las políticas del gobierno.

> **What effect has China's communist government had on life in China today?/¿Qué efecto tuvo el gobierno comunista de China en la situación actual del país?**
>
> _____
> _____
> _____
> _____
> _____

## A NEW JAPANESE EMPIRE/NUEVO IMPERIO JAPONÉS

In 1868, the Japanese restored control of their government to an emperor. Their new ruler took the name Meiji (MAY-jee), which means "enlightened rule" in Japanese. Meiji abolished the old feudal system and based a new government on Western ideas. He created the **Diet,** the elected legislature that still governs Japan. He required all children to attend school.

He built telegraph lines, a postal service, and railroads, and established a national currency. And he built up the military. Between 1890 and 1910, Japan launched military strikes and defeated both the Chinese and Russian armies. In 1910, Japan invaded Korea and made it a colony./En 1868, los japoneses devolvieron el control del gobierno a un emperador. Este nuevo gobernante adoptó el nombre de Meiji, que significa "gobierno iluminado" en japonés. Meiji abolió el antiguo sistema feudal y basó el nuevo gobierno en las ideas occidentales. También creó la **Dieta,** la asamblea legislativa elegida que aún gobierna en Japón. Meiji exigió que todos los niños fueran al colegio. Construyó líneas telegráficas, un servicio postal y carreteras, y estableció una moneda nacional. También formó un ejército. Entre 1890 y 1910, Japón desplegó ataques militares y venció a los ejércitos chino y ruso. En 1910, Japón invadió Corea y la convirtió en su colonia.

> **How did Meiji change Japan when he became emperor?/¿De qué manera Meiji cambió Japón cuando se convirtió en emperador?**
>
> _____
> _____
> _____
> _____
> _____

## CHALLENGE ACTIVITY/ACTIVIDAD AVANZADA

**Critical Thinking: Make Judgments/Pensamiento crítico: Dar opiniones**  Gandhi, Mao, and Meiji all brought large and lasting changes to their nations. Choose one leader, and write a one-page paper that evaluates the long-term results of this leader's actions./Gandhi, Mao y Meiji introdujeron cambios importantes y duraderos en sus naciones. Elige uno de estos líderes y escribe un ensayo de una página en el que evalúes los resultados a largo plazo de las acciones de ese líder.

**DIRECTIONS/INSTRUCCIONES** Write two adjectives or
a descriptive phrase that describe the term given./Escribe
dos adjetivos o una frase descriptiva que describan el
término dado.

1. nonviolence/no violencia _____

   _____

2. civil disobedience/desobediencia civil_____

   _____

3. partition/partición _____

   _____

4. Diet/Dieta _____

   _____

5. People's Republic of China/República Popular de China _____

   _____


**DIRECTIONS/INSTRUCCIONES** Read each sentence and fill
in the blank with the term in the word pair that best completes
the sentence./Lee cada oración y escribe en el espacio en blanco
la palabra del banco de palabras que mejor la completa.

6. A new leader in the Indian resistance, _____ led
   his people to resist the British through nonviolence and civil disobedience.
   **(Mohandas Gandhi/Mao Zedong)**/_____, un
   nuevo líder de la resistencia india, pidió a sus seguidores que se opusieran a
   Gran Bretaña a través de la no violencia y la desobediencia civil. **(Mahatma
   Gandhi/Mao Zedong)**

7. _____ was a powerful Japanese emperor
   who created a new government based on Western ideas. **(Mao Zedong/
   Meiji)**/_____ fue un poderoso emperador
   japonés que creó un nuevo gobierno basado en las ideas occidentales.
   **(Mao Zedong/Meiji)**

8. Tensions between Hindus and Muslims led to the partition of India and creation of the country called _____.
**(Pakistan/People's Republic of China)**/Las tensiones entre hindúes y musulmanes llevaron a la partición de la India y a la creación del país llamado _____. **(Pakistán/República Popular de China)**

# The Postwar World/El mundo de la posguerra

## Lesson/Lección 2

**MAIN IDEAS/IDEAS PRINCIPALES**

1. India and Pakistan were in conflict over Kashmir./La India y Pakistán estaban en conflicto por Cachemira.

2. Many Asian countries have found economic success since World War II./ Muchos países asiáticos han prosperado económicamente desde la Segunda Guerra Mundial.

3. Political shifts in Asia have led to new governments in many countries./ Los cambios políticos en Asia tuvieron como consecuencia el surgimiento de nuevos gobiernos en muchos países.

4. Many Asian cultures blend old and new ideas./Muchas culturas asiáticas fusionan ideas antiguas y nuevas.

## Key Terms and People

**Kashmir/Cachemira** a mountainous region between India, Pakistan, and China/zona montañosa entre la India, Pakistán y China

**trade surplus/superávit comercial** result of a country's exporting more goods than it imports/resultado de que un país exporte más bienes de los que importa

**tariff/arancel** a fee that a country charges on imports or exports/tarifa que cobra un país sobre las importaciones o las exportaciones

**constitutional monarchies/monarquías constitucionales** form of democracy in which a monarch serves as the head of state, but an elected legislature makes the laws/forma de democracia en la que un monarca es el jefe de estado, pero un cuerpo legislativo elegido hace las leyes

**Tiananmen Square/Plaza de Tiananmén** public square in Beijing, China, site of a 1989 protest/plaza pública de Beijing, China, escenario de una protesta en 1989

**human rights/derechos humanos** those rights that all people deserve/derechos que todas las personas merecen

**Corazon Aquino/Corazón Aquino** the winner of a 1986 democratic election in the Philippines/ganadora de la elección democrática de 1986 en Filipinas

**Aung San Suu Ki/Aung San Suu Ki** led a movement for democratic rights in Myanmar/dirigió un movimiento por los derechos democráticos en Myanmar

# Lesson Summary/Resumen de la lección

## CONFLICT IN KASHMIR/CONFLICTOS EN CACHEMIRA

When India was partitioned in 1947, the Hindu prince of the mountainous region of **Kashmir** decided to stay a part of India. Muslims in Kashmir wanted to be part of Pakistan. War broke out. Under a 1949 treaty, the people of Kashmir were to vote on their future. The vote was never held, and Kashmir is still disputed territory./Cuando la India se dividió en 1947, el príncipe hindú de la zona montañosa de **Cachemira** decidió seguir formando parte de la India. Los musulmanes de Cachemira deseaban ser parte de Pakistán, por lo que se desató una guerra. En virtud del tratado firmado en 1949, la población de Cachemira debía votar para definir su futuro, pero la votación jamás se llevó a cabo, y Cachemira todavía es un territorio en disputa.

> **What religions are found in Kashmir?/¿Qué religiones se practican en Cachemira?**
> _____
> _____

## ECONOMIC SUCCESS/ÉXITO ECONÓMICO

With assistance from Europe and the United States, Japan completely rebuilt its economy after World War II. Japan's biggest success has been manufacturing, especially cars and electronics. Many Japanese products are sold outside of the country, and Japan has built up a huge **trade surplus.** One factor in Japan's success has been the use of high **tariffs**—fees Japan charges on goods made in other countries and sold in Japan./Con ayuda de Europa y de los Estados Unidos, Japón reconstruyó su economía por completo después de la Segunda Guerra Mundial. El principal éxito de Japón fue la manufacturación, en especial, de carros y de productos electrónicos. Muchos productos japoneses se venden fuera del país, y Japón ha desarrollado un gran **superávit comercial.** Un factor decisivo en el éxito de Japón fue el uso de elevados **aranceles:** tarifas que Japón cobra sobre los productos fabricados en otro país y vendidos en Japón.

> **What was Japan's biggest success after World War II?/¿Cuál fue el principal éxito de Japón después de la Segunda Guerra Mundial?**
> _____
> _____

In China the Communists took over all businesses. Later they began to allow privately owned businesses and some foreign companies. China's mixed economy is now the second-largest economy in the world./En China, los comunistas quedaron a cargo de todas las empresas. Más tarde, comenzaron a permitir la existencia de empresas privadas y algunas empresas extranjeras. En la actualidad, la economía mixta de China es la segunda economía más fuerte del mundo.

> **Underline what kind of economy now exists in China./Subraya qué tipo de economía existe en China en la actualidad.**

India today is among the world's top ten leading industrial countries. However, millions of Indians live in poverty. The government has worked to bring new industries and better jobs to India./Hoy en día, la India está entre los diez países industriales más importantes del mundo. Sin embargo, millones de indios viven en la pobreza. El gobierno trabaja para desarrollar nuevas industrias y mejores puestos de trabajo en la India.

## POLITICAL SHIFTS/CAMBIOS POLÍTICOS

Since the end of World War II several Asian countries such as Japan have adopted democracy. India is by population the largest democracy in the world today. Thailand and Malaysia are both **constitutional monarchies.** Other democratic countries in Asia include Bangladesh, Mongolia, and Indonesia./Desde el final de la Segunda Guerra Mundial, varios países asiáticos, como Japón, han adoptado la democracia. Por su población, la India tiene la democracia más grande del mundo. Tailandia y Malasia son **monarquías constitucionales.** Otros países democráticos en Asia son Bangladesh, Mongolia e Indonesia.

> **What countries in Asia have adopted democracy or a form of democracy?/¿Qué países de Asia han adoptado la democracia o una forma de democracia?**
>
> _____
> _____
> _____
> _____

The Chinese government controls most areas of life. Opposition is harshly punished. When more than one million pro-democracy protestors gathered in **Tiananmen Square,** the government used force to stop them./El gobierno chino controla la mayoría de las áreas de la vida cotidiana. Los opositores son castigados con dureza. Cuando más de un millón de manifestantes a favor de la democracia se reunieron en la **Plaza de Tiananmén,** el gobierno usó la fuerza para detenerlos.

However, political change has occurred in other Asian countries. In the Philippines, **Corazon Aquino** won an election over the leader of a military government. Another military government in Myanmar is noted for abuses of **human rights.** In response, a reformer named **Aung San Suu Kyi** has led a movement for more rights./No obstante, sí se han producido cambios políticos en otros países asiáticos. En Filipinas, **Corazón Aquino** ganó las elecciones y derrotó al líder de un gobierno militar. Otro gobierno militar en Myanmar era conocido por sus abusos contra los **derechos humanos.** En respuesta, una reformadora llamada **Aung San Suu Kyi** encabezó un movimiento para exigir más derechos.

## BLENDING OLD AND NEW/MEZCLA DE IDEAS ANTIGUAS Y NUEVAS

Asian culture today is a complex blend of old and new. Cities in China have some of the world's tallest buildings. Next to these modern buildings are tiny, ancient temples. In this age of the Internet, elements of other cultures are a part of Asian life./La cultura asiática actual es una mezcla compleja de ideas antiguas y nuevas. Ciertas ciudades chinas tienen algunos de los edificios más altos del mundo y, junto a esos edificios modernos, se encuentran pequeños templos antiguos. En la era de Internet, los elementos de otras culturas forman parte de la vida asiática.

> What has happened to Asian cultures in the age of the Internet?/¿Qué ha ocurrido con las culturas asiáticas en la era de Internet?
>
> _____
>
> _____
>
> _____

## CHALLENGE ACTIVITY/ACTIVIDAD AVANZADA
**Critical Thinking: Predict/Pensamiento crítico:**
**Predecir** Starting a business in Asia? Economic and political conditions will affect your business. Make a list of concerns and tell what research you would need to do to avoid them./¿Establecerías una empresa en Asia? Las condiciones económicas y políticas afectarán tu empresa. Haz una lista de posibles dificultades y explica qué investigación llevarías a cabo para evitarlas.

**DIRECTIONS/INSTRUCCIONES** Match the terms in the first column with their correct definition from the second column by placing the letter of the correct definition in the space provided before each term./Une los términos de la primera columna con su definición correcta en la segunda columna. Escribe la letra de la definición correcta en el espacio que precede a cada término.

_____ 1. Kashmir/Cachemira

_____ 2. human rights/ derechos humanos

_____ 3. Tiananmen Square/ Plaza de Tiananmén

_____ 4. tariff/arancel

_____ 5. constitutional monarchies/ monarquías constitucionales

a. tax on imports and exports/impuesto a las importaciones y exportaciones

b. result of a country's exporting more goods than it imports/resultado de que un país exporte más bienes de los que importa

c. country whose government is known for its abuse of human rights/país cuyo gobierno fue reconocido por sus abusos contra los derechos humanos

d. mountainous region that both India and Pakistan want to control/zona montañosa que tanto la India como Pakistán desean controlar

e. location remembered for crackdown of protesters in China/ubicación recordada por ser el escenario de medidas severas contra manifestantes en China

_____ 6. trade surplus/
       superávit comercial

   f. form of democracy in which a person serves as the head of state, but an elected legislature makes the laws/ forma de democracia en la que una persona es el jefe de estado, pero una asamblea legislativa elegida hace las leyes

_____ 7. Myanmar/Myanmar

   g. all people deserve to have these/todas las personas los merecen

# The Postwar World/El mundo de la posguerra

## Lesson/Lección 3

### MAIN IDEAS/IDEAS PRINCIPALES

1. Unhappiness with European rule led to a call for independence in Africa./El descontento con el gobierno europeo llevó a exigir la independencia en África.

2. British colonies were some of the first to become free./Las colonias británicas fueron algunas de las primeras en ser libres.

3. French colonies followed two paths to independence./Las colonias francesas siguieron dos caminos hacia la independencia.

4. Belgian and Portuguese colonies had to fight for their freedom./Las colonias belgas y portuguesas tuvieron que luchar por su libertad.

## Key Terms and People/Personas y palabras clave

**Ghana/Ghana** former British colony in West Africa, "Gold Coast"/antigua colonia británica en África occidental, la "Costa de Oro"

**Kenya/Kenia** former British colony in East Africa/antigua colonia británica en África oriental

**Mau Mau/Mau Mau** a violent movement for Kenyan independence/movimiento violento que apoyaba la independencia de Kenia

**Belgian Congo/Congo Belga** former Belgian colony in Central Africa/antigua colonia belga en África central

## Lesson Summary/Resumen de la lección

### THE CALL FOR INDEPENDENCE/RECLAMO DE INDEPENDENCIA

Africans' resentment of European control of their homeland grew after two world wars. African soldiers were not thanked for their contributions to the Allied victory. When Britain granted independence to India in 1947, African nations demanded independence, too./El descontento del pueblo africano con el control de su tierra natal por parte de los europeos se acrecentó después de las dos guerras mundiales. Los soldados africanos no recibieron agradecimiento alguno por sus contribuciones a la victoria de los Aliados. Cuando Gran Bretaña concedió la independencia a la India en 1947, las naciones africanas también exigieron su independencia.

> **How were Africans affected by India's independence?/¿De qué manera los africanos se vieron afectados por la independencia de la India?**
> 
> _____
> _____

## BRITISH COLONIES/COLONIAS BRITÁNICAS

In the Gold Coast, Kwame Nkrumah (KWAHM-eh en-KROO-muh) organized strikes and demonstrations and inspired many followers. The British granted the Gold Coast its independence in 1957. Nkrumah became the first prime minister, and the country was renamed **Ghana.**/En la Costa de Oro, Kwame Nkrumah organizó huelgas y protestas e inspiró a muchos seguidores. El gobierno británico otorgó la independencia a la Costa de Oro en 1957. Nkrumah fue el primer ministro, y el país recibió el nombre de **Ghana.**

The British colony of **Kenya,** in East Africa, became independent only after a long and violent struggle. The British used the land to grow valuable crops, such as coffee, and did not want to give the land back. The Kikuyu people of Kenya formed a violent movement called the **Mau Mau** to get rid of white settlers. Between 1952 and 1960, the Mau Mau terrorized anyone they suspected of opposing their goals. In 1963, the British conceded and made Kenya a free country./La colonia británica de **Kenia,** en África oriental, logró su independencia tras una larga y violenta lucha. Gran Bretaña usaba esas tierras para cultivos valiosos, como el café, y no quería devolverlas. El pueblo Kikuyu de Kenia formó un movimiento violento llamado **Mau Mau** para deshacerse de los colonizadores de raza blanca. Entre 1952 y 1960, los Mau Mau aterrorizaron a todos aquellos que, en teoría, se oponían a sus objetivos. En 1963, Gran Bretaña cedió y convirtió a Kenia en un país libre.

> **How did the Gold Coast achieve independence?/¿Cómo logró su independencia la Costa de Oro?**
> _____
> _____
> _____
> _____

> **Underline one reason why the British did not want to give Kenya independence./Subraya una razón por la que el gobierno británico no quería conceder la independencia a Kenia.**

## FRENCH COLONIES/COLONIAS FRANCESAS

Originally, the French wanted to make their colonies part of France. After World War II, France offered its colonies in West Africa more of a role in colonial government. Many leaders

in the French colonies in West Africa chose
to retain political and economic ties to France.
Eventually France granted these colonies full
independence./Inicialmente, los franceses querían
que sus colonias formaran parte de Francia.
Después de la Segunda Guerra Mundial, Francia
concedió a sus colonias de África occidental
una mayor participación en el gobierno colonial.
Muchos líderes de las colonias francesas de
África occidental optaron por conservar los
lazos políticos y económicos con Francia. Con
el tiempo, Francia otorgó la independencia
total a esas colonias.

In North Africa, the colonies of Morocco,
Tunisia, and Algeria were not willing to work
peacefully with the French. The French sent
an army to Algeria to put down the rebellion.
Morocco and Tunisia became independent in
1956. By 1962, France was forced to grant
independence to Algeria./En África del Norte,
las colonias de Marruecos, Túnez y Argelia
no estaban dispuestas a colaborar en paz con
Francia. Los franceses enviaron un ejército a
Argelia para frenar la rebelión. Marruecos y
Túnez se independizaron en 1956. En 1962,
Francia fue obligada a conceder la
independencia a Argelia.

> **What former colony fought against France to gain its independence?/¿Qué antigua colonia luchó contra Francia para lograr su independencia?**
>
> _____

## BELGIAN AND PORTUGUESE COLONIES/ COLONIAS BELGAS Y PORTUGUESAS

Belgium controlled only one major colony in
Africa—the **Belgian Congo.** After World War II,
the Congolese people staged riots in several cities
and even held elections. In 1960, the Belgians
suddenly left and granted independence to the
Congo. Shortly afterward, civil war broke out
between various Congolese groups./Bélgica
controlaba una sola colonia grande en África:
el **Congo Belga.** Después de la Segunda Guerra
Mundial, los congoleses organizaron revueltas

en varias ciudades y hasta llevaron a cabo elecciones. En 1960, los belgas repentinamente abandonaron África y concedieron la independencia al Congo. Poco tiempo después, se desató una guerra civil entre varios grupos congoleses.

Portugal held several colonies in Africa, mostly in the south and east. In Angola, Guinea, and Mozambique, rebel attacks began long decades of bloody war. In 1974, Portugal's military government at home was overthrown and replaced with a democracy. The new government quickly gave up its African colonies./Portugal tenía varias colonias en África, principalmente en el sur y en el este. En Angola, Guinea y Mozambique, los ataques rebeldes dieron paso a largas décadas de guerras sangrientas. En 1974, el gobierno militar de Portugal fue derrocado y reemplazado por una democracia. El nuevo gobierno rápidamente cedió sus colonias africanas.

> **Which African colonies were held by Portugal?/ ¿Qué colonias tenía Portugal en África?**
>
> _____
>
> _____
>
> _____

## CHALENGE ACTIVITY/ACTIVIDAD AVANZADA

**Critical Thinking: Make Inferences/Pensamiento crítico: Hacer inferencias**  What factors might explain why some Africans fought for independence while others protested peacefully? Write a short essay to explain the reasons for the differences./¿Qué factores podrían explicar por qué algunos africanos pelearon por la independencia mientras que otros protestaban en paz? Escribe un ensayo breve en el que expliques las razones de estas diferencias.

| | | |
|---|---|---|
| Algeria/Argelia | Belgian Congo/el Congo Belga | Ghana/Ghana |
| Guinea/Guinea | Kenya/Kenia | Mau Mau/Mau Mau |
| Mozambique/Mozambique | | |

**DIRECTIONS/INSTRUCCIONES** Read each sentence and fill in the blank with a word, or words, from the word bank that best completes the sentence./Lee cada oración y escribe en el espacio en blanco la palabra o las palabras del par de palabras que mejor la completa.

1. The first British colony to win its freedom was _____, formerly called the Gold Coast./La primera colonia británica que obtuvo su libertad fue _____, anteriormente conocida como Costa de Oro.

2. The British East African colony of _____ became independent only after a long and violent struggle./La colonia británica de _____, en África oriental, logró su independencia después de una larga y violenta lucha.

3. The Kikuyu farmers formed a violent movement called the _____ to rid Kenya of the British settlers./Los granjeros Kikuyu formaron un movimiento violento llamado _____ para expulsar a los colonizadores británicos de Kenia.

4. France did not want to give up its control of _____ in North Africa and sent in an army to put down the rebellion./Francia no quería ceder su control de _____ en África del Norte y envió un ejército para sofocar la rebelión.

5. The _____ was the only major colony in Africa controlled by Belgium./_____ fue la única colonia grande controlada por Bélgica en África.

6. Portugal's colonies, Angola, _____, and _____, fought for independence for decades until 1974, when the Portuguese government became a democracy./Las colonias de Portugal, Angola, _____ y _____, lucharon por su independencia durante décadas hasta 1974, cuando el gobierno portugués adoptó la democracia.

# The Postwar World/El mundo de la posguerra

**MAIN IDEAS/IDEAS PRINCIPALES**

1. People in South Africa faced social struggles related to racial equality./ El pueblo sudafricano afrontó conflictos sociales relacionados con la igualdad racial.

2. Many African countries saw political challenges after they became independent./Muchos países africanos enfrentaron desafíos políticos después de independizarse.

3. The economy and the environment affect life in Africa./La economía y el medio ambiente afectan la vida en África.

4. African culture blends traditional and European elements./La cultura africana combina elementos tradicionales y europeos.

## Key Terms and People/Personas y palabras clave

**apartheid/apartheid** South Africa's policy of separation of races/política de separación de razas establecida por el gobierno de Sudáfrica

**townships/municipios** crowded clusters of tiny homes in which South African blacks were forced to live/zonas abarrotadas de pequeñas casas donde los sudafricanos de raza negra estaban obligados a residir

**sanctions/sanciones** economic or political penalties imposed by one country on another to force a policy change/penalizaciones económicas o políticas impuestas por un país a otro para forzar un cambio de política

**Darfur/Darfur** region of Sudan, site of ethnic conflict and violence/región de Sudán, escenario de conflictos étnicos y violencia

**Lagos/Lagos** capital city of Nigeria/capital de Nigeria

**Kinshasa/Kinshasa** capital city of Democratic Republic of the Congo/capital de la República Democrática del Congo

## Lesson Summary/Resumen de la lección

### SOCIAL STRUGGLES IN SOUTH AFRICA/ LUCHAS SOCIALES EN SUDÁFRICA

In the early 1900s, white descendants of Europeans controlled South Africa's government. They set up a policy of separation of races, or **apartheid** (uh-PAHR-tayt). Under apartheid, only whites were citizens. Jobs, education, and housing were limited for blacks. They had to live in isolated **townships,** which were often crowded clusters of tiny homes./A principios del siglo 20, los descendientes de europeos de raza blanca controlaban el gobierno de Sudáfrica. Establecieron una política de separación de razas, llamada **apartheid,** según la cual solo las personas de raza blanca eran consideradas ciudadanos. El trabajo, la educación y la vivienda eran limitados para la gente de raza negra, obligada a vivir en **municipios** aislados que, a menudo, eran zonas abarrotadas de pequeñas casas.

Protests and **sanctions** eventually forced the government to move away from apartheid in the late 1980s. Today all races have equal rights in South Africa. However, white South Africans are still wealthier than the majority of blacks./Con el tiempo, las protestas y **sanciones** obligaron al gobierno a abandonar el apartheid a fines de la década de 1980. En la actualidad, todas las razas gozan de los mismos derechos en Sudáfrica. Sin embargo, los sudafricanos de raza blanca todavía son más ricos que la mayoría de las personas de raza negra.

> **How did the South African government oppress blacks?/¿De qué manera el gobierno sudafricano oprimió a la población de raza negra?**
>
> _____
> _____
> _____
> _____
> _____

## POLITICAL CHALLENGES/DESAFÍOS POLÍTICOS

After gaining independence, many African countries were taken over by military dictators. In Zaire—formerly Congo—the economy collapsed while dictator Joseph Mobutu became rich. Mobutu was overthrown after a civil war in 1997, and the country became the Democratic Republic of the Congo. Similar civil wars have been fought in many countries. Other countries suffered ethnic conflicts. In Rwanda, the Hutu and Tutsi ethnic groups went to war in 1994. The government, run by the Hutu, killed about 1 million Tutsi in the country. Many more fled the country. In Sudan, tens of thousands of blacks in **Darfur** have been killed by an Arab militia group. Millions more became refugees.

> **What were the two main causes of civil war in post-colonial Africa?/¿Cuáles fueron las dos causas principales de la guerra civil en el África poscolonial?**
>
> _____
> _____
> _____

By the 2000s, more than 30 countries had held
elections. By 2015, democracies thrived
in countries such as Senegal, Ghana, and
Tanzania./Después de obtener la independencia,
muchos países africanos fueron tomados por
dictadores militares. En Zaire, antes llamado
Congo, la economía entró en crisis mientras el
dictador Joseph Mobutu se enriquecía. Mobutu
fue derrocado después de una guerra civil
en 1997, y el país pasó a ser la República
Democrática del Congo. Se sucedieron guerras
civiles similares en varios países. Otros países
atravesaron conflictos étnicos. En Ruanda, por
ejemplo, los grupos étnicos Hutu y Tutsi entraron
en guerra en 1994. El gobierno, a cargo de los
Hutu, mató alrededor de 1 millón de Tutsis.
Muchas otras personas huyeron del país. En
Sudán, decenas de miles de personas de raza
negra fueron asesinadas en **Darfur** por un grupo
paramilitar árabe. Millones de personas optaron
por refugiarse. Para la década de 2000, más de
30 países habían celebrado elecciones y, hacia
2015, las democracias prosperaban en países
como Senegal, Ghana y Tanzania.

## ECONOMY AND ENVIRONMENT/ECONOMÍA Y MEDIO AMBIENTE

Some years after independence, many African
countries have huge debts and little industry or
infrastructure. Cities such as **Lagos,** Nigeria,
and **Kinshasa,** Democratic Republic of the
Congo, offer more jobs and higher standards
of living than rural areas, but they have more
crowding and unemployment. Diseases like
malaria and AIDS have killed millions and slowed
development. Droughts have left farmers unable
to grow crops, and terrible famines have swept
through Africa./Algunos años después de
la independencia, muchos países africanos

> Underline some of the
> diseases that have killed
> millions of people in
> Africa./Subraya algunas
> de las enfermedades que
> mataron a millones de
> personas en África.

tenían grandes deudas y escasas industrias o infraestructura. Ciudades como **Lagos,** en Nigeria, y **Kinshasa,** en la República Democrática del Congo, ofrecían más trabajo y mejor calidad de vida que las áreas rurales, pero tenían más superpoblación y desempleo. Las enfermedades como la malaria y el SIDA mataron a millones de personas y ralentizaron el desarrollo. Las sequías impidieron que los granjeros cultivaran, y terribles hambrunas afectaron África.

## AFRICAN CULTURE/CULTURA AFRICANA

Many elements of European culture can still be seen in Africa. For example, many people in West Africa still speak French or English in their daily lives. Yet many Africans have reclaimed traditional cultures. Artists create masks, musical instruments, and sculptures from wood and bronze, just as their ancestors did centuries ago./En África, aún pueden observarse elementos de la cultura europea. Por ejemplo, muchas personas en África occidental siguen hablando francés o inglés en el día a día. Aun así, muchos africanos reivindican las culturas tradicionales: los artistas crean máscaras, instrumentos musicales y esculturas a partir de madera y bronce, como hacían sus ancestros hace siglos.

> **What is African culture like today?/¿Cómo es la cultura africana en la actualidad?**
>
> _____
> _____
> _____
> _____

## CHALLENGE ACTIVITY/ACTIVIDAD AVANZADA

**Critical Thinking: Solve Problems/Pensamiento crítico: Resolver problemas** Choose one problem facing modern Africans, and write a paragraph proposing a way to deal with it./Escoge un problema que enfrentan los africanos en la actualidad y escribe un párrafo en el que propongas una manera de solucionarlo.

**DIRECTIONS/INSTRUCCIONES** Write a word or descriptive phrase to describe each term./Escribe una palabra o frase descriptiva para describir cada término.

1. apartheid/apartheid _____

_____

2. sanctions/sanciones _____

_____

3. townships/municipios _____

_____

4. Darfur/Darfur _____

_____

5. Lagos/Lagos _____

_____

6. Kinshasa/Kinshasa _____

_____

# The Postwar World/El mundo de la posguerra

## Lesson/Lección 5

**MAIN IDEAS/IDEAS PRINCIPALES**

1. New governments in the Middle East after World War I brought about major political changes./Los nuevos gobiernos de Oriente Medio después de la Primera Guerra Mundial llevaron a cabo cambios políticos importantes.

2. Conflict has challenged many countries in the Middle East./Los conflictos afectaron muchos países de Oriente Medio.

3. The oil industry has been a major influence in the region./La industria del petróleo ha ejercido una gran influencia en la región.

## Key Terms and People/Personas y palabras clave

**shah/Shah** Persian title for a king/título persa para un rey

**embargo/embargo** a limit on trade/límite al comercio

**Taliban/Talibán** a radical Muslim group that rose to power in Afghanistan/ grupo musulmán radical que asumió el poder en Afganistán

**OPEC/OPEP** the Organization of Petroleum Exporting Countries/Organización de Países Exportadores de Petróleo

## Lesson Summary/Resumen de la lección

### POLITICAL CHANGES/CAMBIOS POLÍTICOS

In the Middle East, many governments changed after World War I. Military officers took over the government of Turkey. Their leader removed all elements of Islam and formed a democracy. In Egypt, a 1952 military coup gave Gamal Abdel Nasser power. He fought for control of the Suez Canal, which made him a hero to many Arabs. In 1921, an Iranian military officer took power in Iran. He claimed the old Persian title of **shah.** In 1941, the shah's son came to power. In 1947, the United Nations (UN) voted to divide Palestine into Jewish and Arab states. Only the Jews accepted this plan and they created the state of Israel a year later./En Oriente Medio, cambiaron muchos gobiernos después de la Primera Guerra Mundial. Los oficiales militares asumieron el control de Turquía. Su líder retiró todos los elementos del islam y formó una

> **What did Nasser fight for that made him a hero to many Arabs?/¿Por qué luchó Nasser, lo que lo convirtió en un héroe para muchos árabes?**
>
> _____
>
> _____

> **What country was formed after a vote by the United Nations?/¿Qué país se formó después de la votación en las Naciones Unidas?**
>
> _____

democracia. En Egipto, un golpe de estado en 1952 dio el poder a Gamal Abdel Nasser. Nasser luchó por el control del Canal de Suez, lo que lo convirtió en un héroe para muchos árabes. En 1921, un oficial militar iraní asumió el poder en Irán y reclamó el antiguo título persa de **Shah.** En 1941, el hijo del Shah asumió el poder. En 1947, las Naciones Unidas (ONU) votaron para dividir Palestina en un estado judío y un estado árabe. Solo los judíos aceptaron este plan y crearon el estado de Israel un año después.

## DISAGREEMENT AND WAR IN THE MIDDLE EAST/ DESACUERDO Y GUERRA EN ORIENTE MEDIO

Political changes led to conflict between and within countries. Cultural and religious differences have also caused conflict. The founding of Israel was not well-received in many Arab states. Wars have broken out between Israel and Arab countries since it was founded. In the 1970s, Lebanon had a civil war between the country's Muslim and Christian populations. Syria became involved in the conflict. From 2012 to 2015, many Syrian refugees fled to Lebanon. In 1978, Iran's shah was ousted by an Islamic Revolution led by Ayatollah Khomeini. In 1968, Saddam Hussein became Iraq's president. He was a harsh ruler. He fought with Iran in the 1980s and invaded Kuwait in 1990. The United States, with an alliance of countries, forced the Iraqis out of Kuwait in what is called the Persian Gulf War. When Hussein refused to accept peace terms, the UN placed an **embargo,** or limit on trade, on Iraq./Los cambios políticos causaron conflictos entre países y dentro de ellos. Las diferencias culturales y religiosas también generaron conflictos. La creación de Israel no fue bien recibida en muchos estados árabes. Ha habido guerras entre Israel y los estados árabes

> **What has led to violence in the Middle East?/¿Qué produjo la violencia en Oriente Medio?**
>
> _____
> _____
> _____
> _____
> _____
> _____

> **Why did the UN place an embargo on Iraq?/¿Por qué la ONU le impuso un embargo a Irak?**
>
> _____
> _____
> _____

desde su creación. En la década de 1970, el Líbano atravesó una guerra civil entre los grupos musulmanes y cristianos del país. Siria también participó en el conflicto. Desde 2012 hasta 2015, muchos refugiados sirios huyeron al Líbano. En 1978, el Shah de Irán fue destituido por una revolución islámica dirigida por Ayatollah Khomeini. En 1968, Saddam Hussein se convirtió en el presidente de Irak. Fue un gobernante muy severo. Luchó contra Irán en la década de 1980 e invadió Kuwait en 1990. Los Estados Unidos, en una alianza de países, expulsaron a los iraquíes de Kuwait en la llamada Guerra del Golfo Pérsico. Cuando Hussein se negó a aceptar el acuerdo de paz, la ONU le impuso un **embargo,** o límite al comercio, a Irak.

In the mid-1990s a radical Muslim group known as the **Taliban** rose to power in Afghanistan. The Taliban used a strict interpretation of Islamic teachings to rule. It supported terrorist organizations that shared its beliefs. Among those groups was al Qaeda, the network headed by Osama bin Laden. Al Qaeda was responsible for the September 11, 2001 terrorist attacks on New York City and Washington, D.C. The U.S. toppled the Taliban government. Believing that Iraq helped the terrorists, the United States attacked Iraq and removed Hussein from power in 2003./A mediados de la década de 1990, un grupo musulmán radical denominado **Talibán** asumió el poder en Afganistán. Los talibanes usaban una interpretación estricta de las enseñanzas islámicas para gobernar. Apoyaban a las organizaciones terroristas que compartían sus creencias. Entre esos grupos se encontraba al Qaeda, la red liderada por Osama bin Laden. Al Qaeda fue responsable de los ataques terroristas del 11 de septiembre de 2001 en Nueva York y Washington

> **Why did the United States invade Afghanistan?/¿Por qué los Estados Unidos invadieron Afganistán?**
>
> _____
> _____
> _____
> _____
> _____

D. C. Los EE. UU. derrocaron el gobierno talibán y, con la sospecha de que Irak había ayudado a los terroristas, atacaron Irak y expulsaron a Hussein del poder en 2003.

## OIL IN THE MIDDLE EAST/PETRÓLEO EN ORIENTE MEDIO

Oil was discovered in the Middle East in Persia—now Iran—in 1908. Huge reserves of oil were soon discovered. Many countries there are members of the Organization of Petroleum Exporting Countries, or **OPEC.** This is an international organization whose members work to influence the price of oil by controlling the world supply. Oil has brought great wealth to the region. Many people worry what will happen to the economy when the oil is gone./En 1908, se encontró petróleo en Oriente Medio, en Persia (en la actualidad, Irán). Poco después, se hallaron enormes reservas de petróleo. Muchos países de la zona son miembros de la Organización de Países Exportadores de Petróleo, u **OPEP.** Esta es una organización internacional cuyos miembros trabajan para influir en el precio del petróleo mediante el control del suministro mundial. El petróleo ha reportado una gran riqueza a la región. Muchas personas se preguntan qué le sucederá a la economía cuando las reservas se acaben.

> **Underline the goal of OPEC./Subraya el objetivo de la OPEP.**

## CHALLENGE ACTIVITY/ACTIVIDAD AVANZADA

**Critical Thinking: Make Judgments/Pensamiento crítico: Dar opiniones** What do you think is the greatest challenge facing the Middle East today? Write a letter to the editor of a newspaper. Identify this challenge and suggest what to do about it./¿Cuál crees que es el principal desafío para Oriente Medio hoy en día? Escribe una carta al editor de un periódico. Identifica el desafío y sugiere qué hacer al respecto.

| embargo/embargo | OPEC/OPEP | shah/Shah |
| --- | --- | --- |
| Taliban/Talibán | | |

**DIRECTIONS/INSTRUCCIONES** Use the vocabulary terms in the word bank to write a summary of the conflicts in the Middle East./ Usa el vocabulario del banco de palabras para escribir un resumen de los conflictos en Oriente Medio.

_____

_____

_____

_____

_____

_____

_____

_____

_____

_____

_____

_____

_____

_____

_____

_____

_____

_____

_____

# The Postwar World/El mundo de la posguerra

**MAIN IDEAS/IDEAS PRINCIPALES**

1. Juan Perón and Augusto Pinochet were two Latin American dictators who ruled Argentina and Chile./Juan Perón y Augusto Pinochet fueron dos dictadores latinoamericanos que gobernaron Argentina y Chile.

2. NAFTA influences Latin America because Mexico is part of the agreement./El TLCAN influye en Latinoamérica porque México forma parte del acuerdo.

3. Many Latin Americans have informal jobs and are affected by the lack of education in the region./Muchos latinoamericanos tienen trabajos informales y se ven afectados por la falta de educación en la región.

## Key Terms and People/Personas y palabras clave

**Juan Perón/Juan Perón** army colonel who became president of Argentina/coronel del ejército que fue presidente de Argentina

**Augusto Pinochet/Augusto Pinochet** military dictator of Chile/dictador militar de Chile

**immunity/inmunidad** protection that prevents someone from being arrested, tried, or punished for any crime/protección contra la detención, el juicio o el castigo por un crimen

**North American Free Trade Agreement (NAFTA)/Tratado de Libre Comercio de América del Norte (TLCAN)** formal trade agreement between Mexico, the U.S., and Canada/acuerdo comercial formal entre México, los EE. UU. y Canadá

**informal jobs/trabajos informales** jobs that do not provide minimum wages, schedules, or benefits/puestos de trabajo en los que la gente no gana el salario mínimo, no tiene horarios regulares y no recibe beneficios

## Lesson Summary/Resumen de la lección

**POLITICAL POWER IN LATIN AMERICA/
PODER POLÍTICO EN LATINOAMÉRICA**

In 1946, **Juan Perón** became president of Argentina. He did some good, such as increasing wages for industrial workers. But Perón was a dictator who controlled the military. After his death, military officials ruled Argentina. People who protested the government disappeared. Because of Argentina's actions, the U.S. stopped sending aid./En 1946, **Juan Perón** asumió la presidencia de Argentina. Tomó algunas medidas apropiadas, como aumentar los salarios de los

> Why did the U.S. stop providing aid to Argentina?/¿Por qué los EE. UU. dejaron de enviar ayuda a Argentina?
>
> _____
> _____
> _____
> _____

## Lesson/Lección 6, *continued*/*continuación*

trabajadores industriales, pero Perón era un dictador que controlaba el ejército. Después de su muerte, los militares gobernaron Argentina y las personas que protestaban contra el gobierno desaparecieron. A causa de las acciones de Argentina, los EE. UU. dejaron de enviarle ayuda.

Chile was also ruled by a military dictator, General **Augusto Pinochet.** He came to power during a U.S.-supported coup. This choice turned out to have brutal results for Chile because Pinochet had tens of thousands of people arrested and tortured. Eventually, he was voted out of office but he received **immunity.** This meant that he could not be arrested, tried, or punished for any crime. Chilean courts did decide to try him for human rights abuses, but he died before this happened./Chile también fue gobernado por un dictador militar, el general **Augusto Pinochet.** Asumió el poder durante un golpe militar apoyado por los EE. UU. Esta decisión tuvo resultados brutales para Chile, porque Pinochet arrestó y torturó a decenas de miles de personas. Con el tiempo, se votó a favor de retirarlo del cargo, pero recibió **inmunidad.** Esto significa que contaba con una protección contra la detención, el juicio o el castigo por un delito. Los tribunales chilenos decidieron juzgarlo por su violación de los derechos humanos, pero falleció antes del juicio.

For more than 70 years, Mexico's ruling party acted like a dictatorship. Then people protested and accused it of rigging elections. Some presidents introduced reforms and opposition candidates were elected. But corruption still exists./Durante más de 70 años, el gobierno de México actuó como una dictadura. Luego, las personas protestaron y lo acusaron de arreglar las elecciones. Algunos presidentes introdujeron reformas y los candidatos de la oposición llegaron a ocupar cargos, pero la corrupción sigue vigente.

> Underline the sentence that tells why supporting Pinochet's coup was a bad choice./Subraya la oración que explica por qué apoyar el golpe de Pinochet fue una mala decisión.

## THE ECONOMICS OF OIL, TRADE, AND TOURISM/ ECONOMÍAS DEL PETRÓLEO, EL COMERCIO Y EL TURISMO

Venezuela and some other Latin American nations produce oil. Venezuela earns most of its money from exporting oil and gas. Even with its plentiful oil supply, its economy struggles./Venezuela y algunas otras naciones latinoamericanas producen petróleo. Venezuela obtiene la mayor parte de sus ingresos a partir de la exportación de petróleo y gas. Aun con estas abundantes reservas de petróleo, su economía atraviesa dificultades.

Mexico, Canada, and the U.S. created a formal trade agreement effective in 1994 known as the **North American Free Trade Agreement (NAFTA).** One of its goals was to decrease tariffs so that trade would increase and there would be more job opportunities and higher wages for workers. While NAFTA has achieved some of its goals, some people criticize it and say it has put Mexican farmers out of business and made it easier to exploit Mexican workers./México, Canadá y los EE. UU. crearon un acuerdo comercial formal que entró en vigencia en 1994, llamado **Tratado de Libre Comercio de América del Norte (TLCAN).** Uno de sus objetivos era reducir los aranceles para aumentar el comercio y así crear más oportunidades laborales y mejores salarios para los trabajadores. Mientras que el TLCAN logró parte de sus objetivos, algunas personas lo critican y afirman que ha hecho quebrar a los granjeros mexicanos y ha facilitado la explotación de los trabajadores mexicanos.

Cuba is a communist country, but it has seen some change. In 2014, President Obama announced that the U.S. and Cuba would resume diplomatic relations for the first time in decades. Cuba hopes to benefit from the tourism these changes offer./Cuba es un país comunista, pero ha experimentado algunos cambios. En 2014,

> **Why was NAFTA created?/ ¿Por qué se creó el TLCAN?**
> _____
> _____
> _____
> _____

> **How would Cuba benefit if the United States resumed diplomatic relations?/¿De qué manera se beneficiaría Cuba si los Estados Unidos retomaran las relaciones diplomáticas?**
> _____
> _____
> _____

el presidente Obama anunció que los EE. UU. y
Cuba retomarían las relaciones diplomáticas por
primera vez en décadas. Cuba espera beneficiarse
del turismo que ofrecen estos cambios.

## PAST AND PRESENT SOCIAL STRUGGLES/
## LUCHAS SOCIALES PASADAS Y PRESENTES

Latin America continues to have problems with
income inequality, job inequality, and access to
education. As many as 80 million people live in
poverty. A large number of Latin Americans have
**informal jobs,** jobs that do not provide minimum
wages or offer benefits. Education is limited. Some
students drop out to support family members.
Others continue school, but the education is
poor./Latinoamérica sigue teniendo problemas
relacionados con la desigualdad en los ingresos,
la desigualdad en el trabajo y el acceso a la
educación. Alrededor de 80 millones de personas
viven en la pobreza. Un gran número de
latinoamericanos tienen **trabajos informales,** es
decir, trabajos que no ofrecen el salario mínimo
ni beneficios. La educación es limitada. Algunos
estudiantes abandonan los estudios para mantener
a los miembros de su familia; otros siguen
estudiando, pero la educación es deficiente.

## CHALLENGE ACTIVITY/ACTIVIDAD AVANZADA

**Critical Thinking: Identify Cause and Effect/Pensamiento
crítico: Identificar causa y efecto** Consider the effects of
dictatorships in Latin America. Write a one-page paper
on how you think they are related to income inequality,
job inequality, and access to education./Considera los
efectos de las dictaduras en Latinoamérica. Escribe
un ensayo de una página sobre cómo crees que se
relacionan con la desigualdad en los ingresos, la
desigualdad en el trabajo y el acceso a la educación.

**DIRECTIONS/INSTRUCCIONES** On the line before each statement, write **T** if the statement is true and **F** if the statement is false. If the statement is false, change the underlined term to make the sentence true. Then write the correct term on the line after the sentence./En la línea que precede a cada enunciado, escribe **V** si el enunciado es verdadero y **F** si es falso. Si el enunciado es falso, cambia el término subrayado para que el enunciado sea verdadero. Luego escribe el término correcto en la línea que sigue al enunciado.

_____ 1. The general who became military dictator of Chile after a U.S. supported coup was <u>Juan Perón</u>./El general que se convirtió en dictador militar en Chile después del golpe apoyado por los EE. UU. fue <u>Juan Perón</u>.

_____

_____ 2. The formal trade agreement between the U.S., Canada, and Mexico is the <u>North American Free Trade Agreement</u>, or NAFTA./El acuerdo comercial formal entre los EE. UU., Canadá y México es el <u>Tratado de Libre Comercio de América del Norte</u>, o TLCAN.

_____

_____ 3. The army colonel who became president of Argentina was <u>Augusto Pinochet</u>./El coronel del ejército que llegó a ser presidente de Argentina fue <u>Augusto Pinochet</u>.

_____

_____ 4. Jobs that do not provide minimum wages, regular schedules, or benefits are called <u>NAFTA</u>./Los puestos de trabajo en los que no se gana el salario mínimo, no hay horarios regulares y no se reciben beneficios se llaman <u>TLCAN</u>.

_____

_____ 5. Protection that prevents someone from being arrested, tried, or punished for any crime is known as <u>immunity</u>./La protección contra la detención, el juicio o el castigo por un crimen se conoce como <u>inmunidad</u>.

_____

Name/Nombre_____ Class/Clase _____ Date/Fecha_____

# Contemporary Issues/Problemas contemporáneos

**Lesson/Lección 1**

---

**MAIN IDEAS/IDEAS PRINCIPALES**

1. Both governmental and nongovernmental organizations protect human rights./Tanto las organizaciones gubernamentales como las no gubernamentales protegen los derechos humanos.

2. Human rights abuses affect many groups of people around the world./La violación de los derechos humanos perjudica a muchos grupos de personas alrededor del mundo.

3. The human rights movement has achieved significant victories./El movimiento en defensa de los derechos humanos ha logrado victorias importantes.

---

# Key Terms and People/Personas y palabras clave

**human rights/derechos humanos** the basic rights to which all people are entitled/ los derechos básicos que todas las personas merecen

**Universal Declaration of Human Rights/Declaración Universal de los Derechos Humanos** declaration by the United Nations that defines human rights goals for the world community/declaración de las Naciones Unidas que define los objetivos de los derechos humanos para la comunidad mundial

**Helsinki Accords/Conferencia de Helsinki** the agreement signed by the U.S., Canada, and most European countries to work together for peace/acuerdo firmado por los EE. UU., Canadá y la mayoría de los países europeos para trabajar en conjunto por la paz

**nongovernmental organization (NGO)/organización no gubernamental (ONG)** an organization made up of volunteers that are dedicated to solving a specific issue or problem/organización formada por voluntarios dedicados a la resolución de un conflicto o problema específico

**political dissent/desacuerdo político** a difference of opinion over political issues/ diferencia de opinión sobre temas políticos

**genocide/genocidio** the deliberate destruction of a racial, political, or cultural group of people/la eliminación deliberada de un grupo de personas por motivos raciales, políticos o culturales

# Lesson Summary/Resumen de la lección

## A CHANGING WORLD/UN MUNDO CAMBIANTE

Many people believe that everyone should have certain rights as a human being. These are **human rights,** the basic rights to which all people are entitled. Many international organizations work to guarantee human rights for all people. The UN adopted the **Universal Declaration of Human Rights** in 1948, which defines human rights goals for the world. In 1975, the U.S., Canada, and most European nations signed the **Helsinki Accords** in which they promised to work together for peace./ Muchas personas creen que todos debemos tener ciertos derechos como seres humanos. Se trata de los **derechos humanos,** los derechos básicos que todas las personas merecen. Muchas organizaciones internacionales trabajan para garantizar los derechos humanos para todas las personas. En 1948, la ONU aprobó la **Declaración Universal de los Derechos Humanos,** que define los objetivos de los derechos humanos para todo el mundo. En 1975, durante la **Conferencia de Helsinki,** los EE. UU., Canadá y la mayoría de las naciones europeas firmaron un acuerdo por medio del cual se comprometieron a trabajar en conjunto por la paz.

Many **nongovernmental organizations (NGOs)** made up of volunteers work for human rights or other issues. Groups such as Human Rights Watch work to protect human rights worldwide, but it is an uphill battle./Muchas **organizaciones no gubernamentales (ONG)** formadas por voluntarios trabajan por los derechos humanos, entre otros asuntos. Algunos grupos, como el Observatorio de Derechos Humanos (*Human Rights Watch*), trabajan para proteger los derechos humanos a nivel mundial, pero se trata de una batalla ardua.

| |
|---|
| **What are human rights?/** ¿Qué son los derechos humanos? <br><br> _____ <br><br> _____ <br><br> _____ |

| |
|---|
| **Underline the phrase that tells the purpose of the Universal Declaration of Human Rights./**Subraya la frase que menciona el propósito de la Declaración Universal de los Derechos Humanos. |

## HUMAN RIGHTS ABUSES/VIOLACIONES DE DERECHOS HUMANOS

Human rights abuses exist in many parts of the world. Women, for example, are often refused education and not allowed to take part in government. Generally, they are poorer than men. Some cannot get healthcare. Others are victims of violence. Children also face human rights abuses. Many lack food, housing, healthcare, and proper education. Child labor is also a serious problem./En muchas partes del mundo se producen violaciones de los derechos humanos. A las mujeres, por ejemplo, frecuentemente se les niega el acceso a la educación y no se les permite participar en el gobierno. Por lo general, son más pobres que los hombres. Algunas no pueden acceder a la atención médica. Otras son víctimas de la violencia. Los niños también enfrentan violaciones de derechos humanos. Muchos carecen de alimento, vivienda, atención médica y una educación adecuada. El trabajo infantil también constituye un problema grave.

Also, people have been persecuted for having a difference of opinion over political issues, or **political dissent.** This has occurred in places such as Iran, Pakistan, Cuba, El Salvador, Nigeria, and the former Soviet Union. Ethnic or racial differences also have led to human rights abuses. **Genocide,** the deliberate destruction of a racial, political, or cultural group of people, has occurred in Rwanda, Kosovo, Yugoslavia, Serbia, Syria, Darfur in the Sudan, and other countries worldwide. Many governments also practice religious persecution. Egypt, Iran, Pakistan, Saudi Arabia, China, and North Korea all limit religious freedom./Además, las personas han sido perseguidas por tener diferencias de opinión sobre temas políticos, es decir, por **desacuerdo político.** Esto ha ocurrido en lugares como Irán, Pakistán, Cuba, El Salvador, Nigeria y los países que formaban parte de la antigua Unión Soviética. Las diferencias étnicas o raciales también han causado violaciones de los derechos

> **What are three human rights abuses women face?/¿Cuáles son tres de las violaciones de los derechos humanos que enfrentan las mujeres?**
>
> _____
> _____
> _____
> _____
> _____

> **What do Rwanda, Serbia, Syria, and the Sudan have in common?/¿Qué tienen en común Ruanda, Serbia, Siria y Sudán?**
>
> _____
> _____

> **What is true about Egypt, Saudi Arabia, China, and North Korea?/¿Qué sucede en Egipto, Arabia Saudita, China y Corea del Norte?**
>
> _____
> _____

humanos. En Ruanda, Kosovo, Yugoslavia, Serbia, Siria, Darfur (en Sudán) y en otros países del mundo se han llevado a cabo **genocidios,** es decir, la eliminación deliberada de un grupo de personas por motivos raciales, políticos o culturales. Muchos gobiernos también ejercen la persecución religiosa. Países como Egipto, Irán, Pakistán, Arabia Saudita, China y Corea del Norte limitan la libertad religiosa.

## HUMAN RIGHTS SUCCESSES/LOGROS EN MATERIA DE DERECHOS HUMANOS

Even with all the human rights abuses worldwide, there are some successes. In Europe, more countries opened up their political systems and allowed democratic elections and free speech. South Africa put an end to the apartheid so its government became multicultural./A pesar de todas las violaciones de los derechos humanos que se producen en el mundo, también se han obtenido algunos logros. En Europa, más países abrieron sus sistemas políticos y permitieron elecciones democráticas y libertad de expresión. Sudáfrica puso fin al apartheid y, en consecuencia, su gobierno se hizo multicultural.

For much of the world, access to medical care is limited. Groups such as Doctors Without Borders have worked to aid the sick and victims of disaster./Para gran parte del mundo, el acceso a la asistencia médica es limitado. Algunos grupos, como Médicos sin Fronteras (*Doctors Without Borders*) han trabajado para asistir a los enfermos y a las víctimas de desastres.

Some gains have been made by NGOs in reducing malnutrition, helping to end forced labor for children in Africa, and helping women victims of torture. Some successes have been met with the International Criminal Court in convicting genocide participants, too./Las organizaciones

> **Underline the sentence that tells human rights gains NGOs have made./** Subraya la oración que enuncia los logros que las organizaciones no gubernamentales han obtenido en materia de derechos humanos.

no gubernamentales han obtenido algunos logros;
por ejemplo, han reducido la malnutrición, han
contribuido a terminar con el trabajo infantil
forzado en África y han brindado asistencia a las
mujeres que son víctimas de la tortura. También
se han alcanzado éxitos con la Corte Penal
Internacional, al condenar a quienes han
participado en genocidios.

## CHALLENGE ACTIVITY/ACTIVIDAD AVANZADA

**Critical Thinking: Explain/Pensamiento crítico:**
**Explicar**  Many NGOs work to protect human rights.
Imagine that you are starting a human rights NGO.
Write a statement of purpose and a list of goals./
Muchas organizaciones no gubernamentales trabajan
para proteger los derechos humanos. Imagina que
estás comenzando una ONG a favor de los derechos
humanos. Escribe una declaración de motivos y
una lista de objetivos.

| | | |
|---|---|---|
| genocide/genocidio | Helsinki Accords/la Conferencia de Helsinki | human rights/derechos humanos |
| nongovernmental organization (NGO)/ una organización no gubernamental (ONG) | political dissent/ desacuerdo político | Universal Declaration of Human Rights/la Declaración Universal de los Derechos Humanos |

**DIRECTIONS/INSTRUCCIONES** Read each sentence and fill in
the blank with a term from the word bank that best completes
the sentence./Lee cada oración y escribe en el espacio en blanco
la palabra del banco de palabras que mejor la completa.

1. A difference of opinion over political issues is known as _____
   _____./Una diferencia de opinión sobre temas políticos se
   conoce como _____.

2.  The declaration by the United Nations that defines human rights goals for the world community is the _____./La declaración de las Naciones Unidas que define los objetivos de los derechos humanos para la comunidad mundial es _____ _____.

3.  An organization made up of volunteers that are dedicated to solving a specific issue or problem is a(n) _____./ Una organización formada por voluntarios dedicados a la resolución de un conflicto o problema específico es _____.

4.  The deliberate destruction of a racial, political, or cultural group of people is known as _____./La eliminación deliberada de un grupo de personas por motivos raciales, políticos o culturales se conoce como _____.

5.  The _____ is the agreement signed by the U.S., Canada, and most European countries to work together for peace./_____ es el acuerdo firmado por los EE. UU., Canadá y la mayoría de los países europeos para trabajar en conjunto por la paz.

6.  The basic rights to which all people are entitled are known as _____ _____./Los derechos básicos que todas las personas merecen se llaman _____.

# Contemporary Issues/Problemas contemporáneos

## MAIN IDEAS/IDEAS PRINCIPALES

1. People around the world seek to have a voice in their government through democracy./En todo el mundo, la gente busca tener voz en sus gobiernos a través de la democracia.

2. Democracies face a wide variety of challenges in the twenty-first century./Las democracias enfrentan una amplia variedad de desafíos en el siglo veintiuno.

3. Failed states struggle with crumbling infrastructure and violence./Los estados fallidos se ven aquejados por una infraestructura precaria y por la violencia.

## Key Terms and People/Personas y palabras clave

**Aung San Suu Kyi/Aung San Suu Kyi** outspoken activist for democracy in Myanmar/activista destacada que lucha por la democracia de Myanmar

**secular/secular** free of religious influence/libre de influencias religiosas

**Arab Spring/Primavera árabe** democratic uprisings that occurred independently in Arab nations in 2011/levantamientos democráticos que se produjeron de forma independiente en los países árabes en 2011

**Refugees/refugiados** people who leave their home or country because they fear for their safety/personas que dejan su hogar o país porque temen por su seguridad

**Petro Poroshenko/Petró Poroshenko** Ukraine's president in 2014/el presidente de Ucrania en 2014

**failed states/estados fallidos** countries whose governments are unable to provide stability to their people and protect the borders/países cuyos gobiernos son incapaces de proporcionar estabilidad a sus habitantes y proteger sus fronteras

**infrastructure/infraestructura** the basic items a society needs to function/los factores básicos que necesita una sociedad para funcionar

## Lesson Summary/Resumen de la lección

### DEMOCRACY MOVEMENTS/MOVIMIENTOS DEMOCRÁTICOS

New technology has led to a push for more political freedom and democratic governments. India has the world's largest democracy. Nepal is democratic too. Sri Lanka has begun giving its people freedoms. Pakistan is democratic,

> **Where is the world's largest democracy?/**
> **¿Dónde se encuentra la democracia más grande del mundo?**
> _____

but it is shaky. Myanmar started a representative government. **Aung San Suu Kyi,** democracy activist, became a government official. Thailand has had a series of military coups, but in 2015 the government promised a return to democratic elections. Turkey's government is mainly **secular,** or free of religious influence. But the country faces conflict between religious groups, the Syrian refugee crisis, and terrorism./Las nuevas tecnologías han impulsado a las personas a exigir una mayor libertad política y gobiernos democráticos. La India constituye la democracia más grande del mundo. Nepal también es un país democrático. Sri Lanka ha comenzado a dar libertades a su pueblo. Pakistán tiene un sistema democrático, pero inestable. Myanmar ha establecido un gobierno representativo. **Aung San Suu Kyi,** activista a favor de la democracia, se convirtió en funcionaria del gobierno. Tailandia ha padecido una serie de golpes militares, pero en 2015 el gobierno prometió volver a celebrar elecciones democráticas. El gobierno de Turquía es principalmente **secular,** es decir, libre de influencias religiosas. Sin embargo, este país se enfrenta a un conflicto entre grupos religiosos, a la crisis de los refugiados sirios y al terrorismo.

> Underline the phrase that tells about Turkey's government./Subraya la frase que habla acerca del gobierno de Turquía.

## DEMOCRATIC CHALLENGES OF THE TWENTY-FIRST CENTURY/DESAFÍOS DEMOCRÁTICOS DEL SIGLO VEINTIUNO

World democracies have varying degrees of freedom and voice in government. The U.S. and Canada, most Western European countries, and Australia rank the highest. Countries such as Poland, Lithuania, and the Czech Republic are ranked high too. China, North Korea, Egypt, Syria, Iran, and Yemen are ranked low./Las democracias del mundo presentan distintos grados en cuanto a la libertad y la participación

> Which countries have low degrees of democratic freedom?/¿Qué países tienen bajos niveles de libertad democrática?
>
> _____
> _____
> _____

en el gobierno. Los EE. UU., Canadá, la mayoría de los países de Europa occidental y Australia presentan el nivel de libertad democrática más alto. Algunos países, como Polonia, Lituania y la República Checa, también cuentan con un grado de democratización elevado. Este nivel es bajo en países como China, Corea del Norte, Egipto, Siria, Irán y Yemen.

In 2010, Tunisia's citizens started protesting for freedom. News broadcasts and social media sites carried these protests. They spread to other Arab nations across North Africa and the Middle East. The term **Arab Spring** refers to these democratic uprisings in 2011. Egypt's Hosni Mubarak was ousted, but then the military took over. Libya's dictator Muammar al-Gaddafi was overthrown, but a civil war broke out. Syrian dictator Bashar al-Assad used violence to stop the protests, which led to a civil war and the rise of the Islamic State, or ISIS. Many Syrian citizens have since become **refugees.** Refugees are people who leave their home or their country for safety. Overall, the Arab Spring has had little success./En 2010, los ciudadanos de Túnez comenzaron a protestar por la libertad. Los noticiarios y las redes sociales transmitieron estas protestas, que se propagaron a otras naciones árabes de África del Norte y Oriente Medio. El término **Primavera árabe** se refiere a estos levantamientos democráticos que se produjeron en 2011. El presidente de Egipto Hosni Mubarak fue destituido de su cargo, pero luego el ejército asumió el poder. El dictador de Libia Muammar al-Gaddafi fue derrocado, pero estalló una guerra civil. El dictador sirio Bashar al-Assad recurrió a la violencia para frenar las protestas, lo que desencadenó una guerra civil y el surgimiento del Estado islámico, o EI. Desde entonces, muchos ciudadanos sirios se han convertido en **refugiados,** es decir, personas

> Underline the names of the leaders who were removed from office during the Arab Spring./Subraya los nombres de los líderes que fueron destituidos de sus cargos durante la Primavera árabe.

que dejan su hogar o su país por seguridad. En términos generales, la Primavera árabe ha tenido poco éxito.

Ukraine has struggled to be democratic. Conflicts over whether it should have a closer connection with western democracies or Russia exist. **Petro Poroshenko** became president in 2014, and he remained determined to keep Ukraine democratic. Nigeria has also wanted democracy. However, the militant group Boko Haram, which is connected to ISIS, has challenged the government./A Ucrania le ha costado mucho ser un país democrático. Actualmente enfrenta conflictos en torno a si debería tener una conexión más cercana con las democracias occidentales o con Rusia. **Petró Poroshenko** se convirtió en presidente en 2014 y se mantuvo decidido a conservar la democracia en Ucrania. Nigeria también ha querido la democracia. Sin embargo, el grupo militante Boko Haram, que tiene conexiones con EI, ha desafiado al gobierno.

> **Why are there conflicts in Ukraine?/¿Por qué hay conflictos en Ucrania?**
>
> _____
> _____
> _____
> _____
> _____

## DANGER OF FAILED STATES/PELIGRO DE LOS ESTADOS FALLIDOS

Some countries are considered **failed states** because they have governments that cannot provide stability to their people and protect their borders. These countries face war. They have crumbling **infrastructure,** or the basic items a society needs to function. People in failed states may flee to other countries or take illegal actions to survive. Failed states negatively affect the world./Algunos países son considerados **estados fallidos** porque tienen gobiernos que no logran proporcionar estabilidad a sus habitantes ni proteger sus fronteras. Estos países se enfrentan a la guerra. Su **infraestructura,** es decir, los factores básicos que necesita una sociedad para funcionar, es precaria. Es posible

> **Underline the sentence that describes failed states./ Subraya la oración que describe los estados fallidos.**

que los habitantes de los estados fallidos huyan
a otros países o realicen acciones ilegales para
sobrevivir. Los estados fallidos perjudican
al mundo.

## CHALLENGE ACTIVITY/ACTIVIDAD AVANZADA

**Critical Thinking: Make Judgments/Pensamiento crítico:**

**Dar opiniones** The Arab Spring had some success,
but overall it was a failure. Write a one-page paper
in which you express your opinion for or against the
idea of protest for political freedom and democratic
government. Support your opinion./La Primavera
árabe tuvo cierto éxito, pero en general fue un fracaso.
Escribe un ensayo de una página en el cual expreses
tu opinión a favor o en contra de la idea de protestar
por la libertad política y por un gobierno democrático.
Respalda tu opinión.

## DIRECTIONS/INSTRUCCIONES Write a descriptive phrase to

describe each term./Escribe una frase descriptiva para describir
cada término.

1. Arab Spring/Primavera árabe _____

   _____

2. refugees/refugiados _____

   _____

3. secular/secular _____

   _____

4. Petro Poroshenko/Petró Poroshenko _____

   _____

5. failed states/estados fallidos _____

   _____

6. infrastructure/infraestructura _____

   _____

# Contemporary Issues/Problemas contemporáneos

**MAIN IDEAS/IDEAS PRINCIPALES**

1. Space exploration has led to international cooperation and technological developments./La exploración espacial ha promovido la cooperación internacional y los avances tecnológicos.

2. Computers and the Internet have changed how people work and communicate./Las computadoras y la internet han cambiado el modo en que las personas trabajan y se comunican.

3. Globalization has led to greater cultural sharing around the world./La globalización ha propiciado un mayor intercambio cultural en todo el mundo.

## Key Terms and People/Personas y palabras clave

**International Space Station (ISS)/Estación Espacial Internacional (EEI)** combined space station begun in 1998 among the United States, Russia, the European Space Agency, and Japan/estación espacial combinada que establecieron los Estados Unidos, Rusia, la Agencia Espacial Europea y Japón en 1998

**microchip/microchip** tiny silicon chip that stores large amounts of information/ diminuto chip de silicio que almacena grandes cantidades de información

**Internet/internet** worldwide network of linked computers/red mundial de computadoras conectadas

**telecommute/teletrabajo** doing a job by computer from home/realizar un trabajo por computadora y desde el hogar

## Lesson Summary/Resumen de la lección

### SPACE EXPLORATION/EXPLORACIÓN ESPACIAL

The U.S. and Soviet Union once competed to be the first nation to reach space. The Soviet Union achieved this goal. Over time, space exploration led to cooperation such as in the launching of the Hubble Space Telescope and the building and operating of the **International Space Station (ISS).** The U.S. and Russia each carried sections of the ISS into space to be put together. The European Space Agency and Japan joined the program too. People first went to the ISS in 2009, and during 2015 and 2016 two people spent a year living on it./Hubo un tiempo en que los EE. UU. y la Unión Soviética compitieron para ser la primera

> Underline the sentences that indicate examples of cooperation in space exploration./Subraya las oraciones que muestran ejemplos de cooperación en materia de exploración espacial.

nación en llegar al espacio. La Unión Soviética logró ese objetivo. Con el transcurso del tiempo, la exploración espacial promovió la cooperación, como en el lanzamiento del telescopio espacial Hubble y la construcción y el manejo de la **Estación Espacial Internacional (EEI).** Los EE. UU. y Rusia llevaron por separado secciones de la EEI para ensamblarlas en el espacio. La Agencia Espacial Europea y Japón también se unieron al programa. En 2009, por primera vez llegaron personas a la EEI, y durante 2015 y 2016 dos personas vivieron en ella durante un año.

The U.S. space shuttle program began in 1981. More than 350 people went into space before the program ended in 2011. Now, private companies transport astronauts to the ISS. Also, NASA uses robotic rovers to explore the surface of planets such as Mars. The New Horizons mission, launched in 2006, is exploring Pluto, its moons, and the Kuiper belt objects. In 2015, it flew by Pluto and photographed its features./El programa del transbordador espacial de los EE. UU. comenzó en 1981. Antes de que el programa finalizara en 2011, más de 350 personas habían llegado al espacio. Actualmente, ciertas compañías privadas transportan astronautas hasta la EEI. Asimismo, la NASA utiliza exploradores robóticos para estudiar la superficie de los planetas, como Marte. La misión Nuevos Horizontes (*New Horizons*), lanzada en 2006, está explorando Plutón, sus lunas y los objetos que se encuentran en el cinturón de Kuiper. En 2015, pasó volando junto a Plutón y fotografió sus características.

Space exploration has led to artificial satellites, which are important in communications, GPS systems, and weather forecasting./La exploración espacial ha permitido la creación de satélites artificiales, que son importantes para las

---

> **Why is the New Horizons mission important?/¿Por qué es importante la misión Nuevos Horizontes?**
>
> _____
> _____
> _____
> _____
> _____

comunicaciones, los sistemas de navegación
satelital (GPS) y los pronósticos meteorológicos.

## THE INFORMATION AGE/LA ERA DE LA INFORMACIÓN

Computers from the 1940s were so large they filled entire rooms. Today, **microchips,** tiny silicon chips, store large amounts of information and are very powerful. So computers have changed the way people manage information. The **Internet,** or worldwide network of linked computers, is used by people at home, work, and school. Because of technology changes, where and the way many people work has changed. Some people still work in offices, but others **telecommute,** or do their jobs by computer from home. Technology has changed education too. Books were once the main source of information. Now, students rely on the Internet, may take classes online, and may use tablets to do their schoolwork./Las computadoras de la década de 1940 eran tan grandes que ocupaban habitaciones enteras. Hoy en día, los **microchips,** diminutos chips de silicio, pueden almacenar grandes cantidades de información y son muy poderosos. En consecuencia, las computadoras han cambiado la manera en que las personas manejan la información. La **Internet,** es decir, una red mundial de computadoras conectadas, se utiliza en los hogares, los trabajos y las escuelas. Debido a las innovaciones tecnológicas, el lugar y la manera en que las personas trabajan han cambiado. Algunas personas todavía trabajan en oficinas, pero otras realizan **teletrabajo,** es decir, realizan su trabajo por computadora y desde sus hogares. La tecnología también ha generado cambios en la educación. Los libros fueron alguna vez la fuente principal de información. Ahora, los estudiantes recurren a la internet, pueden tomar clases en línea y pueden usar tabletas para hacer su tarea escolar.

> How has technology changed the way some people work?/¿Cómo ha cambiado la tecnología la manera en que algunas personas trabajan?
>
> _____
>
> _____
>
> _____

## A GLOBAL COMMUNITY/UNA COMUNIDAD GLOBAL

Today, people share traditional culture and popular, or pop, culture. With technology, this exchange happens quickly and over greater distances. Western influence affects many cultures because it dominates worldwide mass media. The widespread use of English is also responsible for global culture. Other Western influences include fashion, food, and the way people see themselves and the world. Some non-Western ideas have spread too. These refer to cultures in Asia, Africa, India, Latin America, and the Middle East. Elements of these cultures include food, martial arts, and herbal medicine. People have become more globally interdependent, so they share a greater sense of connectedness and a greater stake in learning to live peacefully./Hoy en día, las personas comparten la cultura tradicional y la cultura popular o pop. Gracias a la tecnología, este intercambio se produce rápidamente y a través de mayores distancias. La influencia occidental tiene efectos sobre muchas culturas porque domina los medios de comunicación en todo el mundo. El uso generalizado del inglés también contribuye a expandir esta cultura global. Otras influencias occidentales son la moda, la comida y la manera en que las personas se ven a sí mismas y cómo perciben el mundo. Algunas ideas que no provienen de occidente también se han difundido, como las relacionadas con las culturas de Asia, África, India, Latinoamérica y Oriente Medio. Algunos aspectos de estas culturas son los alimentos, las artes marciales y la medicina herbaria. Las personas se han vuelto más interdependientes a nivel global, por lo que comparten un mayor sentido de conectividad y una mayor participación en la tarea de aprender a vivir pacíficamente.

> **What are some non-Western influences on pop or traditional culture?/**
> **¿Cuáles son algunas de las influencias no occidentales que ha recibido la cultura pop o la cultura tradicional?**
>
> _____
> _____
> _____
> _____

## CHALLENGE ACTIVITY/ACTIVIDAD AVANZADA

**Critical Thinking: Describe/Pensamiento crítico:**
**Describir** Consider changes that have occurred in
technology during your lifetime. Write an essay about
how they have affected the way you do schoolwork
or communicate./Considera los cambios que han
ocurrido en la tecnología a lo largo de tu vida. Escribe
un ensayo acerca del modo en que estos cambios han
afectado la manera en que realizas las tareas escolares
o el modo en que te comunicas.

| | |
|---|---|
| International Space Station/<br>Estación Espacial Internacional | Internet/internet |
| microchip/microchip | telecommute/teletrabajo |

**DIRECTIONS/INSTRUCCIONES** Answer each question by writing
a sentence that contains at least one term from the word bank./
Responde cada pregunta con una oración que contenga al
menos una palabra del banco de palabras.

1. What technology changed the size of computers and made them more
   powerful and able to store large amounts of information?/¿Qué tecnología
   cambió el tamaño de las computadoras e hizo que fueran más poderosas
   y capaces de almacenar grandes cantidades de información?

   _____

   _____

2. What technology connects people worldwide?/¿Qué tecnología conecta a
   las personas a nivel mundial?

   _____

   _____

3. Where and how do many people work today?/¿Dónde y cómo trabajan
   muchas personas hoy en día?

   _____

   _____

4.  What major development has come from the combination of the U.S.
    and Russian space station programs?/¿Qué desarrollo importante ha sido
    producto de la combinación de los programas para estaciones espaciales
    de los EE. UU. y Rusia?

    _____

    _____

## Contemporary Issues/Problemas contemporáneos

**MAIN IDEAS/IDEAS PRINCIPALES**

1. Population growth has put pressure on Earth's resources./El crecimiento demográfico ha ejercido presión sobre los recursos de la Tierra.

2. Technology and industrialization have created environmental challenges that affect the entire world./La tecnología y la industrialización han generado retos medioambientales que afectan al mundo entero.

3. Both government action and new technologies can help solve environmental problems./Tanto la acción de los gobiernos como las nuevas tecnologías pueden ayudar a resolver problemas medioambientales.

## Key Terms and People/Personas y palabras clave

**overpopulation/superpoblación** when there are more people than resources to support an area/cuando hay más gente que recursos en un área

**ozone layer/capa de ozono** a layer of oxygen in Earth's atmosphere/capa de oxígeno en la atmósfera de la Tierra

**sustainable growth/desarrollo sostenible** the process of creating economic growth while preserving the environment/el proceso de crear crecimiento económico preservando el medio ambiente

**environmentalism/ecologismo** the movement to protect the natural world from destructive human activities/el movimiento para proteger el mundo natural frente a las actividades humanas destructivas

## Lesson Summary/Resumen de la lección

### POPULATION PRESSURES/PRESIONES DEMOGRÁFICAS

Population growth in some developed nations is slowing. However, less-industrialized nations often have high growth rates, which means they have a hard time providing jobs, education, and medical care. Some areas have **overpopulation,** which occurs when there are more people than resources to support an area, and can lead to migration. Push factors for migration are lack of resources, war, political oppression, and natural disasters. People who leave their country to move to another for safety are refugees. Growth and migration have changed the planet's population density. About

> **When does overpopulation occur?/¿Cuándo se produce la superpoblación?**
>
> _____
> _____
> _____
> _____

half of the world's population lives in rural areas, but many people are moving into cities. Megacities struggle with overcrowded conditions./En algunos países desarrollados, el crecimiento demográfico se desacelera. Sin embargo, los países menos industrializados tienen a menudo tasas de crecimiento altas, lo que implica que tienen dificultades para proporcionar puestos de trabajo, educación y asistencia médica. Algunas zonas tienen **superpoblación,** que sucede cuando hay más gente que recursos en un área, y esto puede causar migraciones. Los factores que impulsan la migración son la falta de recursos, la guerra, la opresión política y los desastres naturales. Quienes dejan su país para trasladarse a otro por seguridad se llaman refugiados. El crecimiento demográfico y la migración han cambiado la densidad poblacional del planeta. Aproximadamente la mitad de la población mundial vive en zonas rurales, pero muchas personas están trasladándose a las ciudades. Las megalópolis tienen que lidiar con condiciones de hacinamiento.

> **Why do refugees leave their country to move to another country?/**¿Por qué los refugiados dejan su país para trasladarse a otro país?
>
> _____

## ENVIRONMENTAL CHALLENGES/RETOS MEDIOAMBIENTALES

The manufacturing and transportation of products create pollution and waste and require sources of energy. Around 80 percent of Earth's energy comes from nonrenewable sources that can damage the environment, as can chemicals and pesticides. Manufacturing processes release chemicals that may deplete the **ozone layer,** a layer of oxygen in Earth's upper atmosphere that protects against the sun's damaging ultraviolet rays./La manufactura y el transporte de productos generan contaminación y deshechos, y requieren fuentes de energía. Alrededor del 80 por ciento de la energía de la Tierra proviene de fuentes no renovables que pueden dañar el medio ambiente,

> **How do manufacturing processes affect the environment and people?/**¿Cómo afectan los procesos de manufactura al medio ambiente y las personas?
>
> _____
> _____
> _____
> _____

Lesson/Lección 4, *continued*/*continuación*

como pueden hacerlo los productos químicos y los pesticidas. Los distintos procesos de manufactura liberan sustancias químicas que pueden reducir la **capa de ozono,** una capa de oxígeno que se ubica en la atmósfera superior de la Tierra y que protege contra el daño causado por los rayos ultravioletas del sol.

Climates can change over time due to natural processes and the effects of human activity. When greenhouses gases buildup, they absorb energy from Earth's surface. This slows energy loss into space, which keeps the planet warm enough to sustain life. Human activities, such as exhaust from factories and cars, have caused an increase in some greenhouse gases so there is additional global warming. Many scientists fear that if global warming continues, deserts may expand and there will be an increase in extreme weather conditions./ El clima puede cambiar con el transcurso del tiempo debido a procesos naturales y a los efectos de la actividad humana. Cuando los gases de efecto invernadero se acumulan, absorben energía de la superficie terrestre y evitan que esa energía se libere demasiado rápido al espacio, lo que mantiene el planeta caliente y permite sustentar la vida. Las actividades humanas, como los gases provenientes de las fábricas y de los carros, han provocado el aumento de algunos gases de efecto invernadero, por lo que hay un mayor calentamiento global. Muchos científicos temen que, si el calentamiento global continúa, los desiertos puedan expandirse y aumenten las condiciones climáticas extremas.

Industrialization, economic development, and increased population strain natural resources. Water pollution and lack of clear water are problems in developing countries. States with large populations and agriculture such as California drain water sources. Clear cutting

> **Underline the sentence that describes what has caused additional global warming to occur./**Subraya la oración que explica a qué se debe el aumento del calentamiento global.

> **What things put a strain on natural resources?/**¿Qué cosas suponen una carga para los recursos naturales?
>
> _____
> _____
> _____
> _____

and strip mining are harmful to forests and resources. Success has been limited by nations needing to achieve **sustainable growth,** the process of creating economic growth while preserving the environment./La industrialización, el desarrollo económico y el aumento poblacional suponen una carga para los recursos naturales. Los países en desarrollo sufren problemas como la contaminación del agua y la falta de agua limpia. Los estados con grandes poblaciones y sistemas agrícolas, como California, agotan los recursos de agua. La tala y la minería a cielo abierto son perjudiciales para los bosques y los recursos. El éxito ha sido limitado dado que los países necesitan lograr un **desarrollo sostenible,** es decir, el proceso de crear crecimiento económico preservando el medio ambiente.

## PRESERVING OUR WORLD/PRESERVAR NUESTRO MUNDO

**Environmentalism** is the movement to protect the natural world from destructive human activities. A major step toward helping the environment was taken in 2015, when 195 countries negotiated a global climate treaty in Paris. Businesses and individuals are also doing their part by recycling, purchasing "green" products, reducing emission levels of greenhouse gases from cars, and transforming renewable resources into energy./El **ecologismo** es el movimiento que busca proteger el mundo natural frente a las actividades humanas destructivas. En 2015, se dio un gran paso para ayudar al medio ambiente cuando 195 países negociaron un tratado mundial sobre el clima en París. Las empresas y los individuos también están contribuyendo al reciclar, al comprar productos "verdes", al reducir los niveles de emisión de gases de efecto invernadero provenientes de los carros y al transformar los recursos renovables en energía.

> **Why do you think so many nations would be willing to work toward helping the environment?/¿Por qué piensas que tantos países estarían dispuestos a trabajar para mejorar el medio ambiente?**
>
> _____
> _____
> _____

## CHALLENGE ACTIVITY/ACTIVIDAD AVANZADA

**Critical Thinking: Describe/Pensamiento crítico:**
**Describir** Many businesses and individuals work to protect the environment. Write a one-page paper in which you describe ways you have protected the environment or ideas you have to protect it./Muchas empresas e individuos trabajan para proteger el medio ambiente. Escribe un ensayo de una página en el que describas las distintas maneras en que has cuidado el medio ambiente o las ideas que tienes para protegerlo.

**DIRECTIONS/INSTRUCCIONES** Read each sentence and fill in the blank with the term in the word pair that best completes the sentence./ Lee cada oración y escribe en el espacio en blanco el término del par de palabras que mejor la completa.

1. A layer of oxygen in Earth's atmosphere is the _____. **(sustainable growth/ozone layer)**/_____ es una capa de oxígeno en la atmósfera de la Tierra. **(El desarrollo sostenible/La capa de ozono)**

2. The process of creating economic growth while preserving the environment is known as _____. **(sustainable growth/environmentalism)**/El proceso de crear crecimiento económico preservando el medio ambiente es conocido como _____. **(desarrollo sostenible/ecologismo)**

3. The movement to protect the natural world from destructive human activities is called _____. **(environmentalism/overpopulation)**/El movimiento que busca proteger el mundo natural frente a las actividades humanas destructivas se denomina _____. **(ecologismo/ superpoblación)**

4. People who leave their country to move to another for safety are _____. **(refugees/megacities)**/Las personas que dejan su país para trasladarse a otro por seguridad se llaman _____. **(refugiados/megalópolis)**

5. When there are more people than resources in an area can support then the area has _____. **(sustainable growth/overpopulation)**/ Cuando en un área hay más gente que la que los recursos pueden sustentar, se dice que hay _____. **(desarrollo sostenible/superpoblación)**

# Contemporary Issues/Problemas contemporáneos

**MAIN IDEAS/IDEAS PRINCIPALES**
1. Technology has revolutionized modern medicine./La tecnología ha revolucionado la medicina moderna.
2. World health is threatened by a widespread outbreak of diseases./La salud mundial está amenazada por un brote generalizado de enfermedades.

## Key Terms and People/Personas y palabras clave

**genetics/genética** the study of genes and how they affect the development of living things/el estudio de los genes y cómo afectan el desarrollo de los seres vivos

**cloning/clonación** the creation of identical copies of DNA/la creación de copias idénticas de ADN

**biotechnology/biotecnología** the use of cells, bacteria, and plants to make products/el uso de células, bacterias y plantas para fabricar productos

**pharmaceuticals/fármacos** manufactured medical drugs/drogas medicinales manufacturadas

**3D printing/impresión 3D** a way of manufacturing three-dimensional objects/ una manera de fabricar objetos tridimensionales

**epidemic/epidemia** the spread of an infectious disease between many people in a community or region/la propagación de una enfermedad infecciosa entre muchas personas en una comunidad o región

**pandemic/pandemia** when a disease affects many people over a wide area/ cuando una enfermedad afecta a muchas personas en un área extensa

**AIDS/SIDA** acquired immune deficiency syndrome/síndrome de inmunodeficiencia adquirido

## Lesson Summary/Resumen de la lección

### TECHNOLOGY TRANSFORMS TREATMENTS/LA TECNOLOGÍA TRANSFORMA LOS TRATAMIENTOS

Technology has led to innovations in medicine that have helped patients recover and live healthier lives. Scientists study **genetics,** or genes and how they affect the development of living things, since thousands of diseases have a genetic link. They have found ways to make changes to an organism's genes, which is genetic engineering. This helps them find causes of diseases and develop drugs to treat them. Scientists hope to correct genetic problems before people get genetic diseases./La tecnología ha dado lugar a innovaciones en la medicina que han ayudado a pacientes a recuperarse y llevar vidas más saludables. Los científicos estudian la **genética,** es decir, los genes y cómo estos afectan el desarrollo de los seres vivos, ya que miles de enfermedades tienen un vínculo genético. Han encontrado maneras de realizar cambios en los genes de un organismo, lo que se conoce como ingeniería genética. Esto les ayuda a encontrar las causas de las enfermedades y a desarrollar medicamentos para tratarlas. Los científicos esperan poder corregir los problemas genéticos antes de que las personas padezcan enfermedades genéticas.

**Cloning,** or the creation of identical copies of DNA, is part of genetic engineering. It allows scientists to reproduce organisms that are identical to existing ones. **Biotechnology,** or the use of cells, bacteria, and plants to make products, is related to genetics too. It is used in diagnosing or predicting a disease. Another use is in making **pharmaceuticals,** or manufactured medical drugs./ La **clonación,** es decir, la creación de copias idénticas de ADN, es parte de la ingeniería genética y permite a los científicos reproducir organismos que son idénticos a los existentes. La **biotecnología,** es decir, el uso de células, bacterias y plantas para fabricar productos, también está relacionada con la genética. Se utiliza para diagnosticar o predecir una enfermedad. También se usa en la fabricación de **fármacos,** o drogas medicinales manufacturadas.

Technology such as virtual reality (VR) can be used to help train surgeons. It is also used in robotic surgery and telesurgery. Medicine has

> **Why do scientists study genetics?/¿Por qué los científicos estudian la genética?**
> _____
> _____
> _____
> _____
> _____
> _____
> _____

> **Underline the sentences that tell the purposes of biotechnology./Subraya las oraciones que mencionan los propósitos de la biotecnología.**

also adapted **3D printing,** a way of manufacturing
three-dimensional objects. This has made it
possible for doctors to make prosthetic limbs.
In the future, researchers hope to print tissues
of organs for organ replacement./Algunas
tecnologías, como la realidad virtual (RV), pueden
ser utilizadas para la capacitación de cirujanos.
También se utiliza en la cirugía robótica y la
telecirugía. La medicina también ha adaptado
la **impresión 3D,** una manera de fabricar objetos
tridimensionales. Esto ha permitido a los médicos
crear prótesis para las extremidades. En el futuro,
los investigadores esperan poder imprimir tejidos
de órganos para el trasplante de órganos.

> **How do researchers hope to someday use 3D printing?/¿De qué manera esperan los investigadores utilizar algún día la impresión 3D?**
> _____
> _____
> _____

## DISEASE AND TREATMENT/ENFERMEDAD Y TRATAMIENTO

Poor health is a standard for much of the
world. Reasons for this include lack of proper
healthcare and sanitation, little food to eat, and
unclean drinking water./La mala salud es un
problema habitual en gran parte del mundo.
Algunas de las razones son la falta de asistencia
médica e higiene adecuadas, la escasez de
alimentos y la contaminación del agua potable.

> **Underline the reasons that poor health is a standard for much of the world./ Subraya las razones por las que la mala salud es un problema habitual en gran parte del mundo.**

An **epidemic** occurs when an infectious disease
spreads between many people in a community
or region. A **pandemic** occurs when a disease
affects many people over a wide area. Examples
of pandemics include strains of influenza and
tuberculosis. Two epidemics have occurred in
recent years. In 2014, an Ebola outbreak occurred
in West Africa. Ebola is caused by a virus and
can lead to death by organ failures, coma, and
bleeding. By 2016, more than 11,000 people had
died from it. In 2015, another viral disease called
Zika began in Brazil and then spread into other
parts of South and Central America. Zika seems
to have the greatest effect on unborn babies. It has

**Lesson/Lección 5,** *continued*/*continuación*

led to a birth defect where a baby's head and brain are smaller than expected. International travelers appear to spread Zika to new areas./Una **epidemia** se produce cuando una enfermedad infecciosa se transmite entre muchas personas en una comunidad o región. Una **pandemia** se produce cuando una enfermedad afecta a muchas personas en un área extensa. Algunos ejemplos de pandemias son ciertas cepas de la gripe y de la tuberculosis. En los últimos años se han producido dos epidemias. En 2014, hubo un brote de ébola en África occidental. El ébola es causado por un virus y puede causar la muerte por insuficiencia orgánica, coma y sangrado. Para el año 2016, más de 11,000 personas habían fallecido a causa de ella. En 2015, otra enfermedad viral llamada zika comenzó en Brasil y luego se extendió a otras partes de América del Sur y Central. El zika parece tener un mayor efecto en bebés nonatos. Ha causado una malformación congénita por la cual la cabeza y el cerebro del bebé son más pequeños que lo esperado. Los viajeros internacionales parecen haber propagado el zika a nuevas áreas.

> **How are Ebola and Zika similar?/¿En qué se asemejan el ébola y el zika?**
> _____
> _____
> _____

A major global health issue is **AIDS,** or acquired immune deficiency syndrome. About 70 percent of the people infected with the virus that causes AIDS, human immunodeficiency virus (HIV), live in sub-Saharan Africa. There is no cure for HIV, but it can be controlled with medicines. Some progress has been made in slowing the spread of AIDS, and scientists hope that a vaccine will soon be developed./El **SIDA,** o síndrome de inmunodeficiencia adquirido, constituye un problema grave para la salud mundial. Alrededor del 70 por ciento de las personas infectadas con el virus que causa el SIDA, el virus de inmunodeficiencia humana (VIH), vive en el África subsahariana. No hay

> **Underline the area where most people who contract AIDS live./Subraya el área donde viven la mayoría de las personas que contraen SIDA.**

cura para el VIH, pero puede controlarse gracias
a ciertos medicamentos. Se han logrado algunos
adelantos para frenar la propagación del SIDA,
y los científicos esperan desarrollar una vacuna
dentro de poco.

## CHALLENGE ACTIVITY/ACTIVIDAD AVANZADA

**Critical Thinking: Explain/Pensamiento crítico:**
**Explicar** Imagine that you are a world health worker.
Write a paragraph explaining some ways you would try
to put an end to epidemics and pandemics./Imagina
que eres un professional que trabaja por el cuidado
de la salud mundial. Escribe un párrafo en el que
expliques algunas maneras en que tratarías de
poner fin a las epidemias y a las pandemias.

**DIRECTIONS/INSTRUCCIONES** Match the terms in the first column
with their correct definition from the second column by placing the
letter of the correct definition in the space provided before each
term./Une los términos de la primera columna con su definición
correcta en la segunda columna. Escribe la letra de la definición
correcta en el espacio que precede a cada término.

_____ 1. pharmaceuticals/
fármacos

_____ 2. cloning/clonación

_____ 3. pandemic/pandemia

_____ 4. AIDS/SIDA

a. the use of cells, bacteria, and plants
to make products/el uso de células,
bacterias y plantas para fabricar
productos

b. the study of genes and how they affect
the development of living things/el
estudio de los genes y cómo afectan
el desarrollo de los seres vivos

c. the spread of an infectious disease
between many people in a community
or region/la propagación de una
enfermedad infecciosa entre muchas
personas en una comunidad o región

d. manufactured medical drugs/drogas
medicinales manufacturadas

_____ 5. biotechnology/
biotecnología

e. acquired immune deficiency syndrome/
síndrome de inmunodeficiencia
adquirido

_____ 6. 3-D printing/
impresión 3D

f. the creation of identical copies of
**DNA**/la creación de copias idénticas
de ADN

_____ 7. genetics/genética

g. a way of manufacturing
threedimensional objects/una manera
de fabricar objetos tridimensionales

_____ 8. epidemic/epidemia

h. when a disease affects many people
over a wide area/cuando una
enfermedad afecta a muchas
personas en un área extensa

# Contemporary Issues/Problemas contemporáneos

**MAIN IDEAS/IDEAS PRINCIPALES**

1. Over the past 50 years, the economies of developed and developing nations have changed./Durante los últimos 50 años, las economías de los países desarrollados y en desarrollo han cambiado.

2. Globalization has led to free trade as well as new political and economic problems worldwide./La globalización ha dado lugar al libre comercio así como a nuevos problemas políticos y económicos en todo el mundo.

3. Developing nations face a set of economic challenges and sometimes receive aid from international organizations./Los países en desarrollo enfrentan una serie de retos económicos y a veces reciben ayuda de parte de organizaciones internacionales.

# Key Terms and People/Personas y palabras clave

**developed nations/países desarrollados** countries with the tools needed to produce manufactured goods/países con las herramientas necesarias para producir bienes manufacturados

**developing nations/países en desarrollo** countries that are not fully industrial/países que no son totalmente industriales

**gross domestic product (GDP)/producto interno bruto (PIB)** the value of goods and services produced each year by a country/el valor de los bienes y servicios que se producen cada año en un país

**standard of living/nivel de vida** how well people in a nation can meet their needs and wants/qué tan bien la gente en una nación puede satisfacer sus necesidades y deseos

**inflation/inflación** a continuing increase in the prices of goods and services/aumento continuo en los precios de los bienes y servicios

**recession/recesión** a time of very slow economic activity/época de actividad económica muy lenta

**free trade/libre comercio** the ending of trade barriers among nations/el final de las barreras comerciales entre las naciones

**securities/valores** investments in companies or governments/inversiones en empresas o gobiernos

**World Bank/Banco Mundial** organization that offers loans for large projects in developing nations/organización que ofrece préstamos a países en desarrollo para proyectos a gran escala

**International Monetary Fund (IMF)/Fondo Monetario Internacional (FMI)** organization that offers emergency loans to countries in financial trouble/organización que ofrece préstamos de emergencia a los países con problemas financieros

# Lesson Summary/Resumen de la lección
## CHANGING ECONOMIES/ECONOMÍAS CAMBIANTES

Nations with strong free-market economies are
**developed nations.** They have the tools to be
experts in producing manufactured goods.
Countries that are not fully industrial are
**developing nations.** Over time, some companies
moved manufacturing jobs to developing nations.
They could keep prices low./Las naciones que
tienen economías de libre mercado fuertes son
**países desarrollados.** Estas naciones poseen las
herramientas para ser expertas en la producción
de bienes manufacturados. Los países que no son
totalmente industriales son **países en desarrollo.**
Con el tiempo, algunas empresas trasladaron
los empleos del sector industrial a países en
desarrollo, ya que podían mantener bajos
los costos.

> **What is the difference
> between developed and
> developing nations?/¿Qué
> diferencia existe entre los
> países desarrollados y los
> países en desarrollo?**
>
> _____
>
> _____
>
> _____
>
> _____

The shift in where products are made has
improved many economies. This has affected the
**gross domestic product (GDP),** the value of goods
and services produced each year by a country.
GDP helps measure a nation's **standard of living,**
or how well people can meet their needs and
wants. **Inflation,** a continuing increase in the
prices of goods and services, is a problem that
may occur during a strong economy. A time of
very slow economic activity is a **recession.** People
may lose their jobs and a nation's GDP will
decrease./Los cambios relativos al lugar donde se
fabrican los productos han favorecido a muchas
economías. Esto se ve reflejado en el **producto
interno bruto (PIB)** de las naciones, es decir, el
valor de los bienes y servicios que se producen
cada año en un país. El PIB ayuda a medir el
**nivel de vida** de una nación, o en qué medida los
habitantes pueden satisfacer sus necesidades y
deseos. La **inflación,** el aumento continuo de

> **What is the relationship
> between GDP and standard
> of living?/¿Cuál es la
> relación entre el PIB y el
> nivel de vida?**
>
> _____
>
> _____
>
> _____

los precios de los bienes y servicios, es un problema que puede producirse en una economía fuerte. Una **recesión** es una época de actividad económica muy lenta, durante la cual las personas pueden perder sus puestos de trabajo y el PIB del país disminuye.

## ECONOMIC INTERDEPENDENCE AND GLOBAL TRADE/INTERDEPENDENCIA ECONÓMICA Y COMERCIO GLOBAL

Multinational corporations manufacture and sell products globally. Developing nations want these corporations to invest because investment creates jobs and expands their economies. Developing nations can improve their infrastructure and better meet their citizen's needs./Las empresas multinacionales fabrican y venden productos en todo el mundo. Los países en desarrollo buscan que estas corporaciones inviertan, dado que las inversiones crean puestos de trabajo y amplían las economías. Además, esto permite que los países en desarrollo mejoren su infraestructura y satisfagan mejor las necesidades de sus ciudadanos.

> **Why do developing nations want multinational corporations to invest in them?/¿Por qué los países en desarrollo quieren que las empresas multinacionales realicen inversiones en ellos?**
>
> _____
> _____
> _____

Many countries want **free trade,** which removes trade barriers among nations. A trade bloc strengthens economies too. The EU and NAFTA are such groups./Muchos países quieren el **libre comercio,** que elimina las barreras comerciales entre las naciones. Los bloques comerciales, como la UE y el TLCAN, también fortalecen las economías.

Most nations have stock exchanges for buying and selling **securities.** These are investments in companies or governments. Beginning in 2007, housing prices in the U.S. rose and banks made housing loans. Some people borrowed too much money. They could not pay for their houses and lost them. Investors lost money. Because the U.S. has such a significant role in the global economy,

> **How did the housing crisis in the U.S. affect other countries?/¿Cómo afectó a otros países la crisis inmobiliaria que se produjo en los EE. UU.?**
>
> _____
> _____
> _____

other countries had economic crises. By 2010,
things had improved for some countries, but
not all./La mayoría de las naciones tienen
mercados bursátiles para vender y comprar
**valores,** es decir, inversiones en empresas o
gobiernos. A partir de 2007, el precio de las
viviendas de los EE. UU. aumentó, y los bancos
otorgaron préstamos para comprar viviendas.
Algunas personas pidieron en préstamo
demasiado dinero. Como no pudieron pagar
el costo de sus viviendas, las perdieron. Los
inversionistas perdieron dinero. Debido a que los
EE. UU. desempeñan un papel muy importante en
la economía mundial, otros países sufrieron crisis
económicas. Para el año 2010, las cosas habían
mejorado para algunos países, pero no para todos.

## ECONOMIC AID FOR DEVELOPING NATIONS/ AYUDA ECONÓMICA PARA LOS PAÍSES EN DESARROLLO

Developing nations struggle for economic
stability. So developed nations provide aid to
them through international organizations. The
**World Bank** offers loans for projects such as for
infrastructure, healthcare, or education. The
**International Monetary Fund (IMF)** offers
emergency loans to countries in financial trouble.
Developed nations want to help developing
nations because they are sources of raw materials
and potential markets for goods. All nations
benefit if the economies of developing nations
are strong./A los países en desarrollo les cuesta
mantener economías estables. Por lo tanto, los
países desarrollados les proporcionan ayuda a
través de organizaciones internacionales. El
**Banco Mundial** ofrece préstamos para proyectos
vinculados con la infraestructura, la salud o la
educación. El **Fondo Monetario Internacional**
ofrece préstamos de emergencia a países con

> **Underline examples of the types of projects funded by the World Bank./**Subraya ejemplos de los tipos de proyectos financiados por el Banco Mundial.

problemas financieros. A los países desarrollados
les interesa ayudar a los países en desarrollo
porque estos son fuentes de materias primas
y representan mercados potenciales donde
comercializar bienes. Todas las naciones se
benefician si las economías de los países en
desarrollo son fuertes.

## CHALLENGE ACTIVITY/ACTIVIDAD AVANZADA

**Critical Thinking: Explain/Pensamiento crítico:**
Explicar  Imagine that you live in a developing nation.
Write a short letter to someone in a developed nation.
Describe how globalization has helped your standard
of living./Imagina que vives en un país en desarrollo.
Escribe una carta breve a alguien que vive en un país
desarrollado. Explícale cómo la globalización ha
mejorado tu nivel de vida.

**DIRECTIONS/INSTRUCCIONES** On the line before each statement,
write **T** if the statement is true and **F** if the statement is false. If the
statement is false, change the underlined term to make the sentence
true. Then write the correct term on the line after the sentence./En
la línea que precede a cada enunciado, escribe **V** si el enunciado es
verdadero y **F** si es falso. Si el enunciado es falso, cambia el término
subrayado para que el enunciado sea verdadero. Luego escribe el
término correcto en la línea que sigue al enunciado.

_____ 1. How well people in a nation can meet their needs and wants is its gross
domestic product./El producto interno bruto de un país refleja en qué
medida la gente de una nación puede satisfacer sus necesidades
y deseos.

_____

_____ 2. An organization that offers emergency loans to countries in financial
trouble is the International Monetary Fund (IMF)./Una organización
que ofrece préstamos de emergencia a países con problemas
financieros es el Fondo Monetario Internacional (FMI).

_____

_____ 3. Nations that have developed all the skills and tools to be experts in producing manufactured goods are <u>developing nations</u>./Los países que han desarrollado todas las habilidades y·herramientas necesarias para ser expertos en la producción de bienes manufacturados son <u>países en desarrollo</u>.

_____

_____ 4. The value of goods and services produced each year by a country is its <u>gross domestic product (GPD)</u>./El valor de los bienes y servicios que se producen cada año en un país es <u>el producto interno bruto (PIB)</u>.

_____

_____ 5. The ending of trade barriers among nations is <u>free trade</u>./El final de las barreras comerciales entre las naciones se conoce como <u>libre comercio</u>.

_____

_____ 6. <u>Recession</u> is a continuing increase in the prices of goods and services./<u>Una recesión</u> es el aumento continuo en los precios de los bienes y servicios.

_____

_____ 7. Investments in companies or governments are <u>free trade</u>./Las inversiones en empresas o gobiernos se llaman <u>libre comercio</u>.

_____

_____ 8. An organization that provides loans for large projects in developing nations is the <u>International Monetary Fund</u>./<u>El Fondo Monetario Internacional</u> es una organización que proporciona préstamos para grandes proyectos en países en desarrollo.

_____

_____ 9. <u>Recession</u> is a time of very slow economic activity./<u>La recesión</u> es una época de actividad económica muy lenta.

_____

_____10. Countries that are not fully industrial are <u>developed nations</u>./Los países que no son totalmente industriales son <u>países desarrollados</u>.

_____